Working to Preserve Our Heritage

The Incredible Legacy of
Greek-American Community Services

Working to Preserve Our Heritage

The Incredible Legacy of Greek-American Community Services

John Peter Psiharis

Greek American Press
Chicago, Illinois

Copyright © 2023

All rights reserved. No part of this book may be reprinted, reproduced, distributed, electronically stored, or transmitted in any form or by any means (conventional, digital, or electronic) without the written approval and consent of the author, except as permitted by U.S. copyright laws or for brief quotations in reviews, research, or media reporting.

As an independent project, this book is not authorized, endorsed by, or affiliated with the Greek American Health Services Foundation, the Greek American Rehabilitation and Care Center, or the Coalition of Limited English Speaking Elderly. The views, recollections, and opinions expressed in this book, unless otherwise noted, are those of the author, and not the aforementioned organizations or their members.

Published by: Greek American Press
An Imprint of Psihco, LLC, Chicago, Illinois

Website: GreekAmericanPress.com

First Edition

Published in the United States of America

Library of Congress Control Number: 2023916650

ISBN: 979-8-9890724-0-8 (print)
       979-8-9890724-1-5 (eBook)

This book is also available as an eBook

Elaine Thomopoulos and John Psiharis at Greek-American Community Services office, 3911 North Monticello Street, Chicago, IL. Circa 1987. John Psiharis collection.

Cover pictures:

Front: The Hellas Dance Group performs during a Greek-American Community Services cultural program. DePaul University, Chicago, IL. November 15, 1987. John Psiharis collection.

Back: John Psiharis and Elaine Thomopoulos at the National Hellenic Museum, Chicago, IL. September, 2018. Photo by Margaret Frasier. John Psiharis collection.

To all who played a part in the accomplishments chronicled within, and to those who will carry the torch into the future, I dedicate this book to you.

Hellenism in the Heartland

The "Hellenism in the Heartland" series, published by Greek American Press, chronicles the legacy of Greek-American Community Services (GACS) and the early histories of the Greek-American Nursing Home Committee (GANHC) and the Coalition of Limited English Speaking Elderly (CLESE). It also offers a glimpse into Hellenic life in Chicago during this era (1980s-2000s); a time of increased cultural appreciation and awareness, renewed ethnic pride, and unprecedented achievement.

Authored by John Psiharis, who was GACS co-founder, president, and executive director; with the active involvement of Dr. Elaine Thomopoulos; who served as GACS co-founder, vice president, administrator, and cultural arts program director; this series includes photos, ephemera, detailed timelines, and who's who listings for each organization. John and Elaine's experiences, recollections, and files, provide a comprehensive history of GACS and insider accounts of how the GANHC achieved what some thought impossible, the fulfillment of the community's long-held dream of establishing a Greek-American nursing home.

The first in this series, *Working to Preserve Our Heritage: The Incredible Legacy of Greek-American Community Services,* meticulously details the dynamic history of GACS, which in its day, celebrated, promoted, and preserved Greek American cultural heritage though far-ranging public programs in the arts and humanities, touched the lives of thousands through its social services, introduced adult day care as a viable care option for the community, helped build better interethnic understanding and cooperation, and gave birth to the committee that established Chicago's Greek-American Nursing Home. The early years of the Coalition of Limited English Speaking Elderly (CLESE), an organization GACS played a key role in launching, are also described.

Breaking Ground: The Inside Story of Chicago's Greek Nursing Home Movement, the second in the series, recounts the groundbreaking efforts of the GANHC to establish a Greek American nursing home. This book, in intimate detail, tells the story of how this monumental project came to fruition. John and Elaine's involvement as co-founders and board members throughout this time provides a unique vantage point for this narrative. It is scheduled for release in 2024.

The third, *Hellenes in the Windy City: The Greeks in Chicago - 1980-2000,* co-authored by John Psiharis and Elaine Thomopoulos, is a snapshot of Greek life in Chicago during the time of GACS, including profiles, photos, and ephemera of some of the more prominent individuals and organizations of the era. It is planned for late 2024.

BREAKING GROUND: THE INSIDE STORY OF CHICAGO'S GREEK NURSING HOME MOVEMENT (2024 Release)

On a cold and snowy evening in December 1982, motivated by the lofty Hellenic ideals of *philotimo* and *philoxenia,* a diverse and dynamic group of Greek Americans founded Greek-American Community Services and launched a groundbreaking movement that established the second nursing home in the United States to be owned and operated by and for the Greek community.

Forty years after that first meeting, and 20 years after the opening of the Greek American Rehabilitation and Care Centre, John Psiharis, with substantial involvement from Dr. Elaine Thomopoulos, recounts the history of this monumental undertaking through their unique perspectives as co-founders of Greek-American Community Services and the Greek-American Nursing Home Committee, where they served as board members from inception through 2006.

From that first meeting through construction and opening, this book details the struggles and successes in achieving this monumental goal. The early years, rallying the community behind this effort, site selection, obtaining zoning and approvals, raising funds, obtaining financing, groundbreaking, construction, and opening festivities are all covered. There were setbacks as well, ranging from Chicago politicians who offered an environmentally contaminated property in place of a promised location, to internal disagreements, opening pains, and crushing debt that needed to be urgently fixed. This diligent group persevered and navigated these severe challenges to accomplish the dream.

Of the nursing home, a newspaper of the day proclaimed: "The creation of this center united the Chicagoland Greek Americans as no other project or cause has in these times." Today, the nursing home is consistently rated as one of the best in the state of Illinois.

COMING SOON

HELLENES IN THE WINDY CITY: THE GREEKS IN CHICAGO 1980-2000

The 1980s through 2000s were momentous times for some 240,000 Greek Americans living in Chicagoland. After decades of working to establish themselves in the U.S., the fruits of their labors were becoming apparent. Greeks had become the highest educated and second wealthiest ethnic group in the U.S.

It was a time of progress, promise, assimilation, ethnic pride, and accomplishment. In Chicago, Greek Americans owned countless restaurants and stores as well as many other businesses of all types and sizes. They excelled in medicine, law, government, academics, the sciences, and the arts and humanities. Churches and organizations were integral to Greek-American society. It is noteworthy that this era gave birth to two massive Chicago-based community projects, the National Hellenic Museum and the Greek American Rehabilitation and Care Centre.

John Psiharis and Elaine Thomopoulos, co-founders of Greek-American Community Services and the Greek-American Nursing Home Committee, join forces as co-authors, to chronicle Chicago's Greek community during this pivotal time in its history. Pictures and ephemera add to this story as do extensive listings of business owners, professionals, politicians, academics, artists, and others of the era. Biographies of a number of individuals and organizations that were influential in the community at this time are also included.

Contents

Hellenism in the Heartland...viii

Table of Contents...xii

About the Co-founders...xiv

Acknowledgments...xvi

Foreword...xviii

Part 1

The Genesis...

Charting the Course...1

Part 2

Greek-American Community Services

Serving the *Omogenia*...11

Yes, We CAN...16

Working to Preserve our Heritage...31

Assessing the Needs of our Elders...37

Strains on Ethnic Pride Conference...47

Building Bridges into the Broader Community...55

The Dawn of Day Care...67

Two Steps Forward...One Step Back...93

Northwest Chicago Senior Care Comes of Age...103

Cultural Enrichment in the *Omogenia*...114

Hellenic Alliances...122

Honoring Those Who Preserved the Heritage...135

Greetings & Salutations...171

The A-Team...184

A Building Becomes a Home...192

Settling in...196

A Tornado Strikes...207

Chronicling our Heritage...218

O Cosmos...231

Ya'Sou 2...273

Joining Forces...277

A Stitch in Time...283

Energy Assistance Program...293

Benefits Eligibility Check List...295

The Check Isn't in the Mail...298

Possibilities Unfulfilled...311

Part 3

Greek-American Community Services Who's Who

Advisory Board and Board of Directors...321

The Team...336

The Back Bench...351

The Cheerleaders...359

Special Supporters of GACS...361

Part 4

Chronological History of GACS 1982 – 2002...367

Part 5

The Coalition of Limited English Speaking Elderly

CLESE...437

Chicago's Ethnic Communities Come of Age...446

CLESE Transcends Barriers...450

Index...463

About the Co-Founders

John Psiharis was co-founder, president, and executive director of Greek-American Community Services from inception through 2002 and served on the Greek-American Nursing Home Committee from inception through 2006. He was a founding member and two-time past president of the Coalition of Limited English Speaking Elderly.

John's professional activities have included serving as coordinator of community services for the Community Advocacy Network of Lutheran Social Services of Illinois, senior services director at the Hyde Park Neighborhood Club, and executive director of the Bosnian and Herzegovinian American Community Center. He is currently the executive director of the Irving Park Community Food Pantry; a position he has held since 2008.

John was appointed by three Chicago mayors (Washington, Sawyer, and Daley) to serve as a member of the Chicago Community Development Advisory Committee and completed a three-year term as chairman of the Chicago Department of Cultural Affairs City Arts-Social Services Grants Committee. He was a board member of the Chicago Council for Justice for Cyprus and twice elected community representative to the William Howard Taft High School Local School Council, from which he is an alumnus. He holds a Bachelor of Arts in Human Services degree from the National College of Education (National Louis University) and pursued graduate studies in public administration at Roosevelt University.

John is co-owner of Big Helpers, Inc., a Chicago-based award-winning business he co-founded in 2004, and is founder/owner of Psihco, LLC, and publisher of its Greek American Press imprint. He served as a consultant to the Loyola University of Chicago School of Education, Metropolitan Asian Family Services, America's Disabled, Fuji Television Network of Japan, and several other organizations and businesses.

John's writings have appeared in *Ergon,* the *Greek Press*, *Greek Star*, *Hellenic Chronicle*, *The National Herald,* and *WindyCityGreek.com*. He has written chapters in *Organizing a Volunteer Program Serving the Elderly, The ABCs of ADCs,* and *Modern Greece*.

Elaine Thomopoulos was co-founder, vice president, and administrator of Greek-American Community Services from inception through 1990. She was also a consultant to the Cultural & Arts Program and held the position of Cultural & Arts Program director on a part-time basis from 2000-2002. Elaine was a member of the Greek-American Nursing Home Committee from inception through 2004 and served as second vice president through much of that time.

Elaine earned a Ph.D. in psychology from the Illinois Institute of Technology and was the first director of social services for the Hellenic Foundation. She served as project director of both the Community Advocacy Network and its Assyrian Project for the Elderly, programs of Lutheran Social Services of Illinois. Elaine was a consultant to the Assyrian Universal Alliance Foundation and Chicago project director of "Innovative Approaches to Dissemination of Caregiver Information through Ethnic and Religious Groups," a joint project of the American Jewish Committee Institute and Catholic University.

Elaine was the project director for the "Greek-American Women of Illinois" project sponsored by the Greek-Women's University Club and funded by the Illinois Humanities Council, and the Berrien County Historical Association's "Greeks of Berrien County, Michigan Project," which was funded by the Michigan Humanities Council.

Elaine was managing editor of special issues "Books" and "Scientists" for *The National Herald*, a Greek American newspaper. She has also published articles about Greeks and Greek Americans in scholarly journals, as well as newspapers and magazines.

Elaine served as editor of *Organizing a Volunteer Program to Serve the Elderly* and *Greek-American Pioneer Women of Illinois*. She is the author of *Images of America: St. Joseph and Benton Harbor, Resorts of Berrien County, The History of Greece,* and *Legendary Locals of St. Joseph and Benton Harbor*. Most recently she was editor of *Modern Greece*, published in 2021.

Acknowledgments

I extend my deep appreciation to Dr. Elaine Thomopoulos. Elaine's memories and contributions of photos, documents, ephemera, editing prowess, and advice were instrumental to this project. It has been great to once again have the opportunity to work together with her on this book and other projects. I especially enjoyed our Thursday lunches at the Greek Islands, coffees and delicacies at Artopolis, and visits to the National Hellenic Museum to work on this and other projects. Even though work on this book has come to an end, I look forward to our continuing collaboration in future endeavors.

I also posthumously recognize John Rassogianis for his help with this project. John was integral to GACS and GANHC throughout the years covered in this book. John's recollections added an extra dimension, and his contributions, photos, and editing help are much appreciated. John passed away in October 2022, shortly before this book was completed. Although he didn't see the finished product, John was able to read, edit, and contribute to much of the manuscript. I am grateful to have had the opportunity to work with him one last time.

Thank you to Steve Frangos for his help including providing labels from the *Heartland of Hellenism* and *O Cosmos* exhibits and feedback on this undertaking.

Many of the photos included in this book are from my collection of photos, documents, press clippings, and memorabilia, including items given to me over the years by Frieda Aravosis, Alex Cantos, Tessie Cantos, Bessie Choporis, Ann Prusinski, and John Rassogianis. Other documents, press clippings, and ephemera are from Elaine's collection. Additional photos were provided by John Rassogianis.

A big thank you to Jeremy Bucher, collections manager, Margaret Frasier, former collections manager, and the National Hellenic Museum, for their support of this project and access to the museum's archives related to Greek-American Community Services and the Greek-American Nursing Home. Of particular assistance were archival records, documents, and photos from the *Greek Star, Greek Press*, James Michael Mezilson, Theano Papazoglou Margaris, Ann Prusinski, and Elaine Thomopoulos collections.

Thank you to David Aaron Harbin for providing information and invitations related to the Greek Night events he organized and to Elaine Columbus for sharing photos and news clippings related to a fundraising benefit for the GANHC she co-chaired.

Thank you to Bruce Dean, Barbara Javaras, Dr. Eleni Katsarou, Kathy O'Neill, Constantine Tzanos, and Jerry Vasilatos, for helping to identify people in various photographs; and to Craig Shutt and Toni Enderle for lending their Photoshop skills to improve the quality of several photos in this book.

I also extend my gratitude to Ricardo Rodriguez, who is also my business partner and CEO of Big Helpers, Inc., for his support and guidance during this years-long effort. His advice, ideas, talents, skills, and encouragement are greatly appreciated.

I extend love and appreciation to my past and present feline family members who kept me company and provided needed affection, attention, and distraction throughout this years-long process: *Dickens, Dison, Hero, *Morris, *Pepper, Shell, *Soafire, Thomas, *Tornado, *Tyson, and Zora.

Much of the collective archives that Elaine and I have related to Greek-American Community Services, the Greek-American Nursing Home Committee, the Greek-American Rehabilitation and Care Centre, and the Coalition of Limited English Speaking Elderly will be turned over to the National Hellenic Museum after this project comes to an end so that these items may be available into the future.

Foreword

The idea for this series of books first came about when I discovered several envelopes with photos in a box that I hadn't seen in quite some time. As I looked through the snapshots and thought about the people and stories behind each picture, I realized that in the coming years, few would know who these people were, or their part in the story of Greek-American Community Services (GACS) and the nursing home movement. Much of what they worked so hard to achieve would be unknown to future generations. In large and small ways, they gave unselfishly of their time, talent, and treasure, and in so many other ways, to this legacy.

A few weeks later, I attended a meeting at the Greek-American Rehabilitation and Care Centre (GARCC). It was my first visit to the facility in several years, and I was impressed by how far they had come. As I contemplated the Wall of Honor on prominent display in the lobby, I again realized that the stories of those who were memorialized on this Wall will be lost to those in the coming decades who will assume responsibility for the GARCC. I expect that future generations will continue to benefit from the GARCC but will never know the challenges encountered and sacrifices made by so many to realize the long-held dream of opening the nation's second Greek American nursing home. The first Greek nursing home, the Hellenic Nursing Home for the Aged in Canton, Massachusetts, opened in 1973 and is run by the Hellenic Women's Benevolent Association. It is now known as the Hellenic Nursing Home and Rehabilitation Center.

Nationally, there were three Greek-operated retirement homes. The oldest, St. Michael's Home, currently located in Long Island, New York, was established in 1958 and is owned and operated by the Greek Orthodox Archdiocese of America. Hollywood House, operated by the Hellenic Foundation, opened in 1973 and catered to seniors in Chicago. The building was sold in 2007 to the Heartland Alliance for Housing which provides affordable housing to lower-income seniors.

On June 6, 2023, the *Chicago Tribune* reported that Heartland Alliance for Housing, which managed some 800 units of affordable housing, including Hollywood House, went into receivership. The organization blamed restrictions on rent collections imposed during the COVID pandemic and price inflation related to labor, utilities, and other expenses. Their buildings had a good number of building code violations as well. The American Hellenic Educational Progressive Association (AHEPA) opened a senior housing facility in St. Louis and eventually established properties in other parts of the country.

Initially, I created a Facebook page as a means of sharing some of these photos and the stories behind them but soon realized that this was not enough. Facebook only allowed brief descriptions of photos that were a snapshot in time and not the story of the organizations or their accomplishments.

It became apparent that these memories needed to be preserved and set into context for the story of GACS to be properly told. Further, this is not just the story of GACS; it is also a glimpse into Chicago's Greek community during the latter part of the twentieth century. As a co-founder of both organizations, executive director of GACS throughout much of its existence, and as a member of the GANHC board from inception through 2006, I grew to realize that there was no one more appropriate to tell this story and that if I didn't do this, no one else could or would.

Elaine Thomopoulos was also there from day one. She was co-founder of both organizations and at various times served as GACS vice president and administrator when we shared leadership of the organization from inception through 1990 and continued to lend her support after leaving the administrator role. In later years, she served as a consultant and director of the Cultural & Arts Program. Elaine was a board member and second vice president of the GANHC from inception through 2004. Since we were involved in different facets of these organizations, we each had unique experiences and memories to contribute to this project. Forty years after the founding of GACS, I am overjoyed to have had this opportunity to once again connect with Elaine and to be able to share the story and legacy of GACS in such a comprehensive manner!

I first met Elaine when I was 12 years old and volunteered at the Hellenic Foundation while Tessie Cantos, my uncle's wife, who with her husband Alexander, raised me, worked as the job placement counselor and office manager. Elaine, as director of social services, was her supervisor. I helped to coordinate a health education lecture series, health fairs, and a summer youth tutoring program as both a volunteer and later as a paid part-time staff member.

In 1982, Elaine left the Hellenic Foundation and became project director of the Community Advocacy Network (CAN), a program of Lutheran Social Services of Illinois (LSSI) focused on helping senior citizens access needed benefits or services through trained volunteers. CAN operated the Assyrian Project for the Elderly, teen-chore and telephone reassurance programs, community workshops, in-service training, and other programs. I followed Elaine to CAN. Tessie remained at the Hellenic Foundation for several years after that.

John Psiharis tutors unknown girl during a tutoring session. *Hellenic Foundation Newsletter,* April, 1978. Elaine Thomopoulos collection.

In 1983, as a CAN volunteer, I began to help with fundraising and then was hired part-time to be the coordinator of development where I helped organize fundraising events such as Hike/Bike-a-thons, house party benefits at Elaine's house, and a membership drive. I then became the coordinator of community services at CAN.

As Elaine and I worked together at CAN, we had occasional conversations about the Greek community and the social service and cultural needs within it. The Hellenic Foundation was doing a good job of meeting many of the community's needs, but there were areas of concern that were not being addressed. At a certain point, a vision of what would become GACS emerged.

Over lunches at Demetrios, Mr. James, Mr. Steer, The Alps, and several Chinese and Thai restaurants that were near CAN's Portage Park office, the concept took shape. In the coming weeks, we contacted people we thought would be interested and invited them to an exploratory meeting to discuss this in greater detail. I arranged with Pol Gavaris, proprietor of the Elysion Restaurant, to use the back room of his restaurant for a meeting on December 14, 1982. It was the first of several meetings that resulted in the founding of Greek-American Community Services and set into motion what became the Greek-American Rehabilitation & Care Centre in Wheeling, Illinois.

In 1985, the nursing home endeavor spun off from GACS into its own organization, the Greek-American Nursing Home Committee (GANHC), with many of us serving on both boards. In 2002, 19 years after the founding of GACS, the nursing home opened its doors.

Over the coming years, GACS offered an impressive array of cultural programming that lived up to its motto of "Working to Preserve our

Heritage." Be it film festivals, conferences, and traveling museum exhibits or lectures, classes, and demonstrations, the acclaimed GACS Cultural & Arts Program reached across the state and touched the lives of thousands who attended or participated in the many programs that were offered.

Concern for the elderly was apparent early on with the establishment of a volunteer friendly-visiting program, English-as-a-Second Language (ESL) classes, and community education lectures held during the St. Demetrios Young at Heart senior citizen's group meetings. GACS coordinated Greek community participation in a groundbreaking needs assessment of Chicago's ethnic elderly. Services were enhanced when the Community Advocacy Network (CAN), initially a program of Lutheran Social Services of Illinois, merged with GACS in 1987 and added to the services the organization offered to seniors.

In 1990, GACS launched Northwest Chicago Senior Care, first located at Alvernia Place and subsequently at 3940 N. Pulaski Road. At the time, it was the only adult day care center on Chicago's northwest side and the first in the nation focused on serving the Greek elderly. GACS briefly launched a chore/housekeeping program, helped usher in Chicago's Benefits Eligibility Checklist (BEC), and assisted thousands to receive assistance in paying their utility bills. Although they did not come to fruition, GACS, explored, considered, or initiated planning for a meals-on-wheels program, a Golden Diner's congregate dining program, and several other initiatives.

Along the way, GACS worked with most Greek organizations and established dialogues and close working relationships with many ethnic communities in Chicago including Assyrians, Blacks, Chinese, Hispanics, Italians, Jews, Koreans, Latinos, Polish, Ukrainians, Vietnamese, and others.

Additional efforts to collaborate with ethnic communities were apparent with the creation of the Coalition of Limited English Speaking Elderly (CLESE), of which GACS played a key role and was a founding member. CLESE grew into an unprecedented coalition of leaders of organizations representing most ethnic groups that resided in the metropolitan Chicago area and became a national model of inter-ethnic cooperation that was replicated in other parts of the country. The collaborative spirit and common purpose of CLESE members led to major improvements in service provision to limited and non-English speaking elderly.

In later years, GACS encountered financial difficulties as a result of continued late payments from the state, limitations in fundraising due to the GANHC capital campaign kicking into high gear and the impending opening of the nursing home, a concurrent drive to raise money for the construction of the National Hellenic Museum, and efforts by the Greek Orthodox Diocese of Chicago to establish a monastery and retreat center in Racine, Wisconsin. It was under these challenging circumstances that the GACS Board made the difficult decision to close its doors. Eventually, the owed funds were received and outstanding bills were settled.

Although disheartened, there was no time to rest. All eyes were focused on the impending opening of the nursing home. After years of blood, sweat, and tears, the home was about to become a reality.

With zero dollars and little experience, this group set out to accomplish what many thought was not possible; building a Greek American nursing home for the elders of our community that treated them with dignity and respect and honored their culture, heritage, life experiences, preferences, and language. It would be a home that would care for them irrespective of one's ability to pay.

After years of laying the groundwork, fundraising, and considering several suitable locations; we thought we found the ideal place, North Park Village on Chicago's northwest side. Despite several years of intensive efforts and expense, the project ultimately became a victim of Chicago's "pay to play" politics. The land the city originally offered was substituted for a piece of property that held leaking underground fuel tanks that posed a toxic environmental hazard. The land that the GANHC had initially been offered and bid on went to a politically connected developer.

As they say, everything happens for a reason. After the North Park Village fiasco, the committee cast a wider net into the suburbs where it was believed this project would receive better consideration. Soon, we came across the eight-acre site in Wheeling, Illinois where the Greek-American Rehabilitation and Care Centre is now located.

Buying the land was the easy part! The GANHC needed to secure a Certificate of Need (CON) from the state, obtain zoning approvals, establish and nurture community support, launch a multi-million-dollar fundraising campaign, arrange financing, finalize designs, select contractors, manage the construction process, hire staff, identify residents, and of course, open and operate a nursing home.

Along the way, there were victories and setbacks as we navigated uncharted waters. Each milestone that was achieved presented a new round of opportunities and challenges. Through it all, the GANHC galvanized support for what was an unparalleled community-wide effort that united generations of Greek Americans in a common purpose.

It had been a long-term vision to establish a Greek Village on the GANHC campus in connection with the nursing home. We envisioned a community that encompassed skilled nursing care, assisted living, independent living, adult day care, a senior center, intergenerational programming, and meals-on-wheels prepared from the nursing home kitchen, with opportunities for joint activities and programming within this spectrum. We foresaw purchasing the surrounding land as it became available to create this campus. I'm delighted that in 2018, the GARCC moved a big step closer to fulfilling this dream when it purchased the former Wheeling Senior Center and an adjacent professional medical center building.

This series of books includes individual and shared recollections that Elaine Thomopoulos, John Rassogianis, and I had, as well as a detailed chronological history of GACS and the GANHC. There are also listings of key people and supporters for each organization. Four decades have passed, and for certain events or people, there are vivid memories and for others, they are foggy at best. Extensive research helped fill in the details and in some cases unlocked other memories or events.

In researching and writing this book, Elaine and I have scoured our collective files related to GACS, GANHC, and CLESE and reviewed hundreds of photos, documents, press clippings, notes, board and committee meeting minutes, appointment calendars, correspondence, and publicity materials that helped to tell this story. A few matters, conversations, or details deemed confidential at the time are not included but may be touched upon in the book based on information that was partially or subsequently available in the public domain, or discussed during an open board of directors meeting. No client names were used, except for those that had been mentioned in public or the media at the time.

Many of the photos were taken by Instamatic, Polaroid, pocket, or disposable cameras that were not of the quality that we are accustomed to today. Additionally, over the years, the condition of some of the photos deteriorated. When possible, the photos were enhanced to improve their quality. With each of these photos, a determination was made that the documents, people, or activities depicted in the picture were of enough significance to be included, even if the photo wasn't top-notch.

One conundrum encountered time and again was the spelling of names. Some names were spelled in more than one way and years later it is difficult to confirm the correct spelling. Examples of this include: Yannis and Yiannis, Yorgos and Yiorgos, Kosta and Costa, Dimitrios and Demetrios, Spiro, Spyro, and Spero, Rigas and Regas, Maniates and Maniatis, Soteria and Sotiria, and the list goes on. In quoted texts, the names are spelled as they appeared in the newspaper article or document being cited. When possible, letterheads, correspondence, ad books, and online searches were used to determine the spelling used in the narrative. Unfortunately, with an undertaking of this nature, it is inevitable that despite these painstaking efforts, errors will occur.

Another mystery that we have been unable to solve with certainty, was the name of the GACS traveling museum exhibition. The name of the funded project was "*O Cosmos*: The Private Lives and Public Celebrations of the Greeks in Illinois 1880s – 1980s." There are also references to the years listed as 1886-1992. There is also mention of the "Heartland of Hellenism: The Greeks in Illinois 1880 to 1950" exhibit. The years in the title for this exhibit were listed as 1886-1924 or alternately as 1886-1954.

Neither Elaine nor I remember the reason for the different names or why there are discrepancies in the years. I also consulted Steve Frangos, the grant writer and researcher for this project, who has no recollection of this. One possibility is that Heartland was a precursor, or preview, to the larger *O Cosmos* exhibit. Another is that *O Cosmos* was the overall project name which included the Heartland exhibit and several distinguished lectures. There is a reference to the first possibility in a press release so it is probable that is the case. The differences in years could be typographical errors that were made at the time. Beyond that, we did not find any more information on this. It appears that the Heartland exhibit evolved after work had begun on the *O Cosmos* project.

Other discrepancies are now apparent with the benefit of hindsight. For example, Crystal Palace Banquets is variously listed as being in Des Plaines, Park Ridge, and Mount Prospect. As of this writing, Crystal Palace is located in Mount Prospect. I have included the location as it appeared in the source material. There are instances where there is conflicting information concerning titles, dates, and venues of various events. Again, I have relied on the source material being cited.

Although every effort was made to be as accurate and comprehensive as possible, there are gaps. For instance, most of my copies of GACS meeting minutes and other files, as described elsewhere in this book, are gone and no other copies have surfaced; thus a wealth of information that would have been helpful may be lost forever. My files related to the early years of the GANHC are also gone. Elaine wasn't able to locate her copies for this period either. For the GANHC, this is particularly evident between 1988 and 1994. These years were busy times for the GANHC as it was considering or working on the Foster and Pulaski, Dunning, North Park Village, and Rosehill cemetery properties. The committee spent considerable time and expense on the North Park Village property and it is a shame we don't have more information from this period. The National Hellenic Museum only had a handful of items related to this period.

We reviewed what the National Hellenic Museum had archived, and as of July 2023, they had little from the period we were looking for. It is worth noting that visiting the Museum was difficult in 2020, 2021, and 2022, due to COVID-19 pandemic closings and restrictions so our ability to access their archives was limited. There were similar restrictions (rightfully so) in being able to visit the nursing home during this period, which had an impact on my ability to access records and take updated pictures. Although additional details in certain areas would have been helpful, they do not detract from the overall story.

Listings in the "Who's Who" sections are based on roles within the organizations and people may be listed more than once under different categories or with both organizations. Unfortunately, the passing of years has caused some details to fade. In those cases, I have included the name but may not be able to recall details about their involvement. Although the listings of donors, staff, and volunteers are extensive, they are not all-inclusive. The list is based on our collective memories so many years later and information available from files, media, and ephemera that Elaine and I had in our collections. Additional information was gleaned through research from a variety of sources. I have strived to be as accurate and inclusive as possible, but given gaps in available records or memories, some may have been missed. If that is the case, I apologize in advance. Many played a role in the story of GACS and GANHC in large and small ways and they all receive appreciation.

The profound legacy of GACS in adhering to the Hellenic ideals of *philotimo** and *philoxenia** occurred during a time of cultural renaissance in our *omogenia*. It was rooted in exploring, understanding, celebrating, and preserving the Greek American experience and in providing help to the elders who paved the way and those in need.

Greek-American Community Services…

- Connected Greek Americans in Illinois and beyond, through cultural appreciation and preservation, and social service endeavors.
- Spearheaded efforts to explore, preserve, celebrate, and understand the Greek American experience through unique and far-ranging programs in the arts and humanities involving many of the community's best, brightest, and most talented artists, scholars, and humanists.

- Collaborated with other Greek American churches and organizations to bring humanities, arts, and educational programming to the community.
- Initiated greater inter-ethnic and multi-cultural cooperation, communication, and understanding.
- Participated in efforts that led to significant improvements in social service delivery systems for vulnerable ethnic elderly.
- Provided vital support and assistance to countless individuals that improved or enhanced their quality of life and well-being with a particular focus on older adults.
- Supported efforts to establish adult day care for the elderly as a viable care option in the eldercare continuum.
- Helped nurture an unprecedented multi-ethnic coalition focused on the needs of limited and non-English speaking elderly.
- Launched a movement that established the second nursing home in the United States to be owned and operated by and for the Greek community.

Philotimo

"*Philotimo*, at its core, is about goodness, selflessness, giving without wanting anything in return and the force that drives individuals to think about the people and the world around them." *(1)*

Philoxenia

"The Greek word *Philoxenia*, literally translated as a 'friend to a stranger,' is widely perceived to be synonymous with hospitality.

For Greeks, it is much deeper than that. It is an unspoken cultural law that shows generosity and courtesy to strangers.

Philoxenia today can be as simple as a smile, helping a stranded motorist, buying a meal for a homeless person, or opening your home to friends and family." *(2)*

---

(1) "Philotimo, One Greek Word Packed with So Much Meaning, It Can't Be Defined." *Greek City Times*. October 22, 2018. Accessed July 31, 2023. https://greekcitytimes.com/2018/10/22/philotimo-one-greek-word-packed-with-defined/.

(2) Kokkinidis, Tasos. "Philoxenia: The Ancient Roots of Greek Hospitality." *Greek Reporter*. July 6, 2023. Accessed July 31, 2023. https://greekreporter.com/2023/07/06/philoxenia-the-ancient-roots-of-greek-hospitality/.

Part 1
Charting the Course

On a cold and snowy evening in December 1982, a small and eclectic group of Greek Americans gathered over coffee in the back room of the Elysion Restaurant in Chicago's Budlong Woods neighborhood to discuss unmet needs within Chicago's Greek community. The conversation was lively and wide-ranging with an array of concerns and ideas being discussed.

It became apparent that the needs of the community's older adults were of primary concern. They had come to this country from the *patrida* (homeland) and worked hard to acclimate to their new surroundings, raise families, and earn a living. As they entered their golden years, they found themselves not only dealing with the usual problems of growing older but also those confronted by most immigrant elders. Seniors were culturally and socially isolated. Many spoke little or no English and were unfamiliar with American culture and customs. When in need of help, other than the Hellenic Foundation, there were few places that they could go to and find someone who spoke their language and shared their cultural values.

All agreed that the Hellenic Foundation was providing valuable services to the community; however, there were still areas of concern that were not being addressed. Key among them was the need for a nursing home that would focus primarily on the needs of the Greek elderly. Other areas of discussion were the need for an array of community services and cultural programs that focused on the Greek American community. The Hellenic Foundation did not offer cultural programming. Research in identifying the specific needs of the community was also deemed important since it would enable us to better understand and respond to areas of concern.

The initial guest list for this meeting included: Dr. Theodosis Kioutas, a medical doctor who was active within the Greek community; Thalia Jameson, a teacher at Chapin Elementary School; Helen Geocaris, wife of the highest-ranking Greek American elected official in Chicago (John Geocaris, 40th Ward Democratic ward committeeman); Jim Heliotes, a supervisor with the Chicago Department of Streets and Sanitation; Polyzoes "Pol" Gavaris, proprietor of the Elysion Restaurant; Charles Mouratides, editorial director, *Lerner Newspapers*; Jean Kaporis, a community elder who was actively involved in her church (Annunciation

Cathedral); Ethel Kotsovos, a social worker who had worked for the Hellenic Foundation; Anna Manos, a legal secretary; and Toni Panos, a medical secretary who was active in several Greek organizations including the Daughters of Penelope. A snow storm that evening reduced attendance.

Since this is the meeting that started it all, the complete minutes are reprinted below.

Greek-American Community Services of Chicago
Planning Committee Meeting

Tuesday, December 14, 1982, Elysion Restaurant, 2800 W. Foster Ave
The meeting was called to order at 6:45 p.m.
Present: John Psiharis. Elaine Thomopoulos, Dr. Theodosis Kioutas, Jim Heliotes, and Pol Gavaris.

John opened the meeting by proposing that an agency to serve the Greek-American community should be organized. He sighted the lack of services being provided to Greek Americans and the need for our community to become united. He stated that the proposed agency would not duplicate services already offered but will supplement them, and in no way compete with the Hellenic Foundation.

Dr. Kioutas thought that services were scant and agreed. Dr. Kioutas brought up cases to illustrate his point that the Greek elderly-especially those in nursing homes- do not have adequate services:

Mrs. H – moved from Hollywood House to Lake Land Nursing Home. Hollywood House could not care for her adequately. Now she is isolated at the nursing home and has no one to talk to or no way to communicate with the staff.

Mrs. D. – who had lived in Hollywood House – is currently in Illinois Masonic Hospital. She will have to move to a nursing home. She has spinal arthritis and cannot function on her own.

Dr. Kioutas felt that a nursing home should be considered as a goal for G.A.C.S.C.

Pol and Jim felt that Hollywood House was primarily for the richer Greeks and that no facilities existed for those that could not afford the high rents.

According to Elaine, the only other known agency helping Greeks in the U.S. (besides the Hellenic Foundation) is H.A.N.A.C. in New York. She suggested that we should not limit services to Chicago.

The consensus is that we should not limit the board to being of Greek background but that our services be directed to the Greek-American community. Pol felt that we should also get involved in cultural affairs.

John reported on his conversation with Father Kaloudis (Holy Trinity) who said that he was eager to help us and may be interested in providing us with office space. We would have to submit a written request to their Board. If they approve it, then the Bishop would also have to approve it.

Dr. Kioutas suggested that we contact a few board members in advance to explain our ideas (Chris Demopoulos and Mike Pontikes). He also suggested that we ask Father Kaloudis to act as an advisor.

After discussion, it was the consensus of the group that we should wait until after we are incorporated before we talk to anyone. After incorporation, we should talk to the Hellenic Foundation about how we can work together. Jim added that Holy Trinity is in the 36th Ward.

John stated that we must first write bylaws before we can incorporate. Dr. Kioutas suggested that his wife Anna (an attorney) could help us with the legal wording.

John and Elaine were selected to write a rough draft of the bylaws, to be reviewed at our next meeting.

Other people to be asked to join include Sam Kostogiannes, nominated by Pol, and seconded by Jim. Approved. Pol will ask. Thalia Jameson, nominated by John, seconded by Elaine. Approved. John will ask. Other names mentioned as people who may be interested in this project include Chris Demopoulos, President, Holy Trinity (Dr. Kioutas and John), Gus Contos, C.P.A. (Jim and Pol). Peter Panagoulias, a professor (Dr. Kioutas and Pol).

Recommendations included the following:

1. Co-chair people – rather than one officer will serve as chief executives.
2. Dr. Kioutas suggested: Officers should have two successive two-year terms at most in the same position. John felt that there should not be a restriction if the officers are doing a good job.
3. Pol suggested that we include non-board members to serve on committees as consultants. If these people perform well, they may be placed on the board. All agreed.
4. The purposes of the organization may include:

> i. Health and consumer education (lectures, health fairs, Tel-Med, etc.)
> ii. Legal Assistance
> iii. Immigration and Naturalization
> iv. Housing for Greeks
> v. Education (tutoring, etc.)
> vi. Social Services (not those done by the Hellenic Foundation)
>
> All agreed that the agency should remain non-political.
>
> Jim reported that according to the 1980 census, 23,000 Greeks reside in Chicago and that 1,500 registered voters live in the 40th Ward.
>
> Pol allowed us to use the restaurant as the mailing address for correspondence
>
> The next meeting will be held on Friday, January 14 at 6:30 p.m.
>
> The meeting was adjourned by John at 8:45 p.m.

According to Elaine's handwritten notes of the January 14, 1983 meeting:

> The meeting convened at 7:15 p.m. In attendance were John Psiharis, Elaine Thomopoulos, Polyzoes Gavaris, Jim Heliotes, Sam Kostogiannes, and Steve Kapsalis. Absent: Thalia Jameson.
>
> John opened the meeting by stating we needed to raise some funds to cover initial fees, such as filing fees and postage for the various applications needed for incorporation. Jim Heliotes suggested that once elections are held and a treasurer is selected, each board member should contribute $25.00. The motion was approved.
>
> Sam suggested that we have seven officers: a president, two vice presidents, a secretary, an assistant secretary, a treasurer, and an assistant treasurer. The motion was approved.
>
> The idea of having two co-chairmen rather than one principal officer was discussed and John was asked to look into it. Sam suggested that we look into designing a logo for GACS.
>
> It was decided that the selection of new members of the planning committee will be accepted into the group only after his/her nomination is approved by all members of the planning committee. This should occur before the new member attends their first meeting.

> The remainder of the meeting was devoted to reviewing the by-laws submitted by John and Elaine. Dr. Kioutas said his secretary would be willing to type the second draft of the by-laws, and that John should call him Monday afternoon to make arrangements. His wife will then review for legal wording. The next meeting will be on Tuesday, February 8, 1983, at 6:30 p.m. Meeting was adjourned at 10:15 p.m.

By the end of the meeting, there was agreement that our group should move forward with these conversations and plan to establish a not-for-profit organization that would address these needs. The initial name considered was Greek-American Social Services. After Pol mentioned that the acronym would be GASS, we chose Greek-American Community Services instead. The hyphen between Greek and American was discussed and it was decided to keep it since our goal was to link these two cultures. It was also decided that services, although Greek-focused, should be available to anyone who needed assistance. Dr. Kioutas spoke of it as a way of enhancing the image of the Greek community within the broader community in the same way Catholic Charities, Council for Jewish Elderly, or Lutheran Social Services of Illinois did.

It was agreed that our scope would not be limited to the Chicago region. We planned to expand our footprint into other areas of the country when the opportunity arose.

During subsequent meetings, discussions continued and initial participants invited others to join the conversation. The logistics of creating an organization became a primary topic. Although most of us were involved in various organizations in one fashion or another, few had an understanding of what needed to take place for us to become a full-fledged organization. A board of directors was created and officers were elected. Bylaws would need to be written and incorporation papers filed.

Article I of the bylaws defined the purpose of the organization as follows: "Greek-American Community Services has been organized to operate exclusively for charitable purposes, in providing services to the Greek Communities including but not limited to:

1. Community Services
2. Social Services
3. Housing
4. Cultural
5. Research regarding Greece and its heritage and other programs designed to meet the growing needs of the Greek American Community as decided by the Board of Directors from time to time."

In February, officers were elected and the bylaws were reviewed. I was elected president and Elaine became vice president; however, we worked in tandem as equals. Anna Manos agreed to serve as treasurer, and Helen Geocaris assumed the duties of secretary. John Geocaris offered us a desk in his ward office on Lawrence Avenue above the Family House restaurant, which was used as our initial address. Stationary was ordered from Liberty Press.

At the March 8 meeting, the Board voted to adopt the by-laws, and the Articles of Incorporation were signed for submission to the state of Illinois. A summer tutoring program was also discussed.

Once the documents were completed, they were submitted to the Illinois Secretary of State and the Cook County Recorder of Deeds. A complicated application to the Internal Revenue Service to request 501c (3) tax exemption would then need to be completed. A bank account was established at Commercial National Bank. The initial treasury was composed of $100 donations from each board member.

The minutes of the May 11, 1983, GACS Board meeting at the Elysion Restaurant, as submitted by Elaine:

> The meeting was called to order at 7:00 p.m. Members present included Pol Gavaris, Thalia Jameson, James Heliotes, John Psiharis, Elaine Thomopoulos, Toni Panos, and Anna Manos. Dr. Kioutas and Sam Kostogiannes were out of town. Pol Gavaris had to leave the meeting early. Pol reported that Steve Kapsalis is no longer interested in serving on the board. Elaine volunteered to contact Sam Kostogiannes to find out if he is still interested in serving on the board. It was noted that he has missed several meetings.
>
> John Psiharis moved that the Greek-American Community Services incorporate. Elaine Thomopoulos seconded the motion. The motion was passed unanimously.
>
> John Psiharis moved that Anna Manos be accepted as a new member of the board. Thalia seconded the motion. The motion passed unanimously.
>
> Elaine Thomopoulos moved that Terri Tzakis be accepted onto the Greek-American Community Services Committee if she is interested. She reported that Terri was recommended by Thalia Jameson and is active in *Soteria*. Thalia Jameson seconded the motion, and the motion was passed unanimously.

GACS Articles of Incorporation. September 2, 1983. John Psiharis collection.

Thalia Jameson nominated Stella Adinamis Cuthbert. John seconded the motion which was passed unanimously. Sonia Arvanites was nominated by Elaine Thomopoulos and seconded by John Psiharis. The motion passed unanimously.

Bill Zane was nominated by Elaine Thomopoulos, and seconded by James Heliotes. The motion passed unanimously.

Elaine Godellas was nominated by Elaine Thomopoulos, and seconded by John Psiharis. The motion was passed unanimously.

Lou Mitchell was nominated by Toni Panos, second by John Psiharis. The motion was passed unanimously.

The Greek-American Community Services unanimously agreed that we should express our thanks to Pol Gavaris for the use of the Elysion Restaurant banquet room. It was agreed that meetings be held on Tuesday, Wednesday, or Friday and that if by chance the restaurant was ever not available, our alternate site would be the 40th Ward Office at the N/W corner of Maplewood and Peterson.

Elaine Thomopoulos suggested that copies of the board members' addresses and minutes of our meetings be distributed to the committee members.

Elaine Thomopoulos moved that we develop a prospective member application form. John Psiharis seconded the motion, which was passed unanimously. John Psiharis, Elaine Thomopoulos, and Anna Manos volunteered to design this form. John Psiharis was selected to collect money for incorporation. The meeting was adjourned at 8:30 p.m.

The GACS Nursing Home Committee was established during a June 28, 1983 meeting held at the Elysion Restaurant. According to the meeting minutes, the members present were: Charles Mouratides, Jim Heliotes, Anna Manos, Elaine Thomopoulos, Toni Panos, and John Psiharis.

> Elaine presented a detailed report on her visit to the Hellenic Nursing Home in Boston three years ago.
>
> Charles Mouratides suggested being a liaison with existing nursing homes. Elaine pointed out the problem of control regarding administration. Jim Heliotes suggested contacting hospitals regarding the nursing home idea to rent facilities in hospitals. Elaine pointed out her contact about four years ago with Swedish Covenant Hospital and how expensive it is since Medicaid only pays part of the expenses. Elaine suggested the St. Peter and Paul Northside group and the Japanese American Service Committee who have already explored the idea.

Possible hospitals to contact include Swedish Covenant, Ravenswood, Northwest, Thorek, Bethany, Edgewater, and Forkosh. Charles suggested exploring if they can offer "free care."

Elaine Thomopoulos, John Psiharis, and Charles Mouratides will be on the Nursing Home Committee. John will ask Dr. Kioutas if he is interested in being on the committee and serving as chairman. The consensus was that we explore the nursing home as a goal.

Other suggestions were: Preventive health programs as a possibility. John said that the Illinois Consultation of Ethnicity in Education offers consultation on how to set up speaking engagements and media coverage. Anna Manos volunteered to help with the tax-exempt forms.

The notice for the August 23 meeting, handwritten by Elaine, included the following: "John Yonan, Executive Director of the Assyrian Universal Alliance Foundation will speak about the proposed purchase of a nursing home by the Assyrian Foundation including how this is financed. He will also discuss the possibility of there being a Greek wing in this nursing home."

GACS was officially incorporated as a not-for-profit corporation within the State of Illinois on September 2, 1983. Once that was granted, we were able to apply for a 501(c)3 tax exemption. The IRS granted the final determination that GACS was exempt in January 1986.

A meeting notice that I sent for the October 11, 1983 board meeting stated "Our guest speaker will be Mr. William Smith, Jr., attorney at law, who is considered to be one of the top nursing home lawyers in the state. Mr. Smith serves as legal counsel to the Illinois Association of Homes for the Aged, the Evangelical Retirement Homes of Greater Chicago, and the Life Care Services of Des Moines, Iowa. He will discuss the legal and financial aspects of obtaining financing and running a nursing home. The agenda will include the following: Approval of minutes from the last meeting; guest speaker – Mr. William Smith, Jr; an update on articles of incorporation; discussion on touring nursing homes; discussion on tax-exemption papers; discussion on future plans; old business; new business. Dr. Kioutas joins Elaine and me in urging all Board members to attend this very important meeting. The input and presence of every board member is imperative to the success of GACS. It's time to move towards making our dream of a united Greek community a reality."

Harry Milakis, an experienced fundraiser with the City of Hope, helped GACS to develop a fundraising plan and joined the nursing home committee to lend his expertise to that project as well. During an early meeting, he helped synthesize our lofty vision into what became the GACS motto, "Working to Preserve our Heritage." An early Christmas fundraising appeal letter that Harry crafted included a bookmark emblazoned with the GACS name and motto bordered by the Greek key. Unfortunately, Harry passed away from cancer too soon, but his motto lived on throughout the years of GACS.

In the coming months, we continued the process of establishing the organization and began to look at ways we could put our mission into practice. In the coming years, these initial efforts would lead to groundbreaking achievements in the Greek American community.

Despite lackluster support from some in the community's "leadership," which made it more difficult to raise funds or move the organization's vision forward, Greek-American Community Services persevered and blossomed into a respected and successful organization that launched pioneering social services, innovative cultural programs and laid the groundwork for establishing the first Greek American nursing home in the Midwest and the second in the nation.

This is the story of how a determined group of individuals from different walks of life came together to establish GACS and in turn, enrich the lives of thousands within the *omogenia*. GACS, honoring the ancient Greek axiom of leaving the community better and stronger than we found it, set the bar. Now it is up to future generations to preserve, nurture, and build upon this legacy of accomplishment.

Throughout the two-plus decades that are the focus of this book, the story of GACS provides a backdrop of Chicago's Greek community during a time of assimilation, ethnic pride, and increased cultural awareness. This is a testament to all who played a part in Greek-American Community Services and the Greek-American Nursing Home Committee through their generous donations of time, talent, and treasure, and in many other ways, that helped transform Chicago's Greek American community in the later years of the 20th century.

Part 2
Greek-American Community Services

Serving the *Omogenia*

St. Demetrios Young at Heart Senior Citizen's Group meeting. In center are (L-R): Catherine Burbules (vice president), John Psiharis, Alderman Patrick O'Connor, Barbara Psilakas (president), and Kathy Byrne, following a GACS sponsored presentation during a club meeting. February 1987. John Psiharis collection.

Early on, GACS organized monthly community education lectures focused on health topics, screenings, benefits, and legal matters, in cooperation with the St. Demetrios Church Young at Heart Group. This senior citizens club met twice weekly (Tuesdays and Thursdays) in the church's Panousis Room to socialize, play bingo and cards, and share coffee and desserts. About 80 seniors attended the meetings.

The lectures were presented in the Greek language by doctors, pharmacists, lawyers, and other professionals. Programs included screenings and lectures on topics such as diabetes, cholesterol, and the importance of a will. A few of the speakers were: Fran Mitilianos from the local Social Security office, Helen Georges from the Illinois Department of Public Aid, Roxanne Xenakis from the Chicago Department on Aging Levy Senior Center; Jim Demos and Genia Saveas from the Chicago Department of Human Services; Dr. Peter Chiakulas and Dr. George Dalianis on podiatry and Dr. John Panton on cataracts and glaucoma. Mary Ann Conrick of the Chicago Hearing Society provided hearing screenings and a lecture entitled "I Can Hear, But I Can't Understand," and Dr. Demetrios Trakas spoke on "Stress and Aging: What You Should Know."

Other programs included: Nestor "Lefty" Chakonas, a Chicago Police Department commander, who provided safety tips and distributed safety alert bracelets to the seniors. Theo Theodoratos and Barbara Nicpan, director of the Levy Center, spoke on "City Services Available to Senior Citizens through the Chicago Department on Aging and Disability." Angelike Mountanis from the Hellenic Foundation annually spoke to the seniors about the Circuit Breaker Senior Tax Assistance program and assisted them in completing the application. Tom Chiampas, a community representative for the Chicago Transit Authority (CTA), came annually to help seniors obtain CTA senior citizens' reduced fare cards. John Geocaris, the 40th Ward Democratic Party committeeman, and Alderman Patrick J. O'Connor visited on occasion to discuss matters of concern with the seniors. Kathy Byrne, daughter of former Chicago mayor Jane Byrne, visited on a campaign stop during her mother's campaign for re-election. Dr. Kioutas was a frequent visitor speaking on various health matters and providing updates to the seniors on the progress of the nursing home project. One example was a lecture he gave on hypertension followed by blood pressure screening from Vital Measurements Home Health Care. Another program was a brown bag lecture on pharmaceuticals by pharmacist George Akrivos. Participants were asked to bring any medications and supplements they were taking in a brown bag so that he could advise them about any possible side effects or concerns. In December 1986, GACS hosted glaucoma and cataract screening by doctors John and Peter Panton.

During this time, GACS co-sponsored a literacy program for senior citizens at St. Demetrios Church. The ESL program was operated by the AUAF and funded through a grant from the state of Illinois that Elaine had written for them. The Literacy Volunteers of Chicago was also a co-sponsor. The classes preceded the twice-per-week Young at Heart senior citizen's group meeting. An undated draft document, handwritten by Elaine, reported that 15 Greek elderly registered to take part in the classes. Some were in the country for over 40 years; others had just recently arrived. Participants were in their 60s, 70s, and 80s. Volunteer tutors taught in both one-to-one and small-group settings. Included in the report were quotes from two of the senior participants: "When asked why she wanted to learn to read and write English, an 84-year-old woman replied, 'So I can respond to my granddaughter's letters. and can write more than what I do now, 'I love you.' Another explained, 'When I was a new bride of 24 years of age, my husband would not let me attend school. Now, again I have an opportunity to learn.'"

During the holidays the Pan Laconian Federation supported our efforts to provide Thanksgiving and Christmas food boxes that were delivered by GACS volunteers to needy families. Alice Buzanis organized a food drive out of her mother's store. Her mother Kiki owned Chic Alterations and Designs, a small dressmaking store at 4910 North Lincoln Avenue which served as both the collection point and staging area for the drive. The food was put into boxes and delivered by volunteers to needy families that were known to GACS. About 25 households annually received holiday meals.

I recall delivering a few of these boxes in my car and have a vivid memory of carrying food to an attic unit above the third floor of a three-flat to an elderly lady near Argyle and Rockwell. When she opened the door I noticed that her apartment was empty and dark except for a folding chair and table and burning candles under an icon of the Virgin Mary. A rollaway bed was in the corner. A Greek radio program played in the background. She was advanced in years but was very proud of her home. She was close to 90, had poor eyesight, and wore thick-lensed glasses. She offered to make me coffee which I respectfully declined because I had other deliveries to make. It seemed as though she never had visitors and didn't want me to leave. The neighbors below were her only contacts. They checked in on her and did grocery shopping for her when they could. I'll never forget her tears of joy and thanks for the food, and more importantly, the visit.

On May 17-18, 1985, Elaine was invited to be a discussant for a paper entitled "The Significance of Language and Cultural Barriers for the Euro-American Elderly," at the National Conference on Euro-American Elderly held at The Catholic University of America in Washington, D.C. It was sponsored by the U.S. Department of Health and Human Services Office of Human Development Services – Administration on Aging. Elaine recalls, "I took both Diana and Chris to the conference, although I had a babysitter when I was a respondent to the presentation. What a fun time.

Diana really helped in taking care of her baby brother and navigating the subway system. During the dinner, Chris crawled under the table. They were very accepting of the children."

GACS launched a friendly visiting program to visit isolated elderly living in nursing homes throughout the area. Fran Argiris, R.N., served as supervisor of the program on a volunteer basis. Since there was no long-term care facility that catered to the Greek Community, these elders were often socially and culturally isolated from their fellow residents. Many did not speak the language and had difficulty communicating even the most basic of information or needs to nursing home staff. The food was not what they were accustomed to. Although scattered throughout the city, several nursing homes had larger populations of Greeks including Continental Care, Regency Nursing Home, Glen Crest, Buckingham Pavilion, Norridge Nursing Home, Warren Barr Pavilion, and a few others. Program volunteers made regular visits to these north-side nursing homes to bring some goodwill and cheer to the lives of these elders. When possible, volunteers brought the residents items of interest such as Greek language newspapers and magazines, crocheted items, or a Greek delicacy. Elaine remembers, "The Hellenic Foundation had previously had such a program but because of the federally funded CETA program being discontinued, they lost the workers that had staffed that program and no longer offered it."

A volunteer timesheet circa 1986 or 1987 listed the following friendly visiting volunteers: Tom Alex, Fran Argiris, RN (program supervisor), Olga Bancroft, Spyridon Dimas, Nicholas Festos, Helen Georges, George Gianis, George Gianis, Marion Kappas, Alexander Kouvalis, Jane Lamont, Anna Manos, Evangeline Mistaras, Athanasia Papadopoulos, Sophia Pappageorge, Barbara Psilakas, and Ernest Stavropoulos.

Other volunteers and their roles as described on the timesheet included: Francine Bleavings (typing), Tessie Cantos (clerical, typing, calling; works from home), Steve Frangos (consultant in humanities grant writing, program development; cultural), Ethel Kotsovos (social worker, drives, consulting to friendly visiting program), Harry Milakis (fundraising consultant), John Psiharis (executive director, founder, immediate past president), and Elaine Thomopoulos (administrator, founder, immediate past vice president).

Minutes from the April 7, 1986, GACS board of directors meeting, taken by Secretary Helen Geocaris, provide a sense of what was happening at the time and explain the leadership changes that occurred:

> The meeting was called to order by John Psiharis, President at 6:35 pm at the Elysion Restaurant, 2800 W. Foster Avenue.

In attendance were: John Psiharis, Anna Manos, Helen Geocaris, Helen Georges, Evangeline Mistaras, Jean Kaporis, Christine Burbulis, Thalia Jameson, and Elaine Thomopoulos (late).

John Psiharis gave a brief report on the progress of the organization. His report is as follows:

Greek-American Community Services is finally tax-exempt under section 501 (c) (3) of the Internal Revenue Code.

Grant applications have been submitted to the following:

a) Illinois Humanities Council for $10,000 to organize a two-day conference entitled 'Strains on Ethnic Pride, Conflicts Between the New and Old Immigrants in the Greek and Assyrian Communities,' a joint venture with the Assyrian Universal Alliance Foundation. John reported that 34 high-caliber speakers will participate and an active planning committee developed the program. The committee included several humanists. Extensive media coverage is planned. He hoped that GACS could go ahead with this program even if funding is not approved by IHC. A decision will be made in May.

b) Chicago Department of Human Services through the Community Development Block Grant program, for $24,700 to initiate a youth tutoring program using high school tutors to help grade school children.

c) Illinois Department on Aging for $17,000 to write and publish a manual on model programs serving the ethnic elderly. The manual would focus on ten different ethnic communities. Social service organizations within these communities that agreed to write parts of the manual are Metropolitan Chicago Coalition on Aging, Assyrian Universal Alliance Foundation, Council for Jewish Elderly, Japanese American Service Committee, Lutheran Social Services of Illinois, Casa Central, Korean American Community Services, Lithuanian Human Services, and the Association of Indo-Chinese Refugees.

d) Progress is being made in preparing a $35-40,000 proposal for the Chicago Department on Aging and Disability for a Greek/Assyrian nutrition site.

e) A grant for $2,800 was received from the Chicago Department of Cultural Affairs to organize a fall film festival on the Greeks in America. DePaul University's Greek club and Andy Kopan are helping to organize the program.

John called upon Anna Manos to give the Treasurer's Report. As of April 7th, GACS has a balance of $573.00 in our checking account.

John reported that the new GACS Friendly Visitor Project is getting off the ground. Already one volunteer is visiting two clients twice a week. An orientation meeting for those interested in becoming friendly visitors will be held on Saturday, April 19th at 10:00 am at the Elysion.

A discussion arose as to the need for an office for GACS. Yet finances prohibit paying for rent at this point. Board members were asked to investigate free or low-cost facilities.

Christine Burbulis moved and Toni Panos seconded a motion for GACS to explore obtaining joint office space with the Greek-American Nursing Home Committee. This arrangement will benefit both organizations. Currently, the Committee is looking into the National Bank of Greece building. John Psiharis called for the question and the motion was unanimously approved.

John reported that in his position he has become overwhelmed filling the positions of both president and executive director. He called upon Helen Geocaris to read the letter of resignation he sent to her.

Toni Panos moved and Helen Georges seconded the nomination of John Psiharis to the position of executive director. John accepted the nomination. The nomination was unanimously approved.

John reported Elaine's desire to not succeed him as president. She intends to work with John in program development. Helen Geocaris or Anna Manos did not wish to ascend into the position, the system outlined in the GACS bylaws.

After considerable discussion, John called for nominations from the floor. Helen Georges moved and Helen Geocaris seconded the nomination of Evangeline Mistaras as president. Evangeline accepted the nomination. John called for the vote. Evangeline was elected unanimously. She was congratulated on her position as was John in his new position.

The meeting was adjourned by John Psiharis at 7:20 pm so that the Greek-American Nursing Home Committee could meet at 7:30 pm.

Yes, We CAN

The Community Advocacy Network (CAN), a program of Lutheran Social Services of Illinois (LSSI), was established in 1980 and initially funded by a three-year grant from the Retirement Research Foundation. Erica Karp was the director of the program during its first two years. Through several offices, CAN trained community volunteers to advocate on behalf of their elderly neighbors for benefits and services to which they were entitled. CAN volunteers also provided friendly visiting and telephone reassurance to the homebound elderly. A teen chore program, in collaboration with area high schools, linked teenagers who wanted to earn money with senior citizens who needed snow shoveling, grass cutting, leaf raking, etc. The motto of CAN was "Neighbors Helping Seniors." The program was based at LSSI's northwest side office at 4840 W. Byron Street and maintained an office in South Shore at the Bryn Mawr Community Church (Ollie Bridges, Coordinator),

CAN was in a time of uncertainty. After an impressive record of accomplishment, the three-year Retirement Research Foundation grant funding for this project had come to an end, and they chose not to continue funding the program beyond that period.

Elaine began as director of CAN on June 1, 1982. I followed later that year, first becoming coordinator of development and then coordinator of community services, mainly focused on CAN's offshoot program, the Assyrian Project for the Elderly (APFE). The APFE was a joint program operated by the Assyrian Universal Alliance Foundation (AUAF) and LSSI, which served as the fiscal agent for the program. At first, the program was based at the LSSI/CAN Byron Street office but eventually moved to the AUAF office. I remember that most Assyrians spoke minimal English, and beyond a couple of words that I was taught, I did not speak Assyrian; but in some cases, I could communicate with APFE clients in Greek. Many Assyrians came to the U.S. through Greece. It could take months or even years to be processed to enter the U.S., and many learned some Greek in the interim.

CAN held an emergency staff meeting on April 21, 1983, at its office in LSSI, 4840 W. Byron St., Chicago, IL. In attendance were: Elaine Thomopoulos, Ann Parks, Dolores Hartowitcz, Ollie Bridges, Erica Karp, John Psiharis, and Nancy Sakurai. From the meeting minutes: "Elaine reported that the Retirement Research Foundation grant request was denied. All staff was to be laid off on April 30. Grants pending are $102,250. If any come through, some or all of the staff may be called back. The group decided to continue CAN on a volunteer basis and set up an office schedule. Ollie agreed to continue the south side office. A meeting of the volunteers was planned to update them. It was hoped an upcoming Bike-a-Thon would raise $2,000. A bazaar was planned at our south side location in June. Food and bake sales were the focus of the fundraiser."

In 1984, the APFE project was funded through a City of Chicago Department on Aging and Disability Ethnic Access grant. Elaine remembers, "When Chris was a baby, I wrote the grant for the DAD Ethnic Access program. I remember sitting on the lawn in front of LSSI with him, working on the grant, because they no longer wanted me to bring him into the building while I was working. He was born on Dec. 30, 1983."

Elaine continues, "After the Ethnic Access grant came through, CAN staff, which included Elaine Thomopoulos, Malcolm Karam, John Psiharis, and Dyana Aziz, were paid through LSSI. They were the lead agency and received the funds from the Department of Aging and Disability. We hired Malcolm for that program. After its completion, is when CAN merged with GACS. By the time we had the 'Strains on Ethnic Pride' conference in 1987, we had merged."

When city funding ended in June 1985, the AUAF continued the program under their auspices. Through a major donation from board president Helen Schwarten and her brother John Nimrod, vice president, the AUAF purchased the building at 7055 N. Clark Street which housed their office.

Once the grant concluded, LSSI was reluctant to keep CAN in operation even if other funding was obtained. Since CAN had active volunteers that were serving clients, Elaine and I discussed the idea of merging CAN into GACS. Given the circumstances, this would be a "win-win" situation. CAN would continue to function under a different umbrella organization and GACS would enhance its service offerings. CAN provided similar services to those offered by the GACS Community Services Program such as friendly visiting, telephone reassurance, and nursing home visits. The GACS board agreed, and we moved forward with the process. CAN would be known as an agency of GACS with an advisory board of CAN volunteers and supporters, to guide the program and fundraise to cover its expenses.

LSSI reluctantly agreed to allow the program to operate on a cash-and-carry basis for a few months until the transition to GACS could be completed. An advisory board was created to help guide this process. In addition to Elaine and myself, the board included: Robert Ahrens, former commissioner of the Chicago Department on Aging and Disabilities (DAD); Marguerite Euchler; Luke Fitzgerald, Northeast regional director of the DAD (Levy Center); Erica Karp, past director of CAN; Ethel Kotsovos; Stephanie Kryzminski; Bill LaMagdeleine, Northwest regional information and referral coordinator for the DAD; Frank Manago; Judith Matthews, Chicago coordinator for Project AYUDA of the National Association for Hispanic Elderly; Amydelle Shah, R.N.; Mary Trankina; and Rose Vuco, R.N., owner/president Vital Measurements Home Health Care.

CAN Board members assemble to hear a report by Director of Development John Psiharis (left) at new headquarters.

CAN Has A New Home and Name

The Community Advocacy Network, CAN, has a new name and a new home. Reorganized, the agency will continue to develop volunteers to serve older and disabled people at its new office, 3919 Monticello St.

The original CAN program was organized in 1980 in order to develop volunteers to serve the community's elderly population. The experience resulted in the agency, which developed a model program for volunteers and published a manual entitled "Organizing a Volunteer Program Serving the Elderly," was initially funded by a major foundation.

It continued operating after the grant expired in 1983. By expanding the number of volunteers and the hours served and fundraising CAN survived. Director of Development, John Psiharis reports an open house is scheduled soon.

Anyone interested in becoming a volunteer for this worthwhile organization may call 539-2323, or stop in at the office between 9:00 AM and 2:00 PM, Monday through Thursday.

Prime Times published by Blue Cross & Blue Shield of Illinois. May/June, 1987. Pictured (L-R): Frank Manago, John Psiharis, Stephanie Kryzminski, Gwen Sten, Marguerite Euchler, Amydelle Shah, Rose Vuco, Elaine Thomopoulos, and Christopher Thomopoulos. Elaine Thomopoulos collection.

It was decided that the name of the program be changed to Community Aging Network to better reflect what the program did - serve older adults. The advisory board would guide the program and raise funds. GACS programs for seniors (friendly visiting, community lectures, etc.) would operate under the CAN banner. CAN found office space at Parkview Lutheran Church, 3911 N. Monticello Ave. The church had recently closed its school and rented out two of its classrooms to CAN for $30 per month. Furniture and records from CAN's office on Byron Street were moved to the new office. The pastor of the church at the time, Phillip O. Stein, was

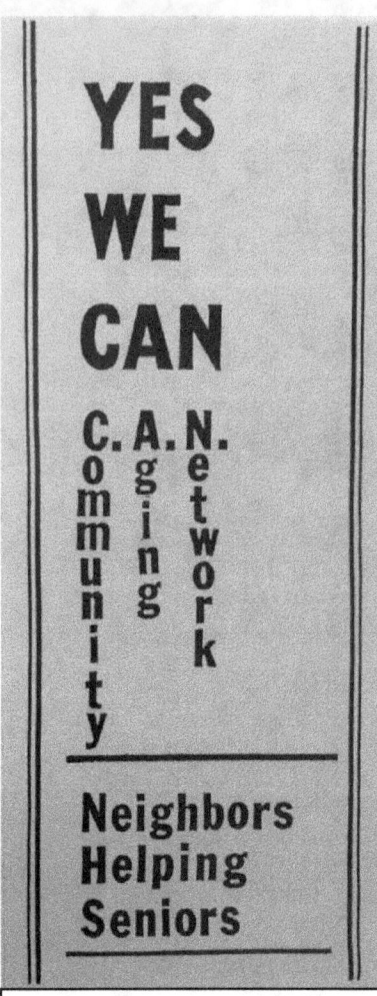

CAN brochure, circa 1987. Elaine Thomopoulos collection.

supportive of our work. The GACS mailing address remained at 4817 W. Montrose Ave., Chicago, IL 60641 c/o Vital Measurements Home Health Care.

The CAN south side office, renamed Bryn Mawr Senior Intercessors, continued to operate under GACS auspices at the Bryn Mawr Community Church at 71st Street and Jeffery in South Shore. Ollie Bridges coordinated services to CAN clients on a volunteer basis. At some point, Ollie's health began to fail, and the south side office closed.

A grant proposal, which did not get funded, dated January 9, 1987, and submitted to the Retirement Research Foundation seeking support for the telephone-friendly visiting program, summarized CAN activities up to that point. Neither Elaine nor I recall the idea of CAN incorporating on its own. It may have been discussed at the time of this grant but never came to fruition. CAN remained part of GACS throughout its existence. An excerpt from the grant:

The Community Aging Network (C.A.N.), located in Chicago, trains volunteers to assist senior populations within their neighborhoods. C.A.N. began operation six years ago and has had a long and successful tradition of serving as the link between senior citizens and available services. It was originally funded through a grant from the Retirement Research Foundation. Each year C.A.N. volunteers have assisted over 700 elderly individuals in obtaining benefits and direct services. During the past fiscal year, 50 volunteers provided 2,474 hours of direct service of one-to-one contact with clients, and an additional 2,913 hours of non-direct services. Fourteen workshops were also given to participants who acquired skills for use in their service to the elderly. C.A.N., through funding from Concordia Mutual Life, published a book, "Organizing a Volunteer Program Serving the Elderly". C.A.N. makes

CAN staff at 3911 N. Monticello Street office. Seated: Shirley Bernstein. Standing (L-R): Mary Trankina and Gwen Sten. Circa 1987. John Psiharis collection.

Chicagoland residents aware of the problems of the elderly and trains volunteers to enable their older neighbors to obtain services and benefits for which they are eligible.

To better secure funding from such sources as United Way, local government agencies, and private foundations, C.A.N. has decided to incorporate as a separate 501(c)3 organization. This will provide C.A.N. with opportunities that were previously unavailable in such a large and complex organization as Lutheran Social Services of Illinois.

To continue serving clients and raising funds in the transition period, the C.A.N. planning committee decided to affiliate with Greek-American Community Services on an interim basis. This affiliation will prevent service cutbacks. Greek-American Community Services is a not-for-profit tax-exempt organization. After meeting all requirements, C.A.N. will establish itself on its own.

On April 25, 1987, GACS hosted a volunteer appreciation luncheon at the Monticello Street office. Volunteers from GACS, CAN, and the Bryn Mawr Senior Intercessors were recognized. Elaine and I provided updates about GACS and CAN, and Ollie Bridges reported on the efforts of the Bryn Mawr Senior Intercessors. Certificates were presented to the volunteers, entertainment was provided by Francis J. Stack, and a door prize raffle was held.

Minutes of an August 10, 1987, GACS board meeting held at the Elysion Restaurant, and taken by Lena Xydes, as acting secretary, record the following in attendance: Evangeline Mistaras, Elaine Thomopoulos, John Psiharis, Lena Xydes, John Rassogianis, and Athanasia Papadopoulos:

> Administrator, Dr. Thomopoulos, reviewed the activities currently sponsored by CAN. A total of 900 elderly people have been serviced thus far; a total of 5,000 hours of service have been given by volunteers; a $1,000 gift in honor of Marguerite Euchler, one of our volunteers, was given by United Way. She was also honored at the Dinner Dance.
>
> The Fabric Arts program continues successfully as 35 members attend – including non-Greek participants. Instruction includes crochet, knitting, needlepoint, etc. at the Levy Center.
>
> The Community Education Program has been successful. Presentations by qualified guests at St. Demetrios were made in the following areas: Hearing loss, hypertension, Circuit Breaker information, Foot care, Food stamps acquisition, etc. Some programs were given bilingually to facilitate understanding for Greek participants.
>
> Executive Director, John Psiharis, continued with the following:
>
> 1. Interesting information relative to starting a primarily Greek Adult Day Care Center. Efforts were made to study existing successful centers e.g. "The Greater Opportunity" [sic] in Skokie. Board members are encouraged to participate on this task force or to nominate interested individuals.
> 2. Areas to study are the coalition of ethnic groups i.e., Assyrian, Korean, Chinese, etc. in order to jointly serve the elderly and receive grants to be shared in providing services and activities.
> 3. Summer jobs were provided for 2 youths (high school and Jr. College) who worked 25 hrs per week in an eight-week program. This was funded by the city of Chicago and was very helpful in providing clerical help to our office.
> 4. The Chicago Council of Fine Arts has granted us a $1,200 grant to organize and promote Greek Arts and Culture…music, and dance. (Sonia Arvanitis has been interested in working in this area). The program would perhaps sponsor weekly classes and feature Greek music from the 1880s to the 1980s.
> 5. The issue of providing temporary housing for Greek students of American institutions was raised by Mr.

Roussogianis[sic]. An effort should be made to provide a link between GACS and the Greek youth of our area.

6. President Evangeline Mistaras announced our participation in the Christ Lutheran Church Flea Market on Oct. 17. The St. Andrews Women's Philoptochos Society is purchasing two tables at $20.00 each. This will benefit both the Philoptochos and the GACS and CAN treasury.
7. Mr. Peter Maroutsos' financial statement for the month of July was presented. (He is a CPA and is recommended by CPAs for the Public Interest – a nonprofit agency). Expenditures for July were $987.99. Income for the month of July was $203.23. The fund balance end of the month was $2,742.12.
8. A social work student attending school at N.E. University will be conducting her internship at CAN from September through April.
9. It appears that the 1st Heritage Award [sic] was successful and (although planned over a brief period of time) left us a profit of $2,200. The future events will be even more successful if each person attempts to update and increase our mailing list.
10. 1988 Heritage Award Dinner plans are in the planning stage. Peter Lallas has expressed interest in being the Chairman once again with his wife as Co-Chairman. They were appointed to do so. The theme for 1988 could be honoring several people who contributed to our Greek Heritage in several fields, i.e. art, music, and athletics.
11. The possibility of offering an annual scholarship to a university student pursuing Greek studies was again mentioned. John, Evangeline, and Elaine will pursue this.
12. The use of the new Terra Museum on Michifan [sic] Ave. has been again suggested for a reception/tea/dinner etc. for a guest honoree. Lena Xydes again mentioned Leon Marinakos as a person to be recognized by our organization.
13. The present Board of Directors has to be reorganized and vacancies filled. There are four vacancies at present. Names suggested wrre [sic]:
    a. Andy Kopan
    b. Ethel Kotsovos
    c. Leon Marinakos
    d. Faye Pantezelos
    e. Dr. George Christakes
    f. Dr. Peter Chioros
    g. Peter Maroutsos
14. John Psiharis emphasized the need to organize our activities along two areas – Program Area and Resource Area for more effective participation.

15. Mr. Psiharis also suggested our participation in the Chicago Access Corporations' Cable program. The program provides a free 6-week training program for eight participants of our own, featuring areas of our interest and produced by these eight participants whom we must identify. There are presently twenty-four stations in their network.
16. It was agreed that our programs i.e. lecture/movie presentations, dancers, etc. be videotaped in the future do[sic] they become part of history and be shown in the GACS cable television program, in the proposed Greek Museum/Library.
17. Our Christmas appeal in 1986 was successful and should be repeated this year.
18. The joint Greek-Assyrian Conference on "Strains on Ethnic Pride" will be held at Loyola University (Lake Shore Campus). Volunteers are needed to work on the logistics of the event.

The next meeting was set for Tues. Sept. 15. Volunteers will meet at 6:30. Board members will meet at 7:30.

Meeting adjourned at 9:30 – Motion by J. Roussogianis [sic]. 2nd. L. Xydes.

In 1987, CAN became a host site for Project AYUDA, a program of the National Association for Hispanic Elderly. The program provided federally-funded Title V senior workers to nonprofit organizations. Program participants were over the age of 60 and had lower incomes. They worked 20 hours per week and were paid directly through the program. GACS retained this agreement, and we had three participant slots assigned to us. AYUDA workers during this period were: Elizabeth "Betty" McClelland (office secretary), Gwen Sten (office worker), Gladys Tichnell (office worker), Florence Kubacki (office worker), and Spyridon Dimas (friendly visitor/chore housekeeper). GACS remained a Project AYUDA host agency throughout much of its existence. AYUDA workers also served as activity aides in the adult day care center. They included Margaret Nikolopoulos, Carmen Vilato, and Rafael Gallardo.

Elaine remembers Betty McClelland: "I recall that as a secretary, even though she could barely make out what you said because of a hearing problem, she is the only secretary I had, and I had many, who never made a mistake and would correct my grammar or spelling mistakes. She was perfect, so much so that I need not have proofed any of the typing she did. She was worth much more than the modest salary she received through the government-sponsored program. Betty also had a hobby of collecting miniature shoes and made delightful public presentations to various audiences throughout the city. This was as a volunteer and not part of her work at GACS."

In 1987, CAN hosted Shirley Bernstein, a social work intern from Northeastern Illinois University who was focusing on gerontology. Under Elaine's supervision, Shirley provided one-to-one counseling and support to isolated and homebound seniors. One of Shirley's projects was to organize a public education program on Alzheimer's disease. The lecture was held at the university and featured the president of the Alzheimer's Association of Illinois as a guest speaker.

CAN fundraising during this time included an ongoing sustaining membership drive and a "Give Your Can to CAN" drive which collected and recycled aluminum pop cans. I remember Spiro Dimas sitting in the Monticello Street office crushing pop cans with his feet as he drank coffee and completed his paperwork. Volunteers and a few neighbors provided their empty cans to CAN.

Hike-Bike-a-thons were held for a couple of years along Chicago's lakefront. Participants walked or rode between Foster Avenue and Oak Street beaches. About 40 to 50 walkers participated. Angelo Karavites, a successful McDonald's franchisee with several locations, donated freshly squeezed orange juice and cold water from his restaurant on the corner of Foster and Sheridan. Elaine hosted several potluck house parties at her home in Oak Brook as another means of raising money. Guests would buy a ticket and bring food to share. We had some amazing food at these events!

At first, the advisory board continued CAN's annual rummage sale at Christ Lutheran Church near the busy Belmont and Central shopping district. It was well attended and financially successful. But the amount of effort needed to collect, set up, price, and dispose of everything afterward was consuming. Bernice Corbett chaired the rummage sale and spent hours coordinating pickup schedules and logistics.

At Betty McClelland's suggestion, the event became a flea market where we sold space and tables to vendors who had the responsibility of setting up and tearing down. We had tables with donated merchandise and plants that were donated by Nick Poulos, a cousin of Elaine's who grew them as a hobby in his greenhouse. We also sold hot dogs, beverages, and desserts. My Aunt Bessie (Choporis) baked and donated cakes that we served during the market. A door prize raffle was held. In all, these events proved to be well attended and successful, although one year we were rained out and the event did not do as well. The flea market fundraisers continued for a couple of years.

Bike-A-Thon
Hike-A-Thon

SATURDAY, JUNE 25th

STARTING TIME: BETWEEN 8:30 A.M. and 2:30 P.M.

STARTING POINT: Foster Avenue Beach

NO LIMIT TO THE MILES YOU CAN RIDE OR WALK!

FOR THE BENEFIT OF:

THE COMMUNITY AGING NETWORK AND
GREEK AMERICAN COMMUNITY SERVICES

CONTACT:

C.A.N./G.A.C.S.
3911 N. MONTICELLO
CHICAGO, IL 60618

539-2323

GETTING READY

Obtain pledges from people you know for specific amounts (e.g., 25¢ - 50¢ - $1) for every mile you ride or walk. There is no limit to how many miles you can walk/ride.
Fill out both G.A.C.S.'s copy and participant's copy.
Check your bicycle if you are riding - wear clothes and shoes that are comfortable.
Sign the consent and release form; parent or guardian must sign for those under age 18. No one can participate unless they have turned this in at the beginning of the event.

DAY OF THE EVENT

The event begins near the Foster Avenue Beach right off Foster Avenue and proceed South to Ohio Street Beach.
You must bring the pledge card to have it validated.
You MUST stop at any checkpoints during your ride/walk to have your sponsor sheet validated. You are allowed to ride as many times as you can between Foster and Ohio. The distance between the two beaches round-trip is approximately 20 miles.
Begin anytime between 8:30 a.m. and 2:30 p.m.
Bring a snack. Drinks will be available at some checkpoints.
Use receptacles for garbage.
Do not speed. Rest if you are tired. This is not a race.
Riders and pedestrians must follow all traffic rules.

AFTER THE EVENT

Go back to the people who pledged for you; show them your verified card; collect pledges.
Turn your money in to G.A.C.S. as soon as you have collected it. The address is 4817 W. Montrose, Chicago, IL 60641. If you have any questions, call 539-2323.

Checks can be made payable to either G.A.C.S. or C.A.N.-G.A.C.S.

All those who have turned in $20.00 or more in pledges will receive a certificate of appreciation in the mail.

T H A N K Y O U !!

Bike/Hike-a-thon pledge sheet. June 25, 1988. John Psiharis collection.

GACS was the first organization in the 42-year history of the United Way Heart of Gold Awards to have volunteers awarded this honor for two consecutive years. In May 1987, Marguerite Euchler won the award which was presented at the Chicago Marriott near Water Tower Place. Elaine and I accompanied Marguerite to the breakfast.

In August 1987, the GACS newsletter reported:

Marguerite was nominated by GACS for her dedication and devotion to helping make the lives of countless elderly a little bit brighter. Marguerite, 77, volunteers weekly to help staff the office. She provides information, referral, advocacy, and other types of assistance to CAN clients, including instructing the elderly in our literacy program. She is actively involved in recruiting and training new volunteers, publicity, and fundraising efforts.

Marguerite, who has actively volunteered for numerous organizations over the past forty years, suffers from deteriorating vision. Rather than feel sorry for herself, she has chosen to re-direct her energies towards helping those less fortunate than herself. Today, in addition to CAN, Marguerite volunteers for Martha Washington Hospital and a local food pantry.

In July, Marguerite was featured in an interview on WBBM-AM radio, where in part, she discussed her involvement with CAN/GACS.

In 1988, Astrid Lewis was honored at the 42nd Annual Volunteer Recognition Event, held on April 22 at the Hyatt Regency Hotel. Sponsored by The Volunteer Center, United Way/Crusade of Mercy, and the Maurice L. and Hulda B. Rothschild Foundation. The entry about Astrid in the program booklet said this:

Welcome to
The 42nd Annual
Volunteer Recognition Event
featuring

Heart of Gold
and
Voluntary Action
Awards

Friday, April 22, 1988
Hyatt Regency Hotel
151 East Wacker Drive
Chicago, Illinois

Sponsored by
The Volunteer Center
United Way/Crusade of Mercy
and
The Maurice L. and Hulda B. Rothschild Foundation

"Heart of Gold Awards" breakfast program. April 22, 1988. Elaine Thomopoulos collection.

> Astrid Lewis has been a volunteer at Greek-American Community Services for five years. Her job entails telephone visiting with homebound elderly clients regularly, providing support and good cheer to them. Calls are made anywhere from two to seven days a week and each call lasts at least an hour on average. Although Astrid is homebound due to multiple illnesses, she logs 45 hours per month visiting with clients over the telephone. For most of her clients, she is their only link to the outside world, for all of them, she is a friend.
>
> Astrid initially began as a volunteer friendly-visitor at Greek-American Community Services. She visited isolated shut-ins in nursing homes or their own homes. As time progressed, her health problems prohibited her from going out to visit clients, however, she wanted to remain busy and productive. Through her, Greek-American Community Services developed the concept of friendly visiting over the telephone. Her dedication and spirit inspire other Community Aging Network volunteers to perform above and beyond the call of duty. Over five years she has volunteered more than 2,750 hours.

In May 1989, GACS received a Venture Grant of $18,800 from United Way of Chicago. The two-year grant funded a part-time program director position for the Community Aging Network. As envisioned, the staff person would also help GACS clients in need. Ethel Kotsovos, after leaving her position as a social worker at the Hellenic Foundation, assumed this role and would remain with GACS for the next decade. Through this grant, 14 volunteers were recruited and hundreds of clients were served.

An article in the July 23, 1989 issue of the *Greek Press* announced the grant:

> Greek-American Community Services (G.A.C.S.) announced the receipt of funding through the United Way of Chicago Venture Grant Program.
>
> The grant will be used to strengthen and enhance the many services G.A.C.S. offers to Chicago's elderly through its agency and the Community Aging Network.
>
> Joining the staff to coordinate direct services to older adults is Ethel Kotsovos. Mrs. Kotsovos is a professionally trained social worker with many years of service to those in need. Most recently, she was employed by the North Shore Senior Center Adult Day Care for Alzheimer's Patients Program in Winnetka. Before that, she served as a social worker for the Hellenic

Accepting the United Way of Chicago Venture Grant. (L-R): John Psiharis, Ethel Kotsovos, Eugene Tracey, president of People's Gas and chairman of United Way of Chicago, and John Rassogianis. May 1989. John Psiharis collection.

Foundation. Mrs. Kotsovos was also a social worker for various suburban school districts for 14 years. She has been active in G.A.C.S. and its sister organization, the Greek-American Nursing Home Committee, as well as in other community organizations.

Services offered through C.A.N. include information and referral, advocacy, telephone visiting, home help, friendly visiting, transportation/escort, translation, a teen-chore program, and a literacy project. Services are available free of charge to anyone over age 60 regardless of their ethnic or religious background.

G.A.C.S., organized in 1982, provides a variety of community services, cultural programs, and research activities to benefit the community. Last year, over 2,000 people participated in G.A.C.S. activities.

For information, or to volunteer, please call Mrs. Kotsovos at (312) 539-2323.

Around this time, Elaine and I received an unexpected invitation from Dr. John Nicholson to visit him in his Hyde Park high-rise condominium on East End Avenue. Dr. Nicholson was a prominent Eye, Ear, Nose, and Throat (ENT) doctor who through shrewd investments, including stock in McDonald's, IBM, Xerox, and other major companies during their early days, had become wealthy. In retirement, he became a philanthropist and pledged support for several causes close to his heart. The meeting over coffee took place at his dining room table with stunning views of downtown and Lake Michigan as the backdrop. During the meeting, he pledged support for GACS and the GANHC.

Dr. Nicholson had arranged substantial bequests to Northwestern University, the University of Chicago, and DePaul University to establish scholarships supporting Greek American students pursuing degrees in medicine and engineering. He also provided large donations to the Hellenic Museum and Cultural Center and the Greek-American Nursing Home Committee. The Nicholson bequest to GACS was announced in the July 9, 1989 edition of the *Greek Press*:

> Greek-American Community Services recently received a $10,000 bequest from philanthropist John Nicholson for the establishment of a student endowment fund. The purpose of this fund is to further the career goals of Greek American youths with the goal of encouraging youth to aspire to higher education and the professions.
>
> News of this magnificent gesture was announced in a joint statement by President Evangeline Mistaras and John Rassogianis, both educators and officers of G.A.C.S. The announcement was made during a board meeting held in the downtown Chicago office of educator and G.A.C.S. board member, Dr. Michael Bakalis.
>
> Tentative plans call for area Greek American students to participate during an annual Career Opportunity Day. Inspirational speakers from the business and professional world would present conferences and symposia geared to develop student career guidance goals. The importance of a college education would be stressed. Various members of the board expressed profound gratitude and enthusiasm for the Nicholson bequest.
>
> The G.A.C.S. Heritage Award is presented annually to outstanding community leaders whose exemplary achievements have made an impact on our Hellenic heritage.

Neither Elaine nor I recall details about what was done with the bequest, and we haven't come across anything in our research to shed light on this. I have a vague memory of a student-related event at DePaul University that Elaine Kollintzas helped arrange which may have been connected to this project. At one time, after his passing, we were asked to provide documentation of our use of the funds to a law firm that was handling his estate, so the program was carried out in some fashion.

Working to Preserve Our Heritage

In 1986, after three years in operation, it became apparent that Greek-American Community Services needed an executive director. The growth of the programs, along with the need to write grants, raise funds and promote the activities of the organization had increasingly demonstrated the need. In some cases, funders required an executive director. Elaine and I shared responsibilities for running the organization up to that point with Elaine focusing more on the cultural programs and I focused on the community programs. Both Elaine and I were interested in making this transition, and after discussion, we decided to continue to share the executive role. Elaine assumed the position of administrator, and I became executive director. Evangeline Mistaras was elected president to replace me, and Athanasia "Sandy" Papadopoulos became vice president replacing Elaine. Evangeline was the head reference librarian at Northeastern Illinois University and was active in the Hellenic Museum and Cultural Center, St. Andrew Greek Orthodox Church, and the Modern Greek Studies Association.

Elaine and I became aware of grant opportunities available through the Chicago Office of Fine Arts (COFA), now part of the Chicago Department of Cultural Affairs. One, the Neighborhood Arts Program (NAP), provided funding of up to $1,500 to artists who worked with underserved populations. The second, City Arts, provided grants to non-profit organizations in support of various arts, education, and enrichment activities, generally up to $3,000.

For the Neighborhood Arts Program grant, Elaine and Steve prepared a proposal to preserve and teach the traditional needlework arts of Greece. Called *stavrovelonia,* this art form highlighted the intricately detailed needlework that created beautiful wall hangings, tablecloths, and similar items. These skills were often passed down through the generations by grandmothers to mothers who then taught their daughters the delicate stitches that were the basis of this art. Steve Frangos was instrumental in writing the proposal.

A team of three artists with decades of combined experience in this art form agreed to take part in the program. In addition to teaching, Tessie Cantos would serve as the coordinator of the program, manage the grant funds, and handle recordkeeping and paperwork. Penny Kalogiannis, a cross-stitch artist, was the lead instructor, and Tasia Economou acted as an assistant instructor. The targeted participants were senior citizens who were culturally underserved and in need of socialization.

The classes began in September 1986. They were held at the Levy Center, 2019 W. Lawrence Avenue, a senior citizens center operated by the Chicago Department on Aging. Thirty-eight seniors enrolled in the program. All materials and supplies were provided at no cost to the participants. After the classes, the artwork that was created by the participants was displayed in the Levy Center lobby for all visitors to see.

At about the same time, work began on a grant proposal for the City Arts program. GACS requested funding to host a series of films that focused on the Greek American experience. Evangeline, as a librarian, helped to select and locate the films. The program was a three-part film series entitled "The Greeks in America: A Celebration of Films." Before each screening, a buffet luncheon was served, enabling guests time to get acquainted with the filmmakers, speakers, and each other. After each show, an audience discussion and question and answer period with the filmmakers was held.

The program description as outlined in the City Arts grant proposal explained: "The film festival will focus on the struggle of the Hellenic people in assimilating into American society and at the same time preserving their heritage and identity. The difficulties and joys that are captured on film by Greek American filmmakers will serve as a starting point for discussion following the films. The filmmakers themselves will be invited to discuss these films immediately following the screening."

The first film, *America, America,* set the tone for the series. The award-winning film by famed director Elia Kazan had not been seen for quite some time. Since Kazan was unable to attend, Dr. Charles Moskos, a noted sociologist at Northwestern University and author of *The Greeks in America,* was the speaker.

The second of the three showings featured two films by Doreen Moses: *A Village in Baltimore: Images of Greek-American Women* (1981), and *One on Every Corner: Manhattan's Greek-owned Coffee Shops* (1986). Doreen was in attendance and participated in the discussions that followed the screenings. Father Chris Kerhulas of St. Basil Greek Orthodox Church provided commentary. Father Chris wrote film reviews for the *Greek Star* and *Orthodox Observer* newspapers.

"The Greeks in America: A Celebration of Films," program booklet cover. Artwork by Mark Quartullo. September, 1986. John Psiharis collection.

The final film shown in November was *Goodnight Socrates*. This award-winning documentary focused on the impending loss of much of Chicago's Greektown in light of the construction of the University of Illinois at Chicago campus. Thousands of Greeks who resided in this area, along with many Italians and other ethnicities, were forced to relocate when Mayor Richard J. Daley chose the area to house the new campus. The writer of the film, Maria Moraities, a professor in filmmaking at Northeastern Illinois University, spoke after the showing. Before each screening, the audience heard a brief presentation about GACS. With the support of Dr. Andrew Kopan, a professor of education at DePaul University, the Hellenic Society of DePaul University co-sponsored the film series and provided the venue for the event. Elaine Kollintzas, assistant director of alumni relations at DePaul University, was the liaison. About 100 people attended each screening, and a program booklet for the series was created. Advertising in the booklet helped to underwrite the costs of both the book and the series.

Elaine and I recall that at the Schmidt Center, where many of these events were held, some steps were not marked. When the lighting was turned down for the movies, there were always a couple of people who tripped or fell on the steps. We posted volunteers at each entry door to warn people as they entered.

By all measures, the film series proved to be a success and helped to establish that GACS had the capability and capacity to organize and promote events of this scale.

In 1987, GACS successfully applied for Neighborhood Arts Program (NAP) funding from the Chicago Office of Fine Arts to continue the Fabric Arts of Greece Project. We also submitted a request for City Arts funding to showcase and demonstrate *Karagiozis,* a form of Greek shadow puppetry theater, and provide other cultural enrichment opportunities for older adults. Demetra "Dee" Manzara, a master in this art form, agreed to lead a series of classes for senior citizens that were held during the St. Demetrios Young at Heart Senior Citizen's Group meeting.

One cultural enrichment activity was an appearance by the Korean Senior Players Group Farmers Dancing Band during a Young at Heart Group meeting. The band, sponsored by Korean American Senior Center, enthralled a packed room of seniors with their lively performance and colorful costumes.

The grant application provided this description: "The Korean Senior Player's Group, under the direction of Bangcho Eun, performs special Korean folk dances with Oriental instruments such as drums, gongs, and horns. More than 20 seniors, from ages 55 to 85, dance, accompanied by traditional music and dressed in traditional Korean costumes. They have previously performed at the Illinois State Fair, City of Chicago Department on Aging and Disability regional centers, the University of Chicago Instrumental Fair, and during Governor's Day at the State of Illinois Building Auditorium."

That same year, GACS received a Community Arts Assistance (CAAP) grant from the Chicago Department of Cultural Affairs. CAAP grants were intended to support capacity building, fundraising, and outreach activities that strengthen the capacity of an organization. The funding was to establish an Advisory Board for the GACS Cultural & Arts Program similar to the one that had been established for CAN.

The CAP Advisory Board was led by Sonia Arvanitis and Toni Panos as co-chairs. Members included: Alice Buzanis, Tessie Cantos, Steve Frangos, Polyzoes Gavaris, Helen Georges, Elaine Kollintzas, Antigone Lambros, Fotios Litsas, Very Rev. Nikitas Lulias, Renata Maresia, Alexander Makedon, Peter Maroutsos, Evangeline Mistaras, Georgia Mitchell, John Psiharis, John Rassogianis, and Elaine Thomopoulos. The board met quarterly to review and monitor GACS cultural programs, recommend future programming, and consider grant opportunities. Once he became CAP director in 1990, John worked closely with the committee to plan and implement our cultural programs.

GACS Cultural & Arts Program Advisory Board meeting in the adult day care center at Alvernia Place. Pictured (L-R): Demetra Makris, Diana Harris, John Psiharis, unknown, Dr. Fotios Litsas. Circa 1991. John Psiharis collection.

Another CAAP grant provided funding for the production of a video for the organization. A professional video producer was hired to create the video. Tessie Cantos, Penny Kalogiannis, Tasia Economou, and several participants spoke about the Fabric Arts Program filmed during a class session. The backdrop for the filming of John Konstas, a GACS volunteer and client who spoke about the help he received from the organization, was a flea market for the benefit of CAN. The video was shown on Greek media and public access television and used to promote the organization at GACS and community events.

GACS, through the Cultural and Arts Program, became a regular co-sponsor and beneficiary of a series of Greek Nights that were organized through the years by Melissa Brown and David Aaron Condos and held at several popular Chicago nightclubs. First launched at the trendy Limelight, the nights would move to Park West, Cairo, and Petros Dianna's. These events provided opportunities for Greek Americans to socialize and featured food, fashion shows, art exhibits by Greek American artists, and performances by Greek American musicians.

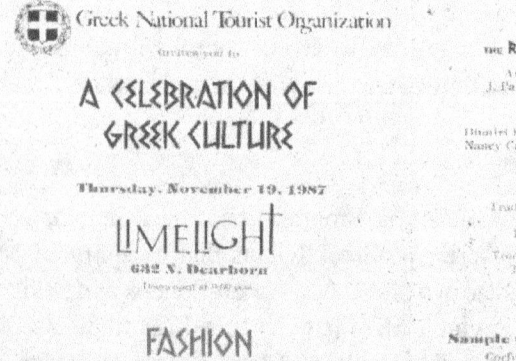

Top: Invitation card for "A Celebration of Greek Culture" event at the Limelight. December 2, 1988. David Aaron Harbin collection. **Bottom**: Invitation card for "A Celebration of Greek Culture" event at the Limelight on November 19. 1987. David Aaron Harbin collection.

GACS received a portion of the cover charge and sold tickets to the door prize raffle that included donated prizes from event sponsors. In addition to raising money, these events provided an avenue for GACS to reach out to younger members of the Greek community.

Assessing the Needs of Our Elders

In 1986, the Chicago Department on Aging and Disabilities (DAD) responded to the concerns of organizations advocating for funding in support of programs for the ethnic elderly. We were asking that a portion of the Department's grant funds be allocated to support and assist ethnic-based organizations serving the elderly who faced language and cultural barriers to accessing essential services.

At the time, mainstream social service agencies lacked staff that could speak the many languages of those seeking assistance. They lacked the cultural understanding and pedigree that was necessary to gain the trust of non-English speaking elderly. These language and cultural barriers often prevented or deterred seniors from receiving the help that they needed.

Up to that point, DAD administered a small program that provided grants to several ethnic providers through its Ethnic Access Grant, including the Assyrian Project for the Elderly. Beyond that, there were virtually no grants focused on ethnic organizations or communities at the local, state, or national levels. Although the Ethnic Access Grant program helped a few communities (including the Assyrian Project for the Elderly), funding was short-term and was a drop in the bucket compared to the myriad of needs of Chicago's many unique ethnic communities.

These concerns found a receptive ear with the newly appointed commissioner of DAD, Robert J. Ahrens. After having helped to establish and run the Commission for Senior Citizens under Mayor Richard J. Daley in 1956, Ahrens returned to oversee the newly created Mayor's Office for Senior Citizens and Handicapped. The office was granted cabinet-level status and renamed the Chicago Department on Aging and Disabilities by Chicago Mayor Harold Washington.

In 1987, DAD launched the city's first comprehensive assessment on the needs of ethnic elderly and tasked Rosemary Gemperle, who worked in their research and planning division, to lead the effort. The Retirement Research Foundation and the Chicago Community Trust provided funding for the project. Twelve ethnic organizations that spoke 10 different languages were selected to take part in the study.

Pictured (L-R): Seated: Carole Bilina (Polish Welfare Association), Sue Kang (Korean American Community Services), San O (Southeast Asia Center), unknown, Qua Tron (Vietnamese American Association of Illinois), Awilda Gonzalez (ASI), Danguale Valentinas (Lithuanian Human Services Council of the U.S.A). Second row: Rosemary Gemperle (Chicago Department on Aging), Peter Laylo (Asian Human Services), Rev.Masaru Nambu (Japanese American Service Committee), Robert Ahrens (commissioner, Chicago Department on Aging), John Psiharis (Greek-American Community Services), Judith Matthews (National Association for Hispanic Elderly), Elaine Thomopoulos (Greek-American Community Services). Rebecca Cruz (ASI), Elena Yiu (Asian and Pacific Islands Research Center), and Rene Lumpkin (deputy commissioner, Chicago Department on Aging) during the unveiling of the Ethnic Elderly Needs Assessment Study at the Chicago Department on Aging office, 510 N. Peshtigo Court. Date unknown. John Psiharis collection.

They were: American Spanish Institute (ASI) (Rebecca Cruz and Awilda Gonzalez); Asian Human Services (Peter Laylo); Cambodian Association of Illinois (Kompha Seth); Chinese American Service League (Bernarda Wong); Greek-American Community Services (John Psiharis and Elaine Thomopoulos); Japanese American Service Committee (Rev. Masaru Nambu); Korean American Community Services (Sue Kang); Lithuanian Human Services Council of the U.S.A (Danguale Valentinas); National Association of Hispanic Elderly (Judith Matthews); Polish Welfare Association (now known as Polish American Association), (Carol Bilina and Bruce Dean); Southeast Asia Center (Peter Porr and San O); and Ukrainian Social Services Bureau.

The University of Illinois Center for Asian and Pacific Studies received funding from the city to prepare the survey instrument. Each organization was to contact 150 older adults and interview caregivers and community stakeholders. Organizations received $8.50 for each completed application

The cover of the Greek language version of the Ethnic Elderly Needs Assessment, circa 1987. Elaine Thomopoulos collection.

plus money for the translation of the survey instrument and related expenses.

The survey instrument was translated into Greek and then back-translated into English by two different people. Fotios Litsas and Nick Ellis did the translations. Elaine remembers that we encountered a problem when some did not understand the translation because of its academic wording. Rewording was needed to ensure the instrument was understood by the seniors being interviewed. Elaine recalls, "Those being interviewed did not understand some of the language being used, words that would have been understood by someone who had graduated high school."

In total, more than 1,500 interviews with senior citizens that hailed from 12 countries and spoke 10 languages were conducted. Ethel Kotsovos coordinated GACS's participation, trained volunteer interviewers, identified seniors, and scheduled interviews.

The director of each organization, a representative of the University of Illinois, and Rosemary were part of the project's steering committee. We met regularly to craft the survey instrument and protocols, determine the questions to be asked, and review the progress of the study. This was a unique collaboration, one that had not been seen before; ethnic leaders, the city, and private foundations came together to assess and document the needs of the limited and non-English speaking elderly.

The results of the study shed light on needs within individual ethnic communities as well as in the city as a whole. For the most part, the results documented what the participating organizations already knew; ethnic elderly had difficulty accessing services and benefits due to language and cultural barriers. Many ethnic elderly were isolated from mainstream society and difficult to reach. Ethnic organizations most able to help these seniors were struggling to get by due to funding constraints and the lack of grant opportunities from government agencies and mainstream funders. Homemaker services, home-delivered meals, and adult day care programs were three services that were underutilized by ethnic elderly.

Additionally, it was found that the majority of case managers who assessed the needs of their clients and linked them to these services often did not speak the language of these seniors. Sometimes ethnic organizations provided translators, however, there was no reimbursement for staff time in such cases. Not all organizations had the wherewithal to cover these costs, especially since the case management units were receiving payments for their role and ethnic agencies were not. The study highlighted the sense of isolation that many older adults experienced as well as their tendency to remain insular within their communities.

Although neither Elaine nor I could locate the full report, which was about 200 pages in length, a fax sent to Elaine from GACS on November 9, 1992, included results for some of the health questions in the survey. This data revealed: More females than males were interviewed. More than 60 percent of those surveyed had attended elementary school, 20 percent had attended high school, and 10 percent attended college. A majority of those surveyed lived with others, primarily their spouse, and to a lesser degree, their children or other family members. More than 80 percent rated their English well and under five percent spoke little to no English. The most frequent health symptoms identified by the respondents (in descending order) were: Light-headedness/dizziness, tiredness, nervousness/tenseness, periods of feeling blue, headaches, loss of strength in arms/legs, unsteadiness on feet, difficulty sleeping, shortness of breath, chest pain/discomfort, leg cramps, coughing a lot, forgetfulness, swelling feet/ankles, bladder control, indigestion or gas, constipation, trouble passing urine, poor appetite, and bleeding (not a cut).

The executive summary of the study by researchers from the University of Illinois at Chicago Asian American Mental Health Research Pacific/Asian Research Center highlighted some additional findings:

Ethnic Groups in the Study

Persons 50 years or older who belonged to one of the following ethnic groups were identified for the survey: Greek, Lithuanian, Polish, Mexican, Puerto Rican, Chinese, Filipino, Korean, Cambodian, Vietnamese, and Ethnic Chinese from Indo-China. The inclusion of these specific ethnic groups was a function of their problematic English language facility, population size, and willingness of an ethnic community agency to commit resources to assist in the study.

Characteristics of Groups

Overall, there are wide variations among the groups as to when and why their elderly came to the United States. Some groups had large percentages of elderly who came predominantly as young adults, of their own volition, in order to seek new opportunities. Others came as refugees, literally driven out of their homeland. Some of the respondents are long-time residents of Chicago, others recent arrivals. Some had done much preparatory work before emigrating, others virtually none. These differences appear to be reliably related to need patterns.

With regard to the important resource of education, a high percentage of Filipinos and Lithuanians have had a college education, while the Ethnic Chinese and Cambodians had virtually no one with a similar level of education. Wide differences exist between groups in the percentage of individuals with the critical abilities to read and speak English. Further, it should be noted that in the unique case of Cambodians, a large percentage of the elderly are illiterate in their native language.

Finances

A key indicator of well-being is employment status. Asians have the largest percentage of elderly who are unemployed, and Hispanics have the smallest. Not surprisingly, the highest percentage of financial difficulties are also reported by Asians. Insofar as satisfaction with their housing is concerned, the majority of the elderly reported satisfaction rather than dissatisfaction, regardless of the size of their rent or mortgage payment.

Neighborhoods

With the exception of Poles, the Europeans, and Hispanics are long-time residents of Chicago. The Asians are, relatively speaking, newcomers. The locations of the respondents' homes show distinct ethnic clustering, even though only five of the eleven ethnic groups surveyed (Greeks, Ethnic Chinese, Lithuanians, Chinese, and Koreans) show large percentages reporting a preference for living in an ethnic neighborhood. Virtually all ethnic elderly felt safe in their neighborhoods. Contrary to popular perceptions, most of the ethnic elderly prefer to live in this country rather than return to their homeland. The Mexicans and Puerto Ricans are the exceptions.

Health

Most of the elderly perceived their health to be 'good' or 'excellent.' Only a minority felt that their health was poor. However, group differences exist in the percentage reporting to be in poor health. The Cambodians, Vietnamese, and Filipinos had a large number of elderly individuals with health problems that restricted daily activities. The Cambodians also stand out as having the most physical health symptoms. Asians, in general, report the most vision, hearing, and chewing problems.

With regard to having access to a health facility, the Chinese have the largest percentage of individuals who said they have no source of health care. They also have the largest percentage reporting not having seen a doctor in the past year. Asians, overall, have the highest percentage who do not receive needed post-hospital care. In the total sample, chore/housekeeping, homemaking services, and the services of a visiting nurse are the most common unmet needs. There is also clear underutilization of dental services. Some 43 percent of the total elderly reported that they had not visited a dentist in the past year.

Mental Health

There are large differences in self-rated mental health across groups. Six out of 10 Chinese, Ethnic Chinese, and Cambodians rated their mental health as "fair" to "poor." At the opposite end of the continuum, the English Speaking Greeks and Filipinos claimed to have very good mental health. Using the Center for Epidemiologic Studies – Depression (CES-D) Scale, Greeks have the lowest percentage of individuals who reported severe depressive symptomatology (12 percent), and Cambodians have the highest (95 percent). Overall, 9 out of 11 ethnic groups surveyed reported a higher percentage of individuals whose mental health had deteriorated – rather than improved – during the past five years.

The Ethnic Chinese and Lithuanians, followed by Mexicans, reported being exposed to the highest number of major stressful life events in the past six months. The Cambodians are the most likely to report low life satisfaction. Since social support has been shown to be linked to mental health, we inquired about friendship patterns. About two-thirds of the elderly in the total sample had two or more close friends. Exhibiting striking deviations are the Chinese and Ethnic Chinese, 70 percent of whom claimed to have no close friends. The groups that have more recently come to the U.S. as refugees are likely to have the lowest percentage of children living nearby. In contrast, Hispanics and "old Europeans" have considerable support in this regard. By and large, the majority of the elderly have at least weekly contact with their children. The overall pattern of mental health measures suggests a strong need for mental health services for the diverse groups of ethnic elderly.

Knowledge and Use of Social Services

Some of the services offered by the City of Chicago Department on Aging and Disability are known to the elderly surveyed, others are not. Generally unknown are the more "personal" services such as homemaker/personal care, home-delivered meals, and in-home chore service. The Chinese and Ethnic Chinese from Indo-China are the least aware of available services.

Of those ignorant of specific services, half said they would use the service now that they have been informed about these services as a result of our survey. Hispanics, more so than Europeans and Asians, are willing to use available services. The availability of children or relatives to perform the much-needed services offered by the Department of Aging and Disability is the single most prominent reason for the ethnic elderly's non-use – actual or anticipatory – of existing social services. The finding of the ethnic elderly's reliance on the informal support network has powerful implications for the future structuring of services to the elderly. Unfortunately, it is also one of the least understood concepts, and most neglected areas of research, pertinent to the underutilization of services by minority groups.

Armed with the results of this study, the organizations could now document the specific needs of older adults within their communities in a quantifiable way that added legitimacy to our efforts to pursue funding for these services. Additionally, the nearly two-year collaboration on this project by leaders of diverse ethnic organizations brought to light the fact that regardless of the language spoken or the part of the world one comes from, there was much more that united us than divided us. The needs and concerns of ethnic organizations serving their elders were pretty much the

> **GREEK-AMERICAN COMMUNITY SERVICES**
> 4817 W. MONTROSE AVENUE • CHICAGO, IL 60641
>
> EXECUTIVE DIRECTOR
> John Psiharis
>
> ADMINISTRATOR
> Elaine Thomopoulos Ph.D.
>
> July 6, 1987
>
> **OFFICERS**
>
> PRESIDENT
> Evangeline Mistaras
>
> SECRETARY
> Helen Geocaris
>
> TREASURER
> Lena Xides
>
> LEGAL ADVISOR
> Stella Adinamis-Cuthbert
>
> BOARD OF DIRECTORS
> Christine Burbulis
> Helen Georges
> James Heliotes
> Thalia Jameson
> Jean Kaporis
> Theodosis Kioutas, M.D.
> Charles Mouratides
> Toni Panos
> Athanasia Papadopoulos
> Barbara Psilakas
> John Rassogianis
>
> REGISTERED AGENT
> Polyzoes Gavaris
> 2800 W. Foster Ave.
> Chicago, IL 60625
>
> – REMINDER –
>
> A meeting to discuss forming a Coalition of Ethnic Elderly Service Providers will be held on <u>Wednesday, July 29th at 7:00 pm</u> at the Elysion Restaurant, 2800 W. Foster (northwest corner of Foster and California). Those who wish, may come earlier and join some of us for dinner.
>
> A tentative agenda includes:
>
> * Discussion on the background and purposes of an ethnic elderly coalition.
>
> * Discussion on how such a coalition could help each of our communities.
>
> * Brainstorming on the roles of a coalition
>
> * Deciding where to go from here.
>
> Encloses is a listing of those who plan to attend. Feel free to bring others from your community who might be interested in participating. And above all, please bring your ideas to share with us.
>
> Please call us at 539-2323 for further information.
>
> Sincerely,
>
> Elaine Thomopoulos
> Administrator
>
> John Psiharis
> Executive Director
>
> JP;pl
> encl.
>
> **WORKING TO PRESERVE YOUR HERITAGE**
> A NOT-FOR-PROFIT TAX-EXEMPT ORGANIZATION DEDICATED TO SERVING THE GREEK-AMERICAN COMMUNITY

A reminder sent to those invited to participate in the July 29, 1987 meeting to form a "Coalition of Ethnic Elderly Service Providers." Elaine Thomopoulos collection.

same across the board. Whether their homeland was in Asia, Europe, or Latin America, unfamiliarity with the culture and customs of the United States was a common denominator. We shared common threads from shared experiences, often encountered discrimination, and were less likely to be informed about or access services, programs, or other assistance that could be of help to our communities.

An early effort to bring together ethnic groups for a common purpose occurred on July 29, 1987, when Elaine and I, on behalf of GACS, convened a meeting to discuss forming a "Coalition of Ethnic Elderly Service Providers" at the Elysion Restaurant. The agenda items included:

- Discussion on the background and purpose of an ethnic elderly coalition.
- Discussion on how such a coalition could help each of our communities.
- Brainstorming on the roles of a coalition.
- Deciding where to go from here.

Those who attended were: Laura Arnette, Assyrian Universal Alliance Foundation office manager; Ranjana Bhargava, Chicago Community Trust (Pakistani community); Alice Buzanis, Friendly Visiting Program supervisor, Greek-American Community Services; Gloria Burger, Polish Welfare Association assistant director; Bill DeMagdelaine, coordinator of information and referral for the Chicago Department on Aging and Disability; Sue Kang, Senior Citizens Unit director, Korean American Community Services; Theodosis Kioutas, M.D., Greek-American Nursing Home Committee chairman; Ethel Kotsovos, Greek-American Nursing Home Committee board member; Daria Kulezysky, a member of the Ukrainian Social Services Bureau of Chicago; Judy Matthews, Chicago program coordinator for the National Association of Hispanic Elderly; Evangeline Mistaras, board president of Greek-American Community Services; Masaru Nambu, executive director of the Japanese-American Service Committee; John Nimrod, board vice-president of the Assyrian Universal Alliance Foundation; Peter Porr, executive director of the Southeast Asia Center; John Psiharis, executive director of Greek-American Community Services; Elaine Thomopoulos, Greek-American Community Services administrator; Danguale Valentinas, executive director of Lithuanian Human Services of the USA; and Bernarda Wong, executive director of the Chinese American Service League. In 1987, Sue Kang left Korean American Community Services to found the Korean American Senior Center and continued to represent the Korean elderly as executive director of the new organization.

These conversations continued in the coming months, and in 1989, after the study ended, the steering committee members decided to continue to discuss how we could work together to address common concerns and advocate for increased funding. With the support of the Chicago Department on Aging, which covered some of Rosemary's time, and provided meeting space at their offices at 510 N. Peshtigo Court, the group moved to formalize these conversations and establish a not-for-profit organization to pursue these goals.

The "Rationale for a Coalition of Limited English Speaking People," developed by the steering committee, was described in a January 19, 1989 document:

Many ethnic agencies do work that only community-based agencies with specific language skills and cultural backgrounds can do, helping limited and non-English speaking persons on a one-to-one basis in the neighborhoods where they live. They provide vital personal services not available from other sources.

Generally, bi-lingual staff members are spread so thin acting as interpreters and escorts that there's insufficient time to develop the economic and political base necessary to ensure their future operation.

Even though their nationalities differ, the constituencies of the individual agencies share the same problems: illiteracy, depression, joblessness, dependence on interpreters, poor housing conditions, and racial or ethnic discrimination.

Advocacy programs and technical assistance can be provided through a coalition of ethnic agencies while enabling the community agencies to gain some of the advantages of size without losing the small, ethnic community identity that makes them so effective in meeting the needs of their limited-and non-English speaking neighbors.

Proposed Purpose:

1. Provide information on private and public funding grants.
2. Assist in developing funding proposals.
3. Provide interpreters pool and escorts on an as-needed basis, paid by the hour.
4. Develop a program for providing chore/housekeeping services by native-language-speaking workers.
5. Develop a program for responding to the mental health needs of individuals.
6. Conduct English-language classes.
7. Provide assistance in interpreting and disseminating results of the Ethnic Elderly Needs Assessment.
8. Share information pertinent to the member agencies (clearinghouse).
9. Assist new agencies to form.
10. Advocate to City, State, and Federal governments on behalf of the ethnic agencies.
11. Sponsor health screening and referral to medical practitioners.
12. Education of social service providers.

Initially called the Illinois Coalition for Limited English Speaking People, the name was changed to the Coalition of Limited English Speaking Elderly (CLESE) before incorporation in 1989. The founders were

Rebecca Cruz, Judith Matthews, Peter Porr, John Psiharis, Kompha Seth, Danguale Valentinas, and Bernarda Wong. The initial board of directors of CLESE was composed of the 12 members of the Ethnic Elderly Needs Assessment Steering Committee.

Strains on Ethnic Pride Conference

After the successful "Greeks in America" film series and the ongoing Fabric Arts of Greece project, GACS began to plan for our next cultural program. Elaine had become aware of a grant opportunity offered by the Illinois Humanities Council (IHC). The proposal was to organize a conference that would focus on the differences and conflicts between the waves of Greek immigrants and compare and contrast those experiences with those of the Assyrian community.

The Assyrians were selected in large part due to the relationship between GACS and the AUAF that evolved during the Assyrian Project for the Elderly. Elaine had begun to work for AUAF in developing programs and writing grants to fund these programs. They were also one of the newest immigrant/refugee groups in Chicago. Steve Frangos remembers that one of the reasons he thought the grant would be funded was that at the time, few knew who the Assyrians were, and the state would likely fund a project that provided a greater understanding of their history and culture.

Elaine recalls: "Steve worked on this grant on my computer in the basement of the 53 Regent Drive house. What an experience! I think it was the year the Chicago Bears won the Super Bowl, and we were working on the grant rather than watching the game. I did buy a cake to celebrate. We had about 150 people in attendance at the conference. The conference was not so much about generational differences, but about the strains felt between the first wave of immigrants and their children, and the second wave of immigrants, although we did cover so much more, including generational differences."

Steve, Elaine, and I wrote the proposal. The initial idea evolved from a one-day event into a two-day conference that would include 40 speakers who addressed the theme of the conference; "Strains on Ethnic Pride: Conflicts Between the New and the Old Immigrants in the Greek and Assyrian Communities." The Illinois Humanities Council funded the project for the maximum grant amount of $10,000. The event was held in the Centennial Forum Building at Loyola University's Lakeshore Campus. In this beautiful setting overlooking the lake, speakers and participants explored tensions between the various generations of immigrants within these communities.

The aim of the conference as detailed in the grant proposal to the IHC stated:

> The proposed conference, 'Strains on Ethnic Pride: Conflicts Between the Old and New Immigrants in the Assyrian and Greek Communities of Illinois,' will focus on one of the most pressing contemporary issues of ethnicity in America – how different waves of immigrants from the same ethnic group are in open conflict over the proper ways of expressing their identity. Individuals of an ethnic group possess more alternatives for expressing their identity than the ones they finally choose. Such cultural and social selections vary not only from ethnic group to ethnic group or even within a particular group but between each generation of all immigrant Americans as well. The complexities of the ethnic reality, far from dry academic case studies, are live compelling community issues faced every day by these people. The resulting tensions and open disagreements over competing versions of being ethnic in America – which are the direct consequence of these cultural and social selections in the new land of America – are so intense and volatile that the resolution of these problems often seems virtually impossible.
>
> This conference will directly address these conflicts as they enact and so express the varying ways of being Assyrian and Greek in Illinois. The community organizers of this proposal feel assured that such a public forum where the contrast and comparison between Assyrians and Greeks are a central feature will allow the respective communities to see beyond their own specific disagreements to the larger issues which inform and in part give structure to the social conditions over which the intra-community disputes now range.
>
> The conference will be scheduled over two days. Eight topical areas spanning community institutions and expressive forms will be the thematic areas around which the panelists will organize their presentations. The structure of each panel will remain the same: there will be two to four speakers per panel each allotted twenty to thirty minutes for their paper. A chairperson will direct and conclude the panels, acting as a discussant summarizing the themes and issues of the speakers. Immediately following the chairperson's summary, there will be a minimum of thirty minutes of open floor discussion and debate. Community concerns dictate the Ethnic Family panel (scheduled for the entire afternoon on Sunday) be an extended

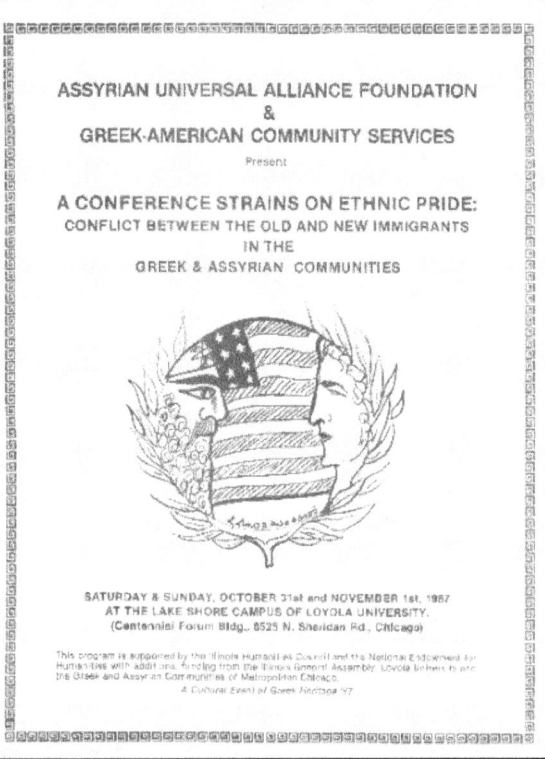

"Strains on Ethnic Pride" conference program book cover. October 31, 1987. Elaine Thomopoulos collection.

forum. The discussion period following this panel will also be extended.

Given the desire to have the panels represent both the Assyrian and Greek communities, it seems too complicated to have any language other than English spoken during the conference presentations. However, in response to community sentiments, a distinguished lecture will be held on the second evening of the conference. The two lectures will be held simultaneously, one in the Assyrian language and the other in Greek. This will of course exclude various persons attending the conference. But English will do the same. The thematic topic of the distinguished lectures will be the ethnic's sense of estrangement in the new land.

In Greek, this notion is covered by the term *xenitia* and in the Assyrian experience, the work *kariboota* describes this sense of loss. Therefore, to provide some balance to the otherwise entirely English language program this one has been conceived.

> **ASSYRIAN UNIVERSAL ALLIANCE FOUNDATION/
> GREEK-AMERICAN COMMUNITY SERVICES**
>
> Invite You to attend our
>
> **STRAINS ON ETHNIC PRIDE
> CONFERENCE AND DANCE**
>
> Featuring:
>
> ASSYRIAN AND GREEK ENTERTAINMENT
> GEORGE CHAHARBAKSHI AND HIS BAND
> ALSO DANCE FEVER PRODUCTION
>
> on Saturday, October 31, 1987
> at LOYOLA UNIVERSITY LAKE SHORE CAMPUS
> (Centennial Forum)
> 6525 North Sheridan Road, Chicago
>
> DINNER: 7:00-8:00 p.m.
>
> Donation
> $20.00 per person in advance
> $23.00 at the door
>
> "Strains on Ethnic Pride" conference dinner ticket. October 31, 1987. Elaine Thomopoulos collection.

The conference directors were John Nimrod, Elaine, and myself. Elaine assembled and led a planning committee for this grant that met regularly to discuss and plan the conference and work on the detailed grant proposal. Members of the planning committee included: Homer Ashurian, Dyana Aziz, George Christakis, Ph.D., Robert DeKelaito Steve Frangos, Bessie Kallas, Malcolm Karam, Alexander Karanikas, Ph.D., Elaine Kollintzas, Andrew Kopan, Ph.D., George "Yorgos" Kourvetaris, Ph.D., Fotios Litsas, Ph.D., John Nimrod, John Psiharis, Helen Schwarten, Elaine Thomopoulos, Ph.D., and Constantine Tzanos. Dr. Christopher Kornaros (Illinois Benedictine College) was the project evaluator who submitted a report to the IHC.

The conference theme was explored in such areas as literature, education, family, religion, fraternal organizations, media, politics, and gender. The weekend conference featured panel discussions that included prominent scholars and humanists who candidly explored the challenges each community faced. A Saturday evening dinner dance featuring Greek and Assyrian foods was held in the campus student center overlooking the lake. The dinner featured demonstrations of Assyrian and Greek dancing featuring Fatin Shabo, Steve "Mixmaster" Broumas, and the Orpheus Dance Troupe. An arts and crafts show featuring Greek and Assyrian artists and crafters was on display throughout the conference. A commemorative program booklet with advertising was created and distributed to those attending the conference. Babysitting was available for children over the age of 18 months for one dollar per child/hour.

Conference registration fees were $5 for early registration and $6 at the door. The dinner was $20 in advance, $23 at the door, or $10 for the dance only. The admission revenue, program advertising, dinner dance, and raffle proceeds covered expenses above the IHC grant.

Conference speakers and moderators included Dr. Henry Allen, Dr. Michael Bakalis (Loyola University School of Education) (conference master of ceremonies), Constance Callinicos, Dr. George Christakis (City Colleges of Chicago), Harriett Condes, Robert DeKelaito, Rebecca Kamber Elias, Steve Frangos, John C Geocaris, Senator Adeline Geo-Karis, Dr. Arian Ishaya, Peter Jasim, Dr. Joel John, Malcom Karam, Dr. Alexander Karanikas, (Professor Emeritus, University of Illinois), His Grace Mar Aprim Khamis (Bishop of the Holy Apostolic Assyrian Church of the East), Dr. Theodosis Kioutas, M.D., Dr. Andrew Kopan (DePaul School of Education), Robert Koshaba, Dr. Yorgos Kouvetaris (Northern Illinois University), Antigone Lambros, Dr. Fotios Litsas (University of Illinois at Chicago), Dr. Alexander Makedon (Northeastern Illinois University and Chicago State University), Theano Papazoglou Margaris, Charles Mouratides, Dr. Eden Naby (University of Wisconsin – Madison), Dr. Arthur Nikelly (University of Illinois – Champaign/Urbana), Senator John Nimrod, Sam Parhad, Nick Petros, Nick Philippidis (*Greek Star*), Dr. Peter Potamianos, Anna Tellios-Razes, Sotiris Rekoumis, David Roth (Illinois Ethnic Consultation), Rev. Emmanuel Sada, Hannah Sue Samuels, Peter Talia, and Lincoln S. Tamraz.

In addition to Loyola University, event co-sponsors included: Ashurbanipal Library, Assyrian National Aid Society, Congress of American Hellenic Organizations, Greek Women's University Club, Hellenic Cultural Organization, Hellenic Medical Society, Hellenic Museum and Cultural Center, Hellenic Professional Society of Illinois, Hellenic Society of DePaul University, KRIKOS, Northeastern Illinois University Greek Club, and the United Hellenic American Congress. Tape recordings of the conference were given to the AUAF for deposit in the Ashurbanipal Library, a library focused on Assyrian culture and history.

At its conclusion, this groundbreaking conference drew high marks for its candid and engaging conversation about the strains between the earlier immigrants and those who came later within our communities as well as a broader comparison between the Greek and Assyrian cultures. This example of cross-cultural cooperation would become a model for future GACS Cultural & Arts Program undertakings.

PROGRAM
STRAINS ON ETHNIC PRIDE: CONFLICT BETWEEN THE NEW AND OLD IMMIGRANTS IN THE ASSYRIAN AND GREEK COMMUNITIES.

CAMPUS OF LOYOLA UNIVERSITY
(Centennial Forum Bldg., 6525 N. Sheridan Rd., Chicago)

SATURDAY, OCTOBER 31

8:30-9:15 Registration and coffee—Centennial Forum

9:15-9:30 Welcoming remarks—Senator John Nimrod
(Crown Center)

9:30-11:00 HISTORICAL OVERVIEW: ETHNICITY IN ILLINOIS, THE ASSYRIAN AND GREEK EXPERIENCE. This panel will provide the social and historical background of the Assyrian and Greek communities of Illinois necessary to understand the nature of conflicts between the various waves of immigrants. Far from recounting the historical incidents the myriad forms in which the conflicts arose will be critically analyzed. The civic and cultural contributions each ethnic group has made in Illinois will be presented.
(Crown Center)
    Sam Parhad, M.A., Publisher of Assyrian Torch, author George Christakes, Ph.D. City Colleges of Chicago, Professor of History Eden Naby, Ph.D. Harvard University, Middle East Studies; Nick Petros, Co-chairperson. Robert DeKelaita Co-chairperson.

11:15-12:45 RELIGION AND ETHNICITY
(Crown Center) The relationships between ethnicity and religion is the central focus. The diversity of religions within the Assyrian community will be compared with the Greek experience in Chicago. The ethnic communities in Chicago had not only a new society to learn about but new faiths as well. The church as the arena for community disputes will be analyzed.
    Peter Potamianos, Ph.D., Educator
    Steve Frangos, Ph.D., Candidate, University of Indiana
    Dr. Joel John
    His Grace Mar Aprim Khamis, Bishop of The Holy Apostolic Assyrian Church of the East Presented by Rev. Emmanuel Sada
    Peter Talia, Ph.D., Chairperson, Minister and author

12:45-1:45 Lunch will be available cafeteria style at Centennial Forum Lake Shore Dining Room second floor.

2:00-3:30 POLITICS OF ETHNICITY
(Crown Center) The politics of ethnicity will encompass both the involvement of individuals in the politics of the old country as well as the role ethnics played in Chicago and Illinois government over the years. What were the goals of Assyrians and Greek ethnics in politics? How did the ethnics use politics toward those political ends? How successful were the Assyrians and Greeks in achieving those goals? In what fashion have the waves of immigrants contributed to the role of ethnics in American politics? The issue of an Assyrian homeland needs consideration, also, some commentary on Greek-American involvement in the Cyprus crisis needs to be discussed.
    Hon. Michael Bakalis, former State Supt. of Public Instruction, Dean of Education, Loyola.
    Hon. John Nimrod, former State Senator, state and local official township committeeman.
    Lincoln S. Tamraz, Past National Commander Amvet's, co-chairperson
    Hon. Adeline C. Geo-Karis, co-chairperson

3:45-5:10 FRATERNAL ORGANIZATIONS
(Crown Center) The role of fraternal organizations among many ethnic groups is second only to the place of the church in community life. How did fraternal organizations assist assimilation? How did the nationalistic concerns for the homeland find expression in the fraternal organization? As the new immigrants came on the scene how did the dynamics of these groups change in emphasis, or did they?
    Malcolm Karam, Past President Assyrian American National Federation ***Fotis Litsas, Ph.D., Prof. of Modern Greek Studies, University of Illinois.
    Theodosis Kioutas, M.D., Chairperson.

5:25-6:25 DISCUSSION GROUPS
(Damen Hall)
History—Rm. 438
    Georgs Christakes, Ph.D.
    Eden Naby, Ph.D.
    Sam Parhad
    Robert DeKelaita
    Nick Petros

Religion—Rm. 439
    Rev. Emmanuel Sada
    Peter Talia, Ph.D.
    Henry Allen Ph.D.
    Steve Frangos
    Dr. Joel John
    Peter Potamianos

Fraternal Organizations-Rm. 440
    Malcolm Karam
    Fotis Litsas
    Theodosis Kioutas, M.D.

Politics—Rm. 441
    Hon. John Nimrod
    Hon. Michael Bakalis
    Hon. Adeline Geo-Karis
    Lincoln Tamraz

7:00-8:30 CONFERENCE DINNER, FEATURING GREEK AND ASSYRIAN FOODS
(Rambler Room—Centennial Forum)

8:30-? CONFERENCE DANCE
ASSYRIAN AND GREEK DANCING
Featuring—FATIN SHABO & BAND
STEVE "MIXMASTER" BROUMAS
(Rambler Room—Centennial Forum)

SUNDAY, NOVEMBER 1

2:00-3:30 LITERATURE OF ETHNICITY
(Crown Center) Ethnic literature provides a profound understanding of the general clash of values every immigrant experiences. The conflict between the waves of immigration is well documented within the pages of ethnic literature. The literary traditions of Assyrians and Greeks in America as represented in Chicago will be addressed in this panel.
    Alexander Karanikas, Ph.D. Prof. Emiratus, University of Illinois, Alexander Makedon, Ph.D. chairperson, Northeastern Illinois University/Northern Illinois University. Additional speakers to be announced.

2:00-3:30 ETHNIC FAMILY
(Flanner Auditorium) Immigration to America has always affected the family. Conflicts among the waves of immigration are especially painful since they often involve the closest of family members separated by immigration. Tensions of living in two worlds—the old country traditions of the homeland and the American community—are often so great that frustrations erupt into frightening generational splits.
(Flanner Hall)
    Arthur Nikelly, Ph.D., Psychologist, Univ. of IL
    Arian Ishaya, Ph.D., Social Anthropologist;
    Yorgos Kourvetaris, Ph.D., Prof. N.I.U.
    Robert Koshaba Chairman Human Services AANF
    Constance Callinicos, author;
    Anna Tellios-Razes, Social Worker (Chairperson)

3:45-5:15 ETHNIC MEDIA
(Crown Center) The waves of immigration to America were paralleled by incredible changes in technology. How have changing forms of media in America and overseas influenced how ethnics in Illinois interact and perceive the world around them? Did the ethnic media only mimic the new forms of the wider American society or have the ideas generated in the ethnic media have profound influences beyond the parameters of their own communities?
    Khoshaba Jasim, past editor Assyrian Star
    Nick Philippides, editor, Greek Star
    Charles Mouratides, former editor, Lerner Newspaper
    Harriette Condes, Educator
    Antigone Lambros, Co-chairperson
    Peter Jasim, Co-chairperson

3:45-5:15 EDUCATION
(Crown Center) Retention of the home language is one of the most debated issues between the old and new waves of immigrants, the parochial schools of the old country are today augmented by the bi-lingual programs found in the Illinois public school system. How these two forms of language school also provide or lack the social context immigrant parents believe is fundamental to language learning will be analyzed in this panel's presentation.
    Andrew Kopan, Ph.D. Professor DePaul University
    Hannah Sue Samuels, Educator/Librarian
    Sotiris Rekoumis, Educator, Co-chairperson
    Rebecca Kamber Elias, Educator, Co-chairperson

5:15-5:30 COFFEE BREAK

5:30-6:30 DISTINGUISHED LECTURERS
(Flanner Hall) Theano Papazouglou-Margaris, Author (presented in Greek)
(Crown Center) Eden Naby, Ph.D. Professor, Presently at University of Wisconsin (presented in English)

6:45-7:45 PANEL DISCUSSION
(Crown Center) Has the conference done what it set out to do? How does this apply to the other ethnic communities. David Roth Chairperson, Midwest Director, Institute for American Pluralism.

"Strains on Ethnic Pride: Conflicts Between the New and Old Immigrants in the Assyrian and Greek Communities" conference program. October 31, 1987. Elaine Thomopoulos collection.

Dr. Christopher Kornaros, a professor of politics at Illinois Benedictine College, was the project's independent evaluator. His final report to the Illinois Humanities Council, dated November 11, 1987, included the following evaluation of the program:

> It was an exceptional opportunity for me to be asked to attend this important conference as an outside evaluator.
>
> I don't know who initiated this conference but I know it was a great idea. The Greeks and the Assyrians have much in common. Both peoples lived under foreign control and the Assyrians are not yet free people.
>
> The speakers representing the Assyrian communities stated over and over that they came to the United States to become free and live among free people away from their homeland because their homeland was not their own. They came to the
>
> United States to stay, not to go back. The theme of the conference strongly centered around the following ideas:
>
> 1. The reasons why people from these two backgrounds came to the United States.
> 2. Who were these people when they came to the United States?
> 3. How educated or uneducated were these people?
> 4. What they brought in the 19th Century, in the turn of the Century, in the post-WWI period, and the post-WWII period.
> 5. How were these people able to integrate themselves into American society?
> 6. If there were conflicts between the new and the old immigrants, the children of the immigrants, why were these conflicts present?
>
> The first topic dealt with an overview of the history of Greek and Assyrian immigrants in Chicago and beyond. Speakers in their presentations dealt with this topic in historical terms. Much of the information of the speakers representing the Assyrian and the Greek points of view came from scholarly works dealing with ethnic questions. Specific studies researching on the Greeks and Assyrians were used. These studies represent mainstream and respected studies.
>
> In addition, speakers used material from interviews, published accounts in newspapers, and personal knowledge and experiences about the two communities. One element that appeared to emerge out of these presentations was the point that the Assyrians came to stay, the Greeks came for economic

reasons and many of them would return to their homeland once they accumulated some savings.

Turning to the topic of religion, one important element that clearly emerged from the Assyrian presenters was the point that the Assyrians adhere to several religious denominations, unlike the much more homogeneous Greeks. I could not help but think as I listened to the speakers, based on their own speeches, that much of the religious diversity that exists in the Assyrian community has been motivated by their eagerness to be integrated as much as possible into American life by adopting mainstream American religious denominations. Few Greeks followed that course.

For Greeks, however, by the time of the third generation, many religious practices are weakened. Data were presented which indicated that there are about 50% intermarriages between Greek-Americans and other Americans. Many intermarriages take place between Greek Americans and Jewish people.

One speaker discussed the 'Crisis Within the Greek Orthodox Church.' Unfortunately, time did not permit him to clarify his main point. One element that seemed to emerge in his presentation was that the Greek Orthodox hierarchy is not very sensitive to feedback from the community. The speaker also seemed to imply criticism because the Greek Orthodox Church did not make the services entirely in English but rather in both languages.

Regarding the topic of politics, the speakers themselves were or presently are political figures and therefore, relied heavily on information derived from their personal experiences with both communities.

The Assyrians and the Greeks were involved in American politics and influenced American politics not because of their numbers but rather because of their educational backgrounds, professionalism, and success in business.

Fraternal organizations helped the Americans to understand the Assyrians and the Greeks through their efforts to 'educate' non-Assyrians and non-Greeks to understand the cultures and aspirations of these people and not to consider these alien to cultural pluralism of the American society.

The discussion groups that followed provided more information and a very lively exchange of ideas by people who knew about what they were talking.

Turning to literature, it is very interesting to note that there is an area where much of the friction within both communities between the old and new, especially the foreign parents and the American-born children, appeared to be intense. That was depicted in the literature in the form of fiction, poetry, and history. This presentation, I think, clarified a great deal for the audience, and even touched deeper their inner feelings. Literature represented heavily the dramatic in life, the physical and psychological suffering.

The ethnic family represented the culmination of the problem and the cultural conflict between the old and the new. Though it seemed that the Assyrians were a little ahead of the Greeks in dealing with that complex problem.

Numerous publications occurred in both communities and became the bridge between the old and new and the bridge between the Assyrian and Greek communities' larger American community.

Education was originally thought to be used to teach children the language of their parents. Later, education took the form of bilingual programs but that did not seem to succeed very well.

The formal program ended with two distinguished lectures representing the Assyrian and Greek communities. Then, an informal discussion followed and the conference ended. As stated before, the program had too many speakers. It could be a little better organized and should have more opportunities for the audience to participate. Yet, notwithstanding these minor lapses, I think the program was a great success.

Thanks to all who contributed to make this program possible. I hope that such efforts be encouraged by enlightened foundations or other organizations. It is a service to the American heritage.

Building Bridges into the Broader Community

Due in part to the success GACS achieved and the relationships we had built, Elaine and I were invited to take part on committees and boards within the broader community. In addition to our extensive involvement in the GANHC and CLESE, Elaine was on an advisory board for the Travelers and Immigrants Aid Society, a member of the Metropolitan Chicago Council on Aging's Respite Care Committee, and was active with the Illinois Ethnic Consultation. She was also active with the American Jewish Committee where she served as Chicago coordinator for a federal grant on caregiving and coordinated an ethnic women's coalition. At

Chicago Mayor Eugene Sawyer and John Psiharis. February 1989. John Psiharis collection.

times, I was on the advisory boards of Ravenswood Community Mental Health Center and Belmont Community Hospital.

In 1986, I was appointed by Mayor Harold Washington to serve as a member of the Community Development Advisory Committee (CDAC). This committee's role was to monitor and advise the city about the allocation and use of Community Development Block Grant (CDBG) funds that were allocated to the city of Chicago. At the time this amounted to nearly $80 million per year. Two years later, I was reappointed by Mayor Eugene Sawyer and then twice by Mayor Richard M. Daley. I served on the CDAC for eight years.

CDBG funds were administered by the U.S. Department of Housing and Urban Development (HUD) and were allocated to cities based on the percentage of low and moderate-income populations they had within their municipalities. These funds were used for services and programs that benefited this population and were sometimes used to pay for city services for communities designated as low or moderate-income according to census tracts.

There were about 30 members of the CDAC, and its membership consisted mainly of nonprofit and community leaders. The CDAC coordinator, Carolyn DeLoache, was based within the Chicago Department of Planning. Meetings were held on the third Tuesday of every month at 3:00

Community Development Advisory Committee Certificate of Appreciation signed by Mayor Richard M. Daley, Paul Vallas, and Valerie Jarrett. December 21, 1993. John Psiharis collection.

p.m. at City Hall. The subcommittees met monthly and sometimes more frequently during the annual grant review period.

Although advisory in nature, the committee was federally mandated to review and monitor CDBG-funded programs and approve the proposed budget. The decisions were non-binding but were submitted to the mayor and city council for review, reported to HUD, and placed in the public record. Each member served on a subcommittee that reviewed funding requests and priorities from their respective city departments and grantees under their purview and provided recommendations to department heads, the budget office, and the full CDAC. The subcommittees also monitored funded programs and heard reports from department heads.

For most of these years, I served on the Public Services Subcommittee. The committee oversaw the lion's share of Chicago's CDBG budget allocated to 14 city departments including Human Services, Aging, Disabilities, Employment and Training, Human Relations, Police, Fire, Streets and Sanitation, Libraries, Chicago Housing Authority, Board of Education, and Cultural Affairs (including the Mayor's Office of Special Events). Most of the money was awarded in grants to hundreds of delegate agencies that provided services while the rest was used to subsidize services provided by the city. Other committees included the economic development and housing sub-committees. Given their more defined

(L-R): Alderman Roman Pucinski, Mayor Richard M. Daley, and John Psiharis during a CDAC Holiday Reception hosted by the mayor. I was discussing the nursing home project with the mayor, and he invited the alderman to join the conversation when this picture was taken. Date unknown. John Psiharis collection.

scope, these committees were able to be more hands-on by actually reviewing proposals submitted by applicants.

Due to the large and diverse portfolio of departments that reported to the committee, we primarily focused on overall budget numbers and priorities and did not usually review specific proposals from delegate agencies. Some departments, such as the Department of Human Services, had hundreds of delegate agencies receiving CDBG funding. Every August, the Public Service Committee set aside two eight-hour days (usually back to back) for department heads to meet with us. It took this long just to hear from each department about their priorities for the coming year and have some dialogue with them. It would take another full-day meeting for us to consider their proposals and prepare our recommendations to the full CDAC for ratification.

One program the committee nurtured was the First Aid Care Team (FACT) program, a partnership between the Chicago Fire Department, the Chicago Housing Authority (CHA), and the City Colleges of Chicago. The Hull House Association, as delegate agency for this program, coordinated advanced first aid training for CHA residents who were then employed to work at CHA buildings, city events, and neighborhood festivals. Opportunities to apply for paramedic training were also available.

I recall a hearing where we were grappling with federal budget cuts and had recommended reducing CDBG funding for a Mayor's Office of

Special Events program that provided free Jumping Jacks for block parties in low and moderate-income neighborhoods. The committee felt that CDBG funds could be better used to offset federal cuts to child and elder care services and that other sources of funds could be tapped for this recreational activity. For several days, I and others on the committee received a slew of phone calls from many who disagreed. It must have been a coordinated effort. Since our role was advisory, I do not remember the outcome and whether in the end the program was funded by CDBG or another source.

I was the first Greek American to serve on this committee. Dean Maragos was appointed several years later but he served on a different sub-committee. In addition to city department heads, the committee worked with Sharon Gist-Gilliam, the mayor's budget director and city's chief operating officer; Valerie Jarrett, Chicago's director of planning and development, who later became a senior advisor to President Barack Obama; and Paul Vallas, who succeeded Sharon as budget director, and went on to a distinguished career in public service including chief of staff to the mayor and CEO of the Chicago Public Schools. Paul was a Democratic party candidate for governor of Illinois in 2002, narrowly losing to Rod Blagojevich. In 2015 he was an unsuccessful candidate for lieutenant governor in Governor Pat Quinn's reelection campaign and went on to lead the New Orleans public school system during its rebuilding process after the devastation of Hurricane Katrina and was CEO of the School District of Philadelphia. Paul was a candidate for Chicago mayor in the 2019 municipal election, which Lori Lightfoot won. In February 2023, he was the top vote-getter in a field of nine candidates for mayor but lost to Brandon Johnson in the April runoff election.

Members of the CDAC had varied backgrounds and represented all parts of Chicago. Patrick Salmon, the chairman of the CDAC, who was appointed by the mayor, was the executive director of the Back of the Yards Neighborhood Council. David Truitt, an affordable housing advocate from Uptown, was co-chair. The chairman of the Public Service Subcommittee was Steven Bishop, vice president of government relations for the United Way of Metropolitan Chicago. Nancy Johnstone, executive director of Youth Guidance, served as co-chair. Committee members included: Freddy Calixto, executive director of Project BUILD; Michael Brickman who became deputy mayor for education under Mayor Daley; Darlena Wilkerson, administrator of the Donor's Forum of Chicago Emergency Fund; Bill Fredrickson who represented the North Park Neighborhood Association; Arlene Knudson, Director of Pegasus Players; and Joann Merritt of the Hull House Association. Gertrude "Pudgie"

Thompson from the Department of Human Services staffed the subcommittee.

On February 10, 11, and 12, 1989, during his reelection campaign, Mayor Sawyer invited me to join him and other ethnic leaders during "Unity Weekend," a three-day citywide tour of several Chicago communities. We rode in "City One," a converted CTA (Chicago Transit Authority) bus. The bus was sponsored by Citibank and used by the city to provide tours to business and governmental visitors. It had a bathroom, a television, and a mobile phone. There was carpeting and comfortable seating. Boxed lunches and ample beverages were provided.

On Saturday, the caravan visited events at Olive Harvey College, Operation P.U.S.H., the Rofei Zedek synagogue in Hyde Park, Temple Menorah, Illinois Institute of Technology, Grand Manor Banquet Hall (a Polish community banquet), St. James Church of God in Christ, American Indian Center, Ukrainian Cultural Center, and culminated with an Asian Lunar New Year's celebration at Chicago O'Hare Holiday Inn Hotel. On Sunday, the delegation visited several churches including Iglesia Palestina, Mount Olivet Baptist Church, Cristo la Victoria, Iglesia de Dios, and Iglesia Asamblea Cristiana. The following Tuesday (February 14), the Mayor hosted a reception for the delegation at the Holiday Inn Mart Plaza.

I recall it was snowing one of these days, and we had fallen behind schedule due to bad traffic. Although we had a police escort, it didn't help much when the weather was bad. At one point the bus briefly got stuck in the snow. It was quite an experience being with the mayor for a weekend and visiting events throughout the city that I would have never experienced otherwise.

I remember a stop at Operation Push in the Kenwood neighborhood. A standing-room-only crowd greeted us as we entered the room, and the Reverend Jesse Jackson gave an impassioned speech in support of Mayor Sawyer, ordering that the doors remain closed until each person in the room made a donation. He began the bidding at $1,000 and worked his way down. I don't recollect how much was raised, but a good amount of money was raised through this aggressive yet effective fundraising technique.

I was appointed by Lois Weisberg, commissioner of the Chicago Department of Cultural Affairs, to serve as chairman of the City Arts Grants Social Services subcommittee for a three-year term. This committee reviewed requests for City Arts grants that came from social service agencies (as opposed to arts organizations) and made funding recommendations to the Department. Mary E Young served as the director of cultural grants, Johnathon Stillwell was the City Arts grants director and

Juana Guzman was the Neighborhood Arts Program coordinator. They provided staff support to the committee and sat through our meetings.

In the days before the Internet and online applications, serving on a grant review committee was a labor-intensive experience. We received paper copies of each grant submission delivered to us in a large box by courier. The committee reviewed about 100 applications and each application consisted of several pages of narratives, budgets, and an array of attachments that could make each application up to 50 pages or longer. Some requests were slick and professionally prepared while others were handwritten. I kept the box in my office and grabbed a handful of applications every day to review and score. Sometimes, I would take a few proposals with me and go to Little Mike's for coffee to read them because the office was hectic and noisy when ADC clients were participating in various activities. Funded projects included an array of arts programming for children, seniors, ethnic communities, and others. A few that I remember include art classes for children of domestic violence victims, origami classes for Japanese children, cultural programming for refugee children, community murals, dance classes for seniors, service learning projects, and arts programming targeted toward crime and gang reduction efforts.

Each year, the committee met for three full days in early November to review and score the submitted proposals. A continental breakfast, lunch, and refreshments were provided so that we didn't need to break. Committee members were each tasked with presenting an equal number of proposals to the group. As chairman, I did not present any requests but instead guided the discussion and decision-making process for each proposal. After each grant was presented, panelist scores were tabulated and a vote was taken on whether or not to fund the program. Allocation amounts, based on the total funding available, were finalized by DCA. Since GACS was an annual recipient of this grant, I abstained from GACS-related discussions and left the room when our proposal was under review.

As committee members, the grantees invited us to their events and performances. Throughout the year, as time allowed, we attended as many as we could. It was an enlightening experience to visit all parts of the city and observe the impact of the funding we provided. I remember attending the opening of a play written and performed by at-risk youth at the Better Boys Foundation, classes on origami at the Japanese American Service Committee, art classes for refugee children at a resettlement agency, and events at the American Indian Center, Erie Neighborhood House, and Gads Hill Community Center.

In early 1987, I was contacted by the Mike Dukakis for President campaign. The three-term Massachusetts governor was planning to run for the Democratic nomination for president and his campaign in Boston was reaching out to Greek American leaders in Chicago (and other early primary states) for assistance and support. I agreed to help, and along with others, worked to engage Chicago Greek Americans in the campaign. I served as an ethnic coordinator, delegate candidate, and 11th congressional district coordinator, and as a member of the Greeks for Dukakis efforts. Mike Bakalis served as Illinois chairman for the campaign. Alice Buzanis was also involved in the campaign and ran as an alternate delegate. Together, we traveled to several states on behalf of the campaign including Iowa, Wisconsin, Michigan, Indiana, and Ohio. Alice and I traveled to the campaign headquarters in Boston several times and the 1988 Democratic convention in Atlanta, Georgia. I remember Alice's mother and father, Kiki and Alex, driving to the convention from Chicago and how excited they were to be able to be part of the historic festivities. Others who I recall being active in the campaign include Andrew Athens, Nick Flevaris, Elaine Kollintzas, John Kulidas, Leo Louchios, and John Rassogianis. Pol Gavaris provided the back room at the Elysion for meetings, and voter registration days, and hosted a delegate meet-and-greet event that I helped organize.

I remember accompanying reporters from Voice of America on a very cold evening as they visited Lawrence Avenue Greek stores and *kafenios* to gauge feelings about Dukakis and consulting for the Fuji TV Network of Japan to coordinate Tarō Kimura's visit to Chicago to report on support for Dukakis within the city's ethnic communities, which included visits to Japanese American Service Committee, Chinese American Service League, Greek Town, and several others locations. Kimura was an anchorman for Fuji TV.

For me, one of the most memorable moments from the campaign (and there were many) occurred when Alice and I had the opportunity to meet Malcolm Forbes, who had flown into Chicago to interview Governor Dukakis earlier in the day. The governor had come to Chicago to speak to a Chicago Council on Foreign Relations luncheon and attend other events.

The campaign plane, a Boeing 737 chartered from Presidential Airways, jokingly referred to by campaign insiders as "Sky Pig," was undergoing emergency repairs in the private plane area at Midway Airport. The nickname referred to the untidy cabin conditions with stuff strewn throughout the plane. Secret Service protocol required the governor's plane to take off first. While the traveling press was in the Butler Aviation terminal filing their stories, the governor and a number of his staff engaged in an impromptu game of touch football on the tarmac. As this was

John Psiharis with Governor Michael Dukakis, Circa 1988. John Psiharis collection.

John Psiharis wilh Malcom Forbes at Midway Airport in Chicago. Circa 1988. John Psiharis collection.

happening and his plane awaited departure clearance, Mr. Forbes stood on the tarmac watching the fray, alone and unnoticed. Alice and I wandered over and introduced ourselves. We found him to be friendly and engaging. After some small talk, he invited us onboard to tour his plane, a dark green Boeing 727 with "Forbes Capitalist Tool" emblazoned in gold letters on its tail. He graciously walked us through the cabin filled with photos of the Forbes family dating back to when he was a child, photos of him with Elizabeth Taylor, and others, and other memorabilia. The fixtures were gold-plated. He had come to Chicago to interview the governor and was departing on a trip to Greece and Turkey, with his photographer, to gauge sentiment for Mike Dukakis' candidacy in these countries.

Others I met or came into contact with (often with Alice) include Kitty, Euterpe, and Olympia Dukakis (the governor's wife, mother, and cousin), Senator Lloyd Bentsen (vice presidential nominee), Madeleine Albright, John Chancellor, Tom Cruise, Sam Donaldson, Mark and Mary Herlihy-Gearan, Richard Gere, Kitty Kurth, Brigitte Nielsen, Robert Novak, Anne Roosevelt, Mike Royko, and George Stephanopoulos, among others.

The campaign rekindled a sense of ethnic pride that resonated amongst many Greek Americans, even those who were not usually Democrats. It galvanized a renewed interest in Greek culture, heritage, and all things Greek. This cultural renaissance could be seen in the heightened interest and participation in the community's cultural events. The governor had raised over $50 million, at the time, a record. A large amount of this was either donated or raised by Greek Americans.

A similar situation happened three years later when representatives of former Massachusetts Senator Paul Tsongas' presidential campaign asked if I would help with his campaign. I ended up running as a Tsongas delegate, assisting the campaign to locate office space, coordinating delegates in the region, and helping with ethnic outreach. I helped to organize an election rally with Tsongas delegates that was held on the floor of the Chicago Board of Trade and chaired an after-rally delegate fundraiser at the Cairo nightclub. I joined others in accompanying Paul to a speaking engagement at Northwestern University and to other locales and was asked to represent the campaign at a United Hellenic Voters Association endorsement session held at Thirteen Colonies Banquets. I recommended several delegates to the campaign, including Elaine, who became a Paul Tsongas delegate for her west suburban congressional district. Elaine won in her area, and with her son, Christopher in tow, went to the July 1992 convention in New York City. My congressional district was carried by Bill Clinton so I did not attend the convention.

(L-R): Nicole Tsongas, John Psiharis, and U.S. Senator Paul Tsongas at the Chicago Southside St. Patrick's Day Parade. March 1992. John Psiharis collection.

In 1988, 1990, 1992, and 1994, GACS conducted voter registration and outreach through volunteers who were trained and certified as voter registrars by the Cook County Clerk's Office. GACS volunteers were responsible for registering hundreds of voters. Pol Gavaris allowed GACS to have registrars at the Elysion and others went to events or out into the community to register voters. I recall GACS volunteers walking down Lawrence Avenue stopping into storefronts and *kafenios* to do voter outreach.

At various times, I was invited to attend meetings or serve on committees involving the Greek community, adult day care or ethnic elderly matters, and other areas of concern. I recall participating in a task force established by Senator Alan Dixon, an ethnic advisory committee for Illinois Attorney General Neil Hartigan, and participating in a two-day focus group on multicultural and ethnic issues facilitated by the Chicago Community Trust. I was an escort for Senator Paul Simon as he visited Greek restaurants and businesses in Lincoln Square and served on the Greeks for Carol Moseley Braun for the U.S. Senate Committee.

Top: U.S. Senator Alan Dixon and John Psiharis. Date unknown. John Psiharis collection. **Bottom:** John Psiharis and Illinois Attorney General Neil Hartigan. Background: John Rassogianis, Jim Mezilson, and unknown. Date unknown. John Psiharis collection.

The Dawn of Day Care

GACS had considered launching an adult day care center since its earliest days. It would be the first step toward a Greek nursing home and help prevent premature or unnecessary institutionalization of older adults. GACS established an Adult Day Care Task Force in 1987. In addition to GACS, the committee included representatives of the Chicago Department on Aging, Lutheran Social Services of Illinois, United Charities, and the Alzheimer's Adult Day Care Center. The first meeting was held on July 6, 1987, at the Elysion Restaurant. Over dinner, we heard from Pauline Yoshioka and Rose Jordan who were with the Greater Opportunities Adult Day Care Center in Skokie. The task force met periodically and made site visits to several adult day care centers to see them in operation.

The ADC Task Force established the following purpose statement for the ADC:

> The center will address the following needs both within the Greek community and the community at large:
>
> - Reduce isolation and depression among vulnerable elderly.
> - Provide respite to families and caregivers experiencing stress in caring for an older adult.
> - Offer a cost-effective alternative to in-home services or nursing home placements.
> - Provide participants with a safe, professional, and caring environment that respects their abilities, life experiences, and wishes; cares for them with dignity; is sensitive to the special needs of Greek-Americans, and offers socialization, health care, and companionship.

Ethel Kotsovos had worked in an adult day care center run by the North Shore Senior Center and was a passionate advocate for establishing a similar center in our community. I had completed a college internship at the Greater Opportunities Adult Day Care Center in Skokie and thus also believed in the benefits of this program.

The idea of seniors being in a communal setting, socializing, and being cared for in a safe and caring environment was a priority for GACS. Adult day care enabled seniors to stay at home with loved ones and still gain socialization, health care, and other assistance while reducing the need to admit loved ones into nursing homes prematurely.

The state saw this as a way to reduce the amount the state paid out through its Medicaid program to nursing homes for care needed by these patients.

Researchers had determined that upwards of ten thousand adult day care centers would be needed nationally to deal with the large numbers of baby boomers that would come of age in the coming decades.

In May 1989, an Emergency Request for Proposals (RFP) for adult day care services on the northwest side of Chicago was issued by IDOA. The only provider in the region, Norwood Park Home, had recently closed its adult day center. GACS was based on the northwest side and had established a track record through CAN and our other programs. The deadline for submission was in June. There wasn't much time to put it together.

When GACS received word of IDOA's RFP, we scrambled to prepare and submit the proposal in short order. Frequent meetings were held at the GACS offices on Monticello Street. The non-air-conditioned offices were uncomfortable given the heat, humidity, and lack of air circulation. In addition to Elaine and myself; Evangeline, Dr. Kioutas, John, Toni, and Ethel attended the meetings to work out the details. The proposal was submitted on time, and there was a 50-50 chance it would be approved.

One such meeting was held on June 14, 1989. Minutes from this special Board meeting, which was held at the GACS/CAN office indicate Evangeline Mistaras, John Rassogianis, Elaine Thomopoulos, Dr. Kioutas, Sandy Papadopoulos, and John Psiharis were in attendance. Special guests were Ethel and Jane Stansell, the director of Alzheimer's Family Care Center. The long meeting started at 7:30 p.m. and finished at 10:25 p.m. Recommendations gleaned from Jane's presentation included:

> This is the worst time to start a day care center in the City of Chicago. There is no chairman of the Chicago Department on Aging A.D.S. task force, no way of licensing such centers, and no way of getting a building permit since there are no requirements to contrast a permit application.
>
> She suggested we seek a three-month contract extension from IDOA to preserve the contract – September 30th ideal target date. The board approved this action, and John P. to follow up. A contract is in effect until IDOA decides to re-open the bidding. Some centers have operated for seven years based on their original contract.
>
> Sixty days after the center opens, IDOA will send an auditor out for a full five days. He will examine everything with a fine-tooth comb. It is imperative that there be paper trails and documentation for everything. Must have a written policy for everything.

We need to establish consistent admission and discharge criteria. However, IDOA may not regulate private pay policies.

Operating revenue comes from the contract and private pay clients. Can apply for a Veterans Administration contract which will pay more than CCP. At present, there is no V.A.-approved ADC in Chicago. ADC policy should allow for this option.

Non-operating revenue - need a minimum of four months' worth (six-to-eight months ideal) to cover general operating expenses and start-up costs until we begin to level off.

Furnishings – no fabric-covered furniture. Can get donated furniture for [sic] damaged warehouses or Marshall Fields.

In naming the center, don't stress GACS in the title as it implies non-Greeks can't come. ADC should have its own identity.

ADC services are considered maintenance and not rehabilitative and thus are not covered via third-party insurance.

A minimum of two full-time staff equivalents is required for centers with twelve or fewer clients.

Instead of stressing a sliding fee scale, we should say something like this," We will accept all people regardless of their ability to pay."

Jane's Center requires 25 clients per day to break even. Her fee is $37.00 per/day.

Not only are we responsible for arranging, but we must also pay for transportation for CCP clients. This can be done through the CTA special services program.

The problem with C.T.A. is they are unpredictable. A client must be in our center for at least 5 hours to obtain the full C.C.P. rate. If the bus is late or arrives too early, we can only bill for a ½ day.

1/3 of A.D.C. clients experience dementia [sic].

Transportation for Jane's center breaks down like this: 1/3 by families, 1/3 through her van, and 1/3 through C.T.A.

Clients have freedom of choice. Thus CCP clients from any part of the city or suburbs may select our center – market all over the area. However, GACS is only responsible for transporting those living in our service area.

Insurance is very expensive. Jane estimates $5,000 per year/per vehicle just for her van. ADC is a 'high risk' program. It is best to expand coverage for the ADC on an existing policy than to purchase a new policy.

Jane suggested we switch to Tri-R Vending for catering.

The state is over-anxious in auditing ADCs. They will give black marks for almost anything. Black marks indicate we are out of compliance. Out of Illinois' sixty-six ADCs, twenty have zero black marks and the standard deviation is two black marks. Fourteen ADCs are located in Chicago.

Jane believes most A.D.C.s fail for two reasons:

1. They don't market enough. You must market non-stop. Some agencies just wait for the C.C.U.s to send people over. Don't do it! We must be aggressive. The ADC Director must have time to do this.

2. When the center faces cutbacks. Don't cut staff. Cutting staff forces the person responsible for marketing and outreach (A.D.C. Director) to work indoors. If she/he's inside serving food, or driving clients around, there is no one marketing.

In looking for an A.D.C. director – the best candidate is an A.D.C. director from another center.

2nd preference – someone who has worked in an A.D.C.

3rd preference – those involved or active in the aging network.

Don't advertise in the Chicago Tribune.

12 hours of pre-service training is required for each A.D.C. employee.

Jane is available as a consultant to G.A.C.S., at a cost of $50.00 per/hour. She estimates it would cost between $1,500 and $1,800 to have her do a complete job. Her policies are a complete set, approved by the I.D.O.A, and can be purchased and modified by G.A.C.S. for our own purposes at a cost of $300. Her fee goes to her center. Board action should be taken on this.

After Jane left, the discussion on the A.D.C. continued.

John R. and [sic] John P. and Evangeline worked on a fundraising appeal letter and fact sheet. Both were approved.

Dr. Kioutas reported that George and Emily Alexander will set up the appointment with Dr. Nicholson.

John P. reported that he visited the Bethesda Home, 2833 N. Nordica, and that they have an ideal facility – 3,000 plus square feet with an adjacent kitchen, separate entrances, and removed from the rest of the nursing home. He met with the Administrator and Board President. Both were interested but it was up to their board to decide on June 26th. No estimate on the price.

John R. and Dr. Kioutas submitted their lists as to who should get appeal letters. John P. will have office staff prepare by the next meeting.

Next meeting, Wednesday, June 21, 1989, 7:30 P.M. at 3911 N. Monticello, 2nd floor.

The meeting adjourned at 10:25 P.M.

About eight weeks later, we were notified by IDOA that our application to offer adult day care services on the northwest side of Chicago as of September 1, 1989, had been approved. Our service area boundaries were the Chicago River on the east, the city limits to both the west and north, and Fullerton on the south. GACS immediately requested a three-month extension to January 1, 1990, since much needed to happen to open the center. Key among these tasks was to find a location and hire and train staff.

GACS would receive $30 per day/client from the state for each day a state-subsidized client attended the center. The reimbursement included the cost of transportation. Clients qualified for the program if they had assets of $12,000 or less, not including a house or car. Co-payments were determined using a sliding fee scale based on monthly income with the first $500 being exempt. GACS established the private pay rate for adult day care clients who did not qualify for state subsidy at $35 per day. A full day of care was four or more hours. If a client attended for less than four hours, GACS received $17.50 from the state. Private pay clients that didn't attend for the full day paid a prorated hourly rate.

It was estimated that GACS needed to raise $30,000 to launch this program and $100,000 to sustain the program over the first few years. This included rent and related costs, furnishings, training, and initial staffing. It was known that the state, which we expected would make up the largest percentage of the client mix, was a frequent late payer, so we needed a cushion to allow for delayed payments.

Once we were notified that the contract was approved, fundraising kicked into high gear with a sense of urgency. The effort began with a community-wide appeal for donations and articles which appeared in community media outlets including the August 6, 1989 issue of the *Greek Press*. This article entitled "Urgent Appeal for G.A.C.S. Funds" read:

Greek-American Community Services has been awarded a grant by the Illinois Department on Aging to establish and operate an Adult Day Care Center on Chicago's Northwest side beginning this summer.

In this program, the Greek-American Community Services will give daily relief to caregivers by offering treatment, care, recreation, and companionship in a warm supportive environment.

Start-up funds in the amount of $100,000 from our Community must be raised in the next 60 days. They are essential to get this pioneering effort off the ground to meet the provisions of the state contract.

'Failure to raise these funds will force G.A.C.S. to return the grant to the State. We cannot let this happen,' stated John Psiharis, G.A.C.S. Executive Director.

'This will be the first comprehensive adult day care center on the Northwest side of Chicago. We are trying to position ourselves to locate in either the Holy Trinity or St. Demetrios areas,' he added.

Members of the site selection committee are Dr. Theodosis Kioutas, Ethel Kotsovos, Peter Maroutsos, Evangeline Mistaras, Athanasia Papadopoulos, John Psiharis, John Rassogianis, and Elaine Thomopoulos. G.A.C.S. President Evangeline Mistaras reported that a decision on an appropriate site will be announced shortly.

Ethel Kotsovos stated 'Donations to this worthy project may be made in someone's honor or a special occasion such as a name day, birthday, graduation, or anniversary. Or they may be made in the form of memorial opportunities,' she added.

Please send contributions to Greek-American Community Services Adult Day Care Center Steering Committee, 4817 W. Montrose, Chicago, IL 60641, or call the GACS office at (312) 539-2323.

In August, the Eclecteon Fine Arts Society hosted a benefit for the adult day care center at Ravinia. The event featured award-winning violinist Leonidas Kavakos and the Chicago Symphony Orchestra. It was a potluck fundraiser on the Ravinia picnic grounds and was well attended. Over $1,000 was raised. The event was organized by Don Dadas, Sandy Ganakos, and Dee Tzakis.

Eclecteon Fine Arts Society recently held a benefit evening at Ravinia, featuring award winning violinist Leonidas Kavakos with the Chicago Symphony Orchestra. This successful evening benefitted the newly established Greek-American Adult Day Care Center, scheduled to open in October, sponsored by the Greek-American Community Services. Pictured l to r: Don Dadas, Chairman of Eclecteon's Board; Leonidas Kavakos, featured artist; Sandra Ganakos, President of Eclecteon Fine Arts Society; Dee Tzakis, Past President of Eclecteon Fine Arts Society.

The *Greek Press*, August 27, 1989. Elaine Thomopoulos collection.

Also in August, GACS organized a house party fundraising event at Nick and Elaine's second home in Bridgman, Michigan. Modeled on our prior house party fundraisers they hosted at their Oak Brook home in support of CAN; this one benefitted the new adult day care center. Both Elaine and John's families had roots in southwestern Michigan dating back decades. Many Chicago area Greek American families maintained homes in Michigan or visited those who did. New Buffalo, Stevensville, Bridgman, St. Joseph, Union Pier, and Benton Harbor were popular destinations for many Greek families; some had vacationed in these parts since their youth.

Guests were greeted with a Tiki Torch-lit event featuring an assortment of homemade and locally donated food selections. Two Thomas R. Dawkins limited edition photographic paintings entitled "Blueberries" and "Raspberries" and plants donated by Nick Poulos were raffled off that evening.

In addition to the party, John planned an eventful weekend for those who wanted to make it a weekend getaway. All activities were optional. Among the activities that were planned: Lunch at Tabor Hill Winery, tomato, peach, and blueberry picking excursions, a shopping outing in St. Joseph's, a beach day at Wako Beach, Dune climbing, peach picking at Shafer's, and apple or pear picking at Johansens. A small group went to Sunday morning church services at Annunciation Greek Orthodox Church in Benton Harbor while others gathered for breakfast at Bob's Big Boy, a longtime local favorite. The event was well attended and both a fundraising and friend-raising success. Fatouros Greek Harbor (New Buffalo), Greek Islands Restaurant (Bridgman), Olympus Restaurant (Bridgman), J and J Truck Stop (New Buffalo), and Santaniello's Glenlord Restaurant and Pizzeria supported the event by donating food and helping to publicize the event through their businesses. John prepared a five-page informational flier detailing the weekend schedule, area lodging and bed, and breakfast inn options, and travel directions from Chicago.

Elaine remembers: "The event at my home in Bridgman was attended by many local Greeks, and they helped in planning the event. I noticed quite a few who were on the committee." The committee for the Michigan event was chaired by John Rassogianis and co-chaired by Sophia Fatouros. Committee members included: George and Emilee Alexandrou, John and Pitsa Arvan, Angelo and Kiki Arvanitis, Sonia Arvanitis, George Bacos, Alice Buzanis, Bill and Dena Dalianis, Harry Dalianis, Deno Fatouros, Nick Fatouros, Nicholas G. Festos, Paul and Pauline Franks, Christopher Hager, Tolis Hovardas, Michail and Louisa Kerhulas, Dr. Theodosis Kioutas, Ethel Kotsovos, Chris and Tasia Lepeniotes, Peter Maroutsos, Evangeline Mistaras, Toni Panos, Athanasia Papadopoulos, John Psiharis, Nick Poulos, Elaine Thomopoulos, and Rev. Theodore Vegalis.

During one fall meeting of the Adult Day Care Committee, I remember us discussing ways to raise the balance of the money needed to open. John pulled out his trusty worn-out pocket-mini-sized address book and called Kay Valone, director of Phos Missions. During that call, Kay pledged several thousand dollars from her mission, putting us back on track. Kay also publicized the center in her "View from the Pew" columns in the *Greek Press* newspaper.

Although fundraising efforts were successful, the goal had not yet been reached. To address the shortfall, GACS held one final fundraiser before the year's end. A cocktail reception was held on December 14, 1989, at the Neon Greek Village nightclub on Halsted Street. The tickets were $50 each, and guests were treated to a special performance by Vasilios Gaitanos. The event was well attended and enthusiasm was in the air since the new center would be opening in three weeks.

The cocktail party was coordinated by Alice Buzanis, GACS director of development, and Manolis Alpogianis, GACS special events coordinator. Alice and Manolis assumed these positions as volunteers. Alice was a good friend, who had been active in the Dukakis campaign and worked as the director of development for the Illinois Democratic Party. Manolis and his brother George would go on to launch America's Dog, a local chain of hot dog restaurants. His family owned Kappy's, a well-known pancake house located in Morton Grove.

GACS Fundraising Committee meeting in the adult day care center at Alvernia Place. Pictured (L-R): Evangeline Mistaras, Manolis Alpogiannis, Alice Buzanis, John Psiharis, and John Rassogianis. Circa 1990-1991. John Psiharis collection.

Additional support from the community included over $1,000 raised by Fannie Manos and Venetia Papamichos, two elderly residents of Hollywood House who went door to door in their apartment building and approached fellow parishioners across the street at St. Andrew Greek Orthodox Church, to collect donations in support of this project. A few years later, their efforts were recognized by Illinois Governor Jim Edgar when he presented Fannie and Venetia with awards during a multicultural senior citizens day event.

Other donations came through special fundraising appeals made by board members and supporters. Several Philoptochos societies and organizations contributed in support of the center. The Hellenic Medical Society, American Hellenic Society of Berwyn, Martin L. and Wyleen T. Coyne Foundation, Walgreens Foundation, and the Assumption Women's Club come to mind but there were others as well.

The priority was to locate a facility to house the program. The state required 40 square feet of common space per client and GACS had a goal of 30 clients per day; at least 1,200 feet of common space was needed. The facility was also required to be accessible to disabled participants and have adequate bathroom facilities (one per every 10 clients). Common space did not include the kitchen, offices, bathrooms, storage areas, and closets.

We wanted to be centrally located within the service area so there was easy access to those who lived anywhere within the program boundaries. Janet Logan, an assistant commissioner with the Chicago Department on Aging, joined the adult day care planning committee to help us find a suitable location that would pass muster in terms of codes. Jane Stansell, director of the Alzheimer's Family Care Center and President of the Illinois Adult Day Services Association, also provided additional consultation. GACS board members toured the Council for Jewish Elderly and the Japanese American Service Committee adult day care centers to get a better idea of what was involved in running a program.

Among the locations we considered were:

- A warehouse with offices located near Holy Trinity Church (Diversey and Austin Avenues). Although this location had ample open space, it would have required a lot of renovations to comply with adult day care center codes.
- A corner storefront on Belmont near Harlem was considered but was deemed too far west from where we wanted to be within our service boundaries.
- A newly built building at 3940 N. Pulaski Road (Irving Park Road and Pulaski) was also considered. The owner offered to build it out to suit our needs, but committee members were concerned about the minimal parking and heavy traffic around the building. The building only had windows in the front and appeared to be "boxy." Also, the rent was higher than what GACS hoped to pay.
- Jim Kozonis offered us reduced rent at three of his strip malls that had vacancies. One on Milwaukee Avenue near Bryn Mawr was deemed too far northwest. The second, in the Veterans' Square Mall, adjacent to the Jefferson Park Terminal was of interest but was slated to undergo a multi-year building and underground parking expansion that would have put us in the middle of a construction zone for too long. We were interested in his strip mall on Irving Park and Kildare, but there were no vacancies at that time.
- At the suggestion of Bill LaMagdeleine, we considered locating within the Bethesda Home. Although the nursing home was further west than we would have liked, there were opportunities for joint activities, lunch, and snacks from their dietary department, and perhaps even subcontracting staff in some way. It seemed promising. For some reason, after several weeks of discussion, the nursing home decided they did not want to sublet space to an outside organization, and the state required that we have a designated space rather than a shared space.

After suggestions from several people to check out the old Alvernia High School building, the committee found an adequate (but not ideal) space. Ethel Kotsovos advocated for this location over the others under consideration. Some ADC committee members had concerns about the complexity of accessing our space, but given the strict timeline we needed to adhere to, this became our most viable option. The space was on the fourth floor and required an elevator ride and a long walk down a hallway to get to the center. Wheelchairs were placed by the elevator for anyone who required assistance.

Since time was running out to meet the state deadline to open, a decision was made to locate the adult day care center there, at least temporarily, until a permanent facility was chosen. The building, located at 3901 N. Ridgeway Avenue/3900 N. Lawndale Avenue (near Irving Park and Pulaski) had been Alvernia High School, a girls' high school that opened in 1924. Like many Catholic schools with dwindling student enrollment, the school was forced to close in 1989.

The School Sisters of St Francis, the Milwaukee-based order that operated the school, renamed the building Alvernia Place and envisioned turning this building into a community center that would serve as a "non-profit incubator," housing organizations that provided services to the community, with the vision that the tenants would complement each other and work together to strengthen and enhance their collective efforts.

GACS signed a three-year lease at Alvernia Place. New neighbors included: Northeastern Illinois University Teachers Center which shared the third floor with GACS, Search Developmental, Kid Watch Child Care, Outward Bound, and Call to Action. Dominic Lobello was the enterprising manager of the building who worked to maximize the building's financial potential to cover the exorbitant costs of operating a large and aging building. A devout Catholic and a member of the Knights of Columbus, Dominic represented the order and mentioned that the sisters were particularly excited to have an adult day care program as part of the building's mix. Alvernia Place now had organizations that ranged from infants to senior citizens.

The space the center occupied was formerly the school's arts and crafts room. The room was bright with a row of windows that emitted plenty of sunlight. The cheerful green space was filled with built-in wooden cabinets that were perfect for storage, two sinks, and ample space for seniors to gather collectively as well as breakaway space if some quiet time is needed. GACS also rented the adjacent band room to provide office space

Top: Entrance to Alvernia Place from Ridgeway Ave. **Bottom:** ADC room at Alvernia Place. Circa 1989. John Psiharis collection.

for the staff. It had been leveled off, but one step remained and during our time there, many of us tripped over it, forgetting that there was a step in the middle of the room.

Ethel and I went shopping for furniture at used office furniture warehouses where we purchased many of the furnishings at very good prices. This included 30 colorful green and blue side chairs and a matching sofa as well as tables and chairs for the activity area. Pol donated cases of water and juice glasses, silverware, and dishes from his restaurant. A community member donated a hospital bed which we maintained in the nurse's office in the event a client needed to rest or did not feel well. Donations of a refrigerator, television, stereo equipment, electric piano, and arts and crafts supplies were also received. Bill LaMagdelein obtained a donation of a new exercise bicycle.

The main issue with this location was that it was on the fourth floor. Despite the elevator, it was a bit of a walk to get to the room. A wheelchair was available to assist clients as needed. Other drawbacks were that we did not have street visibility, and new visitors would sometimes get lost within the building trying to find the center. Eventually, a building directory was placed on the corner of Lawndale and Byron Streets with a listing of occupants and arrows directing guests to the appropriate entry doors.

Notes from an October 10, 1989 meeting of the GACS Adult Day Care Organizing Committee revealed the varied tasks at hand.

> In attendance: John Psiharis, Bill Magdeleine, Elaine Thomopoulos, Dr. Kioutas, Ethel Kotsovos, Luke Fitzgerald, and Rose Vuco.
>
> John reported that IDOA granted an extension to January 1st for the ADC to open. Dr. Kioutas has been exploring the possibility of getting some sponsorship from a hospital. Lincoln West and Martha Washington responded that they are not interested. He has a meeting with the administrator of Belmont Hospital.
>
> Advertisements for an ADC director have been placed. We are preparing a grant request to the Chicago Community Trust to hire a consultant to train staff and establish policies for the ADC. Elaine suggests adding fundraising to the role of the consultant. We are paying a reduced rent of $500 per month from October through December since the ADC hasn't opened yet. We will begin paying the full rent on January 1st. Bill has obtained a donation of a new refrigerator and will arrange pickup. Ethel has received eight inquiries on ADC to date. Two women in their eighties who live at Hollywood House have raised $650 for the center. Their goal is $1,000. Luke Fitzgerald suggests approaching United Methodist Homes and Services for possible partnerships and Bankers Life and Casualty for financial support. Alice Buzanis to coordinate the cocktail party. Rose Vuco to contact the Portage Park Chamber of Commerce. Bill will organize a fundraiser and appoint a committee. We need to focus on fundraising.

Minutes from an ADC Organizing Committee meeting held on November 16, 1989, at the new Alvernia Place location included the following synopsis: "Dana Ferdinand received the flyer printout from Erica Karp and will keyline the figures and get the flyers photocopied in time for the health fair being held over the weekend at Irving Park Lutheran Church. Since the last meeting two $100 donations came in from Elaine Thomopoulos and Leanord Carlson. John reported we were still waiting to hear about financial support from Belmont Hospital. A cocktail party will be held on December 14, 1989. Tickets are $50 each. Letters will be sent to those who may donate $1,000 and to prominent Greek Americans who could serve as honorary chairpersons. Bill got 5,000 raffle tickets printed for $66. So far, $115 in tickets have been sold. Prizes to date include a boat trip, bottles of wine, and a dinner for two at Casa Nieves Restaurant."

In terms of staffing, GACS at the minimum needed to hire a nurse and activity director. IDOA policies required at least two staff members (one a nurse). The nurse could be an R.N. or an L.P.N. under the supervision of an R.N. Fran Nichols (Argiris), a retired nurse who had previously worked at Hollywood House, became the center's nurse. As a volunteer, Fran was the supervisor of the GACS Friendly Visiting Program. Ethel Kotsovos, in addition to her role as director of CAN, conducted intakes and provided social work services to ADC clients and their families.

After interviewing several applicants, Ann T. Prusinski, who had worked as an activity aide for St. Joseph's Nursing Home, was selected to be the activity director. Ann remained with the adult day care center throughout its 12-year existence. Dr. Kioutas acted as the center's medical director and provided consultation and in-service training to the nursing staff. He also conducted periodic health education discussions with the clients. Ann and Amy took classes to become certified food-service sanitation managers.

Search Developmental, a day program for the developmentally disabled, provided freshly prepared lunches and snacks at their cost to our participants from their kitchen. The aroma of the meals being cooked each day would permeate the building and the food quality was high. We paid a reasonable rate for the meals and snacks which were prepared onsite. Intergenerational activities were a frequent part of the schedule for both Kid Watch and GACS with the seniors and children gathering for music, art projects, intergenerational storytelling, and poetry activities at least once per week.

> **NORTHWEST CHICAGO SENIOR DAY CARE**
> **of the ALVERNIA PLACE**
> **CASH RAFFLE**
>
> 1st Prize $300.00
> 2nd Prize $200.00
> 3rd Prize $100.00
>
> **All proceeds Benefit N.W.S.D.C.**
> DONATION: $1.00 PURCHASE • SIX FOR $5.00
> GRAND DRAWING AT THE CENTER of the ALVERNIA PLACE
> 3900 N. LAWNDALE AVE. • CHICAGO, ILLINOIS
> JAN. 14th, 1990 – 2:00 P.M. till 5:00
> WINNERS NEED NOT BE PRESENT - RAFFLE TICKET HOLDERS ADMITTED FREE
>
> No. 193
>
> NCSC raffle ticket. January 14, 1990. John Psiharis collection.

On January 8, 1990, the GACS adult day care center opened its doors. Initially, the center was open on Wednesdays with plans to add additional days as the client base grew. The first client was Mary, a retired Greek school teacher from Solon School (St. Andrew church). Soon thereafter, George, a retired cook, who laid claim to owning the first air-conditioned restaurant in Chicago, and Zoe, also a retired teacher, joined the participant ranks. In time, other clients both Greek and from the broader community enrolled. Within a couple of months, as the census grew, the center expanded its days to include Fridays. At about the midyear point, Mondays were added, followed thereafter by Tuesdays. Thursdays were added after we moved to Pulaski, and the center was officially open five days per week.

On January 14, GACS hosted an open house to introduce the program (and the organization) to the community. Refreshments were donated by local restaurants and a raffle was held to raise funds. There were cash prizes and I believe a couple of the winners donated their prizes back to the center. A donation of a Schwinn exercise bicycle was unveiled and the center staff was introduced during the event.

Additional money was needed to help cover the center's operating expenses until enough clients were enrolled to sustain the program. Dr. Kioutas, with the support of Dr. Angelo Creticos, chairman of the hospital's medical staff, approached Illinois Masonic Medical Center to request support for the center. The administration, led by Harvey Morowitcz, vice president of operations, and Michael Swarzman, vice president of new initiatives, agreed to provide $2,000 per month to support the center. They offered their public relations staff and paid for the design and printing of a brochure. Illinois Masonic also referred potential clients who lived too far from their adult day care program within Warren Barr Pavilion, their nursing home near Chicago's Gold Coast. In all, Illinois Masonic provided more than $30,000 in support to the adult day care program.

A grant request submitted to the United Way of Chicago Priority Grant program on February 21, 1990, requested $290,517 over three years in support of the adult day care center. The funds would be used to employ a program director, support outreach efforts to increase client census, and offer a transportation component. The grant reflected our early thinking related to transportation and mentioned that GACS would either contract with a transportation provider or cover the transportation costs of the CTA Special Services Taxi Access Program, which provided door-to-door taxi service to special needs passengers for a nominal fee.

At the time of submission, the center had only been open for six weeks and had three enrolled participants. Although GACS did not receive this grant, excerpts from the application clearly articulated the need for this program and the development plan that was envisioned at the time. The components included in this request were ultimately funded through subsequent grants received from the Chicago Community Trust and the Retirement Research Foundation.

> N.C.S.C. is the first comprehensive adult day care center on Chicago's northwest side. The other two programs located in the service area are Alzheimer's Family Care Center (which only serves those experiencing mid and later stages of dementia and an activity program which is an offshoot of the Norwood Park Home). G.A.C.S. maintains a contract with the Illinois Department on Aging to offer adult day care services through the Community Care Program.
>
> Even though the Northwest service area boasts one of the largest populations of older adults in the metropolitan Chicago area, the community, bounded by North Avenue on the south, the city limits on the north and west, and the Chicago River-North Branch, has had to shuttle client to facilities located in other parts of the city.
>
> Census data indicates that 107,735 people aged 55 and over and 76,675 people aged 65 and over are living within the area. With the continued aging of our society, longer life expectancy rates, and the gradual aging of the baby boom generation, it is safe to assume that 1990 census data will document an even larger number of older adults living in the area.
>
> These trends indicate a vast amount of growth in the older adult category in the coming years. Yet there is no apparent parallel growth in services designed to serve this population.
>
> As people live longer, their health problems tend to compound and become more severe. These health problems usually affect older adults' mental health as well. This usually leads to social

isolation, depression, or substance abuse. Likewise, they are forced to adapt to the realities of aging: loss of friends or spouses, living on a fixed income, and loss of mobility.

Those who are fortunate enough to have their families to care for them are confronted with the added issue of depending on those who have, for so long, depended on them. No longer is the parent the breadwinner, housekeeper, and cook, but now the recipient of the same kind of care.

This role reversal places a tremendous burden on the entire family unit. Adult children, already working and raising their own families, must now also care for Mom or Dad. When the parent is not adequately able to care for himself or herself, the family out of love, loyalty, and ethics assumes the role of caregiver.

Families face few alternatives in getting help or respite in caring for a parent. They can choose to stop working or opt to leave a parent home alone. Neither option is desirable.

Home health care is a costly alternative that does not aid in reducing isolation or increasing socialization. Nursing home care, even more costly, is often not necessary since the family is capable of offering care in the evening hours. Why institutionalize a loved one for 24 hours, when you only need care for 8 hours?

Caregivers who are not working, often experience an equally high degree of stress; not even a brief respite, i.e. to go shopping, to go to the beauty shop, or lunch with friends can be achieved without inconveniencing others.

Adult day care offers a win-win situation for all involved. Caregivers gain the peace of mind of knowing that their loved one is in a safe and secure environment – thus caregiver stress is reduced. The older adult wins because he or she is in an environment where he is challenged, able to socialize, eat a well-balanced meal; and is cared for by a professional team trained in caregiving, treated with the respect and dignity that he or she is entitled to as an individual, and most importantly able to get out of the house and away from the family. Adult day care is also an inexpensive and cost-effective alternative – fees average $3.75 per hour (based on 8 hours of service). For eligible clients, the Community Care Program will subsidize G.A.C.S for all or part of the fee.

Thus, N.C.S.C. offers accessible and inexpensive alternatives for both the elderly and their families by allowing the older person to remain independent and in his or her community,

> reducing caregiver stress and aiding in the healthy integration and adjustment of the family unit.
>
> Within the northwest side, according to 1980 Census data, 3.6% of 28.400 families are below the poverty level; an additional 2.5% are between 100 and 124% of the poverty level. In the northeast service area (G.A.C.S. will attract some clients from there), 6% of 19.000 families are below the poverty level and 2.6% are between 100-124%.
>
> Most elderly clients are on very fixed incomes, having only Social Security to depend on. Additionally, those that will be served through this center are expected to be in an even more critical financial situation since they may have faced large medical expenses.
>
> Clients who are eligible for a subsidy under the Community Care Program are in financial need. It is expected that by year three, 65% of those served will be C.C.P. clients.
>
> G.A.C.S believes that those seeking assistance through N.C.S.C. will be doing so in large part because other more expensive alternatives to care are not accessible to families.

Another section of the grant entitled "Capacity to Deliver Planned Program" described GACS activities up to that point. Neither Elaine nor I recall details of the advocacy effort that was mentioned below and don't think it ever came to fruition. Excerpts from the six-page response are included here:

> Since its inception, G.A.C.S. has had a long-standing commitment to helping older adults – both within and outside the Greek community. This is demonstrated by the long and successful track record the agency has achieved since its inception in 1983.
>
> G.A.C.S. approaches the older adult population with programs designed to minimize premature institutionalization by offering supportive measures that enable the client to remain in his or her own home or community for as long as possible.
>
> Services offered by the Community Aging Network (C.A.N.), an agency of G.A.C.S., work towards this goal. Each year nearly 800 elderly clients receive assistance in the following areas: information and referral, advocacy, transportation, and escort to medical appointments, the Social Security Office, etc., home help, friendly visiting, telephone visiting, translation, literacy sessions, volunteer opportunities, and a teen home chore program. In 1989, C.A.N.'s efforts were supported through a United Way of Chicago Venture Grant.

Clients come from all backgrounds and walks of life. Several characteristics include: more female than male, slightly fewer 'young old' than 'old-old' clients; primarily north side residents, though clients are from throughout the city; 24% live in United Way targeted communities, 36% of clients are of Greek descent.

Clients are assisted through trained volunteers; many of whom are themselves over age 60, and 43 percent live in United Way target communities. Several of our older volunteers are themselves homebound and make friendly visiting telephone calls daily to other homebound clients.

G.A.C.S. offers other programs targeted at the elderly. These include a Fabric Arts Project held at the Levy Senior Citizens Center and funded by the Chicago Office of Fine Arts. Each week 30 elderly participants attend. Though the immediate goal is to teach and produce works of artistic value that enable a participant to creatively express herself, an additional benefit is the socialization aspect of the program.

G.A.C.S offers monthly community education programs to limited and non-English speaking elderly. Attendance varies from 60 to 100 attendees. The topics are health education, consumer awareness, benefits and entitlements, and cultural activities.

G.A.C.S. relates daily with a variety of social service agencies, hospitals, city departments, and churches to serve its caseload. Often the program has been the point of last resort to serve a client for larger service providers.

G.A.C.S. is an active participant in the aging and ethnic service provider networks. Presently G.A.C.S. representatives participate regularly in efforts to better serve the elderly. Also under consideration is an advocacy effort in which G.A.C.S. will play a key role and which Robert Ahrens, former commissioner of the Chicago Department on Aging and Disability, initiated. The G.A.C.S. executive director is a founding member and president-elect of the Coalition of Limited English Speaking Elderly.

Offering quality care to the elderly is a philosophy that G.A.C.S. has adhered to since day one. To this end, G.A.C.S. has established the Greek-American Nursing Home Committee, presently a sister organization with its own legal identity but many shared board members. The Committee is well on its way to meeting its goal of establishing a nursing home. To date, several hundred thousand dollars are in-hand or pledged. Presently, the committee is negotiating with the City of Chicago for a parcel of land in North Park Village. The proposal has the backing of the neighboring alderman. Mayor Daley expressed his verbal support at a recent meeting with committee representatives.

G.A.C.S. has been working to establish an adult day care center since 1986. A task force of board members, staff, and interested parties researched, visited, and received consultation from other adult day care programs located in Chicago, Skokie, and Elmhurst. They worked diligently to realize this goal and were rewarded on January 8, 1990 – when Northwest Chicago Senior Care opened its doors. G.A.C.S.'s interest in adult day care stems from the desire to prevent or at least delay institutionalizing elderly clients in an unfamiliar environment which especially for non-English speaking clients can be devastating.

The program creates a three-pronged approach to caring for the community's elderly. First, the Hellenic Foundation offers a retirement residence for the high-functioning elderly at Hollywood House, 5700 N. Sheridan. The adult day care center is the second level of care for those who cannot fully care for themselves but do not need nursing home placement. Finally, when the nursing home is open, those in need of extended care will be serviced.

The narrative goes on to describe agreements with other ethnic organizations to service their elders. Neither Elaine nor I recall these agreements, but they come as no surprise given our relationships with these organizations, and, Carole, Sue, and Judy were members of the NCSC advisory committee:

Within the Greek community, G.A.C.S. has raised a majority of its donations from individuals and organizations. A $1,000 donation was received from the Phos Mission. The board and staff are speaking to many church groups and fraternal organizations to receive support. Two radio hosts have donated their time to raise awareness and funds through radio-thons. Hundreds of individuals have expressed their support or pledged to help.

Within the ethnic communities, G.A.C.S. has full support and working agreements with the Polish Welfare Association, Korean American Senior Center, and the National Association for Hispanic Elderly to serve their limited English-speaking clients. G.A.C.S. will recruit staff and volunteers who speak these languages so that these traditionally underserved communities can also benefit from this program. Already through the efforts of the Polish Welfare Association, two feature-length articles have appeared in the *Polish Daily Press.* Representatives from these organizations serve on the N.C.S.C. Organizing Committee.

From the community at large, G.A.C.S. has received an outpouring of support. Illinois Masonic Hospital has pledged to donate $2,000 per month to the Center; Norman Ross featured the Center in a five-minute segment of the Channel 7 News with Linda Yu. WGN-TV mentioned the Center on a noon newscast. Regular articles have appeared in the neighborhood press. The social meeting of a Lutheran church made an unsolicited donation. The Chicago Department on Aging and Disability Copernicus Center staff have played a vital role in opening the Center.

An organizing committee composed of ethnic representatives, service providers, day care professionals, and business people (see attached) has been meeting regularly to plan strategies for reaching the community at large, raising funds, dealing with logistics, operations, public relations, and outreach. The Committee arranged an open house in January that some 100 neighborhood residents attended. A second open house will target service providers, referral sources, and area clergy and the third will target the Greek community.

These efforts of networking with individuals and organizations in each of these communities will continue to grow and strengthen in the coming years.

On May 31, 1990, the *Hellenic Chronicle* lauded the opening of the center. An editorial entitled "The Young and the Elderly" reported on the opening of the adult day care program as well as a newly launched child care center in Roslindale Massachusetts:

> It appears logical to combine these two ideas with a mutually beneficial result. The elderly could serve as "grandparents" to the young and help them feel needed again. The children, perhaps not having grandparents of their own, could derive much love and knowledge of our traditions from the elderly. Such undertakings would provide a great service to their respective communities and should be investigated for feasibility wherever possible. We wish communities considering such ventures much success.

On July 1, an *Agiasmos* (Blessings of the Waters) service and open house were held at the new center. The Very Reverend Nikitas C. Lulias, Chancellor of the Greek Orthodox Diocese of Chicago, officiated. Michael Swarzman and Dr. Angelo Creticos were in attendance representing Illinois Masonic Medical Center. Kay Valone from Phos Missions and

NCSC brochure cover. Circa 1990. John Psiharis collection.

other community members were present. Tours were given, and refreshments were served. Pre and post-event publicity provided additional visibility for the new program.

We reached out to the Hellenic Foundation to discuss the new program and explore ways that we could work together but these efforts were not successful. Instead, I soon received a call from Jean Blaser, Manager of the IDOA Community Care Program, reporting that a Freedom of Information Act request for our RFP and contract had been made by Cynthia Yannias on behalf of the Hellenic Foundation. Jean asked me why Cynthia didn't just ask us for a copy and mentioned that in her many years at IDOA, it was rare for one provider to request another's information. Rather than embrace this new initiative as a benefit to the elderly in our community, it seemed to us that Cynthia viewed the ADC as competition, and I was told that Foundation staff were discouraged from making referrals or supporting us in any tangible way.

There was some reluctance by non-Greek families and case managers to utilize GACS because of the impression that it was for Greeks only. The program focused on the Greek elderly, but the overriding goal was to provide professional and caring service to anyone in need. After consideration and in light of these concerns, GACS named the adult day care program Northwest Chicago Senior Care Center. The name was intended to provide a message to the broader community that all were welcome. It was designated as an agency of GACS in the same way the Community Aging Network and the Cultural Arts Program were.

ΝΕΑ ΠΡΟΓΡΑΜΜΑΤΑ
ΣΥΛΛΟΓΟΥ
ΕΛΛΗΝΟ-ΑΜΕΡΙΚΑΝΙΚΩΝ ΥΠΗΡΕΣΙΩΝ

Ο Σύλλογος Ελληνο-Αμερικανικών Υπηρεσιών με πολλή χαρά ανακοινώνει τη δημιουργία των εξής Κέντρων Φροντίδας Υπερηλίκων.

Northwest Chicago Senior Care Center

Κέντρον Ημερησίας
Φροντίδας Υπερηλίκων.

NCSC Greek brochure cover in Greek. Circa 1990. Elaine Thomopoulos collection.

With the help of Michael Bruckner, a public relations and marketing consultant from Illinois Masonic, a brochure was developed. It consisted of four parts. Each bore the name and sunburst logo of Northwest Chicago Senior Care along with the wording "An Agency of Greek-American Community Services." One brochure was in English and focused on the broader community with little mention of the Greek component. The second was in English but geared to Greek families and caregivers and focused on the Greek elements of the center. Two inserts were designed. One was in the Greek language and summarized key information about the program for those who could not read English. Fotios Litsas and Dr. Kioutas worked on the translations. The final component was a "how you can help" insert which provided a response card and detailed opportunities for people to submit donations or inquire about volunteering. Illinois Masonic donated the printing of the brochures. These were high-quality professionally designed brochures.

An article by Dean Geroulis, staff writer for the *Pulitzer-Lerner Newspapers,* entitled "Greek-American Agency Redefines its Community," appeared in their March 20 - 21, 1990 newspapers and provided a synopsis of where we were at this point.

> Several years ago, a handful of energetic and ambitious Greek Americans decided it was time to offer more to their community and reach out to their ethnic American neighbors.
>
> They were young and old, but with a common thought: 'We saw a lot of needs within the Greek community that were not being

met,' said John Psiharis, executive director and one of the founders of Greek-American Community Services.

In 1983, these men and women incorporated a unique social service organization – unique in that Greek people are reluctant to seek assistance from outsiders such as social service agencies. 'Greeks are very proud people,' said John Rassogianis, a member of the Greek-American Community Services Board of Directors. 'They don't like to ask for help.'

Traditionally, Greek families take care of their own. But in the United States, even traditional Greek families have experienced some alienation and deterioration of the extended family unit.

Even when family members do look out for their own, they often are not aware of what services are available for the elderly or are unable to get in touch with agencies that offer those services because of the language barrier. 'A lot of elderly are lonely out there,' Psiharis said.

Working out of the Alvernia Center, 3901 N. Ridgeway, the organization wants to complement the work of the Hellenic Foundation. That group manages apartments for seniors and provides one-on-one counseling for Greek families.

Greek-American Community Services, meanwhile, took over the Northwest Side's Community Aging Network, established a cultural program that has been operating statewide, and in January opened an adult day care center for Northwest Side senior citizens. Information on all of these programs is available from the Alvernia headquarters, telephone 539-2323.

In addition, a sister group, the Greek-American Nursing Home Committee, is working to establish a facility in Chicago. The nursing home would not be limited to Greek Americans, but the atmosphere would be one where elderly Greeks can live in familiar surroundings.

'None of the programs are limited to Greek-Americans', Psiharis emphasized. Although carrying an ethnic label, the organization wants to be known as a social service organization for all people, much like Catholic Charities and Lutheran Social Services.

Probably the organization's most ambitious program to date is the day care center for elderly adults. Psiharis said it may be the only facility of its type serving the Northwest Side. There are only a few clients now, but the directors are already thinking about branching out into more locations and expanding services for future clients.

Hot lunches, exercise programs, field trips, and presentations are on the agenda as the day care program grows.

Less than half of the seniors served by the Community Aging Network are Greek according to coordinator Ethel Kotsovos. With a team of several volunteers, CAN helps seniors confined to their homes. The program offers visits, telephone reassurance, rides, and shopping and helps seniors fill out forms to take advantage of the services and benefits available to them.

Kotsovos also recruits high school students as volunteers to 'acquaint young people with what happens when you get older and can't get around anymore.'

Even the cultural program works with organizations representing other ethnic groups. 'In order to understand our identity, we believe it's helpful to look at other ethnic groups,' said program coordinator Elaine Thomopoulos. The cultural program recognizes Greek-American artists, musicians, writers, and poets. Unlike the programs for the aging, the cultural heritage program is not limited to the Northwest Side. It has had presentations in various parts of the state, targeting Greek communities as well as others.

The focus has been on the Greek immigrant experience in the United States, a subject not dealt with by other organizations. The cultural program recognizes Greek-American artists, musicians, writers, and poets. It sponsors lectures and readings from Greek and American audiences and has joint presentations with other ethnic organizations. Presentations and presenters are not shy about being critical of the Greek community and generating discussion, either.

Much of this is new in the Greek American community. Rassogianis quipped that, for one of the oldest European cultures, Greeks were among the last to start exploring their roots and developing programs to share their experience with others.

Funding for most older adult programs emanated through Title III of the Older Americans Act. These funds were allocated to each state based on a formula and administered through state departments on aging. The states in turn allocated funding to each of the counties where a governmental or quasi-governmental agency acted as the Area Agency on Aging (AAA). Chicago maintained a special designation as a separate entity. The Chicago Department on Aging was the AAA for Chicago and it, in turn, had five service regions: Northeast, northwest, central west, southeast, and southwest. Each region had a senior center and a designated Case Management Unit (CMU). CMUs assessed older adults and referred them to appropriate providers for services. Catholic Charities was the CMU for the northeast and northwest service regions. Agencies that were service providers could not be CMUs in the same regions since there was a potential for conflicts of interest. In later years, they were referred to as Case Coordination Units (CCUs).

Ethel and I met with case managers at Catholic Charities Northwest Case Management Unit to discuss the program. We offered to host their next meeting at the center so that case managers could see the program firsthand. The Northwest Providers Council, a monthly roundtable meeting of service providers to seniors that was coordinated by the Chicago Department on Aging, also met at the center. CLESE, which rotated its meeting locations amongst its member agencies, held several meetings at GACS. Our Cultural &Arts Program hosted several lectures at the center which brought community members into the center.

A November 14, 1990 article by Jerome Kirn entitled "Greek American Group Cares for Senior Citizens at Alvernia Place," for the *Chicago Leader-Post Newspaper* proclaimed, "Adult day care is an idea whose time has come, almost."

> In an edition of *Newsweek* magazine, it was reported that there are now more than 2,000 centers that serve the needs of senior citizens which reflects an increase from a 'handful' in the early 1970s.
>
> Psiharis feels contributions to adult day care would be a worthwhile investment. 'In this area, we have several large employers. How many of their employees miss days, leave early, come in late, or are distracted all day long because they're worried about mom or dad or their husband or wife home alone? Or how many of them have to rush home because when they call, there's no answer? My view is that these kinds of programs are similar to employee assistance programs like ones for drug and alcohol problems. It's a service to their employees, and in the long run, I think the corporation would benefit.'
>
> 'What we promote here is the treatment of our people with care and dignity, and we think that's important. We believe in respecting their age, their accomplishments, and who they are as individuals. Sometimes people call adult day care a babysitting service, but that's far from the case. Our people are independent, and they're never forced to do anything they don't want to do.'

By the end of the first year, nearly 100 inquiries were received and over 20 assessments had been completed. Although the active caseload had grown to nine, the lack of transportation to and from the center hampered our growth, as did the need to raise awareness in the broader community about the benefits of adult day care.

Two Steps Forward…One Step Back

By the end of 1990, Northwest Chicago Senior Care Center was open Monday through Friday. While some clients came every day, others attended once, twice, or three times per week depending on their individualized care plan. Our expenses increased in proportion to the added days and growing patient census. As this was a labor-intensive program, the more clients we had, the more staff we needed to care for them.

It quickly became apparent that an impediment to the center's growth was the lack of a van to transport participants. Most clients were dropped off and picked up by family members. Those that didn't have rides were transported by Ethel Kotsovos or other volunteers in their cars.

In the spring of 1991, I approached the Chicago Community Trust (CCT), one of the city's largest foundations, about the possibility of getting a grant to purchase a van to transport adult day care center clients. Michael Marcus, CCT senior program officer, and Barb Koremenos, an intern with the Trust, arranged a site visit to the center. They were impressed with GACS and the adult day care center and encouraged us to submit a grant request. As we discussed during the visit, the grant request had three components: A direct grant of $20,000 to purchase a van, $5,000 for insurance and to pay for a driver, and an additional $15,000 in matching funds to help cover the operational costs of the adult day care center. The second year would provide $15,000 in funding for the adult day care center and help to cover the cost of the driver and insurance. With Michael's guidance and institutional support, the grant was approved.

Around this time, Norman Ross, a contributing reporter for ABC 7 Eyewitness News (WLS-TV), who specialized in profiles of people and organizations doing good work, became aware of the adult day care center and wanted to do a story on us. Before retirement, Norman had been a senior vice president for public affairs with First National Bank of Chicago. He was a highly regarded member of local media and the Chicago business community. Ross and his film crew came to the center to tape the segment and interviewed John, Amydelle, and me. The report aired about a week later and was well received. It helped increase awareness about the center within the broader community and generated inquiries from the public.

One unexpected outcome of the broadcast was a phone call I received from Irene Antoniou. She had seen the segment, read our newsletters, and wanted to learn more about us. Irene was a passionate advocate for the arts, having served as president of the Lyric Opera of Chicago Women's Board and as a member and eventual chair of the Illinois Arts Council. Irene had a keen interest in the adult day care program given that she had been caring for an aging mother who would have benefited from the Greek American center. Irene particularly liked that GACS combined both of these interests and told me she would be donating. The check received a few days later, was for $1,000. In the coming years, Irene became a benefactor of GACS.

The Chicago Public Schools needed an additional school in the area and they now saw Alvernia Place as a perfect opportunity. In the spring of 1991, we were notified that the Chicago Board of Education intended to buy Alvernia Place and convert it into a public high school. They had threatened the nuns with eminent domain actions if they did not sell them the building.

Despite the intervention of then-Cardinal Joseph Bernardin, the city held firm in its position. Attorneys for the Order advised the nuns to sell to avoid the protracted legal battle and expense of a court case. Alvernia Place tenants, except for Kid Watch Child Care, were told we would need to move by September 30th.

After having just settled into Alvernia Place, GACS again needed to search for a new location. Several locations were considered including storefronts located in Veterans Square Mall (a strip mall located at Jefferson Park–Lawrence and Milwaukee Avenues-owned by Demetrios Kozonis), a location at Milwaukee Avenue and Sunnyside that became too expensive, a German social hall on Montrose near Hamlin that had no windows and was quite depressing and a two-story storefront on Irving Park just west of Cicero that had been a television and appliances store.

We also revisited the location at 3940 N. Pulaski, in the Old Irving Park neighborhood, which had been considered the last time and remained vacant. It was about three blocks from the Alvernia location. The advantages to this location included that it was street level, it was a newly constructed building, and the owner was willing to build it out to our specifications. The negatives included the fact that it was located near an extremely busy intersection and the parking lot layout was less than ideal. To further complicate the parking, a lighted billboard sign was based in the lot and took up valuable parking space.

The building was located on the west side of Pulaski between Irving Park and the entrance/exit ramps to the Kennedy Expressway, which created a

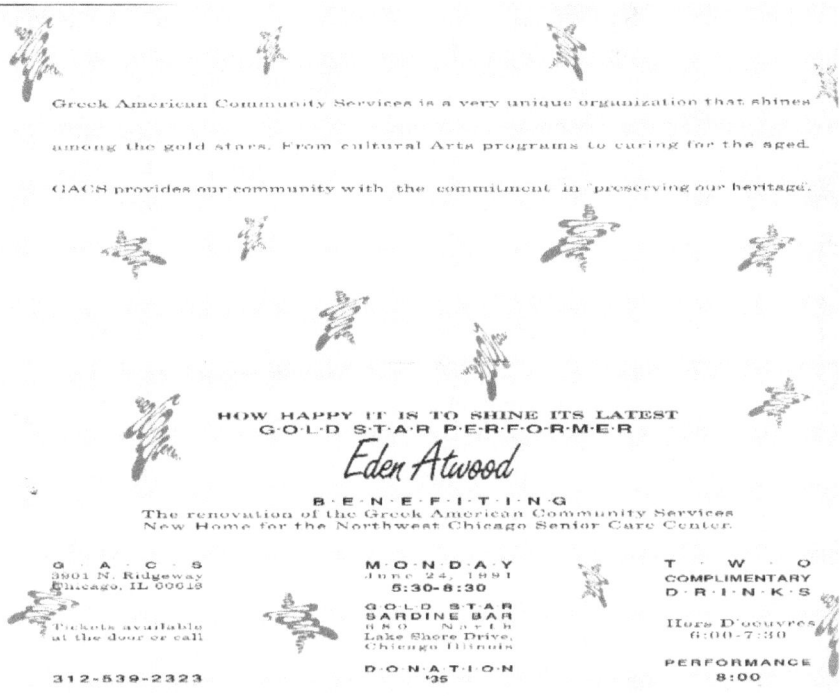

Gold Star Sardine Bar fundraiser invitation. June 1991. John Psiharis collection.

near-constant backup of traffic. The plus side was that it was convenient to get to, given the expressway on/off ramps and the Irving Park and Pulaski intersection. Three bus routes and the Blue Line and Metra train stations were all less than one block away. GACS would occupy the first floor. The second floor, with six studio suites, was occupied by several small businesses including a printer and photographer.

A three-year lease was signed which included the right of first refusal if the building were sold. Roula Alakiotou, a prominent Chicago architect, designed the interior and also donated the assistance of her firm, Roula and Associates. She created an open floor plan that allowed for flexible use with breakout space and offices along the south wall. A hard-wired fire alarm system was installed. Tiles and carpeting were laid and a kitchen area was added.

The final design included an open area that was about 1,800 square feet, three accessible bathrooms, a nurse's office, food service areas, five offices, and a meeting room that could also be used as a breakout activity area for adult day care clients. A large coat closet to accommodate thirty-plus participants and their belongings was created under the staircase to the second floor. A reception area at the entrance was used to greet visitors and monitor the front door. A garage area in the back was converted into an open space with wall shelving added for storage.

On June 24, GACS raised an impressive amount at a cocktail party held at the Gold Star Sardine Bar, a trendy but tiny jazz lounge located at 680 N. Lake Shore Drive. The bar was co-owned by Bill Allen, a co-owner of Treasure Island Food Stores. The evening featured a special performance by Eden Atwood, their guest performer. A raffle with a grand prize of a round-trip ticket to Greece donated by Olympic Airways raised additional money.

On July 1, with the help of a small cadre of volunteers, GACS officially moved to the new location. Several volunteers helped to drive things between the old and new locations as Nick Stathopoulos, Bob Blum, John, and I rolled file cabinets on dollies through the side streets from one location to the other! The fact that the move was only a few blocks away was a big plus, but it was still difficult given a heatwave. Alvernia Place felt like a furnace with its long hallways and lack of air conditioning. The humidity was extreme, making moving a far greater challenge than anticipated.

Shortly after GACS set up shop in the new building, we received word that the Chicago Community Trust approved our grant request to purchase a new van and related expenses as well as a challenge grant of $15,000 which provided a dollar-for-dollar match.

I went shopping for a van and was able to negotiate a deal with Haggerty Dodge for a sky-blue twelve-passenger 1992 Dodge Ram van. In addition to a discounted price, the dealership donated lettering and an alarm for the van. The van was adorned with the NCSC logo, address, and phone number. In keeping with an idea that came to us after visiting the Council for Jewish Elderly adult day care center and seeing their vans labeled "Shalom," we added *Ya'Sou* to the front and rear of our van. We saw it as the perfect name since it had a dual meaning in Greek. On one hand, *Ya'Sou* is a friendly, informal greeting of hello while it is also a toast or salutation meaning "to your health."

Kathryn Adinamis reported on the new van in her April 9, 1992 "The Eye" column in the *Greek Star*:

> The Greek-American Community Services recently announced the creation of a transportation component for its adult day care center, Northwest Chicago Senior Care (NCSC), located at 3940 N. Pulaski Road in Chicago. NCSC offers daytime care to

Pictured with the *Ya'Sou* 2 van in front of GACS shortly after it was purchased. (L-R): **Top**: John Psiharis, Evangeline Mistaras, and John Rassogianis. **Bottom:** John Rassogianis, Evangeline Mistaras, John Psiharis. Date unknown. John Psiharis collection.

frail isolated and forgetful older adults in a safe and caring environment. The center offers an opportunity for socialization and stimulation as well as professional care from a nurse, activity therapist, and social worker. A hot lunch and snacks are served. Throughout the day clients participate in a myriad of activities and programs.

Nurse Eileen Casey (third from left) with ADC participants (as the *Ya Sou* vans are boarded in the background) after a lunch outing to Zephyr's Café. Date unknown. Photo by John Rassogianis. John Rassogianis collection.

According to GACS Executive Director, John Psiharis, the addition of a 12-passenger van to the center will enable the program to reach out to older adults and families who lack the means to get to and from the center. Psiharis expressed his appreciation to the Chicago Community Trust, one of Chicago's largest and most respected community foundations for the funding to purchase the van. The center is supported by the Illinois Department on Aging, Illinois Masonic Medical Center, and individual contributors.

Once the van was procured, GACS held an *"Agiasmos,"* or Blessing of the Waters Service and Open House. Very Rev. Nikitas Lulias, chancellor of the Greek Orthodox Diocese of Chicago, presided. Father Nikitas blessed both our new home and the *Ya'Sou* van. Refreshments were provided by Costas Zografopoulos of Master Caterers. An open house for providers and case managers was held on another day so that they could have an opportunity to see the new location

With the van ready to go, we hired Robert Blum to be the van driver and Ray Manasingh to be the van attendant. Ray was an Earn Fare participant and when funding allowed, we hired him onto our payroll to continue in this role. Bob had worked at Alvernia Place in building maintenance. He was a student at Wilbur Wright Community College working towards a degree in physical therapy. Bob and Ray also assisted with activities throughout the day. They remained with the center throughout most of its existence.

Once the van was in operation, attendance at the center increased, validating our belief that providing transportation was a key component of adult day care. The rough boundaries for transportation were Harlem Avenue on the west to Chicago River on the east and Devon Avenue on the north to Diversey Avenue on the south; however, there were some exceptions made to accommodate clients when possible.

With Chicago Community Trust funding winding down, GACS submitted a grant request to the Retirement Research Foundation requesting three years of funding for ADC outreach. The $110,800 grant request was approved and began in October 1992. Among the line items funded were the salary of the social worker and costs related to outreach activities.

An announcement in the October 22, 1992 edition of the *Greek Star* reported:

> Greek-American Community Services has received a grant from the Retirement Research Foundation in the amount of $110,000 to be utilized within a three-year time frame in support of its adult day care center, Northwest Chicago Senior Care, located at 3940 N. Pulaski Rd., Chicago.
>
> According to John Psiharis, Executive Director of GACS, funds will be restricted to initiating an extensive outreach program that will identify individuals and families that can benefit from adult day care. They would be eligible for enrollment at the center. The effort will be coordinated by the center's social worker, Ethel Kotsovos, who will also offer information and referral, casework, and counseling services to clients and their families.
>
> 'This grant could not have come at a better time,' added Psiharis. 'The ultimate purpose of the grant is to increase the number of participants enrolled and the fees they generate. By the end of the third year, we expect our center to be well on its way to becoming self-sustaining. We truly want to express our

appreciation to the Retirement Research Foundation for their timely and generous support.'

'We are undergoing reorganization,' stated John Rassogianis, Director of the Cultural and Arts Program of the agency. 'We are expanding our governing board, welcoming new clients, and creating new committees to deal with our added responsibilities. In fact, we're preparing to add two more days at the day care center. We are going to open five days a week.'

Amydelle Shah, R.N., became the center's nurse and supervisor after Fran left. In her eighties, Amydelle was an inspiration to many in their golden years. She went motorcycle riding with her granddaughter, hot air ballooning and traveled extensively in both the United States and Europe. She hosted a cable access television program and wrote a column in *Prime Times*, a senior citizens newspaper published by Blue Cross-Blue Shield. Previously, Amy had been a volunteer for the Community Aging Network, regularly calling clients to check on their well-being before joining the staff.

Amydelle brought a wealth of experience to her role, having been a director of nursing for several decades at both the Chicago TB Sanitarium and Henrotin Hospital. She was also a nursing instructor for the City Colleges of Chicago, certified in medical records management, and took art classes regularly. Amydelle was an avid traveler and enjoyed painting. She donated several paintings that were hung in the center and taught art and painting classes for ADC participants.

Amydelle was short in stature. One morning, on her way to work, a CTA bus driver did not see her as she was crossing the street, and drove into her, knocking her to the ground. She refused treatment on the scene, but I drove her to the emergency room as a precaution. All was okay, and Amy insisted on working the rest of the day. Staff joked that Amydelle could get hit by a bus and still go to work. She remained at the center through most of its time. Amydelle uniquely motivated clients. Amy encouraged clients to do something by saying "I'm older than you are, and if I can do it, you can do it too."

Maria Villalobos (Toledo) was hired to be the secretary/administrative assistant. Initially, as an Earn Fare employee, I was mindful of her abilities, and when funding permitted we added her to the staff. Several years later, Maria transitioned to a new schedule where she worked part-time for GACS and part-time at the Greek-American Nursing Home Committee office located in Dr. Kioutas' medical office.

Over time, we hired three part-time workers through Project AYUDA, a Title V senior employment and training program operated by the National

Association for Hispanic Elderly onto our payroll. Carmen Vilato, Margaret Nikolopoulos, and Rafael Gallardo. They were popular with the clients. Margaret and Carmen's duties included leading or assisting with activities and preparing and cleaning up after snacks and lunch were served. Rafael was a *Ya'Sou* van driver.

A cadre of volunteers helped within the adult day care center in many ways. They include Maria Maniates, a retired city health inspector and a registered dietician who reviewed and approved the monthly snack and lunch menu cycles to ensure they met proper nutritional guidelines. Maria also oversaw our participation in IDOA's Child and Adult Care Food Program (CACFP), Phil Williams became a regular with his marionette performances as well as showing old-time movies from his vast collection of movie classics on VHS tapes. Evangeline visited weekly to lead a reminiscing group with center participants. Jackie Peterson assisted in bookkeeping and monthly invoicing of state and private pay clients. Connie and Dee Andrews, two sisters who were retired human resources executives from Sears, assisted in many ways including administratively and organizing programs. When Sears moved its corporate headquarters from Sears Tower to its newly built campus in Hoffman Estates, the sisters were able to obtain a large donation of office furniture from their former corporate headquarters. Sears even delivered the furniture to GACS. The new furnishings greatly enhanced the organization's new offices.

In 1991, I approached the Veterans Administration (V.A.), now known as the U.S. Department of Veterans Affairs, which was looking for vendors to provide adult day care on the north side of the city. I contacted the local V.A. at Edward Hines, Jr. Hospital who visited the center and approved us for referrals. The next step was for GACS to go through the federal contracting process and site visits from their nurse, safety officer, social worker, and administrators which took a few months. Once approved, the center was able to provide services to approved veterans. Initially, GACS received $40 per day plus $5 for transportation for each veteran served. We continued to serve veterans throughout the ADC's existence. There were usually a couple of veterans within the census at any time. For a short period, five veterans were attending at the same time. I was told that GACS was the first Greek American organization in the nation to have a contract with the U.S. Department of Veterans Affairs.

GACS offered adult day care services across the spectrum of options (state-subsidized, private pay, and V.A.). By far, the majority of the participants were state pay (some with co-payments). The balance was private pay, followed by V.A. clients. GACS joined other adult day care centers in advocating for more private insurance options for adult day care programs. The efforts yielded some success but did not have an impact on our center. Private pay families in some cases were able to deduct the cost of adult day care from their taxes as dependent care expenses. There was an increased focus on Long Term Care Insurance and GACS had several clients who were privately insured. We also had clients whose care was paid for through the Cook County Public Guardian's office and bank trust accounts.

A December 1992 GACS fundraising appeal letter from Evangeline and me, introduced "Vasso," an actual client, whose name was changed to protect confidentiality:

> Vasso and her fellow participants at the Greek-American Community Services Adult Day Care Center join us in wishing you a Joyous, Merry Christmas and a Healthy, Happy New Year!
>
> Please help us to help Vasso and all her friends here at the center. Vasso is just one of the participants in our adult day care center. Only two years ago, her life was far different from what it is now. She is now 85 years old, and a widow for over fourteen years. Two years ago Vasso's daughter noticed her forgetfulness. This was the beginning of a series of minor events that led to a realization that she would be unable to live alone. Vasso began to take her medicine sporadically. She paid less attention to her diet. With her growing isolation, she became more and more depressed. Her problems and the concerns of her family multiplied. Once, Vasso could not even locate her home.
>
> Vasso's daughter saw only one choice, a very painful one, yet the only choice she could make was to place her mother in a nursing home.
>
> Fortunately, her daughter heard about Greek-American Community Services from a friend. After visiting the center for only one hour and consulting with staff, she found the answer to her family's concerns for her mother's safety and well-being. A solution was in hand.
>
> Thankful that a new door and a new life had opened for Vasso, her daughter's relief was evident. In this instance, adult day care, as in many other cases, was an alternative to nursing home placement.
>
> With each coming day, Greek-American Community Services strives to provide ongoing support by assisting families such as Vasso's through its adult day care program, as well as other social and cultural programs and services. Last year, our efforts touched the lives of five thousand people!

Our elderly devoted their lives to making our lives better. Now it's our turn, our responsibility, to help them. This holiday season, we hope that you will generously support our efforts. In that way, we will be enabled to help people such as Vasso. May God bless you during this holiday season and throughout the coming year.

Northwest Chicago Senior Care Comes of Age

John Psiharis with the ADC nurses. Pictured (L-R): Carmen Vilato, Amydelle Shah, John Psiharis, Eileen Casey, Eleanor Huber, and Kathleen O'Leary, at a volunteer dinner, during which, Carmen and Eileen received the Executive Director's Awards. Date unknown. John Psiharis collection.

The staff and volunteers worked hard to establish a routine for the center and its operations.

Amydelle, as the center's supervisor, Dr. Kioutas, and I created the policies and procedures for the center with the gracious help of other adult day care centers. Jane Stansell provided a copy of her center's policy book as a reference. The policies were detailed and comprehensive and covered an array of topics such as medication storage and administration procedures, notes, logs and charts, supplies lists, and emergency preparation. We arranged for regular fire drills, CPR training and TB testing, and ongoing professional development for staff and volunteers.

The center developed procedures related to food service. These included: proper food handling and food temperature controls, inventory lists for supplies, and planned menu cycles for each quarter of the year with portion sizes that were approved by a registered dietician.

At Alvernia Place, Search Developmental, a day program for the developmentally disabled located on the second floor, prepared our meals onsite in the former high school's kitchen. Once GACS moved to Pulaski, we determined that the amount of money needed to install a full kitchen with venting and up-to-code was beyond our budget. Add in the cost of food and utensils, a paid cook, and the expense of preparing meals on-site seemed prohibitive. Instead, we arranged for catering and utilized the kitchen area to prepare and serve the meals and snacks that were delivered daily. We intended to add the kitchen later.

For the first few years, GACS contracted with Plum Catering which handled food service for childcare centers. They wanted to break into the adult day care segment and offered a discounted price to use us as a reference. After a noticeable decline in food quality and a price increase, we switched to Open Kitchens, which at the time supplied the majority of meals provided to seniors through the city's Meals on Wheels program, as well as many of the Golden Diners sites.

The meals were of a higher quality than before and the price was a bit less due to the larger scale of meals they prepared daily. Each morning we received a delivery of lunch and two snacks. We separately purchased milk, usually donated by Tessie Cantos, which was required to be served whether or not the client wanted it, as well as toast, cereal, oatmeal, muffins, or bagels for the morning snack; decaffeinated coffee, and other incidentals. At least monthly, participants went out for lunch, and during the warmer months, boxed lunches were prepared for visits to the lakefront or nearby Independence Park. Whenever possible the center served lunches donated by Greek-owned restaurants and food purveyors including the Harris, Greek Islands, Little Mike's, Pegasus, and Roditys restaurants, Master Caterers, and others. Through the efforts of Eleni Bousis, Goya Foods executives donated and served the fixings of a great freshly prepared lunch on a few occasions.

The nurse on duty interacted daily with each participant to assess their conditions, dispense medications, assist clients in the bathroom, and monitor their overall health. She communicated with the participant's family and physician as needed and participated in the initial intake process. When the supervisor wasn't there, the nurse on duty was designated the acting supervisor. The position at one time or another was filled by Fran Argiris, Amydelle Shah, Eileen Casey, Eleanor Huber, Lorraine Lisowski, and Linda Mirza. All were registered nurses (RNs).

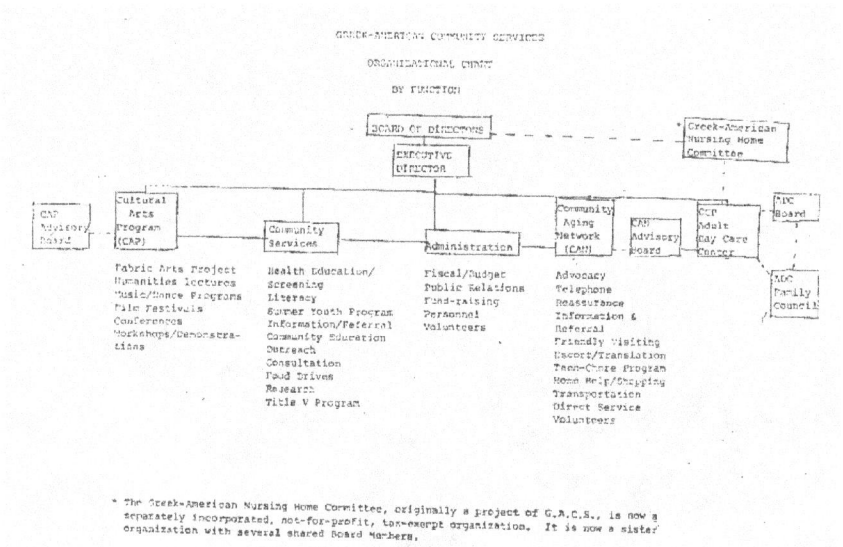

GACS organizational chart. Date unknown. John Psiharis collection.

The social worker handled outreach and coordinated the intake process. She was the primary point of contact for the families and provided one-to-one or small-group assistance as needed. The social worker coordinated the ADC's family support group and arranged for the transportation of the participants. Ethel Kotsovos and Despina Massouras held this position. When Amydelle stepped down from the supervisor role, she remained a rotating nurse and stepped in as an intake worker when the social worker wasn't available.

Ann Prusinski was the activity director of the center throughout its existence. Ann planned and coordinated a monthly calendar of activities and supervised the activity aides and volunteers who helped. The activities included everyday routine tasks like reality orientation, current events, weekly movies, and a monthly outing. They held monthly participant council meetings in which the clients discussed center matters, determined where they wanted to go on their monthly field trip and participated in planning the month's activity calendar. The supervisor, social worker, and nurse on duty also attended.

The intake process began with the social worker who met the potential participant and their primary caregiver(s). An intake packet was initiated, which included an assessment of their ability to accomplish activities of daily living, psychosocial assessments, and general information on the clients and their preferences, dietary restrictions, hobbies and interests, emergency contacts, etc. The nurse completed a health assessment and a medical form was faxed to their doctor who listed any medications that might need to be taken at the center and provided authorization for her to

Children visitng with ADC participants. The artwork on the walls were painted and donated by Amydelle Shah and was based on her travels. Date unknown. John Psiharis collection.

dispense these medicines. Clients were asked to bring an extra change of clothing which was kept at the center in case it was ever needed. We also took a face picture of each client which was affixed to the inside front cover of the client's chart.

A typical day at Northwest Chicago Senior Care began at 7 a.m. when Ray and the drivers would meet with Ann to go over the route list and make any last-minute changes. By 7:15 a.m., the vans departed on their routes. One route usually went north and west of the center while the second went south and east. Ray accompanied whichever route had the most clients on a particular day. While Ann made coffee, the activity aides arrived as families began to drop off participants on their way to work.

The team prepared morning snacks for those who had arrived. Sometimes it was decaffeinated coffee and toast, bagels, or English muffins accompanied by a piece of fruit. Other times it was cereal or oatmeal. The morning news was on television in the background so clients could watch the news or socialize as the day got started. The nurse dispensed the medications for the day into medicine cups labeled with the participant's name and the name and dosage of the medicine. The social worker was the point of contact with families and communicated with family members, case managers, and others regarding any participant concerns.

Once the morning snacks were served, there was a current events session where Ann read through the day's newspaper with the participants and encouraged conversation about the topics of the day, followed by the gossip and advice columns, and the day's horoscopes. Next was an exercise class in which participants were encouraged to participate to the extent possible. The sessions included stretching, bending, chair aerobics, and walking around the center to music. During nice weather, participants exercised on the patio or took outdoor walks.

While the exercise class was occurring, Ray, sometimes with the assistance of clients that wanted to help, arranged and set the tables and chairs, filled water glasses, and placed the napkins and utensils. At 11:00 a.m., as participants were seated for lunch, an assembly line of staff plated and served the meals.

Food temperatures were taken and recorded to confirm it was safe to serve. The food came fully cooked in large trays and was transported in insulated containers designed to retain proper food temperatures from the time of delivery, which was earlier in the morning, until serving. The nurse monitored the process to ensure portion sizes were correct and participants that were on special diets didn't get something that was not allowed. Once everyone was served, the staff joined the clients at lunch. It was a time when we all came together as a group. The WGN-TV midday news played in the background and once participants finished eating, they moved to the living room area to watch the news and wait for the others to finish and for medications to be administered.

At 12:45 p.m., the first afternoon activity began, usually followed by a second activity around 1:30 p.m. and ending at 2:45 p.m. Depending on the day of the week and the week in the month, the activities varied but included: music, art, bingo, intergenerational activities, pet therapy, men's group, classic movies, arts and crafts, games, looming, bowling, trips to the park, special interest groups and outside visitors. On Wednesdays, those who were interested joined the Fabric Arts Program classes. At 2:15 p.m., the afternoon snack was served, usually fruit of some sort, or fruit juice and another type of snack. On movie days, popcorn was served. On other days, wheat crackers with cheese or granola and yogurt were offered. The café room was available for clients to visit and music was played in the background. The library room also functioned as a quiet area that provided a place of retreat for participants. The arts and crafts room was open to participants when it wasn't being used for a class.

At about 3:00 p.m. participants began to board the *Ya'Sou* vans for their rides home. Those who were picked up by family members remained behind until their rides arrived. While waiting, clients, often joined by Tornie, enjoyed watching the *Wheel of Fortune* and *Jeopardy* television

ADC participants are boarded onto the *Ya'Sou* vans for their trip home with Ray Manasingh and Bob Blum (in the background). Date unknown, John Psiharis collection.

game shows. While that was happening, staff completed their charting, filled out paperwork, and prepared for the next day.

Reporter Beth Burmahl wrote a profile for the *Jefferson/Portage/Bel Cragin Times* in the January 27, 1994 edition entitled "Adult Program Keeps Clients from Doldrums:"

> A typical afternoon might consist of bowling, a movie, a sing-a-long, and a little dancing, with a hot meal squeezed somewhere in between. On another day, a parade of pets might prance through the front room, or a roomful of rowdy youngsters on a reprieve from kindergarten might pay a visit.'
>
> The wide span of activities could be a lineup at a well-planned family picnic. But the roomful of seniors who enjoy the activities of the adult day care program at Greek-American Community Services, 3940 N. Pulaski, don't have to wait for summer to get in on the fun.
>
> With a little creative handiwork, the roomy, first floor of the center is easily converted into a small video theater, a dance floor, and a makeshift bowling alley (a ball and bowling pins lined against the wall), or a mini-zoo.
>
> The pets come compliments of the Warren Park Nursing Pavilion, which boasts a small pet center for residents. The children come from the Kid Watch intergenerational program which matches seniors with area youngsters. All the activities

add up to an interesting educational way for seniors to occupy days that might otherwise be filled with eight hours of television.

'We challenge their minds and their memories' said program founder John Psiharis. 'And it's for all seniors.' Some of the seniors even get up and cut the rug. 'We have one woman who used to be in Vaudeville, and she gets up and starts dancing when we play our songs.'

The participants were excited when a donation of a Video Cassette Recorder (VCR) was received. It expanded programming possibilities. Each week, Phil Williams, an ADC volunteer, and classic movie buff brought in a video from his vast collection of classic movies to share with the clients. He also showed recordings of television programs featuring Bob Hope, Lucille Ball, Jack Benny, Milton Berle, Burns and Allen, Roy Rogers and Dale Evans, and others. Phil video-recorded several GACS events and parties with his camcorder. In time, through donations, we were able to amass an impressive video library of our own.

A monthly birthday party was held for those who celebrated during that month. Family members of the celebrants were invited to the party which usually involved cake and ice cream. During the summer months, we sometimes ordered boxed lunches and went to the lakefront, Independence Park, or other venues for a picnic lunch. We also held cookouts where we grilled hot dogs or hamburgers, corn, etc. on our rear patio.

The vans made it possible for ADC clients to go on at least one field trip per month. Participants discussed and voted on where they wanted to go. The trips usually involved going to lunch at places like Big Top, Buffalo Bills, Dapper's, Grecian Taverna, Harris, Jeff's Red Hots, Little Mike's, Margie's Candies, Mr. K's, Mykonos, Old Country Buffet, Pizza Hut, Zephyr's Ice Cream Parlor, and restaurants in Greektown. In December, a traditional trip to Harlem Irving Plaza provided clients with the opportunity to shop for holiday gifts for their loved ones. Participants visited Brookfield Zoo, Chicago Batonic Gardens, Chicago Cubs baseball games, Hellenic Museum and Cultural Center, and Lincoln Park Zoo, and went to Mayor Daley's Senior Citizens Picnics and a taping of the *Jenny Jones Show* at NBC Tower.

One such outing was described by participant Ann Mullen in the May 1997 edition of *Greek American Community News*, the center's participant newsletter.

> On Wednesday, March 25th we all went to Zephyr's for lunch. It was a nice trip and a nice sunny day. We had a lot of fun. Bob

had music on and it was very cheerful. We looked at a lot of different houses on our way to the restaurant.

We had a good time at the restaurant too. The lunch was very good and one of the owners, Lou Bacayanis, treated us to a delicious ice cream sundae. Then we all had a good time on the way back to the Center.

We're looking forward to two van trips in May.

Each year, the ADC arranged two outings to Chicago Cubs games at Wrigley Field. One was for any clients who wanted and were able to go. The second was an outing for the men's group led by Bob and Ray. In November, participants attended a Thanksgiving luncheon cruise on Lake Michigan aboard the *Odyssey*. In December, a shopping trip to the Harlem and Irving Plaza was arranged so that participants could shop for Christmas gifts for family members. Afterward, they went for lunch at Pizza Hut across the street. Whenever possible, family members were invited to join the trips

Throughout the day participants were tended to medically as necessary. This included assisting them in the bathroom, dispensing medicines, checking vitals and blood sugar levels, and one-to-one visits with the nurse or social worker to discuss matters of concern to the participant or family.

Visits to the center included performances from the Sweet Adelines, a senior citizen's women's singing group, the Lincoln Park Zoo Traveling Zoo, Tree House Animal Shelter, and a group that reenacted classic radio programs. Periodically, residents of the Norwood Park Home Kitchen Band, led by their administrator, visited and performed. This led to the creation of a kitchen band that practiced regularly and was invited to perform at Norwood Park Home. Special guests who visited the center included U.S. Senator Paul Simon; Congressmen Dan Rostenkowski, Michael Flanagan, Frank Annunzio, Sydney Yates, and Rod Blagojevich; State Senator John Cullerton; TV personality Norman Ross, and others. On his visits, Annunzio brought a box of his trademark shopping bags swag for the clients. Mike Bakalis filmed a commercial in the center during his campaign for governor.

One year, a number of the more active participants took part in the experimental Liz Lerman Dance Exchange in partnership with the Columbia School of Dance. Each week, a number of our participants took part in dance and movement classes for seniors led by dance students. John drove the participants to the gatherings which were held at Lawrence House Retirement House and the Columbia School of Dance. We also hosted a few of the classes at GACS. The project culminated in three public performances that John and a few of the clients took part in. I recall attending one performance and was amazed at what our clients achieved.

Intergenerational programming was a priority and participants interacted with children in a variety of ways. This included visits from Plato and Socrates schools where children would sing for the participants, work on art projects or play games with participants. ADC clients prepared and shared popcorn with the young visitors. Visits from children in the Kid-Watch program at Alvernia Place were regular occurrences. After we moved to Pulaski that relationship continued with the children visiting our seniors and working on art projects together. During the summer months, they gathered halfway between the centers at Independence Park.

An ADC monthly caregivers support group co-led by the nurse and social worker was available to families and caregivers. A family council was created and grew to include many of the center's families. The council supported our dinner dances, and they launched an annual rummage sale that was held at the center.

A newsletter was produced by center participants under the guidance of Amydelle Shah, who in addition to nursing, wrote a monthly column in *Prime Times,* and had done other writing as well. A May 1997 newsletter featured remembrances of Casimer "Casey" Misiewicz, a long-time participant, who was popular with clients and staff. It included articles written and edited by center participants. Among the topics in this issue were "Memories of Christmas '1996,'" reports, discussion group topics, field trip plans, and announcements about new clients and those who had recently left the center.

A genuine sense of community existed within the center. Higher functioning clients looked after those who required more assistance or orientation. Participants became friends with each other and often talked by phone or sometimes visited each other on their own time. Family members got to know each other while picking up their loved ones or through the family support group. If a client became ill or was in the hospital, staff and clients would call or visit. When a death occurred it was not uncommon for participants to attend the wake or funeral.

Between October 1, 1992 – March 30, 1993, The ADC received 45 inquiries and completed 15 intakes. There were 13 admissions and 4 closed cases. There were 24 enrolled participants with an average daily census of 17. An interim grant report to the Retirement Research Foundation dated April 11, 1994, detailed the progress made:

> Contact with the Greek media (radio, television, and print) elicited positive feedback and an eagerness to cooperate. In

February, two GACS Board members agreed to work on preparing a taped "infomercial," to be broadcast on Greek radio. It is expected that the tape will be ready in the next month or two. Although it will be primarily used as a public service announcement, the United Athenian & Piraeus Societies of Illinois have agreed to underwrite any advertising costs. Their interest in the center was also exemplified during our Christmas party when they purchased clothing and other such items (sweaters, shoes, etc.) and distributed them as gifts to the clients.

Contacts and presentations began with presentations to three church Philoptochos societies (friends of the poor). The churches are St. Andrew's, Annunciation Cathedral, and St. Demetrios. Three additional churches are scheduled for April. Most members of these societies – each Greek church has one – are middle-aged women active in philanthropic efforts who are often themselves concerned about their aging parents. The presentation at St. Andrew's yielded an unexpected $300 contribution to the program.

Another component of the church outreach program involves sponsoring the social/coffee hours at each church on a given Sunday. This will allow us the opportunity to reach most of the parishioners directly (other than through the priests and women's clubs). Ten churches have been identified, and GACS board members each adopted a church, agreeing to coordinate and underwrite the associated costs. This initiative will begin appropriately enough on Mother's Day and extend into June.

An interim report to the Retirement Research Foundation covering the period October 1, 1994 – March 31, 1995, provided updated statistics. There were 46 inquiries, 15 intakes, 12 admissions, eight closed cases, and six support group meetings. There were 36 enrolled participants with an average daily census of 21.

By April 1995, ADC enrollment had grown to 37 and the average daily census had grown to 24. Wednesdays were the busiest day of the week with an average census of 28 and Thursdays were the least busy with a census of 12. Monthly billings had risen from $2,407 in July 1992 to $11,903 in March 1995. At the time GACS was receiving $24.65 per client/per day for CCP clients while the actual cost of care was $45 per client/ day. Grants and fundraising made up the difference.

On May 1, GACS submitted a $91,000 grant request to the Retirement Research Foundation for three more years of funding for the adult day care center. The grant, which was approved, supported continued outreach efforts and the social worker position. The proposal included two letters in support of the request addressed to Marilyn Hennessy, president of the RRF, from Luke C. Fitzgerald, Northwest Regional Director of the Chicago Department on Aging, and Rosemary Gemperle, executive director of CLESE. Luke's letter, dated April 24, 1995. read:

> I am writing this letter to express support for Greek-American Community Services Organization [sic], as they are submitting a reapplication for funding from the Retirement Research Foundation. There [sic] organization has always been known for its long history of providing quality services to families and elderly individuals in the Greek community throughout Chicago.
>
> The Chicago Department on Aging has a long-standing relationship of over 15 years with the Greek-American Community Services Organization. Over the past five years, we have supported their efforts and helped develop and implement this specialized adult day care program for the elderly of Northwest Chicago. It is important to note that although this program was particularly sensitive to the needs of Greek seniors, the program has been and continues to be used by people from a variety of ethnic backgrounds. Five years after its inception, the adult day care program is providing services to many needy Chicago senior citizens and is a model for quality adult day care services.
>
> It is imperative in these times of fiscal restraint that the elderly and their families have alternatives for continued independent living. The services of Northwest Adult Day Care not only benefit their clients but also relieve the burden of putting one's loved one in an [sic] nursing home. I urge the Retirement Research Foundation to approve continued funding of this important program.

In her letter, dated April 20, 1995, Rosemary wrote:

> This letter is to support the efforts of the Greek-American Community Services in serving the elderly through their Adult Day Care program. I have worked closely with John Psiharis for many years, and have seen the Day Care program expand from 8 clients to 38: from 3 days a week to 5: from no vans to 2 vans (and now a need for a third). And, as you probably know, they now own the building.
>
> John and his staff at GACS seem tireless in their continuous efforts (and success) at tapping into the resources of the Greek community – both for their Adult Day Care program and the forthcoming nursing home. GACS has also used those resources to benefit CLESE, by obtaining volunteer entertainers and restaurants for our fundraisers.

> The Greek-American Community Services' generosity extends to other ethnic agencies serving the elderly. They have provided consultation to agencies considering establishing Adult Day Care programs, and they continue to give assistance to a Korean Adult Day Care program that opened two years ago.
>
> The commitment of the Greek community to GACS, and the dedication and benevolence of GACS staff and volunteers make the agency viable and worthy.
>
> I am happy to support them and encourage your positive consideration of their request.

An unaddressed and undated letter of support from Rosemary, also in the grant folder, read in part:

> I have worked closely with John since 1987 when he represented the Greek community in an ethnic elderly needs assessment that I coordinated for the Chicago Department on Aging. Subsequently, with the incorporation of the Coaltion of Limited English Speaking Elderly, John became a Director of the Board and has served the Coaltion either as a Board member or committee member since 1989.
>
> I came to rely upon John as the person on the Board who knew the most about how a not-for-profit should run. He is knowledgeable about administrative, legal, legislative, and fundraising issues. Because of his competence and the trust they had in him, the Board of Directors selected John to serve as president two times, He is the only individual to have served twice.
>
> John has a friendly but serious demeanor that encourages the kind of respect you'd like to see in a leader. I have seen in John a tenacious commitment to whatever organization, campaign, or fundraising event he's involved with. His sensitivity to older people and his grasp of the inner workings of an organization are reasons I encourage your serious consideration of this application.

Cultural Enrichment in the *Omogenia*

The GACS cultural program, under Elaine's direction, resulted in a plethora of groundbreaking programs within Chicago's Greek American community. In addition to the Fabric Arts of Greece project that was ongoing and funded by the city, GACS organized several cultural programs each year through funding that was received from the Chicago Department of Cultural Affairs and the Illinois Arts Council. These grants included:

- "Greeks in America: A Celebration of Films" (1986), (City Arts); Greek Music and Dance (1987), (City Arts); The Greek-American Experience Through Multi-Disciplinary Arts (1987), (Illinois Arts Council); Cultural Enrichment Program for Greek Elderly (1988), (City Arts); Greek-American Poets and Musicians (1989-1990), (City Arts); Greek Dance (1991), (Illinois Arts Council); GACS Music Program (1992), (City Arts) and Arts Therapy with ADC Participants (1995), (City Arts).
- GACS received funding through Department of Cultural Affairs Community Arts Assistance Program grants to establish the Cultural & Arts Program Advisory Board (1987), and to create a GACS Cultural & Arts Program video (1988).
- Beginning in 1986, Tessie Cantos as an individual artist, received annual Neighborhood Arts Program grants for at least six years, to administer the Fabric Arts Program. The program transitioned to CDBG funding in the mid-1990s and continued through 2002.

Details on some of these programs include:

- The 1987 Greek Music and Dance Program, funded through grants from the Illinois Arts Council and the Chicago Office of Fine Arts, featured well-known musicians such as James Stoynoff, music historian Neni Panourgia, and Nick Pappas and the Hellas Children's Dance Troupe. It was held at DePaul University.
- The 1988 Cultural Enrichment Program for Older Adults, funded through the Chicago Office of Fine Arts, offered more than 80 elderly participants such diverse programs as Greek Shadow Puppetry (*Karagiozis*) with Demetra Manzara, a lecture on Greek iconography by Shirley Kontos, and multi-cultural enrichment experiences that included a field trip to the Oriental Institute and a performance by the Korean Senior Citizens Farm Band.
- The Greek-American Poets and Musicians program in 1989-1990, funded by grants from the Illinois Arts Council and the Chicago Office of Fine Arts, allowed GACS to present six literary arts events featuring poets, writers, and historians. Included were readings by Theano Papazoglou Margaris, Harry Mark Petrakis, and Ioannis Dalapas.
- The 1991 Greek Dance program, funded by the Chicago Department of Cultural Affairs and Illinois Arts Council grants, included a Greek Dance Demonstration and Workshop

with over 200 in attendance and a series of weekly dance classes that introduced the rudiments of Greek dance to participants.
- The 1992 Greek Music Program included an April 12 afternoon of classical music entitled "Contemporary Musical Trends as Emerged Out of Byzantine and Macedonian Sounds" in the Waldorf Room of the Chicago Hilton and Towers. The event was organized by KRIKOS and co-sponsored by GACS. A lecture hosted by the Hellenic Professional Society of Illinois followed.
- A 1994 City Arts-funded program focused on Greek Rembetika music (urban folk music especially popular with the poor ranging from the late 19th century to the 1950s) included performances by well-known Chicago performer Vasilios Gaitanos and the Deni's Den Orchestra, featuring the first public performance of musical compositions by Thanassis Zervas and was held at Deni's Den.
- In 1995, GACS received a City Arts grant of $2,500 to enhance arts programming with ADC participants. Janet Lewis, who had a master's degree in gerontology and specialized in art therapy with older adults, provided twice-per-week projects with small groups of ADC clients. The creative and expressive art techniques utilized included mosaics, painting, sewing, looming, and ornament making.

The proposal GACS submitted to the Illinois Arts Council for funding of the music and dance classes in the 1990-91 grant cycle described the program:

> Folk dance seminars will be held in (1) Chicago at the Annunciation Cathedral on 9/26, 10/26, and 11/24, (2) Westchester at Holy Apostles Church on 4/25, 5/23, and 6/20, and in (3) Springfield at Lincoln Land Community College on 6/30, 7/28, and 8/10. Each of the seminars will consist of three two-hour classes. <u>Class one</u> will feature the Greek Island folk dances, <u>Class two</u> will feature dances from the mainland of Greece such as Tsamb, Kos, Kalamatianos, Zonaradiko, and Koftos. <u>Class three</u> will feature dances from the areas of Pontos (the Black Sea area, Cappadocia) such as tiki, spoon dance, and Easter dance. The seminars will be co-sponsored by the Greek Orthodox Diocese of Chicago. Each class will be conducted in three parts: (a) A brief introduction/discussion by Very Rev. Nikitas Lulias of the music, style, and types of dances common to the region being studied. (b) A ½-hour presentation of these

dances, by the Apollo Dance Troupe, accompanied by the display (with a narration of costumes native to the region). (c) Actual dance instruction by Rev. Lulias and Dr. & Mrs. Contos (assisted by the dance troupe). (1 hour). In total, about 250-300 people will be reached through the classes with an additional 5,000 people reached through a video of the program presented on TV.

Father Nikitas Lulias will thoroughly explain and discuss the music, style, and types of dances common to each of the regions. He will explain the history of the dance, going back to ancient times (as illustrated in ancient Greek vase paintings). He will show how they integrated into the everyday life of the Greek peoples of the mainland, the Islands, and Asia Minor. Differences in the dance of the different regions will be illustrated through actual performances by the Apollo Dance Troupe. The various costumes will be explained and modeled. The role of dance in our modern Greek-American community will be discussed.

The project complements the long-range plan for Greek-American Community Services through several means. First, the program continues the GACS mission of "Working to Preserve Our Heritage," by offering audiences a rare glimpse of Greek folk dancing history and techniques. Second, the project is a cooperative effort with several segments of the community joining forces to sponsor this effort. Third, the project, thus audiences, can become involved in the artistic discipline being highlighted. Finally, the program offers communities that are often culturally deprived an outstanding opportunity to explore and experience the artistic forms which are the subject of the program. Too often Chicago is saturated with cultural activities from Greek organizations, while the suburbs and downstate areas rarely see such programs.

Elaine recalls: "I remember the dance troupe at DePaul. We realized that the dance troupe could not fit on the stage we had booked. We hastily moved it to the adjacent auditorium."

Additionally, GACS received funding from the Illinois Humanities Council (IHC) in support of various programs that addressed Greek American cultural issues in the context of the humanities. Elaine recalls that we had a 100 percent track record in obtaining grants from the IHC. Each cycle, GACS received the maximum grant amount of $10,000, and each program saw an increase in attendance compared to the prior year. In addition to covering organizing costs, the grants provided publicity expenses, travel costs, and nominal honorariums for the speakers. These

The Hellas Dance Group performs during a GACS event. DePaul University. November 15, 1987. John Psiharis collection.

programs were "Strains on Ethnic Pride: Conflicts Between the New and Old Immigrants in the Greek and Assyrian Communities" (1987), "Greek Americans in the Workplace, 1888-1988" (1988), "Ethnic Identity and Leadership Development: The Greeks in Illinois" (1990-1991), and "*O Cosmos*: The Private Lives and Public Celebrations of the Greeks in Illinois" (1994-1997).

The GACS Cultural and Arts Program often invited speakers from other ethnic communities to foster opportunities for greater cultural understanding, dialog, and cooperation. Years later, Steve Frangos believes that the multi-ethnic focus of these programs was key to GACS's track record in obtaining grants since it was more difficult for the state to turn down a proposal involving several ethnic communities working together. Most lectures featured one or more speakers who spoke in the Chicago area as well as in another part of the state. The idea was that the lectures would not only occur in Chicago where there were ample opportunities to attend Greek American events but would also be presented at venues in other parts of the state where cultural activities were minimal at best.

GACS cultural programs spanned the state with lectures or other events being held in Aurora, Berwyn, Bloomington, Champaign-Urbana, Chicago, DeKalb, Des Plaines, East Moline, Elgin, Elmhurst, Evanston, Glenview, Homer Glen, Kankakee, Libertyville, Lombard, Orland Park, Palatine, Rockford, Springfield, Stone Park, University Park, and Wauconda.

Co-sponsoring organizations for these programs included: the American Jewish Committee, Apollo Dance Troupe, Assyrian National Council of Illinois, Assyrian Universal Alliance Foundation, Chinese American Service League, Copernicus Foundation, Greek Women's University Club, Hellenic Cultural Organization, Hellenic Link-Midwest, Hellenic Professional Society of Illinois, American Hellenic Society of Berwyn, Hellenic Society of DePaul University, Illinois Ethnic Consultation, Italian Cultural Center, KRIKOS, Lincoln Land Community College, Northern Illinois University, and Southeast Asia Center.

The success and depth of the Cultural & Arts Program led GACS to pursue funding from the city's Community Development Block Grant (CDBG) program. GACS requested CDBG funding from the Chicago Department of Cultural Affairs to support the hiring of a part-time Cultural & Arts Program Director. Given the number of cultural activities offered by GACS and the coordination and organizing that was required for each one, this position was much needed. We also transitioned the Fabric Arts Program to CDBG funding.

In June 1990, Elaine resigned from her position as GACS administrator, and John Rassogianis was hired for the newly created CAP director position. He had shown his passion, enthusiasm, and abilities as a volunteer and board member when he helped organize cultural activities and assisted in the adult day care center. John was also involved in helping to plan the "Strains on Ethnic Pride" conference. He was the publicity chairman and a board member of the Greek-American Nursing Home Committee. He relinquished his GACS board membership when he took on the paid position. John had two master's degrees, one in education and the second in Spanish. After teaching high school in St. Charles, he became a substitute teacher for the Chicago Public Schools which provided him with some schedule flexibility. John focused on organizing and publicizing Cultural and Arts Program activities as well as coordinating GACS publicity efforts. In later years, John also directed our Benefits Eligibility Checklist (BEC) outreach efforts and the Low Income Home Energy Assistance Program (LIHEAP).

Elaine recalls, "I planned many of the programs before John R. took over and forged some of the relationships with Greek organizations and other ethnic organizations mainly through my contacts with David Roth and the Illinois Ethnic Consultation. I worked together with John in planning lectures, such as the one at the Italian Cultural Center. Steve, you, and I worked on the grant proposals. Mary Maniatis from Assumption Church designed our brochure artwork for the Humanities-funded programs free of charge."

John continued to build upon the close working relationships that Elaine established with fellow Greek organizations that offered cultural programs. They were the Greek Women's University Club, Hellenic Cultural Organization, Hellenic Professional Society of Illinois, and KRIKOS, which later became Hellenic Link-Midwest. We had an informal alliance with these organizations, in that they would co-sponsor many of our cultural programs by publicizing the events to their members and helping to cover costs. GACS in turn co-sponsored their programs. In some cases, we helped cover the expenses. This arrangement helped increase attendance at all events. The events were mostly held on Sunday afternoons so that people could attend after church. Some of the events were held in hotel meeting rooms while others were at Greek venues including GACS, the Macedonian Society, or area churches. A few of the lectures were held at other ethnic or community centers as a means to enhance intercultural understanding. These included the Italian Cultural Center (Stone Park, IL), Copernicus Foundation, and the Irish Heritage Center in Chicago.

A June 1, 1994, article by Karen Wagner in the *Northwest Leader* newspaper entitled "Greek Center Offers Services for Seniors," touched on the uniqueness of our cultural programs:

> Every March 25, on Greek Independence Day, the center holds a celebration with music, poetry reading, and dancing. Each week about 20 women attend a fabric arts class where they learn the fine art of Greek needlework. The center has also sponsored various lectures and conferences that focus on the Greek-American experience.
>
> The organization is one of three full-time social service agencies for the Greek-American community in the Chicago area. What is unique about GACS, say Psiharis and Cultural and Arts Program Director John Rassogianis, is their relationship with other ethnic organizations.
>
> The two say it's important that they are in contact with Polish, Italian, Assyrian, and African-American groups, as well as those of other ethnicities. By working together, they said, not only is there the means for discussion but perhaps solutions. 'We're promoting a tremendous amount of dialogue,' commented Rassogianis, who plans the various lectures with other ethnic groups, including one comparing the failures and accomplishments of the Greek and Italian communities.

Steve Frangos was key to the success of our cultural grants from the Illinois Humanities Council and the Illinois Arts Council. He was a doctoral student in cultural anthropology at Indiana State University in Bloomington. Steve could be described as a brilliant eccentric. His research and knowledge of Chicago's Greek community and Greek music genres were impressive. He collaborated with Dino Pappas in Detroit who was a well-known music collector and researcher of early Greek American music. Dino had a collection of 30,000 records, including old Greek recordings that mentioned Chicago in their lyrics and those that were recorded in Chicago. Steve also worked with Dr. Andrew Kopan, the foremost historian of the Greeks in Chicago, to preserve and document Greek American history. Steve understood the language and terminology the grant reviewers were looking for and could properly frame the proposals to reflect that.

Elaine and I recall Steve going off-grid a day before the deadline to submit an Illinois Humanities grant request. Steve lived in a farmhouse in a remote part of Grayslake. He had no phone and this was before the advent of cell phones. Elaine, with her infant son Christopher in tow, journeyed to Grayslake in search of Steve and our grant. On her way there, she went to the police station to get directions to his house. Eventually, she located him and got the grant.

This was the pre-computer age when 15 or even 30 copies of a typed grant proposal (each copy could be more than 50 pages with supporting documentation and attachments) had to be received in the IHC downtown offices by a deadline. A lot of time was spent typing, copying, and assembling the proposals. It took several hours and cost a good amount of money at a local Kinko's copy store, rushing to get the copies made, collated, and stapled to meet the submission deadlines.

Steve played a role in helping us to secure other grants including music and dance programs and the initial Fabric Arts Program grant. He also was the lead researcher of "*O Cosmos*: The Private Lives and Public Celebrations of the Greeks in Illinois 1880 – 1990," an Illinois Humanities Council-funded traveling museum exhibition created by GACS.

Hellenic Alliances

Since its earliest days, Greek-American Community Services cooperated with many organizations within Chicago's Greek community. Some of these relationships grew into steadfast alliances while others, regardless of efforts made on our part, never came to fruition, or if they did, were minimal in impact.

The closest relationship GACS had by far was with the Greek-American Nursing Home Committee. GACS had been the parent organization, and after separating, we continued as sister organizations. Many of the board members served on both boards. There was an effort by a few on the nursing home committee, in particular Helen Georges, to distance the committee from GACS. Although this created some tension early on, the ties between the two organizations were strong and remained so throughout the existence of GACS.

Beyond founding the Greek-American Nursing Home Committee and nurturing it through its first few years of operation, GACS and the GANHC worked together in many ways. GACS board members that were also on the board of the nursing home committee included: Emily Alexandrou, Helen Geocaris, Thalia Jameson, Bill Kakavas, Mary Kakavas, Jean Kaporis, Dr. Theodosis Kioutas, Anna Manos, Toni Panos, Dr. Nicholas Papanos, John Psiharis, John Rassogianis, and Elaine Thomopoulos. Elaine served as second vice president of the GANHC for many of these years and I was assistant treasurer for a period. GACS was the regular meeting place for most nursing home board and committee meetings.

Ethel Kotsovos, GACS social worker, at first volunteered and later was paid, to run the Greek-American Nursing Home Committee office located within Dr. Kioutas' medical suite on California Avenue near Lincoln Avenue. Before her staff role, Ethel was a GANHC board member.

John Rassogianis, a GACS board member and then Cultural & Arts Program director, was a board member of the nursing home committee and its publicity chairman. In that capacity, he generated many press releases and other publicity activities to help inform and update the Greek community. John also represented the GANHC on the board of the Coalition of Limited English Speaking Elderly (CLESE).

Maria Toledo (Villalobos) eventually became the secretary/administrative assistant for both organizations, dividing her time between the GACS and GANHC offices.

The GACS *Ya'Sou* vans were used on several occasions to transport residents from Hollywood House to GANHC fundraisers and to shuttle riders between the GACS center and GANHC events in Wheeling.

A 1994 study conducted by GACS for the GANHC Certificate of Need, coordinated by Ethel, found that there were 340 Greek elderly nursing home residents scattered throughout 85 facilities and that another 400 were expected to need adult day care or nursing home care within the next three years. The results of the survey were also used by the GANHC to document the need for a nursing home in fundraising, publicity, and obtaining zoning.

The study further detailed data gleaned from the 1990 census by Northeastern Illinois University. There were approximately 240,000 Greek Americans in the Chicago metropolitan area. It found that 21 percent or 50,400 were over age 60 and 23 percent, or 11,592 were non-English speaking.

One of these individuals was Efthimios Vlahos. Mr. Vlahos was an adult day care client for several years. In his 90s, Efthimios was alert but physically frail and actively participated in center programming. A favorite activity for him was to teach Greek to Ricardo Rodriguez, a non-Greek volunteer who eventually became a GACS board member. Efthimios prepared weekly lessons and engaged in conversational Greek with Ricky. He also joined in with fabric arts participants during their Wednesday classes. Efthimios was an ardent supporter of the nursing home project and had hoped to be the first resident of the new facility. He frequently inquired about the latest progress and any news on the project. Efthimios and his family attended several GANHC fundraisers, and he was profiled in the *Groundbreaker*, the GANHC newsletter. For some of us,

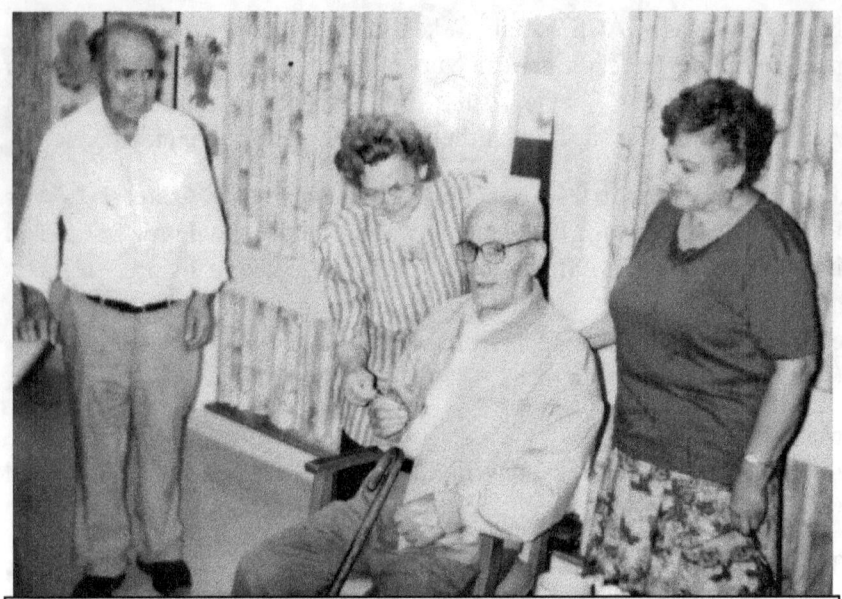

A GACS visit to Efthimios Vlahos. (L-R): Unknown, Margaret Nikolopoulos, Efthimios Vlahos, and Toni Panos. Circa 2001. Photo by John Rassogianis. John Rassogianis collection.

Efthimios epitomized the need for a nursing home. He was a face for the home we were working to establish. Unfortunately, his health declined, and he was admitted into an area nursing home. He died in February 2002 at the age of 95, just weeks before GANHC admitted its first residents in early March. GACS and GANHC members, and several of his friends from the center, visited him at the nursing home and attended his wake.

A profile of Efthimios in the Fall 2001 issue of *the Greek-American Nursing Home Committee Newsletter*, read in part:

> Efthimios Vlahos is 95 years old and has anxiously been waiting for the Greek American Rehabilitation and Nursing Centre to open. He would like to be the first resident.
>
> Mr. Vlahos is very social, loves the companionship of friends, and looks forward to having a conversation with anyone around him who is pleasant, but he cannot. He would like to have a Greek meal regularly, but he cannot. Mr. Vlahos has been in a very fine nursing care facility for several years. All his physical needs are met. He longs for "parea" (companionship). His English is limited, and he has no one to speak with in his native tongue most of the time. He can't wait to be transferred to our nursing home.
>
> After the death of his wife Maria, Mr. Vlahos followed his sons, George, Elias, and Constantine to America in 1969. He had passed some very hard times in his village of Kalavrita. First

the Italians, then the Germans, and lastly the "Antartes" (the leftists in the civil war). His homes were burned twice because he was anti-Communist. He served as a soldier twice.

Mr. Vlahos and his sons are donors and their Society Kalavriton made a generous donation to the nursing home project. Now, all he wants is to be in a dignified, orthodox, and Hellenic environment. He is on our waiting list.

Another example of the need for the nursing home project was Mrs. Stella C. Coroneos. Profiled as "Someone You Should Know," in the Spring 2000 issue of the *Greek-American Nursing Home Committee Newsletter*:

> Mrs. Coroneos has been a resident at Alshore Nursing Home in Chicago for seven years. She is 98 years old. Her life involved many changes and family tragedies.
>
> She was born in Smyrna, Turkey, however, she and her family were forced to escape to Greece. She married in Greece and came to the United States with her husband in the 1930s. They had one son who passed away while at university when he was only 21 years old. She has been a widow for over 30 years.
>
> Mrs. Coroneos began working after she lost her husband. While in Greece, she was one of the recipients of training in needlework at the "Vasiliki Pronia" (Queen's Charity). She was very talented and was able to support herself and save some of her earnings.
>
> In 1993 she fell and broke her hip. She became unable to care for her daily needs, and her doctor recommended she be placed in a nursing home. She states that she misses the friendships that she had, someone to speak with in Greek, and especially to worship in her church and celebrate religious holidays. When the plan to build a nursing care facility to meet the needs of Greek-Americans became known to her, tears came to her eyes, and she said, 'I am sure to find friends there.'
>
> Mrs. Coroneas is visited by a distant relative of her late husband. She has no one else.

In the coming years, the nursing home movement gained the support of several influential and wealthy members of the community who were initially involved with GACS. These included GACS Advisory Board members Irene Antoniou, Eleni Bousis, Aphrodite Demeur, Demetrios Kozonis, Loukas Pergantas, and Chris Tomaras. Dr. John D. Nicholson bequeathed money to both organizations. GACS submitted testimony to the Illinois Health Facilities Board in support of the nursing home project. Once the home opened, GACS referred potential residents and employees to the home.

In 1986 GACS launched a quarterly newsletter that was sent to donors, volunteers, businesses, churches, volunteers, and community members. Evangeline Mistaras prepared the newsletter and used her dot matrix printer to print out the camera-ready copy. GACS had received a grant from the Playboy Foundation for the printing of the newsletter. We delivered the copy to their offices in the Playboy Building where the newsletters were printed and mailed. The newsletter continued for several years but for some reason came to an end.

GACS established and maintained good relationships with the community's cultural organizations. We often co-sponsored various cultural programs that were originated by one of the other organizations. Co-sponsoring an event usually meant promoting and helping to organize the event as well as sharing proportionally in the expenses. Together, this arrangement helped to bring about an array of high-quality cultural and arts programs that the community would normally not have access to. These organizations included: The Greek Women's University Club (GWUC), Hellenic Cultural Organization (HCO), Hellenic Professional Society of Illinois (HPSI), and KRIKOS.

We discussed establishing a clearinghouse/hotline for events in Chicago's Greek community to avoid or at least minimize schedule conflicts. GACS coordinated this through funding from our annual CDBG grant. Organizations were asked to call or fax their event details to John before scheduling major activities to minimize schedule conflicts. Although successful to some extent, there was no consistent buy-in or participation by all, which continued to result in more than one event being scheduled on a particular day. At some point, we discontinued this service.

GACS maintained good relationships with many Greek fraternal organizations including the Cretan Federation, Pan Arcadian Federation, Pan Laconian Federation, Pan Macedonian Federation, Pan Messinian Federation, and the Hellenic Ladies Society of Constantinople. Dr. Kioutas, John, and I served as board members for the Chicago Council for Justice in Cyprus, which often held its meetings at GACS. In the early years, GACS and the Pan Laconian Federation co-sponsored holiday food drives for needy families. Pol Gavaris was active in the Federation and spearheaded this drive.

Relations with the Church could best be described as lukewarm. Although some parishes were supportive, Bishop Iakovos, who was later designated Metropolitan of Krinis, was not particularly supportive of GACS, and at this point was ambivalent about the GANHC. He only wholeheartedly embraced the nursing home project after the property was purchased, and

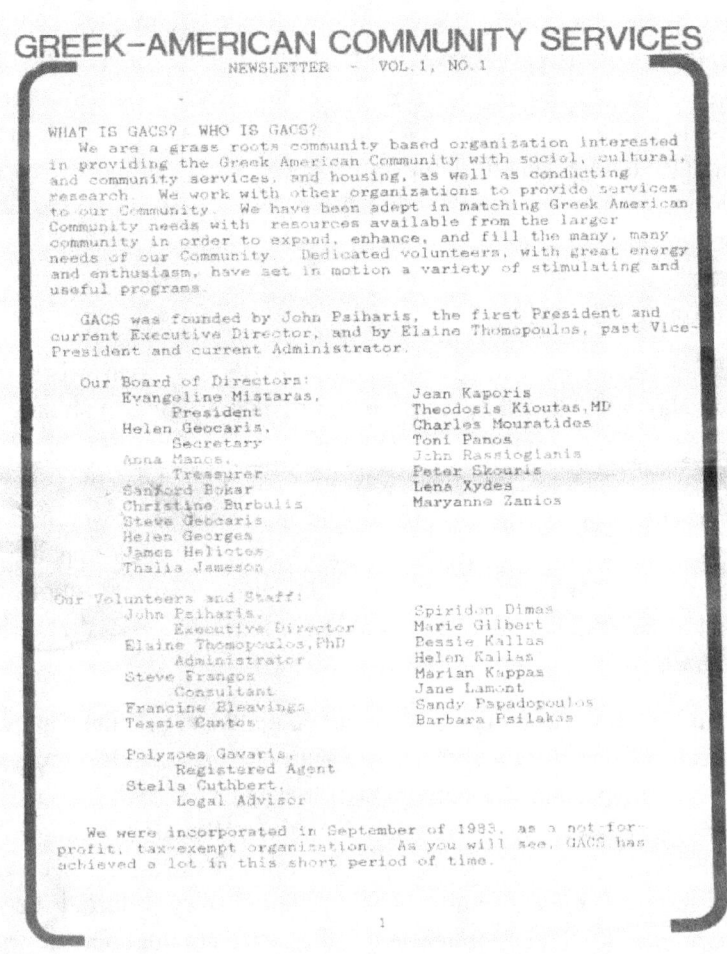

GACS Newsletter front page. Volume 1. Number 1. Circa 1986. Elaine Thomopoulos collection.

it became apparent that we would succeed with or without his involvement.

The Very Rev. Nikitas Lulias, chancellor of the Greek Orthodox Diocese of Chicago during the early years of GACS, was supportive of both organizations. He served on the Cultural & Arts Program Advisory Committee and coordinated a statewide dance program. Father Nikitas also attended our events and dinners and officiated the *Agiasmos* ceremonies during our open houses.

In my view, the powers that be within the community, or at least those who perceived themselves as leaders within the community, were against GACS because they saw it as competition with the Hellenic Foundation.

The Bishop, who was honorary chairman of the Hellenic Foundation, seemed to embrace these views. Although some churches supported GACS efforts at the parish level, no tangible support was received from either the Archdiocese in New York or the Diocese of Chicago. The Diocesan Philoptochos Society did donate to GACS periodically. Individual churches and Philoptochos societies that supported us were usually inspired by members within the parishes who supported GACS and/or the nursing home committee. They included: Annunciation Cathedral, Assumption, Holy Trinity, St. Andrew, St. Basil, St. Demetrios, and St. George.

By far, the most complicated relationship GACS navigated was with the Hellenic Foundation. Many of us believed that Cynthia Yannias, their executive director, unnecessarily created an "us versus them" mentality and seemed threatened in some way by GACS. Instead of embracing opportunities to work together, I was told by several who were involved with the Hellenic Foundation, that Cynthia fostered an environment where GACS was a competitor and not a potential partner. They mentioned that she felt there should be one community organization - the Hellenic Foundation.

GACS believed the organizations should co-exist and that the community was better off because there was more than one organization focused on aiding and supporting the community. It made no sense for GACS to duplicate programs that were already being offered by the Hellenic Foundation and it would be best to develop a seamless service system within the Greek community where clients were referred between organizations based on their needs. In short, we were not competitors, but unfortunately, opportunities to collaborate for the common good of our community were not possible in this environment. This was frustrating to many of us because there were areas that we could have worked on together for the benefit of the community that were never explored.

Soon after the ADC opened, Elaine, Ethel, and I met with Electra Tarsinos, who briefly served as the Hellenic Foundation's director of social services. Electra was essentially a go-between for Cynthia and Angelike Mountanis, who was the director of the Foundation's Hellenic Family and Community Services program. On a part-time basis, Electra commuted from her home in Princeton, Illinois to work in the city. Electra was also good friends with Ethel Kotsovos; they had gone to college together. We discussed how our two organizations could work together; however little came of this since there was no desire to cooperate on their part.

At this time, many of the Greek "establishment" in Chicago were not supportive of GACS or the GANHC, although some became supportive as time went on. This was apparent in our dealings with the United Hellenic American Congress (UHAC), which claimed to be an umbrella organization for the Greek community. Founded and led by Andrew Athens, UHAC distinguished itself in lobbying for issues impacting Greece, Cyprus, and/or the Greek-American diaspora. UHAC supported the Hellenic Museum and Cultural Center, and the Hellenic Foundation, and helped launch International Orthodox Christian Charities (IOCC), of which Andrew Athens was a founding member. After UHAC purchased the *Greek Star*, the newspaper also functioned as their house organ, highlighting UHAC activities and priorities.

After a period of minimal communication with UHAC and the Hellenic Foundation, Andrew Athens, with little notice, invited the leadership of both GACS and GANHC to meet with the UHAC executive committee members in a hastily arranged meeting held on July 3, 1992, at the UHAC office on Michigan Avenue. GACS was represented by Evangeline, Elaine, and myself. The GANHC was represented by Dr. Kioutas and Helen Georges. Dr. Kioutas, Elaine, and I wore two hats during this meeting representing both GACS and the GANHC. In addition to Andrew Athens, UHAC participants included Bill Vranas, Frank Kamberos, and Helen Alexander, executive secretary of UHAC. George Collias, board president, and Cynthia Yannias represented the Hellenic Foundation. His Grace Bishop Iakovos was also in attendance.

Once pleasantries were exchanged, Evangeline, Elaine, and I spoke about GACS while Dr. Kioutas and Helen discussed the nursing home. Cynthia and George then spoke on behalf of the Hellenic Foundation. They felt that the nursing home project should not move forward and argued there was little need for a Greek American nursing home and that it wouldn't be financially viable. They felt that Hollywood House was sufficient for the community. In terms of GACS, Cynthia felt that GACS was taking money away from the Hellenic Foundation since they were also seeking community support. She felt there was a finite amount of money within the Greek community and that GACS and GANHC support was in effect reducing the amount of the pie available to them. The bishop was not enthusiastic about GACS and suggested that the GANHC consider a wing in a nursing home instead. He felt that a project of this magnitude would take years to achieve, if ever.

We in turn expressed our view that GACS attracted new dollars and grants to the community in support of services and programs that did not currently exist. Our community was enriched by these services. We did not see this as a competitive environment but one that should encourage cooperation and collaboration.

Evangeline articulated what was referred to within GACS as the "Mistaras Doctrine." This vision of Chicago's Greek community included a troika of services to the elderly. The Hellenic Foundation would provide housing for independent seniors and homemaker services; GACS would offer mid-range services to the elderly through the adult day care center and the GANHC would offer intermediate and skilled nursing care as well as rehabilitation assistance. She viewed these three co-existing organizations to be the community's safety net for its elders.

The end result was that no meaningful UHAC or Hellenic Foundation support or cooperation was forthcoming for GACS or GANHC as a result of this meeting. Worth noting is that we did not acquiesce. We conveyed that our organizations would go on with or without the support of UHAC, the Hellenic Foundation, or the church. The tone of the meeting reflected the fragmented state of Chicago's Greek community and a lack of unity, even though UHAC boasted that its role was to serve as an umbrella organization.

We were surprised but not surprised about the outcome of the meeting. Over coffee at a nearby downtown diner after the meeting, we discussed what had just happened. The overall feeling was that the individual churches would be supportive of the nursing home and that the Bishop would come along eventually since he would not publicly want to be seen as an obstruction when the churches under his jurisdiction were supportive. The Bishop's main focus was creating a Diocesan Retreat Center near Kenosha, Wisconsin. He was raising money for this and had requested the churches within the Diocese to support this effort. With or without the support of UHAC and the Hellenic Foundation, we resolved to move forward.

In 1993, Dr. Michael Bakalis briefly served as executive director of UHAC. That period was refreshing but short-lived. He formed a social services committee to encourage dialogue and cooperation related to social services. Mike hosted a couple of meetings with GACS and the Hellenic Foundation at UHAC's office. I recall that Cynthia and I attended these meetings and perhaps others did as well. I do not remember much about what was discussed or the outcomes of these meetings, but the fact that we were talking was positive.

At the time, the annual Greek parade was organized by UHAC, and our request to waive the entry fee to have our *Ya'Sou* vans in the parade was turned down. As I recall, the fee was significant, and GACS board member Kostas Zografopoulos, the owner of Master Caterers, arranged with the parade coordinators for GACS to pass out water and cookies to parade marchers from the back of the *Ya'Sou* vans. Kosta provided the cookies,

Top: John Psiharis and Toni Panos pose with the *Ya'Sou One* van on Wacker Drive during staging for a Greek Independence Day parade. **Bottom:** Toni Panos and John Psiharis distribute cookies and water to young parade marchers. Dates unknown. Photos by John Rassogianis. John Rassogianis collection.

Pictured (L-R): Gus Flesor, John Psiharis, and Peter Spyropoulos at a Greek Independence Day parade. Date unknown. Photo by John Rassogianis. John Rassogianis collection.

water jugs, and drinking cups. By doing so, the entry fee was waived and the vans were able to take part in the procession. Passing out water and cookies made the GACS table a popular stop for parade marchers, and there were many visitors. Adult day care clients and volunteers were invited to ride in the vans along with the GACS board and staff.

An example of GACS thinking outside the box was its research into establishing a Greek United Fund. United Way was a major fundraiser and grantor in the philanthropic field. Several ethnic groups including the Jewish and Black communities had similar models within their communities. Evangeline, Ethel, John, and I saw the potential a Greek United Fund could offer our community. We visited with leaders of United Way of Chicago, the Jewish United Fund, and the Black United Fund to learn about their programs.

The idea was simple. There were some 240,000 Greeks in the metropolitan Chicago area. If each of us donated $10 per year, the result would be $2,400,000 annually to benefit the community's social services and cultural organizations.

Additionally, there were Greek-owned businesses that could either support the fund or offer workplace deductions that could result in additional dollars being raised. It was hoped that churches would support this undertaking as a means of helping multiple organizations through one donation rather than on a more piecemeal basis of passing multiple collection trays during services.

Top: Hellenic Cultural Center committee members visit the Copernicus Foundation. Pictured (L-R): George Michalatos, John Psiharis, unknown, Nick Flevaris, and John Rassogianis. Date unknown. **Bottom:** Hellenic Cultural Center committee members tour the Irish Heritage Center. Pictured (L-R): Unknown, John Psiharis, Bob Dyra, president of the Irish Heritage Center, John Rassogianis, and Nick Flevaris. Date unknown. John Psiharis collection.

The funding would have been distributed amongst GACS, the Hellenic Foundation, the GANHC, International Orthodox Christian Charities (IOCC), and any future organizations that might qualify for membership. A portion of the funds would be reserved for cultural organizations including the Hellenic Museum and Cultural Center, Hellenic Cultural Organization, GACS, and others. A board, with representation from each organization as well as outside stakeholders, would oversee the GUF operations, fundraising efforts, and disbursements. The concept was supported by the GACS and GANHC boards but the Hellenic Foundation was not interested in pursuing this.

A reflection of the solid relationships GACS had with fellow Greek cultural organizations was our participation in discussions with several organizations about the feasibility of establishing a Hellenic cultural center. John and I were invited to join the committee considering this possibility. The idea was to create a central gathering place where organizations could host meetings and events. Classrooms and a community library were part of the plan. At this point, the Hellenic Museum was several years from opening and it had more of a museum focus (rather than a cultural center).

Committee members included: Ted Spyropoulos, president of ENOSIS; Nick Flevaris and George Michalatos representing the Hellenic Cultural Organization and Dr. George Alexopoulos, representing KRIKOS. We toured the Copernicus Foundation, the Italian American Cultural Center, and the Irish American Heritage Center.

After several meetings and tours, the idea fizzled out in part because the nursing home was moving forward with purchasing land and the Hellenic Museum and Cultural Center was in the early stages of acquiring its future location. There was a feeling that with two large-scale projects already in the works, the likelihood of a third undertaking of this magnitude was too much for the community to sustain.

There was a schism within some circles of the community who did not feel UHAC reflected their interests and concerns. With exceptions, it was mostly the immigrant community that supported ENOSIS while those of first and second generations were more likely involved with UHAC.

This division became more apparent when ENOSIS assumed control of the Greek parade from UHAC. UHAC had up until that point held the parade on Michigan Avenue in May. Many Greek organizations felt the parade should be held closer to the 25th of March, Greek Independence Day, and that it should go through Halsted Street, the heart of Greektown.

UHAC believed the weather was better in May and that Michigan Avenue, with the reviewing stand across from the Art Institute, was a prime route for the parade that few other parades were granted. ENOSIS felt that the weather was immaterial and that Greektown was a more appropriate setting for the parade. As ENOSIS members represented many fraternal societies and organizations, they succeeded in taking over the parade and continue today to coordinate this event annually.

Honoring Those Who Preserved the Heritage

Since its earliest days, the motto of GACS was "Working to Preserve Our Heritage." GACS endeavored to do so in both its cultural activities as well as in its services to the community.

In this era, it was common to host fundraising dinner dances and many organizations depended on these annual events for a major portion of their budgets. In some cases, dinners had 800, sometimes even 1,000 or more people in attendance. In addition to the funds that were raised, dinners provided an opportunity for attendees to socialize and gather in support of the cause at hand.

*Greek-American Community Services
requests the pleasure of your company
at the
First Annual Heritage
Awards Dinner Banquet*

*Honoring
Alex Karanikas
Andrew Kopan
Yorgos Kourvetaris
Charles Moskos
Theano Papazoglou-Margaris
Harry Mark Petrakis*

*Friday, May 1st, 1987
Diplomat Banquets
5600 West Fullerton
Chicago, Illinois*

*Cocktails 6:30 p.m.
Dinner 7:30 p.m.   Black Tie Optional*

*Donation $35.00
Music by Perry Fotos Orchestra*

*For additional information call:
Greek-American Community Services Office: 539-2323
or Lena Xydes 764-1076 - Evenings*

Invitation to the First Annual Heritage Awards Dinner.Banquet May 1, 1987. John Psiharis collection.

When GACS considered having a dinner dance to raise funds late in 1986, Elaine suggested that we present an award to someone who had preserved our heritage in some way. Upon further discussion, the award was named the Heritage Award. Lena Xydes, who was GACS treasurer at the time, recommended Peter Lallas to chair the event. Peter was active in leadership roles within AHEPA and St. Andrew Greek Orthodox Church. He was the owner of Carpet Forest, a three-store carpet business with its main location in an old Woolworth's store in the heart of Jefferson Park, on Milwaukee Avenue, north of Lawrence. His wife Evelyn served as co-chair.

As a new organization with a smaller base of supporters, Peter recommended that GACS honor multiple people from different disciplines for preserving the heritage in their own unique ways. It was assumed that each honoree would bring in at least one table of ten, although that wasn't the case. Some honorees would take several tables while others accepted the complimentary tickets and didn't donate anything beyond that. Peter felt that since we were honoring people, the dinners should be elegant, and those he organized were black-tie optional. Peter and Evelyn chaired the dinners for the first two years. Ethel and her cousin Mary Bennos handled the reservations and seating arrangements for most of the GACS Heritage Awards dinners.

On May 1, 1987, with "Working to Preserve our Heritage" as our guidepost, GACS honored six distinguished individuals who had lived up to our motto during the First Annual Heritage Awards Dinner. They were: Dr. Andrew Kopan (noted historian of Chicago's Greek community and education professor at DePaul University), Dr. Yorgos Kourvetaris (sociology professor at Northern Illinois University and Greek researcher), Dr. Charles Moskos (professor at Northwestern University and researcher on the Greek community in the United States), Theano Papazoglou Margaris (noted author on the Greek American experience), and Harry Mark Petrakis (award-winning author on the Greek experience in Chicago). The event was held at Diplomat Banquets (Fullerton and Central) and had an attendance of about 100 guests. A retired Greek Orthodox priest, unknown to most in attendance, offered the opening prayer, further evidence of the meager support GACS received from the Bishop and the Diocese of Chicago.

A report in the August 1987 edition of the GACS newsletter described the evening:

> The First Annual Greek-American Community Services Heritage Awards was a stunning success. A full house greeted the five 1987 Awards recipients; Alexander Karanikas, Andrew Kopan, Yorgos Kourvetaris, Charles Moskos, and Theano Papazoglou-Margaris, as they were honored for their outstanding contributions to recording and preserving the Greek American experience through their works.

Heritage Award presented to Theano Papazoglou Margaris by GACS on May 1, 1987. From the National Hellenic Museum - Theano Papazoglou-Margaris collection.

Peter Lallas, who with his wife Evelyn was co-chair of the event, read congratulatory messages from Governor Michael Dukakis, Governor James Thompson, Mayor Harold Washington, County Board President George Dunne, and Zion City Mayor/Illinois State Senator Adeline Geo-Karis.

In her welcoming remarks Evangeline Mistaras, GACS President, echoed the theme of the evening, GACS's mission of 'Working to Preserve our Heritage.' This motto was presented to GACS by the late Harry Milakis, a devoted member of GACS.

Upon receiving their awards from John Psiharis and Elaine Thomopoulos, the Honorees made short but memorable acceptance speeches. Dr. Alexander Karanikas concluded the presentation by reading the Honor Roll of Greek American writers and poets whose contributions to our community should be recognized.

Greek-American Community Services honor distinguished authors of Hellenic descent for their contributions toward the preservation of the Greek-American experience. Honorees: Dr. Andrew Kopan, Dr. Charles Moskos, Dr. Alexander Karanikas, Dr. Yorgos Kourvetaris, Theano Papazoglou-Margaris, Harry Mark Petrakis. Also pictured: Greek-American Community Services Executive Director, John Psiharis, Dr. Elaine Thomopoulos, Administrator, and Evangeline Mislaras, President.

The *Greek Star*. May 1987. Elaine Thomopoulos collection.

Along with the dinner, a souvenir program album was prepared and distributed to those in attendance. The ad book and a raffle added to what was raised through dinner tickets. In addition to greetings and the menu, the album included full-page biographies of each of the honorees, greeting messages from elected officials and community leaders, and advertising and congratulatory messages purchased by businesses and individuals. We printed up NCR (No Carbon Required) advertising contracts that were distributed to friends, families, and businesses that we patronized. Prices were highest for the outside back cover and in descending order the inside front and back covers and gold or silver pages, full pages, half pages, and quarter pages. Patrons could have their names listed for $10. While at the printers I often ran into those from other organizations who were dealing with their own printing projects.

Over the years, greetings and salutations were received from three U.S. presidents (Reagan, Bush, and Clinton), two vice presidents of the U.S. (Bush and Gore), U.S. senators, governors of Illinois, and mayors of Chicago. Archbishop Iakovos and Bishop Iakovos sent messages as did the Greek and Cyprus ambassadors to the U.S., and the consul general of Greece in Chicago. We also received messages from Senators Paul Sarbanes and Paul Tsongas and Governor Michael Dukakis. A selection of these messages is included in the next chapter.

It became an annual ritual for me, often with John, Elaine, or Maria, to spend several days at the printer putting together the book with Dina Ress, the manager of the print shop. Cosmos Press was the primary Greek printer in Chicago and handled many ad books, invites, and publications for Greek organizations and churches. Dina was great to work with and had a quirky sense of humor. This was a labor-intensive process, and we needed to be there to edit and approve each proof, work on any late-arriving ads, and finalize the layout. On the day of the event, we would pick up the books and take them to the event venue. There were times when the books were still being stapled or packed and when our driver arrived, he had to wait. Despite intense efforts to ensure all ads were included and minimize typos or other errors, mishaps did occur. One year, the front cover that was printed was the cover of the prior year's event!

Because of the snafu with the wrong cover and the fact that we had to pick up the books, sometimes at the last possible minute, and drive them downtown through Friday rush hour traffic; we shifted our business to Graphomania which had recently opened. The print shop was also popular in the community. The owner, Dimitri Pnevmatikatos, published a Greek-language newspaper called the *Hellenic Community News*. Tom Gouliamos, who was a friend and worked there, did the design and layouts of the ad books. Many advertisers supported organizations or churches that utilized one printer or the other, so often their logos and messages were already on file. I enjoyed working with Tom and Dimitri, and we appreciated that the books were delivered without us having to pick them Many advertisers supported organizations or churches that utilized one printer or the other, so often their logos and messages were already on file. I enjoyed working with Tom and Dimitri, and we appreciated that the

Top: Senator Adeline Geo-Karis accepts the GACS Heritage Award on April 22, 1988. Behind her (L-R): John Psiharis, Elaine Thomopoulos, and Peter Lallas. John Psiharis collection. **Bottom**: First Row: Evelyn Lallas, Peter Lallas, Sam Stavrakas, Leon Marinakos, Lena Xydes, Evangeline Mistaras. Second Row: John Rassogiannis, John Psiharis, Yannis Lambros, Antigone Lambros, Dr. Fotios Litsas, Senator Adeline Geo-Karis, Dr. John Nicholson, Ethel Kotsovos, Elaine Thomopoulos. Elaine Thomopoulos collection.

Dr. John Nicholson accepts GACS Heritage Award as Peter Lallas, John Psiharis, and Elaine Thomopoulos look on. April 22, 1988. John Psiharis collection.

books were delivered without us having to pick them His newspaper was widely read and Dimitri included our press releases in his paper.

The second annual dinner followed in a similar vein with the honorees representing various disciplines including business, government, education, culture, and medicine. The event was held on April 22, 1988 at the Fountain Blue in Des Plaines, and Peter and Evelyn chaired the event. Honorees included: Senator Adeline Geo-Karis (Illinois state senator and mayor of Zion Illinois), Yiannis and Antigone Lambros (*Hellenic Interlude* radio program hosts), Dr. Fotios Litsas, (director of the Greek Studies Program at the University of Illinois Chicago, radio host, and writer), Leon Marinakos (honorary consular cultural attaché of Greece), Dr. John D. Nicholson (noted philanthropist and retired eye, ear, nose and throat doctor), and Sam Stavrakas (owner of Cosmopolitan Linens and Textiles and active in AHEPA's south side chapter).

After the second year, for health reasons, Peter and Evelyn Lallas stepped down from chairing the events and GACS tweaked the format of the Heritage Awards dinners. As the new decade was upon us, we made a couple of changes to the event.

First, the event was moved from the spring to the fall. This was to avoid conflicts with Easter, Greek Independence Day, the Greek Parade, and events that are planned around those days. The second change was to designate a theme and then select honorees who are worthy within these areas. We chose the overarching theme of "Greek Americans in the 1990s," as the thread that would tie everything together.

Another change was to remove "black tie optional" from the invitation. Peter believed that since this was an awards ceremony, the tuxedo added a touch of class to the event. However, the dinners were held on Friday evenings and it was difficult for those who were coming directly from work to deal with changing into formal wear.

In the third year, the Heritage Award went to John C. Geocaris (40th Ward Democratic Party committeeman and deputy commissioner of the Chicago Department of Streets and Sanitation), James Mezilson (columnist for the *Greek Press*), and Georgia Mitchell (founder and director of the Hellenic Choral Society). The event was held on September 22, 1989, at Diplomat Banquets. The dinner co-chairs were Michael Lascaris and Congressman Frank Annunzio. Sandy Papadopoulos was the coordinator. John Rassogianis was the master of ceremonies and introduced the honorees as Elaine and I presented the awards. His Grace Bishop Iakovos offered the invocation and benediction. We believed he attended because Georgia was being honored. Spyros Aliagas, Consul General of Greece, spoke. Panos and Stratos Orchestra provided the music.

In honor of Jim's 50th anniversary as a columnist for the *Greek Press*, the newspaper printed his noteworthy acceptance speech in its October 29, 1989 edition:

> EDITORIAL NOTE: In lieu of his regular column, the GREEK PRESS is substituting Mr. Mezilson's remarks made on September 22, 1989, when he was honored by the Greek-American Community Services upon the occasion of his golden anniversary as a columnist. They are as follows:
>
> "Thank you Mr. Chairman – Your Grace Bishop Iakovos. Reverend Fathers Nicholas Nikokavouras and Stavroforos Mamies, Officers and members of the Greek-American Community Services, and dear friends.

Third Annual Heritage Awards Dinner. Pictured (L-R): John Psiharis, Athanasia Papadopoulos, Evangeline Mistaras, James Mezilson, Georgia Mitchell, His Grace Bishop Iakovos, John C. Geocaris, John Rassogianis, Elaine Thomopoulos, Peter Maroutsos, and Toni Panos. September 22, 1989. John Psiharis collection.

When the president of Greek-American Community Services, Evangeline Mistaras, called me some weeks ago to invite me to become one of three honorees this evening, I was flattered and honored. And when I learned the names of my two co-honorees, Georgia Mitchell and John Geocaris, I accepted with no hesitation.

What I did not know initially was that I was expected to speak. Those who know me are aware of the fact that I am not a speaker and not blessed with the oratory of the past honorees. The printed word is my speed.

It is indeed a pleasure to see so many of you here, who have been loyal readers of the column, which began as 'Periclean Patter,' and which endured many name changes over the years. And now known simply as 'Mez.' A name like that has been with me from boyhood, and one used to later identify my news copy from the time I began writing for the old *Chicago Sun*, the predecessor to today's *Chicago Sun-Times*.

In accepting this honor tonight, I want to say that I am doing so as a representative of the legion of columnists who have contributed their talents to the Chicago Greek media with no personal financial remuneration – including myself.

These writers include some of the earliest that I can recall at the moment, such as John Chiakulas, Paul Nicopolos, Irene Harvalis Glyptis, Stella Adams Cuthbert, and Angelo Geocaris, with whom I began this column, before going solo several months later in 1939.

Others include Niki Farmakis Skodon, Dr. Andrew T. Kopan, Urania Damofle, Aphrodite Flambouras, Steven Javaras, Stacy Diacou, Katherine Valone, Nick Poulos, Dean Dranias, Helen Galanopoulos, Kathryn Adinamis, Tom Karalis, Dr. Chadwick Prodromos, Dr. Nicholas Kokonis, Professor Basil Papadakis, and others. And one must not forget the venerable Theano Margaris, who did her writing in the Greek language, and unlike the others, was compensated for her work, but not in the measure that it was worth.

One must not forget the regular staff writers of the Chicago metropolitan press, of which the late John Matsoukas was the first at the *Chicago Daily News*. Later came Peter C. Latsis at the *Chicago American* while I was at the *Sun*, and Nick Poulos at the *Chicago Tribune* and now with the *Atlanta Constitution*.

Today, there are four with the metropolitan media – all with the *Chicago Tribune*: George Lazarus, John Kass, George Papajohn, and Elaine Markoutsas.

Of course, for my part, all of this could not have been done unless given the opportunity by my mentor, the late Paul Javaras, publisher, and editor of the *Greek Press*, who made possible the reintroduction of English columns.

My interest in newspapers began after having graduated from the six-year Koraes Greek-American School. I entered Healy Public Elementary School at the seventh-grade level. At the time, with others, I put out the school newspaper – the *Healyville News* – which was mimeographed by us on a manual duplicator. Also the help of my sister, Fay Machinis, who hustled ads for the paper from the neighborhood merchants to help sustain the paper financially in those Great Depression years.

Writing the column has been a most enjoyable interlude for it has given me the opportunity to report activities from here and Greece, which time span has covered that of several generations. It has served as a bridge from the world of our immigrant parents to that of their children and grandchildren. It has also afforded me the additional gratification of having made a contribution to the welfare of our community in reporting its activities, its accomplishments, its goals, its joys – and unfortunately its sorrows.

My involvement in Hellenic life has carried me forward to the extent that I have been an active participant, having served in different capacities with Greek and non-Greek groups.

In recent years, this involvement has primarily been centered on the creation of the Hellenic Museum and Cultural Center. I have previously spoken out for its formation and although today the Hellenic Museum does not, at this stage, have a permanent home, it is anticipated that in the very near future, it will be a reality.

With the help of the United Hellenic American Congress, its chairman Andrew A. Athens, and its responsive leadership, a physical home for this institution will be found.

Individuals such as Dr. Andrew T. Kopan of DePaul University, have amassed a wealth of material that will serve as a nucleus for this project. He also brings much expertise to this arena, for he has done in-depth research on immigrant life in Chicago and elsewhere and has published books toward this end.

Another activist in this endeavor is Leon Marinakos who serves as honorary Cultural Attache of the Consulate of Greece. His writings, his films, and his slides are all of significant historical value.

The achievements of Greek Americans have been chronicled in the media, periodicals, and books. The trials and tribulations of our immigrant forebears have been recorded in various archives, but are scattered, and not under the control of its Greek heirs.

Much of this material is also slowly being lost by virtue of the fact that death has claimed the original possessors of these materials and it is eventually being discarded by their offspring as unwanted 'junk.' Thus priceless photographs, letters, periodicals, albums, books, objects of the relevant art, and icons, have been lost due to the lack of a general depository.

Hopefully, this will soon be remedied by the Hellenic Museum, and this material is classified and made available to research scholars.

As executive secretary of the Hellenic Museum, I request, Don't get rid of anything before consulting with me. I am available anytime.

I hope that I have played a significant role in the life of the Greek community.

GREEK-LEADERSHIP IN THE 90's
1990 DINNER COMMITTEE
(In Formation)

MICHAEL LASCARIS, Co-Chairman
Honorable FRANK ANNUNZIO, Honorary Co-Chairman
ATHANASIA PAPADAPOULOS, Pharm.D., Event Coordinator

ROULA ALAKIOTOU
MANOLIS ALPOGIANIS
MICHAEL J. BAKALIS
MARY BENNOS
ALICE BUZANIS
ANGELO CRETICOS, M.D.
GEORGE F. DALIANIS, D.P.M.
POLYZOES GAVARIS
HELEN GEOCARIS
MR. & MRS. PAUL KALPAKE

THEODOSIS KIOUTAS, M.D.
ELAINE KOLLINTZAS
ETHEL KOTSOVOS
FOTIOS K. LITSAS, Ph.D.
EVANGELINE MISTARAS
JOHN PSIHARIS
JOHN RASSOGIANIS
JOHN SANDORS
APHRODITE SARELAS
ELAINE THOMOPOULOS, Ph.D.

> Invitation to the Third Annual GACS Heritage Awards celebrating "Greek-American Leadership in the 90s." 1990. Elaine Thomopoulos collection.

Several years ago, Leon Marinakos pointed out that the column has been on the scene for 45 years – now fifty – which represents 20% or one-fifth of the life of this country. And my other good friend, Dr. Kopan, has bestowed upon me the title of 'Dean of Hellenic Journalists' in view of my longevity.

Again, many thanks for the award which I also accept on behalf of the thousands of readers and those others who have supported my endeavors these past five decades.

Thank you and God Bless you.

The theme selected for the 1990 dinner was "Greek American Leadership in the 90s." It was held on September 28, at the Thirteen Colonies Banquets in River Grove and the expense was generously discounted by owners Bill and Mary Kakavas. The honorees were: James Kirie, an

"Greek-American Leadership in the 90s," Heritage Award honorees. Thirteen Colonies Banquets. September 28, 1990. Pictured: **Top:** (L-R): Frank Kuchuris, Very Rev. Nikitas Lulias, Katherine Valone, Hon. James Kirie. **Bottom:** (L-R): Dr. Michael Bakalis, Frank Kuchuris, Evangeline Mistaras, Very Rev. Nikitas Lulias, John Psiharis, Katherine Valone, Hon. James Kirie, Dr. Theodosis Kioutas, and Dr. Elaine Thomopoulos. John Psiharis collection.

elected member of the Metropolitan Water Reclamation District of Greater Chicago and Leyden Township Democratic committeeman (government); Frank Kuchuris, owner of East Balt Commissaries and Mary Ann Baking Company. His companies supplied the majority of buns to McDonald's restaurants in the United States and parts of Europe including France (business); Very Rev. Nikitas Lulias who at the time was chancellor of the Greek Orthodox Diocese of Chicago. He eventually was elevated to Metropolitan and would oversee the Greek Orthodox Church in Asia (religion) and Kay Valone, founder, and director of the Phos Missions and a religion columnist for the *Greek Press* newspaper (media).

In 1991, "Greek American Communicators in the 90s" recognized Kathryn Adinamis, society columnist in the *Greek Star* newspaper; Charles Mouratides, former editorial director of the *Lerner Newspapers* chain of neighborhood newspapers and a GACS Board member; Evangeline Gouletas, co-owner, along with her brothers Nick Gouletas and Victor Goulet, of American Invsco, which owned or managed an array of high profile residential buildings including Lake Point Tower and 111 E. Chestnut. Evangeline was a former first lady of New York, after a brief marriage to Governor Hugh Carey; and Mike Tsolinas, a meteorologist and weather reporter for WBBM-TV Channel 2, the CBS-owned and operated station in Chicago. GACS initiated a National Heritage Award and selected Senator Paul Tsongas as the first recipient. Due to a last-minute change in his campaign schedule, his wife Niki attended in his stead. Mike Bakalis and I presented Niki with the award. The dinner was the first of several to be held at the Knickerbocker-Chicago Hotel. Irene Antoniou arranged for discounted pricing for these events. The surroundings, ambiance, and white glove service were top-notch as guests dined and mingled amongst classic and ornate decor and a dance floor that cast an array of colored lights in concert with the music.

"Greek American Women of the 90s" was the theme of the 1992 Heritage Awards Dinner. Honorees were: Roula Alakiotou an architect with an impressive array of projects in her portfolio including large-scale private and government buildings; Soula Koutsopanagos, owner of the Hellenic Broadcasting Company which operated a 24-hour Greek radio station; Helen Theodosakis, president of the Greek Orthodox Diocese of Chicago Philoptochos Society, and Athena Touloumis, a longtime leader in the Pan Macedonian Society. Athena was instrumental in the organization's women's group as well as in fundraising for the purchase of their building on Western Avenue near Lawrence. GACS presented the first *Efharisto* Award to the Chicago Community Trust. Michael Marcus, senior program officer, and Barbara Koremenos accepted the award on behalf of the Trust.

"Greek-American Communicators in the 90s," GACS Heritage Awards Dinner. **Top:** (L-R): Elaine Thomopoulos, John Psiharis, Kathryn Adinamis, John Rassogianis, and Charles Mouratides. **Bottom:** Evangeline Gouletas speaks before accepting Heritage Award from John Psiharis. Knickerbocker Hotel-Chicago. October 11, 1991. John Psiharis collection.

Heritage Awards Dinner. Chicago Community Trust officials who received the *Efharisto* Award. Pictured (L-R): Seated: Evangeline Mistaras and Barbara Koremenos (Chicago Community Trust). Standing: John Rassogianis, John Psiharis, Athanasia Papadopoulos, Michael Marcus (Chicago Community Trust), and Dr. Theodosis Kioutas. October 1992. John Psiharis collection.

In a welcome letter for the souvenir album, Evangeline and I wrote in part:

> In this year, the United Nations' Year of the Woman, our Board of Directors has selected four outstanding women who represent the enormous contributions countless women have made in all areas of our community.
>
> Tonight we also salute and recognize the Chicago Community Trust with our First Annual *Efharisto* (Thank You) award. Each year, the GACS Board will select an individual or organization that, through their support, had a significant effect on GACS. The award is presented in appreciation of a $43,000 grant the Trust awarded to our Adult Day Care Center which allowed us to purchase our new '*Ya'Sou*' van to transport clients to and from the center as well as in support of general program expenses.
>
> We believe tonight's theme 'Greek-American Women in the 90s,' honors the many women who have devotedly and tirelessly, given their time, talents, and resources for the betterment of not only our community – but our society as a whole.
>
> As we approach the coming of a new century, GACS is well-positioned to continue offering services to our *Omogenia*. We are on the move and getting better every day. This can only be possible with your support. Let us continue to work together in

the coming year to enhance the life, well-being, and culture of our community.

A description of the gala evening that appeared as a full- back page article, prepared and written by John Rassogianis, appeared in the December 17, 1992 edition of the *Greek Star* and read in part:

> Four outstanding Greek-American women were recently honored on Walton Street at the Knickerbocker during the Sixth Annual Heritage Awards Dinner held by Greek-American Community Services. Roula Alakioutou, the architect; Soula Koutsopanagos of Hellenic Communications, Helen Theodosakis, Philoptochos Societies, and Athena Touloumis, Macedonian Society. They were presented by Elaine Kollintzas, board member and Mistress of Ceremonies for the evening after opening remarks by Evangeline Mistaras, president.
>
> High points sweeping through the elegance of time and place included a mini-slide presentation entitled 'GACS on the Move in '92,' by GACS Treasurer Peter Maroutsos while guests feasted on Mediterranean Vegetable Soup, Garden Green Salad, London Broil with Hunter Sauce, Greek Oven Browned Potatoes, Stir fry vegetables and Baked Alaska Flambé. Agency contributions in various areas of social service, especially the adult day care center, Northwest Chicago Senior Care, were delineated.
>
> Dr. Theodosis Kioutas, the prominent chairman of the Greek-American Nursing Home Committee as well as a GACS board member, presented the 1992 *Efharisto* Award to Michael Marcus of the Chicago Community Trust. In his acceptance remarks, Mr. Marcus stated: 'We at the Chicago Community Trust view our grantmaking as a way of investing in our community. There are some investments that don't pay off at all. Some pay off, and some pay off spectacularly. Your adult day care center is a model program. I'm proud to say that our investment has paid off in dividends.' He also thanked Barb Koremenos, whom he assigned to evaluate the center, who brought in glowing reports of its progress.
>
> An announcement by Dr. Dimitris Dernis, who pledged support to underwrite the entire lunch program of Northwest Chicago Senior Care for the next six months, plainly added to the excitement and conviviality of the program. He was accompanied by his colleagues, Dr. Demetrios Giocaris, Dr. George Kayalogos, Dr. Alice Lambrinidis, Dr. Rodolfo Patino, and GACS board member Dr. Peter Chioros. The lunch program will be underwritten by Broadway Medical Center.

Dr. Theodosis Kioutas presents GACS *Efharisto* Award to Marilyn Hennessey, president of the Retirement Research Foundation, as Dr. Michael Bakalis and John Psiharis look on. October 22, 1993. John Psiharis collection.

Northwest Chicago Senior Care clients and their families are invited to make use of this multi-medical specialty group.

Heritage Awards Committee members included Dr. Athanasia Papadopoulos, Chairwoman: Connie Andrews, Dee Andrews, Potoula Anglezis, Mary Bennos, Tessie Cantos, Connie Gountanis-Rigas, Ethel Kotsovos, Presbytera Despina Massouras, Nikoletta Papadopoulos, John Psiharis, John Rassogianis, and Elaine Thomopoulos. His Grace Bishop Iakovos was represented by Rev. Emmanuel Vergis and his Presbytera.

Centerpieces were donated by Helen Bousis, Lisa Palivos, and Vicky Palivos. Music was provided by Panos and Stratos Orchestra. The magnificent and colorful dance performance was courtesy of the Orpheus Dance Group.

On October 22, 1993, the seventh annual event, held at the Knickerbocker Hotel, honored "Greek American Entrepreneurs in the 90s," Chris Tomaras, founder and owner of Kronos Central Gyros, and Ted Spyropoulos, owner of T.G.S. Petroleum were recognized. Both were heavily involved in leading and supporting many Greek causes at the local, national, and international levels. The second National Heritage Award was awarded to George Stephanopoulos, Communications Director and Senior Advisor to President Bill Clinton. Although he confirmed his attendance two days before the dinner and arranged for family members to attend the event with him, a crisis of some sort at the White House prevented him from coming at the last minute. Instead, he recorded a videotaped message which we played that evening and his uncle accepted the award on his behalf. Mike Bakalis was the master of ceremonies. The *Efharisto* Award was presented to the Retirement Research Foundation. Marilyn Hennessey, RRF President, and Sharon Markham, Senior Program Officer, represented the Foundation. Vasilios Gaitanos gave a special performance to the guests.

In a welcome letter to dinner guests that appeared in the souvenir album, Evangeline and I wrote:

> We are honoring the very essence of the success of our community – the entrepreneurial spirit which has helped to make Greek Americans one of the most successful ethnic groups in the nation. We honor two men who exemplify the very best in this arena. Although they were eminently successful in their own right, they nevertheless chose to give much back to the community.
>
> We also recognize a distinguished Greek-American who has become one of the most influential men in the nation – at the age of 32! He exemplifies the very best qualities of Greek Americans, and it is, thus, very appropriate that we present him with our second National Heritage Award.
>
> Tonight we are also extremely pleased to honor the Retirement Research Foundation with our second annual *Efharisto* (Thank You) award. An Efharisto is given to an individual or organization that through their support, has had a significant lasting impact on GACS. The award is being presented in appreciation of a $110,800 three-year grant in support of our adult day care center.
>
> For those of us who have been involved from the beginning, it is hard to believe that it has been ten years since our founding. Time sure does go by fast. Our success, though, is due to the education and support of many, both within and outside our community. It is to these special friends that we say thanks.
>
> Tonight's theme, *Greek-American Entrepreneurs in the '90s*, honors the countless men and women who have in large or small degrees worked to achieve the American dream. It also characterizes the entrepreneurial spirit of those of us associated with GACS. We would like personally to congratulate and thank this year's honorees for living up to the GACS motto of 'Working to Preserve Our Heritage.'

"Greek American Organizations of the 90s" was the theme of the eighth annual dinner held on October 21, 1994, at the Ambassador West. The organizations honored were: The Greek Women's University Club, Hellenic Cultural Organization, Hellenic Link Midwest (formerly KRIKOS), and the Hellenic Professional Society of Illinois. Dr. Kioutas made the presentation of the *Efharisto* Award to Illinois Masonic Medical Center for their support of the ADC. Charles Mouratides introduced the honorees, and Sandy as Dinner Chairperson, and I presented the awards. Peter Maroutsos was the master of ceremonies. Very Rev. Nikitas Lulias, Chancellor of the Greek Orthodox Diocese of Chicago, offered the invocation and benediction. Music by the Linardakis Band. It was during this event that Jim Kozonis announced that GACS had closed on the building purchase that afternoon. Several donations and pledges were received from those in the audience in response to the building announcement.

A welcome letter that Evangeline and I wrote for the evening read in part:

> Tonight marks the beginning of our second decade of services to the community. We are especially grateful to all our supporters who have made this possible.
>
> We are honoring the very essence of our community – the volunteer organizations which have helped our *omogenia* to celebrate our rich cultural and ethnic heritage, preserve our language, and maintain our identity. We honor four organizations that exemplify and represent the most active in this genre.
>
> Tonight we are also extremely pleased to honor the Illinois Masonic Medical Center with our Third Annual *Efharisto* (Thank You) Award. An Efharisto is given to an organization or individual that through their support has had a lasting impact on GACS. With this criterion in mind, there is no one worthier of this award than Illinois Masonic. In 1990, when we had a dream of establishing an adult day care center but had scant resources to open our doors, the hospital stepped in and saved the day.
>
> Through their financial support, more than $25,000, and with their technical and professional services, single-handedly ensured that our center would succeed. Today, four years later, the center is a thriving and active hub of activities, care, and friendship among our 35 elderly participants and their families. To Illinois Masonic, we say thank you for recognizing and responding to our pleas for assistance. We treasure the partnership that has evolved between our two organizations.

Gerald Mungerson, president of Illinois Masonic Medical Center, displays the GACS *Efharisto* Award presented during the Heritage Awards dinner at the Ambassador West. Seated (L-R): Evangeline Mistaras, Gerald Mungerson, Dr. Theodosis Kioutas. Standing: John Rassogianis, Loukas Pergantas, John Psiharis, Nikki Pergantas, and unknown. October 21, 1994. John Psiharis collection.

Tonight's theme, 'Greek Organizations in the 90s' is meant to honor and recognize the countless men and women who have in large or small degrees given their time and resources to build numerous cultural organizations throughout our history. Large and small, these organizations have left a lasting legacy for us to cherish. It is to the generations that follow, who are charged with maintaining and expanding these efforts for us to appreciate.

Tonight's theme, 'Greek Organizations in the 90s' is meant to honor and recognize the countless men and women who have in large or small degrees given their time and resources to build numerous cultural organizations throughout our history. Large and small, these organizations have left a lasting legacy for us to cherish. It is to the generations that follow, who are charged with maintaining and expanding these efforts for us to appreciate.

We would like to personally congratulate the honorees for living up to the GACS motto of 'Working to Preserve our Heritage.'

Top: Hellenic Cultural Organization officers display their Heritage Award. Seated (L-R): Evangeline Mistaras, Dr. Eleni Katsarou, Dr. Theodosis Kioutas. Standing first row: Voula Katsaros, Jenny Gotsis, Toula Hlepas, Toni Panos. Back row: Peter Hlepas and John Rassogianis. October 21, 1994. **Bottom:** Greek Women's University Club officers display their Heritage Award presented during the October 21, 1994 Heritage Awards dinner at the Ambassador West. Seated (L-R): Presbytera Theano Rexinis, Barbara Javaras, Jean Leontios. Standing (L-R): Peter Maroutsos, Evangeline Mistaras, Kostas Zografopoulos, Anna Moreno, Sandy Petropoulos, unknown, Athanasia Papadopoulos, John Psiharis, Theodora Nicolandis, and Dr. Irene Panagiotou. Photos from the John Psiharis collection.

Top: Hellenic Professional Society of Illinois officers during the Heritage Awards Dinner. Seated (L-R): Sandy Petropoulos, Elaine Barkoulies Columbus, Frank Columbus. Standing: Peter Maroutsos, Kostas Zografopoulos, Tony Aslonides, John Psiharis, Christos Takoudis, Evangeline Mistaras, John Rassogianis, Dr. George Alexopoulos, Toni Panos, Alexander Rassogianis, and Athanasia Papadopoulos. Photos from the John Psiharis collection. **Bottom:** KRIKOS-Midwest officers during the October 21, 1994 Heritage Awards dinner at the Ambassador West. Seated (L-R): Kakia (Katerina) Xenos, Dr. George Alexopoulos and Christos Takoudis. Standing: Peter Maroutsos, Kostas Zografopoulos, Evangeline Mistaras, John Rassogianis, John Psiharis, and Athanasia Papadopoulos. John Psiharis collection.

(L-R): Helen Angelopoulos, *Greek Press* publisher; Sotiris Rekoumis, *Hellenic Life* publisher; Dimitris Pnevmatikatos, *Hellenic Community News* publisher, and Dr. Theodosis Kioutas. October 13, 1995. Photo by John Rassoganis. John Rassogianis collection.

The 1995 Heritage Awards dinner recognized the role and contributions of the print media to the vitality of the community. Themed "The Greek American Newspaper in the 90s," the event, held on October 13 at the Ambassador West Hotel, recognized the community's print publications: *Greek Press, Greek Star, Hellenic Community News,* and *Hellenic Life*. The *Efharisto* Award was presented to Chris Tomaras for his support of GACS in so many ways. Guests included: Nicholas Zafiropoulos, consul general of Greece, and Lolita Didrikson, Illinois state comptroller. Father George Massouras offered the invocation. The music was by the Linardakis Band. Kosta Zografopoulos was the master of ceremonies. Charles Mouratides introduced the honorees, and Sandy and I presented the awards.

An article that appeared in the October 9, 1995 edition of the *Greek Press* entitled "GACS Presents 'Efharisto' to Chris Tomaras," read in part:

> Mr. Tomaras, a shining light, and inspiration in our community has had a long and distinguished history on both the national and local levels of supporting activities designed to enhance our community. A member of the GACS Advisory Board, Tomaras is being recognized for his outstanding support of Greek-American Community Services over the last several years.
>
> Key among these was his raising of $17,000 at our 1993 Heritage Awards Dinner Dance, Also, in May 1994, he

generously underwrote the costs of an Advisory Board fundraiser at the Metropolitan Club in Sears Tower. The event, chaired by community leaders Loukas Pergantas and Eleni Bousis, raised $30,000.

'The generosity, leadership, and support of Mr. Tomaras, Mr. Pergantas, Mrs. Bousis, and the other members of our Advisory Board enabled GACS to achieve its dream of purchasing a permanent home for our vital services,' stated GACS Executive Director and Founder John Psiharis. 'This year's award is our way of saying *Efharisto* (Thank you) to a man whose actions speak louder than his words.'

Tomaras, founder and past chairman of Kronos-Central Products, Inc., launched a business that revolutionized food service in restaurants and brought gyros to the forefront of American culture. He is the founder and chairman of 'From Athens to Atlanta Committee,' a national organization dedicated to enhancing Greece's role in next year's Olympic games. He is involved in numerous civic and charitable organizations including the Neo Kyma Messinia, the Athenian-Piraeus Society, and the Illinois and U.S. Chambers of Commerce. He was also elected Supreme President of the Pan-Messinian Federation of the U.S. and Canada. Among the many honors he has received are the prestigious Ellis Island Award and a GACS Heritage Award.

A welcome letter from Sandy, as GACS president, and myself as executive director, was printed in the souvenir album and said in part:

> This evening we honor and recognize the remarkable and ongoing contributions of one of the foundations of our community – the Greek print media. We salute four publications that have withstood the challenges associated with publishing an ethnic newspaper and have served as vital links within our community.
>
> Tonight, we are also extremely pleased to honor Mr. Chris Tomaras with our Fourth Annual *Efharisto* (Thank You) Award. An Efharisto is given to an organization or individual that, through their support, has had a lasting impact on GACS. With this criterion in mind, there is no one worthier of this award than Chris Tomaras. Just two years ago, responding to our efforts to raise money to purchase our building, Mr. Tomaras used the occasion of his Heritage Awards acceptance speech to raise one thousand dollars a minute for seventeen minutes. The $17,000 he raised in one night set the momentum for a successful conclusion of our capital campaign. But he did not stop there, in May of 1994, he generously hosted a special

Advisory Board fundraising event at the Metropolitan Club. Under the chairmanship of Loukas Pergantas and Eleni Bousis, the event raised an additional $30,000. His leadership, vision, charisma, and support have inspired us all. Tonight we say thank you, Chris, for all you have done. We look forward to your continued friendship and support in the years to come.

Tonight's theme, the 'Greek-American Newspaper in the 90s', is meant to honor the personal sacrifices and dedication of the men and women who have worked to keep our community informed. The Greek print media has served as the focal point of our *omogenia's* activities and people. By bringing news of the motherland and from throughout the country, they have informed and educated generations of readers.

In 1996, for the tenth Heritage Awards dinner, we chose to honor several of our key supporters with the theme "Greek-American Benefactors." The event was held on November 1st at the Knickerbocker Hotel. In place of Heritage Awards, GACS presented four *Efharisto* Awards. The honorees were Irene Antoniou, chair of the GACS Advisory Board, member of the Illinois Arts Council, and president of the Women's Board for the Lyric Opera of Chicago; Eleni Bousis, a member of the GACS Advisory Board, board member of the GANHC, and co-chair of several of our fundraisers; Dr. Theodosis Kioutas, a founding member of GACS and president of the Greek-American Nursing Home Committee and Loukas Pergantas, owner of Four Star Auto Body Shop, member of the GACS Advisory Board and co-chair of several of our fundraising events. Given the theme, it was not a Heritage Awards dinner; the souvenir album was printed in green ink, rather than the traditional blue. Peter Maroutsos was the master of ceremonies, and the *Efharisto* Awards were introduced by Mike Bakalis and presented by Sandy, and me. The invocation was given by Very Rev. Demetrios Katsavelos, and music was provided by the Linardakis Band.

In the welcome letter to dinner guests printed in the souvenir album, Sandy and I wrote:

> Each year, as you may know, GACS honors outstanding individuals who have worked to preserve or promote the betterment of our community as a whole. To date, we have never strayed from that path. We honored individuals and groups who have helped to make our *omogenia* a better place, regardless of their support of GACS, as a matter of fact, an unwritten rule evolved that we would not honor our own – but reach out to the greater community.
>
> Tonight, however, this being our tenth annual dinner, we are breaking our unwritten rule by recognizing four outstanding and vital benefactors of Greek-American Community Services.

Tenth Annual Heritage Awards Gala

The Greek-American Community Services celebrated its Tenth Annual Heritage Award banquet on November 1 at the Knickerbocker Hotel in Chicago by presenting awards to four outstanding members of the community.

Recipients of the Efharisto Awards were Theodosis Kioutas, M.D., Irene Antoniou, Eleni Bousis and Loukas Pergantas. They were honored for their dedicated service and support of the Greek-American Community Services which is responsible for the Northwest Chicago adult day center.

Pictured from the left: John N. Varones, Executive Director of the Illinois Housing Development Authority; John Psiharis, Executive Director of the Greek American Community Services; Honorees Dr. Theodosis E. Kioutas, Irene Antoniou, Eleni Bousis and Loukas Pergantas, Athanasia Papadopoulos, President of the Greek American Community Services, and Alexander Vroustouris, Inspector General, City of Chicago.

Pictured left to right: Dr. Jaime Escobar, Honorary Consul of Bolivia; Mrs. Anna P. Kioutas, Mrs. J. Escobar, Athanasia Papadopoulos, President of the Greek American Community Services; Mark V. Tiniakos of The Greek Press and Dr. Irene Panayotou.

The *Greek Press*, December 8, 1996. Elaine Thomopoulos collection.

Each of these individuals has worked tirelessly to support the purposes and growth of our organization over the last ten years. We are breaking another tradition today by bestowing not one but four *Efharisto* Awards.

Tonight we recognize Irene Antoniou, Eleni Bousis, Dr. Theodosis Kioutas, and Loukas Pergantas. Under Mrs. Antoniou's leadership, GACS created its Advisory Board, which she chairs. The Board consists of nine of our community's best leaders in the business and professional arenas. It served as a springboard for such major actions as the launching of our fundraising campaign to purchase the building we now own. She is highly regarded in many circles and was just this month appointed by Governor Edgar to the most distinguished position of Chairman of the Illinois Arts Council.

Little new can be said about Dr. Kioutas, he is well-known throughout the nation for his many philanthropic efforts. He was a founding member of GACS and was instrumental in the formative stages of our adult day care center. When seed money to start the center was urgently needed, he rose to the occasion by asking the Illinois Masonic Medical Center for help. The result was over $30,000 in financial support and much more in technical assistance and moral support. Tonight, we recognize him for his years of leadership, support, vision, and wisdom.

Eleni Bousis and Loukas Pergantas often work as a team in their desire to serve our community. Tonight we salute them for their ongoing efforts and support for GACS. This formidable team was instrumental in the success of our efforts to purchase our building. They co-chaired a fundraising banquet which in just one evening raised $30,000 for this effort. Likewise, they have always been there for GACS – helping to bring good cheer to our clients and moral support to the staff and board throughout the year.

As no words can adequately convey the impact these four individuals had on the success of GACS, we extend only one – a deeply heartfelt *Efharisto.*

An article that appeared in the October 27, 1996 edition of the *Greek Press* read in part:

> This year, four *Efharisto* Awards will be given to the following dedicated benefactors whose outstanding service and support of GACS have helped provide agency service to the entire community.
>
> Theodosis Kioutas, M.D., the able and highly respected leader of the Greek-American Nursing Home movement, will be

honored for his innumerable contributions to Greek-American Community Services throughout the years as a participating board member. Always a supporter of GACS who helped define the identity of the organization, the indefatigable Dr. Kioutas was the key figure that sought and obtained generous adult day care start-up support from the Illinois Masonic Medical Center.

Irene Antoniou, the founding chairperson of the GACS Advisory Board, has a statewide and national reputation as a successful arts advocate. Her gracious pivotal position on the Advisory Board formed three years ago, enhanced the vitality of the scope of its activities which also led to the purchase of the premises that house the GACS executive and cultural arts offices and Northwest Chicago Senior Care, its adult day care center. She is a recipient of the 1996 Sidney R. Yates Advocacy Award and a vital contributor to the cultural life of the Chicago metropolitan area, especially in her association with the Lyric Opera of Chicago, the Illinois Arts Council, and the National Endowment for the Arts.

Eleni Bousis, another outstanding member of our community, is deeply and intimately involved in a plethora of philanthropic activities which she has assumed with dignity and grace in the general and Hellenic communities. A shortlist of her involvements does not do justice to the scope of her commitments, some of which include serving on the diocesan and Philoptochos boards, Disabled American Veterans, Mayo Brothers Clinic Fight Against Alzheimer's, and Bread and Water for African Relief. She plays a major role in the support of GACS through her membership on the Greek-American Community Services Advisory Board.

Loukas Pergantas, a successful businessman of our *omogenia*, fits in the mold of the original *protoporoi* who entered this country during earlier generations, whose word was their bond, building *periousies,* churches, homes, and schools with very little except firm goals to honestly achieve their dreams through hard work and sacrifice. Coming from a family that has made its mark in the new as well as old worlds and is committed to service, he is another individual who has played a pivotal role by joining with, among others, Chris Tomaras, Irene Antoniou, and Eleni Bousis to form the GACS Advisory Board.

For the following year, GACS tried something different. Some had complained about the costs and effort needed to go to a downtown event on a Friday evening including driving through rush hour traffic and paying a significant price for parking. The Greek community was spread out throughout the metropolitan area, and we tried to accommodate those who

> **GREEK-AMERICAN COMMUNITY SERVICES**
> **HERITAGE AWARDS RECIPIENTS**
>
> **1987**
> Alexander Karanikas
> Andrew Kopan
> Yorgos Koarvetaris
> Charles Moskos
> Theano Papazoglou-Margaris*
> Harry Mark Petrakis
>
> **1988**
> Adeline Geo-Karis
> Yiannis Lambros*
> Antigone Lambros
> Fotios Litsas
> Leon Marinakos
> John Nicholson*
> Sam Stavrakas
>
> **1989**
> John Geocaris*
> James Mezilson
> Georgia Mitchell
>
> * Deceased
>
> **1990**
> James Kirie
> Frank Kuchuris
> Very Reverend Nikitas Lulias
> Kay Valone
>
> **1991**
> Kathryn Adinamis
> Charles Mouratides
> Evangeline Gouletas
> Mike Tsolinas
>
> **1992**
> Roula Alakiotou
> Soula Koutsopanagos
> Helen Theodosakis
> Athena Touloumis*
>
> **1993**
> George Stephanopoulos
> Ted Spyropoulos
> Chris Tomaras
>
> **1994**
> Greek Women's University Club
> Hellenic Cultural Organization
> Hellenic Professional Society of Illinois
> Krikos
>
> **1995**
> Greek Press
> Hellenic Community News
> (Παροικιακός Λόγος)
> Greek Star
> Hellenic Life (Ομογένεια)
>
> **1996**
> Irene Antoniou
> Eleni Bousis
> Dr. Theodosis Kioutas
> Loukas Pergantas
>
> **1997**
> Greek-American Nursing Home Committee
> Hellenic Foundation
> International Orthodox Christian Charities
> Chicago Diocese Philoptochos Society
>
> ---
>
> **GREEK-AMERICAN COMMUNITY SERVICES**
> *CELEBRATING 14 YEARS OF SERVICE TO OUR COMMUNITY*
> *requests the pleasure of your company at the*
>
> **Eleventh Annual Awards Dinner Banquet**
> *Honoring*
> **Greek-American Nursing Home Committee**
> **Hellenic Foundation**
> **International Orthodox Christian Charities**
> **Chicago Diocese Philoptochos Society**
>
> *Sunday, November 16, 1997*
>
> **BRISTOL COURT**
> 828 E. Rand Road, Mount Prospect, Illinois
>
> Cocktails 5:00 p.m. - Open Bar
> Dinner 6:00 p.m.
>
> Donation
> $50.00 per person
> $35.00 Children under 12 yrs

Invitation to the Eleventh Annual Heritage Awards Dinner Banquet. November 16, 1997. Elaine Thomopoulos collection.

preferred not to go into the city. We also held the dinner on a Sunday evening.

The eleventh annual dinner was held on November 16, 1997, at Bristol Court Banquets in Mount Prospect. It was held in November because for whatever reason we got a late start. Unfortunately, an early snowstorm made the commute difficult for many, especially those coming from the

Top: Dr. Theodosis Kioutas accepts the GACS Heritage Award on behalf of the Greek-American Nursing Home Committee, November 16, 1997. Pictured (L-R): Peter Maroutsos, John Rassogianis, John Psiharis, Athanasia Papadopoulos, and Dr. Theodosis Kioutas. John Psiharis collection. **Bottom:** Dr. George Dalianis, chairman of the International Orthodox Christian Charities-Midwest Region, accepts the GACS Heritage Award on behalf of the organization. Pictured (L-R): Peter Maroutsos, Athanasia Papadopoulos, John Psiharis, and Dr. George Dalianis. John Rassogianis (right) is in the background. John Psiharis collection.

Michael Chioros, president of the Hellenic Foundation, accepts the GACS Heritage Award on behalf of the organization. November 16, 1997. Pictured (L-R): Peter Maroutsos, Athanasia Papadopoulos, John Psiharis, and Michael Chioros. John Psiharis collection.

city and attendance was below what had been expected. With the theme of "Greek American Social Services in the 90s," we honored the Greek-American Nursing Home Committee, the Hellenic Foundation, International Orthodox Christian Charities, and the Chicago Diocese Philoptochos Society. A raffle drawing was held that evening with a grand prize of $500 and the first prize of a weekend for two at the Abbey on Lake Geneva. Other prizes included $100 cash and two dinners for two at the Little Bucharest Restaurant.

An article about the dinner written by John Rassogianis appeared on the front page of the December 4, 1997 issue of the *Greek Star* and in the December 21, 1997 edition of the *Greek Press* reported:

> A confluence of such factors as the opportunity to honor the primary service organizations of the Greek-American community, as well as their gracious response in accepting the heritage awards extended to them, produced an inspiring evening of recognition and remembrance during the recent Greek-American Community Services (GACS) 11th Annual Awards Dinner held on Nov. 16 at the Bristol Court Banquet Hall in Mt. Prospect.
>
> Award recipients welcomed by the Greek-American Community Services president, Costas Zografopoulos were: The Greek-American Nursing Home Committee (GANHC), the Hellenic Foundation, International Orthodox Christian

Charities (IOCC), and the Greek Orthodox Ladies Philoptochos Society.

Representing the GANHC, Dr. Theodosis Kioutas brought holiday tidings to the guests by assuring them of the imminent acceptance of the certificate of need, submitted by the GANHC on its first attempt to the state of Illinois for the establishment of a nursing home in Wheeling, Illinois.

The Hellenic Foundation president, Michael Chioros, accepted the second award acknowledging the foundation's nearly 45 years of service and its continuing impact on the lives of the community under the current director, Lea Ames.

With the recent patriarchal visit and season of heightened awareness of the practical humanitarian work done by the Greek Orthodox church, the heritage awards also brought a timely accent to the work of the IOCC and the Greek Orthodox Ladies Philoptochos Society.

Dr. George Dalianis, chairman of the Midwest Committee of the International Orthodox Christian Charities, accepted the award for IOCC, and Susan Regos, president of the Diocese Philoptochos Society, accepted the award on behalf of the society.

Athanasia Vaselopoulos served as dinner chairman with Ethel Kotsovos as reservations chairman. Master of Ceremonies was Peter Maroutsos with John Rassogianis. Special recognition was extended to GACS founders John Psiharis and Elaine Thomopoulos, Ph.D. Rev. George Massouras of the Assumption Church of Chicago said the invocation.

On October 9, 1998, GACS returned downtown for the Twelfth Annual Heritage Awards Cocktail Buffet, this time to the new Embassy Suites Hotel at 600 N. State Street. The hotel was home to Papa Gus, a newly opened Greek-branded restaurant operated within the Lettuce Entertain You Enterprises portfolio of restaurants. The event was held in the hotel's grand ballroom and included Greek delicacies. John Apostolou, owner of Giordano's Pizza, Dr. Dennis Caralis, cardiologist, and Maria Pappas, Cook County Commissioner were honored. The *Efharisto Award* was presented to Michael Reese Health Trust. The Trust was recognized for a $50,000 grant they provided in support of the adult day care center.

Top: Irene Antoniou presents the GACS Heritage Award to Cook County Commissioner Maria Pappas at the 12th Annual Heritage Awards. October 9, 1998.
Bottom: (L-R): John Psiharis, Nicole Tsongas, and Dr. Michael Bakalis during the presentation of the first GACS National Heritage Award. October 30, 1991. John Psiharis collection.

The Advisory Board took on the task of organizing the 1998 dinner. Chris Tomaras chaired the event, and Irene Antoniou and Loukas Pergantas served as co-chairs. Eleni Sotos, Chris Tomaras' assistant, served as a co-chair and handled the event logistics. Rather than the usual sit-down meal, this time, a buffet was planned. A few weeks before the event, a number of us, including the co-chairs, were invited to a private tasting shortly after Papa Gus opened. Held in the private dining room, a number of the restaurant's featured dishes and wines were showcased. The General Manager took us on a tour of the restaurant, kitchen, and banquet facilities, all within the hotel. I recall Chris Tomaras, Eleni Bousis, Loukas Pergantas, Charles Mouratides, John Rassogianis, Eleni Sotos, and I attended, but there may have been others. We were the first Greek organization to host a dinner there, so they had a keen interest in our event. Chris Tomaras generously underwrote the event, so GACS received the full proceeds. A raffle drawing was held at the end of the event. The grand prize was a round-trip ticket to Greece, courtesy of Olympic Airways, $500 in cash, donated by Evangeline Mistaras, and a weekend for two at the Abbey on Lake Geneva, donated by Irene.

In 1992, GACS initiated an award to recognize major benefactors of GACS, the *Efharisto* Award. Efharisto means thank you in Greek so the award was meant to show our gratitude and appreciation to the recipient. Those honored with the *Efharisto* award were: Chicago Community Trust (1992), Retirement Research Foundation (1993), Illinois Masonic Medical Center (1994), Chris Tomaras (1995), Irene Antoniou (1996), Eleni Bousis (1996), Dr. Kioutas (1996), Loukas Pergantas (1996), and the Michael Reese Health Trust (1998). Aphrodite Demeur declined several nominations to receive the award.

The GACS National Heritage Award was created to honor and recognize successful Greek Americans on a national level and the first honoree was Senator Paul Tsongas in 1991. Paul wasn't able to attend due to a schedule conflict and Nicole "Nikki" Tsongas attended the event to accept the award on behalf of her husband. Mike Bakalis and I presented the award to Nikki. Connie Gountanis Rigas and I drove Nikki to and from the event and to other events on her calendar. In addition to everything else, Connie and I both needed to deal with the urgent need of finding a car wash!

The second GACS National Heritage Award was awarded to George Stephanopoulos who was a key player in the election of President Bill Clinton and served at that time as his communications director. I met George during the Michael Dukakis for President Campaign. He had accepted the honor and planned to attend with his father and uncle. At the last minute, he notified us that he could not be there due to unexpected developments in Washington. Instead, his uncle accepted the award on his behalf and George recorded a video message at the White House that was hastily delivered to GACS hours before the event started and was shown that evening. I remember hearing from office staff about their surprise when a courier came to GACS with "a special delivery from the White House!"

Three other National Heritage Award recipients were in the works but didn't materialize due to schedule conflicts. Unfortunately, when dealing with people of this stature, these things happen. Through John's efforts, world champion tennis player Pete Sampras agreed to accept the National Heritage Award. He ended up going to Australia for a tournament. Another time it was Billy Zane, an actor who had appeared in several movies including *Phantom* and *Titanic*. Due to some reshooting that needed to occur for his film, Billy had to fly to Los Angeles and thus could not attend. Chris Chelios, a star player for the Chicago Black Hawks was another prospect for the award, however, his training schedule changed and did not allow him to attend.

The 1998 event was the last Heritage Awards Dinner to be held. After 12 years, we decided to try something different. We were tired of the grind of producing these events year after year. Although successful, they never reached the levels that would compel us to continue them. Had we selected honorees for the 1999 Heritage Awards, two themes considered were: "Greek-American Education in the 90s," honoring Greek American schools including Socrates, Plato Academy, Koraes, and other Chicago area schools; or "Greek-American Educators in the 90s," honoring outstanding teachers. Either way, a red apple was envisioned as part of the centerpiece decorations.

Many events were going on within the community to benefit the nursing home, and it was difficult to compete against the momentum the GANHC worked so hard to create. There was also a lot of fundraising for the Hellenic Museum and Cultural Center. Since these were two mega projects that collectively required several million dollars to accomplish and were long-held community goals that kindled a sense of enthusiasm and ethnic pride, it became more difficult to compete for dollars and attendees.

In all, an impressive array of outstanding Greek Americans who played key roles in the evolution of the *omogenia* were recognized for their contributions to the community. They were leaders who were distinguished in their respective fields and through their vision, time, talents, and treasure, helped to make our community a better place. It was inspiring to us that the award attained a level of prestige and respect within the Greek community.

Greetings & Salutations

Greetings from Chicago Mayor Harold Washington. May 1, 1987. John Psiharis collection.

Over the years, GACS had received greetings and salutations from prominent leaders related to our Heritage Awards Dinners. Those that were received in time were reprinted in the dinner souvenir albums. If not, they were read by the master of ceremonies during the event. In our albums, the messages began with national figures and worked down from there. Select excerpts are included below. They are included here by year and in the same order:

THE WHITE HOUSE
WASHINGTON

April 1, 1988

I am pleased to send warm greetings to everyone attending the annual Greek-American Community Services Heritage Awards Dinner, and congratulations to your honorees.

Americans are a unique people, a colorful tapestry of traditions and cultures woven into one society. The motto graven on our coins -- E Pluribus Unum -- reflects the rich diversity from which America draws her strength and vitality. Greek-Americans are a valued part of that diversity. Your organization's activities reflect the noble traditions of your ancestral homeland and at the same time foster an appreciation of the ideals for which our nation stands. Your dedication to the values of faith, family, work, and country strengthen and enrich American life.

Nancy joins me in sending best wishes and prayers for every future success. God bless you.

Ronald Reagan

> Greetings from President Ronald Reagan. April 1, 1988. John Psiharis collection.

April 16, 1987. Thank you for inviting me to the First Annual Heritage Awards dinner. I regret that a previous commitment on the evening of May 1st prevents me from joining you for what promises to be a memorable event.

Although I cannot be with you, let me take this opportunity to express my congratulations to these outstanding writers who enrich the Greek-American experience. As the son of Greek immigrants, I am constantly inspired by my ethnic heritage and I am grateful to those who work so hard to keep our culture alive.

Michael S. Dukakis

EMBASSY OF GREECE
WASHINGTON, D.C.

April 1, 1988

Mr. John Psiharis
Executive Director
Greek-American Community Service
4817 W. Montrose Avenue
Chicago, Illinois 60641

Dear Mr. Psiharis,

Thank you very much for your letter of March 24, 1988 and for your cordial invitation extended to me to attend the Annual Greek-American Community Services Heritage Awards Dinner to be held on Friday, April 22nd, 1988 in Des Plains, Illinois.

I would have considered it a great privilege to participate in the Awards Dinner, but a previous commitment on April 22nd in Washington deprives me of the pleasure of doing so.

Nonetheless, I wish to express my wholehearted congratulations to you personally as well as to the Officers and members of the Greek-American Community Services for honoring such a distinguished group of Greek-Americans, who truly represent Excellence in various sectors of achievement. May I join you, too, in recognizing the great contributions of the honorees in upholding the name of Hellenism in the important State of Illinois and throughout the United States.

I would be grateful if you could communicate this message to the honorees and participants at your Dinner on April 22nd.

With kindest personal regards, I remain,

Yours sincerely,

George Papoulias
Ambassador

Greetings from Greek Ambassador George Papoulias. April 1, 1988. John Psiharis collection.

April 1988. Each of these outstanding individuals has excelled in a particular field of activity, but all of them are to be admired for their great qualities of heart and mind, their unflinching dedication to high ideals, and their selfless and effective service to the causes of Hellenism in America and in particular to the promotion of the image of Greek Heritage in this great land of freedom and democracy.

        A.J. Jacovides, Ambassador, Embassy of Cyprus

August 30, 1989. As Governor of the State of Illinois, I am pleased to send this note of congratulations to all the members of Greek-American Community Services who have helped preserve the Greek-American experience.

        James R. Thompson, Governor, State of Illinois

August 21, 1989. The Greek-American Community Services organization has made a great contribution to our community and on behalf of the citizens of Cook County, I extend to you my deep appreciation for your dedication and service not only to our Greek community but to all people.

George Dunne, President, Board of Commissioners of Cook County, Illinois

August 23, 1990. Thank you for inviting Kitty and me to attend the Fourth Annual Greek-American Community Services Heritage Awards Dinner and Dance at the Thirteen Colonies in River Grove, Illinois. I really wish that I could be there; unfortunately, because of scheduling conflicts, it will not be possible to join you.

Kitty joins me in extending our warmest best wishes for a most enjoyable evening, and congratulations to the honorees.

I thank you for your tremendous effort and commend Greek-American Community Services for its dedication and strong commitment to the preservation of our Greek-American heritage.

Michael S. Dukakis, Governor, Commonwealth of Massachusetts

Sept 7, 1990. These outstanding citizens of our community are truly deserving of the recognition bestowed upon them for each, in his or her own chosen field of endeavor, has made outstanding contributions towards preserving and enhancing the Greek heritage in America. They have my best wishes for good health and continuing success in the years ahead.

Frank Annunzio, Member of Congress

September 28, 1990. It is most appropriate that Greek-American Community Services, an outstanding organization dedicated to preserving its heritage while enhancing Greek American community involvement, should honor James Kirie, Frank Kuchuris, Nikitas Lulias, and Kay Valone, all persons whose commercial success, philanthropy, and humanitarian efforts reflect the finest ideals of our Greek heritage. I am well aware of the significant contributions of these outstanding citizens in preserving the Greek-American experience. Their energy and compassion have brought great strengths to the many causes we all care about and support and we are greatly indebted to each honoree.

Paul S. Sarbanes, United States Senator

GREEK ORTHODOX ARCHDIOCESE OF NORTH AND SOUTH AMERICA
ΕΛΛΗΝΙΚΗ ΟΡΘΟΔΟΞΟΣ ΑΡΧΙΕΠΙΣΚΟΠΗ ΒΟΡΕΙΟΥ & ΝΟΤΙΟΥ ΑΜΕΡΙΚΗΣ

10 EAST 79th STREET, NEW YORK, N.Y. 10021 • TEL. (212) 570-3500 • CABLE: ARCHGREEK, NEW YORK

October 16, 1992

The Greek-American Community Services
3940 N. Pulaski Road
Chicago, IL 60641

Dear Friends and Members of the
Greek-American Community Services,

It is a joy to greet you as you again gather to celebrate the Greek-American Community Services Heritage Awards Dinner.

Your organization, and others like it, which are found in all corners of this great Nation, provide the firm foundation upon which programs for the good of society are founded.

It is through efforts such as yours that people are helped, education is supported and charities are provided with extra help to better do their work. The United States is made proud and strong by the contributions of volunteer organizations, and individuals who offer their best for the good progress of all.

I join you in honoring four women of outstanding character and talent which have offered so much of themselves in order to make the local community a better place to live for all.

May the Lord bless Roula Alakioutou, Helen Theodosakis, Soula Koutsopanagos and Athena Toulomis with many years of health and continued service to the community.

Invoking the blessings of the Lord on the contiued good work of your organization, I remain,

With paternal blessings,

I A K O V O S
Archbishop of the Greek Orthodox
Church of North and South America

AI:dj

> Greetings from Archbishop Iakovos. October 16, 1992. John Psiharis collection.

October 30, 1992. The Greek community is a vital and important one to the State of Illinois. I admire and appreciate the contributions of your group, both civic and otherwise. Your unity and organization are an inspiration to all Illinoisans.

Jim Edgar, Governor, State of Illinois

October 22, 1993. Thank you for your gracious invitation to attend the Seventh Annual Greek-American Community Services Heritage Awards Dinner. This weekend marks the Feast Day of my Patron Saint, St. Iakovos, and I am unable to join you since my annual Name Day Banquet to benefit our Theological School will be held in New York. For this reason, I would like to take this opportunity to convey my heartfelt

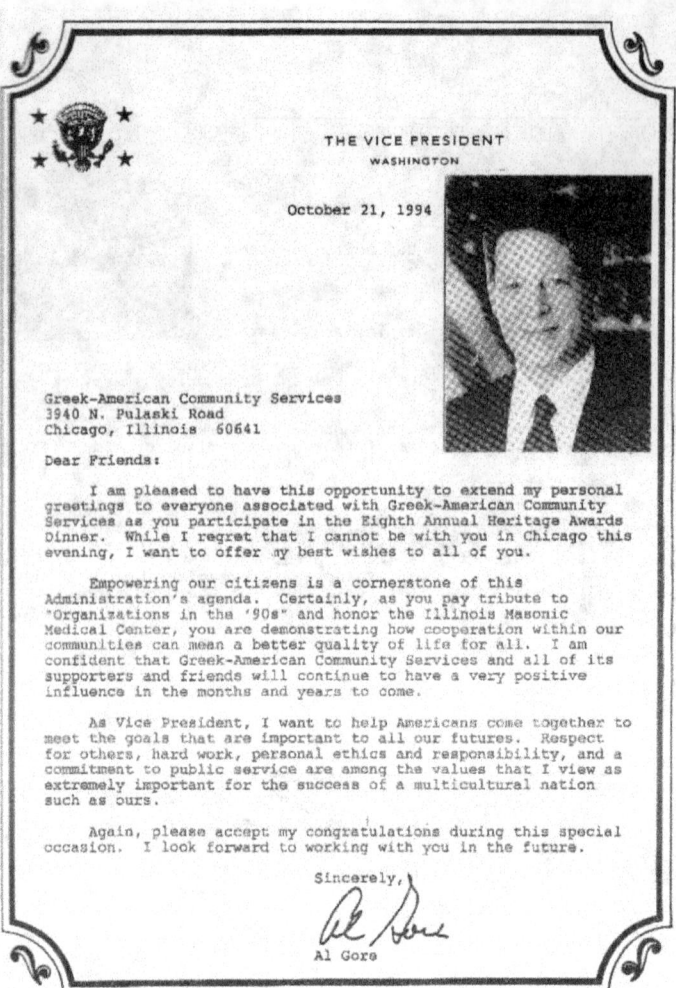

Greetings from Vice President Al Gore. October 21, 1994. John Psiharis collection.

greetings to all those who have gathered for this evening's gala event and to congratulate the honorees, Mr. George Stephanopoulos, Mr. Ted Spyropoulos, Mr. Chris Tomaras, and the Retirement Research Foundation.

Truly, our community has come of age in our new homeland and we have earned for ourselves the respect and admiration of our fellow Americans because of our dedication to hard work and our adherence to the teachings and traditions of our Greek Orthodox Faith and Hellenic Heritage. Your honorees exemplify these qualities and have each made a notable impact in their respective careers. They bring honor to all Greek Americans and are certainly most deserving of this tribute.

Iakovos

Archbishop of the Greek Orthodox Church of North and South America

October 19, 1993. I'm sorry I can't join you on Friday evening for the Heritage Awards dinner. You are honoring some great people who have done our community proud.

Please give my best to them and to all the people who will be present at the dinner. I will never forget the enthusiasm and energy of the Greek community of Chicago in 1988. You were all great to me and Kitty, and we'll never forget it.

Michael S. Dukakis

October 19, 1993. We are most pleased that you have continued the tradition of honoring outstanding members of our Greek-America community. Certainly, they are deserving of the recognition you have chosen to give them for their efforts and labor. Although we would love to share in the evening's gathering, we will not be in the Diocese, as we will attend services and meetings at our holy Archdiocese. Please be kind enough to share our words of congratulations and best wishes with the recipients and those who will attend the dinner.

We hope our Lord and God will bless your efforts so that the older members of our community will continue to benefit from your services. We also pray that St. Iakovos, whose vespers we will celebrate that evening, may intercede for the salvation of us all.

Iakovos, Bishop, Greek Orthodox Diocese of Chicago

October 14, 1993. Please accept my congratulations on your agency's tenth anniversary of providing service to the community. Also, on behalf of the Illinois Department on Aging, I would like to extend congratulations to these individuals being honored for their outstanding contributions towards preserving the Greek-American experience.

Maralee I. Lindley, Director, Illinois Department on Aging

October 14, 1993. Congratulations on 10 years of outstanding service to residents of Chicago's Greek-American community, especially senior citizens. Your organization has helped to make our city a better place for older adults and their families.

Senior citizens are a vital part of the framework that keeps our city strong. As service providers, we must continue to build

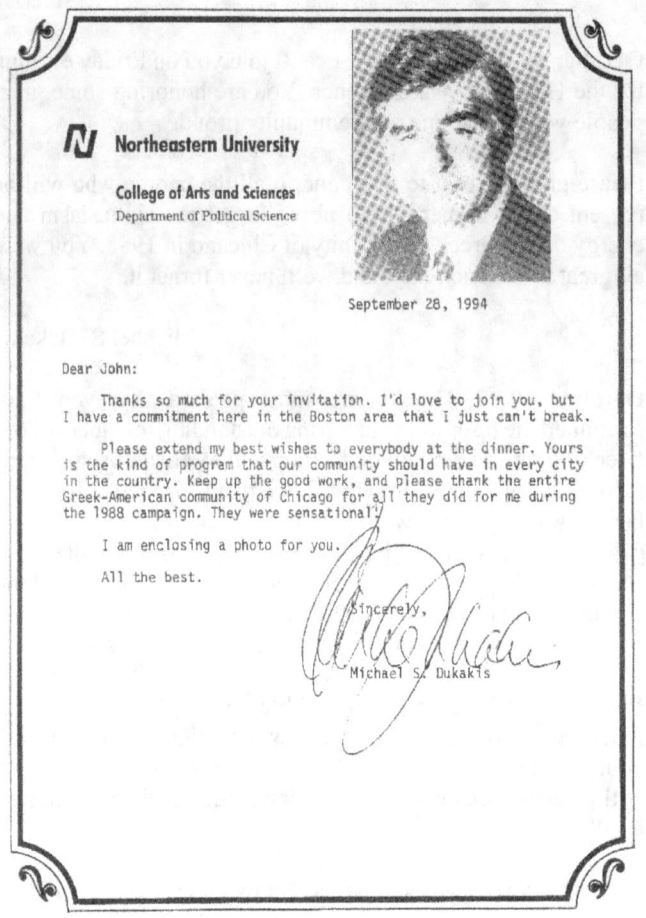

Greetings from Governor Michael Dukakis, September 28, 1994. John Psiharis collection.

partnerships that will help us expand service options for seniors. In doing so, we can guarantee that older residents will receive quality services and programs that will keep them independent and healthy.

Thank you for your support of the Chicago Department on Aging's Benefit Eligibility Checklist program (BEC). We encourage all seniors to receive this free, confidential service to help them identify the services and benefits they are entitled to.

Donald R. Smith, Commissioner, Chicago Department on Aging

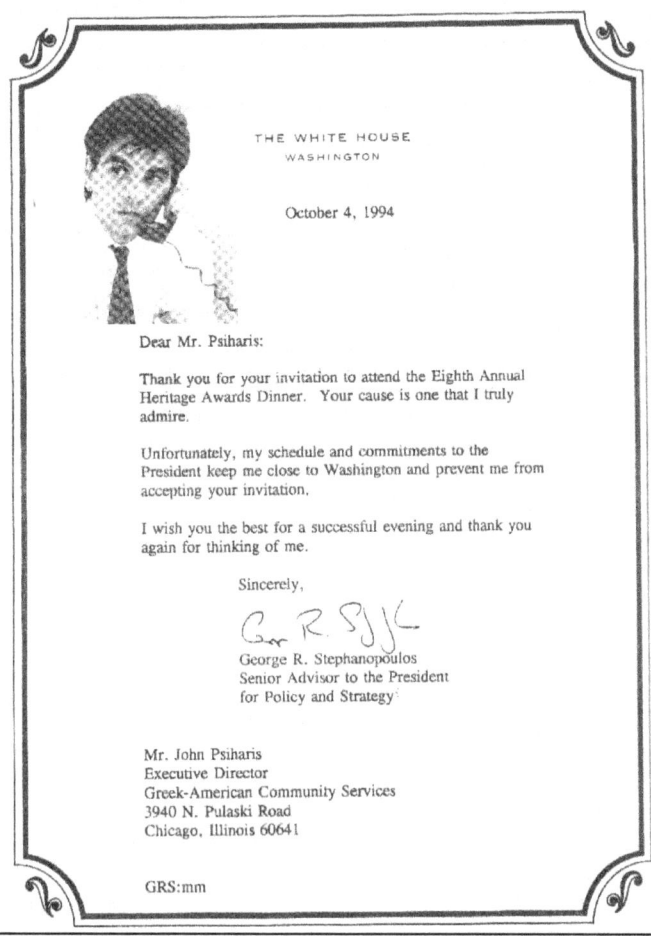

Greetings from George Stephanopoulos. September 22, 1995. John Psiharis collection.

October 4, 1994. Thank you for your invitation to attend the Eighth Annual Heritage Awards Dinner. Your cause is one that I truly admire.

Unfortunately, my schedule and commitments to the President keep me close to Washington and prevent me from accepting your invitation.

I wish you the best for a successful evening and thank you again for thinking of me.

> George R. Stephanopoulos, Senior Advisor to the President for Policy and Strategy

October 4, 1994. On the occasion of the 11th Anniversary of the Greek-American Community Services, I would like to extend to you my warmest congratulations on the high-standard contribution to the care of the Greek-American Community in Chicago over the period of your existence.

It is essential that an organization, such as yours, is given all the financial and moral support required so that it continues to provide all the assistance to the needy in our community.

>John-Alexis Zepos, Consul General, Consulate General of Greece

October 21, 1994. Your organization can be rightly proud of its distinguished record of eleven years of service to the Greek-American Community, fulfilling a much-needed function in support of worthy and noble causes. It is characteristic of the multifaceted and rich contribution that Greek Americans have offered and continue to offer to the cultural, social, economic, political, and spiritual life of this country; a contribution that has earned the admiration and respect of all their fellow Americans.

This year's list of honorees represents an excellent selection of Greek American organizations, all of which have distinguished themselves with their significant contributions and service to the Greek American Community and more broadly.

I warmly congratulate all of the honorees – the Greek Women's University Club, the Hellenic Professional Society of Illinois, the Hellenic Cultural Organization, and KRIKOS – for their well-deserved award and wish them continued success for the good of all. I also commend the organizers for both their choice of honorees and for dedicating this year's event to 'Organizations in the 90s,' a highly appropriate theme indeed.

I would like to congratulate the Illinois Masonic Medical Center, recipient of the 'Efharisto Award,' for its support of the Northwest Chicago Senior Care Center, which provides adult day care for needy seniors and their families.

I would finally observe that the Hellenes of the diaspora, particularly here in the United States, have not only achieved great success in their adopted land but are also a major voice in the national struggles of Hellenism all over the world, working actively to promote these noble causes.

We, in Cyprus, particularly appreciated and are truly grateful for your wholehearted and continuing support for our struggle to regain freedom and restore justice for Cyprus, by ending its twenty-year-long tragedy of division and foreign occupation.

>Andreas J. Jacovides, Ambassador of Cyprus to the United States

October 21, 1994. The Eighth Annual Heritage Awards Dinner acknowledges eleven years of progress at Greek-American Community Services. GACS provides various services to more than 5,000 people in the community each year.

I applaud the hard work and dedication of all those who contribute to the success of Greek-American Community Services. Your support is appreciated by those you serve.

> Jim Edgar, Governor, State of Illinois

September 30, 1994. Greek-American Community Services has made great progress over the past eleven years and represents a growing and influential voice in the Greek/American community.

I want to take this opportunity to congratulate this year's honorees. The work done by each of these organizations has a positive impact that is felt beyond the boundaries of your 'neighborhoods.' The excellent example set by Illinois Masonic Medical Center is being recognized tonight by your Efharisto Award. Please add my congratulations to all the others they have received tonight.

> Dawn Clark Netsch, Dawn Clark Netsch for Governor

October 21, 1994. Tonight's Dinner celebrates eleven years of service to the Greek-American community. By your efforts, you have aided both the young and the elderly. You have helped expand cultural and ethnic awareness. By working to create a strong and caring community, you have helped build a stronger Chicago.

> Richard M. Daley, Mayor, City of Chicago

October 13, 1995. It is with much paternal joy that I greet you this evening as you gather to celebrate twelve years of progress at your Ninth Annual Heritage Awards Dinner.

This group, formed to serve the needs of our Greek American Community, has since its conception helped many needy citizens, whether through the '*Ya'Sou*' vans, the Cultural and Arts Programs, or the Community Aging Network. I thank you for all you have done and continue to do to help those less fortunate than yourselves.

Iakovos, Archbishop, Greek Orthodox Church of North and South America

> PAUL S. SARBANES
> MARYLAND
>
> **United States Senate**
> WASHINGTON, DC 20510-2002
>
> 320 HART SENATE OFFICE BUILDING
> WASHINGTON, DC 20510
>
> October 13, 1995
>
> John Psiharis
> Executive Director
> Greek-American Community Services
> 3940 N. Pulaski Road
> Chicago, Illinois 60641-2930
>
> Dear Friends:
>
> I am most pleased to extend my warmest greetings to those gathered tonight to celebrate the twelfth anniversary of Greek-American Community Services at this the Ninth Annual Heritage Awards Dinner.
>
> Tonight's theme, The Greek-American Newspaper of the 90's, honors the longstanding tradition of service that tonight's honorees The Greek Press, Greek Star, Hellenic Community News and Hellenic Life (Omogenia) have all demonstrated throughout their history. These publications have made significant contributions to the preservation and enhancement of our historic culture. They have provided a valuable forum for the exchange of information within the Greek-American community and also a key source of news on issues of importance such as the brutal invasion and occupation of Cyprus, and religious freedom for the Ecumenical Patriarchate.
>
> I would also like to recognize Mr. Chris Tomaras who is the recipient of the fourth annual Efharisto Award. Mr. Tomaras, in his role as the President of the Pan-Messianian Federation, has provided outstanding leadership and selfless dedication over the years. This award is indeed a tribute to his dedication and commitment to the Greek-American community.
>
> Greek-American Community Services has served the greater Chicago community with distinction and great effectiveness since its founding. The benevolent services that you provide are most important and we are most grateful for your devoted efforts. The staff and volunteers of Greek American Community Service carries on the historic Greek tradition of caring for others, especially, in the tradition of the Greek-American Community in Chicago. Your services for our senior citizens, Adult Day Care, the Cultural and Arts Program--which reaches thousands and is a model for building understanding and cooperation with your neighbors--is a leading example of the very best our community has to offer.
>
> Again, I join in congratulating those being honored at this very important event and salute the leaders and members of Greek-American Community Services for their outstanding leadership and initiative.
>
> With warmest regards,
>
> Sincerely,
>
> Paul S. Sarbanes
> United States Senator

Greetings from Senator Paul Sarbanes. October 13, 1995. John Psiharis collection.

October 1995. There is no doubt that these last twelve years have been productive and rewarding for all those involved in the successful work of Greek-American Community Services and even more so because of the wonderful work you have all put through during this time that clearly represents what goodwill and teamwork can do. Moreover, these achievements, which in no way could be sufficiently stressed, clearly display the prospects that lie ahead.

I would also like to seize the opportunity and extend my genuine congratulations to all the honorees of this year's event, as well as to Mr. Tomaras, recipient of the Efharisto Award and praise them for their exceptional contribution to your wonderful cause.

It is my expectation and hope that the success of this event will further enhance your work and make it more beneficial to all recipients and especially to those of Northwest Senior Care, an initiative that undoubtedly represents a major success in this twelve-year period.

Loucas Tsilas, Ambassador of Greece

October 13, 1995. Congratulations to the honorees, *The Greek Press, Greek Star, Hellenic Community News, and Hellenic Life (Omogenia)*. They are to be commended for providing a forum for Greek-Americans to be included in the sharing of the traditions of our multi-ethnic city while keeping them in touch with news about their native homeland and communities. The Greek-American newspapers of the 90s are a major influence and contribute immeasurably to the Greek-American community's strength and cohesiveness.

Congratulations, also, to Mr. Chris Tomaras for receiving the Fourth annual Efharisto Award. I salute his dedication and commitment to Greek-American Community Services.

Richard M. Daley, Mayor, City of Chicago

September 20, 1995. It's a pleasure to be able to extend my best wishes once again to you and all of the people who will be attending your annual dinner.

Needless to say, I'm not happy with a lot of what is going on in Washington these days. But if the cuts that many members of Congress are seriously considering actually become law, it will be even more important to have organizations like Greek-American Community Services doing the kind of work you do with and for our community.

Michael S. Dukakis
Northeastern University, College of Arts and Sciences,
Department of Political Science

November 1, 1996. The philanthropic and cultural accomplishments which these people achieved through the Greek-American Community Services are a tribute to the dynamism and resourcefulness of the Greek Americans of Chicago.

I am particularly pleased that the proceeds from this event will go to your adult day care center, Northwest Chicago Senior Care, as the welfare of our elderly, is an important expression of our personal and group philanthropy.

Irene Antoniou, Eleni Bousis, Dr. Theodosis Kioutas, and Loukas Pergantas each in their own way have lifted the cultural and philanthropic levels of our community to new heights. Please convey to each of your honorees my deep appreciation for their commitment of time and resources in the best tradition of our shared Greek-American heritage. Likewise, please thank all those in attendance for supporting throughout the year the many good works of the Greek-American Community Services.

Paul S. Sarbanes, United States Senator

November 1, 1996. Your organization is admirable in raising funds through this event to support a variety of social services and cultural programs that benefit nearly 5,000 people per year. I commend Irene Antoniou, Eleni Bousis, Dr. Theodosis Kioutas, and Loukas Pergantas for the leadership roles that they have enacted in the development of Greek-American Community Services over the past ten years.

Jim Edgar, Governor, State of Illinois

September 27, 1996. Thanks so much for your invitation to the Tenth Annual Awards Dinner of Greek-American Community Services. I wish we could join you but I have a major dinner here in Boston that I must attend that evening.

I'm delighted you are honoring four outstanding Greek-Americans who have contributed so much to their community. We are a proud people, and rightly so, and we care about each other. Kitty and I never felt that pride more strongly than when we were in Greece, just two weeks ago, and experienced the warmth and affection that the Greek people have for us and all Greek Americans.

Keep up the good work, and I hope the dinner is a smashing success.

Michael S. Dukakis
Northeastern University, College of Arts and Sciences,
Department of Political Science

The A-Team

In 1992, the GACS Board of Directors was revitalized. According to a year-end report: "After careful review and in response to the continued growth of the organization, the Board adopted a working committee structure with the following committees: Executive, Finance/Budget, Program, Human Resources, and Resource Development. By year's end, the committees began to meet."

The report continued: "In an effort to broaden and stabilize funding for GACS, plans to establish an Advisory Board of well-respected leaders in the community came to fruition. The Advisory Board will devote its efforts to raising annual funds and visibility for GACS."

Since its earliest days, GACS aspired to involve the community's "heavy hitters" in supporting the organization. In addition to whatever unique contributions of talent, knowledge, or experience they would bring to GACS, their involvement would affirm the credibility of the organization as well as provide financial and fundraising support and guidance.

The definition of an A-lister was ambiguous, but you knew who they were within the community. They were successful entrepreneurs who had achieved a degree of success in their chosen fields which afforded them both money and influence within the community. Some were noted professionals or academics who had expertise and respect in their specialty or the broader community. Others were leaders within the Greek Orthodox Church or were active at the parish level, or in the lay hierarchy of the church, and in some cases were anointed Archons of the church or were members of the Archdiocese's Leadership 100 program. A number were leaders within AHEPA or various societies and organizations that existed within the *omogenia*.

The nursing home project attracted some support from prominent individuals, but GACS had a more difficult time attracting the A-listers. A turning point for GACS came when Irene Antoniou expressed support for GACS. Irene had seen the Norman Ross segment that was filmed at the center and had also read our newsletters. The day after the broadcast, Irene called GACS, and during our conversation, I shared our plans to develop an advisory board of community leaders who would help us in fundraising, and equally important, lend credibility to GACS both within and outside the Greek community.

After a lunch meeting with Irene, Mike Bakalis, John Rassogianis, and myself at the Drury Lane Oakbrook, one of the resorts owned by her husband's business, Irene, with Mike's help, agreed to convene a meeting where the idea would be presented to a select group of community leaders we hoped would join the newly formed advisory board. Those invited were notable in their fields and were not particularly aligned with the Hellenic Foundation. It was decided that we would host a dinner meeting at GACS. This would make it possible for the guests to see the center and learn about our programs and aims.

Letters co-signed by Irene and Mike, inviting about 25 people to a joint GACS Board and Advisory Board dinner at GACS in June 1992, were sent. Kostas Zografopoulos, a GACS Board member, catered the event through his business Master Caterers. With his help, the center was transformed. White tablecloths, candles, servers, a bartender, and a dessert table contributed to the success of this elegant yet convivial dinner.

Inaugural meeting of the GACS Advisory Board at GACS. Pictured (L-R): Dr. Theodosis Kioutas, Evangeline Mistaras, Athanasia Papadopoulos, and Kosta Zografopoulos. June 1992. Photo by John Rassogianis. John Psiharis collection.

The guest list included: Roula Alakiotou, Anthony and Irene Antoniou, Dr. Michael Bakalis, Eleni Bousis, Dr. Peter Chioros, Dr. Angelo Creticos, Aphrodite Demeur, Maria Gephardt, Connie Gountanis Rigas, Bill and Mary Kakavas, Dr. Theodosis Kioutas, Ethel Kotsovos, Demetrios Kozonis, Frank Kuchuris, Lou Malevitis, Peter Maroutsos, Evangeline Mistaras, Athanasia Papadopoulos, Loukas Pergantas, Nick Polydoros, John Psiharis, John Rassogianis, Ted Spyropoulos, Elaine Thomopoulos, Chris Tomaras, and Kosta Zografopoulos.

During dinner, I was seated next to Jim Kozonis, and I recounted a conversation I had with our landlord Joe Matushka, a few days earlier. Joe, the developer of the building and our landlord, told me he was planning to sell the property and was giving us the first option to buy it at a reduced price. I mentioned this to Jim during our dinner conversation hoping that he might become interested in helping GACS to buy the building.

Through his businesses, Delko Construction and Mega Properties, Jim developed and owned a good number of properties on Chicago's northwest side; many of them were strip mall locations on Milwaukee and Lawrence Avenues, and Irving Park Road. His hallmark location was Veterans' Square, adjacent to the Jefferson Park Transit Center. The property included underground parking, a strip mall retail space, and a seven-floor office building. Through his political connections, he had several government tenants including the Social Security Administration which

GACS Advisory Board members during a luncheon meeting at the Barclay-Chicago Hotel. Pictured (L-R): Chris Tomaras, John Psiharis, Irene Antoniou, Eleni Bousis, Charles Mouratides, John Rassogianis, and Loukas Pergantas. Date unknown. John Psiharis collection.

occupied the top floors. A congressman and alderman had offices there. Comcast, 7-11, Dunkin Donuts, Subway, and a few other businesses were tenants. As we spoke that night, I immediately sensed that Jim was scoping out the building and running the numbers. After a walkthrough of the building and a few questions, Jim concluded that this was a good deal.

After introductions and dinner, Irene welcomed the guests. Evangeline then spoke. Elaine and I provided overviews of the organization. Dr. Kioutas followed. As conversation and questions ensued, Jim brought up our dinner conversation about the building being for sale and his belief that GACS should buy it. Surprisingly there was agreement. Before you knew it the group had taken on the goal of raising the money needed for GACS to buy the building. Jim would chair the building campaign and Eleni Bousis and Loukas Pergantas joined the newly created Building Fund committee. Ted Spyropoulos joined the building fund committee soon thereafter; however, he was not on the advisory board.

The newly formed Advisory Board selected Irene Antoniou as chair and Chris Tomaras as co-chair. Initial members were: Roula Alakiotou, Dr. Michael Bakalis, Eleni Bousis, Aphrodite Demeur, Maria Gephardt, Jim Kozonis, Frank Kuchuris, Loukas Pergantas, and Eleni Sotos. The next meeting date was set. Irene graciously offered to host the lunch meeting at the Barclay-Chicago Hotel. The group was energized and unified behind the goal of purchasing the building. GACS was grateful to these supporters for their steadfast support. Each year, at least two joint meetings with the GACS board and advisory board members were held over dinner in Greektown. Chris generously covered the costs of the dinner meetings. After having enabled the purchase of the building, the Advisory Board focused its efforts on supporting the annual Heritage Awards dinners.

Even though buying the 3940 N. Pulaski building was not something that could have been imagined a few months earlier; it became a primary focus for the next two years.

First were negotiations with the building owner; Jim led these talks. As a commercial developer and property owner, Jim was well-versed in commercial real estate. He also provided us with legal help through his real estate lawyer, Nicholas Black, and his associate, Dean Kalamatianos. The asking price was $320,000. Our final purchase price was $240,000. Matushka was able to gain a tax reduction for selling the property to a nonprofit at a below-market rate. A contract to purchase was signed soon thereafter. Before we closed we had a soil test taken. Since the building was adjacent to a Mobil gas station there was concern about possible soil contamination. After soil testing, the results were acceptable and the process moved forward.

During the first meeting of the Building Fund Committee, Jim and the others present sketched out a fundraising plan. It called for 50 to 60 individuals to contribute a minimum of $1,000 each to the newly established Building Fund. The additional $40,000 would come from a $100 per ticket raffle, with a goal of selling 500 tickets. There were $10,000 in prizes and the drawing would be held during the annual GACS Heritage Awards Dinner. A radiothon was discussed as an additional means to raise funds.

GACS needed to raise $100,000 to secure financing. After many years my memory is fuzzy, but the mortgage payments were about $2,000 per month. As a nonprofit organization, the property taxes and the water and sewer bills would be waived. The upstairs rents, along with a lighted billboard sign in the front parking lot, and a rooftop sign facing the adjacent Kennedy expressway, provided income that would defray much of the mortgage, to the point that GACS would pay a little more to own the building than the $1,995 per month it was paying in rent for the first floor. The building was about five years old at the time so no major problems were expected for the foreseeable future.

Seated (L-R): Chris Tomaras and Irene Antoniou. Standing: Roula Alakiotou, Jim Kozonis, Loukas Pergantas, and John Psiharis during an Advisory Board luncheon meeting at the Barclay-Chicago Hotel. Date unknown. John Psiharis collection.

To kick off the campaign, most members of the Advisory Board donated at least $1,000 each. Several GACS board members also made generous donations. Organizations that contributed to the building fund included: The Pan Arcadian Federation, Pan Laconian Federation, Pan Messinian Federation, Greek Women's University Club, Hellenic Medical Society of Illinois, Phos Missions, and several others. A special appeal letter was sent to our major donors and mailing list. A GACS Building Fund account was established at Western Springs Savings and Loan, which at the time was owned by Jim Regas, a friend of Jim's, who also donated $1,000 to the effort. These donations yielded over $45,000.

A December 1993 holiday appeal letter signed by Evangeline and me, read in part:

> This holiday year, Greek-American Community Services has much to be thankful for and much more to celebrate. The blessings and support of many have enabled us to reach out to thousands over the last decade. As we celebrate our tenth anniversary, we are asking, once again for your help in support of a very special purpose…**the purchase of the building housing our facilities**. Please help us to maintain a permanent home for our adult day care center.
>
> The two-story building which houses our existing services is for sale. The purchase of the building will enable us to see a reduction in rental costs and to obtain additional office space

> that will allow us to expand our services to the Greek-American community. The space housing our adult day care center was specially designed to meet the needs of our elderly participants.
>
> Since our board announced this special fundraising campaign earlier this year, an outpouring of support from our friends has enabled us to raise a significant amount of our goal.
>
> This Holiday season we ask you to consider making a gift to Greek-American Community Services that will last for years to come. Help us buy a home. Help us to continue helping those in need.
>
> A new year...The second decade of service...1994. Make the promise of the future...a bright, shining, and vibrant one.
>
> We hope that you will join us as we continue to serve those in need and as we develop new programs and innovative approaches to aid our community. We also hope that you will help us realize the dream of owning our own center.

At a subsequent lunch meeting of the Advisory Board held at the Barclay Hotel - Chicago hosted by Irene, a high-end fundraiser was discussed, and the idea evolved into a cocktail reception.

An announcement in the May 12, 1994 edition of the *Greek Star* promoting the fundraiser quoted Eleni Bousis: "We believe the purchase of the Greek-American Community Services building will further entrench the agency and allow us to continue our work long-term." Chris Tomaras agreed, "This reception is about raising money to purchase the building and provide a sense of permanency for the elderly citizens we serve. This indeed is a worthwhile cause."

The "A Touch of Love First Annual Reception Buffet," cocktail party fundraiser was held on May 20, 1994. Chris Tomaras, a member of the exclusive Metropolitan Club located in Sears Tower, offered to host the reception there and underwrote the expenses. It was a venue that few had visited since it was a members-only club, thus there was an appeal. Tickets to the event were $500 each.

A $100 per ticket raffle was also held. It was the raffle originally intended to be held at the Heritage Awards dinner. The fundraiser was chaired by Dimitris and Eleni Bousis and Loukas and Nikki Pergantas. It was well attended, and several significant donations were made or pledged that evening. The Hellenic Ladies Society of Constantinople (now known as the Hellenic Society of Constantinople) donated $5,000. Peter Tselepatiotis presented a check on behalf of the organization he represented that evening and a check from Windy City Gyros, his store.

At the "Touch of Love" cocktail reception. **Top:** Pictured: (L-R): Advisory Board members Chris Tomaras, Eleni Bousis, Aphrodite Demeur, John Psiharis, Irene Antoniou, and Loukas Pergantas. **Bottom:** Officers of the Hellenic Ladies Society of Constantinople present a donation of $5,000 to the Building Fund at the Sears Tower event. Pictured (L-R): Irene Antoniou, Eleni Bousis, John Psiharis, Anna Harisiades, Eva Thomas, Katerina Clifton, unknown, Evangeline Mistaras, Frances Kuchuris, and Loukas Pergantas. May 20, 1994. John Psiharis collection.

In total, about $30,000 was raised as guests enjoyed refreshing cocktails, sumptuous hors d'oeuvres, and a brilliant sunset settling in across the city.

An article entitled "Friends of GACS Gather at Sears Tower for Building Fund Goal" appeared in the June 23, 1994 issue of the *Greek Star* and described the evening:

> The view from the 67th floor on this night was inspiring, setting the tone for the Building Fund goal of GACS that was clearly becoming a reality. Prominent members of the omogenia, personally invited by the Advisory Board, renewed old acquaintances.
>
> In her brief remarks, Ms. Irene Antoniou, Advisory Board Chairwoman, personally recognized the outstanding generous support of Ms. Aphrodite Demeur and Chris Tomaras. She stated, 'Those of us who have been involved with charities over the years know full well that nothing would be accomplished without the assistance of special angels who seem to fall from the heavens when they are needed most.' Ms. Antoniou also expressed special thanks to Ms. Eva Thomas, President of the Hellenic Ladies Society of Constantinople for their $5,000 contribution to the fund. She also complimented Ms. Bousis, Event Chairwoman, and Mr. Loukas Pergantas, co-chair for their exceptional and dedicated efforts and hard work in making 'A Touch of Love' a reality. Ms. Bousis was also complimented on the artwork her daughter, Victoria, sketched on the guest invitations, especially the tiny *Ya'Sou* bus in the background.

The success of this event helped GACS to gather much of the money needed for the down payment. Several individuals made significant donations during this period including Aphrodite Demeur, Alex and Tessie Cantos, and Bessie Choporis. A generous donation from the Argolida Organization O'Danaos was presented by its president, Peter Tselepatiotis. With their assistance, we were able to move ahead with the purchase.

A Building Becomes a Home

At this time, GACS occupied the first floor and there were six studio units on the second floor. Each suite had a bathroom with a bathtub/shower and a kitchen area. The suites were rented to small business tenants including a printer, photographer, and mortgage company. Two adjoining suites on the second floor were rented by shady telemarketers for police associations who nearly destroyed the building with their steady stream of people of questionable character. Once we assumed ownership, we envisioned improvements to both the first and second floors as well as the exterior.

John Psiharis signs the closing papers for the purchase of the GACS building at 3940 N. Pulaski Rd. on the afternoon of October 21, 1994 at Chicago Title and Trust. Photo by Peter Maroutsos. John Psiharis collection.

The building was near one of the busiest intersections on the Northside of Chicago. With two entrances/exits to the Kennedy Expressway (one at Pulaski and the second at Irving Park), a Blue Line stop, and a popular Metra station, it was a very busy area. It was even worse when the Chicago Cubs were playing, the traffic would be backed up in all directions.

Soon after we moved there, the city and state embarked on a project to redesign the flow of traffic to and from the highway. Part of it involved building an extension of the Pulaski exit through to Irving Park to address the problem of cars getting off at Pulaski, only to turn left on Irving Park creating gridlock and accidents. For nearly three years we endured this construction with the building often shaking from the vibrations and noise of the giant machines, traffic nightmares, and even an influx of rats that came out of hiding when the construction began.

The mortgage was financed through Columbia National Bank and Leon Xintaris, their executive vice president, handled this loan himself to ensure that GACS received favorable rates and terms. The bank was already a supporter, donating at least $1,000 each year. Eventually, Columbia was bought out by LaSalle Banks. A few years later, Bank of America bought LaSalle.

The closing occurred on the afternoon of Friday, October 21, 1994. By chance, or perhaps by divine intervention, it was the same day as our Heritage Awards Dinner. While most everyone else was focused on preparations for the dinner, Peter Maroutsos, as treasurer, and I, joined our attorneys at the closing. At about 4:00 p.m., and after many documents were signed, countersigned, and notarized, the building was ours!

That evening, during the Heritage Awards event, Chris Tomaras, during his remarks upon accepting the *Efharisto* award, along with Jim Kozonis, as building committee chairman, announced that the building was now ours. Chris challenged those in attendance to support the drive. Several guests got up to announce pledges. In total, $17,500 was raised in seventeen minutes.

I remember Peter Chioros, Peter Maroutsos, Sandy Papadopoulos, and possibly others, stopping at GACS for an impromptu visit after leaving the dinner dance. We opened a bottle of champagne to toast our ownership of the building. While there, I placed the official change of landlord notice under the doors of each tenant on the second floor. Basking in the moment, we brainstormed ideas for improvements that could be made to the building.

The promised donations were collected from all but one of those who pledged. Danny Boy Terzakis had pledged $3,000 in his usual colorful manner. His claim to fame was as owner of a chain of gas stations called Danny Boy Oil. He also owned several Checkers Drive-In franchises. Danny Boy was notorious within the Greek community for pledging donations that he never intended to fulfill, to get recognition and accolades. On most Friday afternoons he held court at Roditys Restaurant in Greektown. To see him about anything, you needed to go there. Even after John and I made such a visit to have lunch with Danny Boy, the money was not forthcoming.

The impact of the building purchase and the intensified fundraising efforts to benefit the nursing home had on GACS, was described in the May 1, 1995 grant request to the Retirement Research Foundation:

- At the time of our proposal three years ago, it was not anticipated that the Advisory Board, created to assist in raising funds, would assume the project of purchasing our building although it was a very wise, vital, and valuable investment for the long term growth and stability of the center. In the short term, however, this new goal absorbed funds that otherwise would have been used for program expansion.
- Likewise, after ten years of effort by our sister organization to build a nursing home, it was difficult to anticipate that as our RRF grant ended, a community-wide effort to raise $2 million would begin. This effort, though vitally necessary to achieve a dream that eluded our community for 30 years, will

drain a significant amount of funds that otherwise would have benefitted GACS. Once again, a very needed and worthwhile investment in long-term social service goals is affecting GACS in the short term.

- To illustrate the impact of these events, GACS has received approval from the Illinois Department on Aging to begin a Chore-Housekeeping program for the Greek elderly. The restricted contract was awarded, yet our efforts to initiate the program met minimal success. At first, we intended to use existing staff that was overburdened in operating the adult day care center to organize the program. Plans to begin raising funds to hire someone to run the program were delayed after our landlord informed us of his plans to sell the building. Now that this project is complete, the chore housekeeping program must yield to the nursing home capital campaign. In short, an approved contract that would generate committed funds for a valuable program is at present a victim of bad timing.

- A high level of importance is placed on this program, along with an accompanying meals-on-wheels program that we plan to introduce. Both would be the perfect compliments to the adult day care program. In-home services would supplement day service for ADC clients, and homebound clients benefitting from ADC services would be identified.

- During this period, GACS plans to continue intensive outreach efforts to achieve an average daily census of 40 to 50. Given our success over the first three years, this is an attainable goal. The increased revenue, nearly double what is currently collected, will enable the center to achieve long-term financial stability and reduce its dependence on outside funding sources. RRF funding will also enable GACS to explore ways to better serve caregivers. At present, caregiver concerns are varied and far-ranging. A tremendous need for additional one-to-one, family, and group conferences exists. Likewise, again in response to caregiver requests, GACS would like to establish a Saturday care program. Saturday, for some caregivers, is just another workday. For others that work the entire week, it is the only opportunity they have to attend to their own and family responsibilities (banking, shopping, and medical appointments to name a few). GACS would like to address their pressing need by launching a Mini-Saturday program. The program would consist of a shorter day (perhaps five to six hours as opposed to eight), bag lunches (as opposed to catered meals), and more limited transportation services. This program will meet in a cost-effective manner, the needs of this select group of caregivers. A bonus is that an increased number of volunteers may be available over a weekend and since children are not in school, more emphasis could be placed on intergenerational activities.

- As a result of the purchase of our building, GACS will benefit from increased savings. Until the closing date, last October, GACS paid $1,995 per month for the first-floor facility. Today, the entire mortgage for the two-story building is $1,979 per month. In addition, the rental income coming from three second-floor office suites will generate up to $1,400 per month. Thus the out-of-pocket expense for GACS will be about $600 per month versus the previous $2,000.
- In preparation for the establishment of the nursing home, GACS envisions a partnership role in identifying potential residents and their families. Likewise, GACS will explore the feasibility of establishing a satellite day care site at the new nursing home. The potential for reaching a large number of older adults in the northwest suburbs (Palatine, Wheeling, Des Plaines, Arlington Heights, Park Ridge, Glenview, etc.) and the potential cost savings of a combined facility will be carefully examined.
- Launch of the chore-housekeeping and "meals on wheels" program as a means to augment adult day care services, identify potential clients, and utilize the state funds already appropriated to GACS for this purpose.

Twelve years after our first meeting in the back room of the Elysion Restaurant, GACS had a permanent home, and the GANHC was on the cusp of achieving the community's long-held dream of establishing a nursing home!

Settling In

With the keys to the building in hand, GACS had achieved a level of stability. We owned the building and were paying about the same amount each month towards the mortgage as we had in rent. Cook County Treasurer Maria Pappas expedited our tax refund payments and property tax exemptions as she had done for the nursing home. We applied for and received sewer and water tax abatement from the city.

As a condition of the property tax exemption, GACS could not have unrelated income, e.g., rental income from the property. When we took

Front view of 3940 N. Pulaski shortly after GACS purchased the building. Circa 1994. Photo by John Rassogianis. John Psiharis collection.

over there were four tenants in the upstairs units. A telemarketing boiler room for police and fire association memberships occupied two adjoining suites. There was also a photographer, Superior Quick Print, and Sterling Mortgage. They were asked to move as their leases ended.

The telemarketing company was something else. Quite simply, they were the tenants from hell. They had at least 20 telemarketers who worked mostly for commission crammed into two studio suites. Frequently there was a German shepherd that also shared the space. The workers they employed were loud, crude, and disrespectful. The absentee business owner didn't seem to care. Fortunately, they were on a month-to-month lease which was immediately terminated. Given the activities on the first floor including caring for frail elderly, this was a big concern.

I still remember the disbelief I felt as I walked through the two suites they had occupied to survey the damage. There were holes in the walls and dog excrement stains on the carpets. There were grease and tomato sauce stains on the ceiling, broken light fixtures, and a cracked window. The carpet had tears, the blinds were stained and broken, the bathrooms were disgusting and much of the entry hallway outside their offices looked the same. I remember the bathtub being black and the toilet badly stained. It cost a considerable amount of time and money to repair the damage. Shortly after we took over, Sterling Mortgage moved to a location near Six Corners. The other tenants were more complicated. The photography studio was a husband and wife team that did photos for catalogs and sales circulars. Shortly after we took ownership, the husband had a heart attack and was not able to work. They asked for some time, and we granted them three months to make alternate plans.

Superior Quick Print had been the first tenant of the building. They had printing presses, printers, and copiers but I did not know until then that the husband, wife, and daughter were also living in the unit. They were an immigrant family from Pakistan and were current on their rent. They also took care of our routine printing needs (letterhead, envelopes, business cards, flyers, etc.) while Cosmos Press and Graphomania handled the dinner invitations and ad books. Shortly after we assumed ownership the husband suffered a massive stroke and became disabled and needed extra time to move. Eventually, they were able to make other arrangements, but as they moved out, their heavy and large machines tore the hallway carpets and damaged the walls.

Once the move-outs were completed, we worked to improve the building. Locks were changed. Jim Kotsovos, Ethel's husband, owned Argo Painting Company and donated his services in repairing and repainting the first and second-floor walls. Olympic Carpets, a Greek-owned business, replaced the carpeting, and new window blinds were installed to replace those that were broken by the prior tenants.

Two signs on the property were kept for the moment. The first was a two-tier lighted billboard that was mounted on the corner of the parking lot. The prior owner had signed a multi-year rental contract with the media company and there were two or three years left. A benefit that we appreciated was that the sign lit up the parking lot and the front of our building at night increasing our visibility and sense of safety. Since Clear Channel Communications separately paid the electric bills, there was no cost to GACS. Once the lease ended, we planned to have it removed so that the parking lot could be better configured. The Mobil gas station next door was open 24 hours per day and provided additional lighting. We also installed motion-activated sensor lights in the front, back, and on both sides of the building.

The second sign was different. It was mounted to the roof of the building that displayed advertising for Little Bucharest, an area restaurant that specialized in Romanian cuisine. The sign was facing the Kennedy Expressway. It was seen daily by tens of thousands of commuters. The restaurant owner had originally paid for the sign installation as well as $6,000 per year in rent. Since he had paid in advance, we left things as they were for the moment but considered the idea of placing an advertisement for the adult day care center in its place once the agreement came to an end. It wouldn't be costly for us since the fixture was already there, and it would be seen by countless commuters of which a portion would surely be caring for an aging loved one and in our service area. We discovered there was a rule about paid rooftop advertising along the highway, but since we owned and operated within the building, nothing was stopping us from putting up signage about our center.

Shortly after we took over the building, we had a visit from a city inspector who was investigating the rooftop sign. He noticed it as he was driving to work. The inspector wanted to check the structural integrity of the sign as he was concerned that it could become loose in a storm and become a flying projectile onto the highway. This rattled us.

By chance, I was friends with two architects who both worked for the city of Chicago but in different capacities: Zbigniew (John) Gorecki, the city's chief architect for bridges, and Ron Garner who had been the city building commissioner and at the time was chief architect for the Chicago Public Schools. I mentioned the inspector's visit to them one evening as we were having coffee at Jack's Restaurant in Skokie, and they came by to check it out. On a frigid and windy evening, I remember the two of them climbing up to the roof (in their suits, overcoats, and fedora hats mind you) to check on the sign. They assured us that the sign was secured properly. Ron spoke to the building inspector in person about the details and the matter was closed.

An improvement that we quickly made was to fence in the back area to create an outdoor patio for our clients to be able to get fresh air. In nice weather, the participants gathered there for activities or even snacks. A client's family donated wooden planters that were mounted along the fences and added greenery and flowers to the mix. At a subsequent GACS Christmas Party, J.B. Pritzker, a billionaire member of the Pritzker family that owned the Hyatt Hotels, donated patio furniture, barbecue grills, and other items to complete the patio. In November 2018, J.B. was elected governor of Illinois and assumed office in January 2019.

Inside, we updated the look and layout of the facility. A wall of honor was created on the entry wall within the reception area. It included plaques recognizing GACS benefactors and Heritage Awards honorees. After each dinner, Ethel created a photo collage of the event including an invitation, dinner ticket, and a photo of each honoree accepting their award. The frames were displayed in chronological order on the wall. Individual plaques honoring Illinois Masonic Medical Center, Chicago Community Trust, Retirement Research Foundation, Mrs. Aprhodite Demeur, Mr. and Mrs. Anthony Antoniou, Frank Kuchuris, and others were also displayed. The other walls in the entry area displayed colorful scenic posters of Greece that were provided by the Greek National Tourism Office.

Three offices (John's, Maria's, and mine) were moved to the second floor. The social worker and nursing offices remained on the first floor so they could best serve clients. This change freed up space that enabled us to create breakout rooms. My old office became an arts and crafts room and John's became a quiet room where a recliner, bed, and a small library were based. It had subtle lighting and was used when clients wanted to take a break from the hubbub around them or needed to rest because they weren't feeling well. It was also the room where Tornie (Tornado) our cat was based. She was placed in the room at certain times of the day e.g., during lunch, for events, or other reasons. Tornie would sometimes come upstairs to my office when larger events were taking place downstairs. A music area was created around the piano. A copier/printer room did double duty and also served as a smoking room with an air purifier operating. Eventually, the smoking area was moved to the outside enclosed patio, and the room was used as an office for our interns and volunteers.

Although it retained its purpose as a conference room, the room was configured to resemble a café. Greeks of course love their *kafenios* (coffee shops where mostly men gather to sip Greek coffee and play cards or dominoes) and this layout was meant to emulate that environment. A few café-style tables were interspersed in the room with two or three chairs at each table. A large service bar which we inherited from the landlord that was frankly too difficult to move, was in the corner and used for serving refreshments. Clients gathered in small groups to chat, play *Tavli, Kolitsina,* or other card games, watch a Cubs game, or have a cup of decaf coffee or juice. Music was sometimes played in the background. The room could easily be returned to a traditional conference room setting for meetings and classes (e.g., fabric arts and Greek language classes). Through SAE of North and South America, we received a complimentary subscription to ERT, Greece's National TV channel, which played in the

Fabric Arts of Greece Exhibit

At the recent annual Fabric Arts of Greece exhibit sponsored by the Cultural and Arts Program of the Greek-American Community Services, Eugenia Stathakis displayed her beautiful fabric arts work. Attending the event from the left: John Rassogianis, director of the program; John Psiharis, executive director; J.B. Pritzker; Peter Kapsalis; Michael Payne; and novelist and storyteller, Christopher Janus.

The *Greek Press*, January 25, 1998. John Psiharis collection.

background and was available to clients when the room was set up as a *kafenio*.

On the second floor, Maria and I moved into adjoining offices that had been occupied by the telemarketing company, and John's office, previously Sterling Mortgage, was next door. While the printer remained for a while, the former photography studio was vacant. We had the rooms painted and the carpets shampooed. The remaining unit, located in the back, had been occupied by Joe Matushka's nephew who moved out shortly after the closing. That room was turned into a meeting room that was used for meetings such as CLESE training sessions, and neighborhood meetings or gatherings. It was sometimes rented out to organizations in need of meeting space. GACS worked with a community member who was interested in using this room for twice-weekly meetings of an Alcoholics Anonymous group for the Greek community he hoped to start but nothing ever became of this. For a while, the Greek Women's University Club rented space in that room to store old records.

Externally, we placed two planters in the front of the building and had the front and back areas power washed. The adult day care participants cared for the planters. A sloped entry walkway at the front door was created to make it easier for the disabled and wheelchairs to enter and exit. The building was power washed. We added front awnings to the list of upgrades we wanted to make, but it was never accomplished.

A perpetual problem with this building was the first floor having a single front door. Most public buildings have double doors which reduce blasts of hot or cold air and prevent rain from entering whenever the door was opened. Given that we were a community center that accommodated more than 30 adult day care clients, classes, programs, and staff, the door opened and closed often. This was a problem that we had hoped to address at some point since installing a doorway and door would be costly, but it never happened

Another headache was the parking lot. It was a challenge to get into and out of it. The corner that we were located near was one of the busiest and most congested intersections in the city. We were on a short triangular block between the Irving Park and Pulaski Road intersection and the Pulaski entrance and exit ramps to the Kennedy and one-half block from the Irving Park entrance and exit ramps. Additionally, there was a busy CTA Blue Line station and a similarly busy Metra train station. This resulted in all sorts of traffic bottlenecks and frequent accidents out front. During morning and evening rush hours, or when there were Chicago Cubs baseball games, the problem became that much worse.

At maximum, the parking lot could fit six cars comfortably in two rows of three each. The first row was parked in front of the second and drivers needed to back up onto Pulaski and into traffic. There were only a couple of parking spaces on Pulaski and they were usually occupied. Since the two *Ya'Sou* vans needed to park in the lot to load and unload clients, two slots were reserved. Space was also needed for families who were dropping off or picking up participants which meant that parking became even more limited. We tried to deal with this as best as we could. We coordinated amongst ourselves who would be there the longest so that another car could park behind that car. It was annoying because we might need to move a car in the middle of a meeting or phone call. But as they say, when given lemons, make lemonade.

John was notorious for parking his car in the lot and leaving the building to go for coffee at Little Mike's, a haircut, or sometimes even taking the

Blue Line to a meeting downtown, forgetting about his car. He often parked behind another car and blocked them in so that person couldn't leave until John returned. This was before cell phones so it wasn't always easy to locate him if he had left the building. To discourage this, I created a GACS parking ticket. Each time someone blocked another car they were given a "ticket" with a $2 fine. The fines collected went into the client activity fund which was used for adult day care center birthday cakes, parties, etc. Although most of us ended up contributing to this fund now and then, John was by far the leader in that category.

I developed a good relationship with the gas station next door, G&F Mobil. The station was owned by two Assyrian brothers (George and Freddy Oshana) who also owned a Mobil station at Irving Park and Western Avenue. They allowed a couple of our cars to park in the service station lot. For the sake of simplicity, it was mostly our staff that parked there, so their cashiers would know the cars. This in turn freed up space for guest parking in our lot.

G&F rented its repair garage to a Greek mechanic, Spiro Soukeras. Spiro maintained the *Yasou* vans and serviced our cars as well. We established a house account there so that the vans could fuel up when needed. At a certain point, George expanded the station to enlarge the retail space but in doing so eliminated his office. Soon after we took ownership of the building, George asked if any of the offices on the second floor were for rent. In June 1995, we entered into a barter agreement with G&F. Instead of paying rent of $350, we received a monthly credit equal to that on our account for gas. George allowed three GACS cars to park in his lot. It balanced out almost down to the penny in most months. In essence, we got free gas and he got free rent. They also supported our fundraisers.

I had a good relationship with Michelle Milewski who was assistant vice president and branch manager for Midwest Bank and Trust which was located about a block north of us on Pulaski. Although we didn't bank there at the time, we went there every so often to have signatures notarized for forms related to our government funding. She graciously allowed us to use the bank's parking lot when we had gatherings, donated raffle prizes, and even provided gifts for our adult day care clients.

One idea we considered but was too costly to come to fruition was to purchase the mostly vacant building next door which also had a large parking area accessible through the rear alley. A side door would have been added to our building to enable direct access and drop-off. In turn, the existing parking lot in front of our building would have been converted into a gated green garden-type space with grass, planters, and benches.

Within months of taking over the building, a late winter thaw caused a major leak in the roof that dripped into the second-floor offices and then at times into the first floor. A good amount of the reserve fund we had set aside for building upkeep was spent to fix the roof. It took a few attempts and several thousand dollars to locate and repair the cause of the problem. The leak caused some interior damage that also had to be repaired. This caused us to defer other building improvements.

An article by Ken Keenan, staff writer for *Pioneer Press*, which appeared in the November 2, 1995 edition of the *Edison-Norwood Times Review* entitled "A Sense of Purpose for Helping Others:"

> When Greek-American Community Services Executive Director John Psiharis originally founded the organization in 1982, meetings were held at a table in the back of a restaurant.
>
> Today, the group operates out of its own building, runs a successful senior adult day care center, and is responsible for the development of several cultural and community services programs catering to the everyday needs of more than 5,000 Chicago residents.
>
> GACS' top priority is the Northwest Chicago Senior Care Center, located on the first floor of the organization's headquarters – since 1992 – at 3940 N. Pulaski Road, just south of Irving Park Road in the Old Irving Park neighborhood.
>
> Claiming to be the first Greek-American sponsored senior day care center in the United States, it opened its doors to the public for the first time in 1990 at GACS' old Alvernia High School locale and initially serviced one client per week.
>
> 'Back then, we never knew if we'd stay open from month to month,' the 31-year-old Psiharis said while seated at his paperwork-stacked desk in the relative calm of his second-floor office.
>
> 'Now, having been through the struggles, it's a sense of accomplishment knowing that we have the building.'
>
> These days, the day care clientele numbers 25 elderly folks, who are treated to hot lunches, snacks, and various activities such as arts and crafts functions, exercise programs, monthly field trips, game playing, birthday parties, and more.
>
> In fact, the day care center has been so successful that Psiharis and company have purchased some land near Milwaukee Avenue and Dundee Road in Wheeling with the intent of opening a full-time nursing home.

Once the group is granted a license of operation – known as a certificate of need – and once they raise the necessary funds, they will begin breaking ground for the facility.

'One of our primary concerns, when we founded the organization, was to care for the Greek elderly,' Psiharis said. 'But our goal, in addition to helping our own, is to help everyone, to concentrate on the Greek community, but to reach anyone in need.'

Psiharis, a Norwood Park resident and Taft High School graduate, studied human services and psychology and received a bachelor's degree from National Louis University and his master's from Roosevelt University.

He also contributes his time as a community representative on the Taft High School Local School Council, where he's served since 1993.

The fact that he founded GACS (along with original partner Elaine Thomopoulos) at such a young age prompts one to wonder when he began to cultivate such an ambitious undertaking.

'When I was a kid during the summer, I'd do volunteer work with my mom, who was a social services agent,' Psiharis said. 'I was 10 or 12, and I saw how you could help people.'

And help people they do. Besides the senior day care center, GACS founded the Greek-American Nursing Home Committee (a separate entity); the Low Income Home Energy Assistance Program which serves about 1,000 financially strapped seniors a year; and the Community Aging Network (which serves homebound elderly).

They also sponsor several cultural and arts-related programs, among them a traveling museum exhibit called 'The Heartland of Hellenism: The Greeks in Illinois from 1880-1950.'

'The exhibit has been on display at the State of Illinois Building and will travel all over the state.' Psiharis said. 'It contains lots of historical information.'

GACS also founded CLESE (Coalition of Limited English Speaking Elderly) which Psiharis said involves 40 different ethnic agencies.

'It's a group that's really blossomed,' Some people have access problems because of the language barriers.

And there's more: film festivals, conferences, Greek dance classes, workshops, and 75 to 80 different lectures on a wide variety of topics are all part of the GACS game plan.

'We've tried to bridge the gaps between different communities.' Psiharis said. 'So we've had lectures with different ethnic groups participating. We had a two-day conference with about 10 different ethnic groups. I hope that's promoted some cross-cultural communication.'

Providing such an impressive array of programs and services doesn't come without help, and Psiharis was quick to praise those groups and organizations that have contributed to his and GACS' vision.

'We get private grants from foundations and individual contributions from the community,' Psiharis said. 'Several restaurants from the Greek Town area support us. And we developed an advisory board of high caliber businessmen to help build long-term stability.'

As he answered yet another telephone call pertaining to a recent fundraising dinner, Psiharis apologized for the interruption. When asked how many hours he puts in a week, he smiled and said 'A lot. We're very short-staffed and we hope more funding will change that. One of the things I'd like to do in the future is have a traveling social worker.'

Another thing he'd probably like to do in the future is get some rest. But there's always some aspect of this not-for-profit organization's business that needs attention, and Psiharis is always moving, always working toward achieving another goal.

'We started with a group of like-minded people who felt similar needs for the community,' Psiharis said. 'And we've never lost that sense of having to help someone.'

During the summer of 1997, the neighborhood was abuzz with activity as filmmakers were busy filming *Mercury Rising*, a film that starred Bruce Willis and Alec Baldwin. A chase scene was being filmed that took place on the Blue Line and Kennedy Expressway. Filming was done at night and the location for these scenes was a CTA train that was placed about midway between the Irving Park and Addison stations. Traffic scenes were filmed on that portion of the highway as well. Many from the neighborhood came to watch the filming, which lasted late into the evening. The production company approached GACS for the use of its parking lot and building. They parked several trailers for wardrobe, makeup, and other functions, and used the center as a dining area. They paid GACS $3,500 in rent for using our space, and we had the opportunity to see Bruce Willis and members of the cast work on a movie. Not a bad deal by any means!

A Tornado Strikes

Tornie joins in as ADC clients play the "Famous Faces" game. July 25, 1997. Photo by Ann Prusinski. John Psiharis collection.

December 7, 1994, was a day that would live in GACS infamy. A Tornado struck GACS, and it was never quite the same. On that day, a sister of one of the adult day care center participants asked if she could bring in a kitten that she found on her doorstep to visit the seniors. It had been placed in a box along with a note and a few cans of food. The note read "I know you like cats, please look after this kitten since I can't." Margaret had four cats of her own, and those cats did not take kindly to the new arrival who only found safety in the bathroom. The original idea was for the kitty to visit with the clients so that her brother Lenny, who had grown attached to the kitten, could show her off. Margaret suggested that we consider adopting the cat akin to a "resident cat." I was open to the idea but not sure how it would work in our environment. work in our environment. There was a growing body of research that documented the benefits of pet therapy amongst older adults, and I was willing to give it a try.

Within 15 minutes of her arrival, the kitty began to interact with the adult day care clients. Her temperament meshed with the clients, and she was patient and understanding with the seniors. She basked in the attention of the participants, and I noticed she quickly bonded with a few. Until that point, we had arranged for pet therapy that included visits from the Lincoln

Pet therapy in action. Tornie snuggling with an ADC participant. August 28, 1996. Photo by Ann Prusinski. John Psiharis collection.

Park Traveling Zoo, Treehouse Animal Shelter, and a neighbor who brought in her dog to visit every so often. This was different.

I agreed to take her on a trial basis. We would have her stay for a few days and see what happened. Soon thereafter I witnessed magic. A client who would regularly become impatient and agitated in the afternoon with what is known as "sundowner's syndrome" found great comfort in the cat, and others did as well.

A participant council consisting of the ADC clients met monthly as a committee of the whole to discuss center operations, and plan activities and outings for the following month. The activity director led the meeting, and the ADC supervisor, nurse, and social worker also attended. Whenever possible I attended. I asked Ann, our activity director, to bring up for discussion whether or not we should adopt the kitty at the next meeting. The unanimous vote was in favor of taking in the cat.

The clients chose to name her Tornado. The name was prompted by a comment that one of the participants made after the kitty had jumped onto Ann's desk, and the papers on her desk went flying all over the floor. "It looks like a tornado struck," said the participant, and the cat was named "Tornado." Her dark gray coloring matched the name they had selected. We called her "Tornie" for short.

Tornie remained the resident cat and lived at the center for six years before retiring. I would bring her home with me on holidays and most weekends. A couple of years after we adopted her, Tornie came down with a serious illness and needed medical care. The veterinarian suspected that Tornie drank toilet water which had caused an infection. She stayed at the animal clinic for most of the week, and then I brought her home with me for another couple of weeks so that she could rest and receive her medicine. Like a real trooper, Tornie rebounded, and when she returned to the center she was warmly greeted by the participants who missed her and were concerned about her well-being. The clients made her a get-well card and gifted Tornie a bottle of catnip for "when she feels better."

The effect Tornie had on clients and the rest of us was apparent. Tornie was often the center of attention. She would meet and greet arriving participants, seek out attention whenever she could get it, and in return provided love, affection, companionship, and purrs to our clients and staff. She helped create a more homelike and caring environment in an otherwise structured setting. Tornie frequently played fetch with a Pepsi bottle cap and "Cat in the Bag," with a dark green Marshall Field shopping bag. She sometimes chased the ball during ball toss games and would sit by and watch as clients exercised or danced.

Although most clients interacted with Tornie daily, a few were especially close to her including:

Tornie doing what she did best, cuddling. Date unknown. Photo by Ann Prusinski. John Psiharis collection.

- **Ann C.** Ann was a perky, physically fit lady in her seventies who had moderate dementia. As is the case with many who are afflicted with dementia, Ann would experience prolonged and intense anxiety in midafternoon. Studies have shown that this anxiety could be tied to the descending position of the sun at that time of day and it was termed "sundowners syndrome." When it kicked in, our activity staff provided Ann with an empty green Marshall Field paper shopping bag. Ann would put it on the floor and Tornie would willingly jump into it. She would carry Tornie around the center, showing her off to the other clients. Ann's anxiety subsided within minutes of seeing Tornie. We called this routine "cat in a bag."

- **Clara D.** Clara was nearly 100 years old and had a pleasant personality. She was frail, confused, and could not hear well. As with Ann, sundowner's syndrome would usually settle in after 3:00 pm, while she was waiting for her 80-plus-year-old son George to pick her up. Sensing this, Tornie would rub herself on Clara's leg and jump onto the seat next to her so that Clara could pet her. Again, within minutes there was a notable change in Clara's state of mind and alertness.
- **John D.** John was a tall and lanky man who was in his late sixties. He was developmentally disabled and functioned with the capacity of a child. John lived in a group home and was referred to the center because he wanted to be around people of his age. Although pleasant, he was withdrawn and spent a good part of his time observing the group from the back of the room. Tornie befriended John and made it a point to spend time with him every day. She would curl up next to him for a heavy petting session. John spent a lot of time just talking to her. In time, John began to participate in activities and discussions and no longer sat in the back of the room.
- **Bill M.** Bill was a happy and gregarious man in his mid-eighties who had been a security guard for W.F. Hall Printing Company for most of his life. In addition to confusion, Bill had failing eyesight and hearing. He usually thought that the center was his work, and he could often be found sitting next to the front door where he served as our "official greeter." Bill became confused in the mid-afternoon and sometimes walked around the center in search of his daughter Patty. When that would happen, Tornie made her way to Bill and jumped on his lap. He would talk to Tornie and pet her, and in short order, Bill's anxiety dissipated.
- **Eugene H.** Gene was a cheerful developmentally disabled man in his late sixties whose cognitive abilities were minimal. He lived with his sister who had a dog named Rambo that he would always talk about. Gene would say things like "Rambo is a good dog." and "My dog bites the mailman." He seemed to find particular comfort with pets since his limited vocabulary and ability to speak didn't matter. Gene bonded with Tornie and would get upset when for whatever reason he wasn't able to go to the center to see her.
- **Adeline S.** Adeline was a high-functioning senior in her seventies who fell into a deep funk after losing her husband. Her daughter enrolled her in the program so that she could have socialization and ensure that she ate during the day.

Adeline adored Tornie, and the minute Adeline walked through the door in the morning, Tornie would follow her and patiently wait for Adeline to get situated and sit down. Once she was seated, Tornie jumped into her arms and happily purred.

- **Agnes P.** Agnes was a pleasant and sociable older lady whose daughter was an attorney for a major corporation located downtown. She was dropped off early, usually around 7:00 a.m., and didn't leave until after 5:00 p.m. As she waited for her daughter to arrive, Agnes enjoyed watching *Jeopardy, Wheel of Fortune*, and the afternoon news on television. Agnes had a walker to which her daughter affixed a metal basket, akin to a bicycle basket so that her mother could more easily carry her belongings. Each day, the ADC staff placed a large clear green glass of ice water into the basket from which Agnes would drink while she waited. One day after sipping from the glass Agnes placed the glass on the floor. Moments later, Tornie found the glass and began drinking from it herself. On subsequent days, Tornie went to Agnes hoping to get water. We ended up giving Agnes a glass of water for herself and another for Tornie. It became a daily routine for Tornie to go to Agnes for water and then sit next to her while she waited for her daughter to come.

Maggie K. Maggie was a lady in her late eighties who was mentally alert but physically infirm and used a walker to get around. Maggie had a close relationship with Tornie. She often asked her daughter to go shopping for cat food, treats, and toys for her feline friend. After a couple of years of attending, Maggie ended up in the hospital and asked about Tornie regularly. One of the most touching moments I remember about Tornie came when Maggie's daughter told us that her mother's last words to her before passing away were to always look out for Tornie and to make sure she had enough food. In memory of Maggie, the family made contributions to GACS to cover food and litter costs. When Tornie became sick, Maggie's family joined forces with another family to cover her veterinary expenses.

Tornie's relationships with the staff were a bit complicated. From the onset, she viewed me as her pet parent which was important since there could be up to 40 (or more) people in the center on any given day and even more for parties or events, and it was important for her to have someone in the pet parent role. Tornie was also close to John. If John was there late for any reason, he usually went into the "living room" area of the center to sit on the recliner and watch the news. When he reclined, Tornie would jump onto his chest or stomach and settle in for a nap. She wouldn't move until he did. Sometimes on meeting nights, we ordered Chinese food, and a ritual was always that John would give her some of his chicken subgum on a plate which Tornie devoured.

As a social worker who worked with older adults, Ethel recognized the benefits of pet therapy, but did not like pets. She wasn't too happy that Tornie was there, and it seemed from Tornie's point of view the feeling was mutual. Nevertheless, Ethel had an infectious laugh and at times you would hear her laughing at Tornie's antics. Ethel was usually dressed in ¾-length skirts, nylon stockings, and heeled shoes that made noise as she walked on the tile floor. On a couple of occasions, Tornie was not happy with Ethel and pawed at her, tearing her nylons in the process.

Ann, the activity director, cared about Tornie and looked after her throughout the day. Ann had a genuine affection for Tornie. After all, it was her desk that usually fell victim to Tornie's antics with papers flying everywhere when Tornie chose to jump on it. If Tornie didn't engage on her own, Ann routinely brought Tornie into activity groups where there was a good amount of interaction between Tornie and the clients.

The nurses ran the gamut ranging from Amydelle, who despite being an active senior that went motorcycle riding, and hot air ballooning, was afraid of cats ever since she had been bit by one as a child. Kathleen O'Leary became the center's supervisor after Amydelle retired and loved Tornie. She affectionately called her "rug-rat". Kathleen had two cats of her own, so she was feline-friendly. Eileen had a bubbly personality and liked Tornie. Eleanor was okay with Tornie but was uncomfortable with any pets that got too close to her. Lorraine had an abrasive personality, wasn't too friendly, and not surprisingly, didn't care for Tornie. The feeling was mutual, Tornie didn't care much for Lorraine either and kept her distance whenever she was working.

When Tornie did something funny, Maria could be heard breaking into giggles. Bob liked Tornie and took time to chill with her after he returned from his evening route. Bob once rescued Tornie when he found that she had climbed the kitchen cabinets, managed to lift a ceiling tile, and climbed above the ceiling tiles where she was virtually impossible to find.

Another relationship Tornie enjoyed was with Ray. In addition to working as an activity and van assistant during the week, Ray came in over the

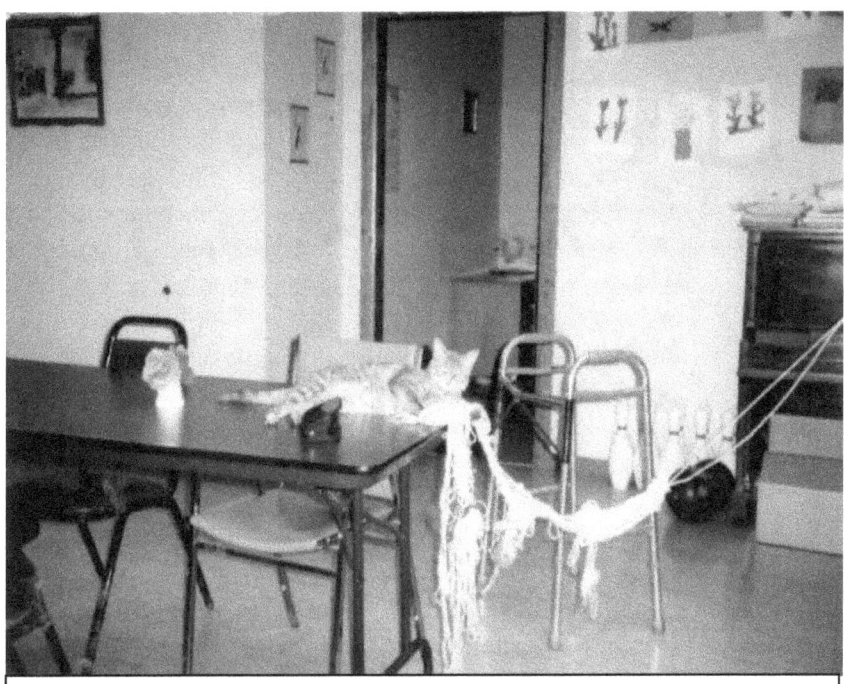
Tornie all tied up. Date unknown. John Psiharis collection.

weekend to clean the center. Since he lived at the Irving Park YMCA, only a few blocks from the center, it was convenient. We set aside leftovers for Ray since he didn't have cooking facilities or refrigeration. Over the weekend, Ray sometimes spent the day at the center. During extreme heat and humidity, he stayed overnight at the center since there was no air conditioning at the Y.

Ray fed and cared for Tornie over the weekends, and they formed a bond with each other. Years later, Ray still recounted the time that he had brought in a barbecued spare ribs dinner from a local restaurant and while he was in the kitchen getting napkins and a plate, Tornie jumped onto the table and grabbed the slab of ribs. When Ray returned to the table, neither Tornie nor the ribs were around. It turned out she took the rack of ribs into the copy room and had herself quite a dinner!

At the board level, there was some resistance to Tornie from Evangeline and Dr. Kioutas. Evangeline was afraid of cats because one had bitten her as a child, and would make comments like "Oh there's that damn cat again," and then snicker and laugh. In addition to being the board president, Evangeline was a frequent volunteer at the center. She saw Tornie interacting with the clients and tolerated Tornie as long as she didn't approach her. When we had board meetings at the center, Tornie would go into her room voluntarily when she saw Evangeline walk through the door.

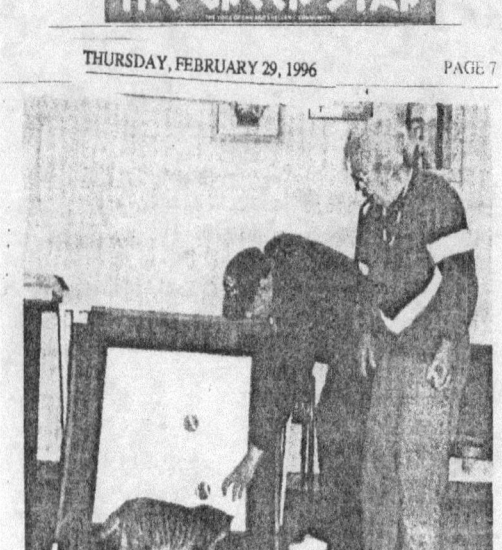

THE GREEK STAR

THURSDAY, FEBRUARY 29, 1996   PAGE 7

Clients at the Greek-American Community Services Adult Day Care Center enjoy a game with new pet kitten Tornado.

Pet companionship arrives at GACS Adult Day Care Center

Pet therapy has arrived at the Greek-American Community Services Adult Day Care Center

Referring to Tornado, a kitten that was recently adopted by the clients, executive director John Psiharis also adds that "she's a quick one."

Clients enjoy the company of the cat and a favorite game is "Cat in the Bag."

Ann Prusinski, activities director at the Greek-American Community Services Adult Day Care Center announces the importance of various new activities for the clients.

"We also have a miniature health club," said Prusinski as she watched clients trying their luck with a hoop game—one of several games that were being played last week.

Donated by Miranda Zaharakis, president of the United Athenian Piraeus Societies, these games are some of the many enjoyable activities provided at the center, 3940 N. Pulaski Rd. (near Irving Park).

"There are numbers on the board.

Whoever gets the most rings around the stick wins, just like horse shoes," she added. Prusinski thinks that the men prefer doing the hoops as well as playing target ball, while chair basketball seems to be a women's favorite.

Discussing the impact of social skill development as well, she adds that "the games assist in a kind of gentle art of competition which they have experienced throughout their lives. And they are designed to promote physical fitness which leads to better hand-eye coordination."

The adult day care center cares for frail, isolated, and forgetful older adults in a safe, caring environment. Hot lunches, activities, and nursing care are offered. Ya Sou vans transport clients to and from the center.

For more information about the center, including the Fabric Arts of Greece classes open to individuals over the age of 60, will start on March 20, call (312) 545-0303.

The *Greek Star*, February 29, 1996. John Psiharis collection.

As medical director of the center, Dr. Kioutas had concerns about clients that might be allergic to cats. Surprisingly, we never encountered that issue. Much of the floor in the main areas was tiled, the furnishings were mainly vinyl, tables, and chairs could easily be wiped down, and carpeted areas were vacuumed daily; there was little opportunity for cat dander or hair to collect. The families of current participants were notified of Tornie being there, and new clients were made aware before they enrolled. There were no problems to speak of at that level.

A family member of a client considering enrolling in the center filed a complaint with IDOA about a cat living on our premises. She wanted her mother to attend our program, but the mother was allergic to cats. IDOA, which administered the CCP program, contacted me to follow up and scheduled a visit.

An IDOA representative, whose name I don't recall, came to the center. Observing the interaction

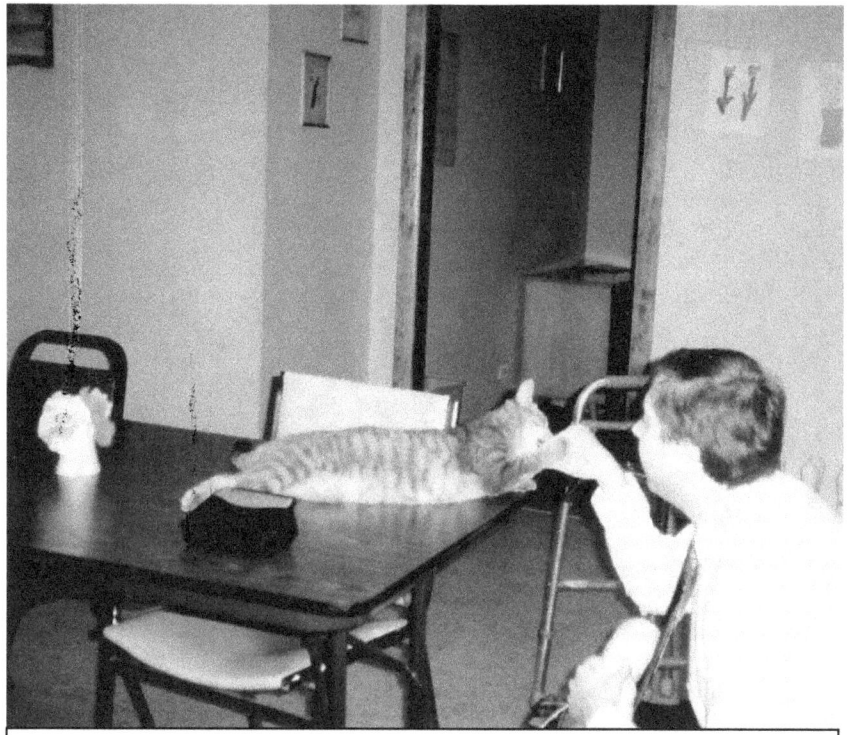

John Psiharis visiting with Tornie. Date unknown. John Psiharis collection.

between Tornie and the clients was all that was needed. At the time, there were no CCP guidelines that prohibited pets from being on the premises, and we were aware of the growing body of research on the benefits of pet therapy. I pointed out, that the impact is even more profound since Tornie resides at the center and interacted with clients daily developing an emotional attachment. She was not a pet that came in every so often to visit but was a full-time "pet therapist" that brought comfort, familiarity, and happiness to our clients. She bonded with them, knew them, and had an emotional and psychological impact far above what a standard pet therapy program could offer. The IDOA visitor spent a couple of hours at the center and observed Tornie and her interactions with the participants and talked with them about Tornie. A symphony of voices talked about how much they liked her and cared about her and how important she was to them. In short, Tornie was part of the family.

About a month later, I received a letter from the Illinois Department of Aging. IDOA recognized the importance of pets and pet therapy and was impressed by the level of interaction between the clients and the cat. They

(L-R): Ethel Kotsovos, John Psiharis, Senator John Cullerton, Ann Prusinski, and unknown during Cullerton's visit to GACS. Circa: 1998. John Psiharis collection.

stated that there were no rules barring pets from living on the premises, as long as there was a distinct space for the pet to be separated from the clients, that she wasn't a threat to the clients in any way, and was current on her vaccinations. They commended us on our attempt to introduce pet therapy into adult day care.

One takeaway I had was observing the humility that Tornie brought to the scene. GACS was her home, and she patrolled it regularly. Although she was loved by the clients and most of the staff who she greeted regularly, visitors and guests usually got the once over from her as well.

I remember prominent people who entered GACS and were greeted by Tornie. Among them were U.S. Senator Paul Simon, J.B. Pritzker, Chris Tomaras, Frank Kuchuris, Irene Antoniou, Maralee Lindley, and Mike Bakalis being met at the front door by Tornie. Congressmen Mike Flanagan and Rod Blagojevich, Illinois Senator John Cullerton, author Christopher Janus, bankers, foundation officers, business owners, and others were similarly greeted by Tornie. It was a humbling moment to see Chris Tomaras in his expensive tailored suit, exit his gold Mercedes with KRONOS license plates, walk in the front door, and get down to his knees to pet Tornie as he entered the center. Whenever Chris visited the center, he made it a point to see Tornie.

"Pet Companionship Arrives at GACS Adult Day Care Center," an article appearing in the February 29, 1996 issue of the *Greek Star*, featured a photo of Tornie playing a ball-toss game with two ADC clients and proclaimed: "Pet therapy has arrived at the Greek-American Community Services Adult Day Care Center." It continued, "Referring to Tornado, a kitten that was recently adopted by the clients, executive director John Psiharis also adds that 'she's a quick one.' Clients enjoy the company of the cat and a favorite game is 'Cat in the Bag.' Ann Prusinski, activities director at the Greek-American Community Services Adult Day Care Center announces the importance of various new activities for the clients. 'We also have a miniature health club,' said Prusinski as she watched clients trying their luck with a hoop game – one of several games that were being played last week. Donated by Miranda Zaharakis. President of the United Athenian Piraeus Societies, these games are some of the many enjoyable activities provided at the center."

Early in January 1999, during a blizzard, I by chance walked into the PAWS pet shelter located within the North Community Bank. Founded by Paula Fasseas, Pets Are Worth Saving (PAWS) had recently opened a storefront shelter within the bank's Clark Street branch. I intended to peek inside the recently opened shelter on the way to my car, but that was not what happened. I went inside. As I visited with the cats, one of them bonded with me immediately. He began hugging me with his paws, licking my forehead and had the loudest purrs I had ever heard. I walked out but then walked right back inside and adopted Dickens.

With Tornie at GACS, I decided I wanted a cat at home too and ended up bringing Dickens home with me. He was one of the first to be adopted from PAWS since it had only opened a month or two before my visit. Today, PAWS is the largest no-kill pet shelter in Chicago.

Tornie was the focus of several newspaper articles and was mentioned in a professional journal article on the merits of pet therapy with older adults. Tornie lived at the center until I left GACS in November 2001. I took Tornie home with me so she could enjoy her remaining years in retirement.

Tornie was the office cat and Dickens was the home cat. Each day when I arrived at GACS, Tornie would greet me and carefully sniff me. She became aware of Dickens through his scent. In the evenings when I returned home, I went through the same process in reverse. It was Dickens checking out Tornie. These cats grew jealous of each other before they ever met. I think they sensed I was cheating with the other. When I eventually brought them together, they had an immediate dislike for each other, since each was used to being the sole cat. There were some standoffs and a couple of fights between them. Tornie stood her ground, and although the two cats didn't like each other, they managed to co-exist and keep their distance. One day, after leaving home, I ended up returning a few minutes later because the car wouldn't start. When I went to the bedroom closet to hang my jacket, I found Tornie and Dickens curled up and sleeping next to each other in the closet. After seeing that, I breathed a sigh of relief that at minimum the cats would be okay with each other if they were home alone.

Tornie remained with me until February 12, 2010, when she passed away at the age of 16. Dickens crossed the Rainbow Bridge on January 10, 2014, at the age of 18. Her impact on my life and the lives of many around me will never be forgotten. She was an amazing cat that touched many in positive and therapeutic ways, whose love was unconditional, and who brought so much comfort, joy, and happiness to many people during their time of need. I am proud to have helped play a role in the evolution of pet therapy with older adults by introducing this in an adult day care environment, but it was Tornie who stole the show!

Chronicling our Heritage

The GACS Cultural & Arts Program had grown to offer an impressive array of programming that showcased and preserved the Greek American experience and helped lead a cultural renaissance within Chicago's Greek community. Essentially there were two facets to these endeavors. The first focused on the arts and was exemplified in a number of our efforts including the Fabric Arts Program, dance classes, film festivals, recitals, readings, etc. The second was rooted in the humanities and explored Greek American life and heritage within the context of the humanities.

A "Greek Americans in the Workplace" program cover designed by artist Mary Maniatis. Circa 1988. Elaine Thomopoulos collection.

(L-R): Dr. Andrew Kopan and Stanley Rosen speak on "The Historical Development of the Greek Immigrant Work Experience in Illinois," at the Copernicus Foundation. March 20, 1988. John Psiharis collection.

After the "Strains on Ethnic Pride," conference came to a successful conclusion, surpassing the projected goals delineated in the proposal to the Illinois Humanities Council, the door was open for us to submit another grant request. Elaine and I met with Francis Pettis and Ellen Malkovich, the executive director, and grants director for the IHC, and developed a good relationship with them. We were encouraged to submit a proposal that fit their subsequent theme.

After conferring with the CAP Advisory Committee and in response to the IHC's theme of labor and the workplace, GACS proposed a series of lectures throughout the state entitled "Greek-Americans in the Workplace 1888 – 1988." This series featured 15 lectures throughout the state related to this theme. Each lecture was done twice, once within the city of Chicago and the second elsewhere in Illinois. These locations included Springfield, Rockford, Aurora, Oak Lawn, Palos Heights, Elgin, Stone Park, University Park, and Elmhurst. We had higher attendance when the programs were held immediately after a church service and when we co-sponsored with other organizations. Many of these programs were designated "Greek Heritage '87" events. Elaine, Steve, and I wrote the proposal.

According to the project description in the grant proposal submitted to the IHC:

The life of the Greek pioneer immigrant is an amazing story of struggle, sorrow, and agony which ended, however, in victory and triumph. The proposed lecture series will address the struggle of the early Greek pioneers in Illinois as they labored at menial jobs in the '*Xenitia*' (strange land). The program will explore the successes and achievements of their children and grandchildren as they became one of the best-educated and economically successful ethnic groups in America.

The Greek traditionally has been associated with the corner coffee shop, produce wholesaler, restaurant owner, barber, or shoe repair shop owner. This program will highlight the Greek Americans' achievements in these areas, but it will also focus on the valuable contributions they have made to Illinois in the fields of business, law, medicine, technology, and academia. Also highlighted will be their struggles to assimilate into mainstream society while at the same time maintaining a sense of identity as Greek-Americans.

Among the lectures in this series:

- "The Historical Development of the Greek Immigrant Work Experience in Illinois," by Andrew Kopan, Ph.D., with comments by Stanley Rosen at the Copernicus Foundation, Chicago.
- "From Peddlers to Bankers: Greeks in American Fiction," by Alexander Karanikas, Ph.D., at DePaul University and Lincoln Land Community College in Springfield.
- "The Greek Professional and Entrepreneur," by Yorgos Kourvetaris, Ph.D., at DePaul University Stuart Center and Rockford College in Rockford.
- "The Greek Work Ethic," by Yorgos Kourvetaris, Ph.D., with a response by Stanley Rosen at the Copernicus Foundation and St. Sophia Church in Elgin, IL.
- "The Greek American Woman at Work," by Elaine Thomopoulos, Ph.D., at the Copernicus Foundation and Diplomat West in Elmhurst. Bernarda Wong, executive director of the Chinese American Service League, addressed the theme as it related to Chinese women at the Chicago program, and San L. O, program director of Southeast Asia Center, spoke of Southeast Asian women at the Elmhurst lecture.

Dr. Alexander Karanikas speaks on April 17, 1988, during a lecture entitled, "From Peddlers to Bankers: Greeks in American Fiction," part of the "Greek-Americans in the Workplace" series, at Lincoln Land Community College in Springfield, IL. John Psiharis collection.

- "The Greek Work Ethic," by George Christakes Ph.D., with comments by Stanley Rosen at Governor's State University in University Park, IL.
- "A Greek-American Storyteller at Work," by Harry Mark Petrakis at St. Athanasios Greek Orthodox Church, Aurora.
- "Immigrant Academia: Greek Intellectuals in Illinois," by Fotios Litsas, Ph.D. at the Copernicus Foundation and St. Nicholas Church in Oak Lawn.
- "The Greek Worker as Portrayed in Literature," an afternoon of readings and observations by award-winning author Harry Mark Petrakis at the Copernicus Foundation.
- "Peripheral Patriots: The Network of Greeks in Antioch and Libertyville in the 1920s," by Steve Frangos at the David Adler Cultural Center in Libertyville and Lake County Museum, Wauconda.
- "The Greek Work Ethic and Comparison with the Italian Experience," a radio presentation by George Christakes, Ph.D., Elaine Thomopoulos, Ph.D., and Dominic Candeloro, Ph.D. WCGO-AM radio.

"The Role of the Greek-American and Ethnic Woman" program cover designed by artist Mary Maniates. April 28, 1991. Elaine Thomopoulos collection.

Excerpts from the final report for the project, prepared by Elaine and submitted to the IHC:

> The Illinois Humanities Council-sponsored program 'Greek-Americans in the Workplace' was very successful. The program accomplished the objectives as set forth in our proposal. Fifteen lectures and one radio program were presented by eight humanists throughout Illinois, including Chicago, Springfield, Elgin, University Park, Aurora, Wauconda, Palos Hills, Elmhurst, and Rockford.

Attendance was taken at each program. It averaged 28 per lecture. We estimated that we reached over 1,500 people through our lectures and the radio presentation.

Attendance was higher when a church organization co-sponsored the event. Attendance was lower when the lectures were held in colleges outside the city (such as Rockford College in Rockford and Governor's State in University Park) where there was no co-sponsorship by another Greek organization. This is in contrast to the lecture at Lincoln Land Community College which drew over 50 people. This lecture was co-sponsored by AHEPA (a Greek fraternal organization) and the local church, as well as the college.

Each of the lectures (with the exception of the one in Elmhurst) was co-sponsored by either a church, fraternal organization, museum, cultural center, or college. Amongst those organizations co-sponsoring the lecture series were: the Lake County Museum, David Adler Cultural Center, Copernicus Foundation, AHEPA, The Hellenic Society of DePaul University, St. Athanasios Church, St. Sophia's Church, SS. Constantine and Helen Church, Lincolnland College, and AHEPA [sic].

Other organizations such as the Greek Women's University Club and the Illinois Ethnic Consultation assisted in publicizing the lecture series. The ethnic media, local community papers, as well as radio stations such as WCEV-AM, helped by providing free publicity. Volunteers helped in all aspects of the program. They included humanists on the organizing committee as well as those who helped with coordination and publicizing the program. An artist designed the program book. This cooperation contributed to the success of the lecture series.

At each of the lectures, there was lively audience participation for at least a half-hour following the presentation. Especially valuable were the contributions made by respondents Stanley Rosen (to Andrew Kopan and George Christakes' lectures) and San O (who responded to Elaine Thomopoulos' lecture). Many in the audience stressed that they were impressed by the 'combination of the two viewpoints' and 'the comparison between cultures.'

The audiences were asked to fill out a questionnaire after each lecture. According to the responses to the questionnaire they were very satisfied with the lectures. Rating the lectures as excellent were 74 percent, and rating the lectures as very good were 22 percent.

Some of the responses to the question: 'I was most impressed by:'

- 'Enthusiastic presentation, very knowledgeable.'
- 'Valuable information on Greek intellectuals.'
- 'His research/lively presentation.'
- 'Quotes of original poets/translation by early Greek immigrants.'
- 'The interaction of the public and the informed speakers.'
- 'The knowledge of the speakers.'
- 'The diversity of subject matter and the presenter's ability to answer the variety of questions with such frankness.'
- 'Audience participation.'
- 'Informative yet casual and easy presentation.'
- 'The extent of his research.'
- 'Keep it up!'

Other comments were:

- 'Keep up the flow of discussion on relevant topics.'
- 'I was impressed with the organization of GACS.'
- 'Should have more of this.'
- 'The exchange of such knowledge as this meeting provides should be encouraged.'

Feedback from the presenters included the following comments:

- 'It seems to me that the main point of the series was a humanities perspective, (1) because Greek-Americans were treated as individuals as well as a group, (2) because the main point of emphasis was the development of humanistic values and activities in the community and for the group as a whole.'
- 'A humanities perspective was clearly evident as the various speakers spoke on their theme. It was effectively done as portrayed by the high level of audience response and questioning. I was very satisfied in my role as a professional humanist.'
- 'The audience asked a number of questions, so I take it they were not only interested in the program but wanted to learn more.'
- 'As a scholar on Greek American themes, I learned much about the Greeks in the Workplace not known before. This subject has not been previously researched so this new information will be a definite enhancement in my work as a scholar and educator.'

- 'The program allowed me to disseminate and elaborate my views on the issue and has stimulated research directions that I hope to pursue in the future'.

Very encouraging is that the response from this lecture series gave us the impetus to undertake another lecture series program: "Ethnic Leadership and American Values," which has been funded through the Illinois Humanities Council. Also, Lake County Museum has expressed an interest in presenting a temporary exhibit on the Greek-Americans of Lake County, as a direct result of this program. Each session was audio-taped so that the information presented can be used in the future by scholars and be available to the general community.

For the first time in memory, GACS was able to take these outstanding Chicago-based programs to all parts of the State. This is key since communities in other parts of the State all feel a lack of such programs, and feel overshadowed or neglected by Chicago's Greek community. Thus through I.H.C. support, we were able to reach out to them and encourage these locales to become involved.

For the following IHC funding cycle, GACS crafted a proposal addressing the theme of leadership. Elaine, Steve, and I, with help from members of the CAP Advisory Board, crafted a traveling lecture series entitled "Ethnic Identity and American Values: Leadership Development in Illinois," for the 1989-1990 year. Although similar in design to our prior programs, this series incorporated a multi-ethnic component. Each lecture would compare and contrast the Greek American experience vis a vis other ethnic communities to create greater cross-cultural understanding, appreciation, and dialogue. The series culminated with an afternoon of recognition of Greek American and ethnic women.

The project abstract, as submitted to the IHC read in part:

> Under the sponsorship of Greek-American Community Services and with the support of a consortium of ethnic organizations, including the Copernicus Foundation, the Italian Cultural Center, the Ukrainian National Foundation, the Mexican-American Women's Business and Professional Organization, and the American Jewish Committee, 17 humanists will discuss the ethnic experience as it relates to leadership development. This will be accomplished by a series of nineteen forums in which we plan to reach 780 people.
>
> Greek-American Community Services has previously conducted two very successful programs funded by the Illinois Humanities Council. We have been asked by our audiences and

other ethnic groups to build upon our past experiences and to bring together a forum for a multi-ethnic exploration of leadership. In the forum, there will be discussions about mutual concerns such as: What is the interaction between ethnic influences and mainstream values? Why has one ethnic group been able to build a nursing home and not another? How can we best train youth for leadership? How can we band together as coalitions for common goals? Some ethnic communities have been successful in training and assuming leadership and others have not been so successful. Each can learn from the other's successes and failures. The new immigrants can learn from the history of the old immigrants. Also, the general community will learn about the ethnic perspective. We can learn from each other and prepare ourselves for the future. Each forum will be presented twice by the same humanists, once in Chicago and once in cities throughout Illinois, including Stone Park, Springfield, Champaign, University Park, Rockford, Aurora, Belleville, and DeKalb. Audience participation is important; at least 30 minutes at each forum will be allocated to audience discussion.

The papers presented at the forums will be collected, edited, printed, and put on deposit at the Chicago Historical Society, and will be submitted for publication. Also, audiotapes will be put on deposit at the Chicago Historical Society. Selected portions of the forums will be videotaped and arrangements will be made with Community Access to cablecast the program to an audience of 6,000 people. *

*Neither Elaine nor I recall any papers or tapes being given to the Chicago Historical Society or cable broadcasts of any of these events.

The lectures organized by GACS under this grant were:

- "Ethnic Diplomats: New Leadership in America in the 21st Century," with David Roth, Midwest Director, Institute for American Pluralism, American Jewish Committee, with a response by Connie Seals, President C-Bren Communications Corp. It was held in the Chicago office of the Illinois Ethnic Consultation which was part of the American Jewish Committee. This was the inaugural event of the series.
- "A Definition of Leadership and the Exploration of Ethnics as Leaders," presented by Michael Bakalis, Ph.D., with a response by Peter Porr, executive director, Southeast Asia Center. The event, held at DePaul University, was co-sponsored by the Hellenic Society of DePaul University, the Hellenic Professional Society of Illinois, and the Institute of

American Pluralism. Mike also spoke on this topic during a lecture at St. Anthony Church in Springfield.
- "Ethnic Leadership and the Development of the American Labor Movement," by Stanley Rosen, Ph, D., professor of Labor and Industrial Relations, the University of Illinois at Chicago, and James Chiakulas, Director of Region 36, Illinois Education Association. The event was co-sponsored by Montay College and the Institute for American Pluralism and held on the college's Chicago campus.
- "Ethnicity and Patriotism," by George Anastaplo, J.D., at the Copernicus Foundation and Southern Illinois University in Carbondale.
- "Leadership Development in the Polish & Greek Communities," by Helena Lopata with a response by Charles Moskos, Ph.D., at the Copernicus Foundation.
- "Problems of Leadership Development within Chicago's Ukrainian Community," by Myron Kuropas, Ph.D., with a response by Yorgos Kourvetaris. The lecture was held at Immaculate Conception Ukrainian Church in Palatine, Illinois, and Saints Volodymyr and Olha Ukrainian Church, Chicago.
- "The Role of Ethnic Arts, Youth Programs and Leadership," by Margie McLain, Executive Director of Urban Traditions, at Assumption Greek Orthodox Church in East Moline Illinois, and DePaul University in Chicago.
- "Leadership in the Italian Community; The Scalabrini Order" by Dominic Candeloro, Ph.D., and the "Failure of the Greek Community to Build a Hospital," by George Christakes, Ph.D. The program was held in the GACS center at Alvernia Place and the Italian Cultural Center in Stone Park.
- "Ethnic Leadership and the Development of the American Labor Movement," by Stanley Rosen, Ph.D., professor of Labor and Industrial Relations, the University of Illinois at Chicago with responses from James Chiakulas, director of Region 36, Illinois Education Association, and Fred Gardaphe, a Ph. D. student at the University of Illinois in Chicago and active in the Italian community. The program was held at the Italian Cultural Center and was preceded by a delicious Italian dinner and a tour of their center and museum which included an exhibit about the Italians in Chicago.
- "A Celebration of the Greek-American & Ethnic Woman," moderated by Evangeline Gouletas, featured Connie Callinicos, author of *American Aphrodite*, Louise Kerr, Ph.D.,

a professor at the University of Illinois at Chicago and a historian of the Mexican community in Chicago, and Bernarda Wong, a founding member and executive director of the Chinese American Service League (CASL). Held at DePaul University, the event was well attended.

A press release prepared by the Illinois Ethnic Consultation promoting the inaugural lecture, "Ethnic Diplomats: New Leadership for America in the 21st Century," described David Roth's talk:

> David will discuss new leadership trends in ethnic and racial communities and the meaning of those trends for Illinois and the nation. He will cite examples of coalitionally-minded ethnic leaders who are highly motivated to play diplomatic roles. Such leaders establish and maintain relations with other communal groups and with organizations and leaders in the civic mainstream. For this reason, he refers to them as 'Ethnic Diplomats.'
>
> Most Ethnic Diplomats pursue careers in business, government, or the professions and many are active in civic affairs. They bring compassionate values from their community into a society that is highly bureaucratic and sometimes overly rigid in its response to human needs. In return, they take back to their communities, skills in using the law to combat discrimination, the social sciences to measure and analyze bigotry, and the arts and humanities to tell powerful personal stories of struggles against injustice.

A final grant report to the IHC detailed, in part, the following accomplishments for this project:

> The program accomplished the objectives as set forth in the proposal. Fifteen lectures were presented by twenty speakers throughout Illinois, including Chicago, Carbondale, Springfield, Stone Park, and Palatine.
>
> Attendance was taken at each program. It averaged 34 per lecture. We estimated that overall, the program reached 750 people. Attendance was higher when a church or organization co-sponsored the event. Attendance was lower at programs held during the winter months or at out-of-town locations (i.e. Carbondale and Springfield).
>
> At each of the lectures, there was lively audience participation and discussion for at least a half-hour following the presentation. Likewise, significant one-to-one and small group discussions with the speakers occurred during the post-event reception. These discussion periods were especially relevant

(L-R): Katherine Lolagos Angee, Nick Festos, and Angelo Angee at a Heritage Awards dinner. Date unknown. John Psiharis collection.

since most of the lectures provided multi-ethnic or multi-cultural perspectives. Thus they contributed to a better understanding and appreciation of the various groups.

The audiences were asked to fill out a questionnaire after each lecture. According to the responses to the questionnaire, they were satisfied with the lectures. Rating the lectures as outstanding were 49 percent, rating the lectures as very good were 42 percent, and rating the lectures as good were 9 percent.

Some of the responses to the question: 'I was most impressed by:'

- 'The high spots were touched as I actually lived by myself as the first American born of Greek illiterate parents.'
- 'The interesting stories and information on other countries.'
- 'General acceptance of ethnic groups.'
- 'Wide variety of ethnic experiences.'
- 'Depth of information.'
- 'Very interesting topic. Kept my interest.'
- 'The mutual cooperation and respect.'
- 'The frankness and knowledge of the Greek Community.'
- 'All the statements are true to everyday life. As the only woman parish council member of my church, many of Dr. Topping's comments hit home.'
- 'The intelligent presentations of both speakers not only in the historical perspective but articulating the present-day dilemma accurately.'
- 'The program was well organized.'
- 'It was high quality all the way around.'
- 'I very much enjoyed the informal discussion following the lecture.'

- 'Stimulating discussion.'

There were few responses to the question, 'I was least impressed by:' Amongst these responses were:

- 'It could have been a little longer.'
- 'I wish more young people were here to listen.'
- 'Wish there was no scheduling conflict with other affairs going on at the same time.'
- 'The Greek communities lack the interest in keeping up with tradition. Especially the 20-40-year-olds. Can you enhance that?'
- 'Schedule during months where turnout would be better.'
- 'Post signs where lectures take place.'
- 'Very important issues on future cooperation for the success of the Greek community were discussed.'
- 'Continue to have these programs. More! More!'
- 'Such discussions are most welcome.'
- 'The problems are there, but not easy to solve. But discussion may help to find some happy solutions.'
- 'Such lectures are very profitable and they help to solve a lot of our problems, but there is a lot of difference between ethnic problems of descendants of free nations and those of occupied nations.'
- 'Let's do it again.'
- 'I hope we will see more and find ways to make changes in our institutions.'
- 'In retrospect – the programs presented by GACS this past year have been timely and interesting – I hope the future programs will continue to be supported by the I.H.C and the N.E for H.'
- 'We need to keep the type of people who attend this type of lecture in touch. I've been searching for you for a while. I made several acquaintances and phone number exchanges.'

We strongly believe that this lecture series met the goals it set out to achieve. The lectures were meant to deliver a multi-ethnic perspective on issues related to ethnic leadership development and offered audiences a rare and unique understanding/appreciation of cultures. Ethnic groups represented in this series included: South East Asians, Jews, Blacks, Polish, Ukrainian, Hispanic, Chinese, and Italian. We believe that these lectures have helped in some way to bring together these diverse groups, exchange ideas, learn from each other, and discuss the future together. The relationships GACS has developed with several of the ethnic organizations will be benefiting us for years to come.

I recall when Drs. Candeloro and Christakes spoke on the Italian community's success in building a nursing home (Villa Scalabrini) and the Greek community's (up to that point) failure to build a nursing home. One lecture was held at GACS and the second was held at the Italian Cultural Center, in Stone Park complete with a spaghetti dinner in their basement before the event. The Center was located in a former Catholic convent. I'll always remember the detailed scale model of the Vatican that occupied most of the second floor and an impressive exhibit on the history of the Italians in Chicago that was on display.

Through Elaine's efforts, a good relationship was forged between GACS and the Italian Cultural Center that resulted in several different collaborations in the coming years. Angelo Angee was the Center's vice president and his wife Katherine (Lolagos) was secretary. Angelo had a colorful, outgoing, and expansive personality and we became friends. In some ways, he reminded me of Rodney Dangerfield. He was a developer who among his projects had renovated the Golden Tiara Bingo Hall on Cicero Avenue near Belmont. Angelo also produced an educational film and a subsequent book on the early history of the United States.

The Angees were masters at event planning. Each year they hosted a Christmas party that started at a Greektown restaurant for dinner. Many different entrees and sides were served family style. Next, we boarded a chartered trolley bus to go to an Italian restaurant in Little Italy for dessert and coffee. Then back on the bus for a tour of downtown Christmas decorations. After that, a walk down State Street to Marshall Field's, to view their window displays and sing carols, before boarding the bus for a ride around the city to look at Christmas decorations, while enjoying champagne and more caroling. We then returned to the original restaurant for a cup of Greek coffee and to retrieve our cars. About 50 people, give or take, attended these annual parties including John Rassogianis, Toni Panos, Nick Festos, George Bakos, and John Sandors. We paid a fixed price and the Angees took care of the arrangements while creating some entertaining and memorable evenings.

O Cosmos: **The Private Lives and Public Celebrations of the Greeks in Illinois**

The final Illinois Humanities Council grant GACS applied for was different from those of the past. This endeavor envisioned a traveling museum exhibit chronicling the Greek experience in Illinois. Entitled, "*O Cosmos: The Private Lives and Public Celebrations of the Greeks in Illinois from 1880 to 1990*," it involved the creation of a 26-panel exhibit that would be displayed at various locations throughout the state along with a concurrent distinguished lecture series addressing the overarching themes of the exhibit.

Although we had a track record for producing high-quality programming through our grants from the Illinois Humanities Council and had mastered the statewide lecture series format, we had never attempted to create a museum exhibition, especially one that would travel throughout the state.

With the help of the CAP Advisory Committee, GACS crafted a proposal that incorporated an exhibit that would travel the state for two years. In addition to research, this project involved the physical construction of the exhibit as well as coordinating logistics such as shipping for a statewide exhibition. A series of lectures related to the exhibit were also planned

Elaine was the project director while Steve Frangos served as a primary grant writer and principal researcher. Steve, whose father owned a construction business in the Grayslake area, handled the construction of the wooden frame and structure as well as preparing the panels for mounting. He wrote most of the labels describing the photos and their context within the overall theme.

The IHC grant application explained the panel themes in this way:

> Each of the four time periods in the exhibition is itself composed of four topical areas. The recurring themes of the exhibition are, in this fashion, extended and enlarged over the sweep of time Greeks have lived in Illinois.
>
> 1. **Public Events: Images Offered**
>   This group of panels will present and analyze the public presentations that Greeks offered as emblematic of themselves. How much was true and how much processed will be presented. Still, it should be noted that after a period of time, the distinctions began to get blurred even for the Greeks. Sometimes the constructed images became the only reality later generations would know.
>
>   In the realms of foreign politics, and issues involving social work projects, Greeks reveal a sophistication that was born out of their overseas experiences and extensive participation in the era's American labor movement.
>
> 2. **Private Life**
>   There were settings or occasions where the Greeks could share their true sense and sensibilities without filtering them through the American environment around them. These included the home, the nuclear or extended family, the extensive but now largely forgotten bachelor groups, the regional societies, and eventually elaborate and exclusive social groups based on economic standing.
>
> 3. **Classic Greek-American: The Arts and the Greek Muse**
>   The life Greeks experienced in America was the subject of dramas, comedy records, *ksenithia* newspaper stories, radio programs, literature, dance performances, musical

reviews, painting, and even the puppet tradition known as *Karagiozis*.

The Greeks used art (and continue to use it) as a means to define and address their life in Illinois. The panels in this category will present these genres, performances, and the artists who offered these interpretations to the community.

4. **Observers Observed**

Who were the American researchers or reporters on the Greeks in Illinois? How did these individuals describe the Greeks? How can we, from our vantage point in history, see the hidden agendas, and the implicit ideological stance, of these individuals? The Greeks were aware they were being studied. The Greeks very often used these researchers for their own ends. Manipulating these outsiders by providing them with specific information. How all this came about will be discussed in this panel.

The period themes were:

1886 – 1915 *Paroika*: The Colony Begins

In 1886, when the first 3,000 Greek men and youths arrived in Chicago they came as temporary workers, intent on returning to Greece as soon as their fortunes were made. When did the Greek laborer in America become an immigrant rather than a temporary worker? Politics in the Balkans and labor battles dominated the attention of the young men. Massive public demonstrations in Chicago by Greeks in 1897 and para-military training on the grounds of Hull House frightened Americans across the country.

The Greeks did not see themselves as immigrants. For centuries Greeks had worked throughout the Ottoman Empire, Europe, North Africa, and the Middle East only to return eventually to their village of birth. A song genre called *Ksenithia* e.g. literally 'the strange land' grew out of this out-migration. The diaspora, e.g. the scattering, as in the scattering of seeds, is how many of these migrant workers looked at and referred to as the scattered colonies of Greeks laboring in the *ksenithia*. What many American scholars saw as immigrants were a people who saw themselves as temporary sojourners with a long history of colonies across the world.

The social networks that are used by the Greeks in Illinois resemble those that evolved over the centuries-by earlier Greek laborers in Europe, the Middle East, across the continent of Africa, and elsewhere. In the very first years of the Greeks arriving in massive waves in Illinois, they begin to establish themselves, often, in the most rural of communities. None of this is even suspected for a moment by the Americans who only 'see' foreigners.

2. 1915-1929 Diaspora: 'Greek Town' in Chicago

Once a majority of the Greeks in Illinois took the position that their stay in America was long-term and/or permanent, they sought to re-create their society and culture in the towns and prairies of Illinois. This active formation and perpetuation of Greek society and culture found expression through a number of avenues.

While it is the establishment of churches throughout Illinois; that is today often thought to be the first priority of an "immigrant" community's agenda, it was only one element of a wider program of action. Chicago is the location for a series of firsts in Greek publications: the first history book, the first poetry book, the first national magazine, and so on. The establishment of Greek schools, the availability of mail-order catalogues written in Greek (but for a whole array of materials from America and around the world), and the appearance of business directories and guidebooks document an awareness about the world that the Americans never suspected. From virtually the moment of their arrival in Illinois, Greeks were attuned to developing themselves, their community, and a competitive business edge through what we would call today, media resources. This was something that even later historians have failed to note.

Greeks were in touch with the wider world through other media forms. Live entertainment in the forms of record companies, drama troupes, and nightclubs abounded everywhere within the community. The Chicago Greek community was recognized as a key location in the worldwide network of Greek entertainment clubs. The major role the Chicago Greeks played as managers and owners of American entertainment in the forms of Taxi Dance Halls, Vaudeville Houses, and movie theaters is glossed over in most historical accounts of Illinois. How the skills and business connections of the Greek entertainment scene helped the Greek managers/owners of strictly "American" entertainment will be explored. How all these social and cultural forms are themselves based on experiences and models developed over the long period of *Turkokratia* or the rule of the Greeks by the Ottoman Empire is kept from Americans. The development in public of a distinctly Greek identity (that is distinct from all other Balkan cultures) is intense.

3. 1929-1956 *Kinotis*: The Passage of Identity

The unintended consequence of the 1922-1924 Immigration Quotas Act was the development of a uniquely American-Greek society and culture, unlike any other diaspora community in the world. The birth of children to immigrants, their life in America, and World War II broadly outline the events of this period. In the late 1940s early 1950s community leadership slowly but inevitably passed from the immigrant generation to their American-born children.

Still, the sojourn in America was never fully accepted. From the late 1920s to just before World War II Greeks took extended trips back to Greece. Within the 1930s, trips back to Greece became a virtual rage in the community. Every family that could afford the trip, and many who really couldn't, returned to their villages. The thought even then was maybe, just maybe, they would repatriate. Commercial records of the period provide us today with the Greek's realization that this was impossible.

1. 1956-1990: *Patridha*: The Many Ways of Being Greek

The Search for Alexander Exhibition, the ongoing political efforts directed at Cyprus, and the church festival are the public personas self-stressed by the Greek-American establishment. What this same group is anxious to downplay at every opportunity is the ongoing clash of identities among the present-day Greeks in Illinois. These unending conflicts are not simply between the American-born and the recent immigrants but also along sharply defined social class distinctions.

With new immigration from Greece dropping off in the 1980s, the community is once again entering an era similar to the post-1922 Immigration Quota period. Social life and events have grown. Still, there are fewer arenas where the various types of persons who call themselves Greek meet. Even church parishes have achieved specific social, economic, and cultural forms that mark them as belonging to one or another of these distinct subgroups.

The thirtysomething generation, born in America or born in Greece, seems to cut across all these lines of different clusters of Greeks, unlike any other subgroup in Greek American history. Where these intra-community distinctions are drawn, what are the specific issues keeping the groups apart, and what may be the eventual outcome will be surveyed in this final group of panels.

An appeal for financial support to supplement the IHC grant, written by Theoni "Sonia" Arvanitis and signed by Doctors Bakalis and Kioutas, was sent to select businesses and organizations in November 1992. It read in part:

> The ancient Athenians made a pledge, a covenant, that was as follows:
>
>> 'We will strive to quicken our sense of civic duty…we will transmit this country greater, better, stronger, prouder, and more beautiful than it was transmitted to us.'
>
> Let us as Greek Americans make a similar pledge to preserve and transmit our heritage to future generations 'greater, better, stronger, prouder, and more beautiful than it was transmitted to us.' And here is how you can make this pledge a reality.
>
> The Greek-American Community Services is proud to present a story told in photographs of our parents, aunts, uncles, *yiayiathes* and *papoulides,* and great-grandparents. It is a historic exhibit that will be displayed in locations throughout the state. The title of this traveling museum is, 'O Cosmos: Public Celebrations and the Private Lives of Greeks in Illinois.'
>
> This is a magnificent opportunity to retain a heritage for our children and grandchildren that will inspire and educate them. It will be a testimony for generations to follow and a living memorial to those before us who worked so hard so that we may lead better lives.

We invite you to be a participant in this most important effort of our OMOGENIA, by considering a donation of $250 or $500.

Your contribution can be in honor of living parents or in memory of beloved grandparents, or other loved ones who left their legacy of our heritage to you.

As a contributor, your name (or your organization's name) will be engraved on a special panel of the display, becoming a permanent part of the exhibit. In addition, you will be among our honored guests during the opening day ceremonies, which will be videotaped.

Mr. Steve Frangos tells us that he got the idea for the title from the common expression among Greeks '*Ti the Lei oh Cosmos.*' Indeed, what will everyone say about our heritage in years to come? Unless we work hard to preserve and cherish what our parents have transmitted to us, there may be little to say!

We are proud recipients of a civilization and culture that has influenced the world. Help us to continue this tradition with your $250 or $500 contribution today.

The exhibit included photos and recollections highlighting the evolution of the Greek community in Illinois including:

- A photo of Georgia Bitzis Pooley and her family. They were the first Greek family to settle in Illinois in 1885.
- A panel entitled "Vlasia Remembered" describes marriage traditions within Greek immigrant households including picture brides and dowries. Death photographs are also explored, all related to a rural Greek village named Vlasia.
- A playbill and photo of Greek immigrant children performing the *Return of Odysseus* in the Hull House Auditorium at the corner of Polk and Halsted in 1899. The playbill states that the play is performed by "Natives of Greece Living in Chicago."
- A rare photo of a 1917-1918 U.S. Savings Bond Drive to raise money for World War I that was organized by Jane Addams at Hull House with the help of young Greeks who attended Hull House.
- A panel of family photographs donated by John Rassogianis that depicted his father and uncles (Constantine, Alex, and George) in Alex's Sweet Shop, their Berwyn, Illinois candy store, circa the 1930s, along with a photo of handmade chocolate lambs made for Greek Easter. There were advertisements for the "Two in One Ice Cream Freezer" and

St. Louis Ice Cream Parlor in Chicago, also owned by John's family.
- A photo of an early 78-record by the Elliopoulos Brothers recorded in Chicago at the turn of the century.
- A panel describing the participation of Greek Americans in Chicago's World Fair includes a photo of a *Chicago Sun-Times* article entitled "A Flying Trip Through Greece – It's Around the Corner."

Below are the panel labels related to the *Heartland of Hellenism* exhibit that Steve Frangos provided from his collection. We do not know if this is the final version or an earlier draft. We were not able to locate any of the exhibit's photos, Steve had captions for some of the pictures that were part of the exhibit and I have included them here. Although this was part of the larger *O Cosmos* exhibition, we do not have any labels beyond Heartland. At least four panels with several pictures and labels on each panel are missing. Given the nature of the content, and that the exhibit is no longer around, I have included what we do have as a means of preserving this history to the extent possible.

The Heartland of Hellenism
The Greeks in Illinois 1886-1924

Introduction

The following museum labels are those of the exhibition entitled: 'The Heartland of Hellenism: The Greeks in Illinois 1886-1924.' This independent exhibition discusses the lives of individual Greek Americans as they exemplify generally accepted historical events known to have occurred for the community at large.

The Heartland exhibition is scheduled to appear at various locations in the downtown area of Chicago, Illinois.

Panel 1: Pioneers

Sailing up the Mississippi and Chicago rivers, Greek travelers first came to Illinois in the early 1840s. As ordinary traders and ship captains, these pioneers were just a few scattered figures in the bustling crowds even then found along the Illinois river towns and in the growing port traffic around Fort Dearborn.

The first panel of the "Heartland of Hellenism: The Greeks in Illinois 1886-1950" exhibit. Top: unknown. Middle: Peter and Georgia Pooley. Bottom: Christos Tsakonas. Circa 1994. Photo by John Rassogianis. John Psiharis collection.

One of these early Greek pioneers was Captain Nicholas Peppas who eventually returned in 1857 to settle permanently in Chicago. Captain Peppas lived on Kinzie Street for more than fifty years and lived to see the massive waves of Greek immigrants arrive in the 1870s and 1880s and form their own community around him. A close friend of Captain Nick was Frank Brown, whose name in Greek was Fotis Kotakis, a barber for many years in Chicago who came from the Greek island of Samos in 1859.

Another of the first pioneers was Constantine Mitchell (Michalopoulos), a captured Confederate soldier. Mitchell was held prisoner by the Union Army in Chicago and after the Civil War decided to settle permanently in Illinois. In the midst of the Civil War, another Greek "Uncle" (or in Greek Barba) Thomas Combiths, a tailor, moved to Chicago. In 1869, his son Frank Combiths was the first child born of a Greek immigrant father in Illinois. Frank Combith's mother was not of Greek descent and there were no Greek women in the entire Midwest for many years.

The First Family

In 1885 the first Greek couple established their home in Illinois. Peter Pooley (Panayotis Poulis), a ship captain much impressed by the development in Illinois, returned to his native island of Corfu, Greece, and married Georgia Bitzi. By 1886, Georgia Bitzi Pooley, a well-educated and dynamic woman, organized the Greco-Slavic Brotherhood for the purpose of founding a common house of worship.

Panel 2: Tsakonas and the Tsintzinians
Christos Tsakonas (1848-1909) called the 'Columbus of the Spartans' arrived in Chicago in 1872 soon after the Chicago Fire. Christos Tsakonas was born in Tsintzina, a secluded mountain village in the very heart of the Parnon mountain range northeast of Sparta. Tsakonas is a singular figure in the history of Greeks in Illinois. It was through the offices of Christos Tsakonas that directly or indirectly over 1,000 young Spartans arrived in Illinois during the late 1870s and early 1880s. Furthermore, these first massive waves of Greek immigrants to Illinois were almost exclusively from the village of Tsintzina.
United States Immigration forms were not prepared for the rural Greek perspective of being from the single village of Tsintzina when they wrote down as 'village of origin' the names of two villages in the Evrotas valley: Goritsa and Zoupena.

Residency patterns that are a consequence of the transhumant lifestyle in the mountainous parts of the Greek mainland result in double or multiple houses all owned by the same family. During the movement of flocks in the summer the family moves to the high mountain pastures and to the house and work buildings used during this season of the year. In the winter months, the flocks and their shepherds move to the lower winter villages. This practice of multiple residences is called <u>diplokatoikia.</u> Tsintzina, situated as it is high up in the Parnon mountains, was even in Christos Tsakonas' time, principally occupied only during the summer months. Goritsa and Zoupena down in the Evrotas Valley were winter villages.

The U.S. immigration forms precluded any of the social conditions and seasonal residency patterns traditional to a transhumant way of life. Consequently, the chain migration of the Tsintzians into Illinois in the 1870s and 1880s was only recently recognized by Greek-American historians.

The historical contributions of Christos Tsakonas and his fellow Tsintzinians in Illinois are profound. Therapnon, the first Greek society in Chicago, was composed principally of Tsinztzinians. Other Greeks mentioned in the membership rosters when not from Tsintzina were from the same region where this village is located, Arcadia. These Greek immigrants were most notably from the villages of Vasaras, Krysapha, Agriannos, Geraki, Arachova, and Vamvachou. In 1891, it was the Therapnon that provided the leadership necessary for the establishment of Illinois' first Greek Orthodox church, Holy Trinity.

Tsakonas and his Tsintzinians also offered a powerful example of cooperative business management not lost upon the subsequent waves of Greek immigrants to Illinois. Through complex and wide-ranging business networks the Tsintzinians began a string of wholesale fruit and candy stores that eventually extended down from Milwaukee, across Chicago, and continued through Ohio into western Pennsylvania.

Up to that time, in no other line of business were Greeks better established or more recognizable to the general American public than the confectionery trade. By the 1920s, there were more than 300 Greek-owned candy and ice cream parlors in Chicago alone.

Panel 3: The Return of Odysseus

The mid to late 1890s were a difficult period for Greek immigrants in Illinois. In 1893 at the Columbian World Exposition, the Streets of Constantinople diorama presented Greeks as mere street vendors in the Ottoman Empire. National newspaper publicity had reported the controversies over the belly dancing at the Chicago Fair and many Americans associated the new immigrants from southeast Europe, the Greeks included, with this scandalous oriental dancing. These events and the negative responses they daily engendered grated on the pride of the Greek immigrants.

In 1897, the year of the brief Greco-Turkish War, Greeks demonstrated in a large rally and parade on Clark Street that frankly upset the majority of Chicagoans. 'Where do the loyalties of the Greek immigrants lie,' writers of the day asked, 'with America or their country of origin?'

An unexpected problem from the Greek immigrant's perspective was that the average citizen in Illinois did not know anything about Greece let alone its classical heritage. Many accounts from the 1890s and early 1900s exist of the Greek immigrants striving to educate the American public about the glories of Classical Greece. The Greeks quickly concluded to use their cultural heritage for political ends. Across the nation there soon developed, in virtually every Greek community, sustained efforts to educate the wider American society not only about Ancient Greece but how the foreigner selling fruit, produce, and penny candy was the direct descendant of this celebrated people.

In Illinois, this agenda found expression on December 7, 1899, when the Greek immigrants presented the classical Greek tragedy, *The Return of Odysseus* at the Hull House Theater. Not only was this the first dramatic production at the Hull House Theater, but the play was also a resounding success. *The Return of Odysseus* received such favorable reviews it proved to be the first unreservedly positively publicly held event by the Greek immigrants of Chicago.

Lorado Taft, a member of the audience on the opening night, made these observations in the *Daily Record* on December 13th.

'The thought which came over and over again in every mind was: These are the real sons of Hellas chanting songs of their ancestors, enacting the lives of thousands of years ago. There is a background for you! How noble it made these fruit merchants for the nonce; what distinction it gave them! They seemed to feel that they had come into their own. They were set right at last in our eyes...The sons of Princes, they had known their heritage all the time; it was our ignorance which had belittled them. And they waited.

The feeling which these humble proud fellow citizens of ours put into the play was at the same time their tribute to a noble ancestry and a plea for respect. Those who saw them on that stage will never think of them again in quite the same way as before...'

A panel from the "Heartland of Hellenism: Greeks in Illinois 1886-1950" exhibit. At top is a photo of the *Return of Odysseus*, play. In the middle is the playbill. On the bottom, the "Liberty War Bond" rally. Circa 1994. Photo by John Rassogianis. John Psiharis collection.

Panel 4: The Families of Men
Before 1930, the vast majority of Greek "families" in Illinois, as in the rest of America, were groupings of male relatives. Fathers and sons, groups of brothers, cousins, men joined by spiritual kinship (*koumbaroi*), and even men from the same village or district in Greece, formed communal households throughout Illinois. Jokes and long-involved stories are still told of these all-male households.

Undoubtedly the rapid rise of Greeks in a number of businesses was due to the strict economy of their communal lifestyle. In Illinois, Greek immigrants soon dominated a whole range of businesses such as fruit and vegetable stores, candy and ice cream parlors, vaudeville houses and movie theaters, shoe-shine parlors, and eventually restaurants. Tight kinship networks in Illinois dovetailed into the new business networks across the state. Brothers who individually owned a number of stores would buy collectively from wholesalers and so underprice their competitors.

The extent of the collective efforts of rural Greek businessmen has long been overlooked. One example would be the many groups or confederations of Greeks in the grocery store business who regularly and collectively purchased huge shipments of canned goods and produce.

As representatives of these all-male family groups, we can cite the experiences of the four Rapanos brothers. The Rapanos family came from the remote mountain village of Planetarou in the Kalavryta region of the northern Peloponnesus. In 1905, Nickolaos Rapanos sold his entire flock of three hundred goats to pay the passage money to America for his oldest son, thirteen-year-old Athanasios. For the next fifteen years, by pooling money Athanasios sent from Illinois with whatever he could raise in the village, Nickolaos would travel back and forth from Planetarou to Chicago. During each one of these extended trips to America, he brought another son to work with Athanasios.

By 1918, Nickolaos and all four of his sons were selling fruits and vegetables from horse-drawn wagons. Sometime between 1920 and 1921, the family had both a storefront grocery store and two teams of wagons. This particular family was no different than many others in Illinois during this era. All five men lived in a two-room apartment on Dewey Street with their horses stabled nearby.

With twelve-hour workdays and five sisters to dower back in the village, tensions ran high. Fistfights were far from infrequent. Soon every one of the brothers had a store. The four brothers purchased their fruit and produce collectively for many years. Whatever disagreements they had privately, in public, as far as the American consumer could see, they each appeared to be no more than another smiling Greek selling produce.

Panel 5: 1917-1918 Liberty War Bond Rally
Few Greek Americans of the post-war generations are aware that the pioneer Greek immigrants were among America's most despised minorities. Newspapers across America carried stories of the newly arriving Greeks as scabs and strikebreakers who frequently resorted to violence as a means to settle public and private disputes. Greeks quickly sought ways to alter the American public's perspectives of their actions.

Here we see the 1918-1919 Liberty War Bond Drive Rally sponsored by the Greeks of Chicago. Rallies such as this one were a mixture of sincere appreciation for all that the Greek immigrants had gained in America along with a desire to have their accomplishments and the value of their traditional culture recognized.

To be 'foreign' does not mean an individual simply speaks another language. The differences in basic beliefs and values are what separate one group from another. The Greek perception that if you are aligned with a powerful group you share in their collective prestige is diametrically opposed to American values and sensibilities. From the American perspective, an individual is to be judged by their personal accomplishments and character.

Greeks were truly perplexed when the Americans did not alter their daily interactions with them after all the much-publicized rallies and parades. It was many years before the Greeks came to recognize that the pride they felt in their discussions of Ancient Greece while weighing bananas for their customers, would be so misunderstood. The public rallies and the elaborate interiors of grocery stores, shoe-shine parlors, and candy stores, along with all the talk of Socrates and Aristotle, were more than irksome to many Americans, it was often laughable.

Panel 6: Death Photographs
The majority of Greeks who came to America in the 1890 to 1924 era envisioned their journey to be of only a short duration. The intention expressed was to work in America just long enough to pay for a sister's dowry or earn enough money for a grove of olive trees and then return home to their village. Out-migration for seasonal or temporary work abroad was then, as now, a centuries-old tradition for Greeks. The *ksenithia,* literally the foreign lands, is so much a part of the Greek historical experience that it permeates all aspects of the culture and society. In hard economic terms, 'Remittances

from Abroad' have always played a decisive role in the economic development of the modern Greek nation-state.

Much is made of the economic advantages that Greeks found when they arrived in the United States. The consensus of most published accounts attributes the decision by the Greek immigrants to make America their permanent home as a pragmatic response to obviously superior economic conditions. These speculations about 'objective' economic motives address none of the emotional realities these young men experienced far from family, home, and country.

In strictly emotional terms, the 1918 Spanish Flu Epidemic which swept throughout the Balkans was especially devastating for many Greeks in Illinois. Entire families, and even whole neighborhoods in the more remote villages, were wiped out by the epidemic. Envelopes edged in black, the traditional sign that the enclosed message spoke of death, streamed into Illinois. With no one to go back to, or at the very least a beloved mother or sister was taken by the plague---some men could simply never go back.

Since 1839, with the introduction of photography in Greece, photographs taken at funerals have served as public documents of these solemn events. Such photographs were often sent to families working abroad. At times of massive catastrophes, such as the 1918 Spanish Flu Epidemic, it was impossible to take such photographs. The sister, mother, and first cousin of one Greek immigrant to Chicago, Zafiri Psychios, are shown in this circa. 1917 photograph taken just outside of the family's home in the rural mountain village of Vlasia in the Kalavryta region of the Peloponnesus. These people are Olga Psychios, Theodora Psychios, and Theodore Baroutis. Between the 18th and the 24th of November 1918, all three individuals died of the Spanish Flu.

This image eventually served as a death photograph with three crosses in pencil drawn above the figures and the dates of their deaths written in ink at the bottom. A much-treasured document, the original photograph reflects the changing emotional responses of its owner to those three deaths in 1918. As the years went by, the three penciled crosses were erased. And when the pain of a beloved sister's death was finally accepted, the date of her death was erased as well. Zafiri always associated this photograph with the fact that he grew hollyhocks in his garden in Rogers Park on Chicago's far north side. Zafiri said it reminded him of the flowers near his family home that his mother and sister always grew.

Panel 7: The Greek Record Company of Chicago, Illinois
In the early 1920s, the very first record company in America owned and operated exclusively by Greek immigrants, The Greek Record

A panel from the "Heartland of Hellenism: Greeks in Illinois from 1886-1950" exhibit. Top: Needlework created by Zafiris Psychios. Middle right: A Greek Record Company of Chicago recording of the Elliopoulos Bros. Middle left: Christos Saramantis and his family in a 1903 photograph. Bottom: The family of Zafiris Psychios, circa 1917. Circa 1994. Photo by John Rassogianis. John Psiharis collection.

Company began to issue a long and distinguished catalog of traditional Greek music. The founders of this famed record label were the two immigrant musicians George Grachis, a violinist, and Spiro Stamos who played the *cymbalon,* which is a traditional Greek stringed instrument similar to an American hammer dulcimer.

Sotiri (Sam) Chianis, the noted musicologist (and a recognized master Santouri player in his own right) observes that the Greek Record Company of Chicago *'...quickly earned a national reputation by featuring prominent folk artists of the era. In addition to Stamos and Grachis, the artists included Amalia (vocal), the singer A. Katsanis (better known by his nickname Mourmouris), Angellos Stamos (vocal), Konstantine Patsios (vocal), Marikia Papagika (vocal), Epaminondas Asimakopoulos (vocal and laouto), Harilaos Papadakis (vocal and Cretan Lyra), and the folk clarinetists Nick Relias and Konstantine Fillis'*

Early in the 1920s *Rast Taxim, To Hanoumeko, Helleniki Rapsodia, Kalamatiano Horos,* and other enormously popular dance records were recorded by the same *compania* featuring George Grachis on violin, Spiro Stamos on *cymbalon,* and Angellos K. Stamos on vocals (c.f. Greek Record Company 513 A/B, Greek Record Company 512 A, and Greek Record Company 514 A).

Panel 8: Greek Muses in America
Introduction

The very moment the young Greek men stepped into Illinois, all the traditional arts of Greek culture and society arrived with these new immigrant laborers. Music, dancing, foodways, icon painting, needlework, wood carving, and a host of other expressive forms were a daily part of the immigrants' new lives. Fueled by the experience of a new way of life in America, many of the traditional arts saw a unique fusion where the rural folk arts were presented and performed in an original Greek-American fashion. Still, each piece of artwork or performance must be approached cautiously. To the untrained eye, what may at first appear to be influenced by the new life in America, is a traditional Greek way of expression.

Vlasia Remembered
The needlework artistry of men is often forgotten in accounts of Greek fabric art in America. This is especially curious since few Greek women were even in America, let alone Illinois, until the 1920s. This splendid example of Greek-American embroidery was completed in 1915 by Zafiris Y. Psychios. Zafiri was born in the mountain village of Vlasia in the region of Kalavryta in the northern Peloponnesus. Zafira came to the United States of America in 1912 at the age of seventeen.

The incorporation of a photograph with embroidery is a design style that evolved out of rural Greek villages. With the introduction of photography into Greece in early February 1839, the villagers were quick to include these new images into their existing artistic creations. Photographs with surrounding embroidery along with elaborate beadwork can be found throughout Greece and in Greek communities around the world.

In this particular photo-embroidery piece we see Zafiri celebrating his continued identification with his home village. What must be obvious to the attentive viewer is the close compositional similarity between a photo-embroidery such as this one, and two other photograph genres seen in this exhibition: the oval plate photographs and the composite photographs.

Panel 9: Composite Photographs and Family Portraits
Countless Greek immigrants were separated from their families for years. Many men never saw any of their families again. In their years of toil in Illinois, some men could simply never accept that this temporary sojourn to Illinois might last a lifetime. In Greek culture, there is no separation between action and belief. The Greek folk saying most often associated with this strongly held point of view is "How can you know what another [person] is thinking?" What a person does is, in fact, what he or she believes. Intentions separate from action are meaningless.

This straightforward belief saw one form of expression in America with the widespread use of composite photography. A simple procedure for any studio photographer was the juxtaposition of any two photographs that could then be photographed as a single image. These composite photographs, as integrated balanced images, vary according to the original photographs and the skill of the studio photographer involved. Sometimes it is difficult to tell a finely worked composite photograph from a carefully orchestrated studio portrait. At other times the crudity of the collected photographs borders on the comical.

The desire for family, its public display, and the denial that any separation was a permanent condition can be seen in these commonly found composite photographs. Christos Saramantis, one of the original founders of Holy Trinity Greek Orthodox Church in Chicago, can be seen in this circa 1903 composite photograph with members of his family back in Greece.

Panel 10: The Greek Heritage in Rural Illinois
The experiences of Greek immigrants and their families in rural Illinois have yet to see inclusion in the historical accounts of ethnic groups in the state. The history of Greeks in Illinois is presented as

an urban experience focusing almost exclusively on Chicago. Demographically the greatest concentration of Greek immigrants to Illinois has settled in Chicago and those towns, suburbs, and villages immediately adjacent to the city. Still unrecorded, except in Greek sources, are the experiences of Greek immigrants in the most rural areas of Illinois.

The most valuable sources for determining the presence of Greek immigrants in rural Illinois are the Greek language business directories, histories, and guidebooks produced since the turn of the century. The original intention of the business directories was to provide a listing of Greek businesses and wholesalers state by state all within one reference source. The success of these directories was immediate.

The idea was simple. If provided a choice, a Greek immigrant would buy from a Greek businessman who in turn would buy from a Greek wholesaler. This scenario, while imperfect in practice, worked well enough for these directories to be produced year after year. The sheer volume of these publications attests to the fact that they received wide attention among Greek immigrants.

Many Greek writers and publishers produced directories, business guides, and even dictionaries that included descriptive sections on cities and states across the United States. Seraphim Canoutos was undoubtedly the most prolific of these business directory compilers, issuing such publications annually from at least 1907 until the late 1920s. Canoutos did not limit himself to business directories but also wrote legal guides, history books, and even a book of manners. From our perspective on history, the present value of these directories resides in the fact that they document page after page of Greek-owned businesses cited with a street address and type of business for every state in America. In the specific case of Illinois, we can chart the presence of such Greek-owned businesses beginning in 1903.

Odigos Tou Laoi, The People's Guide, written and compiled by C.D. Skadopoulos in 1920, is one of the variations on the business directory format. It is a book of manners in section one and section two is a business directory. What makes the *People's Guide* such a valuable historical document is that the majority of businesses cited in the pages are accompanied by photographs of the owners, frequently with a short biography.

Panel 11: The Antioch Café

Not every Greek immigrant living in rural Illinois in the early part

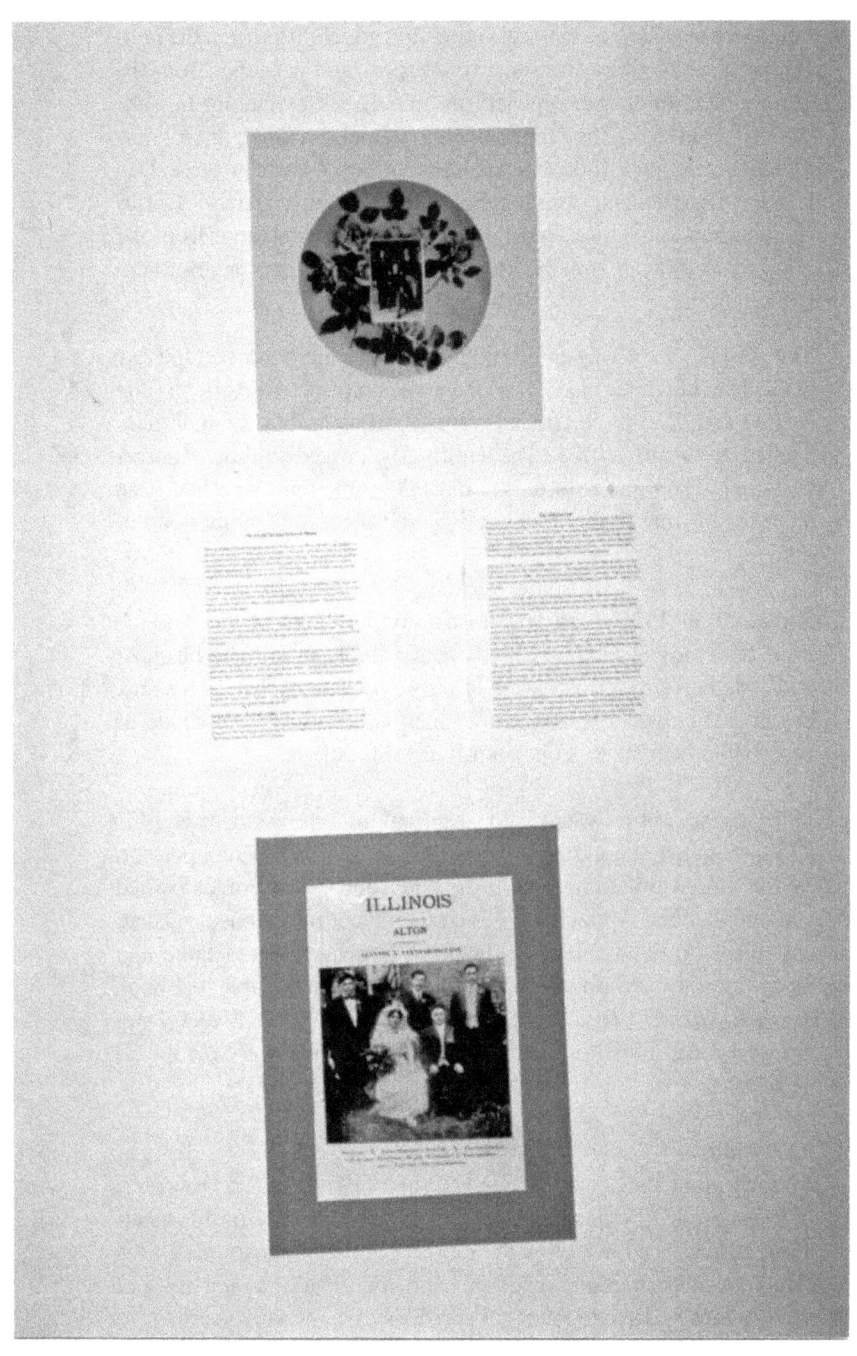

A panel from the "Heartland of Hellenism: Greeks in Illinois 1886-1950" exhibit. Top: An example of a composite photograph. Bottom: A wedding photo from a rural Illinois business directory. Circa 1994. Photo by John Rassogianis. John Psiharis collection.

of the century is included in Greek business directories. of the century is included in Greek business directories. One such case of rural Greeks was three families living in Antioch, Illinois in the mid-1920s. In 1924 three Greeks, two cousins, and a friend, from the same village in Greece, opened the first Greek restaurant in Lake County, Illinois. The three young Greeks called their new establishment the Antioch Café. The three co-owners were Dan Harris (Anastacios Haralambopoulos), Sam Harris (Zafiri Haralambopoulos), and Ted Poulos. All three men came from the village of Vlasia in the Kalavryta region in the northern Peloponnesus.

The Antioch Café was an unmitigated economic disaster. One day in the dead of winter in 1925, a lone man came into the Antioch Café at 6:00 a.m. The three Greeks were all a bustle, but the man only wanted a cup of coffee. The entire day passed without another customer. Then just before 6:00 p.m. the same man who had been there for his morning coffee came in and ordered…another cup of coffee.

Sometime in 1925, Sam Harris sold his holdings in the Antioch Café. Sam moved south to Libertyville, Illinois, going into business with another Greek man who is only recalled by his last name, Pasinis. The two men owned a grocery store on the west side of Libertyville's main street just north of Cook Street.

In 1931 Dan Harris was killed in an automobile accident and his widow sold her share of the Antioch Café to the remaining partner, Ted Poulos. Until sometime in the late 1930s, Ted Poulos owned and operated the Antioch Café. Ted then went into a business that, unlike the Antioch Café, would bring him unexpected fame and recognition throughout the county. In the recently published book *Antioch, Illinois A Pictorial History 1892-1992*, Ted's Sweet Shop, the local confectionery store, is commemorated in a two-page spread of pictures.

'Oh, you mean Ted the Candy Man?' is how longtime residents of Antioch, and Lake County in general, refer to Ted Poulos. For nearly forty years, Ted Poulos received acclaim far and wide for his hand-made candies. Ted was often the subject of newspaper stories for his elaborate Easter baskets made of hand-spun candy or the six-foot candy canes he gave to the local Boy Scout troop every year.

Descendants of all three men still live in Lake County, Illinois. With the phenomenal new growth in this quickly developing county, many people make it a point of stressing how long their families have lived in the area. Just the mention of Ted's Sweet Shop, or even the Antioch Café, and local people smile. The memories of these

Greek immigrants live on in the stories their neighbors still recall. As one person prefaced his comments on Ted's Sweet Shop, 'Well now you're talking about the 'real' Lake County.'

Panel 12 The Picture Brides
The late 1920s and the early 1930s were the eras of the Picture Bride. This was the time when the majority of Greek immigrant women came to the United States to marry. The migration of young men to the United States had resulted in an unprecedented lack of marriageable men for an entire generation of women. Historical events of the day only added to the overall absence of men in the countryside. The Balkan Wars, World War I, and numerous natural disasters such as earthquakes and plagues created such a state of instability and economic hardship that marriage in America seemed, for many young women, the only reasonable option.

Whatever the hardships of everyday life in the rural countryside, few Greek maidens willingly wanted to immigrate. Brothers working in Illinois were more than willing to provide a handsome dowry but finding a suitable groom in the village of equal social and economic standing became increasingly problematic. The exchange of letters between various families in Greece and immigrants in America soon proved a viable means to overcome the lack of suitable grooms. In this growing correspondence, photographs would "just happen" to include, of say, a young Greek standing in front of his candy store on Halsted Street, or a portrait of a young maiden from a rural village. Sometimes these photographs initiated a highly formal exchange of letters between an unwed Greek immigrant in Illinois and a young Greek woman's family in the rural countryside.

After an appropriate passage of time, if all parties agreed then legal dowry contracts, called *prikes,* were drawn up. The formalities involved in such traditional arrangements often created a very complicated series of exchanges. Very often brothers of the young maiden, from let us say Chicago, would send a sizable amount of money to relatives in their home village to fulfill their part of the marriage contract. This money would then be sent to the groom's relatives in Alton, Illinois who were acting on his behalf in these formal exchanges.

Lest anyone think that this was simply a matter of 'buying a husband' the groom was very often required to produce documents. Elaborate legal documents drawn up by officials at the Greek Consulate's offices in Chicago were more frequently required than is discussed today. Testimonies from local parish priests concerning an individual's character and bank documents showing total net worth and/or clear title on the property were commonly requested by the bride's family.

Even after all these careful negotiations, the village women were fearful of the long voyage to an unknown land and a groom they had never even met. Many stories were whispered down by the village fountain where the young maidens gathered every day. Grim accounts of women left at the pier or train station because they were not as beautiful as their pictures made them seem to be.

Panel 13 Spring of 1922: Tasia Comes to Illinois
No single individual's story could possibly represent all the Greek women who emigrated to Illinois during the 1920s and 1930s. Still, one woman's story can illustrate some of the complexities in migration that all women experienced in one form or another. During the early Spring of 1922 Anastacia (Tasia) Rapanos left the rural village of Planaterou in the district of Kalavryta in the northern Peloponnesus for Chicago, Illinois.

Tasia was only able to leave because her brothers had started her emigration paperwork before the quota system imposed by the McCarran-Walter Act. This new legislation blocked her father Nikolaos from accompanying her. Although Nikolaos had made at least three trips from 1907 to 1919 to Chicago for extended periods of work he had never become an American citizen. Consequently, since he had not begun the process of seeking a visa before the McCarran-Walter Act restricted the terms of emigration, Nickolaos could not secure the necessary visa papers.

As far as the United States Emigration officials were concerned Tasia Rapanos was traveling alone. This created a problem. Rural Greek notions of propriety would simply not allow for an unmarried woman to travel alone. So Nikolaos Rapanos made arrangements with a fellow villager, old friend, and distant cousin Sotiri Komberos to escort Tasia.

Tasia joined a group already consisting of four people: Sotiri Komberos, his young wife Demetra, their six-month-old son Yiorgos, and George Kokalis, Demetra's younger brother. So restrictive were the United States emigration laws that young Kokalis had to appear on Sotiri Komberos' travel papers as his son by a previous marriage.

Tasia waited nervously in the port city of Patras to have all her papers processed. Even during her stay in Patras propriety dictated that she be accompanied by her younger sister Olga. Unexpected family responsibilities almost caused Tasia to miss her boat for America!

While Tasia and Olga waited for all the endless paperwork to be completed, Vasso, a third sister, came to bring them back to the village. Eleni, yet another of Tasia's sisters, was having a protracted and difficult childbirth. By the time the three sisters arrived, Eleni and her newborn son had both died. Given the limited conditions in the mountain villages, the funerals took place the next day. Immediately afterward, Tasia, Olga, and Vasso raced back to Patras. Tasia arrived just in time for the final presentation of documents and the boarding.

Within three years of her arrival in Chicago, Tasia was married at Saints Constantine and Helen Greek Orthodox Church and had an elaborate wedding party at Pullman Hall.

Panel 14 The Picture Bride Song
Sometime in the 1920s and 1930s, a folk song was composed that described the dread of these young women. Commonly referred to as the 'Picture Bride Song' this song became so popular it was eventually recorded in Athens as a 78 rpm record with the title "Mother Please Don't Send Me to America." But the record was never sold in Greece. This record was target marketed by Columbia Records exclusively for the Greeks living in America. The famous lyrics of this song are:

>Don't send me to America, Mama
>I'll wither and die there!
>I don't want dollars---how can I say it?
>Only bread, onions, and the one I love!
>
>I love someone in the village, Mama
>A handsome youth, an only son
>He's kissed me in the ravines,
>And embraced me under the olive trees.
>
>Yiorgo, my love, I'm leaving you
>And going far away.
>Ksenithia (the foreign lands).
>They take me like a lamb to be slaughtered!
>And there, in my grief, they'll bury me.

Exhibition Research

Every person of Greek descent whose family or families came to live in Illinois is indebted to the ongoing research of two men: Andrew Thomas Kopan and Peter W. Dickson.

Professor Andrew T. Kopan has an international reputation for his lifetime of research and writing on the Greek communities of

Illinois. Dr. Kopan is the unquestioned Dean of Greek American regional studies for the Midwest. All succeeding generations of scholars owe Dr. Kopan a special debt not only for the high example his continued publications have provided over the years but for his singular dedication to the preservation of archival materials related to the Greek experience in the United States of America.

Mention needs to be made of the specialized and extremely detailed research and writings of **Peter W. Dickson.** Working alone, Mr. Dickson has reconstructed and documented the life and career of Christos Tsakonas. Mr. Dickson's continued research as well as his attention to the preservation of critically important documents related to the experiences of numerous Tsintzinians in America places him in the company of young scholars responsible for the resurgence now underway in modern Greek-American historical studies.

Steve Frangos conducted all the research involved with this project, selected all the photographs, and wrote all the accompanying texts. Mr. Frangos has made extensive use of the photographs and research of Dr. Kopan as well as the writings of Peter W. Dickson. As the viewer will quickly see, Mr. Frangos has most heavily relied upon the work of Dr. Kopan. Nevertheless, the use of those photographs and the interpretive labels that accompany them are those of Mr. Frangos. Any and all errors in fact or interpretation are, of course, Mr. Frangos' sole responsibility.

While the Heartland of Hellenism is a self-contained and independent exhibition display, it is a preview of the research topics that will soon appear in the upcoming museum exhibition 'O Cosmos: The Private Lives and Public Celebrations of the Greeks in Illinois: 1886-1992.' The O Cosmos exhibition is a Greek-American Community Services, Inc. project which is sponsored in part by an Illinois Humanities Council grant award.

Panel Six: Credits
This exhibition could be about any Greek immigrant, his or her family, and their descendants in Illinois. The interpretative labels in this exhibition attempt to mix the specific experiences of individual Greek men and women from Illinois with the generally accepted historical events known to have occurred in the community at large. Undoubtedly other individuals could have been included. For Greeks who have a more developed sense of public self (*egoismo*), than is recognized by the American public, this is a point that requires special citation.

In the ongoing research into the historical experiences of Greeks in the United States of America, many important documents and individuals need to be made available to the growing community of interested scholars. If anyone who is Greek or of Greek descent believes this exhibition has not provided the American public with a balanced presentation, based on privately held documents, the creators of this exhibition urge them to have either the originals or copies of those original documents placed in any of the public institutions in Illinois now seeking to preserve the heritage of Greeks in this state.

Exhibition Physical Panels Design and Construction:
Deno Frangos, master millworker and carpenter for over forty years. Mr. Frangos came out of retirement and devoted his time and considerable skills when no one else was available. His craftsmanship and devotion to family are before you. Mr. Frangos is responsible for the exhibition panels' physical design, construction, and use.

Exhibition Design: Steve Frangos with special help (as usual) from "Elaine." Photographic Reproduction: Steve Schmidt (Mundelein) and Total Image (Grayslake). Title Graphics: Holly Graham. Mounting of the Exhibition: Steve Frangos with Diane Anton Harris. Computer Services and Laser Printing Delaine Frangos.

Sponsors of Greek-American Community Services, Inc.'s involvement in this exhibition project include a number of recognized community figures within the Greek-American community of Illinois who responded to GACS's request for guidance and financial support. As at other times in the past, these men have stepped forward to provide leadership. These individuals are *James Roupas of James Roupas and Associates (Palos Hills), John Koliopoulos of Patio Restaurants, Inc. (Bridgeview), Nick Vern of Nick's Restaurant (Bridgeview), Tom Coutretsis of Tommy's Chicago Bar and Grill (Chicago), and Louis G. Apostol, Cook County Public Administrator.*

Identification Labels for the Individual Photographs by Panel

Panel Number One:

Circa 1870s. Frank Combiths, was the first son born of a Greek immigrant in Illinois. Photograph from the Andrew Thomas Kopan Collection.

Christos Tsakonas (1848-1909) Called the 'Columbus of Sparta,' this one man was responsible for bringing more than 1,000 young Greek immigrants from the villages near the town of Sparta to

Illinois in the 1870s and 1880s. Photograph from the Andrew Thomas Kopan Collection.

Panel Number Two

December 1899 *Return of Odysseus* Hull House Theater program. Photograph from the Andrew Thomas Kopan Collection.

The viewer should note in these select pages from the *Return of Odysseus* program the number of women cited. Photographs from the Frangos Research Collection.

Panel Number Three

1917-1918 Liberty Bond Drive Rally sponsored by local Greek-Americans in Chicago, Illinois. Photograph from the Andrew Thomas Kopan Collection.

1918 Rapanos Family in Chicago, Illinois
Seated from left to right: Nikolaos Rapanos, father, and Athancios Rapanos, the eldest brother. Standing from the left are Haralambos (Harry) Rapanos, Alexandros Rapanos, and Spiro (Sam) Rapanos. Photograph from the Frangos Research Collection.

1917 Olga Y. Psychios, Theodora Psychios, Theodore Baroutis. The photograph was taken in the village of Kato Vlasia, in the district of Kalavryta, in the Peloponnesus. Photograph from the Frangos Research Collection.

Panel Number Four

Completed in 1915 this photo-embroidery was made by Zafiris Y. Psychios. The photograph in the center is of Zafiris Psychios in a costume traditional to his village. The name in Greek on the banner is Vlasia. This is the name of Zafiris' home village of Kato Vlasia which is located in the district of Kalavryta in the Peloponnesus. Photograph from the Frangos Research Collection.

This is a circa. 1903 composite photograph. The figure on the viewer's left is Christos Saramantis. The individuals on the right are unidentified. female members of his family then living in Greece.

Panel Number Five

1919-1920 photograph from page 127 in *Odigos Tou Laoi, The People's Guide* written and compiled by C.D. Skadopoulos.

The "Heartland of Hellenism: Greeks in Illinois 1886-1950" exhibit on display at the Hellenic Museum & Cultural Center. **Top:** The first three panels of the exhibit displayed side-by-side on a wall. **Bottom:** (L): Photos from the Rassogianis family candy store. (R): A *Chicago Sun Times* article on Greeks at the Chicago World's Fair. Circa 1994. Photos by John Rassogianis. John Psiharis collection.

The individuals seen in this wedding photograph are standing left to right: Andonis S. Spiliopoulos, Ioannis S. Giannakopoulos, and Yiorgos Skoutsis, and seated we see the newly wedded couple of Mrs. Elizabeth Giannakopoulos and Ioannis Panagiotopoulos. Photograph from the Andrew Thomas Kopan Collection.

Antioch, Illinois circa. The early 1920s. Sam Harris, Dan Harris, and Ted Poulos. Photograph from the Frangos Research Collection.
Panel Number Six

Circa early 1920s Anastacia (Tasia) Rapanos. The crochet piece that serves as a background for this photograph was also done by Ms. Rapanos. Photograph from the Frangos Research Collection.

May 1922 visa papers used by Anastacia (Tasia) Rapanos to emigrate to the United States of America. Photograph from the Frangos Research Collection.

The exhibit was unveiled in the atrium of the State of Illinois Building (later renamed the James R. Thompson Center). At the invitation of Pat Michalski, Special Assistant to the Governor for Ethnic Affairs, the exhibit was on display from September 12 through 21, 1994. As the building was a major downtown transit center, tens of thousands of visitors and commuters encountered the exhibit while it was on display.

Next, the exhibit traveled to the Hellenic Museum and Cultural Center which at the time was located in a temporary facility at 400 N. Franklin Street in downtown Chicago. Later, the museum moved above the Greek Islands restaurant on Halsted Street before moving into their new facility a block south of there.

Elaine Thomopoulos recalls, "Regarding the *O Cosmos* exhibit at the Hellenic Museum, a couple of hours before it was to be displayed, Themi Vasils, a museum board member, informed us that she thought that it had been hung in the wrong order, even though the panels were numbered. John Rassogianis and I rushed over and rehung the panels in the correct order just minutes before the door opened. There was a wine and cheese opening night reception that was well attended. Drs. Andrew Kopan and Fotios Litsas were featured speakers. The exhibit remained on display at the museum for a couple of months."

An article that appeared in the *Greek Star* announcing the exhibition explained:

Opening night of the *O Cosmos* exhibition at the Hellenic Museum and Cultural Center. Pictured (L-R): Dr. Theodosis Kioutas, Athanasia Papadopoulos, Dr. Peter Chioros, John Psiharis, Irene Antoniou, Evangeline Mistaras, and Elaine Thomopoulos. Circa 1994. John Psiharis collection.

'The 'Heartland' exhibit is a preview of a pioneering effort undertaken by the Cultural & Arts Program of GACS and the '*O Cosmos*: The Private Lives and Public Celebrations of the Greeks in Illinois,' which will be shown at different sites throughout the state of Illinois. This inspiring traveling museum consists of a series of panels depicting the Greek American experience in the state from the late nineteenth century to modern times. It has been made possible through the support of the Illinois Humanities Council.

Selected panel coverage of 'Heartland' will range from snapshots of early pioneers, picture brides, and family portraits to a Greek dramatic production entitled 'The Return of Ulysses' held at the Hull House in 1899. Other representations will consist of the 1917-18 Liberty War Bond Drive Rally, as well as depictions of life in a small-town café and a suburban ice cream shop and candy store.

Many photographs and materials are provided courtesy of the Andrew T. Kopan and Peter Dickson collections. Research materials and narrative were provided by Steve Frangos and Dr. Elaine Thomopoulos, the *O Cosmos* project director.

Years later, neither Elaine, Steve, nor I remember the differences between the *"O Cosmos"* and *"Heartland of Hellenism"* exhibits, and why there were two different names. Heartland panels were a subset of the total panels so they may have been for display in smaller venues.

"The Untold Story of the Greek-American Worker from New Smyrna to Astoria," the first distinguished lecture related to *O Cosmos,* was held on May 31, 1992, in the Swedish Covenant Hospital Auditorium and featured author/professor Dan Georgakas. Over 150 attended this event which was co-sponsored by the Hellenic Professional Society of Illinois.

The second lecture, "The Greek-American Community and Hull House," was held in April 1995 at the Jane Addams Hull-House Museum. The exhibit was concurrently on display in the museum. An article reporting on the event appeared in the June 1, 1995 issue of the *Greek Star* entitled "The Greek Immigrant Experience, Topic for Recent Lecture at Hull House."

> Chicago Greek history buffs recently witnessed a slide presentation entitled 'The Greek-American Community and Hull House,' held at the Jane Addams Hull-House Museum, 800 S. Halsted St.
>
> Making good use of visuals, the presenter, Mary Ann Johnson, Executive Director, surveyed the decades covering the Greek immigrant experience within an overall multiethnic context. Her presentation touched upon the high points of the entire era and expanded on the challenges the newly arrived immigrants faced.
>
> In a revealing portion of her presentation, Ms. Johnson indicated that a paper, written by Andrew Theodore, a Greek citizen of Chicago and Northwestern University student in the late 1920s, opened up her understanding of the Greeks and Hull House. It was originally given to her by *Greek Press* columnist Jim Mezilson.
>
> She quoted Theodore: 'It would not be an exaggeration to say that Hull House gave needed encouraging feelings of security and hope to the Greeks of the largest enclave of Chicago and as a result of them, early immigrants formed the nucleus which later was responsible for the development of the Greek's leadership of various fields in Chicago.'

"The Greek American Community and Hull House," lecture flyer. April 9, 1995. Elaine Thomopoulos collection.

Ms. Johnson related that Theodore, upon establishing residency at the settlement house, had developed a keen appreciation for Nobel Prize recipient Jane Addams. Projecting a scene of the resident dining hall, Ms. Johnson further explained that 'the residents of Hull-House were a cross-section of everyday walks of life but mainly professional people, mostly women who in addition to their daily work devoted spare time they had in the activities and community work. There were university professors, lawyers, bankers, writers, musicians, doctors, social workers, politicians, all motivated to be of help to the community and world in general.'

During the reception that followed, Barbara Javaras, president of the Greek Women's University Club, recounted her experience at Socrates School. 'It was wonderful to network this program and re-establish our roots. We must get as many of these individual stories on tape,' she added. Javaras, along with Katherine Lolagos Angee, recounted stories of their youth in Greek Town which they claimed ranged from Taylor St. to Harrison on Blue Island Ave.

Ms. Angee's father, James Lolagos, owned a small grocery store which later expanded into a thriving restaurant, ultimately branching to extensive real estate holdings in the vicinity.

'I think our next lecture should deal with the Greeks on Blue Island Avenue,' she added.

Ms. Angee related a visual that brought to mind a poignant anecdote of her experience during the outside procession of the *Epitaphios* during a past Good Friday service. 'As they approached, they stopped doing business. Everything froze. Just lighted candles. I can still remember that stillness, that absolute stillness. There was respect. Absolute respect. All you saw was oceans of candles.'

The Sunday afternoon program was sponsored by the Cultural & Arts Program of Greek-American Community Services and co-sponsored by the Greek Women's University Club and Hellenic Professional Society of Illinois. The program was opened by John Rassogianis, CAP Director, and Elaine Barkoulies, HPSI President. The event was videotaped in its entirety by Barbara Javaras, G.W.U.C. President. A coffee followed the presentation amidst historical pictorial panels of the G.A.C.S. *O'Cosmos* traveling museum exhibit specially brought in for the occasion. 'We hope to have a follow-up lecture on this topic soon, while the iron is hot,' stated John Rassogianis. 'We would like to invite at least ten or fifteen individuals to come in and tell their stories,' he added.

The third distinguished lecture featured Dr. Andrew Kopan and Lou Mitchell at the Chicago Historical Society. The sold-out event was preceded by a delicious Greek-inspired meal catered by the Society's newly opened gourmet restaurant. I remember introducing the speakers that evening and it was a very hot day. Dr. Kopan's presentation chronicled the evolution of Chicago's Greek community while Lou Mitchell, longtime owner of Lou Mitchell's on Jackson St, recounted his story and experiences in Chicago. That evening Lou made a generous donation to GACS.

The exhibit was also on display in the Assumption Church Hall. Elaine recalls, "The students at Plato had a chance to see it, as well as the adults." Once the tour had finished, the panels were displayed at GACS. They were hung throughout the building and seen by those who visited. Neither Elaine nor I can remember why the exhibit never went to St. Photios Shrine, as was originally intended.

For this project, Dr. George Christakes was the independent evaluator. His report to the Illinois Humanities Council, dated February 20, 1996, reported:

> The Greek American Communities Service [sic] organization has asked me to review for you the exhibit at Plato Academy of 'The Heartland of Hellenism: The Greeks in Illinois 1886 to 1950.' The exhibit was presented by Greek-American Community Services and was made possible by a grant from the Illinois Humanities Council. I went to the exhibit just before it closed and reviewed it. I must apologize that it took me so long to write to you with the results.
>
> I must admit that I was apprehensive about going to such an exhibit at a school since I thought that they would not have the proper facilities for something like this and would simply have it in a classroom, where it would be difficult to see and crowded. I was pleasantly surprised to find that they had a very large room on the lower level with plenty of wall space and good lighting. Since Plato Academy is right next to a major Greek Orthodox Church it is a place that is easily assessable [sic] to many members of the community who I assume went to see the exhibit after Sunday services. Plato Academy, which has a marvelous energetic director, Catherine A. Antonopoulos Ph.D., is a well-known and active intellectual and cultural center which attracts community members who would view the exhibit as well. I was fortunate that Dr. Antonopoulos took the time to visit with me about the exhibit and share her thoughts about the community and their reaction to the exhibit.
>
> The exhibit itself was very well presented. Mounted on large wallboards it was displayed on two walls of the hall. Arranged chronologically, it actually went back to the 1840s briefly and then concentrated on the advertised period of 1886-1950. It contained a remarkable collection of visual materials about the Chicago Greek American community over the entire span of time and as a historian, I was gratified to see that it was done with a professional flair and good historical explanations. Particularly impressive was the wide range of materials that graphically illustrated the Chicago Greek's experience.
>
> After discussing possible early visitors, the exhibit showed the first Greeks in 1885. The community of course was located in the area of Jane Addam's Hull House and was very influenced, involved, and active in Hull House. This writer vividly remembers interviewing an elderly community member, who when I asked him if he was involved with Hull House, showed me his hand and started to cry as he explained to me that Jane Addams had on numerous occasions shaken his hand. He

regarded her as virtually a saint. One of the reasons for the immigrants' acceptance of Hull House as versus Graham Taylor's efforts was that Hull House instead of trying to change the immigrant's culture and religion accepted them and actually helped give them pride in their culture. This was graphically demonstrated in the exhibit by the original playbill from 1890 of a play at Hull House – *Odysseus*. Hull House was also very active in providing Americanization classes for the immigrants so that they could both adapt to the new land and obtain citizenship.

The new citizens responded as shown in the exhibit by responding to the national crisis of World War I by not only serving in the armed services but by being extremely active in 'Liberty Bond' rallies and drives. Another aspect of immigrant life that was demonstrated was the guidebooks that helped the immigrant Greeks adjust to their new life in the United States. Various business and other directories for immigrants were also displayed.

Daily life was well presented ranging from weddings and other festive occasions, including a marvelous item – the lyrics of the Picture Bride Song (so-called picture brides had sent photographs to Chicago Greeks who actually selected and married the women in the photos). Photos of the picture brides were included as well as various family types of pictures which illustrated the social life of the community. Business was not neglected including photographs of the small businesses which the Greek's [sic] ran including the Rassogeanis [sic] Ice Cream Parlor. Perhaps some shots of the bootblacks that were so important in the early community would enhance the exhibit. Restaurants, as would be expected, were well covered.

By the 1930s, the Greeks were becoming a well-established part of Chicago's community which was reflected by a *Sunday Times* magazine section in 1935 that sketched the Greek American community. The intellectual life of the community could have been better illustrated by including a few issues of *Athene* magazine to demonstrate the rather remarkable wide-ranging intellectual and creative interests of this immigrant community. The Newberry Library has a complete collection of that Chicago magazine.

Steve Frangos, who is a well-known academic commentator on the Greeks in America, selected the photographs and other material and wrote the accompanying text explaining and putting into historical context the various parts of the exhibit. This was very well done and enhanced the value of the exhibit enormously. He relied in his credits on Andrew Kopan and

Peter W. Dickson for many of his comments. I was pleased to see that a professional of Frangos' level was so instrumental in this presentation. The fact that Frangos' explanations provide an excellent overview of the communities [sic] experience in addition to the visual story made the exhibit particularly excellent from an educational perspective.

All in all, I thought that the exhibit was well done and presented in a professional manner in an attractive setting. I would like to see the exhibit shown to more people and would suggest that perhaps it could be packaged for some type of traveling exhibit which could be viewed by more people. My concern would be that the materials should be professionally mounted and packaged so that they would not be at risk of damage.

In 1991, over 800 people attended six Sunday afternoon showings of films by renowned Greek filmmaker Theodoros "Theo" Angelopoulos. The series was co-sponsored by GACS in partnership with the Film Center of the School of the Art Institute of Chicago, the Greek Consulate, and several other organizations. The films were shown at the Film Center and included post-film discussion periods and refreshments. One of the screenings featured a talk by acclaimed Pulitzer Prize-winning *Chicago Sun-Times* film critic Roger Ebert. Angelopoulos attended one of the screenings and GACS co-hosted a reception for him to meet the local Greek community. For each show, we offered transportation to and from GACS on our *Ya'Sou* vans for those who preferred not to drive downtown. The Consul General of Greece hosted a reception for Angelopoulos at his residence, which was also part of the filmmaker's visit to Chicago.

Another CAP event was a screening of the film *Solstice*, a 1993 film by Chicago native Jerry Vasilatos that premiered on the Lifetime cable network during the holiday season. After the showing, a reception with Jerry was held and refreshments were served. The award-winning film was set in Portage Park, and it was fitting that we arranged the screening at the LaSalle Talman Bank Theater just blocks from where much of the film was made. The well-attended event was co-sponsored by Argolis Organization O Danaos, the Greek Women's University Club, the Hellenic Cultural Organization, the Hellenic Professional Society of Illinois, and KRIKOS. An article appearing in the November 17, 1994 edition of the *Greek Star* entitled "*Solstice*, a Film by Jerry Vasilatos Awakens the Holiday Spirit," promoted the screening:

At the GACS screening of *Solstice* at the LaSalle Talman Theater on December 4, 1994. Pictured (L-R): Alexander Rassogianis, A.J. Vasilatos, unknown, Stella Vasilatos, Laura Heckert, Elaine Barkoulies, Jerry Vasilatos, Elaine Thomopoulos, John Psiharis, John Rassogianis, and Yorgos Kourvetaris. John Psiharis collection.

Solstice, an inspiring 48-minute movie arriving just in time for the Christmas advent, will be shown at LaSalle Talman Theatre, 4921 W. Irving Park Rd. Sunday, December 4, at 2:30 pm. Produced and directed by a young man of Greek descent, Jerry Vasilatos, the film is a breath of fresh air with its portrayal of the Christmas Eve sojourn of Nick, the main character, in the tradition of 'It's a Wonderful Life.' Filmed in Chicago, several locations, such as the Music Box Theater and Six Corners are readily identifiable in this holiday drama. Many members of the cast are Greek-Americans. The event is co-sponsored by GACS, Argolis Organization O Danaos, Greek Women's University Club, Hellenic Cultural Organization, Hellenic Professional Society of Illinois, and KRIKOS.

In 1995, GACS received a grant of $2,500 through the Chicago Department of Cultural Affairs City Arts program to enhance arts programming with adult day care participants. The grant enabled us to hire an art therapist to work with the participants in various artistic genres. Janet Lewis, who had a Master's Degree in gerontology, offered twice-per-week projects with small groups of ADC clients. The creative and expressive art techniques our clients were introduced to included mosaics, painting, sewing, looming, and ornament making. Janet had previously completed her internship in the ADC so she was familiar with many of our participants.

On April 21, 1996, GACS co-sponsored a concert entitled *Ziyia* at the Assembly Hall of the International House. The Midwest premiere ensemble featured a five-member band, which included vocalist/instrumentalist Christos Govetas. The concert capped a three-day "Anatolian Heritage Festival, Part 2: The Interior" and also featured Armenian, Assyrian, Kurdish, and Turkish music. The concert included workshops, a culture forum, and a dance party and banquet held on the premises of the International House. The Greek dance instruction portion of the workshop was conducted by Joe Kaloyanidis Graziosi and focused on Cappadocian Greek dances.

Featured performers included George Chittenden, Christos Govetas, Beth Cohen, Lise Liepman, and Dan Auvil, with guest musicians Bob Beer and Joe Zeytoonian. Tickets are $15 each at the door and $13 in advance. The promotional flier, quoting a review in *LAOGRAFIA,* stated: "It is hard to imagine how three Californians and two Bostonians (only one of whom hails originally from Greece) could put together a band that not only plays music from many different regions of Greece, but that also plays it better than any recordings emerging from Greece. But that's exactly what Ziyia has done."

Planning for multiple programs on an ongoing basis kept John busy. A September 10, 1996 letter that John sent to noted author Christopher Janus regarding an upcoming event illustrates the effort involved in organizing one such program:

> It is with great pleasure that I am verifying by letter the date we agreed upon for your lecture which is tentatively entitled 'A Conversation with Christopher Janus.' I have been talking with the new HPSI president, Dr. Anthony Xidis, their past president, Hara Anast, and Elaine Thomopoulos, current Greek Women's University Club president, as well as Barbara Javaras, to complete details of the October 27, 1996 lecture. We are now working on a location for the meeting.
>
> I will be giving Valerie more information as it unfolds in the days to come. I know you would prefer a laid-back informal situation; so can we plan for 25 or more guests? These lectures never draw a huge turnout unless we beat the drums. What do you think?
>
> Again, our wholehearted thanks for so graciously accepting our invitation to speak to us. I think it is inevitable that it will be interesting no matter how much time you will use to put your thoughts together. I think the same format and content that you used at the Hellenic Museum would be just fine. You will always have some solid questions to spice it up!

Noted author Christopher Janus addresses GACS

From left, standing, Leon Marinakos, cultural attache of Greece; Maria Fotinopoulos, Hellenic Professional Society (HPSI) board member; Dr. Anthony Xidis, president, HPSI; John Rassogianis, director, cultural & arts program; and HPSI past presidents Hara Anast and Elaine Barkoulies. Seated, Theodosis Kioutas, Greek American Community Center (GACS) board member, with Christopher Janus, as they gather for a group photo after an interesting question and answer session with Mr. Janus, renowned lecturer and author, at the center. Sponsors of the recent Sunday afternoon lecture entitled "A Conversation with Christopher Janus" were the Cultural & Arts Program of Greek-American Community Services with Greek Women's University Club and the Hellenic Professional Society of Illinois.

Article about the Christopher Janus event at GACS. The *Greek Star*, December 3, 1996. John Psiharis collection.

A press release to promote the event, written by John, entitled "Noted Author to Spend Afternoon at GACS," appeared in the October 17, 1996, *Greek Star*, and read in part:

> A conversation with Christopher Janus will be one of the highlights of the fall season at the Greek-American Community Services Center, located on Chicago's northwest side at 3940 N. Pulaski Rd on Sunday, Oct 27 at 3 pm.
>
> Counted as one of the top-drawer members of the Greek-American community, Janus will touch on a wide range of topics stemming from his many and varied experiences throughout the years. His long and distinguished career is chronicled in *Angel on My Shoulder*, *Rememberances at Eighty*. In *Goodby* [sic] *Miss Fourth of July*, Janus draws on the distant past during his childhood and the joys of the trials experienced by his sister in a West Virginia troubled by the existence of the Ku Klux Klan. The story was made into a movie by Walt Disney.

Meeting some of the most fascinating individuals of the 20th century, such as Albert North Whitehead, and studying with George Santayana, he elected to take the high road for a life of adventure, spanning decades on several continents.

Among his accomplishments was a stint as a reporter for the *New York Times*, participating in investment banking, and serving in the State Department. It is this area of service that brought him the greatest fulfillment in the work of the Greek War Relief.

His memoirs tell it all, meetings with presidents and other well-known personages, and from the perspective of an insider, many of them will come to life during his coming talk. For example, from a humorous yet adventurous perspective, in some of his talks, he mentions his involvement in a South American gold mine, an experience that easily conjures visions, not unlike those gleaned in current adventure movies, but is nevertheless very down to earth.

Going into his second wind, Janus now occasionally lectures and travels extensively. He is an enthusiastic supporter of a movement to build a new library in Alexandria, Egypt, and is working behind the scenes on some interesting projects that may find fruition in the cultural life of Chicago.

The event is sponsored by the Cultural & Arts Program of Greek-American Community Services, the Greek-Women's University Club, and the Hellenic Professional Society of Illinois. The movie 'Goodby [sic] Miss Fourth of July' will be shown after refreshments.

Over the years, in addition to its programming, GACS co-sponsored an array of activities that were organized by other organizations within the *omogenia*. This meant that GACS, and other co-sponsoring organizations, jointly publicized the events to their members and within the broader community. In some cases, especially when collaborating with KRIKOS and HPSI, GACS made a financial contribution towards the expenses of the program. Since many of these programs were held in hotel or banquet meeting rooms, there were room rental and refreshment costs in addition to honorariums, publicity expenses, and postage. These partnerships made possible more frequent and high-quality programs as well as larger audiences.

One example of this was the annual Greek Independence Day events which featured top-drawer programs that were held in larger venues and attended by hundreds of guests. KRIKOS often took the lead in organizing the details and GACS, Greek Women's University Club, Hellenic

Professional Society of Illinois, and Hellenic Cultural Organization co-sponsored.

These reciprocal relationships continued throughout much of our existence and served to strengthen the bonds between the organizations. The arrangement ensured better attendance and enhanced publicity for the events, as well as divided the costs between several organizations. We frequently worked with KRIKOS, GWUC, HPSI, HCO, and at times Orthodox Singles.

In 1996 GWUC, through Elaine's efforts, received a grant from the Illinois Humanities Council to create an exhibition and a related lecture series entitled "Greek-American Women of Illinois: 111 Years of Courage, Struggle, and Triumph." Oral histories of GWUC members were also done.

Elaine served as project director, and she and Penny Sarlas curated the exhibit. Demetra Gianis coordinated the oral histories. GACS was one of many organizations that co-sponsored the project. In addition to those organizations mentioned above, other co-sponsors included: The American Hellenic Society of Berwyn, Assumption Greek Orthodox Church, Copernicus Foundation, DePaul University, Governor's Office of Ethnic Affairs, Hellenic Museum and Cultural Center, Hellenic Link–Midwest, Hellenic Society of Illinois Institute of Technology, Holy Apostles Greek Orthodox Church, Italian Cultural Center, Jane Addams Hull-House Museum, Campus Life Union Board and Hellenic–American Society of Loyola University, Macedonian Society of Greater Chicago, St. Helen's Philoptochos, and the History Department of the University of Illinois at Chicago. GACS hosted two of these lectures at our center ("American Women in Transition," by George Kourvetaris, Ph.D., and Angelike Mountanis, and "Nomads, Migrants, Refugees: Stories of Exile and Home," by Beatriz Badikian).

A post-event press release from the Greek Women's University Club written by Elaine and dated October 13, 1998, described the event:

> Dr. Beatriz Badikian and Dr. Ed Berggren presented an outstanding program at Greek-American Community Services in Chicago on October 11, 1998. The program was presented by the Greek Women's University Club, with the co-sponsorship of Greek-American Community Services and the Hellenic Professional Society of Illinois.
>
> The audience was enthralled with Badikian's moving portrayal of refugee and immigrant life, which was accompanied by the excellent flute music of Dr. Berggren. The reading was based

on her autobiographical work in progress: *Nomads, Migrants, and Refugees: Stories of Exile and Home.*

Badikian explained the stories, essays, and poems are based on her own family's story. She comments that her story is the skeleton and she adds the flesh. Flesh is what she does add, making each of her characters come alive as if they were in the room with us.

Comments from the audience attested to the wonderful experience of that afternoon. 'Beautiful blend of music and prose.' 'A very talented writer and speaker, Ms. Badikian's words vividly portrayed the image, transcending words.' 'I could easily picture the characters in my mind.' 'Spellbinding.'

Ya'Sou 2

Over time, GACS developed a reputation for its annual Christmas parties. The parties included adult day care clients and their families, Fabric Arts Project participants, staff, volunteers, board members, private and public funders, donors, and others that were involved in GACS in some fashion.

The events included a Holiday buffet of food that was often provided by Master Catering. At the request of Eleni Bousis, executives from GOYA, a major manufacturer of Hispanic food items, provided and served an amazing meal to the center during one of these parties.

The parties usually featured children from Plato Academy who performed traditional Greek songs and Christmas carols. Take-home presents were provided to each participant by the United Athenian & Piraeus Women's Society. They coordinated with our social worker to give each adult day care client an appropriate gift. The participants of the Fabric Arts Project gathered to crochet booties, scarves, caps, and other items that were given to the day care clients.

Perhaps the most memorable GACS Christmas party was in December of 1994. It was during this event that Mrs. Aphrodite Demeur, a benefactor of GACS, overheard a conversation I was having with an adult day care participant's daughter about how much their loved one had benefited from the center, but she had been concerned about the time it took to get her home. I explained that since we only had one van, there were two routes and that those who were further away were on the second trip. I added that we needed a second van to alleviate this situation.

Plato Academy children perform during a GACS Christmas party. Date unknown. John Psiharis collection.

A GACS Christmas party. Date unknown. John Psiharis collection.

Mrs. Demeur took me aside and mentioned that she had overheard the conversation and wanted to donate a second vehicle. Her son James Demeur, a successful Burger King franchisee in the western suburbs, had recently passed away, and she wanted to make this donation in his memory. In addition to the van, Mrs. Demeur donated funds to cover insurance costs for the first year and lettering for the van.

That party was also the first time Tornie was around a large-scale activity, having been adopted only a couple of weeks before. Although we had her upstairs in my office and away from the crowds, many wanted to see her, and I remember bringing a few people upstairs to spend time with her.

An article entitled "Plato Academy Choir Entertains at GACS," which appeared in the January 5, 1995, *Greek Star*, described the party:

> Traditional Greek and American Christmas carols, sung by the 30 members of the Plato Academy Choir, resonated throughout the Greek-American Community Services (GACS) day care center during their recent annual Christmas party. They sang many of the standard favorites, some in Greek translation, including the customary Greek staples such as the T*ropario I Yennesi Sou, Archiminia,* and *Ayios Vasilis Erhete.* It was their third yearly visit. 'They made a return visit, and we hope to see them again at Easter,' stated Frieda Aravosis, GACS fabric arts instructor.
>
> The Executive Director's Award, traditionally given at this holiday party, was awarded to two individuals, Elaine Thomopoulos, a co-founder of GACS, and Phil Williams, in recognition of their years of dedicated service to the agency. Williams is a storyteller and visual/audio arts volunteer.
>
> The distribution of gifts, prepared by the United Athenian Piraeus Society, was another important highlight of the party. They were passed out to the 32 adult day care clients present by Miranda Zaharakis, President of the Society, and Betty Karpouzlis. According to Ethel Kotsovos, the organization brought gifts for the third straight year, 'They generously brought head scarves for the women and neck scarves for the men,' she added.
>
> Partygoers feasted on a dinner brought in by Master Caterers. A wide selection of Greek desserts prepared by volunteers and families of clients were available.

In the coming days, GACS purchased a 16-passenger Dodge Ram van through Haggerty Dodge. The shade of blue of our first van wasn't available. The available blue was referred to as Aegean blue and was darker in hue. The van was named *Ya'Sou 2*. In recognition of Mrs. Demeur's support, the conference room/*kafenio* was renamed the James E. Demeur Conference Room, and lettering was affixed to the right-side passenger door that the vehicle was donated in memory of James E. Demeur.

Above: Adult Day Care staff members on the first day *Ya'sou 2* was put into service. Pictured (L-R): Ann Prusinski, Amydelle Shah, Carmen Vilato, Ethel Kotsovos, John Psiharis, and John Rassogiannis. Date unknown. John Psiharis collection. **Below:** ADC clients exit the *Ya'Sou* vans and gather for a picture during a trip to the Chicago Botanical Gardens. Date unknown. Photo courtesy of the National Hellenic Museum - Ann Prusinski collection.

John and I each drove a *Ya'Sou* van to Bolingbrook so that they could be outfitted to provide easier entry for the seniors. Folding steps were mounted to the undercarriage and grab bars were installed on either side of the side entry door. The modifications were covered through a donation from Dodge. On the way back, we stopped to visit Nick Papanicholas, a supporter of GACS, at his Papanicholas Coffee factory in Batavia, to show him the vans. In addition to a guided tour of the sorting, roasting, and packaging operations, Nick donated several cases of coffee for ADC participants and volunteers.

An Open House Reception and Blessing of the Waters (*Agiasmos*) of the *Ya'Sou 2* van was held at GACS on September 19. An announcement in the September 16, 1993 edition of the *Greek Star* read in part:

> *'Ya'Sou 2'*, the Aegean-blue van, was donated by the Demeur family in memory of James E. Demeur, a well-known conscientious and creative real estate entrepreneur. In his all too short life, he carried on and expanded the legacy and vision handed down by his father, the late Dr. Emmanuel Demeur, an Oak Park church, and civic leader. 'He had vision,' stated his mother, Aphrodite Demeur. 'He enjoyed challenges, doing difficult things; he did love life very much…he loved it all.'
>
> With the addition of a second van, the agency now has the capacity to transport up to 25 elderly participants to and from the center at one time.
>
> Selected panels from the *O'Cosmos* traveling museum, including several from the Andrew T. Kopan collection, will be on exhibit during the open house.
>
> Father Dimitri Kantzavelos, Chancellor of the Greek Orthodox Diocese of Chicago, will officiate during the Agiasmos.

Joining Forces

As a provider of adult day care services, GACS was a member of the Illinois Adult Day Services Association (IADSA), previously known as the Illinois Association of Adult Day Care Providers. This statewide group was a resource to centers by offering training programs and other modes of assistance. They also advocated on behalf of adult day care centers with the Illinois Department on Aging, the legislature, and other entities.

Before we opened the adult day care center, GACS staff attended a mandatory week-long pre-service training program that was offered by IADSA. It was led by Jane Stansell and held at the Alzheimer's Family Care Center, which at the time was in a converted house on Milwaukee

GACS membership certificate for the Illinois Association of Adult Day Care Providers. 1992. John Psiharis collection.

Avenue near Bryn Mawr. Their program focused on those who had mid to late-stage dementia and needed individualized care. The center, the first of its kind in the Chicago area, was a partnership with Rush Presbyterian St Luke's Medical Center and the Veterans' Administration. They had a special arrangement with IDOA to receive a higher rate of reimbursement for their clients given the enhanced care and staffing that was provided. Jane was the founding director and a great resource for us. During that week, we observed a caring, professional, and yet homey atmosphere, where clients were cared for individually or in small groups by specially trained staff.

A few years after we opened our center, IADSA, in part due to Jane's leadership as president of the association, was successful in getting IDOA to revise its reimbursement methods to more accurately cover the costs associated with a client's care. Up to that point, centers were paid a daily rate for each client who attended for more than four hours and a half-day rate for those who were there less. GACS received $30 per day/client, and it was meant to cover everything including lunches and transportation. It did not differentiate the actual time the clients were being cared for. A few clients might have been there for five hours, but a majority were there longer, sometimes seven or eight hours.

IADSA advocated for transportation reimbursement. Until that point, IDOA payments were all-inclusive and did not provide any renumeration for transportation costs. Although $2.50 per trip did not come close to the actual cost of transportation, it did help and was a beginning. Transportation was a significant cost. We were very fortunate to have had both of our *Ya'Sou* vans donated, but there were still other costs. A driver and attendant were needed for each van. Insurance for a vehicle of this type and usage was high since there were a larger number of passengers in the vehicle. There were also fuel, maintenance, and repair costs.

In 2001, in response to even more centers being on the verge of closing, IADSA advocated IDOA for a rate increase. An April 27, 2001 memo that I wrote to ADC families and volunteers, appealed for help in obtaining rate increases for ADC services. I wrote, "In cooperation with the Illinois Adult Day Services Association, centers throughout the state are requesting that the Illinois Legislature increase ADC funding to $8.38 per hour (from the current $5.52 per hour) and $6.14 per unit for transportation (from the present $4.15 per unit)." The memo continued, "Adult Day Care programs in Illinois are in a crisis. Last year alone 12 centers were forced to close. This year, without immediate and significant assistance, it is predicted that 7 percent of current centers will also close their doors before the end of the year."

After lobbying by IADSA, CLESE, service providers, and families, including petitions that were circulated by centers throughout the state, IDOA proposed a rate of $8 per hour with a cap on the monthly hours to be determined by the client's case manager based on their individualized care plan. Although these rates still did not cover the full cost of care for IDOA clients, they were an improvement and moving in the right direction. CLESE took part in this advocacy since a number of its members operated adult day care centers. Illinois still ranked amongst the lowest in the nation in terms of state funding for adult day care.

Another time that IADSA mobilized was when the Mayor proposed licensing adult day care centers. Donald Smith, the commissioner of the Chicago Department on Aging, led what most felt were misguided and unnecessary efforts. The Illinois Department on Aging, and in some cases the Veterans Administration visited, inspected, and monitored adult day care programs under their purview. We were also inspected regularly by the Illinois State Fire Marshal. They were funding sources and had a legitimate reason to monitor these programs. The city had no involvement with adult day care programs whatsoever but would add a layer of bureaucracy, redundancy, and expense to centers operating within the city. Most adult day care centers in Chicago were funded by IDOA. Of the two that weren't, one was located in a nursing home, and the other in a hospital.

John Psiharis and CDOA commissioner Donald Smith aboard the Odessey at Navy Pier. Date unknown. John Psiharis collection.

An October 31, 1991 article by City Hall reporter Fran Spielman in the *Chicago Sun-Times* entitled "Daley Plans City Oversight of Senior Day Care" reported:

> Adult day care centers serving Chicago's elderly population would be required to meet strict safety, sanitation, and program standards under an ordinance drafted by the Daley administration.
>
> The city's plan to license non-profit centers that provide daily care for seniors was disclosed by Donald R. Smith, commissioner of the city's Department on Aging, during City Hall budget hearings Wednesday.
>
> Although many of the adult day centers already are inspected under contracts with the Illinois Department on Aging and the U.S. Veterans Affairs Department, Smith said they are not licensed or inspected by the city.
>
> The ordinance expected to be introduced by Mayor Daley in about a month would require adult day care centers to undergo periodic fire, health, and sanitation inspections, Smith said.
>
> The centers would be required to maintain precise staff-client ratios and provide a minimum amount of space. Diverse programs, including periodic outings, would have to be offered so that seniors 'don't sit around all day,' the commissioner said.

Chicago currently has 11 adult day care centers with a capacity to serve 433 seniors. The average daily cost is about $35 per patient – about a third of what most nursing homes charge, officials said.

While the centers currently have plenty of space, Smith predicted they would quickly reach capacity as more women return to the workforce. For many families, nursing homes are either undesirable or too expensive, he said.

Smith predicted that the number of adult day care centers in Chicago would double in five years. The 1990 U.S. Census pegged the city's 60-and-older population at 443,679. Of that number, 137,980 are over 75, and 30,522 are over 85.

Jane Stansell, who runs the Alzheimer's Family Care Center, 5522 N. Milwaukee, predicted the 11 nonprofit centers already in business would pass city inspections 'with room to spare.'

She said the new regulations are needed to ensure that current standards of quality are maintained as more adult day care centers open.

But John Psiharis, who runs Greek-American Community Services, 3940 N. Pulaski, argued that city regulations would be redundant and counterproductive. Psiharis said his agency is already 'overwhelmed with expenses' as a result of state and federal requirements and inspections.

Several meetings were held at the CDOA office about this plan. Representatives from the health and fire departments attended. Codes that included automatic sprinklers, fireproof doors, and all sorts of costly upgrades that would impose severe hardship on centers were discussed.

Many adult day care programs were disgruntled by this effort and the expenses and redundancy that this would create. Some feared they would need to close since the upgrades to their facilities were cost-prohibitive. All ADCs were in facilities that had been approved and were regularly monitored, including annual visits from the V.A., IDOA, and the Illinois State Fire Marshal's office. We felt that if the city wanted to start regulating, they needed to have some skin in the game by funding these costly changes for adult day care programs. After lobbying efforts by IADSA and petitions distributed by adult day centers, and other service providers, the idea was quietly dropped by the city and there was no future discussion.

Note that throughout most of this book, I refer to the Chicago Department on Aging, however, along the way there were name changes and reorganizations. Initially known as the Mayor's Office of Senior Citizens, it eventually merged with the Mayor's Office for the Disabled and became the Chicago Department on Aging and Disability (DAD). At some point, the disabilities portfolio was spun off into a separate department (Mayor's Office for People with Disabilities). and the department was renamed the Chicago Department on Aging. As of this writing in 2022, under Mayor Lori Lightfoot, the department is part of the Department of Family and Support Services (which had been previously known as the Chicago Department of Human Services) as the Senior Services Program.

One example of our involvement in adult day care within a broader context is illustrated in a March 16, 1995, *Greek Star* article:

> John Psiharis, Greek-American Community Services (GACS), executive director, recently returned from Washington D.C., after participating in an invitational policy forum entitled, 'Adult Day Services: The Un-Nursing Home.' The conference, recognized as a mini-conference of the White House Conference on Aging, places a strong emphasis on grass-roots involvement – a policy encouraged by the Clinton Administration.
>
> Psiharis, one of many representatives from 30 states, convened with older citizens and representatives from federal agencies and national associations and organizations. The following issues were addressed: adult day services in the long-term care continuum, the financing of adult day services, long-term care reform, and future directions in adult day services. Policy recommendations were forwarded to the full White House Conference on Aging to be held in May. These special conferences, occurring once each decade, determine major priorities in older adult services and initiatives.
>
> 'Adult day care, as more people age, is becoming the trend of the future,' Psiharis said. 'It is a cost-saving partnership between the family, government, and community-based organizations such as ours. The wonderful thing about it is it is designed to keep elderly people in their homes for as long as possible. That is what we're all about.'
>
> Psiharis also represents GACS as a member of the governing board of CLESE (Coalition of Limited English Speaking Elderly). The coalition supports local community agencies, providing advocacy, technical assistance, and joint programs. He is also a member of the Mayor's Community Development Advisory Committee.

A Stitch in Time

An early Fabric Arts of Greece class held at the Levy Senior Center. Tessie Cantos (center left) assists a participant. Circa 1986. Tessie Cantos collection.

The Fabric Arts of Greece program was one of our first endeavors and remained an integral part of GACS throughout its existence. The program provided socialization to isolated older adults and helped to preserve and share this traditional art form.

Initially, the program was launched through a Neighborhood Arts Program grant offered by the Chicago Office of Fine Arts. The grant targeted individual artists who partnered with community organizations to offer classes or projects to an underserved community.

The Chicago Department of Cultural Affairs came about through a merger of three separate city offices: The Chicago Office of Fine Arts, the Mayor's Office of Special Events, and the Chicago Film Office. Lois Weisberg, who had been the director of the Mayor's Office of Special Events, was appointed commissioner of the newly designated department and served in that role for several years.

The program aimed to preserve and perpetuate the unique Greek art form of *stavrovelonia*, an intricate form of cross-stitching. Examples of this art form could be found in many Greek homes where carefully embroidered tablecloths, doilies, wall hangings, and other textiles were on display.

Although popular with older generations, interest in this art form was waning.

Elaine and Steve crafted a compelling proposal about the importance and uniqueness of this art form and explained how this tradition was passed down from generation to generation in Greek families by teaching this art form to succeeding generations and the works of art that were created and often displayed in prominence within the home.

The classes targeted senior citizens and were held at the Chicago Department of Aging Levy Senior Center located at Lawrence and Damen Avenues. Although this was an instructional class, a secondary goal of the program was to offer participants, some of whom were socially isolated, an opportunity to socialize as well. As envisioned, there would be two sets of eight-week class sessions, one in the spring and one in the fall. The grant funded materials and supplies and a per diem for the artist. Additional time to socialize over coffee or lunch was accommodated before the class. The classes were held on Wednesdays from 1:00 p.m. to 3:00 p.m.

Through word of mouth, Elaine came across Penny Kalogianis who was selected to be the instructor. She had recently come from Greece and was teaching a class in textile arts at her sister's embroidery store on Lawrence Avenue. Penny was willing to teach the class but did not want to take on the responsibilities of being a grantee which included preparing reports and financial accounting of how grant funds were expended. We needed to quickly find an artist to apply for and administer the grant.

Within a day of the deadline to submit the grant, I asked Tessie Cantos if she would be willing to take this on. Although not a professional artist, Tessie was skilled in this art form, which had been passed down to her from her mother and grandmother, and agreed to become the grantee. Tasia Economou, a distant relative and former coworker of Tessie's from the Hellenic Foundation, and a GACS volunteer, joined as a class assistant. Tasia was in her upper eighties at the time. The grant request was approved.

The project description, as initially conceived and submitted to COFA in the May 1986 grant proposal, read in part:

> This project will make available to the public needle-art traditions from all parts of Greece. The fabric art traditions to be taught to the elderly at the Levy Center from August 1, 1986, to March 23, 1987, reveal rural village aesthetics where artistic expression is informed by generations of women providing the daily and holiday needs of their families.

Top: Pictured: (L-R): Tasia Economou, Penny Kalogiannis, and Tessie Cantos during a Fabric Arts of Greece class at the Levy Center. September 1986. **Bottom:** (L-R): Eugenia Stathakis and Tessie Cantos display some of the pieces created by class participants. Circa 1993. Both photos from the Tessie Cantos collection.

Participants in the GACS Fabric Arts Program display handmade Christmas items they made for adult day care center participants. Pictured (L-R): Unknown, unknown, unknown, Mary Strouzas, and Tessie Cantos. December 1992. Photo by John Rassogianis. Tessie Cantos collection.

Since the 1700s, museums, and private collectors from Europe and the Americas have avidly sought to acquire samples from the whole spectrum of fabric arts regularly made by women in the rural villages of Greece.

The thirty-five (35) classes in Greek needle art will be held every Monday from 8:30 AM to 10 AM at the Levy Center's Craft room. The actual classes will be preceded by a two-week exhibition in the Levy Center's main lobby. The exhibition will be drawn from the heirlooms and contemporary work of the class instructors as well as the Greek women who regularly attend the Levy Center. With 450 people per day passing through the Levy Center's main lobby, a potential audience of over 4,500 individuals will see this exhibition. In the course of the year, two smaller exhibits will be presented, again in the Levy Center lobby, to make the public continually aware of the program.

Greek-American Community Services'
Cultural and Arts Program

Presents its

Fabric Arts of Greece Class

Learn or perfect your skills in crocheting, knitting, or embroidery under the direction of skilled instructor Frieda Aravosis.

The 14 week class begins on March 21, 2001

and meets on Wednesdays from 11:30 A. M. to 2:00 P. M.

Classes are held at

Greek-American Community Services
3940 N. Pulaski Road, Chicago.

For further information call 773 545-0303.

The Fabric Arts of Greece class is open to City of Chicago residents over the age of 60 and is free of charge.

You are welcome whether you are a beginner or an expert. Enjoy the friendly group! Learn new skills!

The Chicago Department of Cultural Affairs, Community Development Block Grant Program, and the Illinois Arts Council, a state agency, make the classes possible.

Flyer promoting a display of Fabric Arts of Greece classes at GACS. March 21, 2001. Elaine Thomopoulos collection.

Starting the overall program will be four class sessions (August 1-29) under the guidance of Tasia Economou which will be devoted to presenting the entire gamut of Greek needle arts as preserved and observed in America: crocheting, cut-work, embroidery, knitting, woven fabrics, and even, Eastern Orthodox church vestments. This survey will provide the attending women not only with some essential sense of the overall fabric traditions of Greece but also allow them time to decide which of the classes they wish to attend – if all are not interested in the entire program.

The full range of audience interests is to be served by the careful structure of each of the thirty-five classes. To begin with, there will be five class projects, each to last six weeks: September 5th to October 3rd with Tessie Cantos teaching Pelopponean style crocheting; October 10th to November 7th with Anna Kekatos teaching Thracian style cross-stitching; November 14th to December 19th Penny Kalogiannis teaching {Pelopponean}, style cross-stitching; and Vasia Siapkaris teaching two projects: January 2nd to February 2nd Greek Macedonian embroidery and February 9th to March 16th embroidery for Orthodox Church vestments.

Each of the sessions will be structured with an introductory half-hour showing the class an array of examples of the fabric tradition under review; that session is accompanied by some descriptive historical and social context on the various pieces of needle art. Immediately following these remarks will be an hour of classroom instruction. The final class on March 23, 1987, will be an open house for families and friends of the class participants along with anyone else from the Levy Center who would like to attend.

Our objective with this project is to introduce a new art form to the public through the class and the exhibitions. The project is aimed at teaching twenty (20) people per class session elements of design and overall aesthetics in rural Greek fabric art. Our target audience is hard to reach in both the sense of their being elderly and Greek. We will measure our success with these objectives by the number of those attending this project as well as by the photographs and audio tapes provided with the final report which document the exhibitions and classes.

Thirty-eight participants enrolled in the classes, exceeding our expectations. Participants ranged from first-timers to accomplished artists. The classes provided a means for participants to engage in conversations and get to know each other. Some participants met for lunch before the class. in the Levy Center dining room which served Golden Diner's lunches to seniors.

One enduring relationship that came about through this program was with Luke Fitzgerald, Northeast regional director for the Department of Aging Levy Senior Center. Luke had been in that position for a while, having previously worked with Elaine when she was at the Hellenic Foundation. Luke made the arrangements for our classes to be held at the center. In later years Luke supported CAN and the adult day care center by joining both advisory boards, fundraising, and encouraging referrals.

The Fabric Art Project continued to meet at the Levy Center for its first few years. Tessie coordinated the program with Penny as an instructor and Tasia as a program assistant. Penny eventually returned to Greece and Tasia became less dependable due to her advanced age. Frieda Aravosis assumed the role of assistant. In addition to being a skilled artist in her own right, Frieda had been a program participant and was Tessie's sister-in-law (her brother's wife). The two ran the program through 1993, usually

(L-R): Pat Michalski, Governor's special assistant for ethnic affairs, with Elaine Thomopoulos at the GACS booth in the State of Illinois Center, December 2001. On display were pieces created by Fabric Arts Program participants. Elaine Thomopoulos collection.

assisted by Bessie Choporis, who also had a strong background in these art forms and was Tessie's sister-in-law (her husband's sister).

Once GACS relocated to the Pulaski location, we moved the classes into the center. The classes were held in the James E. Demeur Conference Room, and participants often mingled or visited with adult day care clients. We encouraged Greek ADC clients, as well as any others who may have been interested, to join in on the classes.

At some point, Mary E Young, Cultural and Grants Director for the Chicago Department of Cultural Affairs (DCA) requested pieces of our participant's artwork for a display in the Chicago Cultural Center at 78 East Washington. They were excited to have their works displayed. Unfortunately, several pieces were lost by the city and never returned. When DCA requested pieces for a similar purpose a year or two later, our participants were adamant that they did not want to be part of it.

In March 1994, Tessie Cantos, who coordinated the program since its inception, passed away. Frieda Aravosis then took on the role of coordinator for the project and remained in that role until the program ended in 2002. She was assisted by Bessie Choporis, Beulah Iatropoulos, and Eugenia Stathakis.

A press release announcing the Spring 1995 series of classes quoted Frieda as saying, "It's not too late to come to our group. We have all the materials that are necessary for the program, and we want everybody to come and see what we are doing." John Rassogianis continued. "There seems to be growing awareness of the need to preserve our heritage. *Yiayias and papous* are telling stories to children in our Greek schools, our seniors are learning dance movement exercises to the tune of Samiotissa, and the "sewing club" is helping to preserve the fabric arts skills handed down by our grandparents."

In November 1997, some participants in the Fabric Arts Program purchased a full-page advertisement in the Eleventh Annual Heritage Awards Dinner souvenir album. The dinner recognized social services organizations within the *omogenia*. They wrote: "We the ladies of the Fabric Arts of Greece project of GACS, extend to our honorees our heartfelt congratulations and best wishes for the continued success of all social service agencies of our community." It was signed by the following participants: Frieda Aravosis, Mary Strouzas, Fannie Mitchell, Katina Gouskos, Bessie Selimos, Bertha Funteas, Beulah Iatropoulos, Georgia Sarbieski, Rebecca Vasilakos, Eugenia Stathakis, and Hariklia Mantzavrakos.

In October 1998, examples of artwork created through this program were displayed in the lobby of the James R. Thompson Center in observance of the "United Nations International Year of the Older Adult."

Fabric Arts Program participants displayed some of their work at the Hellenic Museum and Cultural Center. In addition to the display, a roundtable conversation with several participants was held on July 15, 2001, to show and discuss their pieces. Frieda and the participants spoke about their experiences with the art form and how they honed their craft and displayed examples of their creations. The event was well attended.

According to notes that Elaine took of Frieda's talk, she was born in Chicago but moved to Greece at the age of five after her mother died in 1928. When she was in fourth grade, she received one hour of instruction several times each week in crochet and cross-stitch. Frieda's family had a large loom that was used to make items for *prika* (tablecloths, napkins, pillowcases, etc.) as well as pullovers, sweaters, gloves, and other items for the Greek army which was short of supplies. They all felt good to help the war effort. When the war ended, Frieda returned to the U.S. at the age of 18, bringing a number of these items with her. They were dyed with onion skins and were made free-hand by counting threads. There was no

Beulah Iatropoulos discusses several of her works at the Hellenic Museum and Cultural Center. John Dubrovin and unknown look on. July 15, 2001. John Psiharis collection.

stamping and they needed to make the wool first. Although Frieda did some cross-stitching and crocheting in the ensuing years, she devoted more time to this craft upon her retirement after 30 years of working for Brach's Candies.

From December 3–7, 2001, Fabric Arts of Greece Class participants displayed examples of their crocheting, needlepoint, and embroidery in an exhibit at the James R. Thompson Center State of Illinois Building, 100 S. Randolph, Chicago, IL. The exhibit listed the class participants: Anna Arvanitis, Magdalene Bacos, Evelyn Boutzarelos, Phyllis Cain, Emily Cotsirilos, John Dubrovin, Anna Tasia Economou, Margaret Floyd,

Andriana Fotinos, Beulah Iatropoulos, Stamata Kokalias, Bertha Loumbas, Kazimiera Nowak, Mary Poulos, Georgia Sarbieski, Bessie Selimos, Sultana Vougis Smith, Adeline Schmidt, Eugenia Stathakis, Georgia Theodorakos, Ekaterina Sarras, Rebecca Vasilakos, and Frieda Aravosis as the instructor.

An undated CDBG grant request described the FAP: "A model pioneering program for the past twelve years, this project has brought joy and artistic growth with its consequence [sic] social interaction, drawing low-income feeble socially isolated elderly, many of whom are limited English speaking class members, from the many neighborhoods of the city of Chicago. Throughout the years, they have been encouraged to pursue any of the many regional fabric arts of Greece. In the most recent past, they have been specifically assigned Peloponnesian and Thracian style cross stitching, Macedonian embroidery, Peloponnesian style crocheting, and Greek rural knitting. Many participants are of Peloponnesian background."

A draft interim report to the city handwritten by Elaine (year unknown) reported the following:

> The 14-session class on Greek embroidery, cross stitching, and knitting was completed. The class, which included 20 participants met each Wednesday from 11:30 am to 2:30 pm. The program culminated in an exhibit of the participant's work at the Northwest Senior Center with over 200 people viewing the exhibit.
>
> The classes continue to attract all skill levels. The more experienced assist the instructor in teaching those who are just beginning to learn about this art form. This adds to the sense of accomplishment and cooperation that permeates the class. The class not only teaches and perfects the skills of the participants but also decreases their sense of isolation and builds their self-esteem. The audience who viewed the exhibit at the Northwest Senior Center was very enthusiastic about the display. Several were interested in joining our fall classes.

When GACS closed most of its programs in early 2002, the Fabric Arts Project remained intact. Even with no funding, the participants continued to meet weekly for their classes for quite some time. The classes were relocated to the Chicago Department of Aging's Northwest Senior Center (Copernicus Center) at 3160 N. Milwaukee. The participants gathered for Golden Diners lunch before beginning the classes. Elaine, John, and I stopped by to visit on occasion.

Energy Assistance Program

In 1992, shortly after moving into our Pulaski office, we were approached by Michael Payne who coordinated north-side agencies for the Community Economic Development Agency of Cook County (CEDA). CEDA administered the federally funded Low Income Home Energy Assistance Program (LIHEAP) in Cook County.

LIHEAP assisted households with low incomes in paying for their heating expenses. In most cases, it was a credit that was applied to the recipient's gas or electric company account. Some people received checks if, for example, their rent included utility costs.

Advertisement for the Low Income Home Energy Assistance Program (LIHEAP). Circa 1994. John Psiharis collection.

CEDA was looking for a northwest-side intake site for this program. The program provided a stipend of $8 per approved application. Since clients needed to provide proof of their income, residency, and utility bills, which had to be copied and submitted with their application, CEDA provided us with a photocopy machine and a service agreement for the copier. This was before the days of the Internet and computers, and copy machines were vital office machines. Up until this point, GACS didn't have a copy machine. We went to the corner to make copies for 10 cents a page, or to Kinkos or Easy Copy, for larger jobs.

John R took on coordination of the LIHEAP program, enabling us to increase his hours with us. The process was detailed and it took some time to complete an application. The first month (October) was limited to senior citizens, the disabled, or those who had their utilities disconnected. In

November, enrollment opened for everyone else. The funds generally ran out in February.

We underestimated the response to this program when we first agreed to participate. Our initial plan was to have a first come - first serve system on the days we offered the program. We ended up with a line of people waiting to be helped that went to the street and down Pulaski. Once in the center, some without warning sat in with the adult day care clients or even helped themselves to food being served to adult day care participants.

We promptly put a halt to this. I was not comfortable with people off the street coming into contact with adult day care clients. Not only was it disruptive to activities, but it also caused confusion, noise, and some chaos. I was also concerned that we had no idea who these people were, and they might have posed a safety risk or health danger to those elderly who had weaker immune systems or were experiencing dementia. With all the coming and going, there was concern that an ADC client might find an opportunity to wander away unattended.

We decided to schedule appointments instead. The first day of our new approach resulted in all five of our phone lines ringing nonstop all day long. No sooner would we hang up with one call, than another one came through. Maria, John, Ethel, Ann, and I did what we could to answer the calls and set appointments. Later that day I received a call from Illinois Bell, at that time our telephone utility, asking what was happening. The representative asked jokingly, "Are you giving away money or something?" It turned out that the volume of calls coming into GACS was so great that it overwhelmed the 545 telephone exchange and some callers heard an "all circuits are busy" recording.

We quickly realized the need for this program was much larger than was anticipated, and we adapted as quickly as we could. We brought in a few people to help, trained them in how to complete the applications, and paid them a percentage of each application they prepared. They included Bob Blum, our van driver and activity aid, Kathy Rockaitis, a volunteer from the neighborhood, and Floyd "Red" Utley who helped with maintenance at the center. Nick Stathopoulos, a community volunteer, went through training as well. Since Nick was bilingual, our ability to help Greek-speaking applicants was enhanced. Before that, John was the sole Greek speaker in the mix.

At the end of each day, the applications and attachments were tabulated, collated, copied, and then assembled into batches. The emergency applications were prepared in red ink. Batch transmittal forms were completed and the applications were picked up daily by a CEDA courier.

In our first year as an intake site for this program, we helped more than 1,600 households to apply for energy assistance and earned about $12,000 from this program. GACS continued to offer this program in future years with similar results. The same intake people continued their involvement throughout most of these years.

Between July 12-16, 1995, Chicago experienced a record heatwave. The temperature had reached 106 degrees with very high humidity. This was on top of a warmer-than-usual July. The city was in crisis, and by the time the heatwave passed, there were 739 recorded deaths. Most were elderly or low-income individuals who did not have or could not afford the cost of air conditioning.

That summer, CEDA asked GACS to provide emergency cooling assistance. Just before the program began, a semi-trailer truck parked in front of our office to unload cases of box fans. We provided a fan to each applicant who needed one. Hundreds of people came to GACS during this period, and we were able to help them all. The crisis was exacerbated when an electric transformer serving the area caught fire, causing widespread power outages for several days during this heatwave. GACS was fortunate to have been on a different grid so we were not impacted. but across the street from us, the power was out for several days. We opened as a cooling center during daytime hours and had several visitors through this outreach. We received large donations of fresh bagels from the Irving Park Community Food Pantry that we distributed to adult day care participants and LIHEAP clients.

Sadly, one of the casualties of this heatwave was Tina Beniaris. Tina was an older lady who was active within the Greek community, had been a GACS volunteer during special events, and was a participant in the Fabric Arts Project. She lived above George's Restaurant on Foster Avenue near Kimball. She had come in a couple of days earlier to apply for LIHEAP benefits. Although the application had been submitted to CEDA for processing. it had not yet been approved. This underscored how vital this assistance was to those whom we served.

Benefits Eligibility Checklist

Another program that operated under the GACS Community Services banner was the Benefits Eligibility Checklist (BEC), an outreach program that helped senior citizens (classified as age 60 and over) identify and apply for 40 governmental benefits and programs offered at the local, state, and federal levels for which they qualified. It was part of a national effort. The local program was funded by the Chicago Community Trust and the

Retirement Research Foundation and was administered by the Chicago Department of Aging.

Advertisement for the Benefits Eligibility Checklist (BEC) program. Circa 1995. John Psiharis collection.

Among the financial assistance programs BEC screened for were: Qualified Medicare Beneficiary (QMB), Specified Low-Income Medicare Beneficiary (SLMB), Circuit Breaker Pharmaceutical Assistance, State Supplemental Payment (SSP), Supplemental Security Income (SSI), Social Security, Reverse Mortgage, Circuit Breaker Property Tax Relief, Homestead Tax Exemption, Real Estate Tax Deferral, Sewer Service Charge Exemption and Refund, and Railroad Pension. Energy assistance programs on the checklist were: Add-a-Dollar, Illinois Home Weatherization Program, Low Income Home Energy Assistance Program (LIHEAP), and the Illinois Telephone Connection Program. The nutrition/meal programs available were the Food Stamp Program, Golden Diners, and Home Delivered Meals. Health care programs were: Illinois Comprehensive Health Insurance Plan (CHIP), Medical Assistance – No Grant (MANG), Health care programs were: Illinois Comprehensive Health Insurance Plan (CHIP), Medical Assistance – No Grant (MANG), Medicare, Medicare Part A, Medicare Part B, Total-Dent, Dentistry for the Homebound, Emergency Response System, National Eye Care Project, and Public Health Clinics. Housing resources BEC screened for were: CHA Senior Housing, Subsidized Housing for Low-Income Seniors, Home Repairs for Accessible Living (H-RAIL), and the Homescape Program. Legal assistance programs were: Living Will, Durable Power of Attorney for Health Care, and the Community Spousal Impoverishment Program. In-home services offered were the Community Care Program (CCP) and Respite Care Program. Transportation programs they screened for were: CTA/RTA Reduced Fare Program, Chicago Taxi Access Program (TAP), Reduced Auto Insurance, and Reduced City vehicle stickers. Employment resources included: The Job Training Partnership Act (JTPA), Operation ABLE, and the Senior Community Service Employment Program (SCSEP) –Title V.

In the early days of BEC, a concerted effort was made to reach limited and non-English speaking elderly. They were least likely to be aware of programs and services that they were qualified to receive. In addition to language and cultural barriers, this population was difficult to reach and was often insular. In some cases, they shunned mainstream media or had a fear or distrust of the government due to life experiences they encountered in their homeland.

As a result of the relationship we enjoyed with CDOA and our expertise in working with both the Greek community and older adults on the northwest side, we were invited to take part in this program in a unique way. CDOA agreed to pay a part-time Greek-speaking outreach worker to be housed at our center. This person would reach out to older adults to complete the BEC checklist and identify any benefits, services, or entitlements that the senior might qualify for. To my knowledge, GACS was the only ethnic organization to have this sort of arrangement with CDOA at the time.

John agreed to take on this role. At the time he was substitute teaching and was able to work with us on days he didn't get called in. John worked about 20 hours per week at GACS overseeing our Cultural and Arts Program and the publicity for GACS. Additionally, during certain times of the year, he coordinated the LIHEAP program. The new arrangement allowed John to work full-time at GACS. Half of his time was spent on BEC, and the other half focused on other responsibilities.

This arrangement with the city continued for a couple of years. In addition to the low-hanging fruit of our clients, John did outreach events at Greek church picnics, city festivals, area businesses, community events, and partnerships with other organizations. In all we helped hundreds of seniors, possibly thousands, to learn about and receive benefits that they were qualified for and entitled to receive. We created and translated outreach fliers in Greek that were distributed to the churches and other community gathering places. Publicity in both the Greek and local media regularly occurred.

Two of the main program areas under the Community Services Program banner were supervised by John (LIHEAP and BEC). It ended up that in addition to the Cultural & Arts Program, John oversaw most of our community programs. Annually, the community service programs assisted more than 1,500 clients. This was in addition to the adult day care center participants and the Community Aging Network clients. Depending on the types of programming being offered in any given year, the Cultural and Arts Program reached over 1,000 and in some years more (not including the thousands who viewed our traveling exhibit). It is fair to say that GACS reached thousands of people each year in a variety of ways.

A couple of years later, CDOA required John to work from the Copernicus Center, which was the department's Northwest regional office. He often participated in outreach activities at grocery stores, community events, and other public venues. During excessive heat or cold days, John was deployed, along with most CDOA personnel, to do well-being checks on seniors.

The Check Isn't in the Mail

Although GACS had several funding streams including individual donations, special events, program fees, rental income, and foundation grants; the largest share of funding was through government sources. Our contracts with the Illinois Department on Aging Community Care Program in support of the adult day care center, and for a short while, a chore housekeeping program, were our largest and most complicated. GACS maintained a similar contract with the U.S. Veterans Administration (now the U.S. Department of Veterans Affairs) for adult day care services to veterans.

Cultural programs were funded by the Illinois Humanities Council, Illinois Arts Council, Chicago Department of Cultural Affairs, and Community Development Block Grants. Community services programs were funded through agreements with the Chicago Department on Aging, the Chicago Department of Human Services, and the Community Economic Development Agency (CEDA).

Each governmental entity and program had its reporting and billing protocols that required extensive time and effort on our behalf. This was before the Internet and the advent of online invoicing, and the process was labor-intensive, usually including multiple copies of narrative reports, invoices, receipts, attendance sheets, and other forms of documentation. ADC invoicing was monthly while cultural grants were either quarterly or invoiced at the halfway point and project completion.

One would think that invoicing the VA, a federal agency, would be the most time-consuming, but it was the simplest. All they needed were the days each participant attended during the month. The VA paid promptly and we had few problems in dealing with them.

IDOA was another story. It was a nightmare! Maria and Jackie spent a couple of days at the beginning of each month preparing these invoices, not to mention the time Ann spent documenting, adding up the hours of service calendars for each participant, and gathering client signatures, before invoicing could occur.

Completed invoices were mailed to IDOA's Springfield office. Two to three weeks later we received a report on those invoices that were accepted for payment and those that were "rejected." The accepted invoices were forwarded by IDOA to the Comptroller's office for processing. It could take anywhere from a few weeks to several months to receive payment.

The rejects, at times a significant portion of what was invoiced, needed to be dealt with on an individual basis. There were several reasons for a client's invoice being rejected. Usually, Catholic Charities, the Case Management Unit (CMU), was involved. The system required caseworkers from Catholic Charities to visit a senior and assess their needs. If adult day care or chore housekeeping was warranted, the caseworker created a care plan delineating how many hours, or units of service, the client was approved to receive. For lower-income clients, the state covered the full cost of care while those with income exceeding the minimum paid a co-payment. Catholic Charities determined the amount of any co-payment. CMUs submitted their reports and billings to IDOA, and if there were any discrepancies for a particular client, the invoice was rejected.

The social worker handled rejects. Ethel or Des went over the printout line by line to compare them to the care plans. If it was an error on our part, it was corrected and resubmitted. All of this was by mail and involved paperwork so it was a tedious task that took hours of our time each month. If it involved the Catholic Charities-Northeast/Northwest Case Management Unit, she called the caseworker to resolve it. There were times when a client wasn't entered into the system properly, and it could take weeks to correct, and even longer to receive payment. I remember Ethel and me meeting with Sarah Cohen, director of the case management units at her 5801 N. Pulaski office, every so often, to resolve billing issues. We each had thick black three-ringed binders filled with rejects, payment status reports, and other paperwork that we discussed. I usually brought a dozen Dunkin Donuts to these meetings to get us off to a good start.

At the beginning of each month, Maria Maniates began her invoicing challenges. For the Child and Adult Food Program (CAAFP), we submitted monthly invoices to the Illinois Department of Aging. Clients were classified into one of three categories; paid, reduced, or free. The category determined how much GACS received for each meal or snack served.

Since two snacks and one hot lunch were served daily, there was a lot of recordkeeping to do. Pre-computer age, the state provided a spreadsheet form on an oversized piece of paper. It had lines running across the top for each day of the month with smaller boxes identifying each snack and lunch. On the left side, the clients were listed in alphabetical order going down the page. Sub-boxes listed the paid, reduced, and free categories within boxes for each day of the month. Tick marks needed to be in the corresponding boxes for each snack or meal served. We also had to record whether we provided milk to each client. It was a blizzard of tick marks in every direction that required patience, attention, and a magnifying glass to be sure the right mark was in the right box. Years later, I still get eye strain thinking about it! Once completed, the CAAFP invoices were sent to IDOA for processing. After their approval, IDOA forwarded invoices to the Comptroller's office where it took quite a while to process, all for what amounted to a couple of hundred dollars per month. If Maria hadn't volunteered to help with this process, the staff time and effort spent on all this paperwork would have cost more than what we received. Despite her help, at some point, GACS withdrew from this program. It wasn't worth the time, effort, and distraction. IDOA periodically sent staff who spent hours at the center auditing the tick marks and classifications for each client. To me, it was insane that adult day care centers, forced to deal with so much for so little, endured these headaches. All for a couple of hundred dollars per month! This was just one example of how government bureaucracy hindered and distracted providers from their core mission.

The Cultural & Arts Program had its share of invoices and reports that John and Elaine, with Maria's help, managed. By far, the most complex was the quarterly reports to the Chicago Department of Cultural Affairs CDBG. The program narrative reported on what was accomplished during the period of the report and plans for the next quarter, including attachments of publicity, attendance sheets, and photos. The fiscal component required copies of receipts, timesheets, and canceled checks for each expense. These reports needed to be submitted in triplicate. With up to 50 pages for each report, just the effort to photocopy everything took quite a while, and that's assuming the copy machine could make it through the job without a paper jam or overheating.

The Illinois Humanities Council and Illinois Arts Council grants usually required interim and final reports. The IHC report was extensive and required us to engage an outside evaluator who also submitted a report before GACS received the final payment.

Although GACS had several funding streams including foundations, fundraising, rental income, and client service fees; we could not afford to carry the state and city indefinitely. They were notorious late payers, to begin with, and when you add in the persistent reject problem, it was something that few organizations could sustain on an ongoing basis. There were times when GACS was owed more than $30,000 from IDOA and thousands more from the city. Despite this, we needed to meet payroll and pay the mortgage, utilities, and purveyors on time.

For the most part, we were able to navigate when government payments were in arrears within reason. If cash flow was tight, supporters contributed to help us get through. During longer periods, GACS tapped into a line of credit GACS with Midwest Bank.

The state took even longer to process our payments during a period of economic recession in the late 1990s and again after the September 11, 2001 tragedy. I remember that during one of these periods when payments were already in arrears, a state check was lost in the mail. Problems were further compounded when GACS had to wait nearly eight weeks for the check to be re-issued. There were times GACS delayed paying employees until the state checks came because the credit line had been maxed-out. At times, purveyors called or withheld service due to the inability to pay bills on time. It was a frustrating and stressful period not of our own making.

On a couple of occasions, we met with Richard Bradley, our state representative, and Mike Wojick, the local alderman, who made calls to try to expedite payments from the state and city. Some adult day care centers closed as a result of this problem. GACS was owed tens of thousands of dollars for services that had already been provided and the balance owed was increasing by the day. By the time a payment was received, it literally would be gone within minutes as overdue bills from utilities, suppliers, and past-due payrolls were paid. When we received a check, and if I wasn't in, the staff would page me on my beeper to let me know a check had come in. They knew they would finally get paid.

To further complicate the situation, our efforts to raise money from major donors competed with those of our offspring organization, the nursing home. This was a period when the GANHC was aggressively fundraising since the property had been acquired and construction would begin soon. The enthusiasm in the community for the GANHC resulted in large donations being made there, especially for naming opportunities, and less going to GACS. Additionally, the Hellenic Museum and Cultural Center was in the midst of a multi-million-dollar capital campaign to build the National Hellenic Museum. The community was also supporting the Greek Orthodox Diocese of Chicago's new monastery and retreat center in Kenosha that Bishop Iakovos was spearheading. These projects were in addition to fundraising conducted by churches, Philoptochos societies, fraternal organizations, professional organizations, UHAC, AHEPA, the Hellenic Foundation, and others.

Around this time, John went on leave from his position as CAP director due to pressing family matters but returned to the board and became vice president. Elaine stepped into his role and ran the Fabric Arts Program for its duration. In total, the program spanned 14 years. The Fabric Arts Program was funded by CDBG, and Elaine supervised the program and completed the appropriate reports.

A report for the period between October 1, 1997, and March 30, 1998, revealed the following: There were 67 inquiries, 10 intakes, eight admissions, six closed cases, and 180 brochures mailed. During this period, 1,924 units of service were provided (721 private pay, 1.060 state pay, and 143 V.A). In comparison, the prior period had 1,931 units of service (620 private pay, 1,031 state pay, and 280 V.A.). An attached financial summary reported: October ($10,592 billed, 344 units, 21 clients), November ($10,066 billed, 287 units provided, 23 clients), December ($9,827 billed, 310 units, 23 clients), January ($10,043 billed, 308 units, 23 clients), February ($10,875 billed, 335 units, 25 clients), March ($12,067 billed, 161 units, 25 clients), April ($12,365, *, 25 clients), (May *, *, 26 clients). Five new clients, including a Greek lady, were scheduled to begin in June. *This data was not included in the report.

In January 1999, over a long New Year's Day weekend, a blizzard hit Chicago that resulted in heavy snowfall. GACS was closed for the holidays and then due to the snow, was closed for a few more days into the week. The center was plowed in by the snow plows on Pulaski and buried under drifts of snow blown onto the front of the building, making it impossible to open the door. Tornie was with me for the holidays, so she was safe.

While GACS was closed, an assistant to the mechanic at G&F Mobil next door and his brother used George's keys to gain entry to the second-floor hallway. They broke into Maria's office and stole a few pages of checks from the middle of the checkbook, where it wouldn't be immediately noticed. Maria first noticed it when she was reviewing canceled checks from the bank and found several with a vague attempt to forge my signature and the check numbers were not in sequence. When we became aware, we immediately reported it to LaSalle Bank and the police but by that time more than $5,000 was gone. The guys were caught on video trying to cash the checks at a downtown bank. We were prepared to testify, but it turned out they were on video so it wasn't necessary. This could not have come at a worse time given the delayed payments from the state. We eventually got our money back, but it took a couple of months and further contributed to our problems. There was a two-signature requirement on the account with LaSalle for any check over $1,000. The perpetrators didn't know this and only used one signature. Yet LaSalle still honored the checks. I vowed to never do business with LaSalle again. As soon as we were able to, we moved the GACS accounts to Midwest Bank and Trust.

On a couple of occasions, Abe Landa talked to me about the possibility of purchasing our building. He owned a converted house at 3930 N. Pulaski on the corner of Pulaski and the Kennedy Expressway exit. A printer had his business on the first floor and slept in the upstairs attic. Soon thereafter, the printer moved out and Abe and his son Shawn opened a hot dog stand there. Today, after extensive remodeling, it became Hot Woks Cool Sushi, a popular Pan-Asian restaurant that now has several locations in Chicago. Abe had also acquired the building next door to us and wanted our building too. I heard from George Oshana, the owner of the G&F Mobil gas station on the corner, that Abe approached him regularly about purchasing his property as well. Apparently, Abe wanted to buy up the whole block.

I never particularly cared for Abe from when we first met. As he was a neighbor and adjoining property owner, I was friendly with him but let it go at that. I reported his interest in buying the building to the board, and we agreed that the building was not for sale.

Abe then proposed to buy a comparable building and do some sort of exchange. I spent an afternoon driving around the city with him looking at buildings that he had in mind. Some were appealing but were not in areas that made sense for us. We needed to be in a certain geographic area to be in the center of our service area and that was the vicinity of our current location. He showed me a very nice building that had been a medical supply store on Belmont near Harlem and another location at Diversey and Central. Both were far from our epicenter. The third was promising. It was a corner storefront with a parking lot in the back at the corner of Milwaukee and Sunnyside. We expressed interest but it turned out that the property was already under offer.

Months later, Abe again inquired about the building. I again conveyed his interest to the board, and this time, given the finances, some felt that we should hear more. Kosta was designated to speak with Abe. They had a few conversations, and in time an offer was made. I don't recall the numbers at this point, but the deal included one year of free rent for the first floor space, $1,000 per month rent for the second year, and $1,200 for the third. After paying off the mortgage, GACS would net about $50,000.

The board was divided on this. Some saw this as an easy way out of our financial crisis while others felt that we shouldn't go that route. Long-timers like Dr. Kioutas, Evangeline, John Rassogianis, and I were against it. Others, including those who had come to the board more recently and hadn't experienced the struggles that we had, were in my view, too quick to cash out. After a close vote, the board voted to sell the building. Jim Kozonis also objected but there was little he could do given the board's decision. The building was sold and life went on... for the moment.

Once the building was sold, the second-floor offices were moved back to the first floor. This process was underway when Kosta arranged to meet Ray at the center over a weekend while I was out of town. For what Ray later told me were "slave wages and a hot dog lunch," from Abe's hot dog stand next door, Kosta went through the center with Ray, directing him to purge a variety of things. Among the items discarded were a client-curated library in the adult day care center, artwork done by center and fabric arts participants, and a couch that had been donated by Aphrodite Demeur for the room named in memory of her son James. According to Ray, Kosta planned to take Tornie to a pet shelter the following weekend.

After I returned home from the airport, I heard Ray's urgent message left on my answering machine and returned his call. Ray filled me in on his weekend of labor and Kosta's threat about Tornie. I was enraged. I drove to GACS at nearly midnight, collected Tornie and her belongings, and brought her home with me. The next morning, I faxed Kosta my resignation, effective immediately, and disconnected the phone from the wall jack.

After a couple of days, John called me to say that Kosta would resign if I returned. At John's urging, I reluctantly agreed to return. As vice president, John became president upon Kosta's resignation. Kathy Pisheck became treasurer and Michelle Milewski secretary.

In observance of National Adult Day Care Week, Northwest Chicago Senior Care hosted an open house on September 22, 2000. In a press release that appeared in the September 14 issue of the *Greek Star*, I stated, "This is an exciting year for us, as it is our 10th anniversary year. We encourage those who want to know more about us or the critical services we have delivered over the last decade, or our plans for the next 10 years, to drop by and visit."

A GACS December 2000 fundraising appeal letter signed by me, included an insert called "Reflections of a Decade 1990-2000." It included several photos of ADC participants and their families and the backside included memories from ADC staff. It read in part:

> On a windy snow-swept day in January of 1990, Mary walked through the doors of Northwest Chicago Senior Care for the first time. She had the distinction of being the first participant in our new adult day care center.
>
> She was a pleasant lady in her eighties who had taught Greek school for nearly 50 years. The welcoming and caring staff and the friendly environment helped her to quickly adjust to her surroundings. She especially enjoyed teaching Greek to the staff and correcting us when we made a mistake.
>
> Mary was the first of many frail, isolated, and forgetful older adults that have since come through our doors. For most of them, the time that has been spent at our center has had a significant impact on the quality of their lives. The socialization, friendships, and sense of purpose that evolves in the lives of the participants are immeasurable. Healthcare, nutrition, and activities are vital to their sense of well-being. Equally important is the peace of mind caregivers experience knowing their loved one is well cared for during the daytime hours.
>
> As we reflect on the past and look forward to the future, we hope that you will affirm the importance of this program and the impact that it has had on the lives of the elders we serve by making a generous contribution in support of these efforts. Your support will play a critical role in enabling us to continue to offer this needed service in the months and years to come.

GACS entered 2001 with a $1,200 per month rent expense added to the budget. The state was severely behind, and payments were erratic at best. If Abe came into the center to request the rent and the money from the state hadn't arrived yet, he would complain loudly in front of the clients, ranting that GACS couldn't even pay the rent on time, often using intimidating tones and colorful language. If we knew he was coming, John and/or Maria and I would head out the back door and go to Little Mike's for coffee or to the park for a hot dog. Unfortunately, the adult day care staff and clients could not escape Abe's wrath and endured this intimidation.

Tuesday, September 11, 2001, started like any other day. It was a sunny morning and I was leaving home to pick up two of our adult day care clients on my way in since one of the vans was in the shop for repair. After seeing the first plane fly into the World Trade Center. I remember running to the car so I could turn on the radio to hear the latest. While in the car, the second plane hit. By the time I had picked up the clients and driven to the center, the participants and staff were glued to the television. We watched this tragedy unfold together and collectively experienced raw emotion and disbelief at what we were watching. I remember standing outside of the center and being aware of how eerily quiet things were. Being on a flight path, it was eerie to not hear a single airplane in the sky and only a few cars on two usually very busy streets. Within hours, the city was blanketed in American flags displayed from countless windows, rooftops, buildings, and vehicles. GACS proudly displayed American flags in our windows and on each *Ya'Sou* van. I do not recall if GACS closed for any time as a result of this attack but it is likely that it did.

The tragedy and its aftermath caused further delays in government payments to vendors making it even more difficult for service providers to survive. We did better than some because our adult day care center had a more diverse client base. We also had private pay clients who paid the full rate (rather than the state's subsidized rate) and VA clients. The VA paid promptly. We also had grants and thus a better cash flow than some of the other centers. Nonetheless, there were limits to what any organization could endure over a prolonged period, and we were reaching our breaking point.

A special GACS fundraising appeal dated September 14, 2001, described our plight, and the impact delayed payments were having on GACS and other centers throughout the state:

> For over a decade, Northwest Chicago Senior Care, the adult day care center operated by Greek-American Community Services has played an important role in the lives of frail, isolated, and forgetful older adults and the families who care for them. Perhaps the following letter by Mrs. Adory Ramos, a registered nurse by training and daughter of one of our recent participants can best illustrate the effect we have on those we serve.
>
> 'My Dad died February 28, 2001. He was 92 years old. He lived with my family and me for the last 5 ½ years of his life. It's unbelievable how much we miss him, and we console ourselves with the knowledge that he lived a full, wonderful life. It was very sad to see him getting weaker and frailer as he advanced in years, but we know the days he had spent at the day care added life to his years. He enjoyed it so much that not being able to go (during inclement weather and long holiday weekends) was like a punishment for him. He looked so much forward to going every day! Even when I'd see him not looking well, he'd insist on going because he did not want to miss the activities (especially Bingo!) and the exercises.
>
> Sorting his things after he died was particularly painful but gave me a lot of reasons to smile too. Seeing all of the mementos from the day care, like his Bingo prizes, his projects, and the

A closer look at Northwest Chicago senior care center, an agency of the Greek American Community Services

By Danae Voutiritsas

The Northwest Chicago Senior Care Center, an agency of the Greek-American Community Services, opened its doors in January of 1990 to care for people who have needs and require a certain extra something. It is a caring place, which is concerned about people who have "special" needs. It assists families which have many demands placed on them in today's world. The Northwest Care Center is there to help all of those many needs.

A registered nurse is present at all times. The clients receive a healthy lunch and snacks. They also participate at their individual levels in a diverse daily activity program, which includes recreational activities and exercises.

In addition to musical sing-a-longs, arts and crafts, and even pet therapy, the most important activity is interrelating to each other and socializing with one another. The clients are also given more of a reason to enjoy themselves on a daily basis rather than just staying at home. It breaks the monotony that often affects the person who lives alone or is alone during the day.

Transportation is offered for each client from his or her place of residence directly to the center. The Illinois Department on Aging and the Veterans' Administration subsidize many of the clients; if they qualify, they pay very little or nothing.

Having a family member, relative, or friend present at the Northwest Senior Care Center gives one a sense of security; one no longer has to worry or be stressed about the person being cared for. They enjoy plenty of socialization, activities, health care and nutritional meals. The family and the caregiver benefit from the peace of mind that their loved one is cared for while they are at work.

Employers benefit through increased attendance and daily performance of workers who are at peace since their loved ones are being well cared for. The community benefits because the older adult remains at home as an integral part of the family. All benefit from the affordable cost of day care compared to the other elder care options, leaving all involved satisfied and happy.

For more information on adult day care for a friend, loved one or a co-worker, please contact the Northwest Chicago Senior Care Center, 3940 N. Pulaski Rd., Chicago, IL, 60641. Telephone: (773) 545-0303 or log on to www.seniordaycareservices.com.

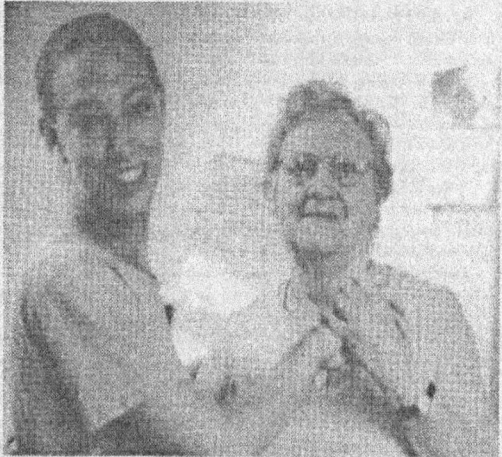
Adeline S. and dance teacher. Photo by Danae Voutiritsas.

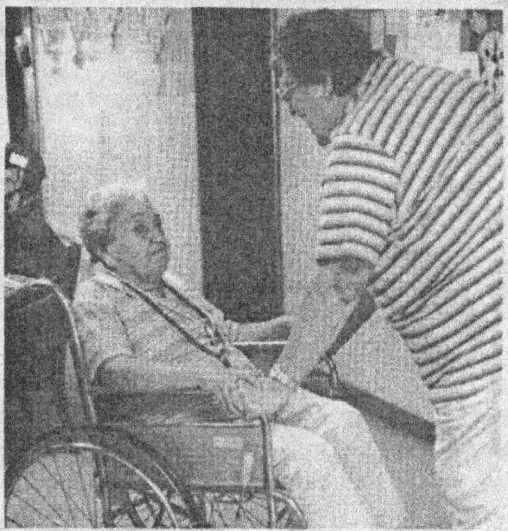
Rose C. and nurse Kathleen O'Leary. Photo by Danae Voutiritsas.

A profile of NCSC prepared by Danae Voutiritsas that appeared on the back page of the *Greek Star*. Circa 2001. Elaine Thomopoulos collection.

different certificates (for Father's Day, Best Athlete, Best in Jeopardy, and every conceivable certificate) that only showed how the day care made every effort to make him feel important. And important he definitely felt. He'd wave his certificate or show me his Bingo prize as soon as he got off the bus! He was like a little boy coming home from school who couldn't wait to show his family his great accomplishments for the day. For that blessed joy, for him and for us, we are eternally grateful.'

This letter is one of many we have received over the years from grateful caregivers and valued clients. Each letter speaks to the vital role our facility has played in the life of an older loved one or a concerned family member. Through the health care services, activities, recreational programs, socialization, exercise, meals, physical therapy, and transportation offered to our participants, we have often been an instrument in preventing or delaying nursing home placement or costly in-home care and in turn, have endeavored to 'add life to the years' of those we serve.

The demand for senior day care is expected to grow at double-digit rates in the coming years as older adults, due in part to modern medical advances, live longer but require more assistance with daily activities.

Likewise, the aging baby boom generation will soon begin to require these services. Those who are enrolled in our program typically require much more personal care and specialized assistance than just five years ago. Despite these increased needs, funding has remained an ongoing and critical concern.

The majority of our participants are enrolled through the Community Care Program (CCP). In essence, this means they are of a low-income status dependent mainly on their social security or a pension to get by. They range in age from 60 to 97 and are affected by a variety of ailments, mobility impairments, or disorientation. They cannot be left home alone while their families work as they may risk injury, wander out of the house unattended, over or under-medicate themselves, forget to eat lunch, fall, or experience other incidents resulting from their physical or mental conditions. If it weren't for our center, the caregiver would either have to quit his/her job or seek costly long-term care or in-home care options.

In-home service does not offer the socialization, health care, and sense of purpose that adult day care offers.

Fabric Arts Program participants meet with Illinois First Lady Laura Lynn Ryan in the Governor's Office. Seated (L-R): Emily Cotsirilos, Eugenia Stathakis, Phyllis Cain, and John Dubrovin. Standing: John Psiharis, Elaine Thomopoulos, Laura Lynn Ryan, Beaula Iatropoulos, and Frieda Aravosis. October 2001. John Psiharis collection.

Today, adult day care programs throughout the state are in crisis. Last year alone, 12 Illinois centers were forced to close. In May 2001, another two centers shut their doors. By year's end, it is expected that over 7 percent of the remaining 94 centers will also cease operations. This is a direct result of inadequate funding from the Illinois Department on Aging's Community Care Program. On average, state funding covers less than two-thirds of the actual cost of care for an older adult and does not take into account rising costs in these uncertain economic times.

Since 1990, our center has served as a valuable resource for Northwest side families seeking relief, peace of mind, and support as they undertake the difficult emotional, and time-consuming process of caring for an aging loved one.

In light of these circumstances, we write to ask for your support to enable us to continue to offer this vital service to a very underserved population. Your donation of at least $100 will help us to sustain this program during these very challenging times and enable us to continue working towards self-sufficiency.

In October, Elaine and I joined Fabric Arts participants who had their work on display in the atrium of the James R. Thompson Center State of Illinois

Building and met with Illinois First Lady Laura Lynn Ryan to show her a few pieces of their works. During the photo op, Elaine and I told Mrs. Ryan about the problems we and other providers were having collecting payments from the state and that these delays could force some providers to close their doors. I asked for her husband's help. She appeared concerned, held my hand in hers, and said "I will pray for you." This was about a month after the 9/11 attacks, and I still remember the somber mood and increased security that permeated the building and how subdued everything seemed compared to the usual hustle and bustle one usually encountered in the State of Illinois Building.

We were very fortunate. Our team cared and remained even if they weren't being paid on time. Ann and Lorraine were both retired and had other sources of income, so they waited. Maria shifted some hours over to the nursing home and eventually expanded to full-time there once the nursing home opened. John worked for the Chicago Department on Aging and had the option to take on substitute teaching jobs to fill any gaps. We always made it a priority to pay Ray first so that he could pay his rent to the Irving Park YMCA.

This situation continued into November, and we were told there was little chance that we would see a payment of any kind from the state until the following February, at the earliest. I was worn out at every level and did not want to endure any more of this. I was tired of telling people they couldn't get paid and hiding from the landlord. Despite our best efforts, we were powerless to change anything to get paid sooner. After 16 years, I resigned from the position of executive director.

John, with agreement from the board, asked Danae Voutiritsas to take on the executive director role and she accepted. I thought John and Danae would make a great team. Elaine and I continued to help from the sidelines to the extent possible.

Given the financial conditions, the board opted not to renew the lease, and instead, GACS closed in the spring of 2002. Katherine Pischeck took the financial and client records. John took a lot of the files and other stuff to store in his garage. Unfortunately, these boxes went missing after a few years. I began a new position as senior services director at the Hyde Park Neighborhood Club, which was in the midst of a makeover. I purchased some of the GACS furniture to use there. John was able to sell both *Ya'Sou* vans through ads in the *Chicago Reader*. Twenty years later, John recalls that one was purchased by a band needing a van to travel cross-country.

About a month after closing GACS, checks started coming from the state. In total, nearly $40,000 came in within a relatively short period. Board meetings were held in the boardroom at Midwest Bank or Little Mike's

Restaurant. The board ensured that to the extent possible all debts were paid and then dissolved the organization.

GACS came to an end but there was little time to rest...the nursing home was about to open. As one set of doors closed, another was on the verge of opening.

Possibilities Unfulfilled

Over the years we considered to some degree or other, many programs, services, and ideas that for one reason or another never came to fruition. I have included some of them here as a way to preserve these efforts and illustrate the thinking that evolved from within. Among those that come to mind:

In 1986, GACS, in cooperation with the Assyrian Universal Alliance Foundation, developed plans to establish a joint Greek and Assyrian Golden Diners Program location. A grant application was submitted to the Chicago Department on Aging. Neither Elaine nor I recall why this project never came to fruition, but it is possible that finding a suitable location was an impediment. It would have built upon our cooperation with the AUAF in other areas (Strains on Ethnic Pride conference, Assyrian Project for the Elderly, and literacy programs for the elderly). A summary of the proposed nutrition program details the plan:

> Our proposal calls for serving 50 senior citizens each day. There will be both Greek and Assyrian participants. The program will be open to all senior citizens over the age of sixty. Greek and Assyrian meals will be served two to three times a week and American meals the remainder of the week. The city will reimburse us for $2.30 per plate that is served. Participants are asked, but not required, to make a voluntary contribution towards the cost of the meals. Lectures, activities, and other programs will be offered to the participants in English, Greek, and Assyrian. This will include health lectures and screening programs, field trips, and if possible, arts and crafts.' Anticipated expenses were $7,800 per year and included a program coordinator at $6,500 (25 hours per week at $5.00/hour), insurance, and publicity costs.

In February 1986, GACS submitted a grant request for $17,406 in response to the Illinois Department on Aging's "Promote Independence Initiative." The funds would be used to write and publish a manual showcasing innovative programs serving ethnic elderly and to launch an ethnic providers' council that would meet every other month. The following organizations had agreed to write a chapter and participate in the council meetings: Association of Refugees from Indo-China, Assyrian Universal

Alliance Foundation, Casa Central, Council for Jewish Elderly, Greek-American Community Services, Japanese American Service Committee, Korean American Community Services, Lithuanian Human Services of the U.S.A., and Metropolitan Chicago Coalition on Aging. The Chicago Department on Aging and Disability and the Illinois Ethnic Consultation would provide technical assistance. Elaine would be the editor of the manual. The plan was to print 500 manuals and to use the proceeds from their sale ($10 per book) to do a second printing.

In January 1987, GACS submitted a grant proposal to the Retirement Research Foundation requesting $76,462 for CAN over two years in support of a telephone visiting program. The program built upon CAN's successful and innovative model of training and supporting homebound elderly to do friendly visits with other shut-ins over the phone utilizing a self-help approach. By the end of year two, it was expected that there would be 60 volunteers phone visiting, and 400 clients. Volunteers would each be assigned up to 10 people to call. The proposal was not funded.

In the spring of 1988, we briefly established a GACS satellite office in Boulder. Colorado. This was in response to interest from Neni Panagouria who wanted to lead the effort. Neni, a Ph.D. candidate in cultural anthropology at the University of Indiana, had participated in a GACS program on *rembetika* in December 1987. During a post-event dinner, Neni mentioned that she was impressed with what GACS had achieved and that she hoped to offer similar programs in Colorado. A conversation ensued and the idea of GACS establishing an outpost in Boulder came about. Since GACS was tax-exempt, operating, and had achieved a track record of successful programming, it would be easier and faster to do it under our auspices, than it was for her to start a new organization. The Boulder office would apply for local and state grants to launch programs.

Neni believed that there was a dearth of cultural endeavors within Colorado's Greek American community and was impressed with the number, variety, and quality of Chicago's cultural and social events. From its inception, GACS maintained a vision of expanding into other parts of the country. This was an opportunity to experiment with a satellite location. We announced the opening in our newsletter and Greek media and began to explore grant opportunities grounded in humanities or arts-based programming. The intent was to partner with local organizations in sponsoring these programs. Neni had begun to invite locals to join a newly established GACS Boulder Advisory Committee. Unexpectedly, Nene moved to another state several months after the outpost was established. As this project depended on her being there to coordinate everything, we ended the effort.

GACS researched and proposed the concept of a Greek United Fund as a united effort to support the community's institutions. As conceived, GACS, Hellenic Foundation, GANHC, and the Hellenic Museum and Cultural Center would benefit through a community-wide fundraising drive and employee deductions program. Ethel, Evangeline, and I met with leaders of the Jewish United Fund, Black United Fund, and United Way in the course of formulating the plan. GACS and the GANHC were interested in exploring the possibilities, but the Hellenic Foundation wasn't, and the idea fizzled as other matters took priority.

John Rassogianis and I had several conversations with Alex Kouvalis, owner of the Patio Theater on Irving Park Road, about showings of Greek films. The idea was that GACS would sponsor and promote a monthly Greek film night and in turn, receive a portion of the proceeds. It turned out that the renovations Alex was making to the historic movie theater took a lot longer than planned, and this never came to fruition.

A big problem in the Greek community during this time was competing events. The community was vibrant and active with a good number of organization and church activities occurring throughout the year. When GACS planned events, we did our best to consult the *Greek Star* Calendar of Events and be in contact with other groups to work out dates, but it wasn't full-proof. In conversations with the Hellenic Professional Society of Illinois, KRIKOS, Greek Women's University Club, the Hellenic Cultural Organization, and Orthodox Singles, we agreed to establish a community-wide calendar of events dubbed the Hellenic Hotline.

As CAP director, John kept the calendar and organizations faxed or called in information on upcoming events so they would be listed. If any schedule conflicts became apparent, there was an opportunity to change a date to minimize competing events. Since GACS had a good number of events each year, we found this to be helpful. This coordination continued for a couple of years, but as leaders within the groups changed and the Internet age dawned, it became less relevant. Expenses for this program were covered through the CDBG grant.

As Northwest Chicago Senior Care evolved, it became apparent that there was a need for Saturday adult day care services. A number of the families being served worked on Saturdays and had to make other arrangements or hire a caregiver to sit with their loved ones. Recognizing that there was a need but not a large demand for this, we considered various ways GACS could provide a scaled-down cost-effective service that met the needs of caregivers. The plan envisioned shorter hours, soup and bag lunches, using only one van to provide transportation, and incorporating volunteers to lead activities. It would be private- pay only for Saturdays since these

GREEK-AMERICAN COMMUNITY SERVICES

WILL OFFER BEGINNING JULY 1, 1993

IN - HOME CARE TO NORTHWEST SIDE ELDERLY

THROUGH ITS CHORE - HOUSEKEEPING

&

HOMEMAKER PROGRAMS

AT NO EXPENSE TO ELIGIBLE CLIENTS IN MOST CASES

Assistance in such areas as shopping, laundry, cooking, housekeeping, medication management, errands and bathing.

For further information, or to enroll in the program, contact the *Community Aging Network*, an agency of *Greek-American Community Services*, at *(312) 545-0303*.

Community Aging Network
3940 N. Pulaski Road
Chicago, IL. 60641

An agency of Greek-American Community Services

Greek-American Community Services does not discriminate in admission to program or treatment of employment in programs or activities in compliance with The Illinois Human Rights Act, the U.S. Civil Rights Act, Section 504 of the Rehabilitation Act, The Age Discrimination and Employment Act, and the U.S. and Illinois Constitutions.
If you feel you have been discriminated against, you have a right to file a complaint at the Illinois Department on Aging.
For further information, call 1-800-252-8966 (voice and TDD).

Flyer promoting GACS Chore-Housekeeping and Homemaker Programs. Circa 1993. John Psiharis collection.

changes would not have been allowed under CCP requirements. As I recall there were always a few families interested in this service but never enough to make it financially viable. GACS needed a certain number of clients participating to break even.

In 1993, GACS received a contract through the IDOA Community Care Program to provide Chore Housekeeping services to the Greek elderly. There were several reasons why we applied: It was the first IDOA CCP-restricted contract for ethnic providers, and it was unknown when the next opportunity to apply would occur. We viewed it as an enhancement and expansion of service to our ADC families, as well as potential nursing home residents. We did not intend to make it a major focus. Instead, we viewed it as augmenting our existing services. The Hellenic Foundation operated a larger program, and we did not want to duplicate or compete with them. Organizationally, the program was placed under CAN, which Ethel Kotsovos directed.

An announcement about this program entitled, "GACS Offers Additional Services," which appeared in the June 6, 1993 issue of the *Greek Star,* reported:

> Greek-American Community Services, celebrating ten years of service, is pleased to announce that it will offer Chore-Housekeeping and Homemaker Services to elderly Northwest Side residents of Greek descent. Services will begin on July 1, 1993.
>
> The program will offer elderly assistance in such areas as housekeeping, laundry, cooking, shopping, errands, medication management, and bathing on a regular basis through an assigned homemaker. There will be no cost to most eligible participants. Funding is assumed by the Illinois Department on Aging Community Care Program.
>
> 'With the addition of these new services we are in fact rededicating ourselves in our commitment to care for the aged,' stated John Psiharis, GACS Executive Director. 'These services complement our existing services to the elderly. We are grateful to the State of Illinois for providing us with this opportunity to expand the services we offer the community.' Greek-American Community Services now operates a highly successful adult day care center, Northwest Chicago Senior Care.
>
> For further information on these services call the Community Aging Network, an agency of Greek-American Community Services at (312) 545-0303.

GACS had a narrow vision for this program and hoped to incorporate it into the existing structure. Ethel supervised the program, and it grew to consume a good amount of her time. As I recall, at most we served 12 clients but the amount of time it took to manage the program detracted from her roles as ADC social worker and CAN program director. The home visits and paperwork required by the program were time-consuming. Interviewing, training, and supervising chore/housekeepers took time and effort, and turnover in these positions was high. There was a constant need to recruit, interview and train new employees to replace others who left. I recall employees moving back to Greece, not being able to meet the physical demands of the position, or quitting because they didn't want to perform essential tasks. We determined that someone was needed to run the program. Payments from the state were in arrears so we needed a cash cushion of several months to carry the receivables. Revenue would increase with proper attention, but our funds were limited due to delayed

ADC payments from the state. We considered fundraising and/or applying for grants to fund the position, but the GANHC had entered the capital campaign phase and the ADC remained our priority. Since these services

were available from the Hellenic Foundation, we decided to end this program and focus our attention and resources in other directions.

In this vein, we worked towards establishing a meals-on-wheels program. The concept grew out of CAN's friendly visiting program when volunteers expressed concern about the lack of nutritional food available to their clients. After some internal conversations, we discussed the idea with CDOA, the possibility of applying for a restricted grant under their Meals on Wheels program to pilot this idea within the community and they were receptive. Master Caterers would prepare Greek-inspired meals for our clients, and the St. Andrew Young Adult League offered to deliver the meals weekly to our clients. This project gained traction and was in the planning phase when Kosta's accident happened and the project was indefinitely postponed.

At some point, CDOA made an effort to establish ethnic Golden Diners sites. Through CLESE, CDOA reached out to ask if we would be interested in establishing a Greek Golden Diners site. They would pay so much per meal and at-will donations from the seniors would cover some of the cost.

Father George Kaloudis at Holy Trinity Church was especially interested in having us. However, the second-floor gymnasium was not wheelchair accessible so it wouldn't work for us. We then reached out to St Athanasios and Ioannis Greek Orthodox Church, the closest church to GACS, located at the corner of Keeler and Berteau. At that time, the church was not part of the Archdiocese. Instead, it reported directly to Constantinople. It was a small congregation and there was interest, but CDOA required that they install wheelchair ramps and make other modifications that made it cost-prohibitive to the church, and nothing materialized.

Given that GACS had two vans that were not in use during certain parts of the day, we considered offering transportation to doctor's appointments or grocery shopping. The suggested name for this service was the *Ya'Sou* Shuttle. We experimented with this on a small scale and found that doctors' appointments often were behind schedule impacting our ability to get ADC clients home on time. So we never pursued it beyond this trial.

"From Your Friends at GACS," a comical fax cover sheet, drawn by volunteer Mark Quartullo, shortly after Evangeline Mistaras donated a new computer and printer to GACS. It depicts the computer room: (L-R) the photocopy machine that was always breaking down, John Psiharis, Evangeline Mistaras, John Rassogianis, Tornie, and the new computer. Date unknown. John Psiharis collection.

GACS was approached by two different cellular companies interested in installing cell phone towers on our property. Our location, adjacent to the Kennedy Expressway, made it an appealing location for cell phone companies. However, we were concerned about the potential health effects of having a cell tower anywhere near the adult day care center and did not pursue this further.

After buying the building, we briefly considered converting the front conference room at GACS into a boutique to sell handmade arts and crafts items made by Greek American artists, including Fabric Arts and ADC participants. Although it was a novel idea and would generate some income for both the artist and GACS, we decided that it was best to keep the room as a meeting room, given the meetings, classes, and ADC activities that utilized the room. We considered using one of the second-

floor studio units for the gallery instead but never moved forward with this idea since there were other priorities at the time.

The idea of converting some or all of the second-floor studios into congregate senior housing was also considered. Upstairs residents could receive health care, socialization, and some meals in the ADC and other synergies were possible. Ultimately, we decided that the second floor was not optimal for this type of housing, and we were hesitant to take on the responsibilities a program of this type entailed. So we did not pursue it.

As Elaine and I collaborated on a paper about GACS for the 2019 National Modern Greek Studies Association Conference, and again on "Working to Preserve our Heritage: A Historical Review of Greek-American Community Services," an article that appeared in the May 2021 edition of *Ergon* magazine documenting the achievements of GACS, we were reminded of an unexplained phenomenon that was often present at GACS; Johnny Q. Elaine recalled this in the *Ergon* article.

> In 2020, Thomopoulos was interviewing staff and friends of GACS to gain more information for this article. Interestingly, four interviewees remembered something very odd: a ghost that was named Johnny. The ghost only did his mischief when the two Johns were together. They were Executive Director John Psiharis and Director of Cultural Arts John Rassogianis. When Johnny made his appearance, chairs would tip over on their own; Thomopoulos, herself, remembers sitting at the Taverna Restaurant on Lincoln Avenue with the two Johns. She witnessed a chair on the other side of the table fall over on its own. One person reported a chair levitating, hitting him. Johnny hid coats and sent little creamers sailing across the room. Having a priest read prayers did not help, according to Rassogianis. Afterward, he found his coat in the trash can. Despite the minor annoyances of Johnny, the dedicated staff, volunteers, and board of directors of GACS achieved a great deal.

Since he was only present when John and I were together, we referred to him as Johnny Q. This way there were John P, John Q, and John R. I remember chairs falling in the middle of meetings, lectures, and during

A photo of a chair that had mysteriously tipped over at GACS with no one near it. Date unknown. John Psiharis collection.

dinner dances and other events. We deduced that this spirit or entity was a youngster who seemed to engage in childish pranks rather than anything harmful. To me, the strangest thing was when coffee creamers would come from nowhere, fly across the room, and burst open upon hitting walls, floors, cabinets, furniture, and sometimes even people. The mystery was intensified by the fact that we did not have these types of creamers in the building. How they got there and managed to fly across

the room remains a mystery. Although initially spooked by this whole phenomenon, in time, we became used to these random occurrences.

John Q was also known to type on the computer. I remember many times when John, Maria, or I were typing reports, grants, or correspondence on the computer, only to find when the letter was printed out the words "the ghost was here" were found inserted randomly into the body of the document prompting us to carefully review everything being printed to be sure an insertion didn't sneak past us.

Although we didn't discuss it publicly, some in our circle were aware of Johnny Q and had witnessed this phenomenon first-hand. I recall times when a random chair fell in the middle of a meeting or lecture, and those of us in the know would lock eyes knowingly, smile, or even laugh while watching the reactions of those who were not in the know and puzzled about why a chair that no one was near tipped over.

Emilee Alexandrou dancing during the Second Annual Heritage Awards Dinner are: (L-R): Sam Stavrakas, Emilee, Helene Stavrakas, unknown, and Elaine Thomopoulos. April 22, 1989, John Psiharis collection.

Greek-American Community Services Who's Who

Many contributed to the success of GACS. They included members of the community and Phil-Hellenes who helped GACS at every stage as financial supporters, grantors, board members, volunteers, event participants, and organizations within and beyond the *omogenia*.

The Advisory Board & Board of Directors

Roula Alakiotou was a member of the GACS Advisory Board and a well-regarded architect. In addition to fundraising and supporting our efforts in other ways, she designed the GACS center. Roula is the principal of Roula and Associates, an architectural design firm that specializes in large-scale public buildings. Roula was a recipient of the 1992 GACS Heritage Award.

Emilee (Argiris) Alexandrou was a board member of GACS. Emily and her husband George were also volunteers, fundraisers, and board members of the GANHC. They were good at fundraising and had a special interest in supporting Little City since they had a special needs son who resided there. Emilee helped with GACS fundraising efforts.

Chris Tomaras and Irene Antoniou during a joint meeting of the GACS Advisory Board and Board of Directors at the Pegasus restaurant. Date unknown. Photo by John Rassogianis. John Psiharis collection.

Irene Antoniou was chairwoman of the GACS Advisory Board and a generous benefactor of GACS. She supported GACS in part because it combined her two areas of interest: the arts and older adults. Irene's husband owned several high-end resorts and hotels including six Holiday Inn hotels, the Knickerbocker Chicago, Barclay Hotel, Drury Lane Oak Brook, Lake Lawn Lodge, and the Abbey of Lake Geneva. Among other roles, Irene was a member and chair of the Illinois Arts Council. She also chaired the Women's Board of the Lyric Opera of Chicago. Irene received the GACS *Efharisto* Award in 1996.

Michael Bakalis, Ph.D., became a board member of GACS in 1989. He helped to plan and convene the GACS Advisory Board and was often the master of ceremonies for Heritage Awards dinners.

Mike had been dean of education at the Loyola University of Chicago and was a professor at Northwestern University during his time on our board. He briefly was a Democratic Party candidate for Governor of Illinois in 2002 until he withdrew from the race. His impressive career in public service included stints as superintendent of public instruction for the state of Illinois, Illinois State Comptroller, undersecretary of the U.S. Department of Education (under President Carter), and Democratic Party nominee for governor of Illinois in 1978. When he became president of Triton College, Mike stepped off the board.

Sanford Bokar was an early member of the GACS board. Anna Manos worked as his legal assistant and invited him to join our board to help guide us during the incorporation and tax exemption application process.

Eleni Bousis was a member of the GACS Advisory Board and a generous benefactor to the organization. Connie Gountanis Rigas, a relative, invited Eleni to join GACS. She joined the GANHC board in 1996 and became GANHC board president in 2003. Eleni was great at fundraising and was involved with many of our Heritage Awards dinners as well as the Advisory Board's cocktail party at the Metropolitan Club. Eleni and her husband Dimitris are the owners of Cermak Produce. She is a founding board member and currently chairs the Hippocratic Cancer Research Foundation (HCRF). GACS honored Eleni with an *Efharisto* Award in 1996.

Christine Burbulis was an early board member of GACS and served on the board until the GANHC branched off and to which she subsequently devoted her time. She had oversight of real estate acquisitions for the U.S. Department of Housing and Urban Development in the Chicago region and was well qualified to chair the real estate committee of the GANHC. Christine resigned from GANHC in protest of the decision to hire SSAS as the project architect over the one she preferred.

Peter Chioros, DPM, was a board member and secretary of GACS. He was in his final years of study at the Scholl College of Podiatry when he first became involved at the behest of John Rassogianis, whose families were close. Peter went into private practice and was affiliated with Swedish Covenant Hospital. He was appointed to the Illinois Department of Professional Regulation and the Illinois Podiatric Medical Licensing Board. Peter was a past president of the Hellenic Professional Society of Illinois. He also provided basic podiatric care to adult day care clients on occasion.

Stella Adinamis-Cuthbert was a GACS board member in the early years, and as a lawyer helped us with bylaws, incorporation, and the tax exemption process. Stella was commissioner of the Illinois Department of Employment Security under Governor James Thompson.

Aphrodite Demeur was a member of the GACS Advisory Board and a generous benefactor to GACS. Her husband was a doctor who over the years had purchased some valuable properties in the downtown Oak Park area. Her son James Demeur was a successful Burger King franchisee who passed away at a young age. *Ya'Sou 2* was named in his memory after Mrs. Demeur donated funds for the purchase of the van. The GACS conference room was also named the James E. Demeur Conference Room. A plaque was placed on the door. Mrs. Demeur shunned recognition for her support and declined a GACS *Efharisto* award. She did receive the GACS Executive Director Award in 1994 since she had no prior knowledge that the award would be presented to her, and it was a surprise.

Polyzoes "Pol" Gavaris was a founding member of GACS and also served as a member of the GACS Cultural & Arts Program Advisory Committee. As the owner of the Elysion Restaurant, he was known and respected within the community. Having been a family friend, Pol was one of the first people I invited to take part in this effort. In addition to financial support, he provided credibility and connections to the Greek immigrant community. Pol was involved in the Pan Laconian Federation, AHEPA, and was a board member of the Annunciation Cathedral and St. Demetrios Church Board of Trustees. At the time, these two churches shared a common board of trustees. For a time, Pol hosted a Greek radio program. He graciously donated meeting space for countless GACS and GANHC meetings and extended that same courtesy to other organizations. We often gathered for dinner in the restaurant before the meetings. When GACS was incorporated, Pol allowed us to use the restaurant as a mailing address, and he assumed the role of registered agent. He did not join the GANHC board after it split from GACS, believing that the nursing home project should have remained with GACS. Pol continued to support GACS throughout its existence but was less able to attend meetings when we moved them from the restaurant to the center.

Helen Geocaris was a founding board member of both GACS and GANHC. Helen, née Alevizos, was married to John C. Geocaris, the 40th Ward Democratic Committeeman. She was the secretary of the GACS board and a member of the GANHC board. Helen was also an officer in the Daughters of Penelope where she helped obtain a significant pledge in support of the nursing home.

Steve Geocaris was a GACS board member for a short period around 1986. He was a City of Chicago Bureau of Electricity employee and the son of John and Helen Geocaris.

Helen Georges was a GACS board member during the early years and served on the Cultural & Arts Program Advisory Committee. She was also a long-serving member of the GANHC, serving as the first vice president of the GANHC for many years. Helen was an administrator for the Illinois Department of Public Aid.

Maria Svolos Gephardt was a member of the GACS Advisory Board. Maria chaired the Cathedral Ball benefiting Annunciation Cathedral for several years and helped with several GACS fundraising events. She was the founder of DanceArt. Maria was a board member of the Hellenic Museum and Cultural Center, the Hellenic Foundation, and a member of the Archdiocesan Council of the Greek Orthodox Archdiocese. Her husband Paul, an attorney for several medical associations, was credited with creating the term "informed consent" as it relates to modern medicine.

Connie Gountanis-Rigas was a GACS board member who joined in the mid-1990s. I first met Connie when we were both involved in the Paul Tsongas for President Campaign. I was impressed with her organizing and leadership skills and invited her to join the board. Connie invited Eleni Bousis, her niece, to support us. Eleni soon joined our Advisory Board. Connie was a guidance counselor for the Chicago Public Schools and remained on the board for several years. I recall Connie and me frantically coordinating a last-minute campaign visit by Nicole Tsongas on March 15, 1992, that involved stops at Diplomat West and the Cotillion. Since we were driving Nikki and her entourage, I remember a desperate last-minute search for a carwash to clean our cars dirtied by road salt and splashing melted snow. When she helped coordinate a visit for the Crown Prince of the Cameroons, Connie invited John and me to the exclusive reception in his honor at the Field Museum.

James Heliotes was a founding board member of GACS. He was a department head within the Chicago Department of Streets and Sanitation and a precinct captain for John Geocaris. Declining health caused him to step down.

Thalia Jameson was a founding member of both GACS and the GANHC. She was a teacher for the Chicago Board of Education at Chappell Elementary School. Her husband operated Jameson Realty. Thalia was actively involved with both boards and was a member of the Annunciation Cathedral and the Soteria Society. Thalia passed away in 1994.

Mary Kakavas was a board member and supporter of GACS. She also served as GANHC board secretary, succeeding Toni Panos. Mary, along with her husband Bill, owned Thirteen Colonies Banquets at Belmont and Cumberland in the Thatcher Woods Mall in River Grove, IL. They were generous and early supporters of both organizations and remained active with them for many years. In total, Bill and Mary donated and raised more than $150,000 for the GANHC and thousands more for GACS. Mary was a member of the Supreme Board of the United Hellenic American Voters of America, AHEPA Chapter #311 – Zoe, and a board member and past officer of the Megalopolis Society.

Jean Kaporis was a founding board member of both GACS and GANHC. She was a member of the Annunciation Cathedral Philoptochos Society, past president of the Laconia Ladies Society, and a founding member of the Soteria Society.

Theodosis Kioutas, M.D., was a founding board member of both GACS and GANHC. He was soft-spoken, but his passion and determination were heartfelt and his accomplishments were many. Initially, as GACS president, I appointed Dr. Kioutas to chair a newly created board committee aptly called the Greek-American Nursing Home Committee. When the committee incorporated as its own organization, Dr. Kioutas continued to serve as its president until 2004, two years after the opening of the Home. His steady and skillful leadership in navigating difficult terrain in a process no one had direct experience or knowledge of was vital to our success.

Dr. Kioutas was on the medical staff of Illinois Masonic Medical Center, Swedish Covenant, and St Elizabeth Hospital and was an assistant professor at the University of Illinois Medical School. He was also the medical director of the Lakeview Nursing Home near Diversey and Halsted.

Dr. Kioutas was involved in many Greek organizations. In addition to GACS and GANHC, he, John R, and I were on the boards of the Chicago Council on Justice for Cyprus and the Congress of Hellenic American Organizations. There were some weeks that we saw each other several times a week at various meetings or events in the community.

Dr. Kioutas enjoyed a high degree of respect and trust within the community and was instrumental in garnering support for both the nursing home and GACS. Dr. Kioutas asked Illinois Masonic Medical Center to support the new adult day care center. The result was more than $30,000 in startup funding for the center as well as public relations and consulting support. Dr. Kioutas was also instrumental in getting grant funding from Washington Square Health Foundation, Michael Reese Health Trust, and Polk Brothers Foundation for the adult day care center. He had a decades-long friendship with Sol Polk, the co-founder of the appliance store chain and the foundation.

Elaine Kollintzas Drikakis was a GACS board member and a member of the GACS Cultural & Arts Program Advisory Committee. At the time, she was the assistant director of alumni relations at DePaul University. When Elaine became executive director of the Hellenic Museum and Cultural Center, she stepped off our board. We were first introduced by Dr. Andrew Kopan who was a professor of education at DePaul. Elaine hosted and coordinated several GACS cultural programs at DePaul in cooperation with the Hellenic Society of DePaul University. The university had a modern auditorium in which we held our film festival, music and dance programs, and several lectures.

(L-R): Ted Spyropoulos, Erika Spyropoulos, and Jim Kozonis attend a GACS Heritage Awards Dinner. Date unknown. Photo by John Rassogianis. John Psiharis collection.

Sam Kostogiannes briefly served as a GACS board member during the first year. He was a captain in the Illinois Secretary of State Police Department and was a frequent visitor to the Elysion Restaurant. Pol invited him to join the board. After he opened a submarine sandwich shop on Irving Park Road near Cicero Avenue in Portage Park he was unable to attend meetings and subsequently resigned.

Demetrios Kozonis was a member of the GACS Advisory Board and served as chairman of our Building Fund which raised the money needed to purchase the center. Jim owned Mega Properties and Delko Construction through which he built and managed an array of strip mall shopping centers located throughout the northwest side of the city. His most impressive development was Veteran's Square, located adjacent to the Jefferson Park Transportation Center. The property included underground parking, an office tower, and an assortment of retail spaces. The Social Security Administration was the anchor tenant in the tower and Comcast and several elected officials had offices there.

Frank Kuchuris was a member of the GACS Advisory Board and a benefactor of GACS. Frank operated baking companies that had been started by his father Louis. These brands included Mary Ann Baking Company and East Balt Commissaries, which supplied buns to McDonald's and other restaurants and retail stores in the United States and France. Frank was honored with a GACS Heritage Award in 1990.

(L-R): Yiannis and Antigone Lambros, and John Psiharis. Date unknown. Photo by John Rassogianis. John Psiharis collection.

Antigone Lambros was a board member of GACS and also served on the Cultural & Arts Program Advisory Committee. She and her husband Yiannis co-hosted the *Hellenic Interlude* radio program, a staple within the community for many years. In addition to the radio program, they operated a successful Greek American import-export business. Yiannis and Antigone were recipients of the GACS Heritage Award in 1988.

Fotios K. Litsas, Ph.D., was a GACS board member and vice president. He was a respected historian and scholar who was the director of the Modern Greek Studies program at the University of Illinois at Chicago. Fotios also hosted a religious radio program, ran the Greek Orthodox Diocese's Sunday schools, wrote newspaper columns, and published many books and monographs.

Fotios' primary interest in GACS was with our cultural programs. He was a member of the GACS Cultural and Arts Program Advisory Committee and helped to translate brochures, forms, news releases, and other items. Unfortunately, he passed away from cancer much too soon in 1998 at the age of 53. Fotios was honored with the GACS Heritage Award in 1988.

Anna Manos was a founding board member and the first treasurer of GACS. She was a legal secretary for Hollobow and Teslitz, a downtown law firm, and was active in the Daughters of Penelope. Anna lived around the corner from the Elysion Restaurant where many of our early meetings were held. She was a close friend of Toni Panos and a member of St. Andrew's church. Anna was also a founding board member of the Greek-American Nursing Home Committee.

Peter Maroutsos, CPA, was a board member and treasurer of GACS and served on the Cultural & Arts Program Advisory Committee. Early on, GACS applied to an organization called CPAs for the Public Interest for help in setting up our accounting systems. Jim Logothetis, a volunteer with the organization, wanted to help us but didn't have the time. Jim was a partner in the accounting firm Ernst and Young, which after several mergers became Arthur Anderson. Peter worked under Jim and was asked to help GACS in his stead. He eventually joined our board and became treasurer. Peter remained involved with GACS throughout much of its existence.

James M. Mezilson was a board member of both GACS and GANHC. He was an elder statesman within the Greek community and was a founder and longtime board member of the Hellenic Museum and Cultural Center, a member of the United Hellenic American Congress (UHAC), and a leader within AHEPA. Jim was active in the church and wrote "Mez," a column that appeared in one form or another in the *Greek Press* newspaper for more than 50 years. When GACS awarded him a Heritage Award in 1989 for his accomplishments within the community, Jim was described as a "Chronicler of Hellenism and dean of Greek American journalists." Jim's journalism career began as a writer for the *Chicago Sun.* He went on to serve as an aide to U.S. Senator Paul Douglas and more recently had worked for Angelo Geocaris who operated a beer distributorship.

Although Jim was a member of both boards, he was more active with the nursing home. In part, this was because he didn't drive and lived on the far Southside. Whenever there was a meeting he would take several buses to and from the meeting which resulted in a two-hour trip each way. This limited his ability to attend meetings at our northwest side location, especially during the winter months.

Michelle K. Milewski was assistant vice president and branch manager of Midwest Bank and Trust located one block north of GACS. I came to know her when we needed to have grants and government contract signatures notarized. Even though we were not customers of the bank, she always helped us. Eventually, we established a line of credit at Midwest. Once we sold the building the requirement for us to maintain our accounts with LaSalle Bank ended and we moved the remaining GACS accounts there. Michelle joined our board and served as secretary. Michelle also provided parking for GACS events at her branch for special events, donated money and raffle prizes, and gave goodies to our adult day care participants.

Evangeline Mistaras was a board member and the second president of GACS (1986-1995). She became president in 1986 after Elaine and I assumed the roles of administrator and executive director respectively. She earned two master's degrees in library science from the University of Chicago. Initially a librarian for the Chicago Public Libraries, she became head reference librarian at Northeastern Illinois University. Evangeline initially began her involvement with GACS as a volunteer friendly visitor and tutoring seniors in English.

Evangeline was a staunch supporter of GACS and the GANHC. In addition to financial support, she volunteered in the adult day care center weekly and represented us within the broader community, and donated our first computer and printer around 1993. Evangeline was a member of St. Andrew Greek Orthodox Church and its Philoptochos Society. She was good friends with Ethel Kotsovos and Maria Maniates, who also volunteered in the adult day care center. A friendship evolved between us, and we often went out to dinner before GACS Board meetings to discuss and plan for the meeting. Evangeline was integral to the success of GACS. She passed away on July 18, 2021, at the age of 93.

Charles J. Mouratides was a founding board member of GACS. He was the editorial director of the Lerner Newspaper Group, a chain of neighborhood newspapers covering the north and northwest sides of Chicago and nearby suburbs. Charles then established a communications firm through which he worked for several Greek organizations including the World Council of Hellenes Abroad (SAE), an organization launched by presidential decree as a means for the Greek government to engage Hellenes throughout the world. Andrew Athens was president and Chris Tomaras oversaw the North American region.

Toni Panos was a founding board member of both GACS and the GANHC. She served on the GACS Board throughout its existence and was on the GANHC board from its inception into the 2000s. Toni was a medical secretary for a doctor in the western suburbs. She was also a member of the GACS Cultural & Arts Program Advisory Committee.

Toni lived in Oak Park, was a member of Assumption Greek Orthodox Church, and was a longtime friend of the Thomopoulos and Rassogianis families. She eventually moved to Lombard which made it difficult for her to attend meetings. Toni was involved in the Daughters of Penelope and helped guide the Daughters' pledge commitments to the GANHC.

Faye Pantazelos was a board member of GACS for a short time. She also served a brief stint on the GANHC board. Faye was recommended to GACS by Peter Lallas, who was related to her. She was vice president of the Bank of Ravenswood, which was eventually bought out by First Chicago and ultimately JP Morgan Chase. Faye was the founder and CEO

John Psiharis and Toni Panos ringing a ship's bell on the Odyssey cruise ship. Circa 1994 or 1995. Photo by John Rassogianis. John Psiharis collection.

of New Century Bank, which subsequently was foreclosed on by the FDIC as a result of the Great Recession.

Athanasia "Sandy" Papadopoulos Vaselopoulos, PharmD. was a board member who served as vice president and as third board president of GACS, assuming that role in 1995. Sandy initially became involved in GACS as a friendly visiting volunteer while she was studying to receive her doctorate in pharmacy from the University of Illinois. After graduating, she became a pharmacist at Lutheran General Hospital. I first met Sandy when she was in high school and volunteering in the Hellenic Foundation's summer youth program. Sandy did so much in so many ways that it is hard to detail everything here. Driving adult day care clients home, visiting elderly residents in nursing homes, donating money to cover mortgage payments when the state was past due in their payments, and soliciting donations from area businesses are just a few of the ways she helped. Sandy chaired several Heritage Awards dinners.

Nicholas Papanos, M.D., joined the GACS board in the late 1990s. He provided medical guidance to the adult day care staff and participated in fundraising efforts. Dr. Papanos also joined the GANHC board and became the medical director of the nursing home once it opened.

Lukas Pergantas was a member of the GACS Advisory Board. He and his wife Nikki co-chaired the Advisory Board cocktail party at the Metropolitan Club and coordinated one of our raffles. Lukas was the owner of the Four Star Auto Body Shop. He was a GACS benefactor who also supported the GANHC and other organizations and churches. Lukas was honored with a GACS *Efharisto* Award in 1996.

Katherine Pischak was a GACS Board member during the latter years. Her mother was a participant in the adult day care center and Kathy was always supportive of the center. As a family member of a participant, she had an understanding of the need for the center from a different perspective. Kathy was an attorney for Quaker Oats Co, which had recently been bought out by PepsiCo. It was nice to have a lawyer on our board. Fortunately, her services were not required beyond providing us with legal guidance in routine matters. Kathy also led a committee of adult day care families that organized rummage sales to benefit the center and obtained several premium prizes for GACS raffles from Quaker Oats, including skybox tickets to Chicago Bulls, Cubs, and White Sox games.

John Psiharis was co-founder and first president of GACS from 1982-1986 and served as executive director from 1986 through November 2001. He was co-founder and a board member of the GANHC from its inception through June 2006 and a founding member, vice president, and two-term president of the Coalition of Limited English Speaking Elderly.

Barbara Psilakas was a board member during the early days of GACS. She was a lively senior who was president of the St. Demetrios Young at Heart senior citizen's group. Barbara lived almost next door to where the Cantos Sheet Metal factory at 4256 N. Olcott in Harwood Heights had been located and I drove her home after evening board meetings.

John Rassogianis was a board member of GACS and became a member of the Cultural & Arts Program and Northwest Chicago Senior Care Advisory Committees. When funding became available, GACS hired him to serve as CAP director. In 2001, after leaving GACS to work for the Chicago Department of Aging on a full-time basis, John returned to the board and became vice president. When Kosta resigned from his position as president, John was the fifth president of the GACS Board (2001-2002). He was also a board member of the GANHC from the late 1980s through 2004 and served on the board of the Coalition of Limited English Speaking Elderly, representing the GANHC for several years.

Ricardo Rodriguez became a board member of GACS in 2001. One of his contributions was creating the first GACS website in 2001. The site, www.seniordaycareservices.com, focused on the adult day care center. It was our first effort at having an online presence when the Internet was in its infancy. If I remember correctly, GACS was one of the first adult day care programs, of those known to us, to have a website. Ricky had an eye for numbers and cost-cutting. He reviewed budgets and cut a significant amount of expenses (at least several thousand dollars), and helped with fundraising and personnel matters. As an example, he led the effort to replace the center's fluorescent lighting with energy-efficient bulbs which led to a 20 percent reduction in electricity costs and helped with routine building repairs. At times, Ricky stepped in to drive ADC clients to and from the center in the *Ya'Sou* van when a driver was unable to work.

Ricky's background was in human resources and he had been an HR professional for Arrow Financial Services and Life Source and as corporate executive administrative assistant to the executive and senior vice presidents at Banco Popular's North America corporate office. When GACS was experiencing severe delays in reimbursements from the state after the September 11th attack, Ricky wrote an impassioned letter and went door to door in our Old Irving Park community to solicit donations from the neighborhood. He raised more than $1,000 through this endeavor and obtained a significant donation from his employer as well.

Aphrodite Sarelas was a GACS board member for several years. A retired social worker, she was a board member of the American Cancer Society and the Fulbright Association. The Fulbright Association's Dee Sarelas Fulbright Service Award is named in her honor.

Peter Skouris was an early board member of GACS. He was an investor who was part of the informal group of local Greeks that gathered at the Elysion Restaurant. Peter had a business background and a special interest in our cultural programs. He moved to Greece soon thereafter.

Ted Spyropoulos was co-chairman of the GACS Building Fund Committee. He was a generous donor to GACS and helped to raise money from the network of fraternal organizations that he interacted with as a founding member and president of ENOSIS. Ted was a distributor of CAM 2 Motor Oil and owned TGS Petroleum. His daughter Mariyana Spyropoulos, as of 2022, was twice elected president of the Metropolitan Water Reclamation District of Greater Chicago (2015 and 2017). She was first elected to the district in 2010. Ted was honored with a GACS Heritage Award in 1993.

Elaine Thomopoulos Ph.D., was co-founder and vice president of GACS from 1982 - 1986. She served as administrator of GACS from 1986 – April 1990. Elaine became a consultant to GACS for the Cultural & Arts Program between 1990 – 2000 and was CAP director from March 2000 - 2002 after John Rassogianis began working full-time for the city. Elaine

Chris Tomaras at a GACS event. Date unknown. Photo by John Rassogianis. John Rassogianis collection.

was co-founder of the GANHC and a board member from its inception through June 2003.

Chris Tomaras was co-chairman of the GACS Advisory Board and a generous benefactor of the organization. He chaired a number of our fundraisers and arranged for his assistant Eleni Sotos to work on GACS matters. Chris was well respected throughout the diaspora and in Greece. He was appointed coordinator for the United States and Canada of the World Council of Hellenes Abroad (SAE), an initiative of the Greek nation to bring together Greeks from throughout the world. Chris was active in many organizations including the Pan Messinian Society and he founded the Pan Hellenic Scholarship Foundation. He was referred to as the "Gyros King." Chris was the founder and owner of Kronos-Central Gyros, a leading purveyor of gyros in the United States, and eventually sold Kronos for a hefty price and then focused on philanthropy. He was honored with the GACS Heritage Award in 1993 and the *Efharisto* Award in 1995.

Lena Xydes was a board member and the second treasurer of GACS. She was invited to join by Evangeline Mistaras and they were both members of the St. Andrew Greek Orthodox church. Lena was a retired music teacher at Senn High School. She encouraged a relative, Peter Lallas, to get involved in GACS. Peter chaired the first two Heritage Awards Dinners.

Konstantine "Kostas" Zografopoulos joined the board in 1994. He became vice president and was the fourth president of the GACS board from 1999 to 2000. His father owned Ruby's, a restaurant on Lincoln

Avenue. Kosta, with his father's help, started Master Caterers. Kosta had an entrepreneurial spirit and built a successful business that catered to many events in the Greek community. He was an active member of the St. Andrews church and became involved with GACS with the encouragement of Evangeline and Ethel. Kosta donated his catering services to both GACS and GANHC for several events and his support was greatly appreciated. At the time, GACS was working with Kosta to establish a Meals on Wheels program for the Greek community.

On the Sunday after Thanksgiving in 1995, upon waking and having my morning coffee while watching the morning news, I heard a story about an overnight car accident that resulted in a serious injury. Minutes later, I received a call from Sandy Papadopoulos. It turned out that Kosta was the person I heard about on the news. While unloading his catering truck in front of his business after a late-night event, a drunk driver crashed into the truck and Kosta was pinned between the truck and the car. He was in critical condition at Cook County Hospital for some time. Some feared that he would not survive. It was touch and go for a while.

The community rallied to support Kosta throughout his ordeal. Prayer vigils were organized and several fundraising activities were held to help cover the mounting medical bills he had incurred. GACS supported these efforts and collected money for the drive from our board, staff, and volunteers. Even a few ADC clients made donations.

Months later, Kosta recovered and began rehabilitation therapy. His legs were lost and he went through months of physical therapy at the Rehabilitation Institute. He devoted a portion of his insurance settlement to launching the Kostas Z Foundation focused on the needs of those who are in wheelchairs.

GACS staff and volunteers at a Volunteer Luncheon held at Central Gyros. Pictured (L-R): Despina Massouras, Maria Toledo, Carmen Vilato, Frieda Aravosis, Toni Panos, Ann Prusinski, Phil Williams, Evangeline Mistaras, Amydelle Shah, John Psiharis, and Alex Cantos. Circa 1994 or 1995. Photo by John Rassogianis. John Psiharis collection.

The Team

These are the people who made all that GACS did possible. They were the staff of the organization. No one worked for GACS for lavish wages or generous benefits packages. They did it from the heart. We recognize their important roles in the history of the organization.

Early on, Fran Argiris and Amydelle Shah were full-time nurses but at some point, they cut back to part-time. Since the nurses were retired, no one wanted a full-time commitment because they also wanted to enjoy their retirement. Eleanor enjoyed square dancing and senior trips, Eileen enjoyed folk dancing and Amydelle often traveled. There are several nurses included on this list, but they were not all on duty at the same time. A nurse was required to be at the center for at least four hours per day.

Cynthia Aarab briefly worked as a nursing assistant and driver. She lived in the neighborhood and had a CNA license as well as a chauffeur's license and drove a taxi cab during her off-hours. Cynthia was hired shortly before I left and worked mainly under Danae's tenure.

Sarantis Alexopoulos was a driver and activity aide for the adult day care center. He had lived at Mount Athos in Greece for a while and was also involved at Assumption church.

Manolis Alpogianis was a volunteer GACS special events coordinator for a series of fundraising events related to the adult day care center launch. Alice Buzanis, as GACS director of development, recruited Manolis, a friend of hers, to take on this unpaid position. Manolis' family owned Kappy's Pancake House in Morton Grove. Manolis and his brother George went on to launch America's Dog, a popular Chicago area chain of fast-food restaurants.

Frieda Aravosis was involved from the earliest days of the Fabric Arts Program and became Fabric Arts Project Coordinator after Tessie Cantos passed away. She was also Tessie's sister-in-law. Frieda was married to Tessie's brother Steve and had decades of experience in the needlework arts of Greece. She remained involved with the program throughout its 14-year history.

Fran Argiris (Nichols), R.N. was the first adult day care center nurse. Before taking on that role, she was a volunteer supervisor of the GACS Friendly Visiting Program. Before GACS, Fran was the resident nurse at Hollywood House where she provided medical care to elderly residents of the retirement home. She had a daughter who was gaining recognition as an opera singer in Europe.

Shirley Bernstein was a social work intern from Northeastern Illinois University with a focus on gerontology. Through CAN she provided counseling and support to isolated or homebound seniors. Shirley also organized an educational program on Alzheimer's, sponsored by CAN, at Northeastern Illinois University.

Robert Blum held several roles at GACS over the years. He was the first driver that we hired after the purchase of the first *Ya'Sou* van. Bob picked up adult day care clients from their homes in the morning and returned them in the afternoon. During the middle part of the day, he divided his time between helping in the center as an activity assistant and leading the men's activity group. Bob also helped clients apply for energy assistance through the LIHEAP program. He was attending college to become a physical therapist. I remember that on one occasion, Bob saved a client's life by administering the Heimlich maneuver to a participant who had choked on an orange slice. He leaped into action and quickly dislodged the orange before some even realized anything had happened. It was at moments like this that we appreciated the CPR training and certification the staff was required to maintain.

I first met Bob after GACS moved into Alvernia Place where he worked in maintenance. It turned out that Bob and I had both gone to Taft High School. He was one year behind me and knew who I was but I didn't know him. It was great to have Bob on our team. He was a great employee and a caring and empathetic person who was popular with both clients and co-workers.

Alice Buzanis was GACS's volunteer director of development for a short time. She organized a few fundraising events including a cocktail party at the Gold Star Sardine Bar, and an event at Neon Greek Village, and obtained a grant from the Chicago Tribune Foundation. When Alice first got involved with GACS, she supervised the Friendly Visitor Program after Fran Argiris transitioned to the adult day care center. Alice also served as a member of the Cultural & Arts Program Advisory Committee.

I first met Alice when she heard about GACS and went to our mailing address to inquire about us. At that time, the address was the Elysion restaurant. We joked that our office was "booth one." Alice, her family, and I became friends. We were involved in Mike Dukakis' presidential campaign. Together, we traveled to Boston, Iowa, Michigan, Ohio, Wisconsin, Missouri, and Indiana on behalf of the campaign and attended the Democratic convention in Atlanta. Alice had worked as director of development for the Illinois Democratic Party, was a candidate for alderman of Chicago's 40th ward, and most recently became principal of Jesse Sherwood Elementary School in Chicago.

Tessie Cantos was the Fabric Arts Program coordinator from its inception through March 1994. In 1986 Tessie was the recipient of a grant through the Chicago Office of Fine Arts, Neighborhood Arts Program. This grant was given to individual artists who were sponsored by a community or arts organization. When funding transitioned to CDBG, GACS became the grantee and Tessie remained the coordinator. Her sister-in-law Frieda Aravosis (her brother's wife) became Tessie's assistant and assumed the coordinator role after Tessie's passing.

After running office operations for Cantos Sheet Metal, her husband Alex's company, Tessie briefly retired when the business was sold. Wanting to become active in the community, she became the second employee (after Elaine) at the Hellenic Foundation. Tessie remained at the Hellenic Foundation for several years as a job placement counselor and office manager. Alex was my father's first cousin. Alex and Tessie were supporters of GACS and the nursing home since the day the idea of GACS was first considered.

Top: Placard that was affixed to the door of the arts and crafts room at the GACS center after the room was dedicated in memory of Tessie Cantos. Circa 1994. John Psiharis collection. **Bottom:** Fabric Arts Program meeting at GACS. Pictured (L-R): Bessie Choporis, unknown, Frieda Aravosis, and John Psiharis. Date unknown. John Psiharis collection.

Spyridon Dimas at a GACS/CAN flea market. Date unknown. Elaine Thomopoulos collection.

Eileen Casey, R.N. worked as a nurse in the adult day care center. Initially, a fill-in nurse until Amydelle cut back her days, she soon took on a regular schedule. I believe Eileen worked at Edgewater Community Hospital until her retirement. She eventually brought in her friend Kathleen O'Leary, also a retired nurse, who later became the center's supervisor.

Bessie Choporis was an instructor in the Fabric Arts Program. An occasional volunteer during the earlier years, she became an assistant instructor when Frieda Aravosis assumed the role of FAP coordinator after the passing of Tessie Cantos. Bessie had years of experience in needlework, crocheting, and knitting. She was my aunt (older sister to Alex Cantos and Tessie's sister-in-law). Bessie was a generous benefactor of GACS, baked cakes for various fundraising events, and donated a dishwasher to the center. Each year, she sent cases of freshly picked Florida oranges and grapefruits to the ADC participants while wintering in Florida.

Spyridon Dimas was the first AYUDA employee we hired in 1983. He was a friendly visitor and chore/housekeeper. Mr. Dimas had a roster of elderly clients whom he would visit regularly. In general, he visited eight clients each week. In some cases, he would visit and chat with clients while checking on their well-being. In other instances, he would shop or assist in meal preparation. A number of his clients were older men who were either widowed, or never married, and for them, he was their only visitor and link to the outside world. When his time had concluded with AYUDA, we hired Spiro onto the GACS payroll.

Spyro had worked as a friendly visitor at the Hellenic Foundation during the time Elaine and I were working there. He had lost part of an arm during the war in Greece but managed as though he had no impairment. Spyro was from Epirus and shared stories about what life was like in his youth.

We were delighted to have him be our first AYUDA hire and he remained with us until returning to Epirus Greece to retire a few years later.

Steve Frangos was a consultant to the GACS Cultural & Arts Program, serving in both volunteer and paid capacities. He was integral to writing many of the humanities and arts grants GACS received. Steve was introduced to Elaine by Dr. Andrew Kopan, a noted Greek American historian. He was pursuing a doctoral degree in cultural anthropology at the University of Indiana-Bloomington. Steve was the primary researcher and builder of the *O Cosmos* traveling museum exhibition and helped us conceptualize the project and write the proposal.

Rafael Gallardo was hired as the second driver when *Ya'Sou* 2 was put into service. Bob drove the larger route which was north and west of the center while Rafael took those who were south and east. Rafael initially came to us through AYUDA and when his enrollment had ended GACS hired him. He was Cuban and wore a wide-brim straw hat. After a couple of years, Rafael moved to Costa Rica to retire. In 2006, I ran into him at a Cuban market on Devon Avenue and he told me he had moved back to Chicago.

Harrula Gikodimos, a graduate student in gerontology from the University of Illinois at Chicago, completed her internship in the adult day care center. Upon conclusion of her internship, Harrula became ADC activity director during a period when Ann Prusinski had taken a leave of absence. Having been familiar with the clients as an intern, she easily fit into the role. Soon after Ann returned, Harrula moved back to Athens, Greece to pursue her career.

Eleanor Huber R.N. worked as a relief nurse referred by Eileen. Eventually, she ended up with regular days. Eleanor was a retired industrial nurse for S&C Electric Company and enjoyed square dancing and tour groups in her off time.

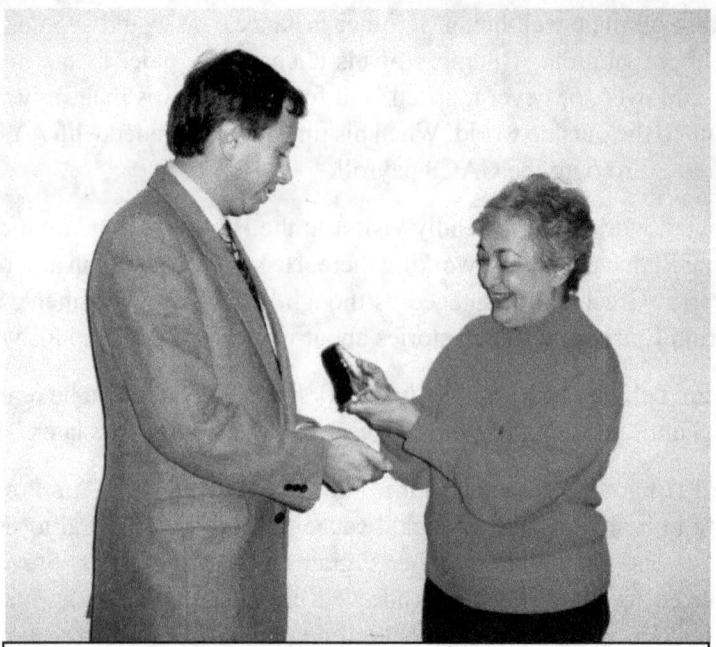

John Psiharis presents the Executive Director's Award to Ethel Kotsovos. Date unknown. John Psiharis collection.

Penny Kalogiannis was the first instructor in the Fabric Arts Program. She had a wealth of experience in the art form and her sister owned a sewing store near Lawrence and Rockwell Avenues where Penny taught classes. A couple of years later she returned to Greece.

Ethel Kotsovos was the GACS social worker and had been involved since the organization's inception as a volunteer. At first, Ethel was hired to coordinate GACS participation in the Ethnic Elderly Needs Assessment Survey. She coordinated the translation and printing of the documents, oversaw the interviewers, and arranged 150 in-person interviews with the Greek elderly. Then through a United Way of Chicago Venture Grant, Ethel transitioned to the part-time role of director of the Community Aging Network. That funding continued for two years and Ethel added hours to her week when she also became the adult day care center social worker. Eventually, Retirement Research Foundation grants funded her position. During the brief period that GACS provided chore housekeeping and homemaker services, Ethel managed that program as well.

Ethel held a bachelor's degree in social work from the University of Illinois Chicago. She often spoke of taking classes at the Navy Pier Campus. Ethel was the first social worker hired when Elaine launched the social services program at the Hellenic Foundation. She was also a member of the Greek-American Nursing Home Committee from its earliest days. After leaving GACS, Ethel became office manager for the

Staff and board members at a GACS Christmas party. Seated (L-R): Lorraine Lisowski, Ann Prusinski. Standing: Cynthia Aarab, John Rassogianis, Ray Manasingh, Kathy Pishack, Elaine Thomopoulos, Antigone Lambros, John Psiharis, and Antonia Papanikolaou (a volunteer). December 2001. John Psiharis collection.

GANHC and then later volunteer coordinator when the nursing home opened. She was active in the St. Andrew Greek Orthodox Church Philoptochos Society and helped run their soup kitchen.

Ethel was well-liked by those she came into contact with and had an infectious laugh that could be heard throughout the center. She was genuine and empathetic with older clients. Ethel was known for having a desk piled high with file folders, enjoying her daily orange and her afternoon chocolate bar. Her husband Jim painted the center on a couple of occasions. Jim and his brother-in-law owned Argo Painting Company which primarily painted public schools.

Florence Kubacki was an AYUDA worker who worked in the GACS office at both Monticello Street and Alvernia Place.

Janet Lewis was an intern in gerontology from National Louis University who completed her fieldwork in the ADC. As an accomplished artist, Janet specialized in art therapy and held classes with both higher and lower-functioning clients. GACS received a City Arts grant in 1995 that enabled us to hire Janet to lead ADC classes in looming, ornament making, watercolor painting, and other art forms. Janet donated a loom to the center for future use.

Lorraine Lisowski, R.N., was a nurse in the adult day care center. She had been a floor nurse at Loretto Hospital before retiring. Lorraine was a friend of Eleanor Huber who suggested her for the job. She began as a relief nurse, coming in on an ad-hoc basis and eventually becoming a regular on the nurses' roster.

Lorraine's husband Ed was retired but worked as an usher during Cubs games. He frequently brought in stacks of coupons for free coffee at Dunkin Donuts or other promotions from Wrigley Field to share with our clients and volunteers.

Both of Lorraine's sons were Catholic priests and she was very proud of them. Her son Brian was a Catholic priest assigned to St. Bede the Venerable Catholic Church, a southwest side parish, and was eventually convicted of pilfering more than $1 million of church funds over five years.

Ray Manasingh wore several hats at GACS, the most notable being as our activity and van aide. He initially came to GACS through the Earn-Fare program and when funding allowed, was hired by the center. Ray was an activity aide in the adult day care center. He helped prepare, serve, and clean up after snacks and lunch service and escorted clients to and from the van. Ray was a down-to-earth, laid-back native of Trinidad who talked fondly of his younger years "on the island."

Despina "Des" Massouras became the adult day care center social worker after Ethel moved to the nursing home office. She completed her internship at GACS while completing her degree in gerontology at National Louis University. Upon her graduation, Des was hired to fill Ethel's position. She stayed in this role for a couple of years but at a certain point tired of the daily commute from her home in the south suburbs, which took up to two hours each way in bad weather or during heavy traffic days, resigned.

Des was married to Reverend George Massouras who was the protopresbyter at Assumption Greek Orthodox Church on Chicago's West Side. As the wife of a priest, a *presbytera* is regarded in Greek circles as the first lady of a church and as such enjoys a level of esteem within the parish. Des was active in church life and was instrumental in obtaining support for both GACS and GANHC from the Assumption Women's Club.

Des had a slight Boston accent, a quick sense of humor, and a smart wit. She would sit with our clients to conduct an activity only to have a chorus

ADC staff table at the 1996 Heritage Awards Dinner. (L-R); Kathleen O'Leary, Maria Toledo, Eleanor Huber, Bob Blum, Eileen Casey, Amydelle Shah, and Ann Prusinski. October 1996. John Psiharis collection.

of laughter follow. Father George and Des were passionate supporters of the nursing home. Des had been involved with the Greek nursing home in Canton, Massachusetts when she lived in Boston. Father George was a member of the GANHC board as the representative of Bishop/Metropolitan Iakovos.

Elizabeth "Betty" McClelland was the first GACS secretary. She was an AYUDA employee who had a background in running an import and export department for a large business. Betty had initially been assigned to CAN while it was still part of Lutheran Social Services of Illinois. When CAN merged with GACS, Betty remained with us. She was an avid collector of miniature shoes and had compiled a nationwide travel resources directory for the disabled. Her late husband had been disabled, and this motivated her to work on this project and to provide help to any disabled person who contacted her for assistance.

Linda Mirza, R.N. was a relief nurse in the adult day care center. She had recently retired as a nurse at the University of Illinois Hospital and was Amydelle's daughter-in-law. We knew her well because, during much of Amy's time with us, Linda would pick up Amydelle on her way home from work.

Margaret Nikolopoulos was an activity aide in the adult day care program funded through AYUDA. She was in her eighties and lived in Portage Park. Margaret was well-liked by the clients and was a pleasure to work with. She was bilingual and often led breakout activities for Greek-speaking clients. At our request, AYUDA allowed Margaret to stay with us beyond the usual assignment period of 18 months and she remained with us for several years.

Kathleen O'Leary, R.N., started as a relief nurse before becoming a staff nurse and then supervisor of the adult day care program. She had been a nursing supervisor for many years at Edgewater Community Hospital before she retired. Kathleen was friends with Eileen and Eleanor who encouraged her to join GACS as a fill-in nurse. She was the ADC supervisor for several years and became a good friend as well. Like Amydelle, she developed a close friendship with Ann. Despite discomfort from several health ailments, Kathleen had a great sense of humor and a genuine concern for the participants. She led a comprehensive review and updating of ADC policy manuals and protocols.

Neni Panourgia briefly served as director of the GACS satellite office in Boulder, Colorado in 1988. She was a Ph.D. candidate in cultural anthropology at the University of Indiana. Neni participated in a CAP program on *rembetika*. During a post-event dinner, the idea of establishing an outpost in Colorado was discussed and launched. Unfortunately, Neni moved out of state due to an unforeseen job change, and the endeavor came to an end.

Ann Prusinski was the ADC activity director throughout the center's existence. She had been an activity assistant at St. Joseph's Home where her mother was a resident. Ann's husband, Julian, was a longtime history teacher at Taft High School and passed away a couple of years after she started with us. Ann was active in her Portage Park neighborhood as well as her church, St Pascal Catholic Church.

Ann planned and coordinated activity programming within the adult day care center. She supervised the activity aides and volunteers. Ann gave her heart to the center and cared deeply about the clients. She loved Tornie, and at times would awkwardly carry Tornie around the center to place her with clients who wanted to visit with her.

Ann was a colorful character who became a close friend of both Amydelle and Kathleen. Ann and Amy frequently went to plays or events together. They traveled on several vacations together both within the US and Europe. Kathleen and Ann frequently went out to lunch or dinner and events. Ann was the only staff member to be with the adult day program from its first day of inception through its last - about 12 years in total. When GACS experienced delays in payments from the state, Ann fronted her own money to GACS so that Ray and the mortgage/rent were paid.

John Rassogianis (L) receives the Executive Director Award from John Psiharis during a volunteer luncheon. Date unknown. John Psiharis collection.

She wanted to help Ray stay current with his rent at the YMCA. I recall that Ann once paid for veterinary care for Tornie.

John Rassogianis first got involved with GACS as a member of the "Strains on Ethnic Pride" conference planning committee the CAP Advisory Board and became a board member soon after. Elaine invited him to participate on the committee. At the time he was a substitute public school teacher which gave him some schedule flexibility. When funding permitted, GACS hired John to be the Cultural & Arts Program director, a position he held for many years. At some point, he also assumed oversight of our community service programs including the Low Income Home Energy Assistance Program (LIHEAP) and the Benefits Eligibility Checklist (BEC). This patchwork funding allowed John to work for GACS on a full-time basis. John also coordinated publicity for GACS and the GANHC.

In addition to his professional qualities and accomplishments, John was known within Chicago's Greek community and had been involved in several organizations including the Hellenic Professional Society of Illinois where he had planned an academic symposium in Michigan. He was a founding member of Hellenes for a Better America. John's father had operated a candy store in Berwyn for many years. Some photos of the

Amydelle Shah and Ann Prusinski at the National Conference on Aging at the Disneyland Hotel, Anaheim, California. Date unknown. Photo by John Psiharis. John Psiharis collection.

shop were donated by the Rassogianis family for the *O Cosmos* exhibit. His mother Anna and brother Alex attended many of our events and fundraisers.

Besides being an integral part of GACS and GANHC, John became a good friend. Our families knew each other and often sat together at events. We worked in tandem to accomplish a great deal and had some great times along the way.

In March 2000, John took a leave of absence because of family responsibilities and Elaine Thomopoulos assumed the position of director of the Cultural & Arts Program. He then returned to the GACS Board as vice president. After Kosta resigned, John became president of the board.

Amydelle Shah, R.N. was a nurse/supervisor of the adult day care center. She was involved in one capacity or another from its inception until 2000. Amy was in her eighties when she took on this role. She was instrumental in establishing policies and procedures for the center that complied with applicable codes and in supervising the center's staff. Because of her age, she had the unique ability to encourage a client to do something they weren't inclined to do by saying "I'm older than you are and I can do it. If I can do it, you can too." Amy initially was a CAN volunteer and continued her involvement when CAN merged into GACS as a member of the CAN Advisory Board.

Gwen Sten at her desk in the GACS/CAN office at 3911 N. Monticello Street. Circa 1987. John Psiharis collection.

Amy had an amazing background. She was part Native American and grew up in Cahokia, Illinois. Amydelle and her husband owned a pharmacy in East Saint Louis. She had been a public health nurse in a rural Illinois county during a syphilis epidemic. Amy served as Director of Nursing for the Chicago TB Sanitarium and Henrotin Hospital, taught nursing to CNAs, obtained a degree in medical records management, wrote a column in the *Prime Times* newspaper published by Blue Cross & Blue Shield of Illinois, hosted a public access television show and became an accomplished artist. She was proud of her Baha'i faith and loved to travel. Amy and Ann became close personal friends and traveled together. They also went out to dinner or other events after work hours.

Gwen Sten was an AYUDA employee who worked in the office as a receptionist and then office manager. Her son Andrew was an actor who was friends with Tim Kazurinsky, studied at Second City, and had done a few television commercials. A few years after Gwen left the AYUDA program, she returned, this time as a participant in the adult day care center. Gwen attended the center for a couple of years and because of that unique connection, always looked out for any clients who needed special assistance and reminisced about her days working in the office.

Gladys Tichnell was an AYUDA worker who worked as a secretary and typist. She had worked as a typist in a large company before retiring. Gladys worked at both the Alvernia Place and Pulaski locations.

Top: Maria Toledo in my downstairs office. Date unknown. John Psiharis collection.
Bottom: (L-R): Antigone Lambros, Maria Litsas, and Danae Voutiritsas. Date unknown. John Psiharis collection.

Maria Toledo (Villalobos) was GACS secretary and office manager from 1992 until she moved to the nursing home staff full-time in 2001. Before that, she worked part-time with GACS and several hours per week at the nursing home office helping Ethel to deal with administrative tasks and correspondence related to the GANHC.

Floyd "Red" Utley handled maintenance at GACS for a few years. He had worked in maintenance at Alvernia Place and when GACS moved to Pulaski, he came in weekly to give the center a thorough cleaning. Red also assisted in completing applications for clients in need of energy assistance. Before Alvernia, he owned a "roach coach" (mobile food truck). Originally from Kentucky, Red enjoyed singing Country and Western music and was friends with Bob Blum.

Carmen Vilato was an activity aide in the adult day care center for some years through the AYUDA program. She was a jovial older Cuban refugee who brought great energy and enthusiasm to working with the clients. Carmen was concerned about her family who still lived in Cuba and was undergoing extreme hardship. She spent most of the money that she made sending medicine, vitamins, and other necessities to her family. At our request, Judy Matthews, AYUDA Coordinator, allowed Carmen to stay with us longer than usually allowed.

Danae Voutiritsas succeeded John Psiharis as executive director of GACS and served in that role from October 2001 until December 2002. She had recently retired as an art teacher at Lane Technical High School. Danae cared for her mother who had Alzheimer's Disease and was supportive of the adult day care center as well as the Cultural & Arts Program events for many years. Danae had a Master of Arts degree from the Art Institute of Chicago and a Master in Education from Loyola University. She held a Ph.D. from the Institute of Design at the Illinois Institute of Technology and did postdoctoral work at the Massachusetts Institute of Technology. Danae was an accomplished photographer and had been selected to travel to Cuba by the U.S. State Department. She was the first woman in 90 years to teach art design, painting, and drawing at Lane Technical High School.

The Back Bench

The success of GACS was built upon the efforts of many volunteers who gave their time, talent, and resources to help us in so many ways. These volunteers included:

Tom Alex was a Friendly Visiting Program volunteer. Before volunteering at GACS, He had been a Hellenic Foundation CETA worker visiting nursing homes. Tom's sons owned the Forest, Bon-Ton, and Derby Street restaurants.

Connie and Dee Andrews were two sisters who started volunteering at GACS after retiring from senior-level positions at Sears Roebuck and Company. Connie was a Human Resources executive, and Dee held a similar position in a different department. Members of the Assumption

Greek Orthodox Church, they were invited to volunteer at GACS by Presbytera Massouras. Connie and Dee helped to organize the office, typed correspondence and reports, and helped in the adult day care center. They baked amazing homemade banana nut bread and other delicacies that they would share with clients. The sisters usually worked on Wednesdays and Fridays from 10:00 a.m. to 3:00 p.m. They attended many of our events and were generous financial supporters of GACS.

The Andrews sisters were key to a big upgrade of the offices. In 1994, Sears moved its headquarters and operations from Sears Tower to a corporate campus they had built in Hoffman Estates. Connie and Dee were able to obtain a truckload of donations of office furniture from the executive suites, enabling GACS to upgrade mismatched and sometimes damaged furniture with something much better. They also helped to facilitate our relationship with James Marousis, president of the Eisenberg Foundation for Charities.

Theoni "Sonia" Arvanitis, M.S.W. was a GACS volunteer on several fronts. She was the co-chair of the GACS Cultural & Arts Program Advisory Committee and helped with fundraising and grant writing. Sonia was the executive director of the Food Justice Program and then moved into development positions with Chicago Access Corporation, Marcy Newberry Association, Highland Park Hospital, and as director of development for Northeastern Illinois University. Sonia was active in the Hellenic Cultural Organization and the GANHC.

Olga "Peggy" Bancroft was a Friendly Visiting Program volunteer. Peggy, Elaine Thomopoulos' sister-in-law, participated in the fabric arts classes and volunteered at a number of our events.

Carol Bilina was a member of the Northwest Chicago Senior Care Advisory Committee. She was assistant director of the Polish Welfare Association (now the Polish American Association) and an early board member of the Coalition for Limited English Speaking Elderly (CLESE).

Ollie Bridges was the coordinator of Bryn Mawr Intercessors. Formerly the Southside office of the Community Advocacy Network, it was renamed when CAN became the Community Aging Network under GACS. As a volunteer, Ollie coordinated a small group of volunteers that provided assistance and support to seniors in South Shore. The office was in the Bryn Mawr Community Church at 71st Street and Jeffery Boulevard. About a year later, Ollie stepped down from the role due to failing health.

Leonard Carlson A.C.S.W. was a member of the Northwest Chicago Senior Care Advisory Committee. He was the retired director of Home Helps for Seniors, a program of Lutheran Social Services of Illinois.

Lu Carravette was a member of the Northwest Chicago Senior Care Advisory Committee. She was the Christian Outreach Coordinator for St. Ferdinand Catholic Church.

Bessie Choporis was a GACS benefactor and volunteer in the Fabric Arts Program. A sister-in-law to Tessie Cantos (her husband's older sister), she assisted participants with their projects. Bessie baked cakes for our events and parties including her famous German chocolate cake. We sold them at fundraisers and served them during agency or ADC events. Bessie donated a new dishwasher to GACS after we purchased the building and frequently sent cases of freshly picked oranges and grapefruits from Florida when she vacationed there during the winter months.

Lori Cohen was a senior citizen who lived locally in the neighborhood and volunteered every so often. She visited the adult day care center to play the piano for the participants. Lori learned about us through Michele Milewski from Midwest Bank and visited us whenever she went to the bank.

Bernice Corbett was a volunteer of the Community Advocacy Network when it was part of LSSI. She helped in transitioning the program to GACS and served on CAN's advisory board. Bernice coordinated our rummage sales and flea markets during this period. She was also president of the Colonial Bank Senior Citizens Club which arranged bus tours for seniors throughout the Midwest.

Mary Cummings was a volunteer in the mid-90s, helping to computerize and maintain the GACS mailing list and helping in other ways. She worked for *Crain's Chicago Business* and was recruited by board member Aphrodite Sarelas, who initially met her at a restaurant.

Amy Dres was a professional dancer was a dance instructor in the Greek Music and Dance program funded by the Illinois Arts Council in 1991.

Tasia Economou was a friendly visiting volunteer during the early days of GACS and then became an instructor in the Fabric Arts Program for several years until health precluded her from participating. Before GACS, she worked at the Hellenic Foundation as a friendly visitor and translator and also led a support group for seniors.

Margarite Euchler was a volunteer with the Community Advocacy Network and transitioned to GACS. She was an office volunteer coordinating the work of field volunteers. Margarite won the United Way of Chicago Heart of Gold Award in 1987 for outstanding volunteer service. For nominating her, GACS received a $1,000 donation, and the volunteer also received a prize. I remember attending the breakfast in honor of the Heart of Gold volunteers in May at the Marriott Hotel across from Water Tower Place with a few others.

Dana Ferdinand was a member of the Northwest Chicago Senior Care Advisory Committee. He was a senior paralegal at United Charities of Chicago.

Luke Fitzgerald was a member of the Northwest Chicago Senior Care Advisory Committee. He was Northwest regional director for the Chicago Department on Aging based at the Copernicus Center. Before that, Luke was director of the Northeast region and was based at the Levy Center. He was a supporter of GACS since its earliest days, helping with the Ethnic Elderly Needs Assessment and hosting the Fabric Arts program at different times at both senior centers.

George T. Gianas was a friendly visiting volunteer and helped with fundraising. He worked as a supervisor for the Illinois State Toll Highway Authority and was a professional violinist in a north-side symphony orchestra. I have memories of seeing George at the Elysion with a cigar in his mouth and a cup of coffee at his side, as he read the latest racing forms.

Diana Anton Harris was a member of the Cultural and Arts Program Advisory Committee and was involved in organizing several programs. She was a dance teacher and choreographer.

Bessie Kallas was a volunteer who helped with GACS activities and did the calligraphy for early GACS Heritage Awards certificates. She was a school administrator and a travel agent.

Sue Kang was a member of the Northwest Chicago Senior Care Advisory Committee. Sue was the director of the Korean American Community Services Senior Citizens Unit and founder and executive director of the Korean American Senior Center. Sue was a founding member, past president, and long-serving board member of CLESE.

Marion Kappas was a GACS Friendly Visiting Program volunteer.

Fran Kapsales was a GACS volunteer who led Greek dancing classes for senior citizen participants of the St. Demetrios Young at Heart Group. In addition to being a Greek dance instructor, Fran owned a hot dog stand in the western suburbs.

Erica Karp, M.S.W. was project director of the Community Advocacy Network from its inception until she resigned about six months before the end of CAN's funding and Elaine Thomopoulos assumed her position. She held a Master's Degree in Social Work and specialized in gerontology. Erica helped implement the transition of CAN to GACS and chaired the CAN advisory board. When the ADC was launched, she provided in-service training and consultation in designing social services and reporting systems and initially led the ADC family support group.

Alexander Kouvalis was a Friendly Visiting Program volunteer. He was an educator who purchased and renovated the Patio Theater.

Stephanie Kryzminski was a telephone reassurance and office volunteer for the Community Advocacy Network and helped with the transition to GACS. She was also the coordinator of CAN's Teen Chore Program which linked area teens with seniors who needed help with snow shoveling and household errands.

Peter and Evelyn Lallas co-chaired the first two Heritage Awards dinners. Peter owned two Carpet Forest stores and was involved with AHEPA. They were active members of St Andrew's church.

Bill La Magdeleine was a member of the Northwest Chicago Senior Care Advisory Committee. He was the coordinator of information & referral for the Chicago Department on Aging Northwest Region. Bill was very supportive of GACS and the ADC and organized a couple of fundraisers to benefit the center. He also obtained donations of an exercise bicycle and a refrigerator for the ADC.

Jane Lamont was a Friendly Visiting Program volunteer who worked at United Way and also assisted in translating our publicity into Greek.

Astrid Lewis was a telephone reassurance volunteer for the Community Advocacy Network and remained through the transition to GACS. She was homebound and lived in the senior citizens' apartment building at Irving Park and Clark. From her home, Astrid kept in contact with many clients who were themselves shut-ins. She was the recipient of the 1988 United Way of Chicago Heart of Gold Award in recognition of her volunteer work with us.

Janet Lewis was an ADC volunteer. A noted artist, she led regular classes in looming and other art forms for adult day care participants. Janet initially came to GACS as a master's degree intern in gerontology from National Louis University. She lived in Evanston. When her internship ended, Janet continued to volunteer as an arts and crafts volunteer.

The Very Rev. Nikitas Lulias was a member of the GACS Cultural & Arts Program Advisory Committee. He had a special interest in the history of Greek dance. Father Nikitas coordinated a statewide dance demonstration program funded through an Illinois Arts Council grant. He officiated the *Agiasmos* (Blessing of the Waters) services held during our open houses and offered invocations and benedictions at several Heritage Awards dinners. Father Nikitas was honored with the GACS Heritage Award in 1990. During his involvement with GACS, Father Nikitas was chancellor of the Greek Orthodox Diocese of Chicago. He later became the Greek Orthodox Metropolitan of Asia.

Alexander Makedon, Ph, D., was a member of the GACS Cultural & Arts Program Advisory Committee. He was a professor at Northeastern Illinois, Chicago State, and Northern Illinois universities.

Demetra Makris was a member of the GACS Cultural and Arts Program Advisory Committee. She was an anthropologist and historian who had gone to Egypt on excavation and had an interest in preserving and showcasing our cultural heritage. Demetra helped organize CAP music programs.

Frank Manago, an artist by profession, was a CAN volunteer who visited shut-in seniors. He lived in the community and visited clients who lived nearby.

Maria Maniates was a longtime volunteer of GACS. She was a friend and neighbor of Evangeline and related to Frieda Aravosis, and by extension knew Tessie Cantos. She was a dietician who had recently retired from her job as an inspector for the Chicago Department of Health where she primarily visited nursing homes and child care facilities to monitor their food services.

Maria functioned as the center's dietician. She reviewed and approved monthly lunch and snack menus including determining portion sizes and planning special menus as needed e.g., diabetic or low-sodium diets.

Maria also helped with the tedious task of timekeeping. Each day and for every client, the arrival and departure times, as well as whether or not they rode in the van, were recorded. We also recorded whether they were served lunch and morning and/or afternoon snacks. Maria audited the timesheets for any missing information and helped to collect or correct whatever was necessary.

For several years, GACS participated in the Child and Adult Care Food Program through which IDOA provided subsidies for the meals we served to our clients. Depending on a client's income, they were categorized as free, reduced, or paid. GACS received a reimbursement based on the number of meals served in each category. As this was in the pre-computer era, all records were on paper, and the worksheet that needed to be filled out involved a grid with tick marks for each snack or meal for each client covering the entire month. It was an incredibly detailed and eye-straining process that Maria mastered. Eventually, GACS ended its participation in the program due to the excessive time and effort required for very minimal returns that took months to receive.

Renata Maresia was a member of the GACS Cultural & Arts Program Advisory Committee. She was vice president of the Hellenic Society of DePaul University and also served as a GACS liaison to the university.

Judith Matthews was a member of both the Northwest Chicago Senior Care Advisory Committee and the Community Aging Network Advisory Board. As Chicago coordinator for the National Association of Hispanic Elderly, she oversaw the AYUDA program, which frequently placed Title V Senior Workers at GACS. Judy was a founding member and served on the board of CLESE throughout its early days.

Harry Milakis was a fundraising volunteer for GACS. He was also a member of the GANHC board and its first fundraising committee chairman. Harry was a development professional who was the regional director for the City of Hope. Before joining the City of Hope, he was director of the Southwest YMCA. During an early GACS meeting to discuss fundraising, Harry crafted the motto "Working to Preserve our Heritage," which endured throughout the years of GACS.

Georgia Mitchell was a member of the GACS Cultural & Arts Program Advisory Committee. She was the founder and director of the Hellenic Choral Society. Georgia received the GACS Heritage Award in 1989.

David Moorehead was a member of the Northwest Chicago Senior Care Advisory Committee. He was president of Corporate Financial Concepts.

Jackie Peterson was a neighborhood resident who wanted to help. She came in weekly to review and calculate client timesheets and prepare monthly invoices to IDOA, the V.A., and the families or guardians of our private pay clients. Jackie also led a current events discussion group with some of our clients.

Jane Stansell was a member of the Northwest Chicago Senior Care Advisory Committee. She was the director of the Alzheimer's Family Care Center. Jane served as president of the Illinois Association of Adult Day Services Providers and provided consultation and in-service training for the opening of the ADC.

Nick Stathopoulos was a GACS volunteer who helped in many ways. He helped with completing applications in the LIHEAP program, assisted with translating, and when needed, drove ADC clients home. I remember

Nick helping us to move from Alvernia Place to Pulaski on a very hot and humid day. He was a board member of the Chicago Council on Justice for Cyprus and was active with the Hellenic Cultural Organization.

Ernest Stavropoulos was a Friendly Visiting Program volunteer. He was also president of the St. Andrew Church Young Adult League.

Mike Tomeczko was a member of the Northwest Chicago Senior Care Advisory Committee. He was a vice president of the Chicago Bank of Commerce and Industry.

Mary Trankina was a volunteer of the Community Advocacy Network and transitioned from CAN to GACS when the organizations merged. She volunteered on Tuesdays and Thursdays while the office was in the Parkview Lutheran Church building.

Rose Vuco, R.N., was a member of both the Northwest Chicago Senior Care Advisory Committee and the Community Aging Network Advisory Board. She was the owner of Vital Measurements, a home healthcare agency. Early on, Rose set aside a small space for GACS in her office at 4817 W. Montrose and allowed us to use her office as a mailing address until we located a permanent office.

Phil Williams receives the Executive Director's Award from John Psiharis. December 20, 1995. John Psiharis collection.

Phil Williams was a volunteer in the ADC. He was a retired woodworker who as a result of a stroke had limited mobility on one side of his body. Phil presented weekly "puppet shows" with stick figures he had created. He also had a vast library of films on VHS tapes which he would show during weekly movie screenings at the center. After each film, Phil led a discussion on the film, and as a movie buff, shared trivia and stories about the films. He video-recorded some of the activities and special events held at the center. It isn't known where these tapes are, or if they still exist, but if they ever turn up they will capture some of the special moments Phil was able to capture on video.

One of the most needed forms of volunteer help was typing. As computers were only beginning to make their way into everyday life and the Internet didn't exist, everything was done on paper, and the ability to type accurately and quickly was a vital necessity. While help with routine correspondence was always needed, typing grants that were many pages in length required extra help.

In the early days, we relied on several people to help with this task. Needless to say, neither Elaine nor I were proficient typists. Marie Gilbert, a retired social worker who had been an intake worker at Lutheran Social Services of Illinois (LSSI), typed a number of our early grants and correspondence. Valerie Scherer, a receptionist at LSSI and a student in the Human Services program at the National College of Education, later known as National Louis University, Mark Quartullo, a high school friend, and Pamela Lekas, also a friend of mine, helped with typing projects.

The Cheerleaders

The three Nicks. (L-R): Nick Thomopoulos, Nick Ellis, and Nick Festos at a GACS Heritage Awards Dinner. Date unknown. John Psiharis collection.

There was a small loosely affiliated cadre of people who by virtue of their relationships with Elaine, John, myself, or each other, were supporters of GACS. They frequently attended GACS events or meetings as guests.

Some were more active than others, but all helped in one way or another and are certainly part of the story of GACS. They included:

George Bacos (Bakoyannis) was a World War II veteran who lived in North Riverside. He attended many of our events and was involved in a rededication of the statue of George Dilboy, a Greek American World War 1 war hero at Edward Hines, Jr. Veterans Hospital. I attended the dedication ceremony. The project was spearheaded by the American Hellenic Society of Berwyn.

Mary Bennos was a volunteer at special events. She was Ethel's cousin and helped her in handling reservations and seating arrangements for our annual dinner dances.

David Aaron Condes was an event planner and promoter. Along with Melissa Brown, he organized numerous Greek Night events at popular venues, often with a portion of the proceeds benefiting GACS. Many of these events were held at the Cairo nightclub at 720 N. Wells Street. Parties were also held at the Limelight, Excalibur, Park West, and Petros Dianna's.

Nick Ellis was an architect and writer who supported GACS by attending events and offering feedback and ideas. He also helped with written Greek translations.

Nick Festos was the owner of Festos Jewelers, a business begun by his father. He was a financial supporter and attended many GACS events. Nick held a patent for an engine analyzer he designed which was purchased by the United States Postal Service to service their postal vehicles.

Tom Geovanis was a professor of humanities at Harry S. Truman Community College and served as a union delegate for the campus. He was president of Hellenes for a Better America. Tom provided appropriate quotations from ancient Greek philosophers that were used in introducing Heritage Awards honorees. The quotes were often included in the biographies of each recipient that appeared in the souvenir program booklets.

James Kledones was a branch manager for Great American Federal Savings. He frequently attended GACS events and donated promotional items from the bank that were used as raffles or bingo prizes in the adult day care center.

Helene Petropoulos was an eccentric older lady who attended some GACS events. I have memories of her at GACS waiting for John R. to take her home. Helene carried a large bag of mail with her and sat at a table shredding each item into tiny pieces with scissors. When John drove her home, she would ask him to drive through a random alley so that she could dispose of her trash anonymously.

Alexander Rassogianis was John's younger brother and a supporter of GACS. Initially a teacher, he later worked as an inspector with the U.S. Department of Labor Occupational Safety and Health Administration (OSHA). Alex attended many of our events.

John Sandors was an elementary school teacher at an inner-city public school and a member of Assumption Greek Orthodox Church. He was known, among other reasons, for passing out pencils during the holidays that were inscribed with "Merry Christmas from John Sandors." John attended many GACS events.

Nick Thomopoulos, **Ph.D.**, supported GACS in many ways. As Elaine's husband, he helped behind the scenes, was an informal advisor, and attended many of our events. Nick was a professor of management science at the Illinois Institute of Technology and had authored several professional textbooks about these topics.

Special Supporters of GACS

Broadway Bank was a financial supporter of GACS. Owned by Alexis Giannoulias, the bank helped underwrite the adult day care center's food costs by donating $2,000 monthly for a year. This support was in partnership with the Broadway Medical Group. Alexis' son Alexi would go on to be elected treasurer of the state of Illinois and win the Democratic party's nomination for the US Senate seat vacated by newly elected President Barack Obama. At this time (summer 2022), Alexi is the Democratic party nominee for Illinois Secretary of State. Broadway Bank failed in 2010 during the Great Recession and was soon taken over by MB Bank. It was seized on the same day that the government took over New Century Bank. In 2019, MB Bank merged with Fifth Third Bank.

Cermak Produce is a chain of Chicago area grocery stores featuring fresh produce that is owned by Dimitris and Eleni Bousis. In addition to financial support, Eleni often brought seasonal fresh fruit to the ADC clients from one of their stores.

The Chicago Community Trust (CCT) is a community foundation covering the metropolitan Chicago area and is a major source of support to nonprofits providing vital services within these communities. The Trust provided seed money during the early phase of the adult day care center and funded the purchase of the first *Ya'Sou* van. They also provided GACS with matching grants over three years in support of the center. The Trust funded the Ethnic Elderly Needs Assessment and provided several grants to the Coalition of Limited English Speaking Elderly. In appreciation of their support, GACS honored CCT with the *Efharisto* Award in 1992.

The Chicago Department on Aging (CDOA) was the city agency focused on serving older adults and was the Area Agency on Aging (AAA) for the region. Its name and structure evolved over the years. Created as the Mayor's Office for Senior Citizens, it merged with the Mayor's Office for the Handicapped to become the Chicago Department on Aging and Disabilities. At some point, the disabilities function was spun off and it became the Chicago Department on Aging (CDAD). Under Mayor Rahm Emanuel, the department was downgraded and merged into the Chicago Department of Family and Support Services (formerly the Chicago Department of Human Services). Over the years GACS worked closely with the department on such matters as the ethnic elderly needs assessment, Benefits Eligibility Checklist, adult day care matters, and CLESE-related concerns. The CDOA Levy and Copernicus regional senior centers at different times hosted the Fabric Arts Program classes, meetings, and other events.

The Chicago Department of Cultural Affairs (CDCA) was the agency that focused on the cultural life of the city. When GACS first worked with them, it was known as the Chicago Office of Fine Arts (COFA) with Madelyn Rabb as the executive director. Mayor Washington merged the Chicago Office of Fine Arts, the Mayor's Office of Special Events, and the Chicago Film Office into a new Department of Cultural Affairs and appointed Fred Fine its commissioner. Upon Fine's retirement, Washington appointed Lois Weisberg, who remained in that position until 2011.

GACS received multiple grants through the Community Arts Assistance Program (CAAP), City Arts, and the Neighborhood Arts Program (NAP) grant programs. GACS also received CDBG delegate agency funding through the Cultural Outreach Program. City Arts grants funded film festivals, cultural enrichment programs for seniors, Greek language classes, and other programs. The Fabric Arts Program was funded first by Neighborhood Arts grants and later through CDBG.

The Chicago Tribune Foundation provided several grants to GACS. For a time, Alice Buzanis worked at the Chicago Tribune and recommended us to the Foundation.

Columbia National Bank of Chicago was a regular supporter of GACS through Leon Xintaris, the bank's executive vice president. Columbia financed the mortgages for GACS and the GANHC land purchase.

Columbia was bought out by LaSalle Banks, which was eventually purchased by Bank of America.

Commercial National Bank located at Lawrence and Western Avenues was the first bank GACS established its accounts with since it was convenient to Anna who was treasurer at the time. The bank supported GACS through donations, advertising in dinner ad books, and underwriting the cost of bi-lingual fliers and publicity.

The Community Economic Development Agency of Cook County (CEDA) is a quasi-governmental organization that provides social services to residents of Cook County. CEDA administered the Low Income Home Energy Assistance Program (LIHEAP). GACS contracted with CEDA to offer LIHEAP services.

Martin L. and Wyleen T. Coyne Foundation provided funding of at least $1,000 per year.

The George M. Eisenberg Foundation for Charities provided annual grants of $10,000 to GACS. Connie and Dee Andrews knew James Marousis, who ran the foundation, and spoke with him about GACS. It turned out that Mr. Eisenberg had a specific interest in funding Greek causes since he had many Greek friends, including James. The foundation reflected Mr. Eisenberg's philosophy, "What we do for ourselves alone, dies with us. What we do for others remains and is immortal." We also approached James about funding the nursing home effort and over time they donated more than $100,000 to the GANHC.

Fel-Pro provided several grants in support of GACS. Located in Skokie IL, they manufactured automobile gaskets.

Goya Foods, a major purveyor of Hispanic food products, donated several community meals to adult day care participants and community seniors. Eleni Bousis was friends with the owners of Goya and made the arrangements. Senior management of the company visited the center and served the freshly prepared lunch to the seniors.

The Hellenic Ladies Society of Constantinople was an association for women whose ancestry came from that region. They were regular supporters of GACS and also donated $5,000 to the building fund drive. In later years, the organization changed its name to the Hellenic Society of Constantinople.

Illinois Arts Council (IAC) is the state agency charged with promoting the arts in Illinois. The Council is appointed by the Governor and legislative leaders. Shirley Madigan, the wife of House Speaker Mike Madigan, served as chair and Irene Antoniou was co-chair. At some point,

Irene assumed the chairmanship of the IAC. GACS received annual grants from the Illinois Arts Council for a variety of programs that included dance classes, folk art events, and music preservation.

Illinois Department on Aging (IDOA) is a state agency focused on serving older adults within Illinois. IDOA administers the Community Care Program (CCP) through which GACS maintained a contract for adult day care services and for some time chore/housekeeping services. IDOA also provided funding to CLESE.

Illinois Department of Public Aid (IDPA) administered the Earn Fare program which assigned unemployed able-bodied public aid recipients to work in community organizations as a condition to receive their benefits. Maria Toledo and Ray Mansingh were among those that came to us through participation in this program. Maria and Ray were eventually hired onto the GACS payroll.

Illinois Humanities Council (IHC) is the state agency focused on promoting humanities in Illinois. Like the IAC, it was led by a council appointed by the governor and legislative leaders. For much of this time, Francis Pettis was the executive director of the IHC. Each year, the IHC designated a theme they were seeking to explore and we submitted proposals related to these themes.

Illinois Masonic Medical Center provided more than $30,000 in funding to help us during the early days of the adult day care center. In addition, they provided us with consultation and furniture and engaged a marketing consultant to design and print brochures. Credit for establishing this relationship goes to Dr. Kioutas who was affiliated with the hospital. Dr. Angelo Creticos, the chief of medicine at Illinois Masonic, was a supporter of GACS and advocated on our behalf. GACS honored Illinois Masonic with the *Efharisto* Award in 1994.

The Mayor's Office of Employment and Training (MET) provided grants for employment and training programs in Chicago. GACS was a delegate agency for the summer youth employment program. For several years, we hosted a group of youth workers who tutored English to senior citizens, helped with activities in the adult day care center, and assisted with outreach for the census. MET later became the Mayor's Office for Workforce Development. GACS did not pursue funding through MET because they were mainly performance-based contracts and to receive payment a participant needed to retain a job and meet certain benchmarks. In short, GACS would have incurred significant upfront costs with the possibility that we wouldn't be reimbursed for the total. and then wait months to receive the payment.

The National Association of Hispanic Elderly operated Project AYUDA, a national senior employment program funded through Title V of the Older Americans Act. Project AYUDA paid lower-income seniors to work part-time in community organizations with the intent that they gain experience to help them obtain employment. In some cases, (including ours), agencies hired program participants onto their payrolls. GACS throughout its existence was a host agency. The AYUDA Chicago coordinator was Judith Matthews who became a member of the Community Aging Network Advisory Committee and was a founding member and board member of the Coalition of Limited English Speaking Elderly. Among AYUDA participants at GACS were Spyridon Dimas, Rafael Gallardo, Betty McClelland, Margaret Nikolopoulos, Gwen Sten, Gladys Tichnell, and Carmen Vilato.

The National Bank of Greece regularly donated to GACS and supported the organization in other ways such as advertising in our ad books.

Olympic Airways donated round-trip tickets to Greece for several raffles and purchased advertising in GACS ad books.

Pan Laconian Federation hosted food drives for GACS. Volunteers distributed food baskets to needy families that were known to GACS. Polyzoes Gavaris was an officer within the organization and served as a liaison between the two organizations.

Polk Brothers Foundation was created by the five Polk brothers who owned and operated Polk Brothers, a Chicago-based retail chain of appliance and furniture stores. The foundation provided grant funding to GACS.

Michael Reese Health Trust was a foundation created with the proceeds from the sale of Michael Reese Hospital. The foundation awarded GACS with a grant of $50,000 in support of the adult day care center in 1998.

Playboy Foundation provided an in-kind grant to print several newsletters and brochures GACS brought the proofs for the newsletter to their plant for printing. When finished, they were shipped to GACS and volunteers prepared the mailings.

Retirement Research Foundation (RRF), now known as RRF Foundation for Aging, is a foundation focused on older adults. RRF, launched by John D. MacArthur, is nationally recognized as a leader in aging and has disbursed millions of dollars in grants. RRF provided over $200,000 in grants to GACS in support of our adult day care center. They also funded the Ethnic Elderly Needs Assessment, CLESE, and a number of its member agencies. Marilyn Hennessy was president of the RRF, and

Sharon Markham and Julie Kaufman were the grants officers we worked with most. GACS honored RRF with the *Efharisto* Award in 1993.

Dr. Scholl Foundation funded the GACS health education program and adult day care center. The foundation was created by the founder of the Dr. Scholl company. Dr. George Dalianis, a podiatrist and GACS supporter, was a board member of the Foundation and helped us to obtain this funding.

United Way of Metropolitan Chicago was a significant funder of Chicago's social services safety net. Becoming a member agency of United Way was coveted since it provided a stable annual funding source for an organization. GACS received Venture Grant funding from United Way in 1989-90. These grants enabled GACS to hire Ethel Kotsovos as a social worker and funded Community Aging Network services. GACS was invited to apply for agency membership. It was a detailed process, and we were told GACS would be recommended. Months later, we were informed that they would not consider any new member agencies for the foreseeable future due to a decline in donations. As far as I know, GACS was the first Greek organization to receive funding from United Way.

Veterans Administration (VA), now the U.S. Department of Veterans Affairs, had a purchase of service agreement with GACS for adult day care services to veterans. Each year, a multidisciplinary team from Hines VA consisting of the supervising nurse, social worker, dietician, activity therapist, and facilities person would visit and meet with their counterparts on the GACS staff to evaluate center operations. The center passed these inspections.

Walgreens Foundation was funded by the Walgreens company. Emily Koulogeorge, a Greek American, was president of the Deerfield, Illinois-based foundation. They funded GACS health education programs for senior citizens and similar endeavors.

Washington Square Health Foundation was a foundation created from the proceeds of the closing and sale of Henrotin Hospital. Dr. Angelo Creticos was chairman of the foundation's board and spearheaded grants to GACS in support of the adult day care center and the GANHC for support of the nursing home project

A Chronological History of Greek-American Community Services

1982

December 14: First meeting of the "Greek-American Community Services of Chicago Planning Committee." Elysion Restaurant. In attendance: John Psiharis, Elaine Thomopoulos, Dr. Theodosis Kioutas, Jim Heliotes, and Polyzoes Gavaris.

1983

January 14: GACS Planning Committee meeting at the Elysion Restaurant. The bylaws of the organization are discussed.

January 25: Presentation by Elaine Thomopoulos, Dr. Kioutas, and John Psiharis to the St. Demetrios Senior Citizens Club about the mission, purpose, and aims of GACS.

February 8: GACS Planning Committee meeting at Elysion Restaurant. Officers are elected. John Psiharis, President; Elaine Thomopoulos, Vice President; Helen Geocaris, Secretary and Anna Manos, Treasurer. Polyzoes Gavaris is the Registered Agent.

February 14: GACS Board meeting at Elysion Restaurant.

March 8: GACS Board meeting at the Elysion Restaurant. Agenda items are voting on the adoption of the by-laws, prospective new members, and Articles of Incorporation to be submitted to the state of Illinois.

April 9: Elaine Thomopoulos speaks on "The Orthodox Woman in her Many Roles," during a Chicago Diocese Philoptochos retreat entitled "The Three Faces of the 20th Century Philoptochos Woman," held at St. Constantine and Helen Greek Orthodox Church in Palos Hills, IL.

April 13: GACS Board meeting at Elysion Restaurant.

May 11: GACS Board meeting at the Elysion Restaurant.

June 29: GACS Board meeting at the Elysion Restaurant. The Greek-American Nursing Home Committee is established as a committee of GACS. Agenda items include the introduction of prospective new members, minutes of the last meeting, progress on incorporation (John Psiharis), Board member application (John Psiharis, Elaine Thomopoulos, and Anna Manos), report on Boston Nursing Home (Elaine Thomopoulos), and new business.

July 26: GACS Board meeting at Elysion Restaurant.

August 23: GACS Board meeting at Elysion Restaurant. John Yonan, executive director of the Assyrian Universal Alliance Foundation, speaks on their efforts towards establishing a nursing home in their community and about the possibility of establishing a Greek wing in the facility.

October 11: GACS Board meeting at the Elysion Restaurant.

December 3: GACS Board and members of the Nursing Home Committee visit the Villa Scalabrini nursing home in Northlake, IL.

December 15: GACS Board meeting at Elysion Restaurant.

1984

January 21: GACS Board and members of the Nursing Home Committee re-visit Villa Scalabrini for a tour of the nursing home.

April 18: GACS Board of Directors breakfast meeting at Elysion Restaurant.

June 26: GACS Board of Directors meeting at Elysion Restaurant.

August 9: GACS Board meeting at Elysion Restaurant.

October 23: GACS meeting to establish a committee focused on the Greek American Nursing Home at Elysion Restaurant. John Psiharis appoints Dr. Theodosis Kioutas as chairman of the Nursing Home Committee and John Geocaris, as co-chairman. Committee members are Christine Burbulis, Jean Kaporis, Helen Geocaris, Elaine Thomopoulos, and Thalia Jameson. Abel Swirsky to serve as a volunteer consultant.

October 24: GACS Board meeting at Elysion Restaurant.

November 14: GACS Board meeting at Elysion Restaurant.

December 3: GACS Board meeting at Elysion Restaurant.

1985

January 10: GACS Board meeting at Elysion Restaurant.

January 15: John Psiharis is invited by Mayor Harold Washington to attend the "Chicago Interfaith Breakfast in Honor of the Birthday of Dr. Martin Luther King, Jr." in the Grand Ballroom of the Marriott Hotel, 540 N. Michigan Ave., Chicago, IL.

January 15: GACS Community Meeting at Elysion Restaurant. John Psiharis and Elaine Thomopoulos provide an overview of GACS. Dr. Kioutas speaks about the newly-formed nursing home committee. Twenty-eight people are in attendance.

February 6: GACS Board meeting at Elysion Restaurant.

February 12: GACS presents a lecture during a meeting of St. Demetrios Church Young at Heart Senior Citizen's Group.

February 19: Dr. Theodosis Kioutas provides an update on GACS and GANHC during a meeting of the St. Demetrios Senior Citizens Club.

March 14: GACS Nursing Home Committee meeting at Elysion Restaurant.

March 27: GACS Board meeting at Elysion Restaurant.

April 2: GACS Nursing Home Committee meeting at Elysion Restaurant.

April 26-28: Elaine Thomopoulos and John Psiharis participate in a panel discussion on the ethnic elderly at the 4th Annual Midwest North Central National Organization of Human Services Educators conference at George Williams College in Lake Geneva, Wisconsin.

May 7: GACS presents a lecture on "Medicines and Side-effects," by pharmacist George Akrivos during a meeting of the St. Demetrios Church Young at Heart Senior Citizen's Group.

May 7: GACS Executive Committee Meeting. Agenda items: New members, film festival, treasurer's report, fundraising (Hike-Bike-a-thon, raffle, neighborhood festival), regular meeting time, and new business. Followed by a meeting of the GACS Nursing Home Committee. Elysion Restaurant.

May 17-18: Elaine Thomopoulos, representing GACS, speaks on "The Significance of Language and Cultural Barriers for the Euro-American Elderly," at the National Conference on Euro-American Elderly. The conference is held at the Catholic University of America in Washington, D.C.

May 29: GACS Nursing Home Committee meeting at Elysion Restaurant.

June 9: GACS presents a lecture on "Cataracts and Glaucoma," by Dr. Demetrios Perros during a meeting of the St. Demetrios Church Young at Heart Senior Citizen's Group.

June 26: GACS Board meeting at Elysion Restaurant.

July 9: GACS presents a lecture on the "Problems of Aging," by Dr. Nicholas Dunkas during a meeting of the St. Demetrios Church Young at Heart Senior Citizens,' Group.

August: Connie Callinicos, Steve Frangos, John Psiharis, and Elaine Thomopoulos meet at Roditys Restaurant to discuss the creation of a museum exhibit focused on the history of Greek-American women.

August 20: GACS Board meeting at Elysion Restaurant.

August 27: GACS presents a free trip to Brookfield Zoo for youth and their families. According to city publicity, "the program is presented by Greek-American Community Services, a newly formed not-for-profit tax-exempt organization." It is sponsored by the City-As-A-School Project of the Chicago Department of Human Services.

September 10: GACS Nursing Home Committee meeting at Elysion Restaurant.

September 23: GACS Board meeting followed by a meeting of the GACS Nursing Home Committee at Elysion Restaurant.

October 8: GACS Nursing Home Committee meeting at Elysion Restaurant.

October 28 – 30: Dominick's Benefit Days to benefit GACS.

November 5: GACS presents a lecture entitled, "How to Use Hospital Social Services," during a meeting of the St. Demetrios Church Young at Heart Senior Citizen's Group.

November 11: GACS Nursing Home Committee meeting at Elysion Restaurant.

November 18: GACS Nursing Home Committee meeting at Elysion Restaurant.

November 26: GACS Nursing Home Committee meeting at Elysion Restaurant.

December 9: GACS Nursing Home Committee meeting at Elysion Restaurant.

1986

January 6: GACS receives a determination letter from the Internal Revenue Service that it is officially a 501(c)3 organization. All donations to GACS are tax-deductible.

January 7: GACS Board meeting at 6:30 p.m. and GACS Nursing Home Committee meeting at 7:00 p.m. Elysion Restaurant.

January 16: GACS Cultural & Arts Program Advisory Committee meeting to discuss the Greek/Assyrian conference and applying for Illinois Humanities Council funding for the project at Dianna's Restaurant.

January 20: GACS Nursing Home Committee meeting at Elysion Restaurant.

January 22: GACS organization meeting at Annunciation Cathedral.

January 23: GACS Cultural & Arts Program meeting at Parthenon Restaurant.

January 24: GACS Board meeting at LSSI-Byron Street.

January 26: GACS IHC grant committee meeting at Elaine's house. That day, the Chicago Bears won the Super Bowl. Elaine serves cake at the meeting to celebrate the Bears' win.

January 28: GACS IHC grant committee meeting at Elysion Restaurant.

January 30: GACS Nursing Home Committee meeting at Elysion Restaurant.

February 17: GACS Board meeting at 6:30 p.m. and GACS Nursing Home Committee meeting at 7:00 p.m. Elysion Restaurant.

February 28: GACS submits a proposal to the Illinois Department on Aging requesting $17,406 to create a manual on innovative programs for ethnic elderly and to create an "ethnic providers' council." Ten organizations agree to take part in the project.

March 5: GACS IHC grant committee lunch meeting at Roditys Restaurant. Present: Steve Frangos, Fotios Litsas, John Psiharis, and Elaine Thomopoulos.

March 7: GACS Nursing Home Committee meeting to discuss fundraising at the home of Helen Geocaris.

March 11: Rosalie Guttman, Elaine Thomopoulos, and John Psiharis conduct a CAN workshop on sensory loss for Little Brothers of the Poor/Friends of the Elderly volunteers.

March 12–13: Nightly meetings of the GACS IHC grant committee at the Elysion Restaurant. The due date for the grant is March 15.

March 14: Elaine Thomopoulos and John Psiharis meet with Electra Tarsinos of the Hellenic Foundation at the CAN office

GREEK-AMERICAN COMMUNITY SERVICES
BOARD OF DIRECTORS MEETING
Monday April 7, 1986

The meeting was called to order by John Psiharis, President at 6:35pm at the Elysion Restaurant, 2800 W. Foster Avenue

In attendance were: John Psiharis, Anna Manos, Helen Geocaris, Helen Georges, Evangeline Mistaras, Jean Kaporis, Christine Burbulis, Thalia Jameson and Elaine Thomopoulos (late).

John Psiharis gave a brief report on the progress of the organization. His report is as follows:

Greek-American Community Services is finally tax-exempt under section 501(c)(3) of the Internal Revenue Service code.

Grant applications have been submitted to the following:
a) Illinois Humanities Council for $10,000 to organize a two day conference entitled "Strains On Ethnic Pride, Conflicts Between the New and the Old Immigrants in the Greek and Assyrian communities" a joint venture with the Assyrian Universal Alliance Foundation. John reported that 34 high caliber speakers will participate, and an active planning committee developed the program. The committee included several humanists. Extensive media coverage is planned. He hoped that GACS could go ahead with this program even if funding is not approved by IHC. Decision will be made in May.

b) Chicago Department of Human Services through the Community Development Block Grant program, for $24,700 to initiate youth tutoring program using high school tutors to help grade school children.

c) Illinois Department on Aging, for $17,000 to write and publish a manual on Model Programs Serving the Ethnic Elderly. The manual would focus on ten different ethnic communities. Social service organizations within these communities that agreed to write parts of the manual are: Metropolitan Chicago Coalition on Aging, Assyrian Universal Alliance Foundation, Council for Jewish Elderly, Japanese American Service Committee, Lutheran Social Services of Illinois, Casa Central, Korean American Community Services, Lithuanian Human Services and the Association of Indo-Chinese Refugees

d) Progress is being made in preparing a $35-40,000 proposal for the Chicago Department on Aging and Disability for a Greek/Assyrian nutrition site

e) A grant for $2,800 was received from the Chicago Department of Cultural Affairs to organize a fall film festival on the Greeks in America. DePaul University's Greek club and Andy Kopan are helping to organize this program.

John called upon Anna Manos to give the Treasurer's Report. As of April 7th GACS has a balance of $573.00 in our checking account.

John reported that the new GACS Friendly Visitor Project is getting off the ground. Already one volunteer is visiting two clients twice a week. An orientation meeting for those interested in becoming friendly visitors will be held on Saturday April 19th at 10:00am at the Elysion.

Discussion arose as to the need for an office for GACS. Yet finances prohibit paying for rent-at this point. Board members were asked to investigate locating free or low cost facilities.

Christine Burbulis moved and Toni Panos seconded a motion for GACS to explore obtaining joint office space with the Greek-American Nursing Home Committee. This arrangement will benefit both organizations. Currently, the Committee is looking into the National Bank of Greece building. John Psiharis called for the question the motion was unanimously approved.

John reported that in his position he has become overwhelmed filling the positions of both president and executive director. He called upon Helen Geocaris to read the letter of resignation he sent to her.

Toni Panos moved and Helen Georges seconded the nomination of John Psiharis to the position of executive director. John accepted the nomination. The motion was unanimously approved.

John reported Elaine's desire to not succeed him as president. She intends to work with John in program development. Helen Geocaris or Anna Manos did not wish to ascend into the position, the system outlined in the GACS bylaws.

After considerable discussion, John called for nominations from the floor. Helen Georges moved and Helen Geocaris seconded the nomination of Evangeline Mistaras as president. Evangeline accepted the nomination. John called for the vote. Evangeline was elected unanimously. She was congratulated in her position as was John in his new position.

The meeting was adjourned by John Psiharis at 7:20 pm so that the Greek-American Nursing Home Committee could meet at 7:30pm.

Respectfully Submitted,

Helen Geocaris
Helen Geocaris, Secretary
Greek-American Community Services

Minutes from an April 7, 1986 GACS Board of Directors meeting. Elaine Thomopoulos collection.

March 17: Elaine Thomopoulos and John Psiharis conduct a CAN workshop on advocacy at the Montrose Baptist Church Providers Cluster.

March 19: Elaine Thomopoulos and John Psiharis speak at the Mid-American Conference on Aging.

March 19: GACS Nursing Home Committee meeting to discuss fundraising at the home of Harry Milakis, Berkeley IL.

April 7: GACS Board meeting at Elysion Restaurant.

April 10: GACS Nursing Home Committee meeting to discuss public relations at the home of Sofia Tasaras, River Forest, IL.

April 19: GACS Friendly Visitor Program meeting at Elysion Restaurant.

April 21: GACS Nursing Home Committee meeting at Elysion Restaurant.

May 5: John Psiharis and Elaine Thomopoulos resign their positions as GACS president and vice president to assume the positions of executive director and administrator. Evangeline Mistaras and Athanasia Papadopoulos became GACS president and vice president.

May 13: GACS presents a lecture on "Headaches," by Dr. Theodosis Kioutas during a meeting of the St. Demetrios Church Young at Heart Senior Citizen's Group. Dr. Kioutas also provides an update on the nursing home.

May 16: GACS Nursing Home Committee meeting at Elysion Restaurant.

May 17: CAN Volunteer Recognition Luncheon at Fourth Presbyterian Church, Michigan Avenue, and Chestnut Street.

May 21: GACS Board meeting at Elysion Restaurant.

May 21: GACS Friendly Visitor Program meeting at Elysion Restaurant (after board meeting).

May 25: GACS participates in the Hands Across America nationwide event.

June-August: GACS, in partnership with the Assyrian Universal Alliance Foundation and Literacy Volunteers of Chicago, operates a literacy program for older adults. Classes are held in the Panousis Room at St. Demetrios Church and staffed by AUAF youth workers funded through the City of Chicago summer youth employment program.

June 16: GACS Board and Nursing Home Committee meetings at Elysion Restaurant.

June 18: GACS Friendly Visitor Program volunteers meeting at Elysion Restaurant.

July 1: Meeting with Paul Karras, Chicago Public Buildings commissioner to discuss North Park Village as a site for the nursing home. Christine Burbulis, Dr. Kioutas, Jim Mezilson, John Psiharis, and Elaine Thomopoulos are in attendance.

July 1: GACS Friendly Visiting Program volunteers meeting at Elysion Restaurant.

July 8: GACS presents a lecture on "Social Security, Medicare, and SSI," by Fran Mitileanos, claims representative for the Social Security Administration, during a meeting of the St. Demetrios Church Young at Heart Senior Citizen's Group.

July 12: GACS Hike/Bike-a-Thon to benefit CAN, along Chicago's lakefront from Foster Avenue Beach to Ohio Street.

July 16: GACS Nursing Home Committee hosts three simultaneous sub-committee meetings for executive, public relations, and fundraising committees at Elysion Restaurant.

July 22: GACS Board meeting at CAN office.

August 5: GACS Friendly Visiting Program volunteers meeting with in-service on communication by Dan Matero at Elysion Restaurant.

August 7: GACS Nursing Home Committee meeting at Elysion Restaurant.

August 21: CAN Flea Market Committee meeting.

August 23: GACS Nursing Home Committee picnic in Michigan.

August 25: GACS newsletter design and layout meeting at the CAN office.

September–December: GACS launches the Fabric Arts Program at the Chicago Department on Aging and Disability Northeast Area Levy Center, 2019 W. Lawrence Avenue, Chicago, IL. Tessie Cantos is the coordinator of the program, Penny Kalogiannis is the instructor, and Tasia Economou is the assistant instructor.

September 4: GACS Board meeting and Nursing Home Committee meetings at Elysion Restaurant.

September 9: GACS presents a lecture on "Foot Health Care" by Dr. George Dalianis, DPM, during a meeting of the St. Demetrios Church Young at Heart Senior Citizen's Group.

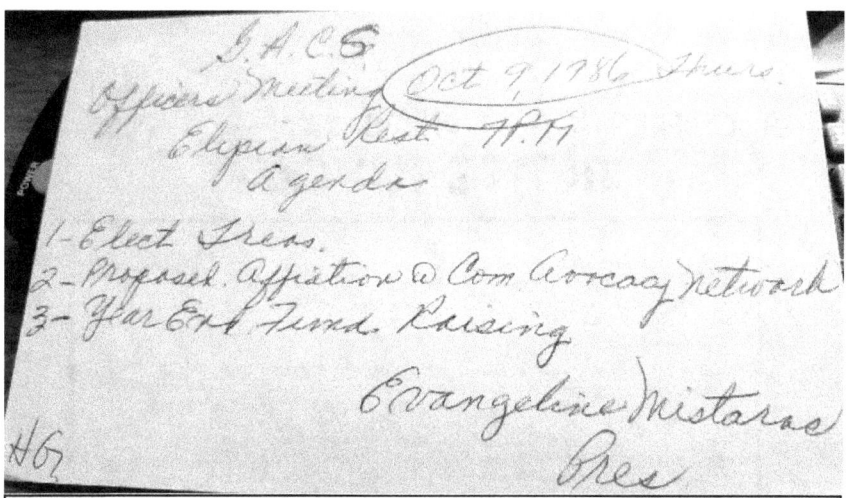

Meeting notice postcard for the October 9, 1986 GACS officers meeting sent by Secretary Helen Geocaris. Elaine Thomopoulos collection.

September 21: GACS hosts the first of a three-part film festival entitled "The Greeks in America: A Celebration of Films," funded through a grant from the Chicago Office of Fine Arts. The afternoon features a showing of *America, America* by Elia Kazan. Guest speaker, Charles Moskos, Ph.D., DePaul University, Schmitt Center.

October 9: GACS officers meeting. Elysion Restaurant. Agenda: Elect Treasurer; Proposed affiliation with Community Advocacy Network and year-end fundraising.

October 13: GACS Nursing Home Committee Meeting at Elysion Restaurant.

October 14: GACS presents a lecture on "Public Aid Programs for the Aged, Blind, and Disabled, Medical Assistance and Food Stamps," by Helen Georges, an administrator at the Illinois Department of Public Aid, during a meeting of the St. Demetrios Church Young at Heart Senior Citizen's Group.

October 15: GACS Strains on Ethnic Pride Planning Committee meeting at Assyrian Universal Alliance Foundation, 7055 N. Clark St., Chicago, IL.

October 19: Part two of the "Greeks in America: A Celebration of Films." Two films by award-winning filmmaker Doreen Moses are screened. *A Village in Baltimore, Images of Greek American Women* and *One on Every Corner: Manhattan's Greek Owned Coffee Shops.* Guest speakers are Doreen Moses and Father Chris Kerhulas from St. Basil Greek Orthodox Church who also reviewed films for the *Orthodox Observer*. DePaul University, Schmitt Center.

THE GREEKS IN AMERICA..
A CELEBRATION OF FILMS
film festival

SUNDAY SEPTEMBER 21, 1986 at 3:00pm "AMERICA, AMERICA" BY ELIA KAZAN a compelling account of the stuggles of a young poor Greek man and his efforts to emigrate to the United States. Based on Elia Kazan's autobiographical novel "America, America."
Guest Speaker: Dr. Charles Moskos, Northwestern University

SUNDAY OCTOBER 19, 1986 at 3:00pm "A VILLAGE IN BALTIMORE, A Look at Greek American Women" BY DOREEN MOSES explores the assimilation process that 4 Greek women go through as they integrate into American culture. The film, made in Baltimore's Greek town looks at such issues as marriage, family life, professional aspirations and traditions.
Guest Speakers: Doreen Moses, the film's producer/director and Father Chris Kerhulas, film reviewer for the Orthodox Observer

SUNDAY NOVEMBER 16, 1986 at 3:00pm "GOODNIGHT SOCRATES" BY MARIA MORAITES brings to life the hardship a family faces as they are forced to leave "Greek town" in the face of construction of the University of Illinois Chicago Circle Campus. The film looks at the family's apprehension as they begin to assimilate into mainstream society and shares such moments at their last Easter in their old neighborhood.
Guest Speakers: Maria Moraites, Writer of "Goodnight Socrates" and Father Chris Kerhulas, film reviewer for the Orthodox Observer

REFRESHMENTS WILL BE SERVED

DePAUL UNIVERSITY AT SCHMITT CENTER

2323 North Seminary Chicago, Illinois   ROOM 154
TICKETS $4.00 per person, $3.00 for senior citizens & students-Available at door.
FOR INFORMATION CALL: 282-6816 or 282-6234, 775-6893 or 655-2077

SPONSORED BY:
GREEK-AMERICAN COMMUNITY SERVICES AND...

CO-SPONSORED BY:
DePaul University Hellenic Society

This project is supported by a grant from the Chicago Office of Fine Arts CityArts I Program made possible by the City of Chicago, the Illinois Arts Council, the MacArthur Foundation, and the Woods Charitable Fund.

COORDINATED BY:

Evangeline Mistaras, President, John Psiharis, Executive Director and Elaine Thomopoulos, Ph.D. Administrator for Greek-American Community Services.

"The Greeks in America: A Celebration of Films" flyer. 1986. Elaine Thomopoulos collection.

October 23: GACS holds a screening of *My Mother, My Father*, at the Elysion restaurant. The film is described as "the best treatment we have seen on the issues confronting children who have a frail older parent." The community was invited and an after-film discussion is moderated by the filmmaker. Sponsored by GACS and the Community Advocacy Network of Lutheran Social Services of Illinois.

November 5: GACS Nursing Home Committee meeting at Elysion Restaurant.

November 7–December 12: GACS Fabric Arts Program classes at the Levy Center, 2019 W. Lawrence Ave. Classes are funded through a grant from the Chicago Office of Fine Arts Neighborhood Arts Program.

November 11: GACS presents a lecture on the Circuit Breaker program by Angelike Mountanis of the Hellenic Foundation, during a meeting of the St. Demetrios Church Young at Heart Senior Citizen's Group.

November 13: Elaine Thomopoulos and John Psiharis attend a board meeting of Parkview Lutheran Church to request office space for CAN.

November 14: GACS meeting to discuss creating a fundraising appeal at Elysion Restaurant. In attendance: Evangeline Mistaras, Harry Milakis, John Rassogianis, Voula Efthemiou, Elaine Thomopoulos, and John Psiharis.

November 16: *Goodnight Socrates*, the final film of the GACS "Greeks in America: A Celebration of Films" series is shown at DePaul University. Guest speakers are Maria Moraites, writer of the film, and Dr. Andrew Kopan, Professor of Educational Policy at DePaul University and noted Chicago Greek historian.

December 2: GACS public relations and newsletter meeting at Elysion Restaurant.

December 9: GACS presents a lecture on eye care by Drs. John and Peter Panton during a meeting of the St. Demetrios Church Young at Heart Senior Citizen's Group.

December 13: GACS submits a grant request to the Sara Lee Foundation for $13,375 for CAN to launch an Older Adult Resource and Referral Program.

December 15: GACS Nursing Home Committee meeting at Elysion Restaurant.

December 18: GACS Board of Directors meeting at the Elysion Restaurant. Agenda items: Office space, fundraising, and dinner dance.

December 18: "Strains on Ethnic Pride" Planning Committee meeting at the Elysion Restaurant.

1987

1987: GACS Friendly Visiting Program volunteers visit 30 isolated non-English speaking elderly regularly.

1987: GACS is a founding member organization of the Illinois Coalition of Limited English Speaking People (ICLESP) which evolved into the

Members present:

Pres. Evangeline Mistaras
Dr. Elaine Thomopoulos
John Psiharis
Lena Xydes
John Roussogiannes
Athanasia Papadopoulos

Administrator, Dr. Thomopoulos reviewed the activities currently sponsored by CAN - A total of 900 elderly people have been visited thus far; a total of 5,000 hours of service has been given by volunteers; a $1,000 gift in honor of Marguerite Zuchler, one of our volunteers was given by United Way. She was also honored at the Dinner Dance.
- The Fabric Arts program continues successfully as 35 members attend-including non-Greek participants. Instruction includes crochet, knitting, needlepoint, etc. at the Levy Center.
- The Community Education Program has been successful. Presentations by qualified guests were made in the following areas: Hearing loss, hypertension, Circuit Breaker information, Foot care, Food stamps acquisition etc. Some programs were given bilingually to facilitate understanding for Greek participants.

Executive Director, John Psiharis continued with the following:
1. Interesting information relative to starting a primarily Greek Adult Day Care Center. Efforts were made to study existing successful centers eg. "The Greater Opportunity" in Skokie. Board members are encouraged to participate on this task force or to nominate interested individuals.
2. Area to study is the coalition of ethnic groups i.e. Assyrian, Korean, Chinese etc. in order to jointly serve the elderly and receive grants to be shared in providing services and activities.
3. Summer jobs were provided for 2 youths- (high school and Jr. College) who worked 25 hrs per week in an eight week program. This was funded by the city of Chicago and was very helpful in providing clerical help to our office.
4. The Chicago Council of Fine Arts has granted us a $1,200 grant to organize and promote Greek Arts and Culture,..music, dance. (Sonia Arvanites has been interested in working in this area). The program would perhaps sponsor weekly classes and feature Greek music from the 1890's to 1980's.
5. The issue of providing temporary housing for Greek students of American institutions was raised by Mr. Roussogianis. The effort should be made to provide a link between GACS and the Greek youth of our area.
6. President Evangeline Mistaras announced our participation in the Christ Lutheran Church Flea Market on Oct. 17. The St. Andrews Women's Philoptochos Society is purchasing two tables at $20.00 each. This will benefit both the Philoptochos and the GACS and CAN treasury.
7. Mr. Peter Maroutsos' financial statement for the month of July was presented. (He is a CPA and is recommended by the CPA's for the Public Interest- a non profit agency). Expenditures for the month of July were $987.99. Income for the month of July were $201.23. Fund Balance end of the month was $2742.12.
8. A social work student attending school at N.E. University will be conducting her internship at CAN from September through April.

9. It appears that the 1st Heritage Award was successful and (although planned over a brief period of time) left us a profit of $2,200. The future events will be even more successful if each person attempts to update and increase our mailing list.
10. 1988 Heritage Award Dinner plans are in the planning stage. Peter Lallas has expressed interest in being the Chairman once again with his wife as Co-Chairman. They were appointed to do so. The theme for 1988 could be honoring several people who have contributed to our Greek Heritage in several fields, i.e. art, music, athletics.
11. The possibility of offering an annual scholarship to a university student pursuing Greek studies was again mentioned. John, Evangeline and Elaine will pursue this.
12. The use of the new Terra Museum on Michigan Ave. has been again suggested for a reception/tea/dinner etc. for a guest honoree. Lena Xydes again mentioned Leon Marinakos as a person to be recognized by our organization.
13. The present Board of Directors has to be reorganized and vacancies filled. There are four vacancies at present, Names suggested were:
   ✓ a. Andy Kopan
   ✓ b. Ethel Kotsovos
   ✓ c. Leon Marinakos
   ✓ d. Faye Pantexelos
   e. Dr. George Christakes
   f. Dr. Peter Chloros
   ✓ g. Peter Maroutsos
14. John Psiharis emphasized the need to organize our activities along two areas- Program Area and Resource Area for more effective participation.
15. Mr. Psiharis also suggested our participation in the Chicago Access Corporation's Cable program. The program provides a free 6 week training program for eight participants of our own featuring areas of our interest and produced by these eight participants whom we must identify..There are presently twenty-four stations in their network.
16. It was agreed that our programs i.e. lecture/movie presentations, dancers etc. be videotaped in the future so that they would become part of history and to be shown in the GACS cable television program, in the proposed Greek Museum/Library.
17. Our Christmas appeal in 1986 was successful and should be repeated this year.
18. The joint Greek-Assyrian Conference on "Strains on Ethnic Pride" will be held at Loyola University (Lake Shore Campus). Volunteers are needed to work on the logistics of the event.

Next meeting was set for Tues. Sept. 15.
Volunteers will meet at 6:30.
Board members will meet at 7:30.

Meeting adjourned at 9:30 - Motion by J. Roussogianis. 2nd L. Xydes.

Respectfully Submitted,

Lena Xydes
Acting Secretary

GACS Board of Directors meeting minutes. Circa 1987. Elaine Thomopoulos collection.

Coalition of Limited English Speaking Elderly. Eleven ethnic communities initially participate.

1987: GACS launches Cultural & Arts Program Advisory Board with funding from a Chicago Office of Fine Arts Community Arts Assistance Program grant. Theoni "Sonia" Arvanitis and Toni Panos are co-chairs. Additional members include Alice Buzanis, Tessie Cantos, Steve Frangos, Polyzoes Gavaris, Elaine Kollintzas, Antigone Lambros, Very Rev. Nikitas Lulias, Renata Marisia, Alex Makedon, Peter Maroutsos, Evangeline Mistaras, Georgia Mitchell, John Psiharis, John Rassogianis, and Elaine Thomopoulos.

January 20: Elaine Thomopoulos, John Psiharis, and Ethel Kotsovos attend a meeting at the Retirement Research Foundation offices to discuss a grant request for CAN with Foundation President Marilyn Hennessey and Sharon Markham, RRF program officer.

January 21: CAN officially merges with GACS and becomes an agency of GACS. The CAN Advisory Board is chaired by Erica Karp. Members include Bernice Corbett, Marguerite Euchler, Ethel Kotsovos, Stephanie Kryzminski, Frank Manago, Judith Matthews, Betty McClelland, John Psiharis, Amydelle Shah, Elaine Thomopoulos, Mary Trankina, and Rose Vuco.

February 10: GACS presents a lecture on "Energy Assistance and Other Programs Available Through the Chicago Department of Human Services," by Angelo Kontaxis during a meeting of the St. Demetrios Church Young at Heart Senior Citizen's Group.

February 21: GACS holds Second Annual Winter-a-Thon to benefit CAN. The event is held at Fullersburg Woods in Oak Brook, Illinois. Participants meet at the home of Nick and Elaine Thomopoulos and then proceed to the forest preserve.

February 24: GACS offers help to senior citizens in completing Circuit Breaker applications at St. Demetrios Church during the Young at Heart Senior Citizen's meeting in the Panousis Room. Theo Theodoratos and Mary Chronis from the Chicago Department of Aging and Disability help in completing applications. Circuit Breaker is a state-run tax and rent rebate program for low-income senior citizens or disabled residents.

March 2: "Strains on Ethnic Pride" Planning Committee meeting. Elysion Restaurant.

March 15: GACS participates in a panel discussion sponsored by KRIKOS-Midwest entitled "Issues and Prospects for the Survival of the Greek-American Community into the 21st Century," at Ambassador

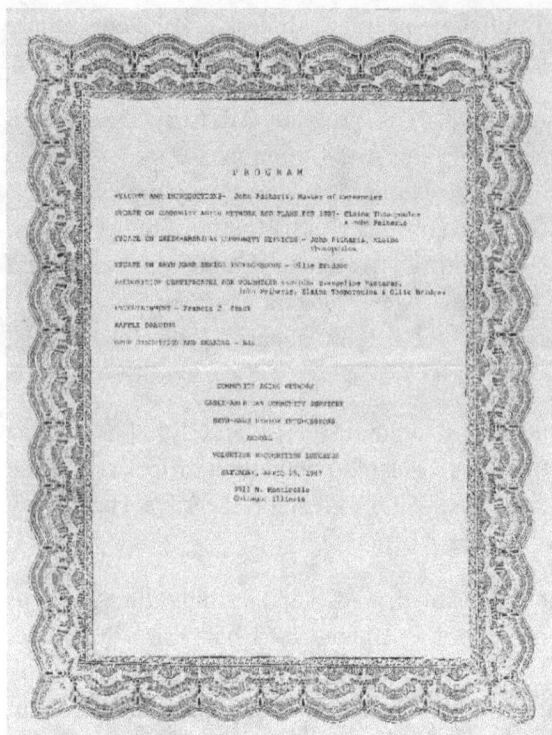
CAN volunteer luncheon program. April 25, 1987. Elaine Thomopoulos collection.

Banquet Halls in Elmhurst. Moderated by Maria Moraitis, professor of film and television at Northeastern Illinois University, the panelists include Dr. Michael Bakalis (Loyola University); Dr. Yorgos Kourvetaris, (Northern Illinois University); Dr. Fotios Litsas (University of Illinois-Chicago); Sotiris Rekoumis (Chicago Public Schools); Nicos Petros (composer and businessman) and Dr. Elaine Thomopoulos (Greek-American Community Services).

April: GACS presents a lecture entitled "I Can Hear but I Can't Understand: Solutions to Hearing Loss," by Mary Ann Conrick, M.A., audiologist and education and outreach coordinator of the Chicago Hearing Society, during a meeting of the St. Demetrios Church Young at Heart Senior Citizen's Group.

April 25: GACS hosts a volunteer appreciation luncheon at the CAN office, 3911 N. Monticello St. GACS, CAN, and Bryn Mawr Senior Intercessors volunteers are honored. The program includes updates by Elaine and John, entertainment, and a door prize raffle.

May: GACS presents a lecture on hypertension by Dr. Theodosis Kioutas, with blood pressure screenings offered by Vital Measurements Home Health Care, during a meeting of the St. Demetrios Church Young at Heart Senior Citizen's Group.

May: Volunteer Marguerite Euchler receives the 1987 Heart of Gold Award from the United Way of Chicago during a May breakfast at the Chicago Marriott – Downtown - Magnificent Mile. Marguerite was an active volunteer for the Community Aging Network, a program of GACS.

May 1: First Annual GACS Heritage Awards Dinner is held at Diplomat Banquets, 5600 W. Fullerton Ave., Chicago. Honorees are: Alexander Karanikas, Andrew Kopan, Yorgos Kourvetaris, Theano Papazoglou-Margaris, Charles Moskos, and Harry Mark Petrakis. Perry Fotos and his Orchestra provide entertainment.

June–August: GACS provides on-the-job training to youth through funding from the Mayor's Office of Employment and Training Summer Youth Program.

June: GACS presents a lecture entitled "Stress and Aging: What You Should Know," by Dr. Demetrios Trakas during a meeting of the St. Demetrios Church Young at Heart Senior Citizen's Group.

July: Service statistics reveal that CAN provided services to 106 clients in July. Twenty-one volunteers gave 360 hours and provided 144 hours of direct service and 216 hours of non-direct services.

July 6: GACS convenes the first meeting of the Adult Day Care Task Force. The group hears a presentation by Pauline Yoshioka and Rose Jordan from Greater Opportunities Adult Day Care Center in Skokie. The group will meet regularly to plan for the establishment of an adult day care center. Task force members include Thalia Jameson, Erica Karp, Dr. Theodosis Kioutas, Ethel Kotsovos, John Psiharis, John Rassogianis, and Elaine Thomopoulos.

July 29: GACS convenes a meeting to discuss forming a "Coalition of Ethnic Elderly Service Providers" at the Elysion Restaurant. The meeting reminder, signed by Elaine Thomopoulos and John Psiharis details the agenda: "Discussion on the background and purpose of an ethnic elderly coalition, discussion on how such a coalition could help each of our communities, brainstorming on the roles of a coalition, and deciding where to go from here."

August 10: GACS board meeting at the Elysion Restaurant.

August 19-November 25: Second-year classes of the GACS Fabric Arts Project are held at the Levy Center, 2019 W Lawrence Ave. Instructors are Tessie Cantos, Penny Kalogianis, and Tasia Economou. The first class has 38 seniors participating. In November, the finished works are displayed in both the Levy Center lobby as well as at the Ethnic Folk Fair in Berwyn.

September 15: GACS volunteers meeting at 6:00 PM, followed by a board meeting at 7:30 PM at the Elysion restaurant.

CAN Flea Market flyer. October 17, 1987. Elaine Thomopoulos collection.

October 4: GACS presents a performance of the Korean Players' Group Farmer's Dancing Band of the Korean American Senior Center, during a meeting of the St. Demetrios Young at Heart Senior Citizen's Group meeting in the church auditorium. Funded through a City Arts Grant from the Chicago Office of Fine Arts.

October 14: GACS presents a lecture on the "Circuit Breaker, Rent Rebate and Pharmaceutical Assistance Program," by Angelike Mountanis, director of Hellenic Family and Community Services of the Hellenic Foundation, during a meeting of the St. Demetrios Church Young at Heart Group Senior Citizen's Group.

October 17: GACS Flea Market to benefit the Community Aging Network is held at Christ Lutheran Church, 3101 N. Parkside, Chicago. Bernice Corbett is chairman of the event. Bessie Choporis donates cakes and Nick Poulos donates plants. Vital Measurements provides blood pressure/pulse testing. Delicious foods, refreshments, and sweets are served. Over 40 dealers occupy the church gymnasium.

October 31–November 1: GACS and the Assyrian Universal Alliance Foundation present "Strains on Ethnic Pride: Conflicts Between New and Old Immigrants in the Greek and Assyrian Communities." This groundbreaking and well-attended two-day conference features over 30 speakers that address this theme through a variety of fields including religion, family life, education, literature, politics, history, media, and fraternal organizations. A dinner is held on the evening of the 31st which is well attended. The conference is at Loyola University of Chicago's Lake Shore Campus. The conference is designated a "Greek Heritage '87" event and a program/ad book is published. The event is funded through a grant from the Illinois Humanities Council.

November 15: GACS Music and Dance Program featuring Jim Stoynoff, Panos and Stratos, Nick Pappas, and the Hellas Dance Group. It is held at DePaul University's Schmitt Center and co-sponsored by the Hellenic Society of DePaul University and funded through a grant from the Chicago Office of Fine Arts City Arts program. Coordinated by Sonia Arvanitis, Evangeline Mistaras, John Psiharis, and Elaine Thomopoulos. Consultants are Steve Frangos and Georgia Mitchell. Part two, on *Rembetika* and New Wave, is to be held on December 6.

November 19: GACS participates in "A Celebration of Greek Culture" at the Limelight, 632 N. Dearborn Ave., Chicago, IL. The event features a fashion show by Zaharoff including furs by Nick Kountzos and make-up by Tom Fanos; an art exhibition by Rodi Karkazis Gallery featuring Ariadne, J, Parmakelis, S. Sorogas, Opy Zouni, and original artwork by Dimitris Betinis, Nancy Canellis, James S. Rousonelos, and the late Ioannis (John) Terzis. Traditional Greek folk music by The Cretan Dancers. The cuisine is made available by Corfu Tasty Gyros, Dianna's, Greek Islands, and Roditys. Gifts and novelty items are available from Columbus Foods and Nikos Imports and Gifts. The event is sponsored by the Greek National Tourist Organization. GACS receives the $5 cover charge and benefits from a door prize raffle.

December 6: GACS program showcasing "*Rembetika* and New Wave Music." featuring Neni Panourgia, (a Ph.D. candidate in cultural anthropology at the University of Indiana), the Deni's Den Orchestra featuring Vasilios Gaitanos, and the Hellas Dance Troupe, directed by George Samaras." The event is held on a Sunday afternoon at DePaul University and is funded in part through a grant from the Chicago Office of Fine Arts City Arts grant. The Hellenic Society of DePaul University is a co-sponsor. Toni Panos and Peter Maroutsos share the master of ceremonies role and Evangeline Mistaras, as GACS president, welcomes the guests.

1988

January 26: GACS Cultural Arts Program Advisory Board meeting at Dianna's. Agenda items: "Review of activities during the past year; discussion and planning for 'Greeks in the Workplace,' an 18-part lecture series; possible meeting with other cultural organizations; selection of a regular meeting time; selection of CAP chairperson, secretary, and other officers; report on the 1988 GACS Heritage Awards Dinner and other business."

March 20: GACS Cultural & Arts Program presents a lecture by Andrew Kopan, Ph.D., professor of education, at DePaul University entitled "The Historical Development of the Greek Immigrant Work Experience in

Illinois. With comments by Stanley Rosen, professor of labor relations, University of Illinois, on the Experience of Other Immigrant Groups," Copernicus Foundation, 5216 W. Lawrence Ave., Chicago, IL.

March 21: CAN presents a free workshop on Alzheimer's Disease entitled "Alzheimer's The Shade of Life Growing Dim" from 2:00 p.m. - 4:00 p.m., at Northeastern Illinois University, 5500 N. St. Louis Ave Chicago, IL in the Ronald Williams Library, Third Floor Classroom. Marge McFadzean, president of the Chicago Chapter of Alzheimer's Disease and Related Disorders Association is the guest speaker. The lecture is coordinated by Shirley Bernstein, CAN intern.

March 27: House Party to Benefit the Community Aging Network at the home of Nick and Elaine Thomopoulos, 53 Regent Drive, Oak Brook, IL. Admission is $6 for adults, $4 for senior citizens, teenagers, and CAN/GACS volunteers, and $2 for children ages 7 to 12, with younger children, admitted free of charge. The party is a "pot-luck" with hors d'oeuvres, main dishes, salads, and desserts requested.

April 16: CAN co-sponsors "To Your Good Health Fair," at the Irving Park Lutheran Church, 3938 W. Belle Plaine Ave., Chicago, IL "The comprehensive Health Fair is designed for both senior citizens and caregivers (free participation). Health screenings include podiatry, audiology, blood pressure, glaucoma, and blood screening. Workshops for caregivers. Co-sponsors: United Charities – Parkside Family Center, Community Aging Network, Lutheran General Hospital – Lincoln Park, Department on Aging and Disability (Northwest Regional Center), Health and Home Management, Inc., North River Mental Health Center, and Lutheran Social Ministry Council."

"From Peddlers to Bankers, the Greeks in American Fiction," flyer. April 17, 1988. Elaine Thomopoulos collection.

April 17: GACS presents a lecture entitled "From Peddlers to Bankers: Greeks in American

Fiction," by Alexander Karanikas, Ph.D. The lecture is held at Lincoln Land Community College, Menard Hall, Room 201, Springfield, IL. Hosted by Lincoln Land Community College. The lecture is part of a series of lectures made possible through a grant from the Illinois Humanities Council.

April 22: Volunteer Astrid Lewis receives the Heart of Gold Award for her volunteer efforts with the Community Aging Network. The award is presented during the 42nd Annual Volunteer Recognition Event at the Hyatt Regency Hotel, 151 E. Wacker Drive, Chicago, IL. Sponsored by The Volunteer Center, United Way/Crusade of Mercy, and the Maurice L. and Hulda B. Rothschild Foundation. Astrid is a homebound volunteer who spent 20 hours per week telephone visiting with other shut-ins.

April 22: GACS Second Annual Heritage Awards Dinner honoring Fotios Litsas, Leon Marinakos, John (Yiannis) and Antigone Lambros, Dr. John Nicholson, Senator Adeline Geo-Karis, and Sam Stavrakas. The event is held at the Fountain Blue in Des Plaines. Peter Lallas is the event chairman.

May: John Psiharis is elected vice president of the newly incorporated Coalition of Limited English Speaking Elderly.

May 1: GACS presents a lecture entitled "From Peddlers to Bankers: Greeks in American Fiction," by Alexander Karanikas, Ph.D. The lecture is held at DePaul University Stuart Center, Room 206. Co-sponsored by the Hellenic Society of DePaul University. The lecture is part of a series of lectures made possible through a grant from the Illinois Humanities Council and is designated a Cultural Event of Greek Heritage '88.

May 10: GACS Board of Directors meeting at the Elysion Restaurant. Agenda: Approval of minutes, financial report, dinner dance report, executive director/administrator report, old business, new business: New board member nomination, and Ill. Board of Elections certification.

May 14: Elaine Thomopoulos presents a lecture entitled "Who Will Take Care of *Yiayia*?" during a conference called "*Yiorti*-A Celebration of Greek Womanhood," sponsored by the Greek Heritage Association of Southern California and held at the University of Southern California at Los Angeles.

May 22: GACS presents a lecture by Yorgos Kourvetaris, Ph.D., entitled "The Greek Professional and Entrepreneur," at DePaul University Stuart Center, Room 206. Co-sponsored by the Hellenic Society of DePaul University. The lecture is part of a series of lectures made possible through

"The Greek-American Professional and Entrepreneur" flyer. May 22, 1988. Elaine Thomopoulos collection.

a grant from the Illinois Humanities Council. It is designated a Cultural Event of Greek Heritage' 88.

June-August: GACS is a host site for 15 summer youth workers ages 14 to 21 funded through the Mayor's Office of Employment and Training. Twelve workers are based at St. Demetrios to tutor senior citizens in English while two serve as office assistants and one is a supervisor.

June 25: GACS holds a Hike/Bike-a-thon originating at Foster Avenue Beach and heading south to Ohio Street Beach and returning to Foster. The proceeds raised were in support of the Community Aging Network.

June 26: GACS hosts a lecture entitled "The Greek Work Ethic," by George Christakes, Ph.D., with a response by Stanley Rosen, professor of labor relations, University of Illinois at the Copernicus Foundation, 5216 W. Lawrence Ave. The lecture is part of a series of lectures made possible through a grant from the Illinois Humanities Council. The event is designated a Cultural Event of Greek Heritage '88.

July 1: GACS launches a sustaining membership drive. Annual memberships are $25 for individuals and $50 for businesses and organizations.

July 17: GACS presents a lecture by Elaine Thomopoulos, Ph.D. entitled "The Greek American Woman in the Work Force." The event is held at the Copernicus Foundation, 5216 W. Lawrence Ave, and is designated as a Cultural Event of Greek Heritage '88. The lecture is part of a series of lectures made possible through a grant from the Illinois Humanities Council.

September 22: GACS presents "John Dalapas Reading his Poetry in Greek," during the St. Demetrios Senior Citizen's meeting in the Panousis

"The Greek Work Ethic" flyer. June 26, 1988. Elaine Thomopoulos collection.

Room. The reading is funded in part through a grant from the Chicago Office of Fine Arts City Arts Program.

October 9: GACS presents a lecture and discussion by Fotios Litsas, Ph.D., professor of Greek studies, University of Illinois, Chicago entitled "Immigrant Academia: Greek Intellectuals in Illinois," hosted by Three Hierarchs Greek Orthodox Church, Champaign, IL.

October 18: GACS presents a lecture by Yorgos Kourvetaris, Ph.D., entitled "The Greek American Professional and Entrepreneur," in Star Science Building #201, Rockford College, 5050 E. State St., Rockford, Illinois. The lecture is part of a series of lectures made possible through a grant from the Illinois Humanities Council. The event was designated a Cultural Event of Greek Heritage '88.

October 23: GACS presents a lecture by George Christakes Ph.D., entitled "The Greek Work Ethic," at Governor's State University in University Park, IL. The lecture was coordinated by Dominick Candeloro and John Kulidas. Elaine Thomopoulos appeared on the University's radio station for an interview related to the topic.

October 30: GACS presents a lecture by Harry Mark Petrakis entitled "A Greek-American Story Teller at Work," at St. Athanasios Greek Orthodox Church, 1855 E. 5th Avenue, Aurora IL. The lecture is part of a series of lectures made possible through a grant from the Illinois Humanities Council. The event is designated a Cultural Event of Greek Heritage '88.

November 19: CAN/GACS Flea Market at Parkview Lutheran Church, 3919 N. Monticello St.

November 20: GACS presents a lecture by Dr. Fotios Litsas entitled, "Immigrant Academia: Greek Intellectuals in Illinois," at the Copernicus Foundation. The lecture is part of a series of lectures made possible through a grant from the Illinois Humanities Council and co-sponsored by the Copernicus Foundation. The event is designated a Cultural Event of Greek Heritage '88.

December 2: GACS participates in "A Celebration of Greek Culture," at the Limelight nightclub 632 N. Dearborn Street, Chicago, IL. The event includes live music, food, dancing, and a fashion show by Zaharoff. A portion of the money collected benefits GACS. The event was filmed by Panos Productions to be shown on an upcoming segment of the *Grecian Spotlight* television program.

December 6: GACS presents Demetra Manzara who lectures and performs *Karagiozi* during a meeting of the St. Demetrios Church Young at Heart Senior Citizen's Group. Funded through a City Arts Grant from the Chicago Office of Fine Arts.

Date unknown: GACS presents "The Greek Worker as Portrayed in Literature, an Afternoon of Readings and Observations," by award-winning author Harry Mark Petrakis at the Copernicus Foundation. The lecture is part of a series of lectures made possible through a grant from the Illinois Humanities Council and co-sponsored by the Copernicus Foundation. The event is designated a Cultural Event of Greek Heritage '88.

1989

February 11-12: John Psiharis is invited to join Mayor Eugene Sawyer and other community leaders to participate in the Chicago Unity Weekend Caravan. Over two days, the caravan visits 15 ethnic communities throughout the city.

February 14: John Psiharis attends the "Unity Thru Love" reception hosted by Mayor Sawyer at the Holiday Inn Mart Plaza, 14th-floor ballroom, 350 N. Orleans.

March 7: GACS presents an eye screening program for senior citizens by Drs. John and Peter Panton during a meeting of the St. Demetrios Church Young at Heart Senior Citizen's Group.

March 25: GACS is a co-sponsor of a theatrical performance entitled *Homage to Ioannis Capodistrias: The Creator of the Modern Greek State*, at St. John Greek Orthodox Church, Des Plaines, IL. The performance is designated a Cultural Event of Greek Heritage 89.

April 16: GACS presents a lecture on "The Greek American Professional and Entrepreneur," by Yorgos Kourvetaris, Ph.D., Professor of Sociology at Northern Illinois University at St. Sophia Church, 525 Church St., Elgin, IL. Refreshments are served by St. Sophia's Philoptochos Society. The lecture is part of a series of lectures made possible through a grant from the Illinois Humanities Council.

April 18: GACS presents a showing of the award-winning film "Goodnight Socrates," during the St. Demetrios Young at Heart Senior Citizen's Group meeting in the Panousis Room of St. Demetrios Church. Maria Moraities, the film's writer speaks after the screening.

May 3: GACS presents a lecture by Steve Frangos entitled "Peripheral Patriots: The Network of Greeks in Antioch and Libertyville, Illinois," at the David Adler Cultural Center, 1700 N. Milwaukee Ave., Libertyville. The lecture is part of a series of lectures made possible through a grant from the Illinois Humanities Council and is designated a Cultural Event of Greek Heritage '89.

June 14: GACS Board of Directors special meeting to discuss ADC at GACS/CAN office. In attendance: Dr. Theodosis Kioutas, Evangeline Mistaras, Athanasia Papadopoulos, John Psiharis, John Rassogianis, Elaine Thomopoulos, Ethel Kotsovos (guest), and Jane Stansell (guest speaker).

June 16: GACS presents a lecture by Steve Frangos entitled "Peripheral Patriots: The Network of Greeks in Antioch and Libertyville, Illinois during the 1920s," at the Lake County Museum in the Lakewood Forest Preserve, Route 176 and Fairfield Road, Wauconda IL.

June 20: GACS presents a lecture on "Communicable Diseases," by Dr. Theodosis Kioutas during a meeting of the St. Demetrios Church Young at Heart Senior Citizen's Group. Dr. Kioutas also updates the audience about the status of the nursing home project.

June 20: GACS presents a lecture by Dr. Fotios Litsas entitled "Immigrant Academia: Greek Intellectuals in Illinois," at SS. Constantine and Helen Greek Orthodox Church, Palos Hills, IL. The lecture is part of a series of lectures made possible through a grant from the Illinois Humanities Council. The event is designated a Cultural Event of Greek Heritage '88.

June 21: GACS Board of Directors special meeting to discuss ADC at GACS/CAN office.

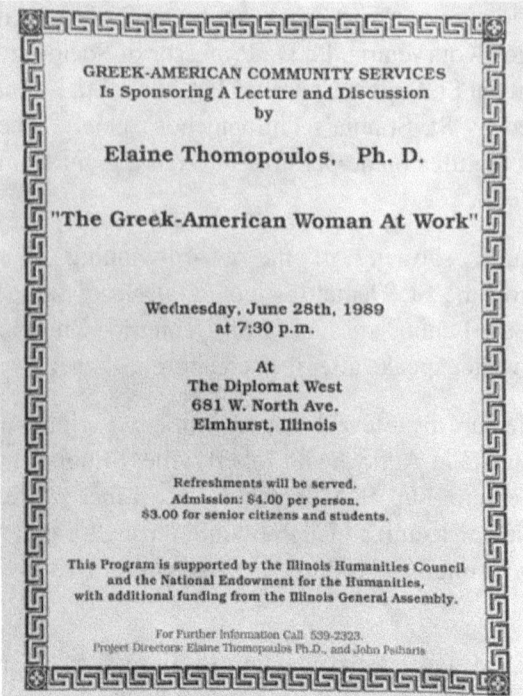

"The Greek-American Woman at Work" flyer. June 28, 1989. Elaine Thomopoulos collection.

June 28: GACS presents a lecture by Elaine Thomopoulos, Ph.D., entitled "The Greek American Woman at Work," with a response by San L. O. Introduction by Toni Panos. The event is held at the Diplomat West, 681 W. North Avenue, Elmhurst IL. Artwork for the program by Maria Maniatis. The lecture is part of a series of lectures made possible through a grant from the Illinois Humanities Council.

July: GACS announces that it is awarded a contract to provide adult day care services through the Illinois Department on Aging Community Care Program for the northwest side of Chicago.

July: GACS Board of Directors elections are held. Evangeline Mistaras, president; John Rassogianis, vice president; Athanasia "Sandy" Papadopoulos, secretary, and Peter Maroutsos, treasurer. Dr. Michael Bakalis is voted on the board.

July 13: John Psiharis, John Rassogianis, and Ethel Kotsovos attend the United Way of Chicago Venture Grant and New Member Agencies Reception held at the United Way office, 104 S. Michigan Ave.

August: The Eclecteon Fine Arts Society hosts a benefit evening at Ravinia, featuring award-winning violinist Leonidas Kavakos with the Chicago Symphony Orchestra to benefit the GACS adult day care center.

August 2: GACS Fabric Arts Project begins the third year of classes at the Levy Center.

August 17: ADC planning committee meeting at Copernicus Center. During this meeting a protest by a large group of seniors against U.S. Representative Dan Rostenkowski, chairman of the House Ways and Means Committee, after he supported increasing Medicare premiums for seniors occurred. He was chased down Milwaukee Avenue by senior citizen protestors.

August 26: Elaine and Nick Thomopoulos host an "August Harvest Wonderland Benefit," at their Bridgman Michigan home to raise funds for the adult day care center. Donations are $20 per person. John Rassogianis coordinates the weekend and serves as an unofficial tour guide. Guests are encouraged to spend the weekend in the New Buffalo area and several optional (both organized and informal) activities surrounding the event take place. Activities include tomato, apple, pear, and blueberry picking; lunch at Tabor Hills Winery; shopping excursions, and beach activities. Sunday morning options include church services at the Annunciation Greek Orthodox Church in Benton Harbor followed by lunch at either Mac's Big Boy or Fatouros Greek Harbor.

August Harvest Wonderland benefit invitation. August 26, 1989. John Psiharis collection.

September: GACS receives Venture Grant funding from United Way of Chicago in support of the Community Aging Network. Ethel Kotsovos assumes the role of CAN program director.

September 22: Third Annual GACS Heritage Awards Dinner at Diplomat Banquets. Honorees are John C. Geocaris, James M. Mezilson, and Georgia Mitchell. Bishop Iakovos offers invocation and benediction. Spyros Aliagas, consul general of Greece, extends greetings to the honorees and GACS on behalf of the government of Greece. Elaine Kollintzas is the mistress of ceremonies.

October 1: GACS presents poetry readings by Beatriz Badikian, Marianthe Karanikas, and John Dalapas. Held in the South Room of the Commons Building at DePaul University, the event is co-sponsored by the Hellenic Society of DePaul University and made possible in part by a grant from the Department of Cultural Affairs, Chicago Office of Fine Arts, City Arts Program.

October 10: GACS Adult Day Care Organizing Committee.

October 23: Drs. George Christakes, Elaine Thomopoulos, and Dominic Candeloro compare and contrast the "Greek Work Ethic in Comparison with the Italian Experience," on WGBO-Radio (broadcast in the South Suburbs).

October 26: GACS Adult Day Care Organizing Committee lunch meeting at Copernicus Center. Lunch is ordered out.

November 12: Nick Lambros discusses his new book, "The Americanization of Odysseus," at GACS in Alvernia Place. The event is part of a series of programs on Greek music and poetry funded by the Chicago Office of Fine Arts grant.

November 14: GACS presents a lecture on benefits available to the elderly by Dr. Theodosis Kioutas, Ethel Kotsovos, John Psiharis, and Elaine Thomopoulos during a meeting of the St. Demetrios Church Young at Heart Senior Citizen's Group.

November 16: GACS Adult Day Care Center Organizing Committee meeting at GACS in Alvernia Place.

November 26: GACS presents an afternoon of music at Deni's Den, 2941 N. Clark St. The event features Tom Zervas, Vasilios Gaitanos, and other musicians and singers who set into music the poetry of Yorgos Kourvetaris. The program is made possible through a grant from the Chicago Office of Fine Arts, Department of Cultural Affairs. Co-sponsored with KRIKOS.

November 29: GACS Adult Day Care Center Organizing Committee meeting at Copernicus Center, 3160 N. Milwaukee Ave. The meeting is from 11:00 am to 1:00 pm and lunch is ordered.

December 5: GACS and the Senior Citizen's Club of St. Demetrios Church present John Dalapas who will read and discuss his poetry in Greek. St. Demetrios Church, 2727 W. Winona, Chicago, IL. The program is part of a series of programs made possible through a grant from the Department of Cultural Affairs Chicago Office of Fine Arts.

December 8: GACS CAP presents Beatriz Badikian and Marianthe Karanikas who will read their poetry on the immigrant experience at the Hilltop Restaurant, 2800 W. Foster Ave., Chicago, IL. The program is part of a series of programs made possible through a grant from the Chicago Office of Fine Arts, Department of Cultural Affairs.

December 10: GACS presents a discussion of Greek American Poetry by Theano Papazoglou Margaris. The Greek language event is held after church services at Holy Trinity Greek Orthodox Church, 6041 W. Diversey Ave. The Holy Trinity Philoptochos Society provides refreshments. The program is made possible through a grant from the Chicago Office of Fine Arts, Department of Cultural Affairs.

December 14: GACS presents a "Benefit for the New Adult Day Care Center Cocktail Reception" at the Neon Greek Village, 310 S. Halsted St. Donation $50. (5:30 p.m.-9:00 p.m.) "An evening filled with Greek music, Greek dancing, hors d'oeuvres, and lots of fun." Vasilis Gaitanos is the featured performer.

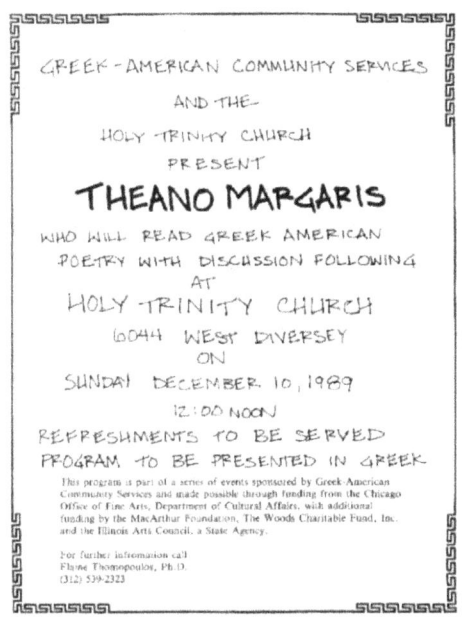

Theano Margaris poetry reading flyer. December 10. 1989. Elaine Thomopoulos collection.

1990

January 2-5: ADC staff attend a one-week (20 hours) pre-service training required before they can work in an adult day care center. In addition to frontline employees, all GACS staff and two board members (Evangeline Mistaras and John Rassogianis) participate. The training is held at the Alzheimer's Family Care Center on Milwaukee Avenue near Bryn Mawr and is led by Jane Stansell and her staff.

January 8: GACS opens Northwest Chicago Senior Care Center at Alvernia Place, 3901 N. Ridgeway Ave. Chicago, IL 60618.

January 14: GACS holds an open house to celebrate the opening of the NCSC at Alvernia Place. About 100 people attend.

February 26: GACS presents a lecture entitled "Ethnic Diplomats: New Leadership in America in the 21st Century," by David Roth, Midwest director, Institute for American Pluralism, American Jewish Committee with a response by Connie Seals, president C-Brem Communications Corp. It is held in the downtown offices of the Illinois Ethnic Consultation, which was part of the American Jewish Committee. This event is part of the "Ethnic Identity and American Values: Leadership Development in Illinois" grant funded through the Illinois Humanities Council. Pre-order lunch for $8, payable at the door.

March: Manolis Alpogianis assumes the role of GACS special events coordinator as a volunteer.

March 16: GACS presents a lecture by Dominic Candeloro, Ph.D. entitled "The Scalabrini Order: Leadership in the Italian American Community," and a response by George Christakes, Ph.D., entitled "The Failure of the Greek-American Community to Build a Hospital." The event is held at the Italian Cultural Center, 1621 N. 39th Ave, Stone Park, IL. A pre-event Italian dinner was offered at $10 per person. Co-sponsored by the Italian Cultural Center and the Institute for American Pluralism. This event is part of the "Ethnic Identity and American Values: Leadership Development in Illinois" grant funded through the Illinois Humanities Council.

March 20–March 21: an article by reporter Dean Geroulis entitled "Greek American Agency Redefines its Community" appears in the *Pulitzer-Lerner Newspapers*.

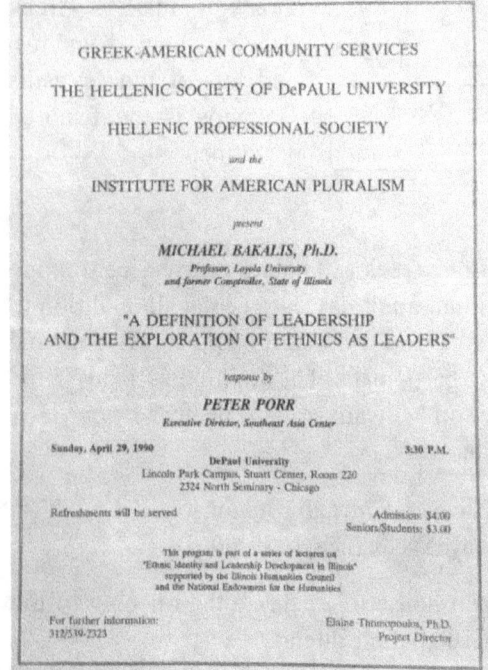

"A Definition of Leadership" flyer. April 29, 1990. Elaine Thomopoulos collection.

March 24: Elaine Thomopoulos, representing the Illinois Humanities Council, speaks during a Northeastern Illinois Historical Council workshop on funding an exhibit at Northeastern Illinois University. Some 230 participants, representing more than 105 organizations from six states were in attendance.

March 25: GACS hosts "John Dalapas Presents His Poetry in Greek," in the Banquet Room of Mother's Day Restaurant, 6326 W. Cermak Road, Berwyn, IL Co-sponsored by the American Hellenic Society of Berwyn. Funded by the Chicago Office of Fine Arts, Chicago Department of Cultural Affairs, and the Illinois Arts Council.

April 29: GACS presents a lecture entitled "A Definition of Leadership and the Exploration of Ethnics as Leaders," presented by Michael Bakalis, Ph.D., with a response by Peter Porr, executive director of Southeast Asia Center. The event is held at DePaul University, Stuart Center, Room 220.

News & Issues

By Mark V. Tiniakos

L-R: Evangeline Mistaras, president of G.A.C.S.; John Rassogianis, director of G.A.C.S.; Dr. Theodosis Kioutas, member of G.A.C.S.; Very Rev. Nikita Lulias, John Psiharis, executive director of G.A.C.S. and Michael Swarzman from the Illinois Masonic Medical Center with his young daughter.

SUNDAY, JULY 1 — Agiasmos services were held at the newly opened Northwest Chicago Senior Care Day Center, an agency of the Greek American Community Services. The Very Rev. Nikitas Lulias performed the agiasmos services attended by many officials of the G.A.C.S. and individuals interested in the services offered by the day center. Following the agiasmos services a reception was held for the guests. The Center, the first of its kind on Chicago's northwest side, offers daytime care to frail, isolated or forgetful elderly in a safe and caring and professional enviornment. In the evening the elderly return to their homes in time for dinner. Each day the Center offers morning and afternoon snacks, a hot lunch and a wide array of activities. A registered nurse is present to administer to their health needs and medication. A social worker is available for any concerns the family may have. The center is supported through a contract from the Illinois Department on Aging, Illinois Masonic Medical Center, client fees and individual contributions from members of the Greek American community. Individual or group tours of the Center are available. For more details contact Ethel Kotsovos at 312-539-____. The Center is located in Alvernia Place, 3901 N. Ridgeway. It is convenient to both St. Demetrios and Holy Trinity communities and is five blocks from the Kennedy Expressway.

Greek Press, July 22, 1990. John Psiharis collection.

Co-sponsored by: The Hellenic Society of DePaul University, Hellenic Professional Society of Illinois, and the Institute of American Pluralism. This event is part of the "Ethnic Identity and American Values: Leadership Development in Illinois" grant funded through the Illinois Humanities Council.

May 31: *The Hellenic Chronicle* publishes a front-page article entitled "Greek-American Community Services Offers Daytime Care to Older Adults."

June: John Psiharis becomes president of the Coalition of Limited English Speaking Elderly.

June 3: GACS presents a lecture entitled "Ethnic Leadership and the Development of the American Labor Movement," by Stanley Rosen, professor of labor and industrial relations, at the University of Illinois at Chicago with a response by James Chiakulas, director of Region 36, Illinois Education Association. The event is co-sponsored by Montay College and the Institute for American Pluralism. It is held on the college campus located at 3750 W. Peterson Ave. This event is part of the "Ethnic Identity and American Values: Leadership Development in Illinois" grant funded through the Illinois Humanities Council.

June 23: GACS presents a lecture by Dino Pappas on "Greek-American Music and Recordings of the 1920s, 1930s, and 1940s" at the Macedonian House, 4544 N. Western Ave., Chicago, IL at 7:30 p.m. The program is funded through a grant from the Illinois Arts Council.

June 24: GACS presents a lecture by Dino Pappas on "Greek-American Music and Recordings of the 1920s, 1930s, and 1940s" at St. Demetrios Church of DuPage, 893 Church Rd., Elmhurst IL at noon. A reception follows the program. The program is funded through a grant from the Illinois Arts Council.

June 30: Elaine Thomopoulos resigns from the position of GACS administrator and transitions into a consulting role with the Cultural & Arts Program.

July 1: *Agiasmos* services are held at the GACS adult day care center. The Very Rev. Nikitas Lulias officiates. A reception and open house follow and include displays of ADC client art projects and pieces from the Fabric Arts Program.

July 1: John Rassogianis becomes director of the Cultural & Arts Program through funding from a City of Chicago Community Development Block Grant.

July 22: GACS board and staff members attend the Patriarchal Divine Liturgy led by His All Holiness Dimitrios, Archbishop of Constantinople and Ecumenical Patriarch, at the Petrillo Band Shell in Grant Park.

September 9: GACS presents a lecture by Michael Bakalis Ph.D., entitled "Definition of Leadership: An Introduction to Ethnic Leadership in Illinois." It is held at St. Anthony Greek Orthodox Church, 1600 S Glenwood Ave, Springfield, IL. Co-sponsored by the Order of AHEPA, Chapter 189, and St. Anthony's Church. This event is part of the "Ethnic Identity and American Values: Leadership Development in Illinois" grant funded through the Illinois Humanities Council.

September 16: GACS presents a lecture by George Anastaplo, Ph.D., entitled "Ethnicity and Patriotism" at the Copernicus Foundation, 5216 W. Lawrence Ave. This event is part of the "Ethnic Identity and American Values: Leadership Development in Illinois" grant funded through the Illinois Humanities Council.

September 26: GACS CAP Folk Dance seminar on Greek Island folk dances at Annunciation Cathedral. The Very Rev. Nikitas Lulias presents, and Dr. and Mrs. Contos and the Apollo Dance Troupe demonstrate. Funded through a grant from the Illinois Arts Council.

September 28: "Greek Leadership in the 90s" is the theme of the GACS fourth annual dinner held at Thirteen Colonies Banquets in River Grove. In keeping with the leadership theme of the cultural programs, this was selected as the theme of the dinner. Honorees are James C. Kirie, Frank Kuchuris, Very Rev. Nikitas Lulias, and Katherine Valone.

October 2. 3, 4: John Psiharis and Amydelle Shah attend the Illinois White House Conference on Aging in Springfield, Illinois. Some CLESE members also attended the conference.

October 7: GACS presents a lecture entitled "Leadership Development in the Polish American Community," by Helena Lopata with a response by Charles Moskos, Ph.D., at the Copernicus Foundation, 5216 W. Lawrence Ave. This event is part of the "Ethnic Identity and American Values: Leadership Development in Illinois" grant funded through the Illinois Humanities Council.

October 12: GACS presents a lecture entitled "Problems of Leadership Development within Chicago's Ukrainian Community," by Myron Kuropas, Ph.D., with a response by Yorgos Kourvetaris. The lecture is at Immaculate Conception Ukrainian Church in Palatine, Illinois. This event is part of the "Ethnic Identity and American Values: Leadership

Development in Illinois" grant funded through the Illinois Humanities Council.

October 14: GACS presents a lecture entitled "The Role of Ethnic Arts, Youth Programs and Leadership" by Margie McLain, executive director of Urban Traditions at Assumption Greek Orthodox Church in East Moline, Illinois. This event is part of the "Ethnic Identity and American Values: Leadership Development in Illinois" grant funded through the Illinois Humanities Council.

October 26: GACS CAP Folk Dance seminar on Greek mainland folk dances at Annunciation Cathedral. The Very Rev. Nikitas Lulias presents. Dr. and Mrs. Contos and the Apollo Dance Troupe demonstrate. Funded through a grant from the Illinois Arts Council.

November 14: The *Chicago Leader-Post* newspapers publish a front-page article entitled "Greek American Group Cares for Senior Citizens at Alvernia Place."

November 18: GACS presents a lecture entitled "Problems of Leadership Development within Chicago's Ukrainian Community," by Myron Kuropas, Ph.D., with a response by Yorgos Kourvetaris, Ph.D. The program is held at Saints Volodymyr and Olha Ukrainian Church, Chicago, IL. This event is part of the "Ethnic Identity and American Values: Leadership Development in Illinois" grant funded through the Illinois Humanities Council.

November 24: GACS CAP Folk Dance seminar on Pontian region folk dances at Annunciation Cathedral. The Very Rev. Nikitas Lulias presents. Dr. and Mrs. Contos and the Apollo Dance Troupe demonstrate. Funded through a grant from the Illinois Arts Council.

November 25: GACS presents a lecture entitled "Leadership in the Italian Community," by Dominic Candelero, and the "Failure of the Greek Community to Build a Hospital" by George Christakes, Ph.D. The program is held in the GACS Adult Day Care Center at Alvernia Place, 3901 N. Ridgeway Ave. This event is part of the "Ethnic Identity and American Values: Leadership Development in Illinois" grant funded through the Illinois Humanities Council.

November 29: GACS Board of Directors meeting at Alvernia Place. Amended bylaws are approved.

December 7: GACS presents a lecture by George Anastaplo, J.D., entitled "Ethnicity and Patriotism." The lecture is held in Lawson #101 at Southern Illinois University in Carbondale, Illinois. This event is part of the "Ethnic

Identity and American Values: Leadership Development in Illinois" grant funded through the Illinois Humanities Council.

December 9: GACS presents a lecture entitled "The Role of Ethnic Arts, Youth Programs and Leadership," by Margie McLain, executive director of Urban Traditions. The program is held at DePaul University Stuart Center- Room 200 and co-sponsored by the Hellenic Society of DePaul University. This event is part of the "Ethnic Identity and American Values: Leadership Development in Illinois" grant funded through the Illinois Humanities Council.

1991

Throughout the year, discussions occur between GACS, KRIKOS, the Greek Women's University Club, and the Hellenic Professional Society of Illinois regarding establishing a Hellenic Hotline to serve as a clearinghouse and coordinating body for events and programs within the Greek American community.

January–February: GACS co-sponsors a six-part retrospective of the films of Theo Angelopoulos. The Film Center at the Art Institute of Chicago organizes and hosts the event.

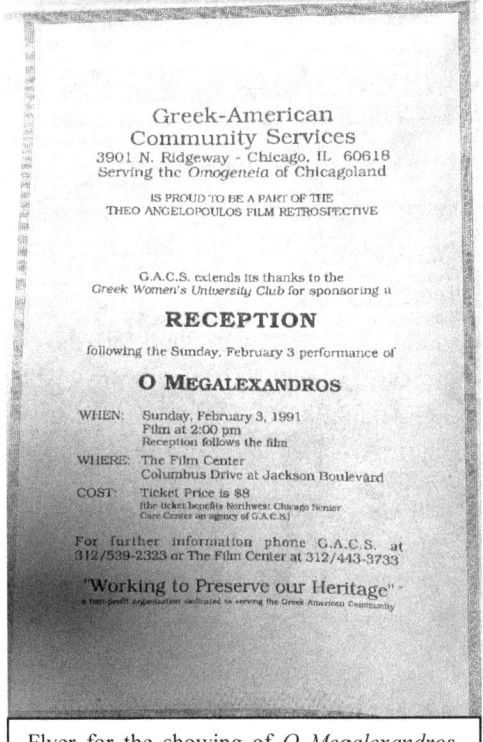

Flyer for the showing of *O Megalexandros*. February 3, 1991. Elaine Thomopoulos collection.

January 18: GACS presents a lecture entitled "Ethnic Leadership and the Development of the American Labor Movement," by Stanley Rosen, professor of labor and industrial relations, at the University of Illinois at Chicago with responses from James Chiakulas, director of Region 36, Illinois Education Association and Fred Gardaphe, Italian community. The program is held at the Italian Cultural Center and was preceded by a delicious Italian dinner and a tour of their center and museum. This event is part of the "Ethnic Identity and American Values: Leadership Development in Illinois" grant funded through the Illinois Humanities Council.

February 3: GACs co-sponsors screening of *O Megalexandros,* as part of the Theo Angelopoulos retrospective held at the Film Center of the Art Institute of Chicago. A reception after the screening is hosted by the Greek Women's University Club.

April 25: GACS CAP Folk Dance seminar on Greek Island folk dances at Holy Apostles, Westchester IL. The Very Rev. Nikitas Lulias presents. Dr. and Mrs. Contos and the Apollo Dance Troupe demonstrate. Funded through a grant from the Illinois Arts Council.

April 28: GACS presents "The Role of the Greek-American and Ethnic Woman," a cultural event that celebrates the conclusion of the GACS lecture series entitled "Ethnic Identity and Leadership Development in Illinois," funded by the Illinois Humanities Council. The event includes opening remarks by GACS Board member Aphrodite Sarelas. Speakers are introduced by Evangeline Gouletas, co-chair of American Invsco. Constance Callinicos addresses the topic with responses by Louis Ano Nuevo Kerr (Hispanic American Woman) and Bernadine Wong (Chinese American Woman). The event is held at DePaul University Schmitt Academic Center, Room 254. Co-sponsored by: Hellenic Professional Society of Illinois and Greek Women's University Club. Supporting organizations: Chinese American Service League, Ethnic Women's Coalition, Hellenic Society of DePaul University, and Mexican Professional Women. Elaine provides lodging to the out-of-town guests at her home.

May: GACS hosts "First Annual Cocktail Reception in Honor of the Adult Day Care Center," in the Pegasus Restaurant Rooftop Garden. Eighty people attend.

May 23: GACS CAP Folk Dance seminar on Greek mainland folk dances at Holy Apostles Church, Westchester IL. The Very Rev. Nikitas Lulias presents. Dr. and Mrs. Contos and the Apollo Dance Troupe demonstrate. Funded through a grant from the Illinois Arts Council.

June 20: GACS CAP Folk Dance seminar on Greek folk dances from the Pontian region at Holy Apostles Church, Westchester IL. The Very Rev. Nikitas Lulias presents. Dr. and Mrs. Contos and the Apollo Dance Troupe demonstrate. Funded through a grant from the Illinois Arts Council.

June 24: Cocktail reception benefitting "The Renovation of the Greek-American Community Services New Home for the Northwest Chicago Senior Care Center" at the Gold Star Sardine Bar, 680 N. Lake Shore Drive. Tickets are $35. More than 60 people attend. Eden Atwood is the featured performer. A special raffle is held with a round-trip ticket to Greece donated by Olympic Airways as the grand prize.

June 30: GACS CAP Folk Dance seminar on Greek Island folk dances at Lincoln Land Community College, Springfield, IL. The Very Rev. Nikitas Lulias presents. Dr. and Mrs. Contos and the Apollo Dance Troupe demonstrate. Funded through a grant from the Illinois Arts Council.

July 28: GACS CAP Folk Dance seminar on Greek mainland folk dances at Lincoln Land Community College. The Very Rev. Nikitas Lulias presents. Dr. and Mrs. Contos and the Apollo Dance Troupe demonstrate. Funded through a grant from the Illinois Arts Council.

August 10: GACS CAP Folk Dance seminar on Greek folk dances from the Pontian region at Lincoln Land Community College. Very Rev. Nikitas Lulias presents. Dr. and Mrs. Contos and the Apollo Dance Troupe demonstrate. Funded through a grant from the Illinois Arts Council.

September: Presbytera Despina Massouras begins an internship in gerontology at the GACS adult day care center and as coordinator of the GACS LIHEAP Energy Assistance Program. She is pursuing a degree in gerontology from National Louis University.

November-December: GACS participates in the Low-Income Home Energy Assistance Program (LIHEAP) by helping low-income individuals obtain financial assistance to pay heating bills. The program serves nearly 600 people during its first two months.

October 11: GACS Fifth Annual Heritage Awards Dinner at the Knickerbocker Hotel – Chicago, 163 E. Walton. The theme of the event was "Communicators in the 90s." Honorees are Kathryn Adinamis, Evangeline Gouletas, Charles Mouratides, and Mike Tsolinas. The first GACS National Heritage Award is awarded to U.S. Senator Paul Tsongas. Niki Tsongas, Paul's wife, accepts the award on his behalf. Special performance by Orpheus Dance Group. Mike Bakalis is the master of ceremonies. Music by Panos and Stratos. Tickets are $40 per person.

1992

March 2: GACS Board of Directors meeting at the center.

April: GACS announces the purchase of a 12-passenger Dodge Ram blue van to transport clients to and from the adult day care center and on field trips or related activities. The van purchase was made possible by a grant from the Chicago Community Trust.

April 6: GACS Board of Directors meeting at the center.

April 12: GACS co-sponsors an afternoon of classical music entitled "Contemporary Musical Trends as Emerged Out of Byzantine and Macedonian Sounds," in the Waldorf Room of the Chicago Hilton and Towers, 720 S. Michigan Ave., Chicago. The event is sponsored by KRIKOS and follows a lecture hosted by the Hellenic Professional Society of Illinois.

April 30: CAN receives the United Way of Chicago - Heart of Gold Award as an outstanding volunteer program during a breakfast at the Palmer House. Evangeline Mistaras, John Psiharis, and Ethel Kotsovos attend.

May 6: GACS has a booth at the Lawrence House Retirement Fair to promote CAN and NCSC.

May 31: GACS lecture on "Greeks in the Labor Movement," by Dan Georgakas at Swedish Covenant Hospital. Co-sponsored with KRIKOS and the Hellenic Professional Society of Illinois. The event is a distinguished lecture for the "*O Cosmos*: The Private Lives and Public Celebrations of the Greeks in Illinois" project. It is co-sponsored by KRIKOS and the Hellenic Professional Society of Illinois and funded by the Illinois Humanities Council. About 150 were in attendance.

June 9: GACS hosts a fundraising cocktail party celebrating the second anniversary of its adult day care center, Northwest Chicago Senior Care, at the Santorini Restaurant, 138 S. Halsted St. Tickets are $15 per person. Eighty-five guests attend.

June 21: GACS holds *Agiasmos* (Blessing of the Waters) and Open House at its new Pulaski Road location. The Very Rev. Nikitas Lulias officiates and nearly 150 guests are in attendance. Refreshments are provided by Master Catering.

June 30: After the fiscal year, GACS has $108,000 in revenues/support.

July 2: GACS Board of Directors meeting at the center.

July 3: GACS and GANHC leaders meet with members of the United Hellenic American Congress and Bishop Iakovos to discuss the two organizations at the UHAC office.

July 10: ADC Kitchen Band participants perform for visitors from Norwood Park Home at GACS.

July 17: ADC clients' field trip to Lincoln Park Zoo.

July 31: Theodoros Skylakakis, an advisor to Greek Prime Minister Constantine Mitsotakis and head of the Office of Planning and

Communication for the Prime Minister visits GACS to meet ADC clients and learn about GACS cultural programs.

August 26: GACS co-sponsors Cairo Greek Night and receives cover charges and door prize raffle proceeds.

September 9: GACS co-sponsors Greek Night at Neon Greek Village and receives cover charges and door prize raffle proceeds.

September 16–December 23: The third year of Fabric Arts classes begins. The program is moved into the GACS center and adult day care clients are invited to participate.

September 16: GACS Board of Directors meeting at the center.

October 1: GACS opens as an intake site for the Low Income Home Energy Assistance Program (LIHEAP). The elderly, disabled, and those who had disconnections can apply after October 1, and others can apply after November 1. The program runs until program funds are exhausted, usually in February or early March. GACS completes roughly 1,000 applications annually during its participation in this program.

October 1: GACS receives a $110,800 three-year grant in support of Northwest Chicago Senior Care from the Retirement Research Foundation. The grant enables GACS to employ social worker Ethel Kotsovos to concentrate on adult day care outreach efforts and helps to cover other center salaries.

October 30: GACS holds Sixth Annual Heritage Awards Banquet at the Knickerbocker Hotel-Chicago, 163 E. Walton. The theme for the evening is "Greek American Woman in the 90s." Honorees are Roula Alakiotou, Soula Koutsopanagos, Helen Theodosakis, and Athena Touloumis. The first *Efharisto* Award is presented to the Chicago Community Trust. Elaine Kollintzas serves as mistress of ceremonies. Bishop Iakovos provides the invocation and benediction. Peter Maroutsos presents a mini slide show entitled "GACS on the Move in '92."

November 5: GACS Board of Directors meeting at GACS.

November 14: Elaine Thomopoulos speaks during a workshop entitled "Cross-cultural Communication in Later Life," held on the Evanston campus of National-Louis University. The event is moderated by Erica Karp. Other speakers include Kimxuyen Le-Kissane, Rebecca Cruz, and Carol Jones.

November 25: GACS co-sponsors a "Grecian Wednesdays with GACS," event at the Cairo, 720 N. Wells St. Hours are 7:00 p.m. and 4:00 a.m. Since it is Thanksgiving Eve, the event is well attended. GACS receives a portion of the admissions and proceeds from a door prize raffle with valuable prizes, including a round-trip ticket to Greece via Olympic Airways.

December 1: ADC begins to offer services on Tuesdays, making it the fourth day per week that the center is open.

December 14: Ethel Kotsovos represents GACS at a meeting to discuss the needs of ethnic elderly at the Chicago Department on Aging.

December 15: John Psiharis attends the Chicago Community Development Advisory Committee Christmas Party at the Palmer House Hotel.

December 16: GACS staff meeting with holiday refreshments.

December 23: GACS hosts its annual Christmas party. Adult day care participants and their families are joined by staff, volunteers, and supporters who gather for the party.

By the end of 1992, ADC enrollment increased from 10 in January to 22 in December. Monthly billings increase from $1,230 in January to $5,057 in December.

1993

January 19: John Psiharis is re-appointed by Mayor Richard M Daley to a third term as a member of the Mayor's Community Development Advisory Committee (CDAC), during a breakfast in the Empire Room of the Palmer House Hotel, 17 E. Monroe Street, Chicago, IL.

January 27: "Greek Night at the Cairo" nightclub co-sponsored by GACS which receives a share of the proceeds from the event.

February 9: GACS Inaugural Board of Directors and Advisory Board dinner meeting at Pegasus Restaurant. The dinner is underwritten by Advisory Board chairman Irene Antoniou.

February 15: GACS Building Fund Committee meets at Jim Kozonis' office, 4849 N. Milwaukee Ave., Chicago.

February 24: "Greek Night at the Cairo" nightclub. GACS cosponsors and receives a share of the proceeds from the event.

March 2: GACS Building Fund Committee meeting at GACS.

March 16: GACS Board meeting at GACS.

> **NEWS FROM ...**
> ## GREEK-AMERICAN COMMUNITY SERVICES
> 3940 N. PULASKI ROAD • CHICAGO, ILLINOIS 60641
> (312) 545-0303 • FAX (312) 545-0388
>
> **1983-1993: CELEBRATING TEN YEARS OF SERVICE**
>
> Ten years ago, a variety of like-minded individuals came together with a common purpose regarding the needs of our Greek community. Thus, *Greek-American Community Services* was born. Today, it is a multi-faceted grass-roots agency serving our *omogenia* and over 5,000 individuals annually with a variety of services, described below.
>
> **ADULT DAY CARE**
> The first Greek-American sponsored senior day care center in the United States opened its doors in January of 1990. Now serving 25 elderly clients and their families, *Northwest Chicago Senior Care Center* provides a team of dedicated staff and volunteers who help to meet the physical, emotional and social needs of the clients. Transportation to and from their homes is provided by our two blue "Ya' Sou" vans. Hot lunches, snacks and an activity schedule that includes arts and crafts, exercise programs and recreational and inter-generational activities are also provided.
>
> **CULTURAL AND ARTS PROGRAM**
> Each year our *Cultural and Arts Program* reaches thousands in Chicago and throughout the state showcasing various timely programs such as: lectures, classes, films, performances and panel discussions that are vital for the survival of our cultural identity. This model program is building bridges of understanding and cooperation with the various other ethnic communities in Illinois.
>
> **COMMUNITY SERVICES PROGRAMS**
> Responding creatively and effectively to the needs of the community, GACS initiated several key programs. For example, GACS arranges an on-going lecture series for seniors. Each winter, nearly a thousand needy individuals and their families apply for financial assistance, which helps pay for their electric and heating bills. Furthermore, GACS serves as a resource to those seeking information and help in a variety of areas such as locating appropriate assistance to meet their needs.
>
> **COMMUNITY AGING NETWORK**
> While our adult day care center strives to care for the elderly in a structured environment, *Community Aging Network* serves the frail, homebound and isolated elderly in their own homes. This is accomplished by offering chore-housekeeping, homemaker services, friendly visiting, information and referral, as well as other forms of assistance.
> **For further information, please call us at (312) 545-0303.**
>
> AGENCIES OF G.A.C.S.:
> ... COMMUNITY AGING NETWORK .... CULTURAL & ARTS PROGRAM ... NORTHWEST CHICAGO SENIOR CARE CENTER ...
> **WORKING TO PRESERVE OUR HERITAGE**
> A NOT-FOR-PROFIT ORGANIZATION DEDICATED TO SERVING THE GREEK-AMERICAN COMMUNITY
>
> **Commercial National Bank**
> Printing donated by: 4800 North Western Avenue • Chicago, Illinois 60025 • 312/989-5100 • MEMBER FDIC

GACS 10th anniversary flyer. Circa 1993. John Psiharis collection.

March 21: GACS co-sponsors the Greek Independence Day event at the Chicago Hilton and Tower with the Hellenic Professional Society of Illinois and KRIKOS.

March 24: "Greek Night at the Cairo" nightclub co-sponsored by GACS which receives a share of the proceeds from the event. The event is well attended given that Greek Independence Day is the following day and many guests are in a party mood.

March 29: United Hellenic American Congress (UHAC) Social Services Committee meeting convened by UHAC executive director Mike Bakalis and held at UHAC's office, 400 N. Franklin St. #215, Chicago.

April 2: GACS receives sales tax exemption renewal from the Illinois Department of Revenue.

April 8: GACS Building Fund Committee meeting at Jim Kozonis' office 4849 N. Milwaukee Ave., Chicago.

April 11: GACS hosts the social hour following Palm Sunday services at St. Andrew Greek Orthodox Church, 5649 N. Sheridan Rd. Evangeline Mistaras, Ethel Kotsovos, and John Psiharis host the event and speak about GACS. The *Ya'Sou* van is parked outside the front doors of the church.

April 29: GACS Annual Volunteer Luncheon, Grecian Taverna, 4761 N. Lincoln Ave., Chicago.

May 2: GACS hosts the social hour after services at St. George Greek Orthodox Church. John Rassogianis and John Psiharis speak about GACS in a packed room.

May 11: John Psiharis, John Rassogianis, and Peter Palivos meet with U.S. Senator Carol Moseley Braun to discuss the need for federal support for both GACS and GANHC. Also in attendance is Jill Zwick, chief of staff, and Paul Cericola, of the senator's staff. The meeting was held at Dirksen Federal Building, 230 S. Dearborn St., Chicago.

May 23: GACS co-sponsors a KRIKOS program entitled "The War in the Balkans" at the Papagus Greek Taverna and Banquets inside the Embassy Suites Hotel. The program is in two parts. The first is "War Crimes in the Balkans: Media Manipulation, Historical Amnesia, and Subjective Morality," by Professor Carl J. Jacobsen, Ph.D. (Carleton University, Ottawa, Canada). The second part is entitled, "Greece and the Balkan Question," by Professor Andre Gerolymatos, Ph.D., director of the Hellenic Studies Center, Dawson College, Montreal, Canada. Drinks and sweets are compliments of Papagus Greek Taverna. Admission: $3.

June 6: GACS hosts the coffee hour following services at Assumption Greek Orthodox Church. Elaine Thomopoulos, Toni Panos, and John Rassogianis represent GACS. The *Ya'Sou* van is parked outside the church.

June 10: GACS Building Fund Committee meeting at the center.

June 14: John Psiharis attends a meeting with Governor Jim Edgar for recipients of Illinois Department on Aging Community Care Program contracts. GACS receives CCP contracts to provide homemaker/chore-housekeeping and adult day care services. Governor's office, 16th floor.

June 16: GACS Board meeting at GACS.

June 23: GACS hosts a cocktail reception in the rooftop garden of the Pegasus restaurant in Greektown. The event benefits Northwest Chicago Senior Care Center. Guests are invited to continue the party by visiting the

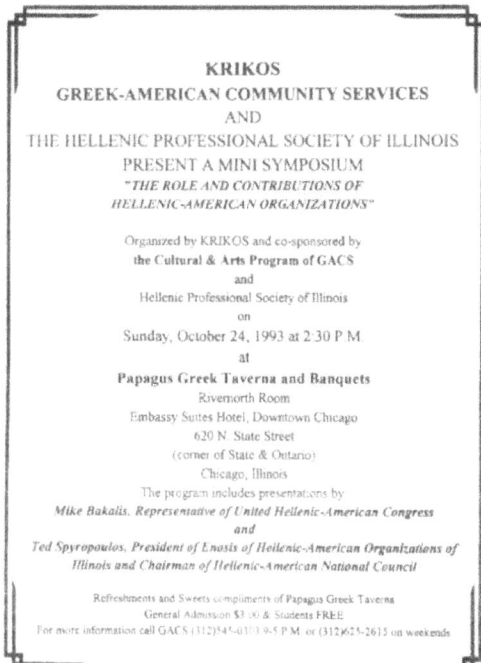

A flyer for "The Role and Contributions of Hellenic-American Organizations." October 24, 1993. John Psiharis collection.

"Greek Night at the Cairo," of which a portion of the proceeds is donated to GACS.

July 1: GACS begins to offer Chore Housekeeping services as a result of a service expansion contract through the Illinois Department on Aging Community Care Program. "Assistance in such areas as shopping, laundry, cooking, housekeeping, medication management, errands, and bathing is available."

July 8: UHAC Social Services Committee meeting convened by UHAC executive director Mike Bakalis and held at the UHAC office, 400 N. Franklin St #215, Chicago.

August 2: UHAC Social Services Committee meeting at St. Demetrios' Church in Elmhurst, IL.

August 4: GACS Board meeting at the center.

September 14: GACS Board meeting at the center.

September 19: GACS hosts an Open House Reception and Blessing of the Waters (*Agiasmos*) for the *Ya'Sou 2* van from 3:00 p.m. – 5:30 p.m. at GACS.

September 29: GACS hosts the first caregivers support group meeting for ADC families at the center. The group will continue to meet regularly (usually once per month) throughout the existence of the ADC program.

October 10: GACS Fabric Arts Project participants take part in a program on Greek Folklore at the Hellenic Museum. Several participants discuss their stories and experiences with the art form, and several examples of their works are on display at the museum.

October 22: Seventh Annual GACS Heritage Awards Dinner held at the Knickerbocker Hotel-Chicago, 163 E. Walton St. The theme was "Entrepreneurs in the 90s." Honorees are Ted Spyropoulos and Chris Tomaras. The first National Heritage Award is awarded to George Stephanopoulos. The *Efharisto* Award is presented to the Retirement Research Foundation. Special performance by Vasilios Gaitanos. Tickets are $50 per person.

October 24: GACS, KRIKOS, and the Hellenic Professional Society of Illinois present a mini-symposium entitled, "The Role and Contributions of Hellenic-American Organizations," at Papagus Greek Taverna and Banquets, Embassy Suites Hotel, 620 N. State St., Chicago, IL. The program includes presentations by Mike Bakalis, representative of the United Hellenic American Congress, and Ted Spyropoulos, president of Enosis of Hellenic-American Organizations of Illinois and Chairman of the Hellenic American National Council. Refreshments and sweets are compliments of Papagus.

1994

January 27: The *Jefferson/Portage/Bel-Cragin Times Newspapers* feature an article entitled "Adult Program Keeps Clients from Doldrums" by Beth Burmahl. The article focuses on the adult day care center and chore housekeeping programs.

March 12: Mike Bakalis, John Psiharis, John Rassogianis, and Alice Buzanis are among those who escort Illinois state comptroller and Democratic gubernatorial candidate Dawn Clark-Netsch on a tour of Greektown restaurants and stores on a Saturday before the March 15 Illinois primary election.

March 14: The family of Tessie Cantos requests memorial contributions be made to GACS upon her passing. Over $8,000 in donations are received and the center's arts and crafts room is named in her memory.

May 20: GACS Advisory Board and Board of Directors host "A Touch of Love" reception and buffet at the Metropolitan Club in Sears Tower. The minimum donation is $500 per person. Hosted by Chris Tomaras and Eleni Bousis, event chairpersons, and Loukas Pergantas, co-chairman.

June: Plato Academy Choir children perform their spring program at the GACS adult day care center and spend the afternoon with center participants.

(L-R): Alice Buzanis, Comptroller Dawn Clark-Netsch, and John Psiharis. Parthenon Restaurant. March 12, 1994. John Psiharis collection.

June 1: *Northwest Leader* newspaper publishes an article by Karen Wagner entitled "Greek Center Offers Services for Seniors." The article describes GACS services with a focus on the adult day care center. The article was reprinted in the August 4, 1994 issue of the *Hellenic Chronicle* newspaper.

June 18: GACS co-sponsors the "Around the World with CLESE" fundraiser featuring food and entertainment from many nations. Held at Ryan Hall, 4432 N. Troy Ave., Chicago. Tickets are $5 per person. GACS arranges for the Orpheus Dance Group to perform at the event and obtains food donations from the Greek Islands, Pegasus, and Rodity's restaurants in Greektown.

June 25: GACS co-sponsors celebrations (including a reception for team members and a public rally) related to the World Cup games held in Greektown and at Soldier Field. Greece would play Bulgaria and there was a lot of enthusiasm for the Greek team at various events in Greektown.

July: GACS has an exhibit booth during the 32nd Biennial Clergy-Laity Conference held in Chicago. The booth is shared by GACS and GANHC and was staffed by both organizations.

August: GACS holds an annual volunteer luncheon at Central Gyros. The Executive Director Award is presented to Ethel Kotsovos and John Rassogianis.

September 7: GACS volunteer and supporter Fannie Manos is honored by Marilee Lindley, Director of the Illinois Department on Aging, with the Community Leader Award at Multicultural Senior Day. Sponsored by Illinois Governor Jim Edgar and the Coalition of Limited English Speaking Elderly. The ceremony is held at the James R. Thompson Center State of Illinois Building. Mrs. Manos turned 87 years old a few weeks after the presentation. She is recognized for her support and fundraising efforts in support of the adult day care center.

September 7–November 30: Fall series of classes for the GACS Fabric Arts Project at GACS. FAP coordinator Frieda Aravosis coordinates the program after the passing of founding coordinator Tessie Cantos. Funded through the Chicago Department of Cultural Affairs.

September 12–September 21: GACS unveils "The Heartland of Hellenism: The Greeks in Illinois – 1886-1950" exhibit at the James R. Thompson Center, State of Illinois Building. Among those in attendance were Roula Alakiotou, Irene Antoniou, Peter Maroutsos, Evangeline Mistaras, Toni Panos, John Psiharis, John Rassogianis, Elaine Thomopoulos, Chris Tomaras, and others.

The exhibit is a preview of panels from the GACS "*O Cosmos*: The Private Lives and Public Celebrations of Greeks in Illinois" traveling museum exhibition that will be shown at various sites throughout Illinois and is supported by the Illinois Humanities Council. During this display, thousands passed through the lobby and viewed it daily.

September 19: GACS kicks off its annual observance of National Adult Day Care Week with the inaugural performance of its newly formed Seniors Community Band. Participants invite their families, friends, and the community at large to this afternoon activity. Refreshments are served after the concert.

October-December: GACS, for the fourth year, begins enrollment of eligible clients into the Low Income Home Energy Assistance Program at GACS. About 1,000 households apply through this annual program.

October 21: GACS assumes ownership of the 3940 N. Pulaski building after final closing papers are signed that afternoon.

October 21: Eighth Annual Heritage Awards Dinner at the Knickerbocker-Hotel Chicago, 163 E. Walton St. The theme, "Organizations in the 90s," honors the community's professional and cultural organizations. Honorees are the Greek Women's University Club, Hellenic Cultural Organization, Hellenic Professional Society of Illinois, and KRIKOS. The *Efharisto* Award is presented to the Illinois Masonic Medical Center. Music by

Linardakis Band. Chaired by Athanasia Papadopoulos. Peter Maroutsos is the master of ceremonies and Charles Mouratides introduces the Heritage Awards recipients. Dr. Theodosis Kioutas introduces Gerald Mungerson, president of Illinois Masonic Medical Center, who accepts the *Efharisto* Award.

November 25: GACS ADC participants enjoy the 4th Annual Thanksgiving Luncheon Cruise hosted by the Chicago Department on Aging aboard the Odyssey cruise ship.

December: GACS "Heartland of Hellenism, the Greeks in Illinois 1886-1954" is on display at the Hellenic Museum and Cultural Center. An opening evening reception is held. Dr. Andrew Kopan and Dr. Fotios Litsas speak about the theme of the exhibit.

December 4: GACS hosts a screening of *Solstice*, a film produced and directed by Jerry Vasilatos, at LaSalle Talman Theater, 4901 W. Irving Park Rd. Jerry hosts a post-screening questions and answers session. Proceeds benefit Northwest Chicago Senior Care Center. Co-sponsors are GACS, Argolis Organization O Danaos, Greek Women's University Club, Hellenic Cultural Organization, Hellenic Professional Society of Illinois, and KRIKOS.

December 21: GACS Annual Christmas Party at GACS. Thirty students from Plato Academy sing traditional Greek and American Holiday songs. The United Athenian and Piraeus Society presents gifts to each adult day care participant. Catering is provided by Master Caterers. Attendance is more than 90 people.

1995

January 4: ADC Caregivers Support Group meeting at GACS.

January 24: GACS Board meeting at the center. Agenda items: Financial report, signature cards, Sandy becomes president. Elect vice-president, executive director report, building report (leases, repairs, tours, and sign), staff attendance, CAP possibilities, ADC (explore Saturday hours), meals-on-wheels program update, Kozonis' tickets, and Evangeline's party.

January 25: John Psiharis is nominated for a fourth two-year term on the Community Development Advisory Committee by Mayor Richard M. Daley during a breakfast in the Empire Room of the Palmer House, 17 E. Monroe St., Chicago, IL.

February 15–February 19: John Psiharis is invited to participate in the "Adult Day Services: The Un Nursing Home," a mini-conference of the White House on Aging in Washington DC.

February 28: GACS Board meeting at GACS. IDOA owes GACS $8,185. A Lazy Boy recliner valued at $587 was donated to the ADC by Bill and Mary Kakavas.

March: GACS co-sponsors *Mr. Greedy*, a Greek comedy theatrical production performed by the St. John's Players at St. John's Greek Orthodox Church, Des Plaines, IL. KRIKOS is the main organizer of the afternoon performance.

March 3: John Psiharis speaks during the White House Conference on Aging Speak-Out session sponsored by the Chicago Department on Aging and held at the Copernicus Center.

March 7: John Psiharis speaks during a Mini-White House Conference on Aging forum organized by CLESE at the Levy Center.

March 16: John Psiharis, Evangeline Mistaras, and Dr. Kioutas attend a Retirement Research Foundation breakfast honoring grantees at the Palmer House, 17 E. Monroe St., Chicago, IL.

March 23: GACS moving day. Offices are relocated to the second floor to expand space for ADC and other uses on the first floor.

March 26: GACS co-sponsors the Greek Independence Day Celebration at the Chicago Hilton and Towers Hotel, 720 S. Michigan Ave, Chicago. The event includes a lecture by Professor John Anton from the University of South Florida entitled "The Muse of Freedom - *To Tragoudi* of the Greek People of 1821" and "Hellas the Unconquerable: It's Spirit in Poetry and Song." Folk dances from Macedonia, Thrace, Epirus, and Peloponnesus are performed by the Orpheus Dance Troupe of the Macedonia Society of Greater Chicago. Co-sponsors include KRIKOS, Enosis, Hellenic Professional Society of Illinois, Macedonian Society of Greater Chicago, and Pan-Euboean Society. The event is designated a "Greek Heritage '95" event.

March 29–June 21: GACS Fabric Arts Project classes resume at GACS.

April 9: GACS presents a lecture entitled "The Greek-American Community and Hull House" at the Jane Addams Hull-House Museum, 800 S. Halsted St, Chicago, IL. The event is a distinguished lecture for the "*O Cosmos*: The Private Lives and Public Celebrations of the Greeks in Illinois" project. It is co-sponsored by the Greek Women's University Club and the Hellenic Professional Society of Illinois and funded by the Illinois Humanities Council. A discussion period after the lecture includes some guests sharing their memories of Hull House.

May 1: GACS submits a grant request for $91,000 over three years in support of the Adult Day Care center to the Retirement Research Foundation.

May 1: John Psiharis attends Mayor Richard M. Daley's inauguration at Medina Temple.

May 6: ADC Caregivers support group meeting at GACS.

May 9: GACS board meeting at the center.

May 13: GACS participates in the annual Greek Independence Parade with clients, staff, and volunteers riding in the *Ya'Sou* vans. Before the beginning of the parade, GACS volunteers pass out cookies and water.

May 15: Elaine Thomopoulos speaks on a panel at a conference hosted by the American Jewish Committee in Washington DC.

May 20: GACS hosts members of a tour group arranged by the Field Museum Education Department. The tour is led by Irving Cutler, Ph.D. According to the tour program flier: "Older Greek, Swedish, Belgian, Polish, and Jewish communities will be highlighted as well as newer communities. Stops will be made at interesting sites along the way for walking and browsing. An ethnic luncheon is included. Tickets are $50 ($43 for museum members)." John Psiharis and John Rassogianis speak about the Greek community in Chicago, GACS, and the nursing home project. Greek hors d'oeuvres and lemonade were provided.

May 23: GACS participates in the annual "Around the World with CLESE" benefit for the Coalition of Limited English Speaking Elderly at Ryan Hall, 4432 N. Troy Ave., Chicago, IL. Varied ethnic entertainment includes the Orpheus Macedonian Dance Troupe. An ethnic buffet featuring food from five continents is provided. GACS provides Greek food donated by Pegasus, Greek Islands, Roditys, and Little Mike's restaurants.

May 24: GACS Advisory Board dinner reception at the center.

June 6: GACS Board meeting at the center.

June 28: GACS ADC clients attend a Chicago Cubs baseball game at Wrigley Field.

July 13: GACS Volunteer Appreciation Dinner at Grecian Taverna.

August 1: GACS Board meeting at the center. Agenda: New phone system installed on both floors. Reports on ADC, Summer LIHEAP program, BEC, CAP, and the Fabric Arts Program.

September 5: GACS Board meeting at the center.

September 6: ADC Caregivers Support Group meeting at GACS.

October 1: GACS receives a three-year grant of $91,000 from the Retirement Research Foundation in support of the Adult Day Care center. According to RRF president Marilyn Hennessey, the Foundation seldom approves two consecutive three-year grants, but they are impressed with our accomplishments and believe adult day care is a significant unmet need.

October 3: Dance Africa Workshop with ADC clients at GACS.

October 3: GACS Board meeting at GACS.

October 9: Dinner Dance Committee meeting at GACS.

October 13: Ninth Annual GACS Heritage Awards Dinner at the Ambassador West Hotel-Chicago, 1300 N. State Parkway, Chicago, IL. The theme for the event is "The Greek-American Newspaper in the 90s." Honorees are the community's four print publications: *Greek Press, Greek Star, Hellenic Community News, and Hellenic Life. Efharisto* Award presented to Chris Tomaras. Guests include Consul General of Greece Nicholas Zafiropoulos and Illinois State Comptroller Lolita Didrikson. Music by the Linardakis Band.

October 18: John Psiharis attends a reception hosted by Governor Jim Edgar at the State of Illinois Building, 16th Floor.

November 2: John Psiharis and GACS are featured in a front-page article in the *Edison-Norwood Times Review* and other Pioneer Press newspapers entitled "A Sense of Purpose for Helping Others."

November 19: GACS presents a lecture by Elaine Thomopoulos, Ph.D., entitled "Greek-American Women Tell Their Stories," at Plato Academy Hall, 601 S. Central Avenue, Chicago, IL. The lecture is in conjunction with the GACS "Heartland of Hellenism, Greeks in Illinois – 1886 -1954" traveling exhibition on display in Plato Hall.

December 11: Bill and Mary Kakavas provide a special Holiday lunch for ADC clients compliments of Thirteen Colonies.

December 13: GACS Fabric Arts Program Christmas party at the center.

December 20: GACS Annual Christmas Party at the center. Thirty children from Plato Academy Choir perform standard Greek and English Christmas carols. The United Athenian Piraeus Society provides Christmas gifts to 32 ADC clients. Executive Director Award is presented to Elaine

Thomopoulos and Phil Williams. Catering is provided by Master Caterers. Greek desserts are prepared by volunteers, clients, and their families.

1996

January: Presbytera Despina Massouras joins ADC staff as a social worker, after completing her internship and graduating with a degree in gerontology from National Louis University. Des replaces Ethel Kotsovos, who transitioned to the role of GANHC office manager.

(L-R): John Rassogianis, film director Pantelis Voulgaris, John Psiharis, and Evangeline Mistaras at the Film Center of the Art Institute, February 25, 1996. John Rassogianis collection.

February 4, 11, 18, and 25 GACS co-sponsors, "Uniquely Greek: The Films of Pantelis Voulgaris," "A mid-career retrospective of Pantelis Voulgaris, one of the most prominent directors in Greek cinema, will take place at The Film Center of the School of the Art Institute of Chicago on Sundays throughout February, and will conclude with an appearance by Mr. Voulgaris on February 25 where he will discuss his latest film, *ACROPOLE* (1995). The films (eight features and three shorts) are in Greek with English subtitles. Sponsored by Olympic Airways and the Consulate General of Greece in Chicago. It is programmed in cooperation with the Hellenic Museum and Cultural Center and the Cultural & Arts Program of Greek-American Community Services." Columbus Drive and Jackson Boulevard, Chicago, IL.

February 5: GACS Board of Directors meeting at the center. Agenda items include review and approval of GACS audited financial statements.

February 9: GACS co-sponsors a lecture entitled, "The Role of Women in the Greek Immigrant Experience," by Nicholas Gage at the Macedonian Society of Greater Chicago, 4544 N. Western Ave, Chicago, IL. The event is part of the "Greek-American Women in Illinois: 111 Years of Courage, Struggle, and Triumph," presented by the Greek Women's University Club and funded by the Illinois Humanities Council. Attendance 125.

February 25: GACS co-sponsors a KRIKOS seminar by Dr. John Anton, professor of philosophy at the University of South Florida. The title of the program was either "Aristotelian Philosophy and its Relevance to the Modern World," or "Aristotle's Political Philosophy – Its Place in Contemporary Life. Is the Wisdom of the Greeks Dated or Timely?" HPSI also co-sponsors the event. River North Room, Embassy Suites Hotel, 600 N. State St., Chicago, IL.

Gov. Jim Edgar congratulates the Greek American Community Services, Irving and Pulaski, for its twelve years of dedication and commitment to the elderly Greek community. From left, are George Palivos; Loukas Pergantas, board member; Eleni Bousis, board member; Gov. Edgar; John Psiharis, executive director of GACS; Constantine Zografopoulos, vice president of GACS and Jim Graham, DCCA.

Northwest Leader Post Newspaper, March 27, 1996. Elaine Thomopoulos collection.

February 26–27: CPR training and certification for staff at GACS.

March 20–June 26: GACS Fabric Arts of Greece spring classes at the center.

March 24: GACS co-sponsors the Greek Independence Day Celebration, "Diaspora Greeks and the Cause of Greek Independence." The event held at the Chicago Hilton and Towers features a celebration speech by Dr. Artemis Leontis and music by Maria Fustalieraki. Dances by Orpheus Dance Troupe. Sponsored by KRIKOS-Midwest and co-sponsored by Greek American Community Services, Greek Women's University Club, Hellenic Professional Society of Illinois, Macedonian Society, and Pan-Euboean Society of Illinois.

April 19: John Psiharis attends a photo opportunity for CLESE with Governor Jim Edgar at the State of Illinois Building, 16th Floor.

April 21: GACS co-sponsors the Midwest ZIYIA Premiere, "Traditional Music of Greece and Asia Minor in Concert," at the International House of the University of Chicago, 1414 E. 59th Street, Chicago, IL. This concert caps the three-day "Anatolian Heritage Festival Part 2: The Interior," held April 19-21, 1996. Tickets are $15 each at the door and $13 in advance.

May 9: GACS Board of Directors meeting at the center.

John Psiharis and President of the Hellenic Republic Konstantinos Stephanopoulos. May 14, 1996. John Psiharis collection.

May 14: John Psiharis and John Rassogianis attend a reception in honor of Konstantinos Stephanopoulos, President of the Hellenic Republic, at Sheraton Chicago Hotel and Towers, Chicago Ballroom. Chicago, IL.

May 18-19: GACS participates in the Skokie Festival of Cultures event. In addition to GACS, the Solon Opa Dance Troupe, and the Orpheus

Dance Troupe participate. About 18.000 people were expected to attend the two days.

May 23: GACS Advisory Board and Board of Directors meeting at Pegasus Restaurant.

May 30: GACS participates in the "Around the World with CLESE" event held at Eden's Banquets, 6313 N. Pulaski Rd., Chicago, IL. In addition to GACS arranging for food donations and a performance by the Orpheus Dancers, John Rassogianis serves as co-master of ceremonies with Santosh Kumar. Tickets: Under 60, $10 in advance, and $15 at the door. Seniors $4 in advance and $5 at the door. Entrance tickets include an ethnic buffet and international entertainment.

June 3: GACS participates in Greektown ceremonies celebrating the arrival and passing-through of the Olympic Torch as it makes its way through the nation en route to Atlanta for the July 19 Olympic Games Opening Ceremonies. Hundreds attend the ceremonies and festivities.

July 15: GACS Board of Directors meeting at the center.

August 21: Northwest Chicago Senior Care Center participants enjoy lunch at the International House of Pancakes in Portage Park.

August 24: John Psiharis attends a private dinner hosted by Governor Michael Dukakis at Pegasus Restaurant as a prelude to the Democratic National Convention to be hosted in Chicago.

September 18: The fall series of GACS Fabric Arts of Greece begins at the center.

September 28: GACS convenes a meeting with Greek cultural organizations at GACS to discuss additional ways of cooperating and jointly sponsoring programs. Organization representatives from GACS, KRIKOS, Hellenic Cultural Organization, Hellenic Professional Society of Illinois, Greek Women's University Club, and Orthodox Singles participate. Topics discussed include sharing mailing lists, email notices, and upcoming events.

October 14: Dr. Kioutas, John Psiharis, and John Rassogianis are invited to a private reception with U.S. First Lady Hillary Clinton to brief her on GACS and the GANHC. Chicago Hilton and Towers, 710 S. Michigan Ave., Chicago, IL.

(L-R): Governor Michael Dukakis, John Gorecki, John Psiharis, and unknown. Pegasus Restaurant. August 24, 1996. John Psiharis collection.

October 15: GACS co-sponsors a lecture entitled, "Theano Margaris, Chronicler of the Greek-American Experience," by Vivian M. Kallen, her daughter, at Ambassador Hall, Elmhurst, IL The event is part of the "Greek-American Women in Illinois: 111 Years of Courage, Struggle and Triumph," presented by the Greek Women's University Club and funded by the Illinois Humanities Council. Attendance 50.

October 27: GACS presents "A Conversation with Christopher Janus" at the GACS center. The conversation is followed by refreshments and a showing of *Goodbye Miss Fourth of July*. Co-sponsors of the event are the Greek Women's University Club and the Hellenic Professional Society of Illinois.

November 1: Tenth Annual GACS Heritage Awards Dinner at the Knickerbocker Hotel - Chicago. The theme is "Benefactors in the '90s." Honorees are Irene Antoniou, Eleni Bousis, Dr. Theodosis Kioutas, and Loukas Pergantas. A raffle in connection with the dinner offers a grand prize of $500 and the first prize of a weekend for two at the Abbey in Lake Geneva.

December 4: GACS staff meeting. Agenda items include the upcoming Christmas party, morning call-ins, transportation boundaries, and doctors' releases.

December 14: John Psiharis attends a fundraiser hosted by the Greek-American Committee to Re-elect U.S. Senator Carol Moseley-Braun at 32 West Penny, South Barrington, IL.

December 20: GACS Christmas Party for ADC participants, staff, volunteers, and supporters at the center.

1997

February 23: GACS co-sponsors a distinguished lecture entitled, "Not Out of Africa: The Greek Achievement and the Myth of Black Athena," by Dr. Mary Lefkowitz, professor of humanities at Wellesley College and author of *Black Athena Revisited* at the Embassy Suites Hotel, 600 N. State St., Chicago, IL. Sponsored by KRIKOS Midwest, Greek Women's University Club, and Hellenic Professional Society of Illinois. Admission is $3. Members are free.

March 16: GACS co-sponsors a lecture entitled, "Women in Greece, Yesterday and Today," by Menie Pavella, with responses by Dr. Vasiliki Toulios and Dr. Elaine Thomopoulos on "Greek-American Women." Moderator Louise Kerr, Ph.D., at the Macedonian Society of Greater Chicago, 4544 N. Western Ave, Chicago, IL. The event is part of the "Greek-American Women in Illinois: 111 Years of Courage, Struggle, and Triumph," presented by the Greek Women's University Club and funded by the Illinois Humanities Council. Attendance 80.

March 18: GACS co-sponsors a lecture entitled, "Greek-American Pioneer Women in Chicago: Georgia Bitzis Pooley and Presbytera Stella Petrakis," by Andrew Kopan, Ph.D., at Saints Constantine and Helen Greek Orthodox Church, 11025 S. Roberts Rd. Palos Hills, IL. Georgia Pooley, the first Greek woman to immigrate to Chicago in 1885, and Presbytera Petrakis, who immigrated to this country in 1916, laid the foundations of philanthropic organizations and social welfare concerns. The event is part of the "Greek-American Women in Illinois: 111 Years of Courage, Struggle, and Triumph," presented by the Greek Women's University Club and funded by the Illinois Humanities Council. Attendance 140.

March 18 and 20: GACS CPR training and certification classes for ADC and other staff held at the center.

March 20: GACS hosts a planning meeting for the "Around the World with CLESE" event.

March 26: GACS Fabric Arts of Greece project begins a 14-week cycle of classes at the center.

March 30: GACS, KRIKOS-Midwest, Council of Hellenes Abroad (SAE) of the Americas, Hellenic Professional Society of Illinois, Greek Women's University Club, Macedonian Society, Pan Euboean Society of Illinois, and Hellenic Council on Education, present a celebration of Greek Independence Day at St. John the Baptist Greek Orthodox Church in Des Plaines. The program includes the theatrical play *The Poet of Freedom, Dionysios Solomos,* by the community theater of "Nefeli," of the Greek community of Toronto. Stage adaptation by Nancy Athanassopoulos-Mylonas, director of Nefeli. Greek dance performance by Orpheus Dance Troupe.

April 6: GACS co-sponsors a lecture by historian and author Helen Zeese Papanikolas, entitled, "Greek-American Women in My Fiction," at the Hellenic Museum and Cultural Center, 168 N. Michigan Ave, Chicago, IL. The program is sponsored by the Hellenic Museum and Cultural Center and the Greek Women's University Club. Other co-sponsors include the American Hellenic Society of Berwyn, Copernicus Foundation, DePaul University, Hellenic Cultural Organization, Hellenic Professional Society of Illinois, Italian Cultural Center, Jane Addams Hull-House Museum, KRIKOS-Midwest, Loyola University of Chicago, Macedonian Society of Greater Chicago, and St. Helen's Philoptochos. The event is part of the "Greek-American Women in Illinois: 111 Years of Courage, Struggle, and Triumph," presented by the Greek Women's University Club and funded by the Illinois Humanities Council. Attendance 110.

April 7: GACS Board meeting at the center.

May 4: GACS co-sponsors a lecture entitled "Greek American Women in Transition" by Angelike Mountanis, director, Hellenic Family and Community Services, Hellenic Foundation, and Dr. George Kourvetaris, Dept. of Sociology, Northern Illinois University, and held at GACS, 3940 N. Pulaski Rd. Co-sponsors include the Greek Women's University Club, KRIKOS, Hellenic Professional Society of Illinois, and Orthodox Singles. The event is part of the "Greek-American Women in Illinois: 111 Years of Courage, Struggle, and Triumph," presented by the Greek Women's University Club and funded by the Illinois Humanities Council. Attendance 80.

May 12: GACS Board meeting at GACS.

June 5: GACS participates in the "Around the World with CLESE" event held at the Central West Regional Center, 2102 W. Ogden Ave., Chicago, IL.

July 8: GACS Advisory Board dinner meeting at Santorini Restaurant.

CHICAGO—Governor Jim Edgar's assistant for ethnic affairs, Pat Michalski, attended the 11th annual awards dinner banquet of the Greek American Community Services Nov. 16. From left, Michael Chioros, president of the Hellenic Foundation, Irene Antoniou, Lea Ames, executive director of the Hellenic Foundation, Michalski, John Psiharis, executive director of the Greek American Community Services, Costas Zografopoulos, president of the Greek American Community Services, Mary Kakavas, board of directors of the Greek American Nursing Home, Bill Kakavas, Fr. George C. Massoutas, Dr. George F. Dallanis, chairman of the Midwest committee of IOCC.

Social service agencies of the Greek-American community receive GACS heritage awards

By John Rassogianis

A confluence of such factors as the opportunity to honor the primary service organizations of the Greek-American community, as well as their gracious response in accepting the heritage awards extended to them, produced an inspiring evening of recognition and remembrance during the recent Greek-American Community Services' (GACS) 11th Annual Awards Dinner on Nov. 16 at the Bristol Court Banquet Hall in Mt. Prospect.

Award recipients, welcomed by the Greek-American Community Services president, Costas Zografopoulos, were: the Greek-American Nursing Home Committee (GANHC), the Hellenic Foundation, International Orthodox Christian Charities (IOCC), and the Greek Orthodox Ladies Philoptochos Society.

Representing the GANHC, Dr. Theodosis Kioutas brought pre-holiday tidings to the guests by assuring them of the imminent acceptance of the certificate of need, submitted by the GANHC on its first attempt to the state of Illinois for the establishment of a nursing home in Wheeling, IL.

The Hellenic Foundation president, Michael Chioros, accepted the second award acknowledging the foundation's nearly 45 years of service and its continuing impact on the lives of the community under the current director, Lea Ames.

With the recent patriarchal visit and season of heightened awareness of the practical humanitarian work done by the Greek Orthodox church, the heritage awards also brought a timely accent to the work of the IOCC and the Greek Orthodox Ladies Philoptochos Society.

Dr. George Dalianis, chairman of the Midwest committee of the International Orthodox Christian Charities, accepted the award for IOCC and Susan Regos, president of the Philoptochos Society, accepted the award on behalf of the society.

Present at the awards banquet were representatives and guests of the various service organizations, as well as staff and guests of the Northwest Chicago Adult Day Care Center, an agency of GACS.

Athanasia Vaselopoulos served as dinner chairperson. Master of ceremonies was Peter Maroutsos. Recognition was also extended to GACS founders John Psiharis and Elaine Thomopoulos, Ph.D.

The *Greek Star* article about the "Social Services in the 90s" Heritage Awards dinner. Circa December, 1997. Elaine Thomopoulos collection.

July 28: GACS Advisory Board dinner meeting at Pegasus Restaurant.

August 6: GACS Volunteer Dinner, Grecian Taverna restaurant.

August 27: GACS Adult Day Care participants visit Tree House Animal Shelter on a field trip.

September 21: GACS co-sponsors a lecture entitled, "Greek, Italian, and Latina Women in Illinois." Elaine Thomopoulos speaks on Greek women, Louise Anno Nuevo Kerr, Ph.D., speaks on Latinas, and Gloria Nardini, Ph.D., speaks on Italian women, at the Italian Cultural Center, 1621 N. 39th Ave., Stone Park, IL. The event is part of the "Greek-American Women in Illinois: 111 Years of Courage, Struggle, and Triumph," presented by the Greek Women's University Club and funded by the Illinois Humanities Council. Attendance 22.

October 19: GACS co-sponsors a panel discussion entitled, "Greek-American Women in Illinois," featuring the Honorable Adeline Geo-Karis, senator; Stella Adams Cuthbert, and Commissioner Maria Pappas at Crown Center, Loyola University Lakeshore Campus, 6525 N. Sheridan Rd., Chicago, IL. Co-sponsored by KRIKOS, Campus Life Union Board, and the Hellenic American Society of Loyola University. The event is part of the "Greek-American Women in Illinois: 111 Years of Courage, Struggle, and Triumph," presented by the Greek Women's University Club and funded by the Illinois Humanities Council. Attendance 140.

October 21: GACS Board meeting at the center.

November 2: A GACS delegation attends the Patriarchal Divine Liturgy led by His All Holiness Bartholomew, Archbishop of Constantinople and Ecumenical Patriarch, at Navy Pier. Some attend a grand banquet at the Sheraton Chicago Hotel and Towers in honor of His All-Holiness that evening.

November 10: John Psiharis speaks about GACS at a meeting of the Old Irving Park Association at Irving Park United Methodist Church, 3801 N. Keeler Avenue, Chicago, IL.

November 10–November 21: GACS co-sponsors a photo exhibit entitled, "Greek-American Pioneer Women in Illinois" at the James R. Thompson Center. The event is part of the "Greek-American Women in Illinois: 111 Years of Courage, Struggle, and Triumph," presented by the Greek Women's University Club and funded by the Illinois Humanities Council. The exhibit was co-curated by Elaine Thomopoulos and Penny Sarlas.

November 16: Eleventh Annual GACS Heritage Awards Dinner. The evening's theme is "Social Services in the 90s." Honorees are the Greek-American Nursing Home Committee, Hellenic Foundation, International Orthodox Christian Charities, and the Greek Orthodox Diocese of Chicago Philoptochos Society. The event is held at Bristol Court Banquets, 828 E. Rand Road, Mt. Prospect Illinois. Tickets are $50 per person.

December 17: GACS Christmas Party at GACS.

1998

January 25: GACS Cultural & Arts Program co-sponsors "Concert of Greek Music and Dance: Regional Rural and Urban Traditions," at the International House, 1414 E. 59th St., Chicago, IL. The event features the Orpheus Dance Troupe of Chicago and music by Jim Stoynoff and Colleagues. Jim plays clarinet, violin, and guitar. Christos Govetas of Seattle performs vocals, laouto, and bouzouki and Joe Zeytoonian of South Florida performs vocals, oud, and percussion. Special guests: Christos Karakostas Zournas and Daoulis Ensemble, direct from Flambouro, Serres region, Eastern Macedonia.

March 6: GACS sales and use tax exemption renewed for five years through April 1, 2003, by the Illinois Department of Revenue.

March 18–June 24: Fabric Arts of Greece classes at the center.

March 29: GACS takes part in the Greek Independence Day Parade along Halsted Street. GACS board members, volunteers, and clients ride the route in the *Ya'Sou* vans

April 22: GACS Volunteer Dinner at Grecian Taverna.

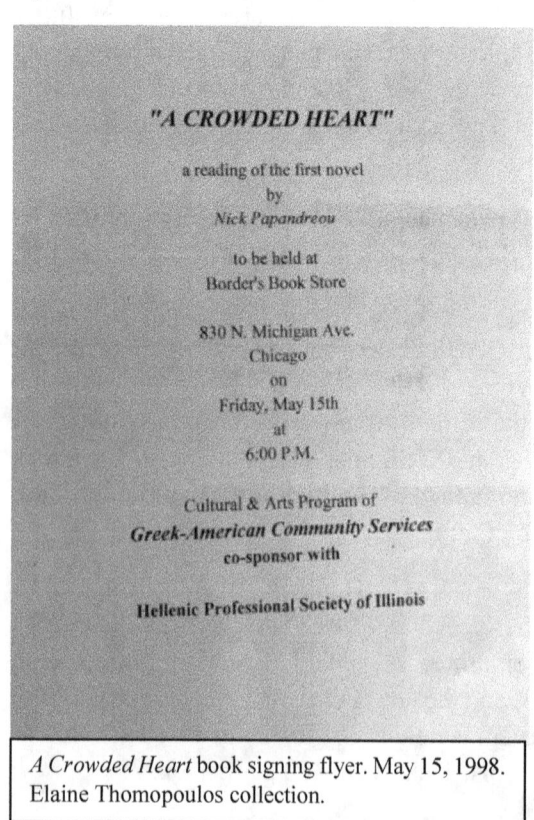

A Crowded Heart book signing flyer. May 15, 1998. Elaine Thomopoulos collection.

May 15: GACS co-sponsors with the Hellenic Professional Society of Illinois, a reading and book signing by Nick Papandreou of his first novel, *A Crowded Heart,* at Border's Book Store, 830 N. Michigan Ave., Chicago, IL. Nick is the younger brother of Greek Prime Minister George Papandreou, the son of former Greek Prime Minister Andreas Papandreou, and the grandson of former Greek Prime Minister Georgios Papandreou.

May 16: John Psiharis, John Rassogianis, and

(L-R): John Psiharis, U.S. Senator Carol Moseley-Braun, Connie Gountanis-Rigas, and John Rassogianis. May 16, 1998. John Psiharis collection.

Connie Gountanis-Rigas, as members of the Greek-Americans for Carol Moseley-Braun Committee, attend a reception with the senator at the home of Peter Palivos in Lake Point Tower.

May 31: GACS Cultural & Arts Program co-sponsors a lecture by Andrew Kopan, Ph.D., entitled "Greek-American Pioneer Women in Chicago: Georgia Bitzis Pooley and Presbytera Stella Petrakis." The event is organized by the Greek Women's University Club and co-sponsored by the American Hellenic Society of Berwyn It is held in the Assumption Church Plato Hall. The event is part of the "Greek-American Women in Illinois: 111 Years of Courage, Struggle, and Triumph," presented by the Greek Women's University Club and funded by the Illinois Humanities Council. Attendance 110.

June 8: GACS Board meeting at the center.

June 16: GACS Advisory Board and Board of Directors meeting at Costa's Restaurant in Greektown. Agenda items: "Welcome by Irene Antoniou, progress reports from John Psiharis and Kostas Zografopoulos, Advisory Board goals, Heritage Awards Dinner, agency needs, expansion of Advisory Board and new members."

July 20: ADC participants' lunch outing to Zephyr's Ice Cream Parlor, 1767 W. Wilson Avenue, Chicago, IL.

A *Greek Press* article September 27, 1998. Elaine Thomopoulos collection.

September 16: The fall session of the Fabric Arts Program begins at GACS. Classes continue for 14 weeks.

September 27: GACS co-sponsors an illustrated lecture by Leon C. Marinakos, Cultural Attaché of Greece (Honorary), entitled "Greek Women: Musings on Antecedents and Realities." The event is held at Embassy Suites, 600 N. State Street, Chicago, IL. It is sponsored by the Greek Women's University Club. Hellenic Link-Midwest is also a co-sponsor. "This presentation explores the reality of Greek women through the ages, starting from mythology, antiquity, the Byzantine era, and the 19th and 20th centuries. It focuses on the need to reassess and reexamine the basic characteristics as to what constitutes womanhood."

September 29: GACS Advisory Board meeting to discuss upcoming Heritage Awards dinner at Chris Tomaras' office.

The Greek Women's University Club
Hellenic Link Midwest and the
Cultural and Arts Program of
Greek-American Community Services

present an illustrated lecture by

LEON MARINAKOS
CULTURAL ATTACHÉ OF GREECE

"GREEK WOMEN:
MUSINGS ON ANTECEDENTS AND REALITIES"

September 27, 1998 at 3:00 P.M.

Embassy Suites, 600 N. State, Chicago, IL.

This presentation explores the reality of Greek women through the ages, starting from mythology, antiquity, the Byzantine era and the 19th and 20th centuries. It focuses on the need to reassess and reexamine the basic characteristics as to what constitutes womanhood.

Leon Marinakos, Cultural Attaché of Greece (honorary), is a lecturer whose activity is rooted in his enthusiasm for the Greek heritage, its impacts and relevance, and fuses two of his many loves: the excitement and lessons of history and a dedication to the power of color photography. He has shared his interest with lectures to academic, fraternal, church and social groups and organizations around the country and in Greece. He has lectured at the Art Institute of Chicago eleven times on artistic, architectural and historical themes of Greek antiquity, the Byzantine world, and Greek-Americana. He was the president of the Classical Art Society at that institution.

For further information contact : Elaine Thomopoulos, Ph.D. (630) 655-2077

Funded in part by the Illinois Humanities Council, the National Endowment of the Humanities, the Illinois General Assembly and the Foundation for Hellenic Studies. The Greek-American Community Services sponsorship is supported by a Community Development Block Grant from the Chicago Department of Cultural Affairs.

"Greek Women: Musings on Antecedents and Realities" flyer. September 17, 1998. Elaine Thomopoulos collection.

October: GACS Fabric Arts of Greece program participants display a selection of their works at the James R. Thompson Center State of Illinois Building in commemoration of the "United Nations International, Year of the Older Adult."

October 7: GACS Advisory Board meeting to finalize Heritage Awards dinner planning at the center.

October 9: Twelfth Annual GACS Heritage Awards Cocktail Buffet at Embassy Suites Hotel, 600 N. State St. Honorees are John Apostolou, Dr. Dennis Caralis, and Maria Pappas. Michael Reese Health Trust receives *Efharisto* Award. Michael Skoubis is the master of ceremonies and the Linardakis Band provided the music.

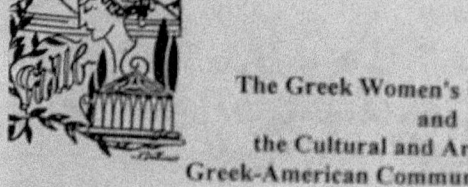

"Nomads, Migrants, Refugees: Stories of Exile and Home" flyer. October 11, 1998. Elaine Thomopoulos collection.

October 11: GACS presents Dr. Beatriz Badikian, who is of Greek and Armenian descent, who reads from her work in progress, "Nomads, Migrants, and Refugees: Stories of Exile and Home," at GACS, 3940 N. Pulaski Rd., Chicago, IL. Her reading is accompanied by Ed Berggren on the flute. The event is co-sponsored by the Greek Women's University Club and the Hellenic Professional Society of Illinois. The event is part of the "Greek-American Women in Illinois: 111 Years of Courage, Struggle, and Triumph," presented by the Greek Women's University Club and funded by the Illinois Humanities Council. Attendance 25.

October 14: John Psiharis attends an Athens Sister Cities Committee meeting at the Cultural Center, GAR Annex.

(L-R): John Psiharis, Nana Mouskouri, and John Rassogianis. November 5, 1998. John Psiharis collection.

Edgar's Office of Ethnic Affairs and the Illinois Department on Aging. Elaine represents GACS and GANHC in the planning leading up to the event.

November 5: John Psiharis and John Rassogianis attend a UNICEF reception honoring Nana Mouskouri. The elegant multi-course dinner is hosted by Evangeline Gouletas at the Cité restaurant in Lake Point Towers. They also attend her November 1 concert at the Auditorium Theater as special guests.

November 18: Chicago Sister Cities reception with Athens mayor. As a delegate agency of the Department of Cultural Affairs, GACS is invited to take part in the planning of this event.

November 19–November 22: GACS co-sponsors "Athens, Greece: A World in a Weekend" with the Chicago Department of Cultural Affairs in celebration of the sister cities' partnership. The weeklong free series of events were held in the Claudia Cassidy Theater at the Chicago Cultural Center. Among the events are film screenings of *Rembetika*, *Never on Sunday,* and *Ulysses Gaze*; traditional music and dance performances involving the Hellenic Five, Orpheus Hellenic Folklore Society, the Apollo Dance Troupe, and the Melissa Thodos Dancers. Other activities include a lecture and readings by Harry Mark Petrakis, a lecture by Leon

Marinakos, and a live broadcast hosted by Antigone Lambros and Jim Stoynoff which features interviews and live performances by Stoynoff, the Hellenic Five, and Greek recording artist Voula Karahaliou.

December 16: GACS Christmas Party at the center.

1999

January 12: GACS Board meeting at the center.

February 9: GACS Board meeting at the center.

March 21: GACS co-sponsors the Greek Independence Day event with the Greek Women's University Club, Hellenic Professional Society of Illinois, and Hellenic Link Midwest at St. John the Baptist Church in Des Plaines. The program includes the play *"Hellenism Will Set Only When the World Ends"* by the Theater "Nefeli" of the Greek community of Toronto and dances by the Orpheus Dance Group. Donations are $8 for adults and $5 for children.

March 31-June: GACS Fabric Arts of Greece classes begin at the center. Frieda Aravosis is the coordinator. This series of classes includes contact with the director of the Orpheus Dance Troupe for suggestions and inspiration on the various styles of dress worn by the troupe dancers. Participants will have access to the 20x15 colored pictures depicting male and female folk costumes, courtesy of the Benaki Museum, Athens, Greece

April 28: GACS and ADC family council rummage sale planning meeting at the center.

May 12: GACS and ADC family council rummage sale planning meeting at the center.

May 26: GACS and ADC family council rummage sale planning meeting at the center.

June 2: GACS and ADC family council rummage sale planning meeting at the center.

June 5: ADC rummage sale at GACS. Some ADC clients and family members volunteer at the event. Bad weather impacts the turnout but it is a successful event, raising more than $1,000.

June 14: GACS Board meeting at the center.

July 13: GACS Board meeting at the center.

September–December 15: GACS Fabric Arts Project at the center.

December 14: GACS Board meeting at the center.

December 15: GACS Christmas Party at GACS and final session of the year for Fabric Arts Project classes. The party hosts 75 guests.

December 19: Several GACS and GANHC members including John Psiharis, John Rassogianis, Dr. Theodosis Kioutas, Toni Panos, Ethel Kotsovos, and others, attend Bishop Iakovos' annual Christmas Party at the Greek Orthodox Diocese, 40 E. Burton St.

2000

January 2: Tenth anniversary of the opening of Northwest Chicago Senior Care Center.

January 19: ADC clients go to Misto's, 1118 W. Grand Ave., which graciously provides lunch to the participants in celebration of NCSC's tenth anniversary. The restaurant is owned by a family member of an ADC participant.

February 1: Dinner meeting with Dr. Theodosis Kioutas, Evangeline Mistaras, and John Psiharis to discuss both GACS and GANHC. Hilltop Restaurant.

March 22–June 28: GACS Fabric Arts of Greece class is held weekly on Wednesdays at noon at GACS.

March 24: GACS representatives including John Psiharis, John Rassogianis, Dr. Theodosis Kioutas, and Toni Panos attend the Consul General of Greece's Greek Independence Day Reception at the Chicago Cultural Center.

May 15: GACS Board meeting at the center.

June 28: GACS Fabric Arts Project participants display their work at the Copernicus Senior Center, 3160 N. Milwaukee Ave., Chicago, IL

June 29: GACS Board meeting at the center.

August 9: ADC clients go on a field trip to the Chicago Botanical Gardens.

September 13-December 20: GACS Fabric Arts of Greece Fall Session begins at the center. The program is in its fourteenth year.

September 22: ADC Open House.

September 27: ADC staff in-service training meeting.

10th Anniversary
Greek - American Community Services

Reflections of a Decade 1990 - 2000

Yes, I wish to support the efforts of Greek-American Community Services by making a contribution in commemoration of the tenth anniversary of Northwest Chicago Senior Care in the amount of $_____.

In honor/memory of _____

Name _____

Address _____

City _____ State _____ Zip Code _____

Telephone ( ) _____

Please make checks payable to: Greek-American Community Services
3940 N. Pulaski Road, Chicago, Illinois 60641 (773) 545-0303
Contributions are tax deductible to the extent allowed by the law.

Reflections of a Decade
1990 - 2000

"I remember our first participant, Mary. She walked through our doors in January of 1990. She was a retired Greek school teacher and took special interest in teaching our staff and volunteers Greek during her visits"
John Psiharis
Executive Director

"I wish to be as witty, energetic and talkative as the senior citizens I met at the Greek-American Senior adult day care center. She is 87 years old and can tell you all the news up to date. She knows all the latest medical findings. She knows and is legally blind"
Lorraine Lisowski, R.N.
Staff Nurse

"I love to play Bingo! When I come to GACS everyday, the first thing I do is wait for my meals, tell all the ladies "I love you" and get to my bingo seat before everyone else takes a place at the table. I am lucky and always win when I play"
Tony, Age 94

"Many people want more activities. This is the best place for them and they get a lot of attention too"
Carmen Vilato
Activity Aide

"When I first saw these participants, I knew immediately that they needed assistance. I was hired for this purpose and someday I may be in the same position they are in now"
Ray Mananingh
Van & Center Aide

"Our eldest client is 96 years old. I love taking care of her because many years ago her daughter took care of my son and now I am taking care of her mother".
Eleanor Huber, R.N.
Staff Nurse

"I've been a volunteer for 3 years and I will never forget Efthimios, a 94 year old Greek man whom looked forward to teaching me Greek every week since I'm not Greek. I learned a lot from him. To this day I am amazed at how alert, friendly and caring he was".
Ricardo Rodriguez
Volunteer

"Since I first applied for the position of Activity Director, I never dreamed I would be with the center for its tenth anniversary. However, the years went by and I can truly say that this has been the most satisfying and rewarding job I have ever had. The staff have been extremely caring and compassionate throughout the years. I have been truly blessed to be able to bring joy and happiness to each of the clients who have passed through our doors. Happy Tenth Anniversary!"
Ann Prusinski
Activity Director

"From day one, the one particular client that I have fond memories from is Casey. As soon as I drove up the driveway to come to work, through the front door, Casey would keep an eye out for my arrival. As soon as I walked up to the door, he would open it for me, kiss my hand and just started talking away. Somehow I think he had a crush on me because of the special attention I received from him. He always complimented me on how nice I looked, "what a nice outfit your wearing today" he'd say. On holidays and my birthday, I would receive a special card from Casey in the mail, wishing me the best. He was always such a gentlemen. He has been missed"
Maria Toledo
Secretary

ADC Tenth Anniversary fundraising appeal flyer (two-sided). Decemeber 2000. John Psiharis collection.

October 15: GACS Open House. The community and service providers attend an open house showcasing Northwest Chicago Senior Care Center. Refreshments are served, tours are provided, and a performance by the ADC Kitchen Band is highlighted.

October 19: GACS Board meeting at the center.

December 4: GACS Fabric Arts of Greece participants display their handmade crocheting, knitting, and embroidery items at the Chicago Department on Aging Northeast (Levy) Senior Center, 2019 W. Lawrence Ave., Chicago, IL.

December 20: GACS Christmas Party at the center.

December 28: Through the efforts of GACS Board member Ricardo Rodriguez, GACS enters the 21st century with a website. The domain seniordaycareservices.com is launched. The email address is adultdaycarecenter@aol.com. GACS was among the first adult day care centers in the area to have an Internet presence. The site includes monthly activity calendars, newsletters, and menus as well as a photo gallery.

2001

March 21–June 27: GACS Fabric Arts of Greece classes are held at the center. It is the fifteenth year of classes.

April 27: GACS executive director John Psiharis, in a memo to ADC families, appeals for help in obtaining rate increases for ADC services from the Illinois Department on Aging.

June: GACS ADC staff undergo annual CPR certification training at the center.

July 15: GACS Fabric Arts of Greece class participants display their work and participate in a panel discussion at the Hellenic Museum and Cultural Center, 168 N. Michigan Ave., Chicago, IL, in conjunction with the HMCC's exhibit "Threads of Life: The Greek Woman's Labors of Love." Transportation between GACS and the museum is provided by the *Ya'Sou* vans.

September 12-December 19: Fabric Arts of Greece program begins the fall series of classes at the center. As in past years, the class for Chicago residents over age 60 is offered free of charge with supplies provided. It is the fifteenth year of the class.

> Celebrate
>
> National Adult Day Care Services Week
>
> Open House
>
> At
>
> **Northwest Chicago Senior Care Center**
> 3940 N. Pulaski Road
> Chicago, Illinois 60641
> (773) 545-0303
>
> Wednesday September 19, 2001
>
> 1:00 pm till 4:00 pm
>
> **Complimentary refreshments will be served. Enjoy!**
>
> **Free Blood Pressure Screening**
>
> Our center has proudly been serving older adults and their caregivers since January 1990!
>
> Adult day care programs offer supervised day time care in a structured environment to older adults, providing peace of mind to those caring for an elderly loved one, often at no cost to the participant. Health care, socialization, activities, meals, physical therapy and transportation to and from the center are all available.
>
> For further information or to arrange a private visit or tour please call (773) 545-0303 or visit our website at www.seniordaycareservices.com
>
> **Northwest Chicago Senior Care is a program of Greek-American Community Services.**
>
> GACS does not discriminate in admission to program or treatment of employment in programs or activities in compliance with the Illinois Human Rights Act; the U.S. Civil Rights Act; Section 504 of the Rehabilitation Act; the Age Discrimination Act; the Age Discrimination and Employment Act; and the U.S. and Illinois Constitutions.
>
> If you feel that you have been discriminated against, you have a right to file a complaint with GACS and the Illinois Department on Aging. For more information call 1-800-252-8966 (voice and TDD).

ADC Open House flyer, September 19, 2001. Elaine Thomopoulos collection.

September 19: Northwest Chicago Senior Care Center Open House from 1:00 p.m. to 4:00 p.m. in celebration of National Adult Day Care Services Week. Complimentary refreshments are served and free blood pressure screening is offered.

November 1: John Psiharis resigns as executive director of GACS and Danae Voutiritsas assumes the position.

November 17: GACS hosts participants of an "Ethnic Chicago" tour organized by the Chicago Historical Society. Guests visit the GACS center

A GREEK-AMERICAN COMMUNITY SERVICES FABRIC ARTS OF GREECE CLASS

For coming events column:

From December 3 to December 7, participants of Greek-American Community Services' Fabric Arts of Greece Class will display their art at the James R. Thompson Center, 100 S. Randolph, Chicago. Participants learn or perfect skills in crocheting, knitting, needlepoint or embroidery in classes held on Wednesdays from 11:30 A.M. to 2:00 P.M. at Greek-American Community Services, 3940 N. Pulaski Road, Chicago. The free classes are open to City of Chicago residents over the age of 60. The Chicago Department of Cultural Affairs, Community Development Block Grant Program, and the Illinois Arts Council, a state agency, make the classes possible. For further information call 773 545-0303.

The *Greek Press*, November 18, 2001. Elaine Thomopoulos collection.

and learn about Chicago's Greek community and the programs and services GACS offers.

December 3–7: GACS Fabric Arts of Greece Class participants display examples of their crocheting, needlepoint, and embroidery in an exhibit at the James R. Thompson Center, 100 S. Randolph, Chicago, IL.

December 4: GACS Fabric Arts of Greece participants display a selection of their creations at the Levy Northeast Senior Citizens Center.

December 19: GACS Christmas party at GACS.

2002

January 14: GACS Board of Directors meeting at the center.

March 19: GACS Board of Directors meeting in the Midwest Bank and Trust Board Room.

March 20–June 26: Fabric Arts of Greece program spring series of classes at Copernicus Center, 3160 N. Milwaukee Ave., Chicago, IL.

March 20: ADC Open House at the center.

April 15: GACS Board of Directors meeting at the center.

May 18: GACS Board of Directors meeting at the center.

June 15: Last day of adult day care services. The ADC closes after 12 years.

June 30: GACS moves out of the Pulaski building.

July 9: GACS Board of Directors meeting in the Midwest Bank and Trust Board Room.

August 12: GACS Board of Directors meeting at Little Mike's Restaurant, 3939 W. Irving Park Rd., Chicago, IL.

August 28: GACS Board of Directors meeting at Little Mike's Restaurant, 3939 W. Irving Park Rd., Chicago, IL.

October 16–December 18: GACS Fabric Arts Program fall series of classes at the Copernicus Center, 3160 N. Milwaukee Ave., Chicago, IL.

November 16: GACS reunion luncheon at Burgundy Restaurant. Among those attending are Frieda Aravosis, Evelyn Boutzarelos, Phyllis Caine, Ray Mansingh, Ann Prusinski, John Psiharis, John Rassogianis, Eugenia Stathakis, and Maria Toledo.

Part 4
The Coalition of Limited English Speaking Elderly

CLESE

An undated rationale and purpose statement developed early on explained the vision for CLESE:

Rationale:

Many ethnic agencies do work that only community-based agencies with specific language skills and cultural backgrounds can do, helping limited and non-English speaking persons on a one-to-one basis in the neighborhoods where they live. They provide vital personal services not available from other sources.

Generally, bi-lingual staff members are spread thin acting as interpreters and escorts and there's insufficient time to develop the economic and political base necessary to ensure their future operation.

Even though their nationalities differ, the constituencies of the individual agencies share the same problems: illiteracy, depression, joblessness, dependence on interpreters, poor housing conditions, and racial or ethnic discrimination.

Advocacy programs and technical assistance can be provided through a coalition of ethnic agencies while enabling the community agencies to gain some of the advantages of size without losing the small, ethnic community identity that makes them so effective in meeting the needs of their limited-and non-English speaking neighbors.

CLESE

Coalition of Limited English Speaking Elderly

FOUNDING BOARD MEMBERS

Carole Bilina
Polish Welfare Association

Awilda Gonzalez
ASI

Tae Sue Kang
Korean American Senior Center

Peter R. Laylo
Asian Human Services of Chicago, Inc.

Judith Matthews
National Association of Hispanic Elderly

Rev. Masaru Nambu
Japanese American Service Committee

Peter Porr
South East Asia Center

John Psiharis
Greek American Community Services

Dangoule Valentinas
Lithuanian Human Services Council

Qua Tran Van
Vietnamese Association of Illinois

o 0 o

Your gift of office equipment, furniture, supplies or financial support is tax-deductible, and will assist CLESE in fulfilling its mission to serve Chicagoland's immigrant, refugee and migrant elderly population.

4750 N. Sheridan Rd., Suite 200
Chicago, Illinois 60640
Tel. (312) 878-7272
989-6927

CLESE MEMBERSHIP APPLICATION

Annual Membership Fees (tax deductible)

☐ Agency Member $50.00
☐ Individual Member $25.00

Name _____

Agency Name (for agency membership) _____

Position Title (for agency membership) _____

Street Address _____
City _____ State _____ Zip _____ Tel. _____

Please make check payable and return application to: Coalition of Limited English Speaking Elderly, 4750 N. Sheridan Road, #525, Chicago, Illinois 60640

Our and send lower portion for membership

C L E S E
Coalition of Limited English-Speaking Elderly

THE MISSION

It is CLESE's purpose to promote, foster, develop, encourage and maintain charitable purposes by coordinating organizations which represent limited and non-English speaking older people to improve the lives of the elderly in the Greater Metropolitan Chicago area through:

* increasing the awareness and understanding of the needs of minority older people and organizations that serve them;

* organizing joint projects to examine and solve service problems related to limited and non-English speaking elderly; and

* reviewing and helping improve and ensure equitable service delivery and public policies affecting limited and non-English speaking older people and their families.

o 0 o

WHO SHOULD JOIN CLESE?

CLESE is for you if you

- are committed to serving limited and non-English speaking older people.

- Need timely information about grant opportunities, special programs for limited and non-English speaking elderly and legislation affecting ethnic minorities.

- Seek to add your voice in educating decision-makers about the needs of ethnic minority elderly people.

- Want to learn more about the needs of ethnic minority elderly.

- Seek to share information with other agencies like your own or are an individual who is concerned with issues and programs that affect the elderly people.

CLESE is a non-profit, tax-exempt organization, incorporated in 1989 by representatives of ten (10) non-profit agencies serving limited and non-English speaking elderly in the Chicago area.

Many ethnic agencies perform work that only community-based agencies with specific language skills and cultural backgrounds can do, helping limited and non-English speaking persons on a one-to-one basis in the neighborhoods where they live. They provide vital personal services not available from other sources.

Generally, bi-lingual staff members are spread so thin acting as interpreters and escorts that there is insufficient time to develop the economic and political base necessary to ensure future operations.

Even though their nationalities differ, the constituencies of the individual agencies share the same problems: illiteracy, depression, joblessness, dependence on interpreters, poor housing conditions, and racial or ethnic discrimination.

Through CLESE, advocacy programs and technical assistance can help improve and ensure equitable service delivery and public policy for the ethnic elderly, thus enabling the community agencies to gain the advantages of size of the larger agencies without losing the small, ethnic community identity that makes them so effective in meeting the needs of their limited and non-English speaking constituencies.

First CLESE brochure. Date unknown. Elaine Thomopoulos collection.

Purpose:

1. Work cooperatively with other ethnic agencies to improve the lives of limited-and non-English speaking elderly.
2. Organize joint projects to examine and solve service problems related to limited-and-non-English speaking elderly.
3. Increase the awareness and understanding of the needs of limited-and non-English speaking elderly and the organizations that serve them.
4. Promote opportunities for equitable receipt of services, including in-home services and mental health services, by limited-and non-English speaking elderly.
5. Promote opportunities for enhancing literacy among limited- and non-English speaking elderly.
6. Provide assistance in interpreting and disseminating results of the Ethnic Elderly Needs Assessment.
7. Serve member agencies and provide opportunities for them to share information, experiences, and resources for their mutual benefit.
8. Provide technical assistance to help new agencies to form and established agencies to grow.
9. Advocate to City, State, and Federal governments on behalf of the member agencies.
10. Promote health screening and referral to medical practitioners.
11. Assist member agencies to help themselves by arranging for empowerment sessions.

Once the Coalition of Limited English Speaking Elderly (CLESE) was incorporated, Rosemary Gemperle left her position at the newly renamed Chicago Department on Aging to become the organization's executive director. At first, she volunteered her time until funding made it possible to pay her a salary. Rosemary's background with CDOA was very helpful in working with various levels of governmental bureaucracies and funders that impacted the work of CLESE and its member agencies.

CLESE initially had a desk and mailing address at the Korean American Senior Center on Sheridan Road near Lawrence. When Rosemary began working in the office, we sub-leased space at the Metropolitan Chicago Council on Aging office at 111 W. Jackson Blvd. Several years later, CLESE relocated a block east to its current offices at 53 W. Jackson Blvd.

CLESE board presidents (in order) during the years covered in this book were: Danguale Valentinas (Lithuanian Human Services Council of the USA); Sue Kang (Korean American Senior Center); John Psiharis (Greek-American Community Services) (two terms); Isaac Toma (Assyrian National Council of Illinois); Awilda Gonzalez (ASI); and Santosh Kumar (Metropolitan Asian Family Services).

In time, the membership ranks grew to include ethnicities and organizations that were not part of the original group. By the second year according to the CLESE website, (accessed in September 2018), membership grew to 20 organizations, and by 2016 CLESE had 51 member organizations.

The CLESE membership roster during the time of my involvement included: Americans by Values (Russian immigrant community), Sabina Pello); ASI (Rebecca Cruz and Awilda Gonzalez); Asian Human Services (Peter Laylo then Abba Pandya); Assyrian National Council of Illinois (Isaac Toma); Assyrian Universal Alliance Foundation (Malcom Karam, John Nimrod and Jeanne Elgarawany); Bosnian & Herzegovinian American Community Center (Zumra Kunosic); Cambodian Association of Illinois (Kompha Seth); Casa Central (Daniel Alvarez); Chinese American Service League (Bernarda Wong and Suey-Lee Chang); Chinese Mutual Aid Association (Yman Vien, Grace Hou, Denise Lamm); Ethiopian Community Association of Chicago (Erku Yimmer); European American Association (John Herman); Greek-American Community Services (John Psiharis); Greek-American Nursing Home Committee (John Rassogianis); Hellenic Foundation (Angelike Mountanis); Japanese American Service Committee (Rev. Masaru Nambu, Jean Fujiu, and Helen Nakayama); Korean American Community Services (Sue Kang and Inchul Choi); Korean American Senior Center (now known as Hanul Family Alliance), (Sue Kang. Elizabeth Cagan, Paul Yun); Metropolitan Asian Family Services (Indian and Pakistani communities), (Santosh Kumar); National Association for Hispanic

Cover of an early CLESE brochure. Date unknown. Elaine Thomopoulos collection.

Elderly (Judith Matthews); Polish Welfare Association (Polish American Association) (Karen Popowski, Carole Bilina, Bruce Dean); Romanian American Community Center (Lilly Olaru); Southeast Asia Center (Peter Porr and San O); Vietnamese Association of Illinois (Qua Van Tran); White Crane Wellness Center (Rob Skeist and Elizabeth Cagan), and World Relief-DuPage County (Liliana Popovic).

A January 1990 listing of CLESE committees included: Membership Committee (San O., chair, Peter Laylo, Awilda Gonzalez, Qua Tran, and Kompha Seth). Search Committee (John Psiharis, chair, Carole Bilina, and Bruce Dean). Site Committee (Danguole Valentinas, chair, and Masaru Nambu) Fundraising Committee (Sue Kang, chair, Judith Matthews, Sueylee Chang, Elizabeth Cagan, Peter Porr).

A program booklet prepared for the "Around the World with CLESE" event held on May 23, 1995, included CLESE's mission statement:

> GOAL: To improve the lives of limited English-speaking elderly by providing leadership, education, and advocacy.
>
> OUR PURPOSE: To bring together organizations and individuals sharing common values and concerns regarding the rights and needs of limited English-speaking older people.
>
> To develop a shared perception that their common concerns are bigger than any single ethnic group or organization and must be addressed on a broader scale through collective efforts.
>
> To encourage member organizations and others to develop and implement advocacy strategies impacting the lives of the language and minority population by:
>
> - Increasing awareness of the needs of limited English-speaking elderly and the organizations that serve them;
> - Examining and solving service delivery problems related to language minority elderly;
> - Reviewing existing public policies and programs affecting the language minority elderly population;
> - Providing technical assistance and informational materials to assure equitable access to supportive services for the elderly.

One way CLESE advocated for the communities we collectively served was our participation in the Illinois White House Conference on Aging, a state conference whose final commendations would flow into the White House Conference on Aging. The national conference, held once every 10

Some of the CLESE delegation to the 1990 Illinois White House Conference on Aging. Pictured (L-R): First row: Yoji Ozaki, unknown, unknown, unknown, unknown, Rebecca Cruz. Second row: Amydelle Shah, Sue Kang, San O, unknown, unknown, unknown, unknown, unknown. Third row: IDOA Director Victor Wirth, unknown, unknown, and John Psiharis. October 1990. John Psiharis collection.

years, influenced U.S. government policies and priorities in matters concerning older adults. CLESE held a community hearing about the needs of ethnic elderly to hear testimony that was then forwarded to the state conference for consideration. On October 2, 3, and 4, 1990, a number of us went to Springfield for the state conference. Rosemary Gemperle, San O, Sue Kang, Peter Porr, Carole Bilina, Kompha Seth, and I (and perhaps others) addressed various concerns impacting limited and non-English speaking elderly. Several CLESE recommendations were included in the final proceedings which were forwarded to the national conference.

A draft of CLESE's "Position Paper on Issues for the 1995 White House Conference on Aging" was faxed from GACS to Elaine on January 6, 1995. It seems there were more pages that we don't have. On the pages Elaine has, there are at least four issues of concern identified. They were: Employment and health care coverage, entitlement programs/benefits, equal access to health care and supportive services and organizations, and delivery and management of community-based long-term care services. For each issue, the paper presented facts, rationales, and recommendations.

CLESE grew into an effective and respected advocacy organization whose combined voices captured the attention of elected officials, policymakers,

CLESE Executive Committee with Illinois Department on Aging Director Victor Wirth. Pictured (L-R): Sue Kang (president), Victor Wirth, John Psiharis (vice president), Awilda Gonzales (treasurer), Peter Porr (secretary), and C. Jean Blaser (IDOA Community Care Program manager). Circa 1990. John Psiharis collection.

and funders that could make a difference in the lives of the thousands of ethnic seniors we collectively represented. Early CLESE successes with the city of Chicago included per diem funding when ethnic organizations were called upon to translate for case managers and reimbursements for translating brochures and other documents into additional languages.

CLESE had established ongoing funding relationships with the Illinois Department on Aging (IDOA), the Illinois Department of Public Health (IDPH), the Chicago Department on Aging (CDOA), and the Suburban Cook County Area Agency on Aging, most of which were pass-through dollars for member organizations who implemented programming within their communities.

CLESE received funding from the Retirement Research Foundation, Chicago Community Trust, Polk Brothers Foundation, and the Alphawood Foundation, among others, to launch programs, increase the capacity of the member agencies, advocate for common interests, and concerns, and provide technical assistance to member agencies.

IDOA funded the lion's share of programs that were identified in the ethnic elderly needs assessment (homemaker services, chore housekeeping, adult day care, and case management). These programs were funded through the Community Care Program. Jean Blaser, Ph.D., was the manager of the Community Care Program and became IDOA's liaison to CLESE.

In appreciation of the uniqueness of CLESE, and the fact that most of Chicago's ethnic organizations were members of the coalition, IDOA directors Janet Otwell, Victor Wirth, Maralee Lindley, and Charles Johnson came to realize the benefits of our coalition. IDOA could reach the majority of ethnic communities in Illinois through CLESE. IDOA regularly provided grants to CLESE to provide technical assistance and training to its membership primarily related to the CCP. This funding allowed CLESE to pay for Rosemary's time as executive director and eventually hire Beth O'Grady as program manager. Several grants for translating IDOA forms and brochures followed. A grant from the Illinois Secretary of State Literacy Program funded English-as-a-Second-Language (ESL) classes for ethnic seniors in three ethnic communities. It grew into a model program that was replicated in other parts of the country.

According to the September 1998 CLESE membership directory:

> CLESE's 37 member organizations represent 24 different countries or ethnic groups. It is the only coalition for the elderly in the U.S. that is so widely represented. Others have coalitions of Asian elderly or Hispanic elderly, but CLESE stands alone as being pan-ethnic. Its members span the alphabet from Arab to Vietnamese. Although CLESE's membership is open to organizations anywhere in Illinois, the reality is that most immigrants, refugees, and migrants are in Chicago and the metropolitan area; and all of CLESE's members are Chicago-based. The 'unofficial' definition of elderly is age 60 and over. (This is the age decreed by the U.S. Congress in allocating funds through the Older Americans Act). Through its member agencies, CLESE reaches an estimated 50,000 elderly.

The directory stated CLESE's goals and objectives:

> GOAL - to assure that older people who are not fluent in English have access to the same programs, services, and benefits as are available to English-speaking elderly.
>
> OBJECTIVES can be described in three categories: Advocacy, Services to the Elderly, and Leadership and Education.
>
> <u>Advocacy</u>

To increase awareness of the needs of the Limited-English-speaking elderly and the barriers preventing their access to services.

Coalition of Limited English Speaking Elderly, Inc.
53 West Jackson Blvd. · Suite 1632 · Chicago, Illinois 60604 · Tel. (312) 922-5890

April 25, 1991

BOARD OF DIRECTORS

CAROLE BILINA
POLISH COMMUNITY

SUE-YLEE CHANG
CHINESE AMERICAN
SERVICE LEAGUE

AWILDA GONZALEZ
ASI

TAE SUP KANG
KOREAN AMERICAN
SENIOR CENTER

PETER LAYLO
ASIAN HUMAN SERVICES

JUDITH MATTHEWS
NATIONAL ASSOCIATION
OF HISPANIC ELDERLY

MASARU NAMBU
JAPANESE AMERICAN
SERVICE COMMITTEE

PETER ROHR
SOUTH—EAST ASIA CENTER

JOHN PSIHARIS
GREEK AMERICAN
COMMUNITY CENTER

KOMPHA SETH
CAMBODIAN ASSOCIATION
OF ILLINOIS

DANGUOLE VALENTINAS
LITHUANIAN COMMUNITY

QUE VAN TRAN
VIETNAMESE ASSOCIATION
OF ILLINOIS

TO: John Psiharis, Sue Kang, Awilda Gonzalez and Yoji Ozaki, Judy Matthews

From: Rosemary Gemperle

SUBJ: CLESE Annual Meeting - May 8, 1991 - 5:00 p.m.
(Ann Sather's Restaurant, 5207 N. Clark)

Following are the plans for the Annual Meeting.

Registration Desk - Elizabeth Cagan. Each attendee will receive a name badge and pocket folder of material.
Cash Bar - 5:00 - 6:00: Dinner at 6:00. Begin program after entree has been served.

John: 1) Ask founding Board members to stand and introduce themselves (name and agency).
       2) Introduce guests. (Rosemary will make list)
       3) Give brief history of CLESE.
       4) Introduce Rosemary

Rosemary: Recap first year

John: Introduce Awilda to give Treasurer's Report

Awilda: Present Treasurer's Report. All CLESE members will have a copy in their folder.

John: Introduce Yoji as representative of the Nominating Committee to announce new officers.

Yoji: 1) Introduce new officers. (Rosemary will write a paragraph on each one.)
       2) Call John forward (as outgoing president) to present gavel to Sue (incoming president).
       3) Ask Sue to say a few words.

Sue: Talk about CLESE plans for the next year and her "dreams" for CLESE - (for instance, possibility of becoming a national organization). Invite members attendance at Board members and participation on Committees. Ask them to use the yellow index cards in their folders to write their suggestions for CLESE. Thank all for coming.

A memo sent to CLESE executive committee members from Rosemary Gemperle outlining the agenda for the 1991 annual meeting. April 25, 1991. The letterhead lists the CLESE board of directors at the time. John Psiharis collection.

To make public presentations, conduct workshops, write articles and letters, present public testimony, and speak out in private meetings and at every opportunity to promote the needs of the Limited-English-speaking elderly.

To ease the process for the elderly to obtain citizenship.

To assure that legal immigrant elderly can participate in federally-funded programs.

<u>Services to the Elderly</u>

To promote the need for culturally appropriate services.

To promote the need for linguistically accessible services.

To provide technical assistance to help community-based ethnic organizations understand programs for the elderly, obtain contracts, and administer the programs.

To coordinate action to remove barriers to appropriate and accessible benefits, programs, and services.

Leadership and Education

To coordinate outreach and screening projects to link elderly immigrants, refugees, and migrants with needed benefits and services.

To identify and respond to the ongoing needs of Limited-English speaking elderly and the community-based ethnic organizations that serve them.

To reach out to newly arrived ethnic groups, and those not yet organized to provide services to the elderly.

To inform mainstream providers of the needs and cultural nuances of the populations they serve.

Due in large part to the effective advocacy of CLESE and its member agencies in documenting how underserved ethnic elderly were by IDOA programs, the Department agreed to issue "Emergency RFPs" (Requests for Proposals) for ethnic organizations. Agencies could apply to offer homemaker, chore housekeeping, or adult day care services to ethnic communities. This was a separate category from their main contracts which were provided to larger mainstream organizations, e.g., Catholic Charities, Lutheran Social Services of Illinois, and United Charities (now Metropolitan Family Services). This change was a major achievement that would greatly benefit ethnic organizations and those they helped. For the first time in the state's history, these vital support services were targeted to limited English-speaking elderly, and special efforts were made to encourage ethnic organizations to apply. CLESE held several workshops for ethnic providers who were interested in applying.

Chicago's Ethnic Communities Come of Age

In large measure, through the efforts of CLESE, the Illinois Department on Aging began to comprehend that many older adults were underserved due to their inability to speak English and a preference for providers who speak their language and share their culture and concerns. The results of

CLESE Board members attend a CCP ethnic providers' presentation with Illinois Governor Jim Edgar and Illinois Department on Aging Director Maralee Lindley in the Governor's Office at the James R. Thompson Center State of Illinois Building. Pictured (L-R): Jeanne Elgarawany, Santosh Kumar, John Psiharis, Sue Kang, Rosemary Gemperle, Gov. Edgar, Awilda Gonzalez, Maralee Lindley, Suey-Lee Chang, unknown, Cynthia Yannias, and Michael Chioros. Date unknown. John Psiharis collection.

the Ethnic Elderly Needs Assessment substantiated this claim and CLESE was uniquely able to lead in this process.

IDOA Director Victor Wirth issued a request for proposals (RFP) for organizations to provide homemaker, chore housekeeping, and adult day care services targeted to limited and non-English speaking elderly. Although focused on serving ethnic elderly, providers could assist anyone in need regardless of their ethnic, racial, religious, or cultural backgrounds.

IDOA provided CLESE with a grant to provide technical assistance to members who were submitting RFPs and subsequent training to those who received contracts. CLESE hired Elizabeth "Beth" O'Grady to provide consultations and arrange the training. Beth was assistant director for several years. Upon Rosemary's retirement, Beth succeeded her as executive director of CLESE and remained in that position until her retirement. Taiqin Dong and Eve Mayer subsequently served as CLESE program managers. Before that, Eve oversaw the Japanese American Service Committee's adult day care program and was familiar with the CCP process.

GACS received a contract for adult day care (for the northwest side of Chicago) in 1989 and was approved for a chore housekeeping contract from IDOA in 1993 to provide chore housekeeping assistance to Greek elderly who lived on the north side of the city.

In addition to GACS, many CLESE member agencies received contracts in that funding cycle. In some cases, existing contracts that a provider had were extended. Agencies included: ASI, Asian Human Services, Assyrian National Council of Illinois, Assyrian Universal Alliance Foundation, Cambodian Association of Illinois, Casa Central, Chinese American Service League, Chinese Mutual Aid, Hellenic Foundation, Japanese American Service Committee, Korean American Senior Center, Metropolitan Asian Family Services, Polish Welfare Association, Southeast Asia Center, and the Vietnamese Association of Illinois.

The presentation of the award letters was done during the CLESE annual membership dinner. IDOA Director Maralee Lindley and Jean Blaser presented the letters to the awardees. At a later date, Pat Michalski, Special Assistant to the Governor for Ethnic Affairs arranged for a photo opportunity with Governor Jim Edgar and leaders of the recipient organizations.

This was a monumental achievement for the ethnic elderly that CLESE helped bring about. IDOA had finally grown to understand that ethnic elderly were best served by providers within their communities. Older adults would now be serviced by homemakers that speak their language, and attend adult day care programs that reflected their cultural heritage. CLESE, and in particular, Rosemary, was instrumental in bringing this about.

In future years, other ethnic communities received contracts through this ethnic provision including European American Association (Romanian community); Hamdard Center (Bosnians); Indo American Center (Indian and Pakistani communities); Lao American Community Center; Urhai Community Service Center (Assyrians); and the White Crane Wellness Center (Asians).

Each time IDOA issued renewals or new contracts in the Chicago area, CLESE was called upon to provide training and technical assistance to providers. This was accomplished through workshops arranged by CLESE and facilitated by member agencies who were CCP providers. ASI and the Chinese American Service League were often called upon to train homemaker agencies while GACS and the Japanese American Service Committee were the adult day care trainers. One-to-one technical assistance was provided as needed to member agencies. CLESE received funding from IDOA and subcontracted with the organizations providing the training to cover their costs.

CLESE Board meeting at GACS. Pictured (L-R): Seated; Zumra Kunosic, Rosemary Gemperle, Awilda Gonzalez, and Sue Lee Chang. Standing (L-R): Sue Kang, Elizabeth Cagan, John Rassogianis, Lucy Le-Kissane, Peter Porr, unknown, unknown, Peter Laylo, Isaac Toma, Bruce Dean, Taiqin Dong, John Psiharis, unknown, Qua Tran. Date unknown. John Psiharis collection.

Another joint effort that transcended the differences between ethnic communities was the need to obtain the most accurate count possible in the US Census. In 1990, census outreach campaigns were commonplace within many of Chicago's ethnic communities. CLESE initiated efforts to increase participation by non-English speaking older adults through its efforts and by supporting initiatives undertaken by member organizations.

Chicago's ethnic communities understood that U.S. Census data severely underreported their populations, and organizations were determined to encourage their communities to participate in the count since funding decisions for a myriad of programs are made by governments at all levels based on census data.

Several community workshops were held to orient and train organizations about the census. Outreach activities to generate awareness and encourage participation were held by many ethnic groups. GACS trained volunteers to conduct outreach, translated materials, publicized the census within the Greek media, and recruited members of the community who could serve as enumerators.

CLESE Transcends Barriers

CLESE was recognized as a model organization at the local, state, and national levels. No other city had an organization like ours, and some wanted to emulate CLESE in other cities. The uniqueness and the unity of purpose amongst organizations representing diverse cultures and languages emanating from all parts of the world were key to our success.

Despite our cultural differences, we worked well together in the spirit of mutual respect, friendship, and collaboration. I considered my involvement with CLESE to be among my high points during this period. The communities we collectively represented were in different stages of evolution ranging from newly arrived immigrants and refugees to those who may have been here for decades or more. We shared ideas, strategies, and information either collectively or one-on-one. We provided training, support, and technical assistance to each other for the common benefit of the elderly. At other times we collaborated on programs, outreach activities, and advocacy efforts. If a member agency was in need, we collectively did whatever we could to help.

CLESE received consistent funding from the Illinois Department on Aging through several grant programs. One grant helped underwrite the executive director position by funding CLESE to offer training and technical assistance to member agencies in need of help with CCP or other IDOA-funded programs.

CLESE was also supported by the city and state health departments, and the Illinois Secretary of State's Literacy Office. Programs that were made possible through these funding streams include outreach, health education and screenings, elder abuse and neglect, Alzheimer's disease demonstration programs, citizenship classes, and refugee programs. CLESE created a model English as a Second Language (ESL) program focused on non-English speaking elderly and was lauded for its success with this. The curriculum was focused on real-life needs and interactions alongside a civics component that helped seniors prepare for a citizenship test if they intended to apply for citizenship.

The CLESE model since inception was to enable and support member agencies to provide services, and not for CLESE to become a service provider itself. Usually, CLESE received a grant which was then subcontracted to the organization(s) participating in that program. CLESE coordinated and monitored the programs, disbursed and accounted for the funds, and reported back to the appropriate funding sources. Beth O'Grady as program manager and later as the assistant director did most of the technical assistance and training. Eventually, Taiqin Dong joined CLESE

Top: The passing of the ceremonial gavel from outgoing president John Psiharis to incoming president Sue Kang. New officers were: Pictured: (L-R): Suey-Lee Chang (secretary), Awilda Gonzalez (treasurer), and Bruce Dean (vice president). May 8, 1991. This was the first term I served as president. Date unknown. John Psiharis collection. **Bottom:** Outgoing president Issac Toma passes the ceremonial gavel to incoming president John Psiharis. This was for my second term as president. Circa 1996. John Psiharis collection.

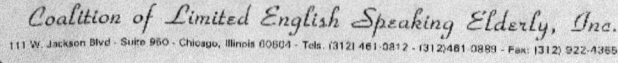

A memo to CLESE members seeking nominations to the Board of Directors. July 24, 1997. The letterhead lists the CLESE Board of Directors at the time. John Psiharis collection.

as a program manager for health programs. Beth was a great person to work with. She was positive, empathetic, and professional and had a great sense of humor. She succeeded Rosemary as executive director upon her retirement. Taiqin was always a pleasure to work with.

In addition to being a founder, I served as president of CLESE on two occasions. The first was when Danguale resigned as president, and as vice president, I stepped in. This was shortly after we came into our own as an organization. After this term, I was asked by the nominating committee to be vice president for another term. Sue Kang was elected president and we made a great team. The CLESE bylaws specified that the vice president was also the president-elect. When I assumed the president's post, Isaac Toma became vice president. Isaac was the president of the Assyrian National Council of Illinois and owner of Ashur's Sports Lounge in Andersonville. Awilda Gonzalez, program director of ASI, became treasurer, and San O, secretary. San was co-founder and program director of the Southeast Asia Center. After Isaac, Awilda became president, followed by Santosh Kumar, executive director of Metropolitan Asian Family Services. CLESE officers served two-year terms.

The ceremonial gavel was passed during the annual membership dinner meeting attended by representatives of CLESE's member agencies, IDOA and CDOA leaders, funders, and friends. The meetings included programmatic and financial reports and presentations of awards to supporters. Each year, the event was held in a different ethnic community restaurant. I recall annual meetings that were in Chinese, Greek, Bosnian, Korean, Swedish, Assyrian, Italian, Polish, and Puerto Rican restaurants. During my terms as president, we had lunch "meetings after the meetings" at a restaurant, usually of the same ethnicity as the member agency that hosted the monthly board meeting. The annual December meeting featured a potluck luncheon following the board meeting. In response to requests, I usually brought baklava and diples as the Greek contribution to the lunch.

Special guests attending the CLESE Annual Meeting, held on May 8, 1991, at Ann Sather's Restaurant, 5207 N. Clark, illustrated the broad relationships the coalition had built and cultivated across a spectrum of federal, state, and local agencies and private funders. As president, I welcomed the guests to the meeting that evening and Rosemary prepared the list of those attending for me to use in the introductions. They were: Eli Lipschultz, regional program director of the Administration on Aging; Pat Michalski, special assistant to Governor Jim Edgar for ethnic affairs; Suzanne Grubb, Nancy Lowder, and Mary Hill (Illinois Department on Aging staff working on the CLESE Home Care Project); Jan Logan, director of planning for the Chicago Department on Aging; Michael Marcus, Community Trust senior staff associate focused on elderly; Marilyn Hennessey, president of the Retirement Research Foundation; and Ron Elling, executive director of the Metropolitan Chicago Coalition on Aging. Next to Ron's name, Rosemary wrote, "Special thanks to Ron for opening his office to us. I don't know where we would have been without him." At the time, MCCOA was providing CLESE with office space within its 53 W. Jackson office.

From the largest of agencies to the smallest of groups, when there were matters of common concern, CLESE members spoke with a unified voice on the matter at hand. CLESE lobbied for increased reimbursement rates for homemakers and adult day care services, funding for translating provided by organizations called upon for help when case managers encountered non-English speaking elderly, and ethnic-specific CCP contracts.

CLESE Board members invite Governor Jim Edgar to the 1996 "Around the World with CLESE" event. Pictured (L-R): Sylvia Salapatas-Poulikakos, Lucy Le-Kissane, Angelike Mountanis, Qua Tran, Santosh Kumar, Awilda Gonzalez, Isaac Toma, Governor Jim Edgar, Rosemary Gemperle, John Psiharis, unknown, Sue Kang, San O, Beth O'Grady, Yoji Ozaki, Alejandro Guerrero. Circa 1996. "Around the World with CLESE" program booklet. John Psiharis collection.

A common concern of many CLESE member agencies was the large number of rejects in invoicing that CCP providers were experiencing. This created financial hardships for organizations due to delays involved in clearing each rejection. CLESE helped agencies to troubleshoot and resubmit invoices to IDOA for payment. One example of that was a meeting CLESE arranged with IDOA at the State of Illinois Building to address rejects. In addition to an IDOA presentation, providers brought their rejects to the meeting to get them processed onsite.

CLESE and its member agencies were presenters at many conferences including the National Council on Aging, the American Society on Aging, and others. Rosemary served as a member of the Illinois Council on Aging and as a member of several boards, committees, or ad-hoc groups. I recall attending or presenting at several conferences with CLESE colleagues including a National Conference on Aging conference at Disneyland in Anaheim, California, and American Society on Aging conferences in Washington DC, Chicago, and Rosemont, IL among others.

CLESE was involved in activities related to several White House Conferences on Aging including hosting a mini-conference at the Chinese American Service League that was attended by the director of the U.S. Administration on Aging.

A CLESE Board meeting at Chinese American Service League with Maralee Lindley, director of the Illinois Department on Aging, in attendance. Pictured (L-R): First row: Unknown, John Nimrod, Rosemary Gemperle, Sue Kang, Yoji Ozaki. Second row: Suey-Lee Chang, unknown, unknown, Isaac Toma, Qua Tran, unknown, Bruce Dean, Maralee Lindley, Lucy Le-Kissane, John Psiharis, Bernarda Wong, Peter Laylo, Rev. Masaru Nambu, Sylvia Salapatas, Karen Popowski, Rebecca Cruz, Awilda Gonzalez, unknown, and Judith Matthews. Date unknown. John Psiharis collection.

For a few years, CLESE hosted an annual gathering in June called "Around the World with CLESE." Although a fundraiser, it was also a cultural and social event for older adults served by member organizations. The events featured traditional ethnic food and entertainment provided by member organizations. To represent the Greek community, GACS arranged for food donations from Hellas Bakery, Greek Islands, Greek Taverna, Pegasus, and Rodity's restaurants which included pastichio, moussaka, dolmades, diples, and baklava. Beyond the "Around the World with CLESE" events, CLESE did not engage in fundraising activities or solicitations to avoid being in competition with its member agencies for donations. Basic expenses were covered by membership dues and salaries and program costs were funded through grants.

On April 24, 2003, CLESE hosted "Vision 2005," an all-day retreat for CLESE member agencies held at the Chicago Yacht Club. Facilitated by Jean Blaser who by then had retired from IDOA, the retreat provided great views and food, and an opportunity for CLESE members to mingle. The invitation asked: "Take a look into the future. What will life be like in 2005, for a 60-year, for a 70-year-old? 80? 90? What will the role of your agency be? What will be the role of CLESE? Join us in welcoming Spring as we gaze across the waters of Lake Michigan and build a vision for the future."

In the summer of 2003, in lockstep with adult day care providers, CLESE became a leading advocate for an increase in reimbursement rates for adult day services in Illinois. CLESE arranged north-side and south-side meetings with state legislators. I participated in a July 18 meeting with state representative Larry McKeon and a July 30 meeting with state senator Carol Ronan and state representative Harry Osterman. In August, CLESE arranged meetings for south side member agencies with then-state senator Barack Obama and Representative Barbara Flynn Currie, the Illinois House majority leader. Since I was then senior services director at the Hyde Park Neighborhood Club and knew these legislators, having worked with them on other matters, I arranged these meetings. U.S. Representative Jan Schakowsky, who represented the 9th congressional district, and of this writing still does, was also a supporter of CLESE and its member agencies and attended various meetings and events.

A talking points memo for these meetings prepared by CLESE ADC providers addressed the crisis in adult day care and the need for additional funding. The "Issue Points" listed:

- Overhead expenses are fixed: however, reimbursement varies according to daily attendance; the population served in ADS programs is very fragile, and their physical/mental/cognitive condition changes unpredictably, therefore daily census is also unpredictable.
- Nursing Expenses ($23-$25/per hour): Depletes a disproportionate percentage of budgeted resources.
- Dietitian (($35-$50 per hour).
- Staffing quota.
- Difficult to cover staff when they attend training seminars/vacation (especially for R.N.s to attend training).
- Occupancy, utilities-meeting all code regulations.
- Medical supplies and office equipment.
- A driver is not needed full-time. It is difficult to find competent drivers for a few hours per day. Some pay up to $18.00/hour-4 hours/day for part-time driver-higher than usual to find a part-time person.
- Cost of cellular telephone/two-way radio.
- Cost of training all staff: including drivers-CPR and First Aid.
- Transportation costs: insurance, maintenance, gas prices-especially in light of current gas price increases.
- General Liability.
- ADS Administrator.

- ADS Program Coordinator.
- Difficult to serve clients & facilitate administrative functions (difficult to afford more staffing as a small agency).
- Difficult to hire peer senior citizens because their SSI would be reduced.
- Especially difficult for small, ethnic, community-based providers to provide bilingual professional staff.
- Many small, community-based organizations and ethnic agencies provide more than minimum requirements: Help in calling paratransit at 6:30 a.m. for seniors; escort to M.D./grocery. shopping/bank; reading official letters from government agencies, etc.; Visit in hospital; bathing.
- Many seniors live at home and do not have a family; ADS becomes a family substitute.
- Culturally we cannot say no to these requests and needs.
- Fastest growing population: Those persons 85+.
- 52% of clients have Alzheimer's/Dementia (increasing needs).
- In Illinois, 51% of adult day services run a deficit.
- In Illinois, the financial performance of adult day services is 85%.
- In Illinois, 277 new adult day programs are needed to meet the current demands.
- In addition to providing services, ADS are faced with the challenge of educating the public and health and social service professionals about the availability and importance of adult day services as a cost-effective option, which keeps individuals (in need of care), in the community for as long as possible. An additional barrier to utilization is dispelling the myth of adult day services as a babysitting service.
- In Illinois, the unit cost per day for adult day services is $58. The average private pay fee is $43 per day. IDOA reimbursement rate: $6.02/hr.
- Healthy People 2010, called for an increase in the availability of long-term care options, including adult day services.

The 2003 CLESE Annual Report presented during the annual Membership Dinner meeting at the Phoenix Restaurant in Chinatown provided an update on CLESE efforts, a synopsis of the report is included below. Charles Johnson, director of the Illinois Department on Aging, was the special guest.

> During Fiscal Year 2003, CLESE participated in three national conferences: the American Society on Aging, the National Alzheimer's Conference, and Teachers of English to Students of Other Languages (TESOL). The presentations emphasized the unique needs of the Limited-English speaking elderly and the essential role of ethnic agencies in linking them with

programs and services. One of the presentations at the American Society on Aging was on how to build and maintain a successful coalition of ethnic agencies. (This was in response to questions from around the country about how other areas could replicate a coalition such as CLESE's).

State conferences included the Governor's Conference on Aging and Human Services (two presentations) and the State of Illinois Elder Rights Conference which addressed the type of elder abuse and neglect occurring in immigrant communities and the intervention required.

Building Better Bones: This osteoporosis prevention and awareness program is CLESE's newest project. With a grant from the Illinois Department of Public Health's Office of Women's Health, CLESE will provide education, risk assessment, and bone density screening to 225 women in two ethnic communities. Two additional ethnic communities are planned for the next fiscal year. The Bosnian & Herzegovinian American Community Center and Urhai Center are sub-contractors on the project.

Illinois Department on Aging: Collaborative projects with IDOA are CLESE's oldest, longest-running grants spanning the administrations of five Department directors. IDOA gave CLESE its first grant, which enabled the organization to begin full-time operations with an office and one staff person. CLESE has received grants from the Department each year since the initial grant in 1990.

Although the emphasis of the IDOA grants varies each year, they always involve the provision of training and technical assistance to the ethnic agencies that have contracts to provide CCP services. The current contract includes assisting providers in understanding the new electronic billing the Department is instituting. The ethnic providers of homemaker and adult day service programs served an estimated 4,000 clients in the past year.

Alzheimer's Disease Demonstration Project: CLESE is in the third year of a 3-year grant to develop models for providing medical assessments, treatment, and supportive services to people with severe memory or behavioral problems. It was funded by the U.S. Administration on Aging and the Illinois Department of Public Health. The five languages identified by the state were: Chinese, Korean, Polish, Russian, and Spanish.

Elder Abuse and Neglect: Funded for four consecutive years through CDBG funds. CLESE subcontracts with ethnic agencies that receive payment when they document the intervention they provided.

Refugee Senior Service Initiative. CLESE is in its third year of a 3-year grant to increase the number of elderly refugees in the publicly and privately funded network of programs and services for the elderly. Funded by the Office of Refugee Resettlement and administered by the Illinois Department of Human Services. CLESE has a contract with the Department to coordinate the activities of eight ethnic agencies that also have contracts with the Department of Human Services to implement the project.

English-as-a-Second Language. Under a contract with the U.S. Department of Education, CLESE completed the development, field testing, and production of curriculum material for English as a second language (ESL) for seniors at nine agencies. Additional funding from the Retirement Research Foundation and the Illinois Department of Human Services.

The report concluded with the following statement:

CLESE's original mission statement, written 14 years ago, is as current today as it was then:

To bring together individuals and organizations with shared values regarding the needs and rights of limited-and non-English speaking older people, and a shared perception that their common problems are bigger than any single ethnic group or organization and must be addressed on a broad scale. To improve the lives of Limited-English speaking elderly, and to promote and encourage organizations that serve them, by:

1. Increasing awareness and understanding of the needs of limited English-speaking older people and the organizations that serve them.
2. Organizing joint projects to examine and solve service problems related to Limited-English speaking elderly.
3. Reviewing and helping improve and assure equitable service delivery, and public policy affecting language minority elderly and their families.

The first Board of Directors went on to delineate how they would fulfill their mission when they wrote:

Time and effort will be expended to develop a structure for the healthy survival of CLESE, by:

1. Developing leadership on the Board of Directors, committees, and staff.
2. Developing a base for continual funding.

3. Developing and cultivating membership.
4. Maintaining accurate financial and legal records.
5. Developing policies necessary to qualify for United Way membership.

CLESE has been true to its mission: The Board is strong, and there are surplus funds to cover expenses when reimbursement is delayed. The lives of ethnic elderly have improved and leadership has been developed. However, the tasks faced by ethnic agencies have grown more complex over the years. For example, the diversity of the older population within each ethnic group has expanded to include: current clients becoming older and frailer, new immigrant elderly sponsored by adult children residing in the U.S.; new retirees with little experience in the U.S. outside the workplace; and undocumented residents (resulting in a change in U.S. immigration policies).

By continuing to work together, the CLESE member agencies will support each other, learn from each other and adapt to changed circumstances with the same determination as in the past.

In November 2003, CLESE held a meeting of ethnic Community Care Program providers with the Illinois state comptroller's office to discuss the state's cash flow problem with providers. They offered to write letters to providers' banks explaining the delayed payments. The comptroller's website would offer updates on the status of payments.

When Rosemary retired in December 2003, the CLESE board held a farewell luncheon in her honor at the Greek Islands restaurant. Beth O'Grady assumed the role of executive director and Taiqin took over Beth's duties. After Beth retired, Marta Pereyra became executive director of CLESE and remains in that position as of January 2022.

On September 23, 2004, CLESE held its Fifteenth Anniversary Dinner and honored Ed Silverman, Illinois Department of Human Services; David Mui, Chicago Department on Aging; Marilyn Hennessey, Retirement Research Foundation; Johnathon Lavin, Suburban Cook County Agency on Aging; and Jean Blaser, formerly of IDOA.

After leaving GACS and assuming the position of senior services director at the Hyde Park Neighborhood Club (HPNC) (2002-2005), I remained on the CLESE Board representing HPNC. I continued on the board during my time as executive director of the Bosnian and Herzegovinian American Community Center (BHACC) (2006). After BHACC, I transitioned into a CLESE individual membership until my term ended at which time I declined re-nomination to the Board.

On September 30, 2014, CLESE celebrated its 25th Anniversary with a gala dinner held at White Eagle Banquets, Niles, IL. Although I would have attended had I known about the event, I did not receive the invitation until a week after the event occurred.

An appreciation, dated April 1, 2021, and posted on the RRF Foundation for Aging website (accessed December 7, 2021), announced the passing of Marilyn Hennessey, former president of the Retirement Research Foundation. In the article, Ruth Ann Watkins, the Board of Trustees Chair, and Mary O'Donnell, the president stated: "Professionally, she was instrumental in the launch of the Coalition of Limited English Speaking Elderly (CLESE), nurturing its growth from 12 to 50 ethnic service providers. Widely acclaimed for its innovative work, the CLESE network annually assists 200,000 older immigrants and refugees and works in 80 different languages."

Further information about CLESE can be found on the organization's website.

INDEX

A

Abbey on Lake Geneva, 166, 169

Jane Addams Hull-House Museum, 262, 272, 412, 421

Adinamis, Kathryn, 144, 148,**149**, 401

David Adler Cultural Center, 221, 223, 389

Ahrens, Robert, 18, 37, **38**, 85

Akrivos, George, 12, 369

Alakiotou, Roula, 98, **146**, 148, 151, **164**, 186, 187, **189**, 321, 403, 410

Alex, Tom, 14, 351

Alexandrou, Emilee, 74, 122, **321**

Alexopoulos, George, 134, **157**

Alexopoulos, Sarantis, 336

Aliagas, Spyros, 142, 391

Allen, Bill, 96

Alpogianis, Manolis, 74, **75**, **146**, 337, 394

Alvernia Place, 35, **75**, 77, **78**, 80, 90, 92, 94, 96, 99, 104, 111, 204, 227, 337, 343, 349, 351, 358, 392, 393, **395**, 398

Alzheimer's Family Care Center, 67, 68, 76, 82, 277, 281, 357, 393

Ambassador West Hotel, 153, 155, **156-158**, 414

America, America, 32, 375, **376**

American Aphrodite, 227

American Hellenic Progressive Association (AHEPA), 135, 142, 185, 223, 302, 324, 325, 329, 355, 397

American Hellenic Society of Berwyn, 360, 394, 421, 425

American Invsco, 148, 400

American Jewish Committee, 119, 225, 226, 393, **394**, 413

Americans by Values, 440

Ames, Lea, **422**

Anast, Hara, 269, **270**

Anastaplo, George, 227, 397, 398

Andrews, Connie & Dee, 101, 152, 351-352, 363

Angelopoulos, Helen, **158**

Angelopoulos, Theodoros "Theo," 267, **399**, 400

Annunciation Greek Orthodox Cathedral, 2, 112, 116, 128, 324, 325, 371,

Annunciation Greek Orthodox Church, Benton Harbor, 73, 391 397, 398

Annunzio, Frank, 110, 142, **146**, 174

Antioch Café, 250-252, 260

Anton, John, 412, 416

Antoniou, Irene, 94, 125, 148, 160, **161**, 162, 163, **164**,**168**, 169, 183, 184, 185, 186, **187**, **189**, **191**, 192, 200, 216, **261**, **322**, 363, **404**, 410, 419, **422**, 425, **426**

Apollo Dance Troupe, 117, 119, 397, 398, 400, 401, 429

Apostol, Louis G., 257

Apostolou, John, 167, 427

Aravosis, Frieda, 275, 288-292, **309**, **336**, 337, 338, 339, 340, 356, 410, 430, **435**, 436

Argiris, Fran, 14, 80, 104, 336, 337, 338

Argolida Organization O'Danaos, 192, 267, 268, 411

Arvan, John & Pitsa, 74

Arvanitis, Angelo & Kiki, 74

Arvanitis, Theoni "Sonia," 8, 22, 34, 74, 236, 352, 379, 383

Ashurbanipal Library, 51

Ashurian, Homer, 50

ASI, 38, 45, **438**, **445**, 448, **452**

Asian Human Services, 38. **438**, 440, **445**, 448

Aslonides, Tony, 157

Assumption Greek Orthodox Church-Chicago, 75, 120, 128, 167, 264, 272, 330, 336, 344, 351, 361, 406, 425

Assumption Greek Orthodox Church-East Moline, 227, 398

Assyrian National Aid Society, 51

Assyrian National Council of Illinois, 119, 439, 440, 448, 452

Assyrian Universal Alliance Foundation, 9, 15, 17, 45, 119, 311, 368, 373, 375, 382, 440, 448

Athens, Andrew, 62, 129, 145, 330,

Athens Sister Cities Committee, 159, 428, 429

Atwood, Eden, 96, 400

Aziz, Dyana, 18, 50

B

Bacos, George, 74, 360

Badikian, Beatriz, 272, 273, 391, 392, **428**

Bakalis, Michael, 30, 51, **52,** 62, 110, 130, **146**, **147**, 148, **152**, 153, 160, **168**, 169, 185, 186, 187, 216, 226, 236, 322, 380, 390, **394**, 397, 401, 405, **407**, 408

Baldwin, Alec, 206

Bancroft, Olga, 14, 352

Barclay-Chicago Hotel, **187**, **189**, 190, 322

Belmont Community Hospital, 56, 79, 80

Bennos, Mary, 136, **146**, 152, 360

Bernardin, Joseph, 94

Bernstein, Shirley, **21**, 25, 337, 384

Big Top Restaurant, 109

Bilina, Carol, **38**, 352, **438**, 441, 442, **445**

Black, Nicholas, 188

Blagojevich, Rod, 59, 110, 216

Blaser, C. Jean, 88, **443**,448, 455, 460

Blum, Robert, 96, 99, **108**, 294, 337, 345, 351

Bokar, Sanford, 127, 323

Border's Books, **424**

Bosnian & Herzegovinian American Comm. Center, 440, 458, 460

Bousis, Eleni, 104, 125, 152, 159-163, **164**, 169, 183-192, 273, 323, 325, 361, 363, 408, **416**, 419

Boutzarelos, Evelyn, 291, 436

Bradley, Richard, 301

Braun, Carol Moseley, 65, 406, 420, **425**

Bridges, Ollie, 17, 20, 21, 352, **380**

Bristol Court Banquets. 164-166, **422**, 423

Broadway Bank, 361

Broadway Medical Center, 151

Broumas, Steve "Mixmaster," 50

Brown, Melissa, 35, 360

Bruckner, Michael, 89

Bryn Mawr Community Church, 17, 20, 21, 352, 380

Buffalo Bills, 109

Burbules, Catherine, 11

Burbulis, Christine, 15, 16, **44,** 127, 323, 368, 374

Burmahl, Beth, 108, 408

Buzanis, Alice, 13, 62, **75,** 79, **146,** 337, 338, 362, 408, **409**

Buzanis, Kiki, 13, 62

Byrne, Jane, 12

Byrne, Kathy, **11,** 12

C

Cagan, Elizabeth, 440, 441, **449, 452**

Cain, Phyllis, 291, 309, 436

Cairo, 35, 64, 360, 403, 404, 405, 407, **435**

Callinicos, Constance, 51, **52,** 227, 370, 400

Cambodian Association of Illinois, 41, 42. 43, 440, **445**, 448

Candeloro, Dominic, 230, 387, 391, 394

Cantos, Alexander, 192, 336, 353,

Cantos, Tessie, 14, 31, 34, 35, 104, 115, **127**, 152, 192, **283**-284, **285-286**, 287, 289, 337, 338, **339**, 340, 353, 356, 374, 379, 381, 408, 410

Caralis, Dennis, 167, 427

Casa Central 15, 312, 440, 448

Casey, Eileen, **98, 103**, 104, 212, 336, 340, 341, **345**, 346, **432**

Catholic Charities, 5, 90, 92, 299, 446

Central Gyros, 152, 334, 336, 409

Cermak Produce, 323, 361, 394

Chakonas, Nestor "Lefty," 12

Chang, Suey-Lee, 440, **445**, **447, 449, 451, 452, 455**

Chiakulas, James, 227, 396, 399

Chiakulas, Peter, 12

Chiampas, Tom, 12

Chianis, Sotiris (Sam), 248

Chic Alterations, 13

Chicago Black Hawks, 170

Chicago Botanic Gardens, 109, 431

Chicago Community Trust, 37, 45, 65, 79, 82, 93, 96, 98, 99, 148, 150-151, 169, 200, 295, 361-362, 401, 403, 443, 453

Chicago Council for Justice for Cyprus, 126, 326, 358,

Chicago Council of Foreign Affairs, 62

Chicago Cubs, 109, 110, 193, 352

Chicago Department on Aging, 12, 15, 18, 32, 34, 37, **38**, 43, 45, 57, 67, 68, 76, 85, 87, 91-92, 113, 178, 268, 279-282, 284, 292, 296, 298, 310, 311-312, 332, 362, 374, 379, 404, 411, 412, 439, 443, 453, 460

Chicago Department of Cultural Affairs, 15, 22, 31, 34, 57, 60, 85, 115, 283, 298, 300, 338, 362, 375, 377, 379, 382, 383, 387, 388, 391, 392, 393, 410, 429, **435**

Chicago Hilton and Towers, 116, 402, 405, 412, 417, 418

Chicago Historical Society, 226, 264, 434

Chicago Leader-Post Newspaper, 92, 398

Chicago Reader, 310

Chicago State University, 51, 356

Chicago Sun-Times, 259, 280

Chicago Symphony Orchestra, 72, 390

Chicago Tribune, 70, 144, 338, 362

Chicago Yacht Club, 455

Chinese American Service League, 38, 45, 62, 119, 220, 228, 400, 440, **445**, 448, **452**, 454, **455**

Chinese Mutual Aid Association, 440, 448

Chioros, Michael, **422, 447**

Chioros, Peter, 23, 151, 186, 194, **261**, 323

Choporis, Bessie, 25, 192, 289, **339**, 340, 353, 382

Christ Lutheran Church, 23, 25, **382**

Christakes, George, 23, **52**, 221, 223, 227, 230, 265, 386, **387**, 391, 394, 398

Cité, 429

Clinton, Hillary, 418

Collias, George, 129

Columbia National Bank, 193, 362-363

Columbia School of Dance, 110

Columbus, Elaine Barkoulies, 157, 264, 268, **271**

Combiths, Frank, 240, 257

Community Development Advisory Committee, 56-60, 404, 411

Community. Economic Dev. Agency of Cook County, 293, 298, 363

Condes, David Aaron, 35-**36**, 360

Condes, Harriett, 51, **52**

Congress of American Hellenic Organizations, 51, 326

Copernicus Center, 87, 292, 298, 354, 362, 390, 392, 412, 431, 436

Copernicus Foundation, 119, 120, 134, 220, 221, 223, 225, 227, 272, 384, 386, **387**, 388, 397, 421

Corbett, Bernice, 25, 353, 379, 382

Coroneos, Stella C., 125

Cosmos Press, 139, 198

Costa's Restaurant, **426**

Cotsirilos, Emily, 291, 309

Council for Jewish Elderly, 5, 15, 76, 96, 312

Martin and Wyleen Coyne Foundation, 75, 363

Creticos, Angelo, 81, **146**, 186, 364, 366

Cruz, Rebecca, **38**, 47, 403, 440, **442, 455**

Cullerton, John, 110, **216**

Currie, Barbara Flynn, 456

Cuthbert, Stella Adinamis, 8, **44, 52, 127**, 143, 323, 423

D

Dadas, Don, 72, **73**

Dalapas, Ioannis, 115, 386, 391, 392, 394

Daley, Richard J., 33, 37

Daley, Richard M., 56, **57, 58**, 59, 86, 109. 181, 183, 280, 404, 411, 413

Dalianis, Bill & Dena

Dalianis, George, 12, **146, 165**, 167, 366, 374, **422**

Dalianis, Harry 74

Daughters of Penelope, 2, 324, 328, 330

Dawkins, Thomas R., 73

Dean, Bruce, 38, 441, **449, 451, 455**

DeKelaito, Robert, 50, **52**, 53

Demeur, Aphrodite, 125, 169, 186, 187, **191**, 192, 200, 273-275, 277, 289, 304, 323

Demeur, James., 275, 289, 323

Demos, Jim, 12

Deni's Den, 116, 383, 392

DePaul University, 15, 30, 33, 51, 115, 117, **118**, 119, 136, 145, 220, 223, 226, 227, 228, 272, 326, 357, 375, **376**, 377, 383, 385, 391, **394**, 396, 400, 421

Dernis, Dimitris, 151

Dickens, 217-218

Dickson, Peter W., 255, 256, 261, 267

Didrikson, Lolita, 158, 414

Dimas, Spyridon, 24, 25, **127, 340**, 365

Diplomat Banquets, 136, 142, 381, 391

Diplomat West, 220, 325, **390**

Dixon, Alan, 65, **66**

Dong, Taiqin, 447, **449**, 450

Dres, Amy, 353

Dubrovin, John, **291, 309, 435**

Dukakis, Michael S., 62, **63**, 64, 74, 137, 139, 169, 172, 174, 177, **178**, 183, 184, 338, 418, **419**

Dunkas, Nicholas, 369

Dunne, George, 137, 174

Dyra, Bob, 133

E

East Balt Commissaries, 148, 327

Ebert, Roger, 267

Eclecteon Fine Arts Society, 72, **73**, 390

Economou, Tasia, 31, 35, 284, **285**, 287, 288, 291, 353, 374, 381

Eden's Banquets, 418

Edgar, Jim, 75, 162, 175, 181, 184, 406, 410, 414 **416**, 417, 429, **447**, 448, 453, **454**

Edison-Norwood Times Review, 204, 414

George M. Eisenberg Foundation for Charities, 352, 363

Elgarawany, Jeanne, 440, 447

Elling, Ron, 453

Ellis, Nick, 39, 360

Elysion Restaurant, 1, 2, 6, 8, 14, 22, 44, 62, 65, 67, 196, 324, 327, 328, 333, 338, 354, 367, 368, 369, 370, 371, 373, 374, **375**, 376, 377, 379, 381, 385

Embassy Suites Hotel, 167, 169, 406, **407**, 408, 416, 420, **427**

ENOSIS, 134, 135, 333, **407**, 408, 412

Ergon, 318

Ethiopian Community. Association. of Chicago, 440

Euchler, Marguerite, 18, **19**, 22, 27, 353, 379, 380

European American Association, 440, 448

F

Fatouros, Nick, 73-74

Fatouros, Sophia, 73-74

Ferdinand, Dana, 80, 354

Festos, Nicholas, 14, 74, 231, **359**, 360

Film Center of the Art Institute of Chicago, 267, **399**, 400, **415**

Fitzgerald, Luke C., 18, 79, 113, 288, 354

Flanagan, Michael, 110, 216

Flevaris, Nick, 62, **133**, 134

Forbes, Malcolm, 62, **63**, 64

Fotinopoulos, Maria, **270**

Frangos, Deno, 257

Frangos, Steve, 14, 31, 34, 47, 50, 51, **52**, 119, 121, **127**, 221, 232, 237, 238, 256, 257, 258, 260, 261, 266, 341, 370, 371, 379, 383, 389

Franks, Paul & Pauline, 74

Fustalieraki, Maria, 417

G

G&F Mobil, 203, 302, 303

Gaitanos, Vasilios, 74, 116, 153, 383, 392, 393, 408

Gallardo, Rafael, 24, 101, 341, 365

Ganakos, Sandy, 72, **73**

Gardaphe, Fred, 227, 399

Garner, Ron, 199

Gavaris, Polyzoes "Pol," 2, 4, 6, **7**, 8, 34, 62, 65, 126, **127**, **146**, 324, 365, 367, 379

Gebhardt, Maria, **426**

Gemperle, Rosemary, 37, **38**, 40, 45, 113, 114, 439, **442**, 444, **445**, **447**, 448, 449, **452**, 453, **454**, **455**, 460

Geocaris, Angelo, 143, 329

Geocaris, Helen, 1, 6, 14-15, 16, **44**, 122, **127**, 142, **146**, 324, 368, 371, 375

Geocaris, John, 1, 6, 12, 51, **52**, **143**, **164**, 324, 325, 368, 391

Geocaris, Steve, 324

Geo-Karis, Adeline, 51, **52,** 137, **140**, 141, **164**, 385, 423

Georgakas, Dan, 262, 402

Georges, Helen, 12, 14, 15, 16, 34, **44**, 122, **127**, 129, 324, 375

Geovanis, Tom, 360

Gephardt, Maria Svolos, 186, 187, 324, 426

Gerolymatos, Andre, 406

Geroulis, Dean, 89, 394

Gianis, George, 14, 354

Gikodimos, Harrula, 341

Gilliam, Sharon Gist, 59

Giocaris, Demetrios, 151

Giordano's Pizza, 167

Gold Star Sardine Bar, **95**, 96, 338, 400

Gonzalez, Awilda, **38**, **438**, 439, 440, 441, **445**, **451**, **452**, 453, **454**, **455**

Goodbye Miss Fourth of July, 270, 271

Goodnight Socrates 33, **376**, 377, 389

Gore, Al, 139. **176**

Gorecki, Zbigniew (John), 199, **419**

Gotsis, Jenny, **156**

Gouletas, Evangeline, 148, **149**, **164**, 227, 400, 401, 429

Gouliamos, Tom, 139

Gouskos, Katina, 290

Governor's State University, 221, 223, 387

Goya Foods, 104, 273, 363

Graphomania, 139, 198

Grecian Spotlight, 388

Grecian Taverna, 109, 406, 413, 422, 424

Greek-American Nursing Home Committee, 16, 29, 30, 45, 85, 90, 100, 120, 122, 123, 124, 125, 151, 160, **164**, **165**, 166, 167, 205, 326, 328, 342, 367, 423, 440

Greek Islands Restaurant, 73, 104, 260, 383, 409, 413, 455, 460

Greek Orthodox Diocese/Metropolis of Chicago, 87, 98, 116, 127, 148, 154, **164**, 177, 277, 301, 328, 356

Greek Orthodox Diocese/Metropolis of Chicago Philoptochos Society, 148, 423, 431

Greek Press, 28, 30, 71, **73**, 74, 142, 144, 148, **158**, **161**, 162, **164**, 166, 183, **201**, 262, 329, **395**, 414, **426**, **434**

Greek Record Company of Chicago, 246-248

Greek Star, 32, 51, 96, 99, 129, **138**, 148, 151, 158, **164**, 166, 183, 190, 192, **214**, 217, 260, 262, 267, **270**, 275, 277, 282, 304, **307**, 313, 315, 414, **422**

Greek Women's University Club, 51, 119, 120, 126, 154, 156, 180,

189, 202, 223, 263, 264, 267, 268, 269, 271, 272, 313, 399, 400, 410, 411, 412, 416, 417, 418, 419, 420, 421, 423, 425, 426, **427**, **428**, 430

Guerrero, Alejandro, **452**, **454**

H

Haggerty Dodge, 96, 275

Harris, Diana Anton, **35**, 257, 354

Harris Restaurant, 104, 109,

Hartigan, Neil, 65, **66**

Heliotes, Jim, 1, 2, 6, **7**, 8, **44**, **127**, 325, 367

Hellas Bakery, 455

Hellas Children's Dance Troupe, 115

Hellenic Broadcasting Company, 148

Hellenic Chronicle, 87, 396, 409

Hellenic Community News, 139, 158, **164**, 183, 414

Hellenic Council on Education, 421

Hellenic Cultural Organization, 51, 119, 120, 126, 134, 154, **156**, **164**, 180, 267, 268, 272, 313, 352, 358, 410, 411, 418, 421

Hellenic Five, 429, 430

Hellenic Foundation, 1, 2, 3, 4, 12, 14, 28, 29, 88, 89, 90, 127-130, 134, **164**, **166**, 167, 185, 188, 284, 288, 302, 313, 314, 316, 324, 331, 338, 341, 342, 351, 353, 371, 377, 382, 421, 423, 440, **447**, 448

Hellenic Interlude, 141, 356

Hellenic Ladies Society of Constantinople, 126, 190, **191**, 192, 363

Hellenic Life, **158**, **164**, 183, 414

Hellenic Link-Midwest, 119, 120, 154, 272, 426, **427**, 430 (see KRIKOS)

Hellenic Medical Society of Illinois, 189

Hellenic Museum and Cultural Center, 30, 31, 51, 109, 134, 137, 145, 170, **259**, 260, **261**, 269, 270, 272, 290, **291**, 301, 313, 324, 326, 329, 411, 415, 421, 433

Hellenic Professional Society of Illinois, 51, 116, 119, 120, 126, 154, **157**, **164**, 180, 226, 262, 264, 267, 268, 271, 272, 313, 323, 347, **376**, 396, 399, 400, 402, 405, **407**, 408, 410, 411, 412, 417, 418, 419, 420, 421, 424, 430

Hellenic Society of DePaul University, 33, 51, 75, 119, 223, 226, 272, 326, 357, 383, 385, **386**, 391, 396, 399, 400

Hennessey, Marilyn, **152**, 153, 379, 414, 453, 460, 461

Henrotin Hospital, 100, 349, 366

Herman, John, 440

Hlepas, Toula & Peter, 156

Hollywood House, 2, 75, 79, 80, 86, 123, 129, 337

Holy Apostles Greek Orthodox Church, 116, 272, 400

Holy Trinity Greek Orthodox Church, 3, 72, 76, 128, 241, 249, 316, 392, **393**

Hou, Grace, 440

Huber, Eleanor, **103**, 104, 212, 336, 341, 343, **345**, 346, **432**

Hull House, 58, 59, 233, 237, 242, 258, 261, 262, **263**, 265, 266, 412

Hyde Park Neighborhood Club, 310, 456, 460

I

Archbishop Iakovos, 139, **175**, 176, 177, 181

Metropolitan/Bishop Iakovos, 126, 129, 139, 142, **143**, 152, 177, 302, 345, 391, 402, 403, 431

Iatropoulos, Beulah, 289, 290, **291**, 292, **435**

Illinois Adult Day Services Association, 76, 277, 278, 279

Illinois Arts Council, 94, 114, 115, 116, 121, 160, 162, 163, 298, 300, 322, 353, 356, 363-364, 394, 396, 397, 398, 400, 401, **435**

Illinois Ethnic Consultation, 51, 55, 119, 120, 223, 226, 228, 312, 393

Illinois Department of Human Services, 459, 460

Illinois Department of Public Health, 443, 458

Illinois Department on Aging, 15, 72, 82, 98, 177, 195, 277, 279, 280, 298, 309, 311, 315, 364, 371, 390, 406, 407, 410, 429, 433, **443**, 446, **447**, 450, 453, **455**, 457, 458

Illinois Humanities Council, 15, 47, 53, 117, 121, 122, 219, 222, 225, 231, 256, 261, 265, 272, 298, 300, 364, 371, 382, 385, 386-390, 393, 394, 396-400, 402, 410, 412, 416, 419, 420, 421, 423, 425, 428

Illinois Masonic Medical Center, 2, 81, 87, 89, 98, 154, **155**, 162, 163, 169, 180, 181, 200, 326, 364, **395**, 410, 411

Illinois Secretary of State's Literacy Office, 450

Immaculate Conception Ukrainian Church, 227, 397

International Orthodox Christian Charities, 129. 134, **164**, **165**-167, 423,

Irish American Heritage Center, 134, 448

Irving Park Community Food Pantry, 295

Irving Park Lutheran Church, 80, 384

Irving Park United Methodist Church, 423

Irving Park YMCA, 213, 310

Ishaya, Arian, 51

Italian Cultural Center, 119, 120, 225, 227, 230, 231, 272, 394, 399, 421, 423

J

Jackson, Jesse, 60,

Jacovides, Andreas, J., 173, 180

Jameson, Thalia, 1, 3, 4, 6, **7**, 8, 15, 4, 122, **127**, 325

Janus, Christopher, **201**, 216, 269, **270**, 271, 419

Japanese American Service Committee, 8, 15, **38**, 61, 62, 76, 312, **438**, 440, **445**, 447, 448

Jarrett, Valerie, **57**, 59

Jasim, Peter, 51

Javaras, Barbara, 144, **156**, 263, 264, 269

Jefferson/Portage/Bel Cragin Times, 108

John, Joel, 51, **52**

Johnson, Charles, 444, 457

Johnson, Mary Ann, 262-264

Jenny Jones Show, 109

K

Kakavas, Bill & Mary, 122, 146, 186, 325, 412, 414, **422**

Kalamatianos, Dean, 188

Kallen, Vivian, 419

Kalogiannis, Penny, 31, 35, 203, 284, **285**, 287, 288, 342, 374, 381

Kaloudis, George, 3, 316

Kamber, Rebecca Elias, 51

Kamberos, Frank, 129

Kang, Sue, **38**, 45, 354, **438**, 439, 440, 441, **442**, **443**, 445, **447**, **449**, **451**, **452**, **454**

Kaporis, Jean, 2, 15, **44**, 122, **127**, 325, 368

Kapsalis, Peter, **201**

Kapsalis, Steve, 4, 6

Karahaliou, Voula, 430

Karam, Malcolm, 18, 50

Karanikas, Alexander, 50, 51, **52**, **135**, 136, 137, **138**, **164**, 220, **221**, 381, **384**,385

Karanikas, Marianthe, 391, 392

Karavites, Angelo, 25

Karp, Erica, 16, 17, 18, 80, 354, 379, 381, 403

Karras, Paul, 374

Katsaros, Voula, **156**

Katsarou, Eleni, **156**

Katsavelos, Demetrios, 160

Kavakos, Leonidas, 72, **73**, 390

Kazan, Elia, 32, 375

Keenan, Ken, 204

Kerhulas, Chris, 32, 74, 375, **376**

Khamis, Mar Aprim, 51

Kid Watch Child Care, 77, 80, 94, 108

Kioutas, Anna, **161**

Kioutas, Theodosis, 1, 2, 3, 5, 6, **7**, 9, 12, **44**,45, 51, **52**, 68, 70, 71, 72, 74, 79, 80, 81, 89, 100, 103, 122, 123, 126, **127**, 129, **146**, **147**, **150**, **152**, 154, **155**, **156**, **158**, **161**, 162, 163, **164**, **165**, 167, 169, 183, 184, **186**, 187,213, 214, 236, **261**, **270**, 304, 326, 364, 367, 368, 369, 373, 374, 380, 381, 389, 392, **395**, 411, 412, 418, 419, **426**, 431

Kirie, James C., 146, **147**, **164**, 174, 397

Kirn, Jerome, 92

Kissane, Lucy Le, 403, **449**, **454**, 455

Kledones, James, 360

Knickerbocker-Chicago Hotel, 148, 151, 152, 160, 322, 401, 403, 408, 410, 419

Kollintzas, Elaine, 30, 33, 34, 50, 62, **146**, 151, 326, 379, 391, 403

Konstas, John, 35

Kontaxis, Angelo, 379

Kontos, Shirley, 115

Kopan, Andrew T., 15, 23, 33, 50, 51, 121, **135**, 136, **138**, 144, 145,

146, **164**, **219**, 220, 223, 255-261 264, 266, 277, 326, 341, 377, 381, 383, 411, 420, 425

Korean American Community Services, 15, **38**. 45, 312, 354, 440

Korean American Senior Center, 34, 45, 86, 354, 382, **438**, 439, 440, 448

Koremenos, Barbara, 93, 148, **150**, 151

Kornaros, Christopher, 50, 53

Koshaba, Robert, 51, **52**

Kostogiannes, Sam, 3, 4, 6, 327

Kotsovos, Ethel, 2, 14, 18, 23, 28, **29**, 39, 45, 67, 68, 72. 74, 77, 78, 79, 80, 91, 92, 93, 99, 105, 123, 128, 132, 136, **146**, 152, 167, 186, 198, 200, 212, **216**, 275, **276**, 294, 299, 306, 313, 315, 330, 335, **342**-343, 344, 350, 360, 366, 379, 381, 389, 390, 391, 392, 402, 403, 404, 406, 409, 415, 431

Kourvetaris. George "Yorgos," 50, **52**, **135**, 136, **164**, 220, 227, **268**, 272, 380, 381, 385, **386**, 387, 389, 392, 397, 398, 421

Koutsopanagos, Soula, 148, 151, **164**, 403

Kouvalis, Alexander, 14, 313, 355

Kozonis, Demetrios "Jim," 76, 94, 125, 154, 186, 187, **189**, 194, **327**, 404, 406, 411

KRIKOS, 51, 116, 119, 120, 126, 134, 154, **157**, **164**, 180, 267, 268, 271, 272, 313, 379, 392, 399, 402, 405, 406, 408, 410, 411, 412, 416, 417, 418, 420, 421, 423 (see Hellenic Link-Midwest)

Kryzminski, Stephanie, 18, 19, 355, 379

Kubacki, Florence, 24, 343

Kuchuris, Frances, **191**

Kuchuris, Frank, **147**, 148, **164**, 174, 186, 187, 200, 216, 327, 397

Kulidas, John, 62, 387

Kumar, Santosh, 418, 439, 440, **447**, 453, **454**

Kunosic, Zumra, 440, **449**

Kuropas, Myron, 227, 397, 398

L

Lake County Museum, 221, 223, 225, 389

Lallas, Peter & Evelyn, 23, 135, 137, **138**, **140, 141**, 142, 330, 334, 355, 385

LaMagdeleine, Bill, 18, 76

Lambrinidis, Alice, 151

Lambros, Antigone, 34, 51, **140**, 141, **164**, **328**, **343**, 379, 385, 430

Lambros, Nick, 392

Lambros, Yiannis, **140**, 141, **164**, **328**, 385

Lao American Community Center, 448

LaSalle Talman Theater, 267, 268, 411

Lavin, Johnathon, 460

Laylo, Peter, **38**, **438**, 440, 441, **445, 449**, **455**

Leontios, Jean, **156**

Leontis, Artemis, 417

Lepeniotes, Chris & Tasia, 74

Liz Lerman Dance Exchange, 110

Levy Senior Center, 12, 18, 22, 32, 85, **283**, 284, **285**, 286, 288, 354, 362, 374, 377, 381, 390, 412, 433, 435

Lewis, Astrid, 27, 28, 355, 385

Lewis, Janet, 116, 268, 343, 355

Lightfoot, Lori, 59, 282

Limelight, 35, **36**, 360, 383, 388

Linardakis Band, 154, 158, 160, 411, 414, 427

Lincoln Land Community College, 116, 119, 220, **221**, 223, **384**, 385, 401

Lindley, Maralee I., 177, 216, 410, 444, **447**, 448, **455**

Lithuanian Human Services Council of the USA, 15, **38**, 45, 312, **438**

Litsas, Fotios, 34, **35**, 39, 50, 51, **52**, 89, **140**, 141, **146**, **164**, 221, 260, 328, 371, 380, 385, 387, 389, 411

Little Brothers Friends of the Elderly, **452**, **454**

Little Bucharest, 166, 199

Little Mike's, 61, 104, 109, 202, 305, 310, 413, 436

Lobello, Dominic, 77

Logan, Janet, 76, 453

Lopata, Helena, 227, 397

Louchios, Leo, 62

Loumbas, Bertha, 292

Loyola University of Chicago, 24, 51, **52**, 322, 382, 421, 423

Lulias, Nikitas, 34, 87, 98, 116, 117, 127, **147**, 148, 154, **164**, 174, 355, 379, **395**, 396, 397, 398, 400, 401, 402

Lutheran Social Services of Illinois, 5, 15, 16, 19, 21, 23, 67, 90, 345, 353, 359, 376, 446

M

Makedon, Alexander, 34, 51, **52**, 356, 379

Makris, Demetra, 35, 356

Malevitis, Lou, 186

Manago, Frank, 18, **19**, 356, 379

Manasingh, Ray, 99, 106, 107, **108**, 110, 212, 213, 304, 310, **343**, 344, 346, 347, 364, **432**, 436

Maniates, Maria, 101, 299, 330, 356

Maniates, Mary, **222**

Manos, Anna, 2, 6, 8, 9, 14, 15, 16, 122, **127**, 323, 328, 367

Manos, Fannie, 75

Manzara, Demetra "Dee," 34, 115, 388

Marcus, Michael, 93, 148, **150**, 151, 453

Margaris, Theano Papazoglou, 51, 115, 136, **137**, **138**, 144, **164**, 381, 392, **393**, 419

Marinakos, Leon, 23, **140**, 141, 145, 146, **164**, **270**, 385, **426**, 430

Markham, Sharon, 153, 366, 379

Maroutsos, Peter, 23, 34, 72, 74, **135**, **143**, 151, 154, **156**, **157**, 160, **165**, **166**, 167, 186, 193, 194, 329, 379, 383, 390, 403, 410, 411

Massouras, Despina "Des," 105, 152, **336**, 344, 352, 401, 415

Massouras, George, 158, 167, 344, **422**

Master Caterers, 98, 104, 130, 185, 275, 316, 335, 411, 415

Matthews, Judith, 18, **38**, 45, 47, 351, 357, 365, 379, 441, **445**, **455**

Mayer. Eve, 447

McClelland, Elizabeth "Betty," 24, 25, 345, 365, 379

McDonald's, 25, 29, 148

McKeon, Larry, 456

Mercury Rising, 206

Metropolitan Asian Family Services, 439, 440, 448, 453

Metropolitan Chicago Coalition on Aging, 15, 55, 82, 132, 312, 361, 366, 439, 453

Metropolitan Club, 159, 160, 190, **191**, 323, 332, 408

Mezilson, James M., **66**, 142, **143**-146, **164**, 262, 329, 374, 391

Michalatos, George, **133**, 134

Michalski, Pat, 260, **289**, **422**, 448, 453

Midwest Bank and Trust, 203, 305, 310, 329, 353, 436

Milakis, Harry, 9, 14, 137, 357, 373, 377

Milewski, Michelle, 203, 304, 329, 353

Mirza, Linda, 104, 345

Mistaras, Evangeline, 14, 15, 16, 22, 23, 30, 31, 32, 34, 45, 68, 72, 74, **75**, **97**, 101, 102, 126, **127**, 129, 130, 132, 137, **138**, **140**, **143**, **146**, **147**, 148, **150**, 151, 153, 154, **156**, **157**, 169, **186**, 187, 189, **191**, 213, **261**, 304, 313, **317**, 329-330, 334, **336**, 356, 373, 377, **378**, 379, 383, 389,

393, **395**, 400, 401, 402, 406, 410, 411, 412, **415**, **426**. 431

Mitchell, Georgia, 34, 142, **143**, **164**, 357, 379, 383, 391

Mitchell, Lou, 8, 264

Mitilianos, Fran, 12

Modern Greek Studies Association, 31, 318

Moraities, Maria, 33, **376**, 389

Moreno, Anna, **156**

Morowitcz, Harvey, 81

Moses, Doreen, 32, 375, **376**

Moskos, Charles, 32, **135**, 136, **138**, **164**, 227, 375, **376**, 381, 397

Mountanis, Angelike, 12, 128, 272, 377, 382, 421, 440, **454**

Mouratides, Charles, 2, 8, 9, **44**, 51, **127**, 148, **149**, 154, 158, **164**, 169, 187, 330, 401, 411

Mouskouri, Nana, **429**

Mungerson, Gerald, 155, 411

N

Naby, Eden, 51, 52

Nakayama, Helen, 440

Nambu, Masaru, **38**, 45, **438**, 440, 441, **445**, **455**

National Association for Hispanic Elderly, 18, 24, **38**, 45, 86, 100-101, 357, 365, 440, **445**

Neon Greek Village, 74, 338, 393, 403

Netsch, Dawn Clark, 181, 408, **409**

Never on Sunday, 429

Nicholson, John, 29, 30, 70, 125, **140, 141**, 142, **164**, 385

Nicolandis, Theodora, **156**

Nikelly, Arthur, 51, **52**

Nikolopoulos, Margaret, 24, 101, **124**, 345, 365

Nimrod, John, 18, 45, 50, 51, **52**, 440, 455

Northeastern Illinois University, 25, 31, 33, 51, 77, 123, 330, 337, 352, 356, 380, 384, 394

Northern Illinois University, 51, 119, 136, 356, 380, 389, 421

Northwest Leader, 121, 409, 416

Northwestern University, 30, 32, 64, 136, 262, 322

Norwood Park Home, 68, 82, 110, 205, 402

O

O, San L., **38**, 223, 390, 441, **442**, 453, **454**

Obama, Barack, 59, 361, 456

O'Connor, Patrick J., **11**, 12

O'Donnell, Mary, 461

O'Grady, Elizabeth, 444, 447, 450, **454**, 460

O'Leary, Kathleen, **103**, 212, **307**, 340, **345**, 346

Old Irving Park Association, 94, 423

Olympic Airways, 96, 159, 169, 365, 401, 404, 415

Olympic Carpets, 198

O Megalexandros, 399

One on Every Corner: Manhattan's Greek-owned Coffee Shops, 32, 375

Orpheus Dance Troupe, 50, 152, 401, 409, 412, 413, 417, 418, 421, 424, 429, 430

Orthodox Observer, 32, 375, **376**

Orthodox Singles, 272, 313, 418, 421

Ozaki, Yoji, **442, 445, 452, 454, 455**

P

Palivos, George, **416**

Palivos, Lisa, 152

Palivos, Peter, 406, 425

Panagiotou, Irene, **156, 161**

Pan Arcadian Federation, 126, 189

Pandya, Abba, 440

Pan Euboean Society of Illinois, 421

Pan Laconian Federation, 13, 126, 189, 324, 365

Pan Macedonian Federation, 126, 148

Pan Messinian Federation, 126, 189, 334

Panos & Stratos Orchestra, 152, 383, 401

Panos Productions, 388

Panos, Toni, 16, 34, **44, 127, 131**, 142, 328, 330-**331**, 379, 383, 431

Panourgia, Neni, 115, 312, 346, 383

Pantezelos, Faye, 23, 330,

Panton, John, 12, 377, 388

Papadopoulos, Athanasia "Sandy," 31, **44**, 68, 72, **127**, 142, **146**, 154,

156, **157**, 158, 159, 160, **161**, 194, 331, 355, **378**, 390, 411

Papadopoulos, Nikoletta, 152

Papagus Greek Taverna, 406, **407**, 408

Papamichos, Venetia, 75

Papandreou, Nick, **424**

Papanicholas Coffee Co., 277

Papanicholas, Nick, 277

Papanikolas, Helen Zeese, 421

Papanos, Nicholas, 122, 331

Papoulias, George, 173

Pappageorge, Sophia, 14

Pappas, Dino, 121, 396

Pappas, Maria, 167, **168**, 196, 423, 427

Pappas, Nick, 115, 383

Parhad, Sam, 51, 52

Parkview Lutheran Church, 19, 358, 377, 387

Park West, 35, 360

Patio Theater, 313, 355

Payne, Michael, **201**

Pegasus Restaurant, **322**, 400, 404, 406, 418, **419**, 422

Pello, Sabina, 440

Peppas, Nicholas, 240

Pergantas, Loukas, 125, 151, **155**, 160, **161**, 162, 163, **164**, 169, 183, 184, 186, **187**, **189**, 190, **191**, 192, 332, 408, **416**, 419, **426**

Perros, Demetrios, 369

Peterson, Jackie, 101, 357

Petrakis, Harry Mark, 115, **135**, 136, **164**, 221, 381, 387, 388, 420, 429

Petrakis, Stella, 420, 425

Petropoulos, Sandy

Petros Dianna's, 35, 360

Petros, Nick, 380

Pets Are Worth Saving (PAWS), 217

Philippidis, Nick, 51, **52**

Phos Missions, 74, 86, 87, 148, 189

Picture Bride Son, 255, 266

Pioneer Press, 204, 414

Pischak, Katherine, 310, 332

Plato Academy, 111, 170, 264, 265, 273, **274**, 275, 408, 411, 414, 425

Playboy Foundation, 126, 365

Pnevmatikatos, Dimitri, 139, **158**

Polish Welfare Association, **38**, 45, 86, 352, **438**, 441, 448

Polk Brothers Foundation, 326, 365, 443

Polydoros, Nick, 186

Pooley, Georgia Bitzis, 237, **239**, 240, 420, 425

Popowski, Karen, 441, **455**

Porr, Peter, 38, 45, 47, 226, **394**, **438**, 441, 442, **443**, **445**, **449, 452**

Potamianos, Peter, 51, **52**

Poulikakos, Sylvia Salapatas, **454**, **455**

Poulos, Nick, 25, 73, 74, 144, 382

Poulos, Ted, 252, 260

Prime Times, **19**, 349

Pritzker, J. B., 199, **201**, 216

Prusinski, Ann T., 80, 105, **207**, **208**, **209**, 212, **214**, **216**, 217, **276**, 294, 310, **336**, 341, **343**,346, **348**, **432**, 436

Psiharis, John, 2, 4, 6, 7, 8, 9, **11**, 14, 15, 16, 17, 18, **19**, 22, 23, 24, **29**, 34, **35**, **38**, **44**, 45, 47, 50, **56**, **57**, **58**, **63**, **65**, **66**, 68, 72, 74, **75**, 79, 90, 92, **97**, **98**, 99, **103**, 109, 113, **118**, 121, 122, **127**, 131, **132**, **133**, 135, **138**, **140**, **141**, **143**, **146**, **147**, **149**, **150**, **152**, **155**, **156**, **157**, 159, **165**, **166**, 167, **168**, 186, **187**, **189**, **191**, **193**, **201**, 204-206, **214 215**, **216**, 217, **261**, **268**, **276**, **280**, 281, 282, **309**, 315, **317**, 318, **331**, 332, 351, **358**, 367, 368, 369, 370, 371, **372**, 373, 374, 377, **378**, 379, **380**, 381, 383, 385, 388, 389, 390, 391, 392, **395**, 396, 397, 402, 404, 405, 406, 407, 408, **409**, 410, 411, 412, 413, 414, **416**, **417**, 418, **419**, **422**, 423, 424, **425**, **426**, 428, **429**, 431, **432**, 433, 434, **435**, 436, **438**, 439, 440, 441, **442**, **445**, **451**, **452**

Psilakas, Barbara, 11, 14, **44**, **127**, 332

Psychios, Zafiris, 246, 247, 248, 258

Pucinski, Roman, 58

Pulitzer-Lerner Newspapers, 89, 394

R

Rapanos, Tasia, 244, 254, 258, 260

Rassogianis, Alexander, **157**, **268**, 361

Rassogianis, John, 22, **29**, 30, 34, **44**, 62, **66**, 68, 72, 74, **75**, 90, 91, **97**, **98**, 100, 120, 121, 122, 123, **133**, 142, **143**, **146**, **149**, **150**, 151, 152, **155**, **156**, **157**, **165**, 166, 167, 169, 185, 186, **187**, **201**, 231, 237. 260, 264, **268**, 290, 304, 313, **317**, 318, 323, 330, 332, 333. **343**, **347**-348, 377, **378**, 379, 381, 389, 390, 391, 393, 396, 406, 408, 409, 410, 413, **415**, 417, 418, 424, **425**, **429**, 436, 440, 449, **452**

Razes, Anna Tellios, 51, 52

Reagan, Ronald, 139, 172

Michael Reese Health Trust, 167, 169, 326, 365, 427

Regas, Jim, 189

Regos, Susan, 167

Rekoumis, Sotiris, 51, 52, **158**, 380

Rembetika, 429

Ress, Dina, 139

Retirement Research Foundation, 16, 17, 20, 37, 82, 99-100, 111-114, **152**, 153, 169. 176, 194, 200, 296, 312, 342, 365-366, 379, 403, 408, 412, 413, 414, 443, 453, 459, 460, 461

Return of Odysseus, 237, 241, 242, 243, 258

Rexinis, Theano, 156

Rigas, Connie Gountanis, 152, 169, 186, 323, 325, **425**

Rockford College, 220, 223, 387

Roditys Restaurant, 104, 194, 370, 371, 383, 413

Rodriguez, Ricardo, 123, 332-333, **432**, 433

Ronan, Carol, 456

Rosen, Stanley, **219**, 220, 221, 223, 227, 384, 386, 396, 399

Ross, Norman, 87, 93, 110, 185

Rostenkowski, Dan, 110, 390

Roth, David, 51, **52**, 120, 226, 228, 393

Ryan, Laura Lynn, **309**, 310

S

Sada, Emmanuel, 51, 52

SAE of North and South America, 200, 330, 334, 421

St. Andrew Greek Orthodox Church, 31, 75, 81, 112, 128, 135, 316, 328, 330, 334, 335, 343, 358, 406

St. Andrews Women's Philoptochos Society, 23, 330

St. Athanasios and Ioannis Greek Orthodox Church, 316

St. Basil Greek Orthodox Church, 32, 375

SS. Constantine and Helen Greek.Orthodox. Church, 223, 255, 367, 389, 420

St. Demetrios Greek Orthodox. Church, **11**, 12, 22, 34, 72, 112, 128, 324, 332, 354, 367, 369, 370, 373, 374, 375, 377. 379, 380, 381, 382, 386, 388, 389, 392, 396, 407

St. George Greek Orthodox. Church, 406

St. John Greek Orthodox Church, 388, 412, 421, 430

St. Sophia Greek Orthodox Church, 220, 223, 389

Saints Volodymyr and Olha Ukrainian Church, 227, 398

Samuels, Hannah Sue, 51, 52

Sandors, John, **146**, 231, 361

Saramantis, Christos, 247, 249, 258

Sarbanes, Paul S., 139, 174, 182, 184

Sarelas. Aphrodite, **146**, 333, 353, 400

Sarlas, Penny, 272, 423

Saveas, Genia, 12

Sawyer, Eugene, **56**, 60, 388

Schakowsky, Jan, 456

School Sisters of St Francis, 77

Schwarten, Helen, 18, 50

Search Developmental, 77, 80, 104

Selimos, Bessie, 290, 292

Seth, Kompha, 38, 47, 440, 442, **445**

Shah, Amydelle, 18, **19**, 80, 93, 100, **103**, 104, 105, 106, 111, 212, **276**, **336**, 340, **345**, 346, **348**, 349, 379. 397, **442**

Silverman, Edwin, 460

Simon, Paul, 65, 110, 216

Skouris, Peter, **127**, 333

Skylakakis, Theodoros, 402

Smith, Donald R., 178, 279, **280**, 281,

Solstice, 267, **268**, 411

Sotos, Eleni, 169, 187, 334, **426**

Soukeras, Spiro, 203

Southeast Asia Center, **38**, 45, 119, 220, 226, 394, **438**, 441, **442**, **445**, 448, 453

Southern Illinois University, 227, 398

Spielman, Fran, 280

Spyropoulos, Ted, 134, 152, **164**, 176, 186, 187, **327**, 333, **407**, 408

Stansell, Jane, 68, 76, 103, 277, 281, 357, 389, 393

Stathakis, Eugenia, **201**, **285**, 289, 290, 292, **309, 435**

Stavrakas, Sam, **140**, 142, **164**, **321**, 385

Stavropoulos, Ernest, 14, 358

Stein, Phillip O., 19

Sten, Gwen, **19, 21**, 24, **349**, 365

Stephanopoulos, George, 64, 152, **164**, 169, 176, **179**, 408

Stephanopoulos, Konstantinos, **417**

Stoynoff, Jim, 115, 383, 424, 430

Strouzas, Mary, **286**, 290, **435**

Suburban Cook County Agency on Aging, 443, 460

Swarzman, Michael, 81, 87, **395**

Swedish Covenant Hospital, 8, 9, 262, 323, 326, 402

T

Takoudis, Christos, 157

Talia, Peter, 51, 52

Tamraz, Lincoln S., 51, 52

Tarsinos, Electra, 128, 371

Tasaras, Sofia, 375

Ted's Sweet Shop, 252-253

Terzakis, Danny Boy, 194

Theodoratos, Theo, 12, 379

Theodosakis, Helen, 148, 151, **164**, 403

Thirteen Colonies Banquets, 64, 146, **147**, 148, 174, 325, 397

Tiniakos, Mark V., **161**

Mark V. Tiniakos, 161

Thomopoulos, Christopher, 13-14, **19**

Thomopoulos, Elaine, 2, 4, 6, **7, 8**, 9, 14, 15, 17, 18, **19**, 22, 34, **38**, **44**, 45, 50, **52**, 68, 72, 73-74, 79, 80, 91, 122, **127**, 137, **138**, **140**, **141**, **143**, **146**, **149**, 152, 167, 186, 205, 220, 221, 223, 260, **261**, **268**, 269, 275, 318, 330, 333-334, 348, 352, 355, 367, 368, 369, 370, 371, **372**, 373, 374, 377, **378**, 379, **380**, 381, 383, 384, 385, 386, 387, 389, **390**, 391, +392, 394, 396, 403, 406, 410, 413, 414, 415, 420, 423, **435**

Thomopoulos, Nick, **359**, 361

James R. Thompson Center, 260, **289**, 290, 291, 309, 410, 423, 427, **435, 447**

Tichnell, Gladys, 24, 349, 365

Toledo, Maria, 100, 123, **336**, **345**, **350**, 364, **432**, 436

Toma, Isaac, 439, 440, **449**, **451**, **452**, 453, **454**, **455**

Tomaras, Chris, 125, 152, 158-159, 163, **164**, 169, 176, 182, 183, 186, **187**, **189**, 190, **191**, 192, 194, 216, **322**, 330, **334**, 408, 410, 414, **426**

Tornado (Tornie), 107, 200, **207**, **208**, **209**, 210, 211, 212, **213**, **214**, **215**, 216-218

Touloumis, Athena, 148, **164**, 151, 403

Tracey, Eugene, 29

Trakas, Demetrios, 12, 381

Trankina, Mary, 18, **21**, 358, 379

Treasure Island Foods, 96

Tsakonas, Christos, **239**-241, 256, 257

Tselepatiotis, Peter, 190, 192

Tsilas, Loucas, 183

Tsolinas, Mike, 148, **164**, 401

Tsongas, Nicole, **65**, 148, **168**, 169, 325, 401

Tsongas, Paul, 64, **65**, 139, 148, 169, 325, 401

Tzakis, Dee, 72, **73**

Tzakis, Theresa, 6

Tzanos, Constantine, 50

U

Ukrainian Social Services Bureau, 38, 45

United Athenian & Piraeus Societies of Illinois, 112, **214**, 217, 273, 275, 411, 414

United Hellenic American Congress, 51, 129, 145

United Hellenic Voters Association, 64, 325, 329, 402, 405, 408

United Way of Metropolitan Chicago, **27**, 28, **29**, 59, 82, 85, 132., 313, 342, 355, 366, 380, 390, 391, 402, 460

University of Chicago, 30, 34, 330, 417, 421

Utley, Floyd "Red," 294, 351

V

Valentinas, Danguale, **38**, 45, 47, **438**, 439, **445**, 452

Vallas, Paul, **57**, 59

Valone, Katherine "Kay," 74, 87, 144, **147**, **164**, 148, 174, 397

Varones, John, **161**

Vasilatos, A.J., **268**

Vasilatos, Jerry, 267, **268**, 411

Vasilatos, Stella, **268**

Vegalis, Theodore, 74

Vern, Nick, 257

Veterans Administration, 69, 101, 278, 279, 280, 298, 366

Vietnamese Association of Illinois, **38**, **438**, 441, **445**, 448

Vilato, Carmen, 24, 101, **103**, **276**, **336**, 351, 365, **432**

A Village in Baltimore: Images of Greek-American Women, 32, 375, **376**

Vital Measurements Home Health Care, 12, 18, 20, 358, 380, 382

Vlahos, Efthimios, 123, **124**-125

Voulgaris, Pantelis, **415**

Voutiritsas, Danae, **307**, 310, 336, **350**, 351, 434

Vranas, Bill, 129

Vroustouris, Alexander. **161**

Vuco, Rose, 18, **19**, 79, 358, 379

W

Wagner, Karen, 121, 409

Walgreens Foundation, 75, 366

Washington, Harold, 37, 56, 137, **171**, 368

Washington Square Health Foundation, 326, 366

Watkins, Ruth Ann, 461

Weisberg, Lois, 60, 283, 362

Western Springs Savings & Loan, 189

White Crane Wellness Center, 441, 448, **452**

White Eagle Banquets, 461

Williams, Phil, 101, 109, 275, **336**, **358**-359, 415

Willis, Bruce, 206-207

Windy City Gyros, 190

Wirth, Victor, **442**, **443**, 444, 447

Wojick, Mike, 301

Wong, Bernarda, 38, 45, 47, 220, 228, 400, 440, **455**

Wilbur Wright Community College, 99

X

Xenakis, Roxanne, 12

Xenos, Katerina "Kakia," **157**

Xidis, Anthony, 269, **270**

Xydes, Lena, 22, 23, 24, 135, **140**, 334, **378**

Y

Yannias, Cynthia, 88, 128, 129, 130, **447**

Yates, Sydney, 110, 163

Yimmer, Erku, 440

Young, Mary E., 60, 289, 408

www.ingramcontent.com/pod-product-compliance
Lightning Source LLC
Chambersburg PA
CBHW080746060526
44119CB00072B/163